The Civilian Conservation Corps in Utah

THE CIVILIAN CONSERVATION CORPS IN UTAH

Remembering Nine Years of Achievement, 1933–1942

Kenneth W. Baldridge

UNIVERSITY OF UTAH PRESS
Salt Lake City

UTAH STATE HISTORICAL SOCIETY
Salt Lake City

Copublished with the Utah State Historical Society.
Affiliated with the Utah Division of State History,
Utah Department of Heritage and Arts.

The Defiance House Man colophon is a registered trademark of The University of Utah Press. It is based on a four-foot-tall Ancient Puebloan pictograph (late PIII) near Glen Canyon, Utah.

LIBRARY OF CONGRESS CATALOGING-IN-PUBLICATION DATA
Names: Baldridge, Kenneth W. (Kenneth Wayne) 1926- author.
Title: The Civilian Conservation: Remembering nine years of achievement Corps in Utah, 1933-1942 / Kenneth W. Baldridge.
Other titles: Civilian Conservation Corps in Utah, 1933-1942
Description: Salt Lake City : University of Utah Press ; Utah State Historical Society, [2018] | Includes bibliographical references andindex. |
Identifiers: LCCN 2018030228 (print) | LCCN 2018031927 (ebook) | ISBN 9781607816522 | ISBN 9781607816515 (pbk. : alk. paper)
Subjects: LCSH: Civilian Conservation Corps (U.S.)—History. | Civilian Conservation Corps (U.S.)—Officials and employees—Utah. | Labor camps—Utah—20th century. | Public works—Utah—20th century.
Classification: LCC S932.U8 (ebook) | LCC S932.U8 B35 2018 (print) | DDC 363.109792—dc23
LC record available at https://lccn.loc.gov/2018030228

Plates reproduced by permission of the Utah State Historical Society.

Printed and bound in the United States of America.

Contents

Figures

Plates following page 250

12. Group of enrollees outside one of the barracks at the Ferron Civilian Conservation Corps camp, F-11.
13. Merchandise available at a Utah Civilian Conservation Corps camp exchange counter.
14. Sign and brick pylon marking the entrance to Zion National Park.
15. Enrollees hauling cut-down trees through a clearing near a Civilian Conservation Corps construction site, Hobble Creek camp.
16. Large rock structure, probably the Shivwits Dam on the Santa Clara River, built by Company 961, camp SE-213 of St. George.
17. Civilian Conservation Corps baseball team from Company 959 of Ferron camp F-11.
18. Crew of men working on a rock retaining wall at their Civilian Conservation Corps construction site.
19. Finished section of a flood-control embankment along the Virgin River in Zion National Park, at the east end of the canyon.
20. Bridge built over Sulphur Creek in Capitol Reef National Park, likely by enrollees of NP-7.
21. Ranger station at Sulphur Creek at Capitol Reef National Park.

Tables

Acknowledgments

To list all those to whom I owe huge debts of gratitude for help in this endeavor would add several more pages to this already lengthy work. Unfortunately, I did not record the names of all those who helped, especially in the early days.

Among the dozens of people who helped were many from various levels within the technical agencies, from archaeologists and historians of the U.S. Forest Service Region Four in Ogden to ranger station office workers in Richfield and Kamas. Others were Civilian Conservation Corps (CCC) historians and personnel of the Bureau of Land Management, U.S. Forest Service, Bureau of Reclamation, and Soil Conservation Service (now Natural Resources Conservation Service).

Many civilians helped me find campsites or gave detailed explanations of work done. Family members of CCC personnel were helpful as they told me of stories related by husbands, fathers, and uncles. JoAnne Chandler of the Green River museum gave me her copy of *Utah Road and Recreation Atlas*, which enabled me to find roads to the backcountry of the state, where I found CCC campsites that I probably would not have been able to locate.

As I said, thanks are due so many people for their kind words, encouragement, and assistance. The late Professor Leonard J. Arrington, then of Utah State University, provided much valuable counsel as well as tangible assistance in the form of material he had gathered for a project of a similar nature. My chairman, Professor Thomas G. Alexander, was a fount of patience and encouragement. The more than seventy ex-CCC "boys" who were so generous with their time in responding to letters and questionnaires and personal visits back in the late 1960s were of great assistance, especially as they provided insight into the workings of the CCC not normally available to the researcher or the public in general. Librarians and archivists of federal, state, and county repositories have been most helpful in making materials available.

At that time five of our six kids were still at home, so then I said, "To a long-suffering wife and neglected children, mahalo." Today I repeat my gratitude to Delma, not only for her encouragement but for traveling with me while visiting CCC campsites and work projects throughout the state on a variety of roads, although after some of them she said, "Never again!"

My next-door neighbors, Kailean and Rylan O'Keefe, were my teenaged tech support, willing to dash over at a moment's notice to bail me out of some computer jam. Finally, my son Steve, author of two books in his own right, was most helpful, especially toward the end, when he took over the editing, shortening, and tweaking, persuading me not to slit my wrists and working closely with the ever-patient Reba to bring this to its completed form. I could never have done it without you, son.

Preface

This is an unusual book. Submitted originally as a doctoral dissertation in 1970 for a Ph.D. degree at Brigham Young University, copies of it have been found since then, primarily, as microfilms in the offices of the U.S. Forest Service and the National Park Service here in Utah. For the most part I carried out my research between 1966 and 1969. In addition to gathering information from the Federal Archives Center in Denver, Colorado, and going through Utah newspapers, probably the most valuable—and certainly the most interesting—is the collection of letters, interviews, and questionnaires received from many former Civilian Conservation Corps (CCC) and governmental personnel contacted during that time. Efforts to find any survivors among those informants have, unfortunately, been in vain, so the information they left behind provides a valuable perspective now lost forever.

In 1943 I was a sixteen-year-old high school student, working on a U.S. Forest Service fire crew in the Groveland Ranger District of California's Stanislaus National Forest under two foremen who had worked with the CCC until the program terminated the preceding year. Bill Fiske and George Bond were similar, yet quite different. Both were sixty-three-year-old ex-cowboys from Coulterville, a small community not too far away. Bill was our fire boss, as he had been with the CCC. Small but wiry, he was a capable, no-nonsense individual, whose top priority was the safety of his young charges. George Bond, our crew foreman, was more laid-back, and his ability to roll his own cigarettes fascinated me and resulted in ten-minute smoke breaks nearly every hour.

From Bill and George I learned a lot about the CCC and their work and was sorry I had missed out on the opportunity to serve. Still, I developed a strong interest in this organization, which persists until the present, highlighted by my writing on the topic for my doctoral dissertation at Brigham Young University in 1971. When contacted by Rebecca Rauch, acquisitions editor for the University of Utah Press, in 2012 and told they wanted to publish my dissertation I was surprised but flattered. I pointed out that it was more than forty years old, but Reba was persuasive, so here it is, having been brought up to date considerably.

The book has been updated with material found within the last four decades, including further research in the Utah State Archives and the archives of the Forest Service and Park Service and visits to as many of the campsites as possible. Also included are interpretations offered in publications that have surfaced since that time. The photographs included herein were not included in the dissertation.

I am happy to report that my extensive research over the years, stimulated more recently, of course, by the publication prospect, has only strengthened my original thesis that CCC activities in Utah from 1933 to 1942 were indeed nine years of achievement.

KEN BALDRIDGE, Ph.D.
Pleasant Grove, Utah
2017

CHAPTER 1

The Beginning

During my army tour I discovered that soldiers with CCC experience always got along better, advanced faster, and were all-around better adjusted.

—Russell C. Christensen, enrollee, camp F-40

About one hundred of the townspeople of Ferron, Utah, were invited to a dance held in the mess hall of camp F-11, located about five miles up the canyon above the little community in Emery County. It was September 29, 1933, and the first six-month enlistment period for the young men of President Franklin D. Roosevelt's "tree army" was coming to an end. Over in Milford, twenty-two Virginia boys from Camp Delano were planning to catch the train east the next night. And in Ogden a few days later, some four hundred enrollees from camps in Brigham City and Bountiful, as well as some from Wyoming, entrained for Fort Dix, New Jersey, to receive discharges from what was still unofficially known as the Civilian Conservation Corps (CCC).[1]

Not all of them left, however. Mark Anderson, civilian superintendent of camp SE-206 in Hobble Creek Canyon near Springville, told the Provo Lions' Club that fifty-six of the 185 New York boys had reenlisted as well as all twenty-five of the older, experienced, local men. They would continue to work on flood and erosion control in nearby canyons until the middle of October, when the Utah men were to join a camp in Washington County and the New York boys were transferred to Florida.[2] Not counting the two operated by the Bureau of Indian Affairs, eleven winter camps had been approved for Utah, and most of those CCC companies that remained in the state were being transferred from potentially snowbound mountain camps to work on erosion control at lower elevations. A striking winter uniform had been prepared for CCC enrollees, although it appears never to have been used in Utah. Complete with visored cap and earmuffs that could be tied under the chin, it made, according to one newspaper account, the "debonair young foresters look like a cross between Daniel Boone and Rebecca of Sunnybrook Farm."[3]

As the first six months of this New Deal experiment came to a conclusion, Utahns paused, as did others across the country, to reflect on the accomplishments of this new agency. So far, most observers had described it in glowing terms, but to determine positively its influence upon the land was impossible at this stage.

Among the most serious of the problems inherited when Franklin D. Roosevelt assumed the presidency in March 1932 was the specter of unemployment, which had been stalking the land the previous three and a half years and which Roosevelt had promised to attack. To the office he also brought what eminent historian David Kennedy called "a lover's passion for conservation."[4] That this longtime interest should provide a means for attacking two of the nation's problems was most convenient and resulted in a marriage made not in heaven, perhaps, but certainly in the White House.

The Civilian Conservation Corps began within a month after Roosevelt became president. One of his first acts after his inauguration on March 4, 1933, was to ask Congress seventeen days later to create an organization to help alleviate the twin challenges of massive unemployment in the country and sorely needed conservation efforts. His idea was to get unemployed youth out of the cities and pay them a dollar a day to work on projects such as the Tennessee Valley Authority or reforestation.[5] Congress responded ten days later on March 31, and S. 598 passed both houses by voice vote to create the agency officially known as Emergency Conservation Work but known throughout its lifetime—and ever since—by the name Roosevelt proposed: the Civilian Conservation Corps. Although there was considerable vocal opposition, especially from Republicans, historian John Salmond states that "the bill was never in danger of defeat" and concludes that "the CCC began its existence on a broad, bipartisan base of support, something it never really lost."[6]

In spite of extensive evidence supporting the claims of external sources for the genesis of the CCC, it is equally certain that credit must be given to Roosevelt for promoting the Civilian Conservation Corps on the level at which it was to function so effectively for nine years. It can certainly be acknowledged that a good idea has many fathers; a poor idea is an orphan. Regardless of the routes by which the beginning of the CCC emerged, whether it was the European response to the advice of professional foresters or philosophers, precedents established by the Hoover administration or various cities and states, or even FDR's own experience as governor or merely a practicing forester on his Hyde Park estate, Roosevelt was responsible for bringing the agency into creation. In addition to being the most popular and successful of the New Deal agencies, it is also the one in which he took the greatest personal interest, due, as Kennedy points out, to "his passionate, even romantic interest in conservation."[7]

Although it appeared initially that President Roosevelt might launch his conservation program without adequate consideration, it must now be recognized that his haste was due to his anxiety merely to strike quickly at the twin problems of unemployment and conservation.[8] On March 15, 1933, therefore, Roosevelt requested that the secretaries of war, interior, agriculture, and labor consider themselves an informal committee to coordinate suggestions and plans for the Civilian Conservation Corps. He asked Secretary of the Interior Ickes to serve in a position of ill-defined leadership of the group.[9]

On March 15, 1933, the committee met and formulated some objectives of the new agency, which the president revealed that same day in a press conference. Work on the bill lasted over the next few days, and the measure, accompanied by a relief message from the president, went to Congress on March 21.[10] Identified as "An Act for the relief of unemployment through the performance of useful public work, and for other purposes," the bill gave the president authority to hire unemployed men for works of a public nature on state and federal lands for "the prevention of forest fires, floods and soil erosion, plant pest and disease control, the construction, maintenance or repair of paths, trails, and fire lanes." Provision also was made for the extension of work onto private and municipal lands when it was felt in the public interest to do so.[11]

Although labor leaders and a few members of Congress and senators of both parties made spirited opposition, assailing the program with labels running the gamut from "socialism" to "fascism" and "forced labor," the measure actually enjoyed generous bipartisan support.[12] Still another factor that weighed into the president's support of his pet program was his feeling, as he once told Harry Hopkins, that every young man would benefit from the opportunity of spending six months or longer in the woods, a position with which few could argue.[13]

Whenever a work organization is created the issue of wages comes up for discussion. When the component of relief is factored in it may become even more problematic. The wage for the regular nonrated enrollees of $30.00 monthly, however, was set in the original bill and was maintained the entire life of the Corps. George A. Yager, secretary of the Utah Federation of Labor, also mentioned the slavery issue by saying that hunger drove men "tantamount to involuntary servitude." William Green, American Federation of Labor president, however, diffused the opposition of organized labor somewhat when he finally announced his reluctant endorsement of the bill.[14]

From the wages received the War Department was to send a monthly allotment of $25.00 home to the enrollee's dependants. Due to the fact that the boys were theoretically only from families on relief, this proved to be a most welcome help for the folks at home. On the other hand, several at Mount Nebo camp F-9 and, no doubt, elsewhere, as well, were sending $27.50 home each month, and four enrollees were sending the entire $30.00.[15]

Considering how hard the boys were expected to work, some people felt that a little higher pay was in order. An enrollee in a southern Utah camp complained about the $30.00 monthly wage. Conceding that the boys were already receiving the equivalent of $3.00 daily in food, clothing, and shelter, he still proposed that the actual cash paid be increased to $60.00 a month. "Any man with a drop of blood in his veins resents working at scab wages," he maintained.[16] From my research it appears that the pay scale was never a very serious issue in Utah camps. Most of the boys felt that they were adequately housed and extremely well fed and their "three hots and a cot" were ample compensation. Besides, the prospect of further pay by promotion through the enrollee ranks was always a possibility.

Surprisingly, most of the senators and members of Congress from the western states opposed the measure. They feared that the radical elements found in the east would soon contaminate the west with their revolutionary ideas and that members of Congress from eastern urban areas would use the CCC as a means of "unloading this undesirable element and shipping them west." Senator Elbert D. Thomas, junior senator from Utah, was virtually the only western Democrat at all enthusiastic over the program and who expected to see positive results. Although passage of the bill was ensured because of the president's insistence, the *Salt Lake Tribune* commented, "It was interesting to note that the preponderance of those who spoke on the bill opposed it."[17] However, timely amendments and the skillful piloting of Senator David I. Walsh of Massachusetts resulted in the final acceptance in both houses.[18]

Although the agency was known officially for four years by the name Emergency Conservation Work, the president signed the CCC bill on March 31, 1933, and the Civilian Conservation Corps was legislated into being. Much was still to be done, however, in the way of organization, and Roosevelt's issuance of an executive order on April 3 should really be considered the beginning of the CCC's existence.[19]

There were those, both in and out of government, who opposed the creation of any agency of a relief nature. Labor leaders were fearful that the low wages planned for the emergency work program would impact negatively upon the existing wage structure. FDR short-circuited this opposition by wisely choosing the highly respected Robert Fechner to head the new agency. Fechner, born in Chattanooga, Tennessee, in 1876, was a vice-president of the American Federation of Labor and on the General Executive Board of the International Association of Machinists. Fechner had come up through the ranks of organized labor since he had quit school in Georgia at the age of sixteen. While assistant secretary of the Navy during World War I Roosevelt had met Fechner when the latter went to Washington, D.C., as a special adviser on labor policy. Although the two men were not particularly close, Fechner had helped persuade the machinists union to back FDR's election in 1932, which certainly kept his name high on Roosevelt's list when he looked for someone acceptable to organized labor to head the new agency. Roosevelt selected Fechner; it was a wise choice.[20]

Coordination of the various aspects of the CCC would probably be regarded today as an impossible task in the prevailing political climate. Getting the four cabinet departments of War, Labor, Agriculture, and Interior to move as quickly as they did and in the same direction was a huge accomplishment even then.

An Advisory Council made up of representatives of the four participating departments assisted in establishing policy. The War Department had the major, immediate task of actually getting the camps set up and the enrollees transported, housed, clothed, and fed. The Labor Department, headed by Madam Frances Perkins, also had an immediate, huge task ahead in enrolling men according to the population-based quota of each state. Soon instructions were on their way; although the existing state welfare agencies did the actual enrolling, the Labor Department established specific guidelines. Enrollment was initially limited to unemployed single men between eighteen and twenty-five who were members of families on relief rolls.[21]

Although the Army administered the camps, the actual work projects for which the CCC is remembered even to this day were to be under what were referred to as the technical agencies, which were part of either the Department of Agriculture or the Department of the Interior.[22] Although there was some reshuffling during the life of the program, from the beginning the technical agencies were the ones responsible for the actual work getting done. They were the ones that had the enrollees during working hours and were responsible for teaching them the skills to turn inexperienced boys into capable, productive men.

On April 18, 1933, news arrived at Fort Douglas, on the bench overlooking Salt Lake City, that Director Robert Fechner had named C. B. Morse, assistant regional forester of Region Four of the U.S. Forest Service, as his representative to serve at the headquarters of the Ninth Corps Area at the Army Presidio in San Francisco. Morse's task was to coordinate the work between the Departments of War, Labor, Agriculture, and Interior in recruiting, training, and preparing the enrollees for work in the camps of the Ninth Corps Area, the largest of the nine such subdivisions into which the Army divided the country, as shown in Appendix A.

The Corps Area was the Army unit that was immediately utilized to administer the CCC organization, and CCC companies were numbered according to the Corps Area in which they were organized.[23] The Corps Area designation of all CCC companies was found in the "hundreds" column of the company number, that is, the third number from the right. Company 1254, for example, was organized at Fort Dix, New Jersey, as the 154th company in the Second Corps Area, whereas Company 1354 would be the 154th company created at Fortress Monroe, Virginia, in the Third Corps Area. When a company was transferred to a camp in Utah, however, it became the responsibility of and was under the jurisdiction of the Ninth Corps Area. Although occasionally a state might request the return of one of "its" companies to its home Corps Area, this happened only rarely.

With very rare exceptions, companies carried the same numerical designation until the company was disbanded. In nearly every circumstance, disbanding a company seldom took place until the waning days of the CCC, when the availability of manpower was preempted by the national military mobilization beginning in the late 1930s.

Each company was under a commanding officer, usually an Army captain, although there were occasionally lieutenants, and on a few occasions, majors were assigned. On rare occasions officers from the other military services were also utilized. A Marine Corps officer commanded the Black's Fork camp the first year of the program, and Lt. Commander Dow H. Casto of the Navy commanded Company 957 in Logan camp F-1. Lt. George L. Edman of the Naval Reserve commanded at least five camps between 1938 and 1940.[24]

Although the needs of the states and the technical agencies were paramount in determining the locations of camps, this had to be done with the approval of the Army through the Corps Area headquarters. Corps Areas were further divided into districts. Headquartered in Salt Lake City, the Fort Douglas District of the Ninth Corps Area handled the CCC for virtually the entire state of Utah as well as portions of Wyoming, Arizona, and Nevada. Very little remained static in the CCC, however, and in later years some of the camps in northern Utah were transferred to the Pocatello District, as explained in chapter 3.[25]

It was here at Fort Douglas, one of the six military bases in the Ninth Corps Area to house a CCC district, where the new enrollees recruited from within the district would be processed before receiving their camp assignments. Companies sent into Utah from out of state would usually also be routed through Fort Douglas, although they were often sent directly to their assigned camps. At either district or corps headquarters Army medical personnel conducted physicals and administered the necessary vaccinations, while the new enrollees went through a conditioning program complete with calisthenics. District headquarters Fort Douglas was also the storehouse from which all the camps in the district received supplies and equipment, except, of course, for those materials that were purchased locally.

In the meantime there had been two, sometimes violent, demonstrations in which unemployed veterans of World War I were involved. Seeking to have Congress approve the bonus previously promised to them, several years after the war veterans occupied sections of the nation's capital. Referred to as the "Bonus Army," the men were violently dispersed under orders from President Hoover, although more violently than he had intended. In 1933, a second "Bonus Army" gathered, but this time the outcome was considerably different.

Newly appointed Veterans administrator General Frank T. Hines soon saw the infant CCC as a possible solution to the pressing needs of the veterans. He wrote FDR on May 6, 1933, suggesting that veterans be accepted for enrollment and placed in special camps where they could be assigned work suitable for their age and physical condition. FDR then issued Executive Order #6129, authorizing the enrollment of 25,000 veterans into the program.[26] It became the function of the Veterans Administration to determine eligibility and make the selection of applicants in order to maintain the quota as authorized by law.[27]

Between this prospect of employment, disputes between left- and right-wing factions within this self-styled "army," and some unconventional wisdom, the Second Bonus March came to an end. At Fort Hunt, at the wise suggestion of FDR's adviser Louis Howe, the marchers were visited by the president's wife, Eleanor. While Howe dozed in her automobile, Mrs. Roosevelt walked alone through the mud into their camp and defused the volatile situation in grand style, and the veterans were most appreciative. She even led them in singing the wartime favorite "There's a Long, Long, Trail A-Winding." As one commented in an oft-quoted statement: "Hoover sent the army; Roosevelt sent his wife."

Although some of his cabinet members decried turning "large groups of jobless and presumably resentful men" loose in America's forests, the new president recognized the so-called dangerous situation as an opportunity.[28] When he offered the veterans of both the Great War and the Spanish-American War positions in the new Civilian Conservation Corps some of the men were insulted at the idea of working for $30.00 a month, but more than 2,600 accepted. Those seven hundred who had not done so by the deadline of May 22, 1933, were provided transportation home; those who accepted became the nucleus of special veterans' companies, still another facet of the new organization, eventually employing more than 225,000 men over the next nine years. Utah gained one company that served two camps as a result. The final nail in the bonus coffin symbolically occurred when Fort Hunt, temporary locale of the second Bonus Army, was turned over to the CCC.[29]

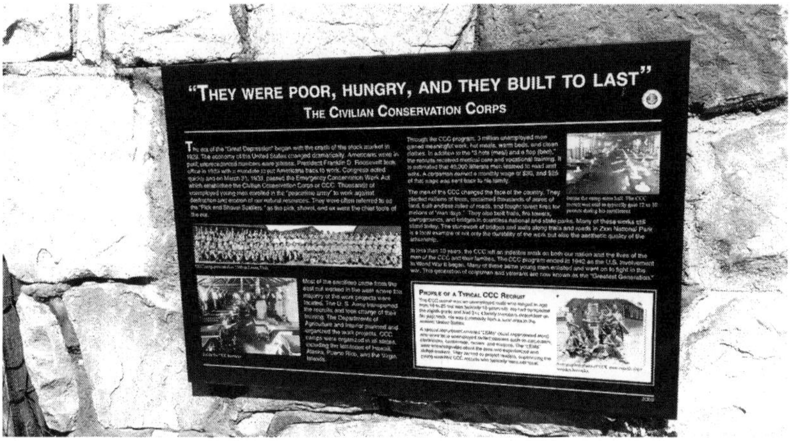

Figure 1.1. Sign, among the many Civilian Conservation Corps signs in Leeds, Utah, identifying the pre–Civilian Conservation Corps situation of enrollees as well as the quality of work they did as members of the Corps.

In the meantime, accommodations for other groups continued through April 1933. Washington announced on April 14 that the Corps would enroll 14,400 Indians in camps on fifty-three reservations in North and South Dakota, Oklahoma, Arizona, New Mexico, and Utah.[30] Still another major step was the announcement on April 23 of the intention to enroll 24,375 “local experienced men,” or LEMs as they soon came to be known. This was very likely an outgrowth of the letter Major Robert Y. Stuart, chief forester of the U.S. Forest Service, wrote to Fechner the previous week requesting that local men be hired to provide adequate supervision of the work being done.[31]

An additional reason for hiring such men locally would be to defuse any possible opposition to bringing outsiders into an area and providing work for them while ignoring the difficulties faced by local residents. Unemployed loggers and former state foresters insisted that they be given an opportunity for government employment, as Salmond describes it, “in areas the foresters considered their own.”[32]

To prevent such unrest from happening, the CCC Advisory Council sent a joint letter to Roosevelt calling for the employment of “technicians,” the short-lived term used initially to identify the LEMs. Roosevelt accepted the recommendation immediately, but disagreement followed, at first between the Forest Service and the War Department, especially, and then between the Forest Service and the Bureau of the Budget over the wages to be paid the LEMs, as well as the camp supervisors hired by the technical agencies.

Although there had been opposition to the bill, no one had seriously denied that the country was in severe economic difficulties. The number of unemployed in the country in 1933 is often set at 12,000,000, but estimates ranged to more than 16,000,000. Of these, experts estimated that five to seven million were young people sixteen to twenty-five who were out of work.[33] More than 1,250,000 men and boys were found in breadlines and on highways across the country, wandering aimlessly in search of employment. The U.S. Children's Bureau and the National Association of Travelers' Aid Societies estimated that more than 200,000 of these were youths.[34] That work was needed by hundreds of thousands of men was apparent.

The apprehension described earlier over the low-wage situation voiced by labor leaders fearing that this would exacerbate the unemployment situation was another problem with which the president had to wrestle. Actually, throughout the life of the CCC, other federal programs such as the Works Progress Administration employed men to do exactly the same work the CCC enrollees were doing, also under Forest Service supervision. Heads of families and individuals on relief were given preference and were, for the most part, able to live at home and work on nearby projects. They were limited to 130 hours a month and could expect to be paid between forty-five and fifty-five cents an hour, netting them approximately $65.00 a month.[35] This is compared with the approximately 170 hours per month for which CCC enrollees were paid $30.00, only $5.00 of which they were to keep for themselves. As mentioned earlier, Utah enrollees complained little about their pay.

In spite of all the rhetoric about what a great thing the CCC was going to be, there were still some communities across the country that did not initially welcome the idea of establishing CCC camps nearby. Based on complaint letters sent to Corps leaders, Neil Maher cites three reasons for local apprehension. The major complaint, even outside the South, was the possibility of having African American enrollees in the vicinity: "In addition, locals criticized new CCC camps for bringing urbanites and foreign-born immigrants into their overwhelmingly rural and homogeneous communities." The third major concern was that the camps would provide a dumping ground for ne'er-do-wells who would be taking jobs from unemployed local men.[36] Although similar concerns were felt in some Utah areas at first, after a short while the opposite became the norm, as communities rose up in protest when it was learned—or even rumored—that established CCC camps were going to be transferred out of their community.[37]

There were few precedents to follow in a program such as this. Some states were better organized than others to cope with the demands of the new organization. Many sent officials to Washington to get instructions from the source. One of these was T. L. Holman, chairman of Utah Governor Henry H. Blood's Emergency Relief Committee, who left Salt Lake City on April 12, 1933, to confer with Fechner, Miss Perkins, and others concerning the new scheme.[38]

CHAPTER 2

The Civilian Conservation Corps Comes to Utah

I wish we could take them all.
—Gus Backman, Salt Lake City relief officer

Times were hard in the Beehive State. Since the onset of the Great Depression, the economic situation had been deteriorating badly. By the end of 1932, unemployment in Utah had spread to 61,000, over one-third of the labor force, higher even than the national average. Over one-fourth of the population of the state was receiving some form of financial assistance.[1]

By 1932 most private agencies in Utah had exhausted their relief funds, and many cities and counties were forced to discontinue their limited relief activities and the work projects in which they were engaged. Even the relief loans of the Reconstruction Finance Corporation were inadequate to stem the descending course of the economy. Executive action by Utah's Governor George H. Dern was limited to ordering an economic survey to determine what effect the depression was having upon the state. Some small road projects were attempted, and eventually the legislature was asked to consider the problem of unemployment. Nothing happened. One student critical of the period states that aside from offering counsel and advice, "the Dern administration was characterized by a no-action policy with respect to unemployment and relief."[2]

Today Utah is considered solidly Republican, as it had been in the 1920s. In November 1932, however, the voters of Utah followed the lead of the rest of the country, with over 56 percent of ballots cast for the Democratic presidential candidate. Of twenty-nine counties in Utah, twenty-two voted Democratic and helped elect New York's Governor Franklin D. Roosevelt as the thirty-second president of the United States.[3] Henry

H. Blood, chairman of the Utah Road Commission, was elected governor, and his predecessor, George Dern, went off to Washington to become secretary of war in FDR's new cabinet.

A student of Blood's administration articulated the question most of his constituency probably had on their minds: "Could this silver-haired, rather frail-looking, sixty-one-year-old man ease their pain by his words today or by his actions in the months to come?" Blood's inaugural address at the capitol building in Salt Lake City on a cold January 2, 1933, was not encouraging. He described the existing economic conditions as more serious than "the state has ever known," with agriculture "in helpless and almost hopeless distress." He stated that the mines in Utah were nearly all closed because the prices of metals were at an all-time low and the decline of purchasing power was having a woeful effect on manufacturing and business in the state. Warning that "stagnation exists in financial circles," he seemed to offer little to look forward to: "Unemployment stalks the city streets.... Men's hearts are failing them for fear, and no one can tell what the future has in reserve."[4]

The change in the statehouse took place as 33,000 Utah families were on relief. Immediately after the election, Governor Blood's office began receiving appeals for assistance. Accounts of personal misery poured in daily, telling of homes lost and hopes destroyed. In Logan the City Commission received a petition from a group of unemployed requesting that a labor project be instituted in order that those out of work would have some means of working off their delinquent light and water bills.[5]

Hopes revived, however, when Roosevelt announced his reforestation plan, and immediately inquiring letters about this new "tree army" began arriving at Governor Blood's office.[6] With no specific information available, the applicants were directed to get their names on file with their county relief agencies and continue to be patient.

In Utah, as across the country, these reports of qualified acceptance of the new scheme came from various sources. The two leading newspapers of the state carried views that reflected the diversity of opinions. The *Deseret News* spoke favorably of the proposal as an emergency measure dictated by the circumstances of the times. It deplored, however, the separation of men from their community and their families. Organized labor criticized the idea of dollar-a-day wages. Opponents expressed contrary opinions on editorial pages. The program was described, on the one hand, as destroying "the wage basis for which labor has been struggling.

On the other hand, conservative people see... shift toward state socialism that... may carry us irretrievably out of the era of individualism." The *Salt Lake Tribune* feared the idea even more and claimed that only one-fortieth of the unemployed would benefit. Some were apprehensive that those enrolled would virtually become wards of the government, and others were frightened by the possibility of wartime discipline being imposed upon civilians. The ideological implications, however, most concerned the editor. "It magnifies the power of elected leadership" and also "becomes a socialistic experiment that may or may not forestall more serious difficulties." He concluded on this cautionary note: "We question the wisdom of pursuing this cause too far."[7]

After passage of S. 598, the first call for 25,000 enrollees across the nation was issued April 3, 1933, and the first man was selected just three days later in Pennsylvania. Some 250,000 junior enrollees as well as 25,000 local experienced men eventually enrolled that first year.[8]

As a result of the vast amount of public lands available and the need for so many conservation projects, Utah began its experience with a total of twenty-six camps, with twenty-five functioning under the Forest Service and one under the National Park Service.[9] During that first summer of 1933, 5,500 men served in the regular twenty-six camps within the state of Utah. Twelve, or nearly half of Utah's camps, were nominally Third Corps Area camps, while the remaining fourteen were divided evenly between companies from the Ninth and Second Corps Areas.[10] Utah's smaller population established a quota of junior enrollees insufficient to man more than seven camps that First Enrollment Period, so it was necessary to bring nearly three times that many from out of state.

The seven Ninth Corps Area companies were all from Utah and staffed six camps in the national forests and the one in Zion National Park. Companies out of the Second Corps Area of New York, New Jersey, and Delaware equaled the number of those from Utah and were assigned to two regular Forest Service camps and the five state camps working on soil erosion control. Nearly half the companies assigned to Utah came from the Third Corps Area of Pennsylvania, Maryland, and Virginia and, like the Ninth Corps Area companies, were all assigned to national forest camps. The Utah quota of men was augmented considerably by those from the ranks of "local experienced men," who actually exceeded the number of Utah's junior enrollees and were considered a necessary component of nearly all the companies, especially those from the eastern states.[11]

Utah's original quota was received on April 20; initial enrollment took place on May 4; construction crews were working on most of the camps by the end of the month. Stretching the length and breadth of the state, the camps were involved in nearly all of the various activities performed by the CCC that First Enrollment Period. From 332 Utah men enrolled in May, the number climbed to 3,694 only two months later and remained in excess of three thousand for the entire six-month period. Actually, Utah came out quite well in terms of men enrolled and was able to exceed the quotas that were set.[12] With the addition of approximately two thousand young men from out of state, the economic, social, moral, and physical impact upon the face of Utah gave some indication of what lay ahead as a result of the new agency.

Camps generally operated in six-month enrollment periods. In March and September, the Director's Office or other Corps officials announced the location of camps for the ensuing period, which began the first of the following month. The date was seldom the deciding factor when a move might take place, however; weather and the completion of ongoing projects were much more likely to be considered. Usually, the work varied little from one period to another, although there were some camps with which particular activities were associated.

There was a certain magic about sending young men into the woods. It was not so much man against nature as it was man in league with nature against the economic troubles that were then stalking the land.

While there were some NIMBY—"Not-in-my-backyard"—attitudes as expressed in chapter 1, feelings were also expressed at the other end of the continuum, fear of eastern states placing their men in camps within their own borders, thus reducing the number available for camps in the west. The text of a wire to President Roosevelt is found in Governor Blood's papers in which concern is expressed over this dismal prospect: "Emergency conservation program has won exceptionally wide approval of our people and failure to man all approved camps in Utah would be disappointing and would react unfavorably as well as upset the very fine program of work which has been planned."[13] Frank Persons of the Department of Labor immediately responded from Washington, D.C., that although the department had no voice in determining just how many camps a state might have, "you and Holman may depend confidentially upon the enrollment of Utah's full quota [of men]...whatever the eventual number of camps in the state."[14]

As the program developed, many of the fears disappeared or, at least, were minimized. Grand County historian Gary Shumway reports that city officials of Blanding, for instance, realizing the benefits that a camp could bring to the community and were "gratified when the federal government decided to place one of the largest CCC camps ever established in the northwest corner of town."[15]

The other side of that coin, of course, lay in the fears of many Utah people who worried about eastern boys coming into the state with whatever practices or looser morals they might bring with them. Even after there had been a fairly clean track record of two years these fears still existed. On May 4, 1935, the Blanding Commercial Club met to discuss whether to approve construction of a CCC camp in the little Mormon community. A "prominent member of the town" voiced what seemed to be the majority opinion that the fear of getting "the girls into moral trouble" outweighed the good that the CCC could possibly do. Finally one holdout reminded the others of how much help Blanding needed in fighting the depression and that "as far as religion and outside influences are concerned he can't understand why we send missionaries all over the world to teach outsiders the gospel if we can't accept outsiders ourselves." He urged acceptance of the camp for the good that could come and that they would "deal with the bad if it arises." Based on interviews over a two-year period by a high school student, the vote was for acceptance of the camp, much to the delight of a pair of eavesdropping teenaged girls, one of whom later exulted in claiming that she "got the best husband in the world" as a result.[16]

Instead of worrying about the impact of the CCC upon the community, the *Washington County News* editorialized from the opposite point of view. Stating that residents should not provide alcoholic drinks for the boys, the editorial pointed out that they were nearly all from Utah and had "mothers, fathers, brothers or sisters or wives" and nearly all had joined up "for the purpose of obtaining some funds to help their loved ones at home."[17]

Utah's congressional delegation provided an interesting contrast in political support for the CCC program. The two congressmen, Democrats J. Will Robinson and Abe Murdock, supported the legislation and worked hard in support of the CCC during its existence. One of its most consistently enthusiastic supporters, Senator Elbert D. Thomas advocated the permanency of the plan from the very beginning until the final days of the organization. Senator William H. King, however, felt differently. Although a Democrat, King followed a brand of conservatism highly unpopular for the times, and it eventually cost him his seat in the Senate.[18]

In Utah, interest in the new program continued to mount, although much information was still lacking. Preston Peterson of the Utah State Road Commission and R. H. Rutledge, regional forester of Region Four of the U.S. Forest Service, had joined T. L. Holman in Washington to represent the state of Utah in the receipt of preliminary instructions. Peterson, however, returned to Utah on April 13, full of praise for Rutledge's efforts.[19]

Just the day before Peterson arrived back in Utah, Governor Blood announced that he, too, would leave soon to confer with those directing the program. In Washington he was soon disappointed to learn that federal road funding was to be cut off, as Roosevelt planned to use all such money to finance the new CCC. As chairman of the Utah State Road Commission before his election as governor, Blood was determined to see federal road funding not only restored but expanded, since he felt that was the most direct way to attack the problem of relief for the unemployed. Because of his connections as former head of the National Association of Highway Officials, he was successful in getting highway funding back where he wanted it to be. Although initially concerned over the CCC siphoning off funding for his beloved highways, Blood came to embrace the conservation program when he learned that enrollees would come from families on relief, which would also be supported by the wages to be sent home.[20]

In the ensuing years Governor Blood was to visit Washington often, advocating the retention or increase of available funds for relief spending. It was always road construction, however, that was to be his chief interest rather than the reforestation program, although he certainly did not deprecate the idea.

Recruits in the east, in the meantime, had commenced training under Army supervision in Virginia, New York, and Illinois. Fort Douglas, the Army base on the eastern bench above Salt Lake City, was designated as a training camp and the headquarters for a CCC district under the command of Colonel Edwin Butcher. Beyond that, however, there was still no news for the anxious unemployed. Fort Douglas was to serve as the district headquarters for most of the CCC experience and initially included all the Utah camps and a few in Arizona and Nevada.[21]

ENROLLMENT

On April 20, 1933, Utah's enrolling officers announced the state's quota of one thousand unmarried men between the ages of eighteen and twenty-five.[22] In addition to the regular enrollees, Utah's quota of 1,300 "local experienced men" hired from the ranks of unemployed carpenters, lumbermen, miners, and others who could serve as role models for the inexperienced junior enrollees further increased CCC ranks in the state.

While the population of the state determined the number of junior enrollees, the quota of LEMs, as the "local experienced men" were quickly identified, was based on the number of camps in the state. To secure their appointments, these men, unemployed but excluded from the normal marital and age requirements, registered with the designated welfare office just like the junior enrollees but were actually selected by the appropriate technical agency.[23]

Enrollment blanks were soon printed, and recruiting agents were to be named on May 3. In most cases county relief committees were assigned to handle CCC enrollments. All applicants had to be listed on county relief rolls and residents of that particular county. Officials initially emphasized that only the junior enrollees would be accepted through the relief offices, but, as mentioned, the LEMs would be selected by the supervising agencies.[24]

However, the following day (May 3, 1933) it was explained that although the relief agencies would receive the applications of the experienced men, their actual selection would be carried out by the technical agencies as had been originally announced. Salmond, on the other hand, cites the *Report of the Director, 1933*, in claiming that originally LEMs were selected under Department of Labor directions and that selection by the technical agencies did not begin until 1935.[25]

LEM enrollment often came very close to the numbers of the junior enrollees. Of the quota of 212 for Ogden and Weber County, there were 117 junior enrollees and ninety-five LEMs, who were told to report on June 15, 1933.[26]

Table 2.1. Utah County Quotas for Initial Enrollment.

County	Quota for Initial Enrollment
Salt Lake	774
Weber	210
Utah	200
Cache	113
Carbon	73
Box Elder	73
Sanpete	70
Garfield	65
Davis	54
Emery	50
Juab	50
Sevier	48
Millard	44
Summit	42
Uintah	41
Beaver	40
Duquesne	40
Washington	40
Wayne	40
Tooele	39
Iron	38
San Juan	34
Grand	30
Wasatch	25
Piute	20
Kane	15
Morgan	11
Rich	11
Daggett	10
Total	2,300

Governor Blood had been named Labor Department representative for the selection of enrollees in the state, and to him the Ninth Corps Area commanding officer offered the cooperation of the Army.[27] Blood, in turn, designated forty-two-year-old Ogden businessman Robert H. Hinckley as his recruiting agent. Hinckley, described by Leonard Arrington as "one of thirteen children of a poorly paid geology teacher at Brigham Young University" had previously been a high school teacher, mayor, auto dealer, and member of the state legislature, where he became acquainted with George Dern. Later, as governor, Dern asked Hinckley to become a member of the Volunteer Relief Committee in 1932. In March, Senator William H. King had recommended Hinckley as the necessary "person of ability and courage" to handle federal and state unemployment funds. Blood had already considered him, and when FDR announced the Federal Emergency Relief Administration in May 1933, Blood appointed Hinckley to direct the program in Utah. As such,

Hinckley fielded requests from Utah counties for federal funds and, in turn, distributed federal money to the counties as he deemed appropriate.[28]

Hinckley and T. L. Holman scheduled enrollment to begin May 1 but were totally unprepared for the horde of nearly four hundred applicants who swarmed into Holman's Salt Lake City office on the designated day. Instead of accepting them, Hinkley and Holman told the hopeful applicants that recruiting must wait until agents had been named in the individual counties to which the 2,300 vacancies had been assigned on the basis of population.

Completion of enrollment was scheduled for May 15, and the Army emphasized that enrollment was completely voluntary, with no coercion or conscription implied. The Corps wanted only men "eager to participate."[29]

By May 4, 1933, Salt Lake City and County were ready to begin receiving the first formal applications for Utah's 140 vacancies of the assigned quota of 774 junior enrollees. With twenty clerks, Gus P. Backman, head of the Salt Lake City Relief Office, signed up four thousand applicants for the 140 spots. Priority, of course, was to go to unmarried men then on relief or whose families had no breadwinners. The 140 men selected received medical examinations in the Federal Building, along with the successful eighty-five of the eight hundred "local experienced" applicants certified by Wasatch Forest Supervisor A. L. Nord. The frustrated Backman was unhappy that so many applications had to be denied.

The men were then transported to Fort Douglas, where they received equipment and clothing, initially surplus from what was then still known as the Great War. Uniforms were issued to cover a six-month enrollment period, and although there was some slight evolution in uniforms over the years, they eventually became quite standard. In 1940 a supply sergeant described the six-month issue as follows:

> 2 prs. trousers W.O.D. or khaki; 2 shirts W.O.D. or khaki; 2 prs. of shoes, service; 2 jumpers working; 2 prs. of trousers, working; 1 belt, web, waist; 1 overseas cap; 1 hat for working; 1 black tie; 6 prs. of socks, either summer or winter issue; 2 prs. of shorts or 3 prs. of John L's; 3 summer tops or 3 John L. tops.[30]

Lieutenants Keith K. Tatum and Grady Epps, assisted by Army noncommissioned officers and cooks, then took over the group, now designated Company 940. With about half the men in barracks and the other half in tents, they began their two-week conditioning program, which included vaccination for smallpox and inoculation for typhoid fever.[31] Utah's first CCC enrollees had begun their service.

On May 6, Holman, Hinckley, and Ernest Winkler of the Forest Service left Salt Lake City to visit communities in the southern part of the state.[32] After organizing county committees for registration and selection, the three men returned to Salt Lake City, only to continue into eastern Utah and the Uinta Basin. By the time they returned to Salt Lake City the three had set up the enrollment process in twenty-seven of the state's twenty-nine counties, and the other counties of Rich and Daggett had received their blanks and instructions by mail; they were ready for the initial May 15 deadline for enrollment.[33]

The response was tragically gratifying as applications exceeded quotas all over the state. Cache County reported 275 applicants for the fifty-eight junior enrollee positions and ninety-two for the fifty-five available openings for experienced men. In Provo there were three hundred applications for the two hundred positions that the entire county was allotted.[34] Registration continued in Salt Lake City as well. Although about one-third of Salt Lake County's quota had already been selected, 549 still had to be chosen.[35] In the southern Utah community of Cedar City, Relief Chairman William R. Palmer scheduled registration for the thirty-eight Iron County vacancies for May 11.[36]

The CCC enrollment touched the lives of many types of people. Mark Baird was one of the first Utah boys to join. Having been temporarily laid off from his job with a railroad, he enrolled in the CCC program to provide an income for a fatherless family of a mother and six children. A father and son combination was found in Mt. Nebo camp F-9. The father, W. J. Powell, had been unemployed for four months and refused to accept charity. When the opportunity arose, he and his son both signed up and were accepted. Theoretically, all enrollees came from families on relief. However, one youth whose family was not on relief joined the CCC in 1933 right out of high school. Perhaps the fact that this farm family was nearly destitute and consisted of eleven children provided extenuating circumstances. Ken Haslam had just graduated from high school in Salt Lake City when he received a letter telling him to report for enrollment. He had not applied, but his Latter-day Saint bishop knew he needed work and had submitted his name. After a physical exam and shots at Fort Douglas, he and his friend boarded the

Denver and Rio Grande Railroad for Price, where they were taken on to Ferron camp F-11 by truck.[37]

William Udink of Ogden was thirty-three when he applied in June 1933 for CCC employment as a "local experienced man." He had immigrated from the Netherlands with his family at the age of thirteen and received his citizenship papers a few years later. He worked for a plumber for two years but was laid off in June 1933, when his employer experienced financial difficulties.

Soon after he applied for CCC enrollment Udink received a form letter from the U.S. Forest Service office in Ogden stating that the Weber County quota for local experienced men had been filled and he was not among those selected. However, he was invited to report to the Federal Building in Ogden the following day and that, if some of those selected failed to appear or to pass the examination, he might be chosen as an alternate.[38] This he did and, with his affairs in order, was selected to go on just a few hours' notice.

The problem of selection was most serious. With so many needy from whom to choose, it was extremely difficult to make objective choices. In general, the work of enrollment went forward with little evidence of any partisan bias or personal favoritism; nevertheless, a few complaints of unfair treatment did trickle into Governor Blood's office occasionally. In early July 1933, a widow with three children wrote an anguished letter stating that relief officials had told her twenty-year-old son he was too young but hired his friend the next day. A Magna youth applied about the middle of June, but when he received no response he wrote an angry letter to the governor stating, "I can see no justice in keeping anyone out who needs a job." He went to Salt Lake City, but "the lady and man in charge didn't even consider talking to me about it." He had been unemployed for three years and felt it unfair when others received work, concluding that "the project is not as successful as it might be in the employment of men." An Orangeville woman also wrote about her son's failure to get CCC work. Blood passed this letter, like the others, on to Hinckley to take whatever action he could, although the governor answered each letter sympathetically, explaining what disposition he was making of their appeal.[39] Another disappointed applicant was my friend William C. Carr, now deceased. Without money and unable to find employment, he applied for CCC enrollment at the relief office in

Provo, where officials turned him away when they learned that he was still a citizen of New Zealand.[40]

MILITARY PERSONNEL

In the meantime, the Army had been making personnel changes as well. In the middle of August, General Pegram Whitworth, commanding officer of the Fort Douglas District, announced the release from CCC duty of ten Regular Army officers ordered back to their home stations. Five of these returned to duty at universities and military academies in the east, one to the University of California at Los Angeles, two to Utah State Agricultural College, and one to a Salt Lake City high school ROTC service. The other officer went back to his post at Fort Monmouth, New Jersey. The Army assigned five other officers to other camps within the district.[41] By this time Reserve officers had been mobilized in sufficient numbers to take over many of the companies.

Blood continued in his efforts to get additional camps while he was in Washington. He talked with James J. McEntee, assistant director of the CCC, who told him that only an executive order from the president could secure additional camps. Blood submitted a request to initiate procedures for establishing more camps through Commissioner Fred C. Johnson, but he was admittedly pessimistic. In addition to getting three camps to carry out the much-discussed range rehabilitation program in the western part of the state, Blood hoped to get an additional camp for the Escalante area.[42]

VETERANS' ENROLLMENT

The veterans' quota for the Ninth Corps Area was two thousand out of the initial 25,000 veterans authorized nationally. Each state was entitled to one veteran for every ten regular enrollees, with preference to be given to veterans with dependants. Utah's quota of one hundred was based on the initial quota of one thousand junior enrollees. The Veterans Administration assigned the distribution to counties on the basis of population. Salt Lake County provided thirty-eight, Utah and Weber counties had ten each, and Cache County had four. The next four most populous counties had quotas of three each; five counties had quotas of two apiece;

and the sixteen smallest counties sent one man each. The Veterans Hospital in Salt Lake City received the applications, and the men were to be sent to the conditioning camps to begin their six months of service.[43]

On June 28, 1933, Utah's one hundred veterans met a similar group from Idaho at Fort Douglas and traveled by train to San Leandro, California, where they joined California veterans and became Company 1925.[44] Their work consisted of building roads in the watershed overlooking the city of Oakland. The camp, administered by the Department of the Interior, was located near Lake Chabot. Although fifty of the men reenrolled for a second period, there was some dissatisfaction, and in January 1934 the Utah men began taking steps to be returned to their home state by requesting Governor Blood's help in having them transferred to Utah. The reasons offered were sound. Most of the men were married, and service in Utah would permit them not only to see their families occasionally but also to render service at home. It was also suggested that access to former employers would offer greater likelihood of getting back into regular employment again. The wheels moved slowly, but move they did, and by the summer of 1934 the men had been relocated to camp F-9 at the southern base of Mt. Nebo, near Nephi, Utah.[45]

ECONOMIC OPPORTUNITIES

The financial advantages of having a CCC camp nearby naturally proved to be an attraction. Each CCC enrollee received three suits of woolen underclothes, two pairs of denim jumpers and trousers, three shirts, a work hat, a raincoat, six pairs of socks, a necktie, a belt, one pair of olive-drab trousers, two bath towels, three face towels, and a toilet kit. Each man was supplied with a straw bed sack and four blankets. Although much of the clothing and other items were left over from the Great War, much had to be purchased new. In Utah, the Army also asked the Chamber of Commerce to help out by supplying towels and toilet articles, including five hundred safety razors, toothbrushes, and combs.[46]

These economic possibilities were recognized by enterprising businessmen, farmers, and the public in general. Although some Provo citizens showed reluctance to accepting a camp there, the majority agreed with Utah County Commissioner Hilton J. Robertson, who reminded his colleagues of the cash benefit of the enterprise.[47]

A delegation from five communities in the eastern part of Millard County in central Utah petitioned the regional forester for a two hundred-man camp to be located on Chalk Creek, a few miles east of Fillmore. They suggested several possible projects, including road- and trail-building, timber conservation, and water projects in the mountain range east of the communities.[48] Another group from Salina and Richmond visited Governor Blood urging that a camp be established in Salina Canyon for flood-control work.[49] The Marysvale Commercial Club also contacted Blood expressing annoyance at not having a reforestation camp assigned to that vicinity. Members expressed hope that a camp might be transferred from the Escalante area since there were supposedly more valuable work projects in the petitioning community: "If you can, you will win the gratitude of many Democrats who are beginning to feel their party has forgotten them. We get neither sympathy nor aid from the two Republican county commissioners."[50]

The purchase of tools, trucks, cars, and heavy equipment added to the attraction of nearby camps, which were initially provided with eight one-and-a-half-ton trucks and one half-ton pickup apiece. The Forest Service office of the Intermountain Region made plans to purchase four hundred trucks, over half for use within the state of Utah. Merchants submitted bids at the Ogden and Missoula, Montana, offices of the Forest Service for 50,000 shovels, enough to supply every man in the camps in the Rocky Mountain area. Also open to bid were two carloads of scrapers, a dozen heavy-duty plows, "large numbers" of grubbing hoes and picks, supplies of fencing materials, carpentry equipment, and building materials. About $2,000 worth of tools was purchased for each camp.

In addition to several smaller companies, the larger Salt Lake City firms of ZCMI, Salt Lake Hardware, Consolidated Wagon and Machine Company, and the Mine and Smelter Supply Company and the Ogden-based George A. Lowe Company received contracts as the principal suppliers. Even poisoned grain, including 440,000 pounds of oats, was purchased to be used in rodent control. The order for nonperishable goods for the month of June 1933 alone was $70,000.[51]

Communities quickly recognized that the distribution of the camps' purchases was worth fighting over. The Bountiful merchants, for example, protested through one of the Democratic precinct chairmen that they were largely overlooked in the matter of providing supplies, since purchasing agents still did most of their buying in the larger city of Ogden, where the Forest Service headquarters were located.[52] Although their annoyance was understandable, there is nothing to indicate that the issuance of contracts was in response to any factors other than low bids.

Of course, in addition to the commercial prospects, many communities sought camps for the work that could potentially be carried out. Many livestock men, especially, could see the possibility of great accomplishments. In August of that first year, David P. Howells entered into correspondence with Governor Blood over the availability of camps for the public domain in the western part of the state, where grazing was of considerable significance. It was the practice to pasture most of Utah's sheep on the western ranges during the winter months, and in the absence of roads in the area, trailing was necessary to get the livestock to their wintering grounds. With trails and water holes in short supply, losses of sheep ran as high as 30 percent in transporting them from summer to winter ranges. Howells felt that when the winter snows drove the camps from the mountains the men could be put to work building roads and developing water holes. Other livestock interests lodged similar appeals, as did the county commissioners of Beaver, Tooele, Millard, and Iron counties. When this was done, however, it drew protests from the areas from which the men were transferred, attesting to the popularity of the camps even at that early stage.[53]

SETTING UP CAMPS

Just where the camps were to be located, therefore, proved to be another somewhat ticklish problem. Initially President Roosevelt insisted that he personally approve the location of every campsite, and Salmond suggested that the retardation of the early progress of the CCC may have been due to this factor.[54] The Director's Office eventually made decisions regarding location, although the establishment of additional camps could only be made by executive order. The Army and technical agencies were soon to be given permission to move camps up to twenty-five miles from their original sites without prior approval from Washington, but the Director's Office continued to maintain very close supervision of camp administration.[55] When states established their own camps, the selection of sites became a matter of state concern in coordination with the technical agency involved.[56]

CCC camps were often "wooden camps," in which semipermanent buildings were built entirely of about one hundred thousand board feet for each, usually by local carpenters working under contract. On the other hand, many of the summer-only facilities were tent camps, in which the men lived in World War I surplus canvas tents, usually six or eight men to a tent.

The wooden camps usually consisted of three or four fifty-man barracks, a kitchen and mess hall, separate offices for the military and the technical service supervisors, a shower and latrine building, garages, workshops, and, eventually, a recreation building. The wooden barracks had double bunks, while camp cots provided sleeping facilities in the more common tent camps. In the later years of the CCC program wooden buildings were constructed so that they could be easily dismantled and moved to other camps where they might be needed.

Tent camps consisted of between twenty and twenty-five tents with lumber frames and floors. The mess hall and shower and latrine facilities, however, were often constructed of wood with concrete floors; sometimes garages, offices, and other buildings were as well.

Tent camps could be erected for about $2,800, while the more permanent structures cost an additional $1,500. Water systems added nearly $1,000 more to the cost of each. Economy must have been emphasized at F-10, where the boys of Company 959 reportedly had to depend upon candles for illumination. However, they began to enjoy the luxury of a gasoline-powered generator when they moved to Orderville for the winter.[57]

The difference between tent and wooden camps was reflected in the awards offered as incentives to maintain camps that were neat in appearance as well as productive in their work. The two types of camps were judged separately to determine which camps would fly the coveted blue, red, or white pennants for the month in which they were awarded.

Officials announced camp locations almost immediately. In addition to the twenty camps authorized for the Forest Service and one for the National Park Service, there was also provision made for five camps on state land for the purpose of fighting soil erosion (see chapter 6).

Arnold R. Standing had had a long history with Dixie National Forest, where he had also served as supervisor when he told an interviewer in 1965 about his role in setting up the five state CCC camps within one and a half weeks. About June 5, 1933, he and Reed Bailey were given the assignment and moved quickly with the help of two or three clerks. The first cadres arrived about June 11, and by June 16, camps were up and running: "We hired about eighty overhead and got the campsites approved and got tools and equipment and trucks purchased and had Army approval and it just meant practically not sleeping for awhile." One month later Standing and U. S. Swartz made an inspection trip of the five camps and found all in order, with approximately two hundred enrollees from the eastern states manning the camps along with about twenty-five LEMs from Utah.[58]

In Utah, Colonel A. F. Danemiller had succeeded Colonel Butcher as commanding officer of the Fort Douglas District. In the last week of May he requested four hundred more LEMs from T. L. Holman's selection office. Within the next three days Danemiller wanted them to report to sixteen new camps scattered through fifteen counties where building was to start immediately. The camps assigned to national forests in Utah were all under construction by May 30, and 475 Utah LEMs were helping the 275 eastern boys get accustomed to life in the Rocky Mountain west. By mid-June several of the first Utah camps were occupied.

By the middle of the month the enrollment process had been largely completed locally, and men were on their way to Utah from out of state. Soon sixty-one advance detachments, each usually consisting of one officer, four sergeants, and twenty-one enrollees, were on their way from Baltimore to Idaho and Utah. Nineteen of these were scheduled for Fort Douglas.[59] Seven of the advance cadres were dropped off at various points along the Denver and Rio Grande Railway line in eastern Utah. Of the nine reaching Fort Douglas in Salt Lake City, four were immediately dispatched to camps on May 25, and the remaining five followed the next day. The Forest Service assigned local experienced men from the northern Utah counties of Cache, Box Elder, and Rich to join the new arrivals at camps in Logan and Blacksmith Fork canyons and other men from the reconditioning camp at Fort Douglas to help construct camps near Salina and Nephi in the central part of the state. Construction began by May 25, and the Civilian Conservation Corps had finally come to Utah.[60]

For much of the summer new enrollees poured in from the east as well as Utah communities as camps continued to open. Typically, enrollees were sent by train from Fort Douglas to the station nearest the camp and then carried by truck the rest of the way. In early June, for example, sixty-eight traveled by train to Marysvale, where trucks picked them up for the ride to F-18 north of Escalante. Another fifty-eight were dropped off in Cedar City and then taken by truck southeast to the Kolob Plateau in the northern part of Zion National Park, camp NP-1, also named Blue Springs.[61]

Construction of the camps themselves was accomplished quickly. As the CCC enrollees arrived from the east, a cadre of workers, either enrollees or local men, moved into each camp, and construction started immediately. One publication quoted a former enrollee's recollection of his experience in this regard:

> I'll never forget the ride up the mountain in this battered old truck. We had an old grizzled army sergeant in charge. When we got to the area, it was just thick wood. "Where's the camp?" we asked. The sarge waved his hands around the trees. "This is it. Break out the axes and chop like hell if you don't want to sleep on the ground." We chopped and built cabins and even a mess hall.[62]

Local labor officials protested to Fechner about the use of enrollees in constructing the camps, and, in fact, George A. Yager, secretary of Utah's Federation of Labor, called for Fechner's resignation if any but union members did the construction work. Fechner, of course, with his background in organized labor, hastened to assure other labor officials that there was no such intention by issuing orders that only skilled mechanics receiving prevailing pay rates were to be used in building camps where over one day's work was involved. Interestingly, a newspaper headline reference to "soldiers" is an example of the occasional confusion caused by misunderstanding of the term *enlisted men*, which, of course, meant soldiers, and the term *enrollees* for the CCC youths.[63] Another source of potential misunderstanding was eliminated by the term *junior enrollees*, which identified the young men subject to the usual age and marital requirements and distinguished them from the local experienced men to whom those restrictions did not apply and who are described in greater detail in chapter 5. This distinction, like many others, was not absolute, and in many newspaper articles the term *enrollees* could include both junior enrollees and local experienced men.

Although the state did lose nine approved state camps that first summer, Utah gained an extra 1,429 LEMs early in July to bring all the established camps up to their authorized two hundred-man strength. Again, the announcement stressed that "only men experienced in timber work, road building, fence construction and other outdoor tasks will be recruited." Once more, county quotas were established. Fort Douglas officers examined Salt Lake County's 480 and dispatched them to camps in American Fork Canyon, Soapstone, and Nebo. Weber County had a quota of 130, Utah County had a quota of 124, and the quotas declined proportionately to little Daggett County in northeastern Utah, with its quota of ten.[64]

In May 1933, the War Department advised Ninth Corps Area officers that companies should be ready to move by June 1 and that twenty-five companies should be dispatched daily throughout the Corps Area until all the men were in their assigned camps. The Ninth Corps Area received one-third of all CCC camps in the country, and most of the enrollees came out of the Second and Third Corps Areas. The War Department instructions provided for thirty-two companies of 175 men each for the Fort Douglas District. General Douglas MacArthur, Army chief of staff, directed that all camps should be operating by July 1 and warned that if camps were not prepared to accept the enrollees when they arrived, the surplus men would be directed to other Corps Areas.[65]

When orders were received in mid-July calling for more than 1,400 men to be at their assigned camps within a week, enrollment procedures moved rapidly. Enrollees from Davis County traveled to F-17 at Pine Valley in the southwest corner of the state, and the Tooele County boys moved out to the Desert Range camp near the Nevada border west of Milford. Officials first asked the counties to provide the transportation for these men, but after checking on the legality of using state relief funds with the state attorney general, Governor Blood ordered Holman to transport the men at state expense.[66]

CAMPS AND COMPANIES

Various letters were used to designate which agency was responsible for the work projects of the camp. Although the first two camps to be numbered in Utah were S-1 and S-2, the letter *F* soon replaced *S* for Forest Service camps, and *S* came to designate state camps. The designation "NP" meant that the National Park Service supervised the work.[67] The camps were numbered while still in the planning stage, and so numbers did not indicate the order of completion.

Each agency had its own system of numbering the camps, but for the most part, the Forest Service and Park Service kept their camps numbered consecutively within the state. For example, Utah's initial twenty Forest Service camps were F-1 to F-20, while the National Park Service's only camp down in Zion National Park was NP-1. Unfortunately, such ease in identification did not always prevail. The five state erosion camps were numbered SE-201, -204, -206, -211, and -212. Gaps occurring in the sequence presumably were the numbers of those of the original fourteen planned for Utah that never materialized. SE-205, however, showed up in the Second Period, along with the sequentially numbered SE-213, along with PE-214 to PE-219. In the Fourth Enrollment Period, camps PE-220 to PE-223 were added to the list.

In some states, the initial letter of the state was used as part of the designation. Wayne Hinton found this to be necessary in his *With Picks, Shovels, and Hope: The CCC and Its Legacy on the Colorado Plateau*,[68] since his book covers parts of Arizona, Utah, Colorado, and New Mexico. But even this, on occasion, could be somewhat confusing. NM-1-C, for example, was a designation for National Monument 1, located not in New Mexico as the initials might suggest but in Colorado.[69] In only one other source did I find a Utah camp so designated.

When a new company was sent to set up a camp, four or five Army enlisted men were usually assigned to assist the company commander and junior officer in getting the camp organized. Normally included among the enlisted men were a first sergeant (not to be confused with enrollees of that rank), a mess sergeant, a supply sergeant, and a cook. Captain Everett L. Upson was on leave from his post as an ROTC instructor at the University of Maryland when he brought Company 1342 from Fortress Monroe, Virginia, to set up F-3 at Kaler Hollow northwest of Vernal, Utah. As was usual practice, he was accompanied by a first sergeant, two other sergeants, and a private first class serving as cook, all from the 2nd Coast Artillery Corps. After a few weeks they returned to other duties, and the two, or occasionally three, commissioned officers were the only military personnel in camp.[70]

Among the various areas of confusion encountered by anyone reading about the Civilian Conservation Corps, the use of the word *camp* could well be one. A regular camp of approximately two hundred men would soon come to be fairly easy to understand, but what, one might ask, was the difference between a stub camp, a fly camp, a side camp, and a spike camp? The answer, very simply, is: nothing. All were various terms used to describe a temporary base located some distance from the camp to which the enrollees were permanently attached, so housed for a brief period in order to avoid long-distance travel to the work site. The phrase "spike camp" is the more common and will be used here throughout.

A spike camp might consist of as few as a half-dozen men under the direction of one of the more senior enrollees or as many as fifty or possibly even more, supervised by one or two foremen. The length of time away from the home camp would depend on a variety of factors, with completion of the project to which they were assigned being the main one in most cases, with weather, perhaps, being a close second.

These spike camps, by the way, came into use as a result of a policy decision that actually created considerable controversy between the Army and the technical agencies. The Army, of course, administered the regular camps and assumed that this authority would also extend to the spike camps, contrary to the expectations of the technical agencies. Fechner agreed with the Army, but Roosevelt, against the Army's bitterly strong opposition, came down on the side of the technical agencies, freeing them from military control providing the spike camps never housed over 10 percent of the regular company strength.[71] That 10 percent figure was occasionally violated, by the way, again, depending upon circumstances. The history of Company 1968 written for the third anniversary of the Corps states that three spike camps worked out of BR-11 in the summer of 1935—two as camp construction companies at DG-27 and SCS-3—all under the command of Army officers, a rather unusual situation.[72]

F-5, AMERICAN FORK CANYON

The first CCC unit to actually make it into a Utah camp was Company 940, organized at Fort Douglas in mid-May 1933. The fortieth camp organized in the Ninth Corps Area, it initially consisted of the first 140 junior enrollees and eighty-five local experienced men from Salt Lake County. After undergoing the conditioning routine at the Army installation, forty enrollees were sent south about forty miles to establish camp F-5 in American Fork Canyon, about twelve miles east of the central Utah

Figure 2.1. One of camp F-5's building projects still in use in American Fork Canyon.

community of American Fork. Here they began the construction of two barracks on May 17, 1933, in the area then and now known as Granite Flat.

Of the eight business firms that submitted bids to the Army quartermaster at Fort Douglas, Chipman Mercantile Company of American Fork and Morrison-Merrill Company of Salt Lake City were the two to which contracts for the materials for F-5 were awarded for $4,632.44. Although construction was completed by June 7, the formal dedication of the new camp did not take place until June 28.[73]

In a manner that became quite typical of all camp dedications, the enrollees of F-5 conducted a flag-raising ceremony at 4:30 p.m., which was followed by athletic events, a program, speeches, and a dance for state and Forest Service officials and a generous representation of the local population from the surrounding area. In the years to come it became customary to invite Governor Blood, although official duties prevented him from attending in most cases.[74] With the dedication the camp officially got under way, but it was not until July 13, however, that seventy-five LEMs arrived from Salt Lake County to fill out Company 940's complement of two hundred men.[75] Although F-5 lasted only that summer of 1933, much was accomplished, as the men built roads, bridges, and trails; poisoned rodents; constructed picnic tables for many campsites; and constructed Forest Service facilities, including the South Fork Ranger Station, which is still in use two miles downstream from the Tibble Fork Reservoir.[76]

With winter coming on, eleven camps were authorized for the Second Enrollment Period beginning October 1. Depending on their perspectives regarding the CCC, most residents of Washington County had reason to be delighted with the final locations selected, with six camps assigned within its borders: four state camps, one regular Forest Service camp (F-24) at Leeds, and NP-2 at Zion National Park. To construct the six winter camps located in the county required forty-one carloads of lumber to provide the one million board feet necessary.[77]

From having only two camps in the First Enrollment Period to having six in the Second, Washington County was a regular beehive of CCC activity. First of all Pine Valley camp F-17 secured its tent flaps for good, and Company 1335 moved south across the mountains to set up F-24 at Leeds. Although NP-1 at Blue Springs was also discontinued, Company 962 came down from the Kolob Plateau back into Zion Canyon and continued what was to be an association with the National Park Service that was to last the entire CCC tenure.

EROSION CONTROL CAMPS

The other four camps were part of the state's erosion-control program and were to spend the winter constructing flood-control barriers along the Virgin and Santa Clara river valleys.[78] From having none of these somewhat unusual camps in the summer of 1933, Washington County now had four.

The first state camp completed of Washington County's four was SE-213 at St. George on the property of Mr. Sherman C. Lamb, just off Bluff Street on what was described as the road to Santa Clara, U.S. 91. Company 961 under Captain Arthur L. Warren was an established unit, having served at F-16 in Duck Creek Period One, and was able "to hit the ground a-runnin'" when it moved in just a few days prior to the dedication of the camp on October 28, 1933. Camp SE-213 consisted of the typical layout of four barracks, an administration building, a mess hall, a laundry, a shower, and a building for housing the Forest Service personnel.[79]

It wasn't long before the camp received its principal work assignment. Engineers visited the camp in mid-November to inspect the site of the proposed flood-control dam on the Santa Clara River above the Shivwits Indian Reservation.

Just a few miles along the highway to the west of St. George lay the site of PE-215 in the small fruit-raising community of Santa Clara. Although committed to erosion control, occasionally an SE or PE camp might be utilized in another assignment, usually to enable it to carry out its primary mission but sometimes to take advantage of its presence just to do some work that needed to be done. Thus Company 1338 began constructing fences and remodeling the Cottonwood Ranger Station in the Dixie National Forest. The enrollees also built a road north from Diamond Valley to Oak Grove to intersect with the road-building work carried on by the company from Leeds camp F-24. In late December 1933, the CCC boys got down to their main erosion-control assignment: building flood-control structures on the upper Santa Clara River.[80]

THE COMING OF WINTER

Toward the end of summer several communities were seeking winter camps, and state officials were hard put to satisfy the various demands. The governor's committee discussed the possibility of establishing camps on the western rangelands, while Governor Blood planned a trip to Washington to present the state's views in person prior to September 20, the deadline for the consideration of winter camps.[81] The people of the Uinta Basin requested that two camps be stationed at Fort Duchesne barracks for the winter in order to carry on surfacing work on U.S. Highway 40. Should that be completed, they hoped that the boys might be used for further road-building to timber and recreation areas. They even suggested the construction of a stadium in Vernal as a possible project.[82]

With nearly four thousand Utah men in the First Period camps, those in charge of state enrollment sought to ensure enough camps to house them for the Second Period.[83] Many rumors circulated. Early in September one of the national forest supervisors announced that camps might be moved to the southern states. This was somewhat close to the truth, as the Corps did dispatch to the Deep South many of the out-of-state enrollees who were serving in companies from outside their own Corps Areas. Three hundred fifty-three of these individual boys, mostly from New York, went to Pensacola, Florida, and Savannah, Georgia, where they worked in winter camps. On the other hand, complete companies that were removed from the state all went to California and Nevada.[84]

In mid-September local officials finally received word that Utah would have eleven regular camps for the winter. The National Park Service kept its one camp in Zion National Park, but the camps under the Forest Service dropped from twenty-five to ten, of which eight were actually camps whose projects were determined by the state.[85] Superintendent Mark Anderson of SE-206 acknowledged that it was very "doubtful" there would be a camp in Utah County that winter. The hope that there might be a camp at the county fairgrounds in Provo would have to wait for the future.[86]

Summer work was winding down, however, as the closing of camps became more certain. Diamond Fork camp F-8 had completed the road from U.S. Highway 6 through Dry Fork to the east end of the canyon leading north toward Hobble Creek. Work on the Diamond Fork ranger station and the ongoing battle against pocket gophers had been quite successful.[87]

All twenty Forest Service camps shut down, and the companies were shifted to lower latitudes and elevations for the winter and were also transferred to other agencies. Of those twenty camps, eleven never opened again. The Forest Service erected new camps at Leeds and Richfield, designated F-24 and F-25, respectively, and prepared to administer the eight state camps to work on the erosion-control projects noted above.

Of course, no one knew whether all of the men would reenroll, but it appeared likely that most of them would. The president himself issued an appeal that the enrollees find work if possible so that a vacancy might permit an unemployed boy to take his place in the Corps. However, if enrollees could not honestly find work, officials encouraged them to reenroll for another six-month period.[88]

In addition to enrollees, camp foremen suffered from the cutback of camps. When an enrollee from SE-213 requested appointment as a foreman in another camp, he was reminded that the cutback would necessitate laying off about 60 percent of the foremen then serving.[89]

The misgivings expressed at the inauguration of the CCC had largely disappeared by October 1933, when the Second Enrollment Period began. Roosevelt was extremely pleased with the results. The *Deseret News*, although agreeing that it was really too early to evaluate, pointed out on August 25 the good already being done to the public lands, to the national awareness, and to the young men themselves. Even the *Salt Lake*

Tribune spoke more favorably of the project and referred to it as a "constructive endeavor."[90]

The reaction of professional foresters indicated their approval. Government officials and laymen joined in voicing their support. Officials of Wasatch and Cache national forests were described as having "fully endorsed the New Deal policy of conserving human beings as well as resources, and most Forest officers welcomed the CCC enrollees because of the program's human elements as well as for the fact that ten years' improvement plans could be fulfilled in a single year."[91] Max Schlegel of F-2 near Hyrum spoke for many hundreds of young men when he compared his attitude at the end of the period with what he had felt when he first heard of the program:

> Oh, yes, I was pessimistic just like a lot of other fellows, at that time down in the dumps. But things are different now. I've been given a chance to reestablish normal relations with life, to recreate faith in the future as well as...to send money home to help those who helped me and...shared what little they had.[92]

There was still the occasional raising of dissident voices, however. One letter to an editor complained that there seemed to be little discipline in the camps and that men apparently could come in from "their wild parties any time of night and in any condition of sobriety."[93] But for every letter of complaint there were many of praise. One of the most loyal supporters of the program was conservationist J. H. Paul, who defended the CCC at every opportunity. In response to a protest over the cost of overhead, he cited the benefits of the program as providing safety from floods and noted that the work done in erosion control, "perpetual supplies" of grass and timber, hydroelectric development, recreation, reforestation, scientific opportunities, and "cultivation of the national esteem" was most beneficial. He commented on the good done to the men involved by concluding that the forests "tend to make man patriotic, religious, esthetic, meditative, romantic, heroic."[94] When one enrollee complained in the *Deseret News* about the pay he was chastised by another reader, "Forget the pay, kid, make the most of the picnic and enjoy it; it's the best thing ever happened to you."[95]

Generally, the boys were pleased with the opportunity. The people of the state were grateful for the program. Governor Blood was satisfied with the camps and declared, "They have been successful both from the standpoint of human service for needy men and accomplishing useful results." At the October conference of the Church of Jesus Christ of Latter-day Saints, Elder Richard L. Evans encouraged the members of Utah's principal church to support the programs of the federal government.[96] It seemed that these sentiments were nearly unanimous.

The accomplishments of the CCC during that first summer were only a humble beginning, but Utahns were generally pleased at what had been done. In addition to the fences, trails, and bridges that had been constructed; in addition to the acres of land that had been replanted, terraced, or reseeded; and in addition to the fire suppression and rescue work that had been carried out by CCC crews, their presence permitted direct financial benefits. Utah merchants profited from government contracts for lumber, equipment, and foodstuffs. More than $125,000 a month was pumped into the state's economy through the wages of the CCC personnel alone. That first fiscal year of 1933–34, the Civilian Conservation Corps was responsible for more than $4.7 million being spent in Utah, more than any of the other federal programs dedicated to agriculture, public works, or just relief in general.[97]

The eagerness of the youths to enter the CCC program is evidenced by the facts of enlistment as previously cited. An enrollee at the Brigham City camp reported his feelings as follows:

> Perhaps I'm no better off than I was before... but somehow I feel different. I haven't a care or worry in the world. I'm earning my way. I'm not on charity, which is something that scared me from the first. I'm giving value received for what I get. Perhaps I may not be getting anywhere, but I certainly feel as if I were on the way.[98]

Even before the summer was over the original fears concerning the Corps had largely been put to rest. The *Deseret News* editorialized in a positive vein that "good reports" were coming out of the 1,428 camps across the country and that the young enrollees were "earning their keep in improving the nation's forests by building roads and bridges, clearing underbrush, protecting the forests against fire and pests and performing other useful tasks."[99]

Forest officials were equally pleased. Ashley National Forest Supervisor James O. Stewart described the coming of the CCC as "like a bolt of lightning out of a clear sky," leading "to the year of greatest activity in [Ashley National Forest] history."[100]

By the end of the First Period the new winter camps were humming; the season's work had been planned and was even then under way; and the specter of winter suffering had been eliminated for many Utah families. Down in Ferron the night of the farewell dance at the end of the First Period there was, no doubt, considerable reflection by those present: townspeople, departing enrollees and their town girlfriends, and those fellows staying on for another period. Many experiences had been gained; many men had found work so that their families could be fed; much work had been accomplished. To be sure, final conclusions were yet to be drawn, but there existed hope in the fact that the Civilian Conservation Corps was now a booming organization. The farewell dance continued; so did the CCC. Things were looking up in the Beehive State as well as the rest of the nation.

And four years later the country showed its overwhelming approval of Roosevelt's New Deal, with the CCC as the most highly popular of the horde of alphabetical agencies that had been created. In 1936 Utah joined forty-five other states in providing Roosevelt a landslide victory over his Republican challenger, Alfred Landon of Kansas.

CHAPTER 3

Administration of the Program

We were interviewed by the company commander when we arrived in Pleasant Grove, and he made the choice of the men he wanted in the key positions such as top sergeant, supply sergeant, company clerk, mess sergeant, canteen clerk and mail orderly; this group of Leaders ran the camp: fed them, clothed them, and supplied most of their needs.

—A. F. Fischio, leader, camp F-43

Director Robert Fechner and the CCC-focused interdepartmental Advisory Council had the challenging task of coordinating the activities of the four cabinet-level departments—Labor, War, Agriculture, and Interior. The Labor Department had the immediate task of getting the unemployed youth of America signed up for the Civilian Conservation Corps in the first place. The Army, under the War Department, was regarded as the only existing government entity capable of getting such a large body of young men organized as the president wished and was assigned the huge responsibility of examining, clothing, housing, transporting, and feeding the enrollees; in fact, the Army supervised every facet of the enrollees' existence except the actual work projects for which the Corps is largely remembered today—if at all.

The Army's Quartermaster Corps provided food, clothing, and transportation and did most of the purchasing in connection with keeping the camps operating. The Finance Office handled the payrolls for the Corps and saw to it that from the enrollee's monthly pay of $30.00, $25.00 was sent home to his family or, if he was an orphan, deposited into his account to be returned to him upon his discharge.

The actual work projects of the young men, however, were supervised by the technical agencies of either the Department of Agriculture or the

Department of the Interior. Here the Army was also back in the picture because it also disbursed funds to the technical agencies for their own CCC personnel and for purchasing equipment to be used in the work projects that have so benefited our country.[1] The Medical Corps, Adjutant General, Signal Corps, and other Army departments carried out other appropriate responsibilities.

The detail of Army supervision within the camps can be noted in a sixteen-page memo issued to new enrollees at Fort Douglas spelling out instructions for the appearance of enrollees, camps, and barracks both inside and out. Also included were assignments for the men should a fire break out in camp, such as "Men in bunks #15 to 24, barracks 3, will proceed to the administration building and insure its protection" and "Men in bunks #37 to 52, barracks 5 will form fire line and bucket brigade."[2]

FORT DOUGLAS DISTRICT, NINTH CORPS AREA

The requirements of the states and the technical agencies were chief in determining camp locations, but they needed the approval of the Army through the headquarters of the nine Corps Areas into which the country was divided (see Appendix A).[3] In Salt Lake City, the Fort Douglas District of the Ninth Corps Area handled the CCC for the state of Utah and parts of Wyoming, Arizona, and Nevada. Very little stayed fixed in the CCC, however, and as noted previously, later some camps in northern Utah were transferred to a new Pocatello District in Idaho.[4]

The Army also had the responsibility of creating the CCC companies, the basic unit of the organization. Originally the camps had a commanding officer, or CO, usually an Army captain but sometimes a lieutenant or even a major. Occasionally a camp might have an officer from the Navy or Marines as a CO. Early in the program, for example, three Marine captains and a first lieutenant were dispatched from San Diego to Fort Douglas to help staff the district.[5] A Marine Corps officer commanded the Black's Fork camp the first year of the program, and Lt. Commander Dow H. Casto of the Navy commanded Company 957 in Logan camp F-1. Lt. George L. Edman of the Naval Reserve commanded at least five camps between 1938 and 1940.[6] Later in the program when officials were attempting to further demilitarize the Corps, the title was changed to "camp commander."

Each company also had a junior officer, sometimes designated as such and other times referred to as the adjutant, welfare officer, mess officer, or later in the program, subaltern. Some camps also had a military doctor on staff, but many camps instead utilized civilian doctors from nearby communities who served under contract. In the later years of the program when military doctors were more apt to be recalled to active duty, civilian contract physicians became the norm. In the summer of 1940, for example, twenty-eight of Utah's thirty-four camps utilized contract physicians, while only four had military doctors.[7] In Tremonton, Dr. George Ficklin, just out of medical school, was happy to be hired to serve Company 736 at SCS-9 for $125 a month. During his daily sick call he treated mostly bruises, colds, sore throats, and minor injuries, but the employment was enough to keep him in his hometown.[8]

In the CCC, the Army district headquarters was a vital hub in the organization. As happened throughout the country, it was here at Fort Douglas, one of the six military bases in the Ninth Corps Area to house a CCC district, where the new enrollees recruited from within the district would be processed before receiving their camp assignments. Companies sent into Utah from out of state would usually also be routed through Fort Douglas, although they were often sent directly to their assigned camps. At either district or Corps headquarters, Army medical personnel conducted physicals and administered the necessary vaccinations, while the new enrollees went through a physical conditioning program. As district headquarters Fort Douglas was the storehouse from which all the camps in the district received supplies and equipment, except, of course, for those materials that were purchased locally.

THE ARMY AND THE CCC

In addition to enrollees, veterans, Indians, and LEMs, still others were anxiously attempting to find places in the Corps. When the program began in 1933 three Army officers were to be assigned to each of the twenty-six camps in Utah. Three hundred applications arrived for the seventy-odd positions available.[9] Initially, the Army assigned many regular officers to CCC duty, but, as rapidly as possible, unemployed Reserve officers were called into active duty for service in the camps.

The figures released by Fort Douglas in July 1933 indicate that there were fifty-eight Regular officers and eleven Reserve officers, including two who were assigned as assistants to the chaplain. Although nothing was said to indicate otherwise, there appears to have been no pattern to the selection, as while most camps had three officers assigned, some camps had only two and a few even had four.[10]

The role of the Army underwent considerable transformation from that originally planned. In congressional hearings, Chief of Staff Douglas MacArthur emphasized that the Army's participation would be limited to looking after the men immediately after enrollment, conditioning and clothing them, and transporting them to their forest camps, where they would come under the supervision of the Department of Agriculture.[11] On April 12, 1933, a *Deseret News* story illustrated the confusion then rampant concerning the Army's position. In a statement about as completely incorrect as it could possibly be, the secretary of the Utah State Federation of Labor, George A. Yager, announced that military control had been abolished and MacArthur had been "scrapped" as head of the project with the naming of labor official Robert Fechner as director. Fechner's comment at this time is also quite interesting in view of future developments:

> The project is a temporary expedient and not to be confused with a public work program. As rapidly as other jobs are found for the men the reforestation projects will be abandoned. The men will be housed in camps not under military control; with the exception of the preliminary work of getting the men to the forest camps, the Army is to have nothing to do with the project.[12]

Although this, ironically, was in keeping with the role as seen by the Army itself, other quarters feared that the Army had plans for enlarging its degree of participation. When the Army's part in the operation increased it was over the mild protests of the War Department and based on the stark realization that the Army was the only agency with the physical capability of performing the necessary task of actually administering the camps.[13]

The Army's Ninth Corps Area, which included Utah, soon processed more CCC men daily than the Army and Navy combined had done in World War I recruiting days.[14] On a visit to Fort Douglas, Colonel Edwin S. Hartshorn, Ninth Corps Area chief of staff, asked for patience from the people of Utah. He explained that the Army was making every effort to get the men into the camps as quickly as possible but that it would be impossible to send them before the camps were ready. In the meantime the 225 men already at Fort Douglas would be cared for and given something to do until camps were ready for them.[15]

The military personnel rotated frequently, although some officers stayed in the state for several years. Assignments were made irrespective of the technical agencies; an officer might command a company in a Forest Service camp one period and be assigned to a Division of Grazing camp the period following.

The CO had a great amount of control in the camps, to be sure, but his rule was not absolute. CCC regulations closely governed his actions, and there were usually enough "barracks lawyers" in each camp to see to their adherence. Army inspectors from Fort Douglas visited each camp in the district at least twice a month, and there were occasional visits from Ninth Corps Area personnel as well. One camp newspaper tells of the visit of the "enrollees' friend," James C. Reddock, special investigator operating out of the Director's Office in Washington. His assignment was to spend his entire time touring camps in the west, looking for ways to improve conditions for the men, and to report any noticeable deficiencies back to the director.[16]

The rapid mobilization of the Civilian Conservation Corps required the utilization of nearly half of the commissioned officers then in the Regular Army. Officers on duty with ROTC detachments and Reserve officers were also called up to man camps as necessary. When the program first got started in the summer of 1933, Utah had fifty-eight officers from the Regular Army and only eleven from the ranks of the Reserves. By 1935, however, Reserves filled nearly all the positions, as Regular officers returned to active duty.[17]

RESERVISTS AND REGULARS

Some officers were ably suited to command men; others were not. Reserve officers from all branches of the military were given the opportunity of service in the CCC, and most regarded it as an opportunity; others accepted the assignment grudgingly. Many officers felt that the camps manned by Utah enrollees were the easiest to handle and that those from the Second Corps Area were the most difficult.[18] Many military men agreed with a local resident who felt that most of the hoodlums of New

York and New Jersey had been rounded up off the streets and shipped west to the CCC camps.

Reserve officers often came directly from civilian life with very little experience in commanding men or carrying out military duties. One ex-foreman described his camp's adjutant as a "shoe salesman from Salt Lake City who didn't know 'straight up' about duty rosters, morning reports, etc." Some found it difficult to operate in a basically civilian environment in which they not only were responsible for more than two hundred young men but also were expected to exercise a limited authority over the men of the technical agency assigned to the camp. This authority had to be administered in a persuasive manner because the men, after all, were civilians and exempt from most of the disciplinary measures suitable for a strictly military situation.

Whether Regular Army officers or Reserve officers were the more competent depends on who was being asked. Raymond W. Cassell was a Reserve second lieutenant when he was assigned to CCC duty early in 1935, where he served as mess officer, supply officer, exchange officer, and even educational officer at one time or another. He was finally appointed commanding officer, even before being promoted to first lieutenant. In 1937 he arrived at NP-2 in Utah and by late in the year was CO of Company 736 at Willard camp SCS-4, where he served for two years. His opinion was that Regular officers were not too keen on CCC duty, as it was "too demanding," and that he and his fellow Reserve officers generally appreciated the opportunity and usually did a better job.

Glen Carlson, on the other hand, felt just the opposite. He served three years in the CCC as an LEM, the first two as a clerk and the last as a senior foreman. In both positions he had close interaction with officers and felt that those from the Regular Army were more skilled in handling men than were those from the Reserve ranks.

Because the Army had responsibility for the enrollees at all times except for the daily seven or eight hours the men were actually working, cooperation between the Army and the technical agency was essential from the very beginning. Much of the time the arrangement worked well, but there were occasional problems.

Graduate student Thora Bergeson taught in the CCC educational program and for her master's thesis surveyed and analyzed the enrollees at four camps in a sociological study of the CCC in central Utah. She compared companies from different parts of the country: Company 940 at camp F-48 in Bountiful, Company 736 at SCS-4 in Willard, Company 536 at SP-2 in Farmington Bay, and Company 3240 at F-38, the Big Cottonwood camp east of Murray. Bergeson commented on the great differences between two of the four camps she observed. In one, there was a "home-like atmosphere" in which the Army and technical staff worked together harmoniously, the wives of the officers and foremen had free run of the camp, the camp commander's wife taught music to the enrollees, and his children ran freely, "inspiring the young men to gentleness and consideration." The other camp—unfortunately unidentified—provided a sharp contrast, for here, as Bergeson noted,

> the entire Army staff and a large portion of the enrollees went on a week's "binge" and left the rest of the camp to run itself.... In the latter camp sex talk and unwholesome practices run ruit [*sic*]. The fact that girls of the town had spent entire nights in camps was known and not disapproved by the officers.[19]

Because of her thorough study of the four camps, Bergeson formed some interesting opinions on the relationship between the Army and the technical agencies. Admittedly her sampling was too small to provide a very accurate analysis of the entire situation, but her views do reflect those held by many, both from the Army and civilian perspectives.

For one thing, Bergeson felt that the duality of leadership was a decided "weakness" and that having the groups share responsibility "resembled the mixing of oil and water." Her claims that "the Army is not entirely in sympathy with the technical staff and the technical staff thoroughly dislikes Army methods" and also that "the camp is often demoralized because of the conflict between the two controlling groups" may be somewhat exaggerated, but, again, one must recognize the limitation of her sampling.[20]

This matter of dual leadership responsibility caused serious difficulties in only a few instances, however, and three decades later most former officers and technical personnel recalled their CCC days as a time of almost uninterrupted harmony between the two. Friction did arise, of course, but it was seldom apparent.

T. Carl Haycock, a ranger with the U.S. Forest Service with many years' association with the CCC, wrote me on May 4, 1968, that the "Army had too much responsibility" and in many cases was "resentful" of the various technical agencies. His most damning indictment was that the Army "wanted to pamper [the] boys."[21]

In other cases, views changed with the passage of time. In 1968 I interviewed J. Whitney Floyd, former dean of the College of Natural Resources of Utah State University and a Utah State forester. Floyd worked with the CCC for two years as a "forest technician," a Forest Service employee who laid out work for the CCC. It was his opinion that during the CCC days most Forest Service personnel objected to Army control and felt that the Army was too conscious of regulations, reports, hours, and so on, whereas the Forest Service men were more interested in getting the work done. Although the Army discipline often bothered the Forest Service personnel, Floyd felt at the time of the interview that much of the criticism by the latter was unjustified and that it was necessary to have the Army "ride herd" on the CCC program just the way it did. Speaking to the public in 1937, Regional Forester Rutledge praised the Army, "When leadership in lieu of discipline was needed, the officers supplied it, a remarkable job was done for which they deserve unstinting praise." One camp newspaper expressed the view, widely held, that the Army and Forest Service worked well together.[22]

Although the Army officers were responsible for maintaining discipline in the camps, they were governed by regulations providing for maximum consideration of the young men away from home in new surroundings. Compared with those imposed for similar violations in military service, the penalties were quite light and might "include admonition, suspension of privileges, substitution of specified camp duties instead of regular work for a week's time, or deduction of cash allowances not exceeding three days per month, or, in extreme cases, discharge from the camp."[23] Seldom was harsh discipline required; most of the problems were limited to occasional thefts in camp or fights in town. Only occasionally did the CO find it necessary to discharge anyone.[24]

As previously cited, enrollees found guilty of civil crimes were usually given dishonorable discharges and sent home. Desertion, continuous misconduct, and "infraction of the rules" were other offenses for which discharge was suggested.[25] One former camp commander recalled discharging the "camp bully" when other methods of control proved fruitless. When six enrollees of F-43 decided that they didn't want to work, they were given administrative discharges and were on their way home within twenty-four hours.[26] Action such as this prompted the following entry in an annual report: "The small minority of boys who, in earlier periods, joined the CCC with no intention of exchanging hard work for their pay and allowances, has practically disappeared because it is now generally understood that the boys must, as the enrollees say, 'put out or get out.'"[27] In many cases, the boys themselves handled the discipline, either somewhat formally, through "kangaroo courts" that were established with the approval of the officers, or by bringing group pressure to bear upon actual or potential miscreants.[28]

The commanding officer of BR-11 warned his CCC boys of another technique of control. At the end of an enrollment period some might wish to reenroll but, instead, would receive written notice that they were not "worthy of enrollment." They received an honorable discharge under such circumstances but received no recommendations on their ability or conduct and were never again permitted to reenroll.[29]

One observer of the period who felt that the Army should get out of the CCC program admitted, "But on the whole, the disciplinary problem has been admirably handled, to the great credit of the Army and the Reserve officers."[30] This sentiment was echoed by a two-and-a-half-year veteran from Ohio who stated, "The company commanders were for the most part tough, competent, and forceful characters who instilled discipline and leadership in their men."[31]

It was in a history of Company 1256 written in 1939 that the writer determined the blame for the problems that plagued the infant organization. The writer quite deftly passed the buck to the Army, before concluding that when the Army overcame its poor beginnings, the company wasn't so bad after all:

> Its existence is proff [*sic*] that the national organization has triumphed over the waste, mismanagement, and inefficiency which were the result of a lack of training personnel in the gigantic problems of housing, feeding, and clothing the members of the new conservation movement. There had been no occasion to cope with these problems previously and their weight was staggering. The administration was tenderly placed in the uneager hands of the U.S. Army and its Reserves. It is known that this allocation of responsibility was justified—the Army soon had things running smoothly and the CCC was ready to do the work of

conserving the potentialities of the youth of America as well as the resources of the country.

Lieutenant George Edman, CO of Company 1968 of BR-11 and later BR-91, had a regular column entitled "Notes from the C.O." in the camp newspaper. He kept the enrollees informed of regulations and constantly encouraged them to avoid violations by talking to him before doing anything foolhardy.[32] Lieutenant Oren Nelson told his company that those enrollees seen throwing bones, sticks, or papers on the ground would receive fifteen minutes extra duty and gave the enrollees the same privilege in regard to the officers and foremen. If an enrollee observed any camp official littering, he was permitted to put the offender to work "with no prejudice held."[33]

With the military in charge of the companies for all but working hours, even when the men returned to noonday lunch, there was no question about who really ran the program. Evans J. Phillips, living in Roosevelt, Utah, in 1968, had served as educational adviser under thirty-five different Army officers over a period of six years in five camps and had an interesting perspective on the issue. He wrote me on May 18 of that year that since military personnel rotated fairly frequently, camp superintendents and foremen often built up loyal followings who were inclined to favor them more than their Army officers.

In cases where conflict between the two groups did erupt, camps were seriously demoralized. In most cases the morale and well-being of the camps were quite good, depending on the capabilities of the two or three Army officers at the camp, the technical staff, and the civilian educational adviser. Quite typical were remarks in period reports such as one in which an individual commented that the good relations between the Army, enrollees, and work agencies "are nothing short of unusual."[34]

The Army assigned companies from the different Corps Areas to the various camps. Once a camp was established as host to, say, a Fifth Corps Area company, all replacements generally came from the Fifth Corps Area, although occasionally Utah enrollees—especially LEMs—would fill the ranks. Every Corps Area except the First had companies in Utah, although the Sixth and the Eighth had less than a half dozen apiece and these all came in after 1939. Actually, there were more companies from the Fifth Corps Area serving in Utah than there were companies from the Ninth. Overall, the number of enrollees serving in Utah was almost equally divided between Utah young men and those from outside the state.[35] In 1937 there were 1,630 Kentuckians in the Fort Douglas District, 1,371 men from Utah, and 1,339 from Ohio. New York, Missouri, Minnesota, and North Dakota also had large contingents.[36] An official report of September 30, 1940, indicates that in September 1940 there were 948 enrollees from Ohio and 658 from Utah, with Alabama (490), South Carolina (474), Georgia (428), and New York (366) next in order.[37]

To illustrate that considerable variation existed in camps, companies, Corps Areas, and even districts, that same report could be cited to offer some supporting statistics. DG-35 at Milford hosted the undermanned Company 1508, out of the Fifth Corps Area. Indeed, of the sixty-six enrollees then in the company, sixty-two were from the four states in the Fifth Corps Area, with Ohio having contributed forty-five of them. The unusual thing is that the other four enrollees in the company were one each from Georgia and Louisiana of the Fourth Corps Area and Arkansas and Missouri of the Seventh Corps Area. Neither company newspapers nor official records suggest why this occurred; my guess is that these four may have been leaders or assistant leaders persuaded to stay behind when their original companies moved on from their earlier stays at DG-35. Company 1508, incidentally, was one of only five of the thirty-four companies then in the state that did not have a single enrollee from Utah. Companies 958, 962, and 1968, on the other hand, consisted entirely of Utah enrollees, while Company 940 with one Missourian and Company 969 with three from the Fourth Corps Area came very close to making that pristine list.

Seldom were companies assigned to a particular agency on a permanent basis. For the most part a CCC company could be assigned one enrollment period to the camp of an agency under the Department of Agriculture, say, the U.S. Forest Service, and then find itself the next period under the Division of Grazing of the Department of the Interior. In addition to the movement of companies, camps were also subject to change, although not quite to the extent of the companies. For example, camp F-43 in Pleasant Grove under Agriculture's Forest Service closed down in May 1938 at the end of Period Ten and was empty for three enrollment periods before reopening in October 1939, as BR-91, a Bureau of Reclamation camp under the Department of the Interior.

MILITARY TRAINING

When the Civilian Conservation Corps began Adolf Hitler was coming to power in Germany and Japan was embarked on creating the Greater East Asia Co-prosperity Sphere. Isolationism was strong in the United States, however, and a politically astute Roosevelt was sensitive and cautious. He wanted his program to succeed and realized that the pursuit of military training would considerably raise the level of controversy. Still, considerable apprehension mounted over the issue of militarism in the CCC. The topic was brought up periodically right from the formation of the program.[38]

The president, the Army, and the Corps itself had consistently tried to convince the skeptics in the country that the organization did not constitute a covert attempt to form a military auxiliary. One publication in 1939 stated,

> It should be emphasized that the CCC's is not in any respect a military project.... A man does not enlist in the Army when he enrolls. The CCC enrollee remains a civilian throughout his entire term of service; he receives no military instruction nor does he become liable to military law.[39]

CCC boys generally practiced no military drills, and marching in formation was seen only occasionally—and then usually only in some camps later in the program. The May 24, 1935, issue of *Yell-A-Gram*, camp newspaper of Company 958, then at F-30, announced "drill regulations" that had come down in a memo from headquarters a few days before. The men were to stand in formation before all meals—presumably outside—and then stand at attention before sitting at each meal, with an orderly at each table to see that the instructions were carried out. Orders were given for a standing inspection to be held weekly in the tents under the direction of the leaders and assistant leaders. On the other hand, this may not have been an example of military training at all but merely of what might have been considered a commonsense approach to the handling of nearly two hundred young men away from home for the first time.

Roosevelt's insistence that the CCC avoid any semblance of militarism called for the boys to "enroll" rather than "enlist." There were occasional salutes given and some use of the title "Sir," but this "seems to be more out of genuine respect for the officer than 'militarism.'"[40] It is true that living together in barracks, learning to take orders, and standing in line for various purposes constituted training that assisted the enrollees who later did enter the military, but to describe these functions as militarism is a strain on reason.

Retired Air Force Colonel Raymond Cassell conceded, however, that militarism might have been perceived by some. Roll call at morning formation, chow call in which enrollees in some camps would march to the mess hall in cadence, response to bugle calls, and standing "Retreat" when the flag was lowered at the end of the day bothered some people, although I found no evidence that this was distasteful to the enrollees.

This last practice, the lowering of the flag, was fairly common. Around five o'clock, many of the camps stood "Retreat" as the flag was lowered, which was the closest concession to militarism until quite late in the entire program. Director McEntee described the ritual as follows:

> It is a formation which makes men feel good. It seems to symbolize unity among them. During the moments while they stand at attention, they know that they are more than individuals; they are a part of that camp; they are a part of a big organization working to preserve the health and wealth of America; they are citizens of the United States.[41]

Although whistles were usually used, some camps were fortunate enough to have buglers, often enrollees who had played the trumpet in high school bands. Ken Haslam was told by his first sergeant at Orderville camp PE-218 that he was to become the company bugler. Haslam took notes as the senior enrollee whistled the various bugle calls and was soon able to fulfill his new assignment. Some camps, therefore, were able to end the day to the haunting melody of "Taps."[42]

The issue continued, however, as it had almost from the very beginning. The program was less than a year old when Assistant Secretary of War Harry H. Woodring stated outright that "I believe that this activity should be expanded and put under the control of the Army." As historian Arthur Schlesinger Jr. has pointed out, Woodring's wish to organize CCC enrollees, World War I veterans, and many of those on relief into "economic storm troops" was "a singularly unfortunate phrase for a nation which was just beginning to dislike Hitler." Although the White House reprimanded Woodring, the Army didn't back off.[43]

In February 1935, three years after his receipt of severe criticism for the way he followed President Hoover's orders in dispatching the "Bonus Army," General Douglas MacArthur again stoked the fires of militarism in the CCC. Shortly before leaving to assume his position of military adviser in the Philippines, he proposed that enrollees be permitted to enlist in the Army Reserves for one dollar a month and at the end of their CCC service be called up for two months of training. This mustered considerable support among veterans' organizations and many members of Congress. In another editorial, the *Salt Lake Tribune* correctly theorized that should the United States become involved in warfare, CCC youths could well become the "nucleus" of an American military force and the two months suggested by MacArthur could well provide some valuable military training.[44]

Echoing the sentiments of MacArthur, Congressman J. J. McSwain, chairman of the House Military Affairs Committee, introduced H.R. 5592, providing for two months of "intensive military training" and the designation of the CCC as an auxiliary reserve force. Opinions in Utah varied over the issue. Dean Milton Bennion of the School of Education of the University of Utah added his name to those of Harry Emerson Fosdick, Roger Baldwin, John Dewey, Oswald Garrison Villard, and others of the 156 educators, clergymen, and publicists who petitioned Roosevelt in protest of the resolution. During the squabble over the proposal the group refuted one of the explanations that had been offered for implementing any military training. In what has to be one of the more telling examples of the shortsightedness of the strong isolationist thinking of the time, this rebuttal was offered: "We fail to comprehend any impending danger, external or domestic, which might be cited to justify this or any other in our military forces at this time."[45]

The *Salt Lake Tribune*, on the other hand, felt that the suggestion had merit and editorialized concerning the motivation of the sponsors of the anti-MacArthur petition. What was their concern since there was no military training going on at the present time? The *Tribune* averred that its own suspicion was based on the fact that the names of the petitioners were on file with the "Committee on Militarism in Education," which, according to a recently published directory, claimed that "this committee is the supporting organization of the communist-organized and controlled 'U.S. Congress Against War.'"[46]

Robert Fechner, Selection Director W. Frank Persons, and the general public, however, vigorously opposed the bill, which died in committee in April 1935.[47] The issue itself, however, did not disappear and was constantly being revitalized. In 1937 the *Tribune* again scolded those who claimed that the discipline administered by the Army constituted military training and insisted that the Army could also teach an "orderly way" of improving one's appearance, pride in oneself, efficiency, and "stirring the individual out of inertia into mental alertness."[48] When war threatened Europe in 1938 and 1939, the clamor for increased quasi-military activity heightened. A Gallup poll of August 1938 indicated that 75 percent of those polled favored the idea of having military training in the camps. CCC officials continued to resist, although Fechner affirmed that the CCC unintentionally, yet by its very nature, prepared men for military life.[49] The *Provo Sunday Herald* disagreed with militarization and described the idea of training only a certain class of young men as "undemocratic" and "a grave mistake" that would disrupt the valuable work program in which the CCC was rightfully engaged.[50]

The CCC vigorously attempted to maintain its avowed purpose of being a *Civilian* Conservation Corps. By now the Army would have been quite happy to be rid of its CCC participation, and thus contention between Roosevelt, Congress, the Army, and the CCC increased considerably. Going against Roosevelt's wishes, Congress granted disability benefits to Reserve officers on CCC duty, after which Roosevelt retaliated by directing the secretary of war to begin on July 1 to replace Reserve officers with civilians due to "the essential civil, rather than military character" of the Corps. However, as Salmond points out, "the change was more apparent than real," as the civilians appointed were to be taken from the rolls of Reserve officers of the Army and Navy. The directive came down that Reserve officers would "revert to the status of civilian employees" by December 31.[51]

The military titles were dropped: the "company commander" replaced the "commanding officer," and the "junior officer" gave way to the "subaltern." The full-time Reserve Army chaplains reverted to civilian status at the same time.[52] There was little actual change, however. The officers wore CCC uniforms instead of Army uniforms, and they were addressed as "mister," but there were few changes in personnel and no changes in the authority and responsibility of the positions.

Still, with each passing month in 1939 the CCC demonstrated greater involvement in preparedness for national defense. The emphasis still centered on noncombatant activities, but the men in the camps became more aware of increased concern regarding the relationship between their daily activities and possible military assignments. The director's report of 1940 indicated this awareness on the national level: "The Corps is ready for rapid expansion if the need arises. . . . The Corps has hastened and is hastening the day when this country will be adequately prepared for any aggressor or combination of aggressors." As the fiscal year ended the Corps was emphasizing every phase of its work and training program that contributed to national defense.[53]

Agitation continued until General George C. Marshall, Army chief of staff and a former CCC company commander, stated that the Army maintained no interest in providing military training for the enrollees, conceding, however, that there might be noncombatant work in which the Corps could be used to good advantage. Shortly thereafter, Senator James F. Byrnes of South Carolina introduced an amendment to a relief appropriation measure that enabled the CCC to provide noncombatant training, that is, educational courses in areas helpful to the Army.[54]

The War Department issued instructions to commanders of CCC districts in a letter entitled "Training for National Defense in Civilian Conservation Corps Camps." It directed officers to provide "intensive training for service operations of direct military value," including courses leading to specialization in motor vehicle operation, mechanics, construction, cooking and baking, clerical work, radio, photography, telephone, first aid, mess management, mapping and map reading, military hygiene, blueprint reading, concrete work, forging and blacksmithing, machine shop practice, and welding.[55]

Still, James M. McEntee, as the relatively new director, felt it necessary to remind the country that the CCC was not becoming part of the military establishment just because the enrollees were going to begin training in marching according to Army infantry drill regulations. The purpose was merely to help in the physical training program of the Corps and to "spruce these kids up."[56]

McEntee pointed out that the CCC had trained more than 20,000 cooks and bakers since the program began and every year nine thousand enrollees received practical training in automotive mechanics and 72,000 were trained in the operation of heavy automotive equipment in "the largest fleet of mechanized equipment in the U.S."[57] He felt that the training of skilled mechanics, welders, electricians, and others constituted a major contribution to the preparedness program and observed that over 70 percent of the CCC tasks were of the same type performed by combat engineers.[58]

PERSONNEL

Camp Superintendent

Although the Forest Service, along with the other technical agencies, had the enrollees for no more than one-third of the day, it was the camp superintendent who was responsible for overseeing the work for which the CCC is remembered today. On him rested the responsibility for that for which the Corps was organized. His status remained constant throughout the program. These men, on whom the success of the work program depended so much, were selected for their positions largely as a result of political influence, especially in the early days of the program. It was fortunate that under this system so many capable men were to be found. What was unfortunate was that many equally capable men were no doubt overlooked. Some men wrote directly to Governor Blood, who in turn recommended them to Regional Forester Rutledge or someone else in a position to secure their employment. The proper procedure, however, for securing a supervisory position was for the applicant to secure the endorsement of the chairman of the Democratic Party in the county where he lived and forward it to one of the Utah congressmen in Washington. His name was then placed on what was called the "Friant list," from which the appropriate technical agency made its selection for the various positions.[59] Other than the commanding officer or company commander—depending on the time frame—the superintendent was the most important figure in camp.

Foremen

The superintendent's right-hand men were the foremen, with between six and twelve usually assigned to each camp to more closely direct the work of the enrollees. Each foreman usually had a crew assigned to a specific type of work assignment, that is, one crew for road construction, another for rodent control, still another for reforestation, and so on. As a result, most camps pursued many different types of projects at the same time. Foremen were paid $1,680 a year, or $1,860 if they were assigned more technical work such as supervising engineering activities. At first, the technical agencies close to the project made the appointment, but before long these selections became subject to Washington approval as well. Foremen usually had a regular crew with whom they worked, often assisted by one or two leaders or assistant leaders from among the enrollees. In 1940 the company newspaper of Moab camp SCS-6 identified five different foremen, each with one or two enrollee assistants. Occasionally a foreman's crew would be split up, with each assistant taking a group for a particular project. For a camp under the Soil Conservation Service, it is no surprise to find five foremen working on the general category of erosion control, although different crews were working on dams, rock work, or cutting trees. Of course other assignments came up from time to time, as evidenced by one crew engaged in grading the hospital grounds in Moab.[60]

Foremen also were generally looked upon with considerable favor by the enrollees with whom they worked. Usually they were older men from the local area, a step above the LEMs, and they occasionally made the transition from the rank of foreman to superintendent. On a few occasions, the foreman position was a stepping-stone for the rare ordinary enrollee who sometimes made it quite a ways to the top spot of superintendent.

The position of foreman, incidentally, was probably the one in which political patronage most often came into play. Fortunately, most of the foremen about whom I was able to learn much seem to have been good, competent men certainly worthy of their positions.

Facilitating Personnel

Just over halfway through the program another group surfaced. These were the few men in each camp designated as "facilitating personnel" or "junior assistant technicians." This rank came into effect after the CCC eliminated the favored status of "local experienced men" on October 1, 1937. In order to keep some of these men in key positions who might not otherwise qualify as regular junior enrollees, they were hired by the technical agency as "Facilitating Personnel, Junior," with a salary double what they received as regular enrollees. These men worked at such assignments as engineer's helper, machine operator's helper, and clerk's helper.[61] This rank, too, was soon discontinued in June 1938, and "project assistants" stepped into the void. Only five were permitted in each company, and they were exempt from the normal requirements of age, marital status, and length of service in the Corps. The technical agencies recommended them for selection, and they generally ranked just below the foremen in matters of authority.[62]

Probably the ultimate in enrollee recognition took place when one was hired by the technical agency for which he worked. Twelve enrollees at BR-11, for example, made that step to becoming "employed by the Bureau [of Reclamation] and are earning a substantial wage through gaining their experience and knowledge while enrolled in this camp."[63]

LEMs: Local Experienced Men

Teaching the fresh enrollees to work in their new surroundings was made considerably easier by the presence of the "local experienced men," or LEMs. Having capable men possessing certain outdoor skills available to provide an additional level of leadership was regarded as essential for the well-being of youths from urban areas of the eastern United States. Having more experienced peers able to help the new, untrained youths become adapted to their new environment and to working alongside them was recognized as a real benefit. The job of the LEM was one of the more complex and misunderstood responsibilities within the Civilian Conservation Corps.

Utah, as did most of the western states, benefited from the fact that so many of the CCC camps were in the western one-third of the United States.[64] Since the LEMs came from areas adjacent to the camps, these men enjoyed greater employment opportunities than men of similar experience in other parts of the country.

In 2006, Patsy Stoddard, editor of the *Emery County Progress*, interviewed county resident Owen Price, who had worked in Emery County camps as a youth. Ninety-two at the time of the interview, Price described the work of the LEMs and the value of their instruction: "It was quite the trick making teamsters out of city kids. But those city boys came along and made pretty good workers. They relied a lot on us farm boys to show those city kids the ropes."[65]

As a researcher it has been quite surprising to me to discover that few of the CCC veterans I've met, either individually or at the annual gatherings of CCC Legacy, have indicated familiarity with the term *LEM*. On further consideration I reached the conclusion that this was probably because the term was no longer used after 1937 and it would have been unfamiliar to those enrolling in the late 1930s. Perhaps even more surprising is that few historians writing about the CCC have managed to accurately describe just where this particular type of enrollee fits into the big picture of CCC participants.

Even John Salmond's epic is not entirely clear on the subject, albeit in a fairly minor detail. Salmond accurately describes the twofold rationale behind the enrollment of 24,375 local experienced men, but his statement that "usually eight... were assigned to each camp" warrants explanation.[66] While that may have been the original intent, numbers varied considerably, usually based on such vagaries as the difficulty of the projects involved, budget considerations, and/or local unemployment conditions. In one admittedly unusual case at least one Utah camp found itself with more LEMs than junior enrollees. This was also the situation with the original Utah quotas, when one thousand junior enrollees were allocated to be followed shortly by a supplemental quota of 1,300 LEMs.

In Iron County in southern Utah, the 1933 registration called for a total of thirty-eight men: five junior enrollees and thirty-three local experienced men.[67] My research indicates that trying to determine a specific number of LEMs in a company is virtually impossible. What is known, however, is that the age and marital requirements were relaxed. LEMs were, however, subject to other restrictions as CCC regulations prohibited them from leaving their home state, so if a company to which they were assigned moved elsewhere, they were transferred to another company remaining in Utah.[68] Two years later, however, this regulation, too, was amended. Although Utah LEMs had never been assigned to work outside the state, they could be assigned to out-of-state companies then working in Utah.

Pennsylvania CCC historian Mike Schultz has written a thoroughly researched book about the Corps in the Allegheny National Forest, and I was able to get his views about LEMs. In an e-mail to me, he stated:

> Each camp on the Allegheny had at least two LEMs.... I don't really believe there was much written down about LEMs, that is, did every camp need 2? Just specifically what were their duties? I think their number was also affected by political persuasion. That's another interesting point about the CCC. The organization was flexible enough that one camp may have more LEMs

than other camps depending on budget, enrollment, and immediate area needs.[69]

Contrary to what was described by some historians, LEMs were neither foremen nor part of the company overhead as described below. So, while the LEMs were expected to provide some degree of leadership in helping the junior enrollees with their work, they were not *official* leaders with any particular rank. However, because of the fact that they were experienced, it was quite common for them to gain the rank of leader or assistant leader and, in some cases, even foreman. At least one historian even misunderstood the term *LEM*; instead, he used the designation LTM, as in "local trained man."[70]

One Nevada enrollee accurately described the LEMs as "men that were qualified to teach us and lead us in the type of work that we were going to do."[71] In the same book, however, the authors incorrectly state that "local men were hired as foremen." While it is true that "local men were hired as foremen" and also true that "local men were hired as [LEMs]," the foremen and LEMs were two different levels of personnel, with the former hired by the technical agencies and, until 1935, LEMs selected under the direction of the Department of Labor, in a manner similar to that for junior enrollees. After 1935, the selection of LEMs was carried out by the technical agencies, and as mentioned previously, the rank itself was dropped in 1937.[72]

It is possible, however, that the differences in perceptions of the LEMs might indicate a difference in jurisdictions, perhaps in Army Corps Areas. In Minnesota, for example, historian Barbara Sommer describes LEMs as "local foremen" who were "allowed to live at home" and "also earned more money." None of these applied in Utah, however. Her statement that they "did not have the same age or marital restrictions as enrollees," on the other hand, seems to have been the universal pattern.[73] In Utah, as mentioned previously, although subject to different methods of initial enrollment, once in the company they were officially just like other enrollees, except that their experience could provide greater opportunity for advancement.

The determining criteria in classifying a "local experienced man" were rather broad. The agencies were usually looking for someone at home in the outdoors, especially in forests, or farm boys with skill in handling horses, able to handle heavy equipment or even to drive trucks.

Extenuating circumstances occasionally entered the picture; for example, if a camp immediately needed truck drivers, "cat" operators, cooks, powder men, or some other particular skill, steps might be taken to lure those with such skills into signing up. In Tooele County the relief manager there hoped to attract some new enrollees by offering those willing to become cooks to enter the Corps even if they were married, that is, as LEMs, while all others were subject to the normal requirement of being single.[74]

Just being an unemployed all-around good worker of good character might qualify a local man, as would his ability to handle men. In announcing Utah's increased allotment of 1,429 LEMs in early July 1933, T. L. Holman, state director of selection, provided another interesting qualification: "Boys who have had experience in scouting and evidence qualities of leadership will also be considered."[75]

That favored status of local experienced men was eliminated on October 1, 1937, to be replaced by yet another designation. As noted, to keep some of these men in key positions, the technical agencies hired them as "facilitating personnel, junior," or "junior assistant technicians," with double the salary. The men then worked as assistants to the camps' engineers, machine operators, and clerks.[76]

This rank was eventually discontinued, however, and five project assistants were assigned to each company. Like the LEMs in whose footsteps they followed, they were exempt from the normal requirements. Project assistants were selected by the technical agencies and usually ranked just below foremen, a responsibility denied the LEMs.[77]

Overhead

Each camp also had a large group of enrollees in positions of responsibility, known collectively as "overhead." These were regular enrollees who were advanced to the position of either assistant leader or leader and usually held down specific responsibilities as clerks, first aid men, truck drivers, and others. In the later years they often had uniforms sporting military-type felt chevrons of gold stripes on a black background with identifying emblems to denote their rank and position. Assistant leaders and leaders earned $36.00 and $45.00, respectively, and also included enrollees who had no specific responsibility but were instrumental in providing leadership either inside or outside the camp.

Both the Army and the technical agency of a particular camp had overhead personnel. Army overhead included the first sergeant or senior foreman, mess steward, canteen steward, cooks, first aid man, supply sergeant or store clerk, truck driver, assistant educational adviser, and barracks leaders, among others, who, like the Army, were involved with running the camp.[78]

The most senior position among the enrollees was designated by various terms in different camps. Although he was usually identified as first sergeant, in some camps he bore the designation of senior enrollee, senior leader, or even senior foreman, a situation often leading to some confusion among researchers. This was especially true when the "senior foreman" title was often logically used to identify the foreman who was most senior among the four or five foremen assigned to a camp. Whatever his title, this enrollee supervised "camp details in the necessary duties of the enrollees while in camp."[79]

The responsibilities of the technical agency overhead, on the other hand, were connected with the work projects with which the company might be involved and usually included field leaders, assistant mechanics, powder men, truck drivers, and others. Crews were usually supervised by foremen assisted by as many as two leaders and five assistant leaders. Often, however, leaders or assistant leaders served in a subforeman capacity, sometimes in charge of a small crew or squad. The authority of these enrollees was generally respected, and the others seemed quite willing to take orders from someone their own age, although there were probably occasions when one's rank had to be firmly established after hours behind the barracks.

Another overhead position with considerable clout was that of the supply sergeant, although in some camps he also served as the canteen steward, resulting in two terms for the same position.[80] In a lengthy article in the camp newspaper of Company 1256, Supply Sergeant Joe Solomon at SCS-6 in Moab was very blunt in describing how he saw one aspect of his duty:

> The dates for ordering clothing will be between the 11th and the 14th of the month, and also between the 27th and the end of the month. Please bear this in mind, as I have other work to do, and do not like to be bothered every other minute of the day.[81]

His instructions also dealt with topics as diverse as when to seek replacements for worn-out clothing or shoes, folding sheets, purchases and services available at the company store, and just where an enrollee might get a haircut, films developed, or his clothes pressed.[82]

While the supply sergeant issued clothing, as canteen steward he also sold candy, soda pop, toiletries, and cigarettes, providing an opportunity for the enrollees to spend the money left over after the $25.00 allotment was sent home. In some camps scrip was issued that could be used instead of cash, perhaps to prevent excessive temptation for a steward who was seeing more money than he was used to. A printed coupon about the size of a monetary bill and bearing the number of the company as well as the coupon's value was the standard form of "money" in such cases.[83] Sometimes profits would be used to buy sporting equipment or rent movies. CCC regulations prohibited outsiders from buying at the canteen, where a pack of cigarettes costing fifteen cents could be quite a temptation.[84]

In addition to the extra pay and prestige, the positions generally entitled the chosen enrollees to a few more privileges, as well as responsibilities. Leaders and assistant leaders were often placed in charge of work projects as well as, in some cases, entire spike camps, which gave them considerable power: "Weekend passes will be granted enrollees in spike camps by the Leader or Assistant Leader in charge of the camp."[85]

These enrollees in leadership positions were generally highly regarded by both the Army and technical agency personnel. One superintendent stated, "At times it has been necessary for some of the Leaders to take full charge of a project and in every case they have made a real go of it."[86]

The number of overhead usually varied from around nineteen for a small company of less than 120 men, to twenty-four for a company of two hundred men, to twenty-seven for a company of more than 213. In the latter situation, ten leaders, evenly divided between the "Army overhead" and the "work section," or those assigned to the technical agency, served in each company. The regulations called for seventeen assistant leaders in such a situation—eight to the Army and nine to the technical agency. These numbers, of course, varied considerably, although circumstances could affect the numbers. For example, in 1939 Company 959 was stationed at F-31 in Veyo and could be considered a typical company, although at the time the company boasted 171 enrollees. Of those, ten were designated leaders, including Senior Leader Lee R. Warren, along with fifteen assistant leaders.[87]

POLITICAL PATRONAGE

The patronage opportunities provided in the selection of foremen and superintendents seem to have been one reason the CCC was so popular in the halls of Congress. To most of those who appealed to him for work, Governor Blood responded that all such requests should go through the Washington office of the appropriate technical agency; in some cases, however, the governor extended his own influence.

Officially, political patronage was to have no part in the selection of federal employees. On November 25, 1933, George A. Yeager, state director of the Federal Re-employment Service, announced to a Salt Lake City meeting of his county counterparts that should evidence of such happening be found, all those involved "will be ousted immediately."[88] Although CCC was not specifically mentioned, there is no doubt that the warning applied to all federal programs, including this one.

The influence of politics is demonstrated by the problems of a young college graduate in Panguitch. The Bureau of Biological Survey had approved his appointment to the position of rodent control foreman at Division of Grazing camp DG-34 in Blanding. His father was a Republican, however, and he waited from March until November 1938 before his appointment was announced. In the meantime, he hauled hay and dug ditches, while many of the unsympathetic townspeople made fun of his bachelor of science degree.[89]

Although there were some superintendents who were "appointed because of their political party instead of skill in supervising boys," such as the "ex-bank vice-president who didn't even know how to shovel dirt," most of them were men who had considerable experience in forestry or the building trades. Some were with the CCC only a short time before finding other employment, but there were many whose names were associated with the program for several years. Frank Hyde was one of these, as were Hyrum Kunz, Richard Greenland, Milton P. Greaves, E. W. Hoopes, George Hick, James M. Orr, R. C. Parkinson, William C. Oakden, George Moyes, Frank R. Worthen, Charles Wehmeyer, Lionel Chidester, and many more.

CIVIL SERVICE OPPORTUNITIES

The availability of Civil Service exams also permitted enrollees to enter government service outside the CCC. Two men who fit into this category in 1937 were enrollees Gerald "Jerry" Quick and Arthur "Pop" W. Robertson of Bountiful camp F-48. They were both veterans of World War I and were the only two men who had been with Company 940 ever since it began in 1933. Quick, after having served as both mess steward and supply sergeant, was then serving as first sergeant, the top enrollee position in the company. Robertson was then serving as supply sergeant. They enrolled on May 5, 1933, in that regular company rather than the veterans' company serving at F-9, Nebo, as was the usual route for ex-servicemen. As veterans they were exempt from the age and marital requirements and because of their positions of responsibility as company "overhead" were allowed to stay in past the usual two-year maximum.

As Quick was preparing to leave for his Civil Service job the camp newspaper gave him and Robertson quite a send-off, stating that "service to the company has meant more to these men than anything else as neither man has a leave of absence marked against him during his four years of service." The regular April anniversary open house that year honored not only the CCC in general but specifically Jerry Quick, who was leaving for his new job as junior general mechanic in the Department of Air Commerce.[90]

PAIRING

From 1935 until 1941 Utah had more than thirty camps each period.[91] Some of the camps were seasonal—that is, they were occupied only during the winter or the summer. Winter, of course, received the major consideration. Two main factors in determining the suitability of a winter camp were (1) the availability of suitable work projects close to the camp and (2) the accessibility of the camp to and from "outside" for supplies and any necessary hospitalization.[92]

After 1934 seasonal camps often paired up, and a company moved back and forth between summer and winter homes. Company 958, for example, moved between F-30 in Hobble Creek Canyon and F-40 (originally PE-220) at the Provo fairgrounds for three years before finally settling at the latter camp for a solid five-year stretch. The Soapstone camp, F-6, was a summer camp nearly every year, usually switching to F-43 in Pleasant Grove during the winter. Companies under Superintendent Hyrum Kunz moved from F-16 at Duck Creek in the summer to Veyo camp F-31 in the winter every year between 1936 and 1941, with one winter side trip to F-39 in Mayfield. Company 962 traveled regularly between its NP-4 winter camp at Bridge Mountain in Zion National Park and NP-3 at Bryce Canyon.

In 1939 and 1940 pairing arrangements were set up for some of the grazing camps, and companies moved from Willow Springs for the winter to Castle Dale in the summer, Simpson Springs to Antelope Springs, Dry Valley to Blanding, Lucin to Park Valley, and Black Rock to Callao. Pairing also involved some short-term alignments of Forest Service camps in Escalante (F-42 and F-44) and Salina (F-12 and F-32). The pairs always stayed within the same technical agency, and usually superintendents and foremen moved right along with the company and the camp officers.

Whether the overall popularity of the Civilian Conservation Corps across the country continued *because* of what happened in the nation's capital or in *spite* of it may be difficult to determine. But a supposedly Asian proverb might be appropriate: "The dogs bark, but the caravan moves on."

CHAPTER 4

Those Who Did the Work

The Technical Agencies

Generally the cooperation between the Army and the work agency was good and they helped each other in getting the job done whatever it happened to be.

—Albert Anderson, supervisor, Fishlake National Forest, camps F-12, F-25, and F-36

Although the Army administered the CCC camps as well as looked after the enrollees in their nonworking hours, the actual work projects of the young men were supervised by the technical agencies of either the Department of Agriculture or the Department of the Interior. And the fact that the two cabinet-level agencies are both conservation-oriented has contributed to the friction between them that exists to the present day.

THE DEPARTMENT OF AGRICULTURE

While the Department of the Interior did have more technical agencies working with the CCC, the Department of Agriculture actually had a greater number of camps. Throughout the United States, however, the proportion of camps nationally in the two departments decreased over the years. In 1933, for example, the Department of Agriculture had 1,264 camps out of a total of 1,468, or 86 percent. In 1935, the peak year of the CCC, Agriculture had 1,907 out of 2,635, or 72 percent. In July 1941, the CCC was winding down somewhat, and of the 1,234 camps, only 793 camps, or 64 percent, were under the Department of Agriculture.[1] During those same three years, in Utah the figures were, respectively, twenty-five of twenty-six camps, or 96 percent, under the Department of Agriculture's Forest Service. In September 1935, twenty-two of the thirty-two CCC camps, 69 percent, were within the Forest Service, Soil Conservation Service, and Bureau of Fisheries, and in July 1941, fifteen were U.S. Department of Agriculture camps out of thirty-four, or 44 percent. So, compared with the situation on the national level, the Department of Agriculture's percentage of camps in Utah was much higher in 1933, nearly the same in 1935, and much lower in 1941.

In addition to the Forest Service, the Department of Agriculture also administered the Soil Conservation Service, now the Natural Resources Conservation Service. Eventually the Soil Conservation Service was to play an increasingly significant role in the CCC after it finally became part of the Department of Agriculture, an interesting story in itself of the turf battles that seem to be part of most organizations, government or private.

Also under Agriculture was the Bureau of Biological Survey, which had a camp at the western edge of Brigham City and another near Ogden. Its history, however, was more complex as it went through several interdepartmental shifts as well as some name changes. In 1939 Biological Survey merged with the Bureau of Fisheries to create the Fish and Wildlife Service under the Department of Commerce before the new agency was finally returned to the Department of the Interior in 1940, where it remains today.[2]

U.S. Forest Service

Within the Department of Agriculture the largest of the agencies and the one with the highest profile was, of course, the U.S. Forest Service, which had the primary responsibility and handled the work projects for about 80 percent of the camps assigned to the department. Most of the work was done on national forest land, although the Forest Service also worked on state forest land, Tennessee Valley Authority land, military and naval land, railroad land-grant land in Oregon and California, public land in Alaska and Puerto Rico, and even private land if the work was considered to be in the public interest.[3]

East of the Rocky Mountain states, there are far fewer national forests than in the west, hence far fewer Forest Service CCC camps. Although figures varied over the years, a 1933 map shows Minnesota with fifteen U.S. Forest Service camps, having the most in the Midwest and east; many, including FDR's own New York State, had none. Of the eleven most western states, only Nevada, with four Forest Service camps, had less than Utah's twenty-six. California had 166.

Administratively, within the forty-eight states existing at the time, the U.S. Forest Service, like the Army, was divided into nine districts, or regions as they were officially known, although the Forest Service regions were not coterminous with the Army's subdivisions. Utah lay in Region Four, also identified as the Intermountain Region, which in addition to Utah included all of Nevada and parts of Idaho, California, Colorado, Arizona, and Wyoming. The Region Four headquarters were in Ogden, Utah, where Regional Forester Richard H. Rutledge had his office.[4]

In 1933 one of his top assistants was Chester B. Morse. Morse had over a quarter century with the Forest Service by then and was a good fit to serve at the Ninth Corps Area office at the Presidio in San Francisco when Fechner selected him as the Ninth Corps Area CCC coordinator with the Forest Service. Another of the assistant regional foresters, Clarence N. Woods, then became Rutledge's principal assistant.[5]

Rutledge always had great respect for the Civilian Conservation Corps. Honoring the fourth anniversary of the organization, he spoke over Salt Lake City radio station KSL on April 2, 1937. Rutledge described the makeup of Region Four and said that there were twenty-three national forests in the region, to which thirty-eight CCC camps were assigned. At that time Utah had only ten camps within its nine national forests; Dixie National Forest in southern Utah had two CCC camps, and the others had one each, just half of the twenty Forest Service camps when the program began four years before.

Within the CCC administration, Director Robert Fechner was Rutledge's immediate boss, and both men required that every camp "justifies its existence and fulfills a useful purpose."[6] It was constantly being emphasized that while the Army ran the camps, it was the responsibility of the technical agencies to plan, design, and carry out the work projects (see Table C.1).

First Enrollment Period

In April 1933, President Roosevelt granted approval for twenty Forest Service camps to be located in Utah. Wasatch and Fishlake national forests were assigned three camps each; two each were allocated to Ashley, Cache, Dixie, Manti, Powell, and Uinta; La Sal had one; and one, camp F-15, was located in the desert in western Utah. F-15 was about sixty miles west of Milford, and instead of being assigned to Humboldt National Forest in Nevada, as indicated in the *Deseret News*, it was administered directly from regional headquarters in Ogden, hence not assigned to any specific national forest.[7]

In May 1933, construction crews were also working on camp F-1 in Logan Canyon in the northeastern corner of the state, also in Cache. A. H. Powell was the work superintendent, and Captain Robert Sharpe commanded Company 957, made up primarily of local men from Cache County as both LEMs and enrollees.[8] The campsite, located at Tony Grove about fifteen miles up Logan Canyon, had been selected previously by Utah State Agricultural College (now Utah State University) for a summer camp for forestry and botany classes. By the middle of June crews were working on several jobs: constructing campgrounds in Logan Canyon, clearing roadside strips, poisoning ground squirrels, building log cribs and rock dams in Logan River to create fish pools, and erecting drift fences. Two crews worked on a connecting road from U.S. Highway 89 south through Cowley Canyon and Herd Hollow into the Left Hand Fork of Blacksmith Fork Canyon, east of Hyrum.

Work on the camp buildings went on simultaneously. The camp as finally constructed consisted of the fairly typical mess hall, recreation hall, four barracks, blacksmith shop, hospital, shower building, and administration building. The boys had even laid out plots for lawns and encircled the buildings with shale walks by the time an open house was held on July 28.[9]

Although F-2 was known as the Blacksmith Fork camp during the First Enrollment Period, another camp opened in Blacksmith Fork a year later. Camp F-2 was situated in the *left* fork of the canyon, and the new F-34 opened in the fall of 1934 in the *right*-hand fork, with the canyon's powerhouse often used as a reference point. The latter camp, however, was identified as the Hyrum camp. Although the different name might have minimized possible confusion, somewhat, newspaper references to the "Blacksmith Fork camp" could easily lead someone to assume that it was F-2 being described rather than F-34.

Avoiding confusion does not appear to have been an agenda item for those responsible for camp numbers, locations, and names. An almost identical situation existed in Utah County east of Springville. During the First Enrollment Period, the Hobble Creek camp was SE-206 located near Pole Heaven Road in the *left* fork of the canyon.[10] With the SE/PE camps

Figure 4.1. Pole Heaven Road, a tortuous connection between Hobble Creek Canyon and Provo Canyon to the north. Identified in the *Utah Road and Recreation Atlas* only as the Squaw Peak Trail, it has no number identifying it as a Forest Service road.

nearly out of the picture by the Third Period, the Hobble Creek camp was then relocated to the *right* fork as F-30, where it remained except when the company rotated between F-30 and the Provo camp.

Although this duplication of camp designations was rare, it was not a completely uncommon practice. In the latter part of May 1933, twenty-five Virginia boys arrived to set up a temporary camp in the city park of Vernal out in the Uinta Basin in eastern Utah. The Army and Forest Service considered Kaler Hollow, Iron Springs, and Bullionville as possible sites for new Forest Service camp F-3, but since "it is impracticable to get to Kaler Hollow at this time and the camp will undoubtedly be made permanent at Bullionville," construction of the Kaler Hollow camp began at Brush Creek at Bullionville approximately twenty-six miles northwest of Vernal.[11]

The misnaming of camps provided confusion multiple times during the life of the Corps. In Ashley National Forest, for example, newspapers might refer to F-3 by its Forest Service designation of Kaler Hollow on one occasion and on another as Bullionville, where it was physically located in the First Enrollment Period. To add to the problem, the camp was subsequently moved from Bullionville west actually to Kaler Hollow, nearly three miles of rough road and about five hundred feet of elevation away. In spite of extensive research in both government documents and local newspapers, Forest Service archaeologist Richa Wilson of the regional office in Ogden and Ashley National Forest archaeologists Tara Hamilton and others in Vernal still express some uncertainty about where F-3 was located in the summer of 1934: "It is not clear if the men returned to Bullionville or to Camp F-3's second location at Kaler Hollow, two miles west."[12] A Forest Service document offers about as good an explanation as any I've heard:

> Camp F-3 at both locations built the road between the camps, and a separate historic site exists at each location so it is not possible that the camps were the same. Historic research leads us to assume that the location was simply modified during the second year of the CCC, and it took local vernacular a while to catch up to the on-the-ground shift, while non-local CCC officials never bothered with distinguishing between the two locales.[13]

Likewise, Woods Cross camp SE-201 was not in Woods Cross but in Bountiful; the next period, however, Woods Cross SE-205 was indeed in Woods Cross. Rock Canyon camp F-40 was nearly three miles away from Rock Canyon, actually closer to Slate Canyon in south Provo; Brigham City camp SE-204 was not in the Box Elder County seat but about five miles away as the crow flies, and it took even longer to reach the campsite at about twelve miles south of the little town of Mantua in Sardine Canyon. While there was a camp about one mile west of downtown Brigham City, it was officially called the Bear River camp, BS-1, later BF-1 and FWS-1—not Brigham City. In other words, the Bear River camp was in Brigham City, and the original Brigham City camp was at Dock Flat.

The Ashley National Forest had one other camp besides the Kaler Hollow camp at Bullionville. This Smith's Fork camp, F-4, was situated on the north slope of the Uinta Range, just south of the Wyoming border. Company 230, one of the earliest to be formed in the Second Corps Area, received twenty-five LEMs from Weber County, Utah, in addition to 185 boys from New York under Captain J. E. Grove. Unfortunately, information on camp F-4 is sparse. Because the nearest post office was Mountain View, Wyoming, some newspapers failed to recognize it as a Utah camp, so it was often overlooked in Utah news coverage, while Wyoming papers, realizing that the camp was indeed in Utah, provided

Figure 4.2. Sign about one mile south of Mantua pointing to Dock Flat, where Brigham City camp SE-204 spent the summer of 1933.

limited coverage. As was so often the case, building roads was the camp's major assignment, under the able direction of Superintendent Leon Pack.[14]

In addition to the initial CCC camp F-5 in American Fork Canyon, the Wasatch National Forest had two others. Soapstone camp F-6 was one of the few original camps to survive after the first year. Company 1346 and Captain William C. Louisell were the first of several companies and commanding officers to serve there.

F-7, located at Black's Fork, southwest of Evanston, Wyoming, was another short-lived camp very similar to F-4. Lasting only that first summer, like F-4, F-7 was also located just south of the state line. The camp also resembled camp F-4, perhaps twenty miles to the east, in several respects in its personnel makeup. Its twenty LEMs were from the Ogden area; the two hundred junior enrollees were from New York; the primary assignment was road-building. Both camps listed the "nearest post office" as being in Wyoming. Although located in Summit County in northeastern Utah, F-7 was only about two miles from the Wyoming line. Because the nearest post office was there, it, too, was sometimes thought of as a Wyoming camp. William E. Applegate was superintendent.[15]

Two camps were located in the Uinta National Forest in central Utah. Diamond Fork was a tent camp located about sixteen miles up the Strawberry Valley in the mountains east of Provo. Here Company 1343 at F-8 worked on rodent control and thinning out stands of lodgepole pine before moving out of the state in October.

Figure 4.3. Camp F-8 at Diamond Fork, located between Hobble Creek and Spanish Fork canyons.

A Utah unit, Company 958, spent the summer at Mt. Nebo camp F-9 on Salt Creek, about eleven miles northeast of Nephi in Juab County, one of the few barracks, or "wooden," camps during the First Enrollment Period. The camp's biggest project was the construction of Red Creek Road, joining Salt Creek and Payson canyons, just a few miles east of the 11,928-foot Mt. Nebo, the highest peak along the Wasatch Front. Other assignments included the typical sheep and cattle trails, flood and erosion control, clearing up recreational areas, and building benches, tables, and restrooms.[16]

Manti National Forest was host to two camps in the First Enrollment Period. Camp F-10 was located in Joe's Valley west of Orangeville, where Company 959 was made up of youths from Emery, Carbon, Sanpete, and Salt Lake counties of Utah. The Ferron camp, F-11, lay about twelve miles through the mountains to the south, where Utah and Virginia boys shared the comforts of smaller six-man tents. Boundary rocks may still be seen at the campsite in Ferron Canyon on the north side of the road, about five miles west of town.[17]

Fishlake was one of the two national forests to have three camps under the initial quota. F-12, another wooden camp, was located near the ranger station about twenty-two miles up Salina Canyon and manned by boys from Utah and Virginia who made up Company 960 and worked under the direction of Superintendent R. C. Parkinson.[18]

Seven miles north of what might be considered the community of Fish Lake, F-13 was set up as a tent camp at a spot called "The Fryingpan." The dedication of the camp took place on July 22, 1933, under the direction of Captain David S. Doggett, company commander of Company 1337, another southern unit. Like the other camps of Fishlake National Forest, F-13 was busily engaged that summer in working on roads and campgrounds, grubbing larkspur bushes, and building check and silt dams for erosion control.[19]

Camps assigned to Beaver County were to be somewhat of an enigma during the entire CCC experience. On May 25, 1933, a detachment of fifty-six men under Captain Robert C. Snidow arrived in the central Utah railroad town of Milford from Fortress Monroe, Virginia, to set up the two camps assigned to the county, F-14 and F-15, with Companies 1338 and 1340, respectively. The enrollees were formed into two cadres of twenty-one each, with Regular Army men to temporarily assist in key positions. While Captain Snidow was assigned to remain with Company 1338, Lieutenant John C. Wade took charge of Company 1340, which was to go to the West Desert camp of F-15 at the Desert Range Experiment Station.

Deep snow delayed the start of Beaver camp F-14, but by mid-June construction was under way. Even before their camp at Tusher Ranger Station in the Beaver Mountains had been completed, the boys were at work surveying their initial project, a road to nearby Kent's Lake.[20]

Two camps were originally assigned to the Dixie National Forest, at Duck Creek east of Cedar City and at Pine Valley, in the extreme southwest corner of the state. The tent camp at Duck Creek, F-16, was dedicated late in June 1933, with Captain W. V. Witcher as commander of Utah Company 961 and J. T. Leigh as superintendent. Less than a month after the camp was set up, it was shifted about three-fourths of a mile west to a site near Duck Creek Springs, about five miles east of Navajo Lake. The thirty-five tents that made up the camp were erected in one row facing the creek.

The other Dixie camp, Pine Valley, was designated F-17 and began on May 25 with the arrival of a small cadre from Virginia to form the nucleus of Company 1335. This would more properly have been listed as a Ninth Corps Area camp, however, as Utah men were added to bring the camp up to its two hundred-man quota; Captain William A. P. Moncure and Superintendent Alma A. Nelson directed the camp. Besides the fairly standard tasks of building roads, culverts, fences, and so on, the crews of F-17 did much of their work at the Pine Valley Recreational Park, where they piled firewood for use the following winter and also constructed bulletin boards, latrines, tables, drinking fountains, and a three hundred-seat stadium. Then on their own time they planted lawns, trees, flowers, and shrubs and laid out rock gardens and gravel walks around their own quarters, which consisted of thirty-six floored tents. In early September the camp played host to Senator Elbert Thomas as he made one of his periodic visits to the CCC installations in the state, accompanied on this trip by Ernest Winkler, assistant regional forester in charge of grazing.[21]

Two Forest Service camps were attached to the Powell National Forest. The Blue Springs camp, F-18, located in Garfield County about nineteen miles north of Escalante near the Box Ranger Station, was commanded by Captain G. W. Morris of Company 1336.[22] Camp F-19 with Company 1339 settled at Grover, in southwestern Wayne County on present Utah Highway 12.[23]

The remaining Forest Service camp for the First Enrollment Period was assigned to the La Sal National Forest. A permanent campsite for F-20 was selected at the Warner Ranger Station approximately twenty-five tortuous miles southeast of Moab. Even before the camp could be established, four soldiers and twenty-one CCC enrollees arrived to form the nucleus of Company 1345 from Fortress Monroe, Virginia. When the group of men detrained at Thompson, two trucks from Moab took them, along with five tons of equipment, to a temporary camp at the foot of Brumley Ridge, near the Grand–San Juan County line.[24] Within a few days the company moved to the Warner site and by mid-July had reached its full two hundred-man strength. Of a hundred-man detachment that arrived a few days earlier, eighteen had come from Grand County, twenty-one from San Juan County, and the remaining sixty-one from other areas of Utah.[25] Although it was designated a Third Corps Area company, most of the enrollees were actually from Utah.

In addition to the twenty-one camps authorized on federal land in the First Enrollment Period—twenty in national forests and one at Zion National Park—five camps were also established for the sole purpose of combating soil erosion, under the direction of state conservation officials. In what might be considered a spin-off of the Forest Service camps, these five were specifically assigned the erosion-control responsibilities first described in chapter 2 and thoroughly explained in chapter 6.

That the CCC work of the First Enrollment Period was well received by Utah stockmen is illustrated by a recommendation that fourteen camps be set up for the Second Enrollment Period, in the winter of 1933–34. A committee headed by S. M. Jorgensen, president of the Utah Woolgrowers Association, identified not only the recommended camps but also how the 3,030 enrollees desired would be dispersed. The very detailed request called for the construction of 394 reservoirs, 690 miles of truck trails, and 234 miles of fence in addition to phone lines, springs, pipelines, and various buildings.[26]

Of the twenty original Forest Service camps set up in 1933, twelve never lasted past the First Enrollment Period, and five more saw only one additional period of occupancy. Only three of the original twenty—F-6 at Soapstone, with seven enrollment periods; F-11 at Ferron, also with seven; and F-16 at Duck Creek, with nine—saw more than two enrollment periods of service.

Second Enrollment Period

As the Second Enrollment Period got under way in October 1933, Utah State Relief Director Robert Hinckley notified the county relief directors that there would be no new enrollments for the period since the First Period quota had been oversubscribed. Of the 3,700 enrolled during the summer of 1933, 2,951 had reenrolled for the winter, but with the Second Period quota being only 2,150, there was already a surplus of about eight hundred men.

The new year 1934 did not appear to offer much more opportunity for hope economically in Utah than had 1933. In the month of January, 13,086 families received relief assistance. The state had received grants for more than $13,000,000 from the federal government for emergency relief and spent an additional $5,000,000 on a massive program of highway construction, a program that Governor Blood had indicated would provide at least part-time employment for ten thousand men.[27]

In the meantime, state officials prepared a list of thirteen camps that they wished to see established in addition to those requested by the U.S. Forest Service and National Park Service.[28] It soon became apparent, however, that such plans were excessively optimistic. Utah's CCC director, Public Welfare Chief Robert Hinckley, notified Blood, who in turn passed the information on to Chief Forester Rutledge, that probably three state camps were all that could be expected. Acting on this information, Blood recommended that camps definitely be established at the mouth of Willard Canyon in Box Elder County, near Bountiful in Davis County, and in Utah County, probably near the site of SE-206 in Hobble Creek Canyon east of Springville.[29] Each camp would spend the summer building flood-control barriers at the mouths of the several canyons that provide access to the interior of the Wasatch Mountains.

In spite of the pump-priming attempts, the misery continued, and many Utahns anxiously awaited the month of April, when the snow line recedes significantly, leaving mountain wildflowers in its wake. And to many unemployed, of even greater significance was the fact that April brought a new enrollment period of the by-then highly popular Civilian Conservation Corps.

After thorough consultation with Forest Service leaders in Ogden, Blood finally requested thirty national and state camps in Utah for the summer of 1934, an increase of four over the previous year. The governor insisted that this was a "very conservative" number that should be granted without difficulty, considering that over three-fourths of the state consisted of federal lands in the public domain: "If the purpose is to check flood and erosion damage and conserve forests the requested number could well be increased many-fold. As an unemployment measure this number of camps is also vitally important as our relief case load is practically twice that of the national average."[30] It appeared, however, that the appeals of Hinckley, the Utah congressional delegation, the governor, and Chief Forester Rutledge did not suffice in stemming the proposed reduction to ten (later nine) Forest Service camps and one National Park Service camp.[31]

Utah was actually entitled to only five Forest Service camps if population remained the sole criterion. Proportionately, Utah had 122 percent of its quota over the first three periods, compared with 101 percent for Washington and 108 percent for Montana, both of which required greater forestry protection. The neighboring state of Colorado with conditions somewhat similar to those in Utah had only 82 percent of its quota.[32]

It took a catastrophe of nature to bring about the first major expansion of the CCC and to increase Utah's planned quota from one thousand men for the Third Period to more than 1,700. In the spring and summer of 1934 drought conditions laid waste to much of the western and central areas of the United States; all of the Rocky Mountain states suffered seriously, with the sole exception of Wyoming. President Roosevelt saw the CCC as an agency that could bring immediate relief, by providing both the labor necessary to restore the physical damage done to the land and employment in the areas that were hardest hit.

Drought Relief

The impact of the drought-relief program can be noted by referring to the situation in Cache County in northern Utah. At the beginning of the Fourth Enrollment Period 215 applications came in for the twenty-nine vacancies available under the regular quota. Three months later the increased quotas were announced, and 108 more enrollees were accepted from the 220 applicants, all from Logan, the only town in the county to qualify by having a population over 2,500. The county Federal Emergency Relief Administration office handled the enrollment in the same manner as the enrollments under the regular quotas.[33]

As Salmond describes the environmental catastrophe of the devastating drought, "Millions of acres of topsoil were lost, crops withered and died, and cattle languished without water."[34] Again, the twin challenges of concern for the land and the resulting spike in unemployment required immediate action. Roosevelt responded by utilizing the CCC as one of four agencies to help alleviate the situation, not only by providing immediate employment but also to carry out work projects in the stricken areas, especially in combating soil erosion and developing irrigation projects. He requested $50,000,000 in additional funding to enroll 50,000 more men for projects in the affected areas, which included most of the states from the Pacific coast as far east as Indiana and Missouri.[35] Utah's allotment called for an additional 741 men, and enrollment took place from midsummer at least into October 1934.[36]

The removal of out-of-state enrollees and the initiation of the drought-relief program permitted the expansion of Utah enrollments in the Third Period. The peak for the entire life of the Corps in Utah was reached at the beginning of the Fourth Period in October 1934, when 4,340 Utah enrollees labored in the camps, over twice as many as had been enrolled only four months earlier.[37] By the end of the period, however, the number had dropped again to 2,577.

Six of the new drought-relief companies were added to Utah to handle the 75 percent increase in the state quota for the Third Period. One National Park Service, two Bureau of Reclamation, and three Forest Service camps were designated as drought-relief camps, identified by the initials "DR." Companies 1964 through 1966 were assigned to DRF-14, DRF-3, and DRNP-2, respectively. Two new Bureau of Reclamation camps were set up that summer and immediately designated drought-relief camps, with Company 1967 assigned to DBR-6 in Sanpete County and Company 1968 assigned to DBR-5 at Currant Creek in Wasatch County.[38]

Later in the summer of 1934, Captain Peterson and a crew of twenty-four men worked to prepare the Kaler Hollow camp for the drought relief enrollees who arrived soon afterward.[39] In addition, other camps absorbed some drought relief enrollees along with those new men accepted under the normal quota.

Probably at no time in the CCC program was there such a high proportion of local men in the Utah camps as there was during the drought relief era. Of the sixteen companies serving in Utah in the Third Period, that is, April 1 to September 30, 1934, ten were Ninth Corps Area companies made up almost exclusively of Utahns. As mentioned previously, two companies, 1338 at F-26 at Maple Springs and 1339 at Blue Springs (Escalante), were nominally Third Corps Area companies, although all the LEMs and many of the junior enrollees were also from Utah.

In July 1934, Uinta National Forest received a drought-relief camp near Mt. Nebo. One factor that made it unique was its composition of World War I veterans, the nucleus of which had been transferred from a camp at Lake Chabot in California, when the Utah members petitioned Governor Blood to secure a transfer to their home state. Richard Greenland served as the superintendent of the Nebo camp, located on the old site of F-9, until the middle of October, when he transferred to Moab and the veterans' company went to a new camp at Veyo.[40]

Camp F-25, which eventually located at Richfield, had an interesting origin. As early as August 1933, the Richfield Businessmen's Association began agitating to have both the Fish Lake and Grover camps assigned to Richfield for the winter instead of moving to California as had been rumored. Mayor W. L. Warner announced a plan to have the CCC camp set up on the county fairgrounds. Captain Doggett, commanding the Fish Lake camp, explained that he agreed with the plan because his men would then be in better condition for work the next summer. He expressed some concern, however, about the availability of federal

Figure 4.4. Scattered wood and concrete are all that remain of DRF-9, manned by a veterans' company northeast of Nephi near Ponderosa campground off the Nebo Loop.

projects, although soon it was decided that a road-building activity into the mountains would be satisfactory.[41]

As late as October of that first year it appeared that both F-13 of Fish Lake and F-19 of Grover might be transferred to the new Richfield camp, F-25. The prospect of having four hundred additions to the community pleased the business interests, as reports said that the government would be spending close to $1,600 in Richfield every day in addition to the money spent by the enrollees. In the meantime, employment prospects increased in the county as the Army hired forty carpenters, four electricians, and four plumbers to complete the $14,000 complex of a mess hall, an administration building, and four fifty-two-man barracks.

At a Richfield city council meeting on October 5, 1933, the city offered a lease for a section of the northern part of the city airport to the government at no cost and even agreed to provide the necessary water through a one-and-a-half-inch pipeline. The suggestion came up that the camp, in return, be given to the city and county after CCC use had terminated and that the pipeline remain in city hands.[42]

By the end of the month, F-25 neared completion. Located right on the main highway, the camp was described as being in the shape of an "inverted goblet." Captain Charles N. Kennedy commanded Company 1339 from Grover; Company 1337 transferred to California as originally planned.[43]

Third Enrollment Period

In addition to the one at Nebo, other Third Period camps were located at Logan Canyon, Kaler Hollow, Soapstone, Beaver Mountain, and Box Canyon. Identified as F-1, F-3, F-6, F-14, and F-18, respectively, these had been reestablished on sites from the previous summer when they had been part of the original twenty Forest Service camps. The remaining five Forest Service camps for the Third Period were all new, although in each case they were manned by companies that had been in Utah since the previous year. Ashley, Uinta, and Fishlake national forests eventually had two camps; each of the other five forests had only one.

In late April 1934, Company 957 had returned from its winter encampment at PE-217 in La Verkin to take up residence again at camp F-1 in Logan Canyon, to be the only camp in Cache National Forest. Some of the men accompanied the trucks on the four hundred-mile journey north, but most traveled by train along with Captain J. F. Gestring, who had been in command of the company since November 15 of the previous year.[44]

Company 960, another Utah contingent with some drought relief enrollees, had been at camps F-12 and PE-219 in the Salina area. In May 1934, the company transferred from PE-219 to Soapstone camp F-6 on the Mirror Lake Road about sixteen miles east of Kamas on the South Fork of the Provo River. Like F-1 and F-3, F-6 was one of the original camps that had operated during the previous summer but had been closed because of the winter snow.[45]

In addition to the 175 men in the main camp at Soapstone, another seventy-five worked out of F-6 at a spike camp at Mirror Lake, about fifteen miles to the northeast in the Uinta Mountains. On October 15, the entire company returned to Salina and took up winter quarters at the previous location of PE-219, although now the number had been changed to F-32, as the SE and PE designations had been terminated.

Company 1339 had spent the winter at F-25 in Richfield, but with the return of milder weather the company moved to Escalante's Blue Springs in Box Canyon, the former site of F-18. Although nominally a Third Corps Area unit, the company had been staffed for the most part with Utah men ever since it had been transferred west from Fortress

Monroe, Virginia, the year before.[46] Under Superintendent J. E. Teague, the men continued the monumental chore of road-building and worked on widening and improving the Hell's Canyon link between Escalante and Boulder.

F-26, the only camp initially assigned to Fishlake National Forest, was a new installation first located in Oak Creek Canyon east of the small community of Oak City in northeastern Millard County. Company 1338 had spent the winter at Santa Clara in camp PE-215 in Utah's "Dixie." Then, on April 23, 1934, a small detachment under a Lieutenant Meade was sent to Oak Creek; the entire company followed by May 5.[47] Later a tent spike camp was set up at Maple Springs in Chalk Creek Canyon some forty miles south. One of the major assignments of this group was the construction of the barracks and other buildings in Kanosh that were to become F-36 the following period.[48]

Located in the Dixie National Forest for the Third Enrollment Period, camp F-27 settled at Panguitch Lake in Garfield County.[49] Company 961, under First Lieutenant William G. Hines, moved up from doing flood-control work at PE-213 in St. George to occupy the new camp. J. C. Tolton continued with the company as superintendent over the work projects, including the construction of a highway from Panguitch to Cedar Breaks.[50] At the end of the summer the company again returned to St. George.

Another SE company moved from Orderville's PE-218 to F-28 in the Manti National Forest. The Gooseberry camp, as it was called, was located about twelve miles east of Fairview at a spot called Beaver Dam in Sanpete County. Company 959 arrived from Orderville in May and shifted to Mt. Pleasant, PE-223, in November.[51]

Besides this Kaler Hollow camp, which opened in July 1934, Ashley National Forest had another camp located in Uinta Canyon north of Roosevelt in eastern Utah. This Uinta River camp, F-29, opened in May and housed Company 1345, which previously had been located at F-20 and PE-214 in the Moab area since coming out from Virginia in May 1933. The company commander, Captain Vernon Peterson, had been with the company since its service at Warner Ranger Station east of Moab. Superintendent Alden Newell, formerly in charge of the work at both Warner and Moab, continued in the same position at the new camp, directing the building of roads to timber and recreational areas in the forest.[52]

The Forest Service actually benefited more than any of the other technical agencies in the allocation of camps. In 1933, with plans on the drawing board ready for implementation when a sufficient labor force was available, the Forest Service could put enrollees to work almost immediately as soon as the CCC was organized.[53] As a result the Forest Service had forty-six of Utah's 116 camps, nearly double the Division of Grazing's twenty-four. Throughout the life of the CCC, eight of Utah's nine national forests had camps in at least eleven of the eighteen enrollment periods; La Sal had camps for only five periods. La Sal had the least number of camps, as well, with only two ever assigned. Fishlake National Forest was the one most blessed, since its seven camps were in the forest during seventeen of the eighteen periods, with F-32 at Salina Creek operating for twelve of those periods, the most of any of the Forest Service camps. Other camps that were almost permanent fixtures were F-40 in Uinta, F-34 in Cache, and F-38 in Wasatch, each open for eleven periods.

THE DEPARTMENT OF THE INTERIOR

Established in 1849, the Department of the Interior, like the Department of Agriculture, is thought of primarily as a conservation agency, although it has many other functions as well. Those agencies that had CCC camps included the National Park Service, the Division of Grazing (now the Bureau of Land Management), the Bureau of Reclamation, the Bureau of Indian Affairs, and, later in the program, the Fish and Wildlife Service.

Anyone familiar with the history of the intermountain west in the territorial period might wonder that there was any amicable relationship at all between the state of Utah and the Department of the Interior. Focusing, for the most part, on Indian affairs and land policy, the federal government was often at odds with Utah residents, as historian Thomas Alexander pointed out in 1977: "A person got along well in the United States if he happened to be an Anglo-American Protestant farmer. If he were an Indian or a Mormon, a cattleman, or a logger, federal policy insisted that his activities be changed to fit within generally acceptable bounds."[54] And since all of those mentioned—Indians, Mormons, loggers, and cattlemen—were extremely affected by what the federal government was doing just one generation later, it is illustrative of the seriousness of the catastrophic social and environmental problems of the 1930s that the federal agencies were welcomed to the extent that they were. The reason for that success Alexander may have partially identified in the final paragraph of his book *A Clash of Interests*:

> Though some central direction is undoubtedly necessary, in view of the problems of administering Interior Department affairs in the Mountain West during the late nineteenth century, it may well be that in a culture such as ours the creative energies of those involved in the day-to-day operation of the affairs of organizations could be put to much more effective use through more local autonomy. If those nearest the problems were allowed latitude in the formulation and implementation of policies to meet the circumstances at hand, more effective administration might well result.

And the fact that it was the *local* advisory boards and the *local* heads of the technical agencies in the 1930s who saw to it that "practical considerations designed to solve immediate problems" succeeded in overriding most "ideological and conflicting political considerations . . . [to] provide more satisfactory answers to pressing needs."[55] Eight decades later many Utahns feel that concept got lost along the way.

The conflicts between the Departments of Agriculture and Interior were exacerbated by the creation of the U.S. Forest Service in Agriculture and the National Park Service in Interior, during the Progressive era of the early twentieth century. Schlesinger describes Gifford Pinchot's feeling that "Agriculture stood as the conservationist citadel, while Interior seemed more and more the appointed avenue by which the stockmen, the oilmen, the mine owners, and the land speculators conducted their raids against the nation's resources."[56] And Pinchot himself stated, "The tradition of the Interior Department is to put private interests first." It would be difficult to determine the harm done to the conservation movement by the fierce competition between the Departments of Agriculture and Interior over the past century, as each department attempted to stamp its imprint on the movement. On the other hand, it may actually have been productive, since, as Schlesinger pointed out in his analysis of the brouhaha, "it also spurred each Department to redouble its efforts in the conservation cause."[57]

National Park Service

The National Park Service (NPS) is generally regarded as the flagship agency of the Department of the Interior, although that honor has not always gone unchallenged. The competing interests of scenery, recreation, historic preservation, and, later, the generation of hydroelectric power have all been factors impacting the direction the NPS attempted to pursue—or tried to avoid—at various times in its history. During the CCC era the Park Service handled the work projects and camps for national parks and monuments and state parks, as well as in the territories of Alaska and Hawaii.

With the intracabinet difficulties with the Bureau of Reclamation, the intra-agency problems between competing NPS factions over what national parks should be, and the interagency challenges with the U.S. Department of Agriculture's Forest Service, it is quite impressive that the national parks ever came to be, in the words of filmmaker Ken Burns, "America's best idea." And now, of course, the national parks and monuments in Utah are suffering from their own popularity with the creation of long lines at the entry stations as the "Mighty Five" struggle to accommodate millions of visitors.[58]

During the CCC period the presence of a camp at Zion National Park was assured from the beginning of the program. Governor Blood and Regional Forester Rutledge were told in May 1933 that a camp would be established in the park to "augment those to be stationed in the twenty forest camps."[59]

Company 962

Zion, established as a national park on November 19, 1919, therefore had one of Utah's original twenty-six camps, with a company of Utah men assigned to NP-1. Company 962, the only one that summer not under the Forest Service, temporarily camped on the canyon floor and constructed some CCC buildings as well as carried out some irrigation projects, but by the last week in June 1933, road and weather conditions had improved sufficiently to permit the company to relocate to its permanent camp at Blue Springs, about forty miles north of park headquarters.[60] Here on the North Fork of the Virgin River near the present Kolob Reservoir, Company 962 under Captain Garth B. Haddock established its quarters.

NP-1 at Blue Springs was short-lived, however, lasting only the First Period, during which crews constructed more than 1,100 checks and dams, dumped brush and rock into 17,000 feet of gullies, and terraced eroded areas on the Kolob Plateau.[61] Company 962, on the other hand, was to become a permanent fixture in the park and served at Zion for most of the CCC's entire existence.

Captain D. M. Shearer replaced Captain Haddock as commanding officer of Company 962 on August 25, 1933, shortly before the company returned from Blue Springs to Zion Canyon and reoccupied the original, temporary site on the west side of the Virgin River. At this point the official records in the archives at Zion Park become somewhat confusing. Identified usually as just the "Zion camp," the site was occasionally called NP-1, probably because it was occupied by NP-1's former unit, Company 962. Actually, it was a new camp, NP-2, as NP-1 no longer existed.

Company 962 spent the winter at NP-2 on the canyon floor, carrying out work projects under Superintendent Frank Rozelle. The beginning of the Third Enrollment Period marked the commencement of a sort of CCC camp "musical chairs" involving NP-2 and NP-4 and even NP-3 and NP-5, along with Companies 962 and 1966 and two companies from out of state. It began smoothly enough in the spring of 1934, when NP-2 was vacated and Company 962 moved to the new camp NP-3 in Bryce Canyon for the summer in what became a fairly regular seasonal rotation.[62]

One of the major accomplishments of the Bryce camp that summer was the preparation of Cedar Breaks for its dedication as a national monument on July 4, 1934. At the dedication itself CCC boys directed traffic, helped stalled automobiles in getting up the hills, and served a barbecue to the huge crowd, which included Governor Blood; Carl R. Gray, president of the Union Pacific Railroad; President Heber J. Grant of the Church of Jesus Christ of Latter-day Saints; and Leo A. Borah of *National Geographic* magazine.[63]

Every summer between 1934 and 1939 Company 962 served at NP-3 in Bryce Canyon National Park. Bryce Canyon, with its picturesque hoodoos and reputation as "a hell of a place to lose a cow," had been a national park since February 25, 1928, but until 1956 was to be under the administration of the superintendent of Zion National Park, who for most of the 1930s was P. P. Patraw.

The national drought-relief program described earlier in this chapter had also just gotten under way, and in late July 1934, Company 1966, one of Utah's five newly created drought-relief companies, moved into the vacant NP-2 site, which was then redesignated DNP-2.

The checkered chapter in Company 962's history really commenced when it returned to Zion Canyon in October 1934 to find some changes in effect. With Company 1966 assigned to DNP-2 on the west side of the Virgin River just inside the park's southern boundary, 962 was to occupy the new NP-4 on the east side of the river, very near to where the Visitors' Center parking lot is located today, at the base of the imposing and picturesque monolith called The Watchman.[64]

As described later in this chapter, Company 962 remained at NP-4 that winter and returned again to Bryce NP-3 for the summer of 1935. October 28, 1935, saw the company return to NP-4, about the time that the first of two major changes took place.

First, a shake-up of NP-2 and NP-4 began in late 1935. What was described as "a new departure in the CCC history of Zion Park" was taking place. Frank Rozelle, of course, had been superintendent of Company 962 since it had been at NP-1 and continued to serve with the company at NP-2 in the winter of 1933–34 and at Bryce Canyon NP-3 the following summer. In October 1935, Daniel Back had just resigned his position as superintendent at NP-2, and foreman Francis Raile was named to replace him. With two camps separated only by the Virgin River, leaders of NPS and the CCC decided that greater efficiency might be possible by administratively combining the two under Frank Rozelle as senior superintendent over both camps. Foreman Owen Johnson was promoted to become superintendent of NP-4 with Company 962, while the newly appointed Raile would continue serving as superintendent of NP-2 and Company 1966.[65]

Those involved regarded the move as a favorable step. The *Parks Post*, the enrollee-produced newspaper of Company 962, lauded the "closer kinship and cooperation between the two camps" and stated that "one unified, coordinated work program functions more smoothly than two separated disjointed ones."[66]

When the drought-relief program came to an end in 1936, this resulted in a "national reduction in companies," and Company 1966 folded on April 12, 1936. NP-2 soldiered on, however, as Company 3238 came in to staff it for two months until, on June 17, the boys from New York and

New Jersey moved up to NP-5 to spend the summer at Cedar Breaks.[67] The easterners lasted only for Period Seven, however, as with the coming of winter Company 3238 moved back to NP-2 on October 10, only to be disbanded four days later. Two weeks after that, on October 27, Company 4779 moved in from North Dakota to man NP-2 for the winter.

In April 1937, Second Lieutenant Cassell became CO of Company 4779 for a very brief period before swapping assignments with Captain John P. Bottonfield of another Seventh Corps Area company, 4777 of Veyo camp F-31. In late May 1937, Company 4779 was still at NP-2, awaiting orders to transfer within the next few days to Grand Teton National Park south of Yellowstone on June 1, 1937.[68]

A First Lieutenant Kroger had returned from Ft. Lincoln, N.D., with 114 new enrollees from North Dakota and Minnesota to replace the eighty-six he had escorted there for discharge. For the most part the new enrollees were full- and half-blood Chippewa Indians, described in the annual report as "a very well-behaved and husky lot."[69]

The second major change took place two years after the first, during the summer and fall of 1937. In a stroke of bureaucratic brilliance someone recognized that greater coordination could be achieved with even further reorganization.

By November 1937, consolidation had been carried to the ultimate when NP-2 was abandoned and Utah LEMs and some building materials were moved across the river to become part of Company 962 and NP-4. Now back to only one camp in Zion National Park, Rozelle resumed his previous position as camp superintendent of NP-4; Johnson was the senior foreman. The record is unclear about what happened to Superintendent Raile; he evidently was no longer at Zion.[70]

NP-2 acquired quite an impressive list of accomplishments during its four years at Zion. Work on the East Rim Truck Trail was carried out to assist primarily in fire protection in the area north of the highway east of the tunnel. Other trail and road construction and maintenance, riprapping along the Virgin River in the canyon, "sloping" of roadsides near the tunnel, constructing stone buildings near the administrative headquarters at the South Entrance, and continuing to fight invasive vegetation and pesky rodents were typical of NP-2's activities.[71]

Camp NP-4 and Company 962 shared a long history on the canyon floor of Zion National Park. NP-4, commonly known as Bridge Mountain camp, lasted until at least 1941 and possibly even into 1942, to become one of the longest-operating camps in the state. From its 1934 opening until 1939 NP-4 was a winter-only camp, and as mentioned previously, Company 962 began its seasonal rotation between NP-3 during the summers and NP-4 during the winters. During the summers of 1940 and 1941, however, NP-4 continued operations at Bridge Mountain as one of Utah's most outstanding camps, with Company 962 until the very end.

An announcement came in February 1935 that Company 1966 would be setting up a "new camp, (NP-5) near the north boundary of Cedar Breaks National Monument." Due to the ten thousand-feet elevation, snow would prevent occupancy until late June, the article warned.[72] It turned out that the camp was not occupied until July 1935, just north of State Highway 14 east of Cedar City. The records, however, are somewhat confusing as to just how it should be identified. The *Kane County Standard* mentioned in July 1935 that "this week a National Park camp was established at Cedar Breaks."[73] From here on it gets murky.

The Cedar Breaks camp was sometimes identified in Park Service records as NM-1, indicating that it was the first national monument camp.[74] In most cases, however, it was known as NP-5, the fifth national park camp in Utah. NP-5, as I refer to it instead of NM-1, was opened in the Fifth Enrollment Period with Company 1966 in the summer of 1935. In an interesting example of interagency cooperation, the National Park Service and Forest Service divided the construction projects. Crews under the Park Service did most of the trail construction, campground development, fencing, and working on roadsides, while the Forest Service oversaw building a road around the rim of the Breaks and another road to the top of Brian Head as well as a parking lot, lookout, and shelter for what is today one of Utah's most popular skiing areas. A fishpond as well as some range improvement in the adjoining Dixie National Forest were also completed by Forest Service crews.[75] In 1936 Foreman Marion Willis transferred from Company 962, then at NP-3, to "supervise the erection of two new log cabins to be added to the administration buildings." During their stay there, enrollees also built an administration building, fireplaces, tables, campsites, and the structure that now serves as the monument's museum.[76]

Both of the CCC camps "assigned to this headquarters . . . are camped in Zion during the winter months"; during the summers one company worked at NP-3 in Bryce, while the other was at NP-5 in Cedar Breaks. Company 1966 moved from Cedar Breaks NP-5 back to NP-2 in Zion on October 8, 1935, where "due to national reduction in number of companies," Company 1966 was disbanded on April 12, 1936. Two months later Company 3238 out of New York moved in, on June 17, 1936, to take its place for the summer.[77]

Here Company 3238 quickly established its routine. Hinton states that the company put out the *Zion Zephyr* and also the *Carry-On Monthly*, presumably at NP-5. Also, teams from DG-30 at Cedar City visited Cedar Breaks twice that summer for sports competitions, lending further support to Cedar Breaks being more than just a spike camp.[78] Changes continued, however, and as mentioned previously, it wasn't long before Company 3238 was disbanded on October 14, 1936, to be replaced by Company 4779.

After the summers of 1935 and 1936, NP-5 was used only as a spike camp in 1937 and 1938, usually by Company 962, then at NP-3 at Bryce Canyon for the summer. Former enrollee George Alma Platt told me in April 1968 of having been sent from Bryce Camp NP-3 in June 1937 "to cook for another sub-camp being sent to Cedar Brakes [*sic*]."[79] The *Kane County Standard* reported in April 1936 that Company 3238 was moving into NP-2 when Company 1966 was disbanded.[80]

After NP-2 shut down at Zion in 1937, only NP-4's Company 962 continued as an NPS company until 1940. In 1935, Utah State Planning Engineer Paul Arentz and Zion National Park Superintendent P. P. Patraw had requested $21,000 for a winter CCC camp to be established at Capitol Reef, about ten miles east of Torrey in Wayne County, to determine what needed to be done two years before it was even designated a national monument in 1937. The 1935 request was denied by Hillary Tolson, assistant director for operations of the NPS, due to a freeze on the construction of new camps. There was, however, some preliminary work done on roads in the area by the Works Progress Administration.[81]

At Patraw's urging, Capitol Reef was made a national monument in 1937, and finally, approval was given in July 1938 to move the Cedar Breaks spike camp to Capitol Reef.[82] Foreman Marion Willis and seventeen enrollees set up a tent camp one thousand feet west of Chimney Rock on the north side of Utah Highway 24 about 2.5 miles west of the tiny community of Fruita. At first the camp consisted of tents and one small frame building that housed a radio for communication with Zion and Bryce. A spring about a quarter mile northwest of the camp supplied water, which was stored in a 2,300-gallon corrugated iron tank. A portable generator supplied electricity. Eventually frame buildings were constructed with material salvaged from razing the abandoned camp at Cedar Breaks. Enrollees built riprap and basket dams along Sulphur Creek and were also involved in road construction in the rugged country south of Highway 24 roughly between Chimney Rock and the town of Fruita.[83]

Enrollees quarried sandstone for a headquarters building, although apparently it was not known at first whether it was going to be a checking station, a residence, or a museum; Hinton described the structure as "early Mormon-type architecture." Whatever it was, before long it was designated a ranger station for awhile but eventually became the superintendent's office, as it is now adjacent to the Visitors' Center. Another major project was building retaining walls along the Hickman Bridge Trail. In October 1938, the camp closed for the year; the spike camp crew returned first to Bryce to help close camp there and then continued on to Zion for the winter.[84]

Spike camps returned every summer to build more roads, bridges, and retaining walls. Then, in April 1942, with World War II under way, NP-6 was discontinued, another one of the few camps to last that long. Historian Bradford Frye offered his summation in 1998:

> The Chimney Rock camp was dismantled after the crews left [and was] later burned down by vandals in April, 1947. . . . The Civilian Conservation Corps provided the first visible effort by the federal government at Capitol Reef National Monument. Not only was the CCC responsible for the improved roads and the construction of the first building and trail, but it also assisted the National Park Service in gathering visitation statistics. In fact, the on-site foreman actually served as the first, unofficial custodian for the monument.[85]

The final National Park Service camp in Utah was NP-7, one of only fourteen camps active in Utah during the eighteenth and final working period in 1942. Located in Moab in far eastern Utah, it served Arches National Monument—today a national park—just across the Colorado River north of the town.

Division of Grazing

A highly significant part of the Department of the Interior's conservation work was carried out on the Utah rangelands by another new agency. Under the provision of the Taylor Grazing Act passed on June 28, 1934, the Division of Grazing (DG) was given the responsibility of administering the public domain in ten western states by "preventing over-grazing and soil deterioration." Most of Utah's unclaimed acres outside national parks and forests lay in the drier regions of the state, and the development of springs, reservoirs, and stock trails by the DG camps was one of the major accomplishments of the Corps. The Grazing Service worked in cooperation with local stockmen, who were represented by an advisory board set up in each of the eight grazing districts that were organized the first year.[86] The advisory board elected a "CCC Project Committee," which worked with the superintendent of the assigned camp in recommending and approving camp projects.[87] Division of Grazing camps received numbers on a nationwide basis, and for the Fifth Enrollment Period camps DG-26 through DG-35 were approved for the state of Utah.[88] Only three, however, began operations during the period: DG-28 at Clover Creek, DG-30 at Cedar City, and DG-34 at Blanding.

During the Sixth Period, beginning October 1, 1935, the rest of the scheduled grazing camps opened, in addition to DG-45 in St. George, which previously had been listed as an Arizona camp. With very few exceptions, the DG companies were all from the Fifth Corps Area. I'm not sure why enrollees from Indiana, Kentucky, Ohio, and West Virginia were considered prime prospects for work in Utah's desert areas.

Of the technical agencies, I would suggest that it was the Division of Grazing that found the most remote parts of the state in which to locate its camps, although nearly all could lay partial claim to that dubious distinction. Of the twenty-four DG camps, nine eventually had towns grow up around them, but in most cases, just barely. While St. George, Milford, Hurricane, Kanosh, Blanding, and other camps were then near the edges of their respective communities, they are now well within the city limits. Even such far-flung DG camps as Park Valley, Callao, and Garrison were within two or three miles of the small towns whose names they bore—but which had little to offer in the way of entertainment opportunities. For nearly complete isolation, the camps of Modena, Simpson Springs, Lucin, Antelope Springs, Jericho, and Dalton Wells would probably head the list, although the latter two were at least on state highways.

Eleven camps, nearly half of the twenty-four, were located in the West Desert; another five were located in desert areas east of the Wasatch

Figure 4.5. Simpson Springs Pony Express monument built by DG-154.

Range. The only camp in the range itself was DG-131 in Kanosh. Originally operating as F-36 from 1934 to 1936, it was taken over by the Division of Grazing for about three years, after which it continued as a spike camp, probably out of DG-29 at Antelope Springs.

The final expansion of the Division of Grazing took place during the Fourteenth Period, October 1, 1939, to April 1, 1940. Six new winter camps opened at Lucin, Simpson Springs, Black Rock, Modena, Willow Springs, and Hurricane. Since they were staffed by companies transferred from other camps, this did not increase the overall total of approximately fifteen DG units. In fact, Clover Creek and Cedar City closed permanently in the summer of 1939, and Henrieville followed suit in November.[89]

Almost without exception, the work of the DG camps varied little from camp to camp: development of springs and stock reservoirs, control of rodents as well as noxious weeds, stringing fence, and building corrals, stock trails, and roads to get to the various projects. In most cases the projects completed then are still in use today. The benefit to the livestock industry over the eight decades since their construction would be nearly impossible to calculate.

Bureau of Reclamation

Similar to the history of other facets of the conservation movement, the Bureau of Reclamation grew out of the Progressive era of the early twentieth century. Initially called the U.S. Reclamation Service, it was created under the Reclamation (Newlands) Act of 1902 primarily for the purpose of providing water to arid parts of the western United States. In 1907 Reclamation became an independent bureau within the Department of the Interior. The present name has been in effect since the restructuring of the organization in 1923.[90]

During the 1930s, E. O. Larson was the headman of the bureau in Utah and was involved in one way or another in nearly every bureau project in the state. As some of the most major of the projects in which the CCC was involved in Utah, the work of the bureau is discussed in greater detail in chapter 7.

State Park Camps

The National Park Service also provided technical supervision of CCC work in state parks across the country. For the first time in history, the federal government cooperated with the states in the development of their recreational programs.[91] The only state park Utah had in 1933 was a city block in Fillmore where the territorial capital had once been located. When the state appeared anxious to develop some of its waterfowl areas on the shores of the Great Salt Lake, SP-1 was set up on the northwest shore of the lake at Locomotive Springs through the cooperation of the NPS and the Utah Fish and Game Department. It wasn't long, however, before SP-1 shut down and SP-2 took its place on the other side of the lake at Farmington Bay. Although the designations of SP-1 and SP-2 suggested that they were state parks, such was not the case; no state parks were built by the CCC as such, although there was one major project that eventually became a state park. Minnesota, on the other hand, had the CCC working on state parks from the very beginning. There were thirty parks in 1935 when Minnesota's Division of State Parks was created, and today some of the CCC's finest work can be found in the state parks of Minnesota.[92]

Somewhat related, however, is the work of MA-1. This was a new type of unit, described as the first in the country, a "Metropolitan Area" camp that opened in Provo in November 1939, under the joint administration of the city of Provo and the National Park Service. This was the only one the state ever had and one of only sixteen in the country in 1941.[93] Eventually, MA-1's labor resulted in what actually turned out to become today's Utah Lake State Park.[94]

Office of Indian Affairs

The Office (later Bureau) of Indian Affairs, another agency of the Department of the Interior, was virtually autonomous in its supervision of the two Indian CCC camps in Utah. Within a few weeks after the CCC was approved, Washington extended the program to include Native Americans who found the Great Depression at least as burdensome as did their white countrymen. Soon it was announced that beginning June 23, the Corps would enroll 14,400 men in sixty-seven camps on fifty-three reservations in North and South Dakota, Oklahoma, Arizona, New Mexico, and Utah.

By September 24, 1933, 12,702 Indians had enrolled, mainly in the western states; eight more camps were added for the Second Enrollment Period.[95] The only requirements that an Indian applicant had to meet were that he be a tribal member seventeen years of age or older, be in financial need, possess the physical strength to do the work required, and be free from contagious disease.[96] In spite of the use of irregular procedures of enrollment, the Indian enrollees received the same compensation.

The organization of the Indian companies was considerably different from that for the regular Corps. They were handled entirely by the Office of Indian Affairs; the Army had nothing to do with the administration of the program, nor did the enrollees come under the supervision of the regular technical agencies.[97] Instead, the office handled the selection of men as well as the supervision of projects through local tribal agencies. Utah's original quota called for the enrollment of two hundred Indians, although this figure was seldom reached.

An arbitrary decision was made that an entire reservation within one state should be considered a camp, although this seems to have been loosely followed.[98] Oklahoma had twelve such camps during the First Enrollment Period, Arizona had nine, and New Mexico and Montana had seven. In 1939 Utah was one of eighteen states with Indian camps; that year approximately one-fourth of Utah's Indian population was in the Corps. Eventually a total of 746 Indians were enrolled in the state.[99]

Admittedly incomplete accounts speak of two camps on the Uinta and Ouray Reservation in Utah. One might possibly be considered only a spike camp, since other accounts speak as if there was only one camp. However, I feel that the matter was settled definitively by L. W. Page, superintendent of the reservation, when he spoke of the good work done by *both* Indian camps. The Indian reservation, the largest completely within the state of Utah, was located in the Uinta Basin south and west of Vernal. Working at what was touted as the only all-year camp in Uinta County, the Indian enrollees were to be assigned the typical CCC work projects in southern Uinta County: road- and trail-building and the development of water holes and springs. The plan was for the camp to last for two years and generate more than $25,000 in spending.[100]

One factor that impacted the limited participation of Native Americans with the CCC in Utah might have involved the ongoing legal problems the Ute Indians of eastern Utah were having in the 1930s over what had been the Uncompahgre Reservation. Lawsuits, hearings, and legislation involving the federal government, white stockmen, and mining interests in the basin not only strained relations with white people but also tied up Indian leadership. Disputes over water rights and the creation of grazing districts under the Taylor Grazing Act were not resolved until the creation of the Hill Creek Extension to the Uinta and Ouray Reservation in 1948.[101]

Few formal Indian CCC camps were actually set up, since the enrollees usually lived at home and worked with the Corps on a part-time basis or traveled about with their families, working on projects on their own reservations.[102] One camp that appears to have been of a more permanent nature, however, was located at the Uinta Power and Light Company's plant on the Uinta River and identified as Uinta Camp number 1, which suggests that there may, indeed, have been two camps. The camp itself was described as being "very modern," with electric lights, an effective water system, showers, a radio, and a functioning recreational program set up that first summer. No mention was made of barracks, however, and although I have found no Indian records to confirm this, I assume that this indicates the camp was just a base of operations with no housing facilities provided.

It was from here that the first work by Indian enrollees in Utah got under way in July 1933, with one group of approximately one hundred men under Project Manager Edward T. Nero and another of fifty men under Foreman Roy Smith carrying out the typical CCC work of building roads, erecting phone lines, and developing springs. Crews worked on a service road along Farm Creek between Whiterocks and John Starr Flat on the northern edge of the Uinta and Ouray Reservation just south of the Ashley National Forest, where it was planned to access Indian timberland. A construction crew under C. J. Langer also cut poles for a telephone line connecting Fort Duchesne with the John Starr Flat Ranger Station.[103]

Inasmuch as most of the Indian lands were located in extremely arid regions, it was felt that the projects would primarily be concerned with soil erosion from both wind and water. Jay B. Nash, director of the Indian program, announced that additional projects would include small ponds for the watering of livestock, the construction of secondary roads and fire trails, and the stringing of telephone lines. Tribal councils were able to participate in the selection of projects and the administration of the program.[104]

The work projects on the reservation were among the most difficult to be tackled anywhere. Truck trail construction required that much hand labor be used to clear small rocks off the roadbed. Fence construction was even more difficult. The Indian agent on the reservation stated that of thirty miles of fence built during the previous year, "only about four miles could be reached by truck and very little of the balance could be reached by wagon."[105] As a result, most of the wire, posts, and other materials and equipment had to be hauled in on packhorses. The posthole diggers that had been purchased for the project proved worthless, as every posthole had to be dug out of rock. One crew camped at an elevation of ten thousand feet for the summer and developed springs and horse trails in the surrounding area where trucks and wagons were of no avail.[106] Fortunately the work was described as being permanent. By July 1938, a total of $351,942 had been spent on the Uinta and Ouray Reservation, with another $70,035 budgeted for the fiscal year ending July 1, 1939. Range management programs were under way, and nearby white cattlemen were being provided with hay raised during the summer as part of a CCC project.[107]

When the program began in 1933 the Shivwits Indians in Washington County in southern Utah refused to have a CCC camp on their reserve,

Figure 4.6. Shivwits Dam on the Santa Clara River, which helps control the sometimes violent river.

Figure 4.7. Spillway at the top of the Shivwits Dam showing the intricate rockwork of which enrollees were capable.

but regular camps were located just off the reservation in St. George, Gunlock, and Santa Clara.[108] SE-213 of St. George built a diversion dam on the Santa Clara River on the reservation, near the site of the old smelting town of Shem.[109]

In the summer of 1935, however, Indians in southern Utah were reportedly working under the direction of Subagent Parwin E. Church on projects to improve the conditions for livestock on the Moccasin Reservation. Fences, troughs, springs, and reservoirs were built, and a survey was completed for a highway that was to cross the reservation.[110]

James S. Andrews, project manager for the CCC in the Uinta Basin, stated that one of the major benefits of the program in the basin was in providing employment for an average of approximately one hundred men over the previous three years. The cash accruing from the wages was of great value in allowing lessees to pay off long-overdue debts and in enabling their families to escape from the relief rolls. Concerning the employment opportunities for the youth, Andrews states,

> I cannot praise the ECW [Emergency Conservation Work] too highly for the excellent training it has afforded the Indian people especially the young boys and girls that have just finished school. No other department in the Indian Service furnishes them the necessary experience required before they can secure a better paying job. Any number of young boys and girls coming from school have enrolled with us and after a few months of experience have gone to better paying jobs, such as clerks or stenographers, tractor drivers, truck drivers, cooks, foremen and camp assistants.[111]

The Corps was providing hope for the Indian, according to J. Harold Thompson, local supervisor of Indian CCC work: "No longer does he sit in his cabin, dreaming of a glorious past and resigned to a government dole in the future. Instead he is out with the CCC gang reseeding the range, building fences and dams, cutting down diseased trees, breaking roads and trails."[112]

President Roosevelt, too, felt quite strongly about the benefits of the Indian CCC program. The development of resources on the reservation and the provision of financial assistance for Indians were two of the factors he especially regarded as most beneficial.[113]

EVOLUTION OF THE PROGRAM

Although the CCC was, without doubt, the most popular and successful of the New Deal agencies, it did not always enjoy smooth sailing and continued to be pilloried by the partisan politics that usually accompanies most acts of American government. Not only was its continuation an issue of contention, but the ideological concept of relief also threatened the Corps.

The major expansion of the Civilian Conservation Corps occurred during the summer of 1935, when the peak of 505,782 was reached.[114] Forty-two camps gained approval for Utah during the Fifth Period, although only thirty-two opened as scheduled. Camps F-38 through F-44 and F-48 at Bountiful were added to the Forest Service roster, and two camps came in under the new Soil Conservation Service.[115]

In May 1935, Roosevelt put the CCC into expansion mode and succeeded in raising the membership quota to 600,000, necessitating that the original maximum age requirement of twenty-five be raised to twenty-eight, and at the same time the maximum time of enrollment was increased from twelve to eighteen months. It looked as though expansion to the desired 600,000 would be easily achieved, especially after the minimum age for enrollment was lowered to seventeen in September 1935, an action that greatly increased the number of applicants.[116]

FDR never saw the goal of having 600,000 in the CCC met. Instead, when the Fifth Enrollment Period ended on September 30, 1935, the Corps had peaked at 502,000, due partly to the creation of the National Youth Administration, which provided another option for unemployed youth, and also, according to Salmond, partly to the "obstinacy" of Harry Hopkins, Roosevelt's new confidant and no friend of the CCC.

Fortunately for Utah, the ripples of the political machinations in Washington seldom impacted the Beehive State, although the threat of camps closing surfaced at the end of many enrollment periods. Actually, Utah had thirty-three camps operating during that climactic Fifth Period, and the number never dropped below thirty until the final period beginning in October 1941. In fact, the highest number of camps in Utah was attained immediately prior to that—during Period Seventeen, April through September 1941—when thirty-six camps were in operation.

When the Seventh Enrollment Period began in April 1936, there were only 1,778 Utah enrollees in the camps.[117] The period of local domination was over, as Utahns fell below two thousand in number for the first time since May 1933. Never again was that figure reached. In July 1937, 43 percent of the approximately 4,600 enrollees in the state were local youths. There should have been even more, as for the first time since the CCC began, there were still not enough applicants in Utah to fill the slots the state was allotted. In Salt Lake County only twenty-one young men had applied for the 173 open positions, and while figures were not yet available, it appeared that other counties might have similar reports.[118] The Seventh Corps Area was becoming more strongly represented in Utah; at the end of the period three trainloads of enrollees returned to Fort Lincoln, North Dakota, and were replaced by other Seventh Corps men who took their places in the Utah camps.[119] There were few changes in the work patterns that year; the projects had been laid out and were being pursued as planned.

Praise for the CCC

It is interesting to note that throughout the entire legislative process the actual value of the CCC was seldom questioned. Salmond described the Corps as being "at the zenith of its great popularity, drawing support from all sections of the community" and "the most popular New Deal agency." He also quoted the *Chicago Tribune* saying that "the merits of the CCC were not an issue" and that the value of the organization was beyond question.[120] Locally, the *Salt Lake Tribune* chimed in with a left-handed compliment by pointing out that the CCC "has suffered less from criticism than many other projects," but it was still hoping to see some military training introduced.[121]

Positive sentiment was echoed across the country; this feeling was indicated in a letter from the Utah Woolgrowers Association to Utah's junior senator: "Without question, the most helpful government agency that has come to the range livestock men in this part of Utah has been the local CCC camp." In fact, the sheepmen were annoyed that some $1,200 in funds supposedly allotted to their local camp in northeastern Utah, DG-31 in Vernal, were apparently being diverted elsewhere, thereby hampering the work locally. The organization sought the senator's help in seeing that the practice cease immediately, since they saw little value in "their" money being spent not only in other Utah counties but especially, in the amount of $50.00, going toward an experiment station in Oregon.[122]

With nearly all concerned being most enthusiastic about the success and value of the CCC, one might wonder why Congress did not grant permanence, as Roosevelt—and, indeed, most of the country, apparently—wished to see happen. The *Salt Lake Tribune* indicated that the CCC "seems fairly certain to become a permanent part of American life."

Fechner stated that after an encouraging visit to the White House he was "preparing the necessary recommendations to Congress to provide for making the CCC permanent with an enrollment of between 300,000 and 350,000 young men."[123]

Salmond offers the following basic reasons. First, Congress seemed to feel "that a permanent CCC would be a gesture of pessimism, a recognition of defeat in the war against unemployment." A second factor was that the Civil Service provisions stripping members of Congress and senators of the powerful opportunity of patronage were not acceptable. Third, if the Corps were to be limited to 300,000 young men, several camps would have to close, creating "local discontent." Perhaps even more significant was the feeling that the legislation had not been sufficiently considered and that the creation of a permanent agency required more serious study. Increased emphasis on education in the camps was another disturbing factor.

Extension of the Program Questioned

Although the Civilian Conservation Corps enjoyed widespread success during the First Enrollment Period, even then there were questions about its continuance. There seemed little doubt that Roosevelt wanted to see the program continued, but in the political arena "it ain't over 'til it's over," as Yogi Berra so eloquently described lingering uncertainty.

The *Herald Journal* of Logan editorialized in rhetoric typical of prevailing attitudes:

> One of the most completely successful of all the items on the New Deal program seems to be the forestry work of the Civilian Conservation Corps.... So well is the project working out that a person is inclined to wonder if it might not be a good thing to make this forest army a permanent affair.... All of this of course would be pretty expensive but it might be money well spent.... [C]ertainly the question deserves serious consideration. This forest army is too good an outfit to be discarded off-hand.[124]

On January 25, 1934, President Roosevelt notified Emergency Conservation Work Director Robert Fechner that the program would be carried on for at least another year. The president asked Congress for $275,000,000, an amount that would provide for continued enrollment at the current figure of slightly more than 300,000.[125] Two weeks later, Utah's Governor Blood received instructions from Fechner concerning the continuation. Fechner invited Blood to make recommendations for the establishment of new camps but warned him to "limit your proposals to cases of real emergency" since the granting of "any great number of new camps" would be virtually impossible.[126] Unfortunately continuance of the program was to be an issue that was discussed the entire nine years of the Corps' existence, and its justification was debated from one congressional session to the next.

The announcement that FDR had extended the life of the CCC was "received with enthusiasm by Forest Service officials." The enthusiasm, in fact, was practically euphoric, as the Cedar City newspaper announced that "another year of the CCC program would develop the Dixie Forest to a point that would have taken years to reach under normal conditions and far beyond the fondest dreams of many of the forest officials."[127]

Although the CCC camps nominally held two hundred men each at full strength, this figure was usually attained only at the beginning of an enrollment period; therefore even with a consistent number of camps the number of enrollees might vary widely. There were, for example, thirty-three camps on October 1, 1936, and thirty-four on October 20, 1938, September 2, 1939, and September 30, 1940.[128] Enrollees for each of those dates numbered 4,524, 6,800, 6,179, and 4,109. From these and other figures it can be seen that five thousand men a year would be a fairly close approximation of the average annual enrollment to serve in Utah.

In July 1937 legislation dropped the maximum age limit, from twenty-eight back to twenty-three, and the relief requirement was removed; enrollment was to be open to any young men between seventeen and twenty-three who needed employment. The Civil Service requirement was removed at House insistence, thereby maintaining the patronage plum members of Congress so enjoyed—and utilized.

For a time in 1938, it appeared that many camps across the country, including six or possibly seven in Utah, would be eliminated because of President Roosevelt's desire to balance the budget. The prospects alarmed many in Utah, including Salt Lake City Chamber of Commerce Secretary Gus Backman. Backman, especially concerned about the future of camps such as F-38 in the Salt Lake City area, wrote frantic letters to Utah's congressional delegation and CCC officials, reminding them, "You will find in the opinion of 99 percent of our people the Forest Service's program of CCC work has been outstanding."[129]

The situation improved, however, in the fall of 1938. Four new camps were added to the Division of Grazing for the Twelfth Period: Hanksville (DG-114) and Green River (DG-115) east of the populated middle strip of Utah and Callao (DG-116) and Garrison (DG-117) in the West Desert.

In 1937 the future of the CCC again surfaced in the nation's capital. To the biannual quarrel over its permanency was added the issue of just where it would be administratively housed, which became another significant bone of contention. In his January 7 budget message of that year Roosevelt asked that Congress "establish the Corps as a permanent agency of the Government." The bill finally introduced would have actually made little change in the day-to-day functioning of the 300,000-man Corps, although it would have required all CCC employees to come under the Civil Service Commission, including the mastery of Civil Service exams by all current employees.

In what Salmond describes as a formality, the Senate Committee on Education and Labor heard only one voice questioning the basic premise of the CCC. Utah Senator Elbert D. Thomas called for the removal of the idea of the CCC being a relief organization and proposed that, instead, the Corps should be regarded as a source of rehabilitation of all socially deprived young men down to the age of sixteen, regardless of their financial status.[130] On the other hand, this was the event in which Utah's other senator, William H. King, broke ranks to be the only Democrat to join with Republican Senator William E. Borah in voting against the Senate proposal to make the CCC a permanent institution. For this and other attacks against the New Deal, King was to suffer defeat in the 1940 election.[131]

That bill, however, brought Robert Fechner's anxieties to a boil, especially over the reorganization of the executive branch of government and the resulting relocating of the CCC. Fechner felt that this implied a change in the CCC's direction away from work relief to a program of welfare and training, a change he vehemently opposed, as did his assistant director and later successor, James McEntee.[132]

After experiencing controversy of long standing, the new legislation pushed Fechner over the edge, and he angrily submitted his resignation, which he soon withdrew even though he had been battling ill health through most of 1939. The increased tension between Fechner and other government officials was to continue until he experienced a heart attack in early December and died three weeks later on New Year's Eve, the last day of 1939. The Senate confirmed James J. McEntee, Fechner's assistant, as the new director on February 27, 1940. McEntee, a close personal friend of Fechner's, had, like him, previously worked as a labor negotiator with the International Association of Machinists.[133]

In spite of the turmoil in Washington the CCC kept plugging along, and in September 1939, Senator Elbert Thomas announced that Utah would have thirty-four camps for the Fourteenth Period over the winter of 1939–40. With sixteen camps closing and ten new camps starting, there would be a net gain of one. Unfortunately, connecting the dots between plans that have been announced and the fulfillment of those plans does not always work out. Myton and Dry Valley, for example, never did open, while some of those shown as closing would be back in Period Fifteen after their regular seasonal closing for the winter. There were, however, six new Division of Grazing camps, including some of the most isolated in the entire Utah CCC experience, such as Lucin, Simpson Springs, Black Rock, Modena, Dry Valley, and Willow Springs, numbered 153 to 158, respectively.[134]

The Twelfth Enrollment Period ended in March 1939, with the Utah enrollments at 848, the first time the number had dropped below one thousand.[135] New enrollments increased the figure to 1,253 the next month, however, as the Thirteenth Period began. The Forest Service gained a new camp, F-50, at Seeley Creek, east of Ephraim in the Manti National Forest, which operated for two consecutive summers.

That year, 1939, Roosevelt made his final attempt to achieve permanence for the agency. Many of the same issues from the 1937 hearings—Civil Service provisions, Fechner's salary, and the concept of permanence itself—were raised again in 1939, but as a result of the increasing tension in Europe and Asia, a new matter was introduced regarding the possibility of military training in the CCC camps. Although both Fechner and the War Department's representative, Brigadier General George P. Tyner, spoke against the plan, many members of Congress demanded that military training be included in any plan for CCC permanence. Nothing came of the idea, however, and the bill that Roosevelt signed on August 8, 1939, made virtually no changes to what had been accepted in the way of numbers in 1937 and actually extended funding until July 1, 1943.

Figure 4.8. Two concrete structures at Seeley Creek camp F-50 built to hold fifty-five-gallon barrels of fuel.

By the middle of 1941, the need for the CCC as a relief organization had declined even further, although $163,470.86 had been allotted that year to Utah dependants.[136] When the year began, there were approximately 300,000 enrollees in camps throughout the nation; the year closed with 174,000, the lowest number the Corps had reached since it began operation.[137]

District Realignment

CCC administrators recommended to the War Department that the Fort Douglas, Boise, and Pocatello district offices be merged for easier administration, a recommendation that immediately drew fire from Salt Lake City officials. The War Department agreed with the proposal, stating that the Army needed space at Fort Douglas for the expansion of an Air Corp unit stationed at the post. Mayor Ab Jenkins and Gus P. Backman of Salt Lake City attempted to find rent-free office space for the CCC operations, and when Boise and Pocatello merged as planned, Salt Lake City was able to continue on its own. The postponement was short-lived, however, and on February 1, 1942, the consolidation of the Salt Lake City office with Pocatello became official. The new district supervised forty-four camps in Idaho, eastern Nevada, Utah, eastern Oregon, and western Wyoming and included 5,500 enrollees.[138] By then the CCC was in its last days.

CHAPTER 5

The Work They Did

[They did] flood control, channel stabilization, road construction, fence construction, fire suppression, farm and ranch development including irrigation and erosion control, drainage, stock water development. Fire suppression both on Forest and on private and other public range lands.

—William Anderson, superintendent, SCS-5

In his press conference of March 15, 1933, President Roosevelt described the work of the proposed but not as yet officially named Civilian Conservation Corps as being that which would otherwise not be done so that it would not conflict with regular public works.[1] As the program grew, the work opportunities also developed. In Utah enrollees worked at nearly every job listed on the sixty-two-item report of work projects. Ideas came not only from the technical agencies responsible for developing projects but from many sources among the interested citizenry as well.[2]

Communities often weighed in on projects that would be of benefit to them. A joint meeting of the Lions Clubs of Richfield and Fillmore came up with the suggestion of a direct, fifty-three-mile route through the mountains connecting the two towns that would cut off about twenty-three miles from the trip on the existing road through Clear Creek Canyon.[3]

A. O. Smoot, chairman of the Commissioners of Utah County, offered one of the first suggestions, almost before the ink was even dry on the CCC legislation. He hoped that the tree-planting program of the federal government might include the planting of trees for a snow fence and for shade adjacent to the dangerous stretch of highway near Point-of-the-Mountain between Salt Lake City and Provo.[4] Although Smoot's idea died on the vine, many others survived to come to fruition. Regional Forester Rutledge outlined the possibilities of the program by stating that

Figure 5.1. Mountain road between Spring City and Skyline Drive in Sanpete County typical of Civilian Conservation Corps road construction projects.

besides reforestation, projects would include the construction of trails, phone lines, campground improvements, fences and cabins, low standard roads, flood-control work, and insect control. While emphasizing that helping young boys gain self-respect and self-reliance was the primary purpose of the program, he said, "At the same time we hope to get some worthwhile work done."[5]

Assignments varied from camp to camp, depending upon the needs of the surrounding area and the technical agency supervising the work. Probably the most common work of the enrollees during those nine years was building roads throughout the state, whether in mountains or the West Desert.

But whether the work was of a routine nature, such as building roads, campgrounds, or reservoirs, or whether it was a more unique assignment, such as the construction of supply houses or deer pastures, the work schedules of the various camps differed only slightly. After the morning routine, which usually included policing the barracks and grounds, enrollees were ready for work call. One superintendent described the beginning of the workday in his six-month report as follows:

> After breakfast, the trucks are placed in line with the tailgates down. Water cans with water for the entire day are placed in trucks by foremen and driver according to the size of the different crews. The men are turned over to the work agency at 7:45

a.m. The men know exactly which truck is theirs and which foreman they have.... Men leave work in time to arrive back at camp 4:00 p.m. giving the camp a full six hour day on the job.[6]

Usually the enrollees had thirty minutes for lunch. The eight-hour day, including travel time and lunch, was rigidly observed. This aspect of the schedule often upset the men of the technical agency, since it seemed that work was just getting started when time came to get ready to return to camp. And at least one enrollee couldn't quite get used to working only limited hours: "Being raised on the farm I was used to a full day's work besides chores at night and in the morning seven days a week and twenty-four hour irrigation turns every week in the summertime.... And they even gave us $5 a month."[7]

It was especially difficult when the work project lay some distance from camp. There was no company stationed in Logan Canyon during the winter of 1934–35, and a spike camp was not deemed feasible; but there was still work to be done, so it was necessary to bring in crews from Blacksmith Fork Canyon near Hyrum, almost twenty miles from the project. Dawn had barely arrived when the trucks left camp F-2, and as soon as they arrived on the job some of the men began preparations for lunch. By the time the enrollees left work to be back at camp by 4:00, only four or five hours of work had been accomplished. Still, as J. Whitney Floyd, Utah State forester and forestry professor at Utah State Agricultural College—now Utah State University—told me, the enrollees were "good, hardworking kids" and always did enough work to justify the trip.[8]

Like F-30 and F-40 in Utah County, camp F-16 at Duck Creek east of Cedar City had a typical variety of assignments. One of the earlier projects in 1933 was the construction of a road from Duck Creek to Mammoth down in Iron County. In the southern end of the state the CCC completed the Duck Creek Recreation Camp, started earlier by volunteer residents. In addition to this enrollees poisoned two hundred acres for rock chucks; built pipelines, fences, phone lines, fireplaces, stoves, and signs; dug water trenches; and cleared roads and trails. In June the boys even spent eight man-days shoveling snow! One of the major projects of F-16 was to complete the Navajo Lake dike project. The Cedar City Chamber of Commerce had been working on a recreational project at Duck Creek and had it about 70 percent completed. Upon request, the Forest

Service took over the project, raised the height of the dike about six feet, and strengthened it with rocks on both sides. Further work on the recreational area included a thousand-seat amphitheater, clearing sixty acres of land in the park, and completing a baseball diamond.[9]

Tree-planting, roads, and campgrounds were typical projects of most of the Forest Service camps. The CCC devoted much time to the development of recreational facilities throughout the forests as well. A picnic and campground for 1,500 people erected in the Fish Lake National Forest was described as "the biggest Forest Service Recreational project in the Intermountain West." This began as a Works Progress Administration project in the spring of 1937, but CCC enrollees later transferred in from the Salina camp to help complete it.[10]

Many of the work projects of the Forest Service differed from those of the Division of Grazing merely due to the difference in the location of the camps. Most Division of Grazing camps rested on the public domain outside the national forests, which was primarily rangeland on the western and eastern borders of the state; the Forest Service camps were confined to projects in the nine national forests in the state. Since most of the timberlands within the state were to be found in the national forests, projects of reforestation, campground construction, and the development of recreational sites stayed restricted to those camps under the supervision of the Forest Service or, in limited cases, the Park Service.

National Park Service reports showed a similar diversity, as enrollees participated in even something as mundane as irrigating. CCC crews in Zion built a diversion dam across the North Fork of the Virgin River to raise the level of the water, which was then diverted into a ditch for irrigating transplanted areas at the South Entrance of the park.

NPS enrollees also constructed cottages and converted an office into a museum and information office as well as an old residence into administrative and technical offices. One project was the remodeling of a building formerly used as a museum at the Grotto Campground into a cottage to be occupied by the campground ranger/caretaker. The purpose was later changed again, and it is now used as a residence for visiting artists, historians, and others involved in research.

During the 1930s enrollees improved campsites there at the Grotto Campground, built equipment, and laid out parking spaces bordered by rock curbs still in use more than seventy-five years later.[11]

Figure 5.2. Pylon marking the south end of Jericho Camp, DG-26, south of Ephraim on US Highway 6, Juab County.

Figure 5.3. Hawaiian visitor Percy TeHira admiring the rockwork at Mutual Dell amphitheater on the Alpine Loop.

Rockwork at Zion National Park became almost a CCC trademark, although most visitors today are unaware of the projects carried out. The majestic sign pylon at the South Entrance and the Grotto Museum at the other end of the canyon are typical of many structures chiseled out of the red sandstone found in great abundance in the park. Garages and maintenance buildings are still in use, though out of sight of the casual visitor, as are cottages built for park personnel along Oak Creek and elsewhere in the park. The amphitheater at the South Campground is a good example of the enrollees' workmanship. Curbs lining the highway through the park, equipment sheds, and culverts are other examples. A rather unorthodox project was the construction of two sets of steps leading nowhere that were constructed for the 1937 Easter pageant staged in the park.[12]

Other amphitheaters built at Mutual Dell and Aspen Grove on the Alpine Loop in Utah County are still in use today, as is the thousand-seat Guinavah amphitheater of locally quarried limestone near Tony Grove in Logan Canyon in Cache County.[13] Bridges, rock culverts, and spillways are additional testimonies of the skill developed by the young men of the Corps.

REFORESTATION, RESEEDING, AND RANGE MANAGEMENT

More than five and a half million man-days passed just in developing forest nurseries, clearing and leveling land, preparing seedbeds, and planting, caring for, and transplanting seedlings. During the nine-year span of the program CCC enrollees planted "the stupendous total of 2,246,100,000 young trees on potential forest lands."[14] Only 3,255,000 of these were in Utah, but this still represented over three million more trees than if the CCC program had not existed. More than 180,000 trees were planted to help protect the watersheds and terraces in Davis County.[15] In one week in 1940, F-31 planted three thousand ponderosa pine and one thousand blue spruce seedlings around recreational areas in the Dixie National Forest in southern Utah.[16] In his story of the work of the CCC, James J. McEntee presents an almost melodious description of the work:

> There is a knack to planting trees. There is a rhythm to it. A tree-planter's tools are a tray of seedlings and a mattock or a planting bar. He swings the mattock with a measured stroke, kneels down and plants a seedling, carefully presses the fresh soil around the roots, humps the earth around it, strides forward the prescribed distance and takes another measured swing with the mattock. The first hundred he thinks are fun. The next

Figure 5.4. Civilian Conservation Corps logo.

> five or ten thousand he thinks are monotonous. After that tree planting is in his blood.[17]

Since the initial days when the terms "reforestation army" and "Roosevelt's tree army" referred to the still-unnamed Civilian Conservation Corps, the idea of planting and protecting trees has perhaps been most closely identified with the program. And indeed there has been a close relationship, as Barbara Sommer describes in her history of the CCC in Minnesota: "Tree planting, for which the CCC is best known today, was only a part—albeit a significant part—of forest camp work. It was and remains the symbol of the CCC."[18]

Tree-planting was an arduous job, usually handled by two-man teams, one enrollee carrying a box of seedlings and the other digging the hole. After putting the seedling into the hole—which had to be deep enough for the roots to all point downward—the boys stomped on the ground, thoroughly tamping the encircling earth. Tree-planting crews in the Willard Basin were described as averaging about two hundred trees per man per day.[19]

The thinning process, on the other hand, required more judgment calls, since the men were to cut out some trees and leave others. Enrollees assigned this task were expected to wade into an overgrown clump of trees and cut down those that were sickly or possibly misshapen. Cutting out underbrush also gave the remaining trees a better chance to grow straight and tall, creating better timber and at the same time reducing fire danger.

In addition to the typical purpose of reforestation, that is, restoring the forests, tree-planting was carried out for aesthetic purposes such as landscaping. In the spring of 1937 Company 940 out of F-48 assisted in beautifying Washington Memorial Grove in Parley's Canyon, where enrollees planted 1,400 Douglas fir trees. Crews from one camp helped landscape the new George Dern Memorial Plot at Mountain Dell Reservoir. The Utah Federation of Women's Clubs announced that shrubs and 2,638 trees would be planted on the two hundred-acre plot. Firs were planted around the Dern Memorial, while hardwoods mixed with firs were planted elsewhere in the park.[20]

After reclaiming good rangeland from plant and animal pests, it was also necessary to see that man himself did not abuse it, necessitating range management provisions. Under the terms of the Taylor Grazing Act of 1934, ranchers were restricted in the number of livestock they could run on a particular area. The Division of Grazing took responsibility for the enforcement of these restrictions, and the CCC erected drift fences to ease the work of range control. Crews actually erected fences for a variety of purposes. The Vernal camp, for example, had one twenty-man crew building fences to control cattle drifting from their summer to the winter range. Another nine-mile drift fence was built to separate ranges assigned to sheep from those reserved for cattle. North of Vernal, enrollees from Manila camp F-35 prepared one thousand log poles for gates and cattle guards for a fence along the boundary of the Manila Grazing District.[21] During the first few years of the CCC program, the Utah camps generally averaged about 140 miles of fence-building a year; the figures increased somewhat beginning in 1939, and the overall average reached 230 miles a year, or a total of 2,069 miles of fence.

Beginning in 1939 the CCC camps, especially those under the Division of Grazing, commenced a vast program of reseeding rangeland that had been denuded, by either rodents, erosion, or overgrazing. Of the 214,290 acres eventually reseeded in Utah, approximately one-third received treatment during the twelve months ending in June 1940.[22] The activities of the Vernal camp constituted a major part of this project. A crew under Foreman Forrest D. Thomas began a reseeding program that covered between ten and twenty thousand acres of overgrazed rangeland.

Figure 5.5. Civilian Conservation Corps–built road to a job site in the west desert east of Garrison. Usually, one of the first tasks of a new camp was the construction of a road to the job site.

The variety of soil and moisture conditions present required a variety of different grasses. Indian ricegrass, filaree, crested wheatgrass, buckbrush, and clover were planted.[23]

The Hanksville camp carried on a similar project about two years later in what was described as the largest single project in that particular area. After eight thousand acres had already been reseeded, preparations proceeded for the reseeding of another ten thousand acres with a mixture of crested wheatgrass, ricegrass, clover, and rye. First, seed was scattered over the land, about four pounds per acre. Next, a tractor pulling a disc harrow followed to cover the seeds and scarify the land, providing contour-following trenches. Money to purchase the seed came from the so-called 25 percent fund, which came from the grazing district's share of the fees paid by range users.[24]

TRAILS, ROADS, AND BRIDGES

Next to the development of watering places for their sheep and cattle, the livestock men of Utah needed roads over which to trail their animals from summer mountain meadows to winter grazing lands and back again. In some cases this required a cut through a mountain pass; in others, a road had to be carved out of the side of a mountain to enable animals to get around an otherwise impassable barrier. Nearly every annual report

Figure 5.6. Rotary Park east of Springville where Hobble Creek Canyon forks. SE-206 was on the left fork, and F-30, on the right.

from the Division of Grazing camps and many newspaper accounts told of roadwork being done in the western desert.

In the winter of 1937, for example, survey crews of the Jericho camp began laying out twenty miles of proposed road from Joy to the Tooele-Juab county line. Other men worked on a sheep trail running from Lookout Pass out to Swasey Springs. In April 1938, an article on the camp described its most important work as the construction of a road into the western part of the county via Sand Pass.[25]

Road-building immediately became an integral part of the work of all the CCC camps, as in nearly every case it was necessary to construct access routes to the projects on which they were working. Company 1254 of Hobble Creek camp SE-206 started the road-building program off right by building a road through Spring Creek and Kolob canyons to erosion-control projects in Little Rock Canyon and then on into Provo Canyon, thereby completing one of the many loop roads provided by the CCC that first summer.[26] And the work certainly went on from there.

Pole Heaven Road between the Left Fork of Hobble Creek Canyon and Provo Canyon was completed; Payson Canyon and Diamond Fork roads were also improved. Another road in southern Utah from Parowan to Cedar Breaks opened up what was to become a national monument. In an oral history interview Glade Sowards describes in detail his memories as a child regarding some of the roadwork the CCC did:

Figure 5.7. Civilian Conservation Corps road constructed in the West Desert, where construction was more difficult than it might seem.

> I remember the road that went from Vernal to Manila.... Instead of just taking dirt and making a fill, the CCC's would take rocks and fit them in by hand and would make a nice retaining wall and then they would put dirt behind it. Then it was very neat and always made a good solid road. A place where the mountain would sluff off, they would dig down to some kind of bedrock and then brick it up with generally rock; I have seen some that was done with old railroad ties and things like this, but generally it was rock that they use. So these boys worked hard.[27]

Box Elder, Tooele, Juab, Millard, Beaver, and Iron counties occupy nearly one-third the area of Utah, lying almost entirely in the arid region between the Wasatch Range and the Nevada line. Since most of this area is desert, the population of the counties concentrates largely along their eastern margins closer to the Wasatch Front. There are, therefore, few roads built out into the empty rangelands in the western part of the state, which are primarily important as wintering grounds for huge herds of sheep and lesser numbers of cattle. It was here that the CCC built most of the stock trails and roads.

Clover Creek camp DG-28 lay in the eastern part of Utah's West Desert in Tooele County. For the first six months of the camp's operation, the enrollees of Company 2517 worked on roads. Six of the first twelve projects planned involved road construction or conditioning, including a road over Johnson Pass out toward the present Dugway Proving Grounds, another north of Faust through Lookout Pass, and another from St. John north toward Grantsville.[28] Farther south in Beaver and Iron counties bulldozer operators of DG-30 and DG-35 scraped their way across the desert between Enoch and Minersville in the vicinity of present State Highway 130. Although most of the work proved quite simple, about four miles of the route lay in clay, which required gravel-capping to provide a satisfactory surface. The completion of this road reduced the distance between Milford and Cedar City to about thirty-five miles and saved ranchers both money and time in getting stock to their destination.[29]

The Milford camp, DG-35, carried on another major project in the same general area the following year. A look at a Utah road map will show that the highway between Milford and Beaver must swing south to avoid the Mineral Mountains lying between the two communities. A half century earlier, soldiers from Fort Cameron had built a trail by way of Granite Pass; this was to be the foundation of the new Beaver Pass Road of the CCC. This shortened the trail by eight miles and permitted livestock men to get to the Milford railhead with one less night on the trail. The eighteen-mile route included ten miles of ditching and grading and eight miles of heavier work. Four miles lay through brush, six miles through oak and mahogany, and eight miles at the higher elevations through heavy growths of cedar. The estimated cost was $6,765; 13,500 man-days were planned.

Another road from Cove Fort through Black Rock built by the same camp proved only slightly less formidable. Engineers estimated that 12,000 man-days and $5,865 would be required to complete the seventy-seven-mile road to be built from Cove Fort through Black Rock and on over Cricket Pass in the Beaver Mountains. Lying south of the dry bed of Sevier Lake, the road eventually intersected with Utah Highway 21 near the Desert Range Experiment Station. The men under Foreman George Payne were expected to meet a variety of conditions, from heavy rock ledges to stretches of clay flats, where the construction would be quite simple.

They encountered problems of vegetation clearance ranging from the simple matter of dry brush to the hard work required to clear heavy timber. Nearly one-third of a million sheep and the men who looked after them would have reason to thank the CCC as they traveled the road each season.[30]

A major thoroughfare in the West Desert is the Garrison–Black Rock Road, much of which was built by enrollees from Black Rock camp DG-155 beginning in 1939.[31] Several thousand acres of winter graze was thus made available to grateful sheepmen. Except for the quite majestic Crystal Peak, the scenery along the road consists of little except desert landscape, sparse juniper trees, and Sevier Lake off to the north as one nears the eastern end of the road. Not as adequately signed as it might be, the well-graveled road roughly parallels Utah 21, lying about twenty miles to the south between Garrison and Milford.

The work of building roads in national forests and national parks was deemed so valuable that when there was a possibility of that type of endeavor being suspended cries of protest were soon heard. The Associated Civic Clubs of Southern Utah mounted the verbal ramparts by wiring Utah Congressmen Abe Murdock and J. W. Robinson, protesting a possible cut in funds for road-building on public lands.[32]

The CCC built miles of roads not originally planned as such. Many of the dams, reservoirs, springs, and other work projects lay in remote areas, often virtually inaccessible. Since it was necessary to get crews on to the job, some form of road had to be roughed out. Although it was not always necessary to build the standard fourteen-foot graded truck trail, superintendents soon found that it paid off in the long run to do so. The money saved in time on the job and in the elimination of many truck repairs justified the construction of truck roads to each project. As a result, the state of Utah now has roads in areas where population alone would be insufficient to warrant them.

CCC camps administered by the Forest Service also built stock trails in national forest areas. In late 1939 about seventy-five men of Company 958, stationed at F-40, began work on the elimination of steep grades on the stock driveway in Spanish Fork Canyon south of Provo. The estimated cost of $3,000 was shared by the Utah County Commission and the state. The stock driveway itself had been completed previously at a cost of $12,800, but steep grades over a five-mile stretch of the route had prevented its complete utilization, since the stockmen found it necessary to drive their animals on the highway, resulting in several being killed.[33] About a year later, the same camp provided the labor for another stock trail from the western part of Utah County to the mouth of Provo Canyon. Utah County and the State Road Commission split the cost of the $25,000 project. The county commissioners signed the work agreement on February 10, 1941, and CCC youths whose labor for the project was valued at $9,000 readied themselves for work and already had eight hundred posts ready for installation.[34]

In some cases building a stock trail consisted of little more than merely leveling a path along which the sheep or cattle could more easily travel. Others, however, required considerably more work. Early in the experience of the Cedar City camp, plans were drawn for a three-and-a-half-mile stock driveway through rugged timber country. Poisonous plants abounded in the area, so the driveway was completely fenced with four thousand aspen poles and 1,800 cedar posts to keep the sheep from noxious weeds.[35]

Division of Grazing camps in Cedar City and St. George worked from their respective ends to construct a stock driveway between the two communities, where huge herds of cattle and sheep had previously been driven each fall and spring on the way to new pastures or shipping points. Since no well-defined route existed, however, property owners along the way often complained of trespassing. Finally landowners, stockmen, and local officials of the grazing district agreed on a route, and the CCC camps went to work. Cedar posts marked the driveway boundaries, so spaced that in level country drovers could see at least two posts ahead of the herd.

In one stretch of the driveway near Hamilton Fort, the signposts stood 650 feet apart, alternating on opposite sides of the trail. CCC crews cleared underbrush and cut off low branches in wooded areas to help prevent loss of stock. The St. George camp, DG-45, completed the twenty-nine-mile stretch from St. George to New Harmony; DG-30 of Cedar City marked the northern portion of the route. Although some hoped that it might be possible to fence the driveway along a three-and-a-half-mile stretch, the grazing district advisory council announced that it was unable to get funds for the wire, so the plan was dropped.[36]

In the eastern part of the state the road- and trail work of DG-34 at Blanding was typical. Several springs had been completed in the area under the drought-relief program in November and December 1936, but in order to use the log troughs at Distillery Springs, the CCC had to blast a seven-foot trail down the face of a sandstone ledge. The trail was eight hundred feet in length and had six switchbacks; however, for just seventy-two man-days and a cost of $142.47 for materials and supervision, another supply of water became available.[37]

San Juan County, in which the little community of Blanding is the most populous, is about the size of Connecticut, Delaware, and Rhode Island combined. Montezuma Creek, which empties into the San Juan River across from Navajo country, lies southeast of Blanding. In the winter of 1935–36, enrollees from the Blanding camp began building a truck trail to open a large sheep and cattle range in such exotic areas as Mustang Mesa and Alkali Canyon. They built eight miles during the Sixth Enrollment Period and another twenty during the Seventh. Two foremen and a crew of seven worked two shifts a day on the project, known as the Blanding-Montezuma Truck Trail.

The project moved slowly. The Recapture Wash proved a major obstacle. The wash was twenty feet deep and sixty feet wide at the spot where engineers decided to place a bridge. The stream was diverted during the Eighth Period, and during the Ninth Period DG-34 crews constructed a truss-type bridge with a span of fifty-four feet. The bridge sat on pilings thirty-three feet long, which sank into the ground eight feet below the surface of the streambed. On September 20, 1937, the bridge was dedicated, and the CCC and grateful stockmen celebrated together at a barbecue. Even though the road lay unfinished, it vastly improved the possibilities of feeding the 30,000 sheep and three thousand cattle that grazed the area.[38]

THE WORK OF COMPANY 958

That the diversity of the work projects envisioned by Rutledge was achieved can perhaps best be seen in a report given by Uinta Forest Supervisor Charles DeMoisy five years later in which he recounted the accomplishments of one CCC company assigned to Utah County.[39] Company 958 was a Utah company that had started out at Mt. Nebo camp F-9, one of the twenty-six original camps in Utah. After serving at Washington camp PE-216 the preceding winter, Company 958 opened camp F-30 in the summer of 1934 up the right-hand fork of Hobble Creek Canyon, east of Springville. After 1938 the company then stayed in Utah County until 1941, seasonally moving between F-30 and the Rock Canyon CCC camp in Provo.[40]

During the summer months while at F-30, Company 958 built campgrounds at Hobble Creek, Payson Canyon, Diamond Fork, Wolf Creek, and Daniels Canyon, among others. They also installed 6,250 feet of

Figure 5.8. Informative sign at Civilian Conservation Corps–built Ponderosa Campground unfortunately fails to mention that it, too, was built by enrollees at F-9.

pipeline for drinking water, and the construction of 137 camp stoves or grills, sixteen tables and benches, and some open-air theaters, including those at Mutual Dell and Aspen Grove on the Alpine Loop, were among their other projects. Enrollees built horse trails in Rock and Slate canyons as well as a stock bridge over Sixth Water Creek, which is what carries irrigation water from Strawberry Reservoir through tunnels into Diamond Fork. DeMoisy told of three miles of range fences completed and the development of seven stock watering facilities.

Battling the pine beetle infestation was a constant job for many camps. Company 958 brought 1,360 acres of lodgepole timber under control near the head of Provo River and on Tabby Mountain. Sportsmen also benefited from the eight miles of stream improvement, including small dams to increase the capacity for fish in Hobble Creek and Diamond Fork.

Surveying; posting forest boundaries; making 541 road, trail, and information signs; fabricating rustic furniture, swings, and teeters for public campgrounds; and erecting camp buildings and forest service warehouses in Heber, Spanish Fork, and Provo, as well as office buildings in Heber and Spanish Fork, all showed up on work reports. Regular work such as that done on these projects was occasionally interrupted, of course, and crews had to spend time fighting wildfires as well as performing other emergency activities, described in chapter 9.

Figure 5.9. Timpanogos Cave National Monument.

This rather lengthy recitation of projects carried out by one CCC company operating out of two camps in Utah County provides some idea of the scope of activities to which Forest Service camps were assigned.[41]

Iron County furnished DG-30 with the powder, fuses, and caps for Company 1508 to blow out a twenty-two-foot cut on Kanarra Mountain south of Cedar City. Between August 2 and October 15, 1937, Ohio enrollees worked at eliminating a gap of one-tenth of a mile to link the two sections of a road winding up the west side of the mountain. The project, described as "one of the most hazardous tasks the camp has worked on," was completed without accident and was expected to benefit fifty stockmen in the area.[42]

During this time the CCC started many of the loop roads now connecting some of the canyons. As soon as crews completed camp F-5 in American Fork Canyon they went to work planting 1,500 pine and spruce seedlings in Deer Creek Canyon and at Altamont. The company carried out rodent-control projects with the use of poison grain. As the season progressed the boys spent several days grubbing noxious weeds and Canadian thistle. Crews were assigned to make improvements in trails, tunnels, and other facilities at Timpanogos Cave National Monument to make additional caverns available for tourists. In addition to these eight-to-four jobs at which they regularly worked, the CCC force constituted a huge fire brigade, units of which could be mobilized at any time for forest fire suppression.[43]

THE SKYLINE DRIVES—NORTH AND SOUTH

Several roads that were constructed by the Corps have become the scenic byways and back ways of the present day. The beautiful Davis County road today known as Skyline Drive leaves the city of Bountiful just north of the Latter-day Saints Temple and winds east and north through the mountains past Centerville Canyon and Bountiful Peak to the head of Farmington Canyon, where it descends back into the traffic patterns that make up today's Wasatch Front. Men from Company 940 working from camp F-48 began building the road out of Parrish Canyon in the summer of 1936.[44] Today one can look out from the road over the metropolitan areas below, as well as see the CCC-built terraces, which are still doing their job.

Still another CCC-built Skyline Drive is found a bit farther south in Sanpete County, roughly paralleling U.S. 89 ten to fifteen miles east of Fairview and Ephraim. In 1977, Carlyle Olleston was interviewed by his daughter and told her of his father, Seth Olleston, who was formerly a ranger in the Fairview District of the Manti National Forest. Seth told his son that he had had a CCC camp that built roads, trails, and firebreaks in the mountains east of Fairview. Although no camp number was given, it was almost certainly F-28, identified as either Fairview camp or Gooseberry camp. He stated that CCC crews built the dam creating the present Gooseberry Reservoir, located about twelve miles east of the town of Fairview north of the present Fairview Sno-Park. These young men were also involved in the construction of Skyline Drive along the crest of the ridge between Oak Creek on the west and Gooseberry Creek on the east, providing views of both valleys.[45]

That Skyline Drive of today still bears the original name and as a result of extensions on both ends now stretches some eighty miles from Tucker on U.S. 6 in southern Utah County across the county line, where it virtually bisects the eastern quarter of Sanpete County from north to south, before fading from the maps in Sevier County in the vicinity of I-70 east of Salina. The present dirt thoroughfare is now identified for the most part as Forest Service Road 150 and also the Great Western Trail.[46]

Figure 5.10. Skyline Drive, built by Gooseberry camp F-28, a rough but still well-traveled road.

Figure 5.11. Sheepherder and his dog sharing Skyline Drive with a tourist passing through.

Roadwork continued in the summer of 1935 as six more miles of truck trails were built in the vicinity as well as connecting roads to other communities. The little town of Ferron, for example, anxiously requested that a CCC company be brought back to F-11 in the summer of 1934 to complete the road project in Ferron Canyon just west of town. The Forest Service had used the initial camp in 1933 in order to construct a road that would connect Ferron with an improved highway on Ferron Mountain; later it was hoped to continue on to Skyline Drive about twenty-three miles west of the community. Emery County had spent $3,000 on a road from Ferron to the boundary of Manti National Forest in order to link up with the new road, which would provide access to the coal and timber resources of the area around Ferron Mountain to the west. The county had spent all its funds, and the uncompleted forest road rapidly deteriorated. Blood, although sympathetic, offered little hope that a camp would be reestablished, at least in 1934. Although there was no camp that year, a company returned in 1935, and the proposed road was eventually completed.[47]

This road up Ferron Canyon proved to be a major undertaking that today incorporates views of an old road dating back to pioneer days and the actual incorporation of parts of that same road into the beautiful drive up the canyon. Several CCC-built structures are outstanding examples of the work of which these young men were capable. About twelve miles west of Ferron at the top of what is called The Narrows they constructed a tunnel under the road through which water could flow to a beautiful and decorative spillway that is known today as the Steven's Creek Dip. Another two miles west a traveler will encounter the Dugway, which could well cause one to wonder how in the world virtually untrained men could hang onto the side of the mountain long enough to build a road to the top. Robert Hyslop, an enrollee on the project, provides a partial explanation as he describes what was the major project of Company 959 after it moved to Ferron from its summer campsite at Gooseberry camp F-28 on October 24, 1935:

> During the construction of the Ferron Canyon road it was necessary... to blast the road through a ledge of solid rock for a distance of approximately three-fourths of a mile at 4% grade. At some points in the ledge it was necessary to hang down on ropes to drill and load the holes.[48]

It was in that same area of Ferron Canyon that a bridge was built that became the source of still another testimonial. In 2003 Ray Wareham of Ferron remembered the CCC with great admiration:

> You can still see a lot of their work. If you go to the head of the Narrows, where the switchback is, look back at that bridge they built. It's been there for 70 years and still as good as the day they

Figure 5.12. Site of F-34, now a Scout camp at the mouth of Blacksmith Fork Canyon above Hyrum.

> made it. It is rocked up and cemented up, with a pipe through it, and they built a lot of them like that.... They also did the first bridge on Ferron Creek, right just above town.[49]

The caterpillar tractor proved virtually indispensable to the road crews. Many of the enrollees sought the position of "cat skinner," since it was regarded as one of the more elite assignments, one in which special favors were sometimes received, such as freedom from KP duty. Two men constituted a "cat" crew: the driver and his helper, who did the greasing and also learned how to operate the huge machine. Many of the camps had two "cats" and usually worked two shifts so that eight enrollees worked on "cat" crews.[50]

Jackhammers were necessary in rocky country. These machines, powered by one hundred pounds of pressure from a big LeRoi Rix compressor, chipped away hundreds of cubic yards of rock in building roads and trails. Horses and scrapers came in handy on some road-building projects, although they were more likely to be found terracing on steep hillsides. The man with the hand tools, however, was the indispensable element. Regardless of the sophistication of the equipment, workers always used the simple shovel to make the finishing touches. And there seemed to be little that hardworking enrollees could not do when they set their minds and hands to it. Down near St. George, for example, a crew of four enrollees, equipped with only picks and crowbars, moved a rock that weighed about three tons a distance of eight feet to get it off the right-of-way of a truck trail then under construction.[51]

Building roads in the desert involved much more than merely leveling the surface of the ground. Supervisors used bulldozers and shovels to excavate dugways, which were then filled with rock rubble to a depth of about two feet to provide a stable Roman-type foundation. Dirt covered the surface. The road through Death Canyon in Millard County was built in this manner. This followed an old emigration road toward Nevada and was planned to serve as an auxiliary road between Delta, Utah, and Ely, Nevada, when it reached completion. Superintendent Paul Arentz of DG-29 reported that twenty-four miles had been completed toward Death Canyon not far from the camp in the Sixth Period, with construction still under way in the Seventh.[52]

Much of the desert area of Utah is crisscrossed by streambeds or washes that are generally dry but can become impassable barriers when filled with floodwaters from a cloudburst occurring somewhere upstream. Various types of structures were used to span these washes or shallow ravines, depending upon the depth and width of the gap. Where a short span had to be crossed, culverts were used. These generally consisted of rock walls and concrete floors, and if the span was only about one foot wide, rock was also used for the top. On wider spans, cedar posts provided the decking. Enrollees first built forms for wing walls and poured in rocks and concrete. The culverts were often built with a slight slope to prevent silt and rock from being deposited on the floor underneath. Crews also used corrugated pipe in the construction by cutting it in two longitudinal sections and then using each half to form the arched top over a regular concrete floor.[53]

Rock dips could be used instead of culverts where crossings were shallow. The enrollees would first dig a trench where the road crossed the stream, place coarse rock on the bottom, and fill it up with finer material. If the volume of water across the road seldom reached serious proportions, the dip could be built with gravel and a little bit of clay. Crews generally built a wall on the downstream side of the dip to prevent erosion. If cement was available, the wall was built of rock and concrete; if

Figure 5.13. Gravel-filled rock dips, the simplest form of stream crossings.

not, rock baskets were used. The top of the wall ran flush with the downstream edge of the dip and extended into the ground two or three feet. To construct a basket, enrollees would first dig a trench about three feet deep and one foot wide, extending the width of the dip. They then tied two strips of heavy wire mesh together and lowered this crude basket into the trench. They filled this with loose rock and then tied the top together with galvanized wire. For further protection an apron was added below the wall. A piece of the same type of fifty-inch wire was laid down the complete length of the wall, and rocks were piled on top to a depth of about one foot. Another strip lay on top, and the two pieces were secured with galvanized wire. This provided a flat rock basket one foot thick and four feet wide across the streambed right next to the wall and about one foot below its top. To prevent the wire basket from being swept away in a heavy flood, workers anchored it by wires to large rocks sunk deep in the ground below the road surface above the wall.

Superintendents reported that these structures worked very well, because during the first flood the voids in the rock wall and apron were filled with the fine gravel and mud brought down by the water, and soon the structures were nearly as solid as if they had been built of rubble masonry. Floodwater occasionally caused some erosion downstream from and even underneath the apron, but this was of little consequence to the dip wall itself.[54]

A regular bridge was necessary if the wash was quite long or deep. Abutments, sometimes as high as eight or ten feet or more, would first be built of rock on either side of the span. Stringers of logs or heavy timbers were placed across the span, and the decking of the bridge would be nailed to these.

FORT PIERCE WASH

Some of the larger bridge-building projects used steel, such as one carried out by camp DG-30 in Cedar City on one of the major spans in southern Utah. The Fort Pierce Wash was a ravine that lay south of St. George and controlled access to the Arizona Strip, that portion of Arizona lying north of the Colorado River. Whenever serious cloudbursts flooded the wash, the people of the strip would be isolated, occasionally for several days at a time. A bridge across the wash just north of the state line was planned to provide permanent relief for the three hundred stockmen, 300,000 sheep, and 20,000 cattle that occupied the area. The CCC, with the help of the Utah State Road Commission, constructed a steel truss bridge 162 feet long and twenty-four feet wide, which was expected to cost $3,500. Crews built cement piers, abutments, and cofferdams in connection with the two-span, three-pillar structure. The bridge was about 10 percent complete by March 1936 and totally finished on September 25.[55]

Even though DG-45 was physically located in Utah, it was actually an Arizona camp and at that time was prohibited from working in Utah. Therefore it was necessary for Cedar City camp DG-30 under Superintendent Harold P. Richards to come down and build the bridge across the wash, while DG-45 of St. George constructed the approaches and other work projects on the Arizona side. The St. George enrollees built a suspension footbridge across the wash to serve them temporarily in case the wash ever flooded while they were away from camp. The 215-foot bridge served them occasionally, and although the men had to leave their trucks behind and walk across, they at least were able to return to the shelter of their barracks for the night.[56] In spite of having to shut the project down when occasional cloudbursts hit the area, the work progressed rapidly during the summer, and the St. George Chamber of Commerce conducted dedication ceremonies on October 24, 1936. One year later this project was one of two especially called to Governor Blood's attention in a letter from Regional Grazier D. D. McKay as outstanding pieces of work.[57]

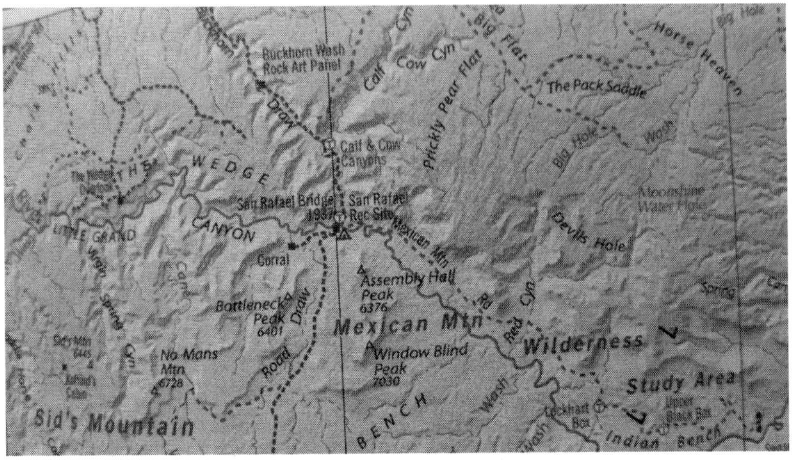

Figure 5.14. Since its swinging days are past, the San Rafael Bridge is more simply identified in the *Utah Road and Recreation Atlas*, and it is not even shown on the official 2017 Utah Highway Map.

SAN RAFAEL SWINGING BRIDGE

The other "outstanding piece of work" to which McKay referred in November 1937 was located in central Utah's Emery County in Castle Valley, so named "because of its castle-like formations on the mountain peaks and rimrocks surrounding the region."[58] In his letter McKay told Governor Blood about the recently completed swinging bridge over the San Rafael River in the arid reaches of the county by Company 529 at DG-27 in Castle Dale.

In an area of steep sedimentary cliffs and very few passable roads, the San Rafael River is a formidable barrier all the way to where it empties into the Green at the Ruby Ranch, some twenty-five tortuous miles south of the town of Green River. For stockmen hoping to get supplies and feed to their herds on grazing lands south of the river, Emery County Road 3-32 was impassable much of the time. Often it was necessary to wait until the river froze over before the sheep could cross; likewise the return trip had to be made before the spring thaw. Three previous bridges had been destroyed when the San Rafael flooded and washed out the supporting piers in the riverbed.

Still, stockmen and county officials requested that another attempt be made, and finally Milton A. Greaves, CCC engineer and superintendent of DG-27 in Castle Dale, developed plans for a suspension bridge across the river at the mouth of Buckhorn Wash to cope with the situation.

The unusual structure was to be fourteen feet wide, built to provide for the passage of two automobiles. It was 160 feet long and suspended from two three-inch cables stretching between two concrete towers on either side of the river, embedded in the earth some fifty feet from either side of the river.[59]

Improving twenty-eight miles of road from Castle Dale to the construction site was one of the first tasks to be completed. Traveling under 1,800-foot cliffs of layered sandstone decorated with Indian rock art must have been an awe-inspiring experience for the enrollees, most of whom were boys from Kentucky.[60]

Engineers found that the rocks on one side of the wash provided a satisfactory foundation but that the other side consisted of sand and gravel, so thirty-six piles were sunk upon which the concrete pillar was built to suspend the cables. Everyone concerned right up to the governor was enthusiastic about the results. The dedication, originally scheduled for March 27, 1937, did not take place until April 24, with some two thousand people in attendance.[61]

With no parts of the suspension bridge subject to the damaging effects of a raging river, the bridge served its purpose for over a half century before being replaced by a concrete structure in the 1990s. The bridge was officially listed on the National Register by the National Park Service on June 3, 1996.[62]

ROADS TO BOULDER

The roads that were built into Boulder in Garfield County would certainly qualify not only as among the most hazardous of the road construction work carried out by the CCC but also as some of the most necessary. The little community, located almost in the center of rural Garfield County, was once arguably regarded as perhaps the most isolated in the United States. Well into the 1920s tax collectors had ignored the village rather than make the treacherous trip to make property assessments. There is no question that it was the last place to have mail delivered by pack mule, which carried mail part of the way between Escalante and Boulder as late as June 1940.[63]

For many years only rough trails had connected the thirty-five families of the tiny community north approximately thirteen miles to the town of Grover in Wayne County. It was about the same number of tortuous miles to the southwest to the larger town of Escalante over trails with such picturesque names as the Cream Cellar Road, McInelly Twist, Claude V. Cut-Off, Thompson Turnover, and Peters' Whip-Up. It was the Death Hollow Trail, however, that, although the most dangerous, was also the shortest and captured the attention of daring souls on horseback or on foot.

The Commercial Clubs of Boulder and Escalante contacted Senator Elbert Thomas as soon as the CCC program was announced and requested that a road connecting the two communities be included among the projects. Thomas and Chief Forester Rutledge approved of the idea and forwarded their recommendations to Governor Blood, who offered further sympathetic treatment.[64] Bringing Boulder into closer contact with the outside world is certainly to be regarded as one of the signature accomplishments of the CCC in Utah, one that occupied the attention of the Corps for several years.

The long ridge west of Boulder known as Hell's Backbone was a formidable obstacle. This landmark, supposedly named by pioneer resident Henry Baker, was a prominent landform that lunged upward from the surrounding rugged country. Sand Canyon flanked the narrow ridge on one side, and Death Hollow, on the other. The Backbone was broken by a crevasse that had to be bridged in order for the road to go through. Although twenty-two other bridges were built over the thirty-eight-mile route, the Hell's Backbone Bridge stands out as one of the major accomplishments of the entire CCC experience in Utah.[65]

Two Escalante men, brothers Oscar and Rufus Liston, packed in much of the cement, lumber, and other building materials to the spike camp near the site. One hundred nine feet long, only fourteen feet wide, and with a frightening drop of 1,500 feet on either side, the bridge was completed in five and a half weeks without serious accident.[66] No doubt the care taken—as illustrated by the following example—had much to do with the admirable safety record.

Arrangements had been made for Leo Munson to freight a compressor up to the site of the bridge. Two huge trees had been carefully felled across the span, winched into place, and hewn flat. When Munson's truck arrived it was seen that although the makeshift stringers were in place, the decking had not yet been completed. However, the stringers were just the right width to accommodate the tracks of a caterpillar tractor and the wheels of the compressor, giving birth to a frightening idea involving the ability and courage of Loral "Sixty" McInelly.[67] Even more significant, however, was the LEM's bulldozing skill and willingness to tackle dangerous tasks that no one else would touch. Historian Jerry Roundy graphically describes the event:

> Equipment can always be replaced, but the life of a man cannot. In order to protect the driver in case of a mishap, a cable was strung overhead between two huge pine trees from which a rope and a shoulder harness was suspended and secured to the driver. Then at least if the caterpillar had gone over the side, the driver would have been left dangling safely (?) in mid-air.... Loral revved up the caterpillar engine and began inching his way out onto the stringers. Once out on the stringers, everything depended on the skill of the driver. He alone was in charge. Those standing on the sideline could do nothing but pray. But Loral was an excellent "cat skinner" and cautiously made his way across the chasm with the compressor as everyone held their breath. As the cat pulled onto the other side, a huge cheer went up from the onlookers.[68]

In the meantime, Company 1339, which had moved into F-18 in the spring of 1934, proceeded with the work between Boulder and Grover and continued widening the road through Box Canyon and improving the work of the previous summer; crews completed that stretch in 1935. In spite of the fact that two roads now linked Boulder with the outside world, the community often still found itself snowbound during the winter. The pack mule still carried the mail, but its days were numbered.

In 1935 work began on a second or "lower road" to Boulder, which would allow all-year access. This route, now Utah State Highway 12, traveled east of Escalante to Calf Creek, climbed out of the canyon to the rim, and then swung north along a sharp ridge of volcanic rock. Here lay a situation similar to Hell's Backbone, where it became necessary to blast the top of the narrow ridge in order to secure enough space to build the road. The route continued over the New Home Bench and on into Boulder. By 1938 only five miles of this "million-dollar road to Boulder" remained to be completed—five miles that had to be blasted through solid rock.[69] Supervisor A. C. Folster of Powell National Forest announced that three thousand bags of cement and two tons of steel were needed to build two more bridges. He explained that Forest Service

Figure 5.15. Chimney and an abandoned swimming pool, all that remain of F-42 in Escalante.

and CCC funds were not available since that portion of the road lay outside the national forest.[70]

In spite of protests by the Associated Civic Clubs of Southern Utah the Escalante camp transferred in the spring of 1939, and work on the "lower road" came to a halt. In September, however, Senator Elbert Thomas announced that Escalante would be one of the eight Forest Service camps operating during the winter, and work shortly began again.[71] By April 1940, only a half mile of the solid sandstone remained to be breached, and Regional Forester C. N. Woods stated that by summer it would be "possible to reach Boulder by road any time of year for the first time in history."[72]

Roads remain as one of the most visible reminders of the work done in Utah by the CCC, although most Utahns know little of the builders. Without exception, every camp participated in road construction to some extent. Some camps built a few roads besides those necessary to provide access to work projects; other camps had road construction as their principal reason for existence. Most, however, merely listed road construction as one of the variety of projects in which they engaged.

Whether it was road construction, planting trees, or building reservoirs, most of the work was that which new enrollees had not previously encountered, especially those from the eastern states. It was well and good for the leaders of the technical agencies to come up with worthwhile projects; it was another matter to utilize the young men who would carry them out. Fortunately, as Superintendent D. H. Beck of NP-2 acknowledged in one of his reports, the enrollees were teachable:

> Their construction experience was practically nil, so our first task was to teach the boys how to work and how to use tools. The time required to complete a unit of work six months ago compared with the time required to do a similar unit of work at this time shows a decrease of at least 50%. This together with a glance at the work accomplished shows that the boys have really been on the "job."[73]

STILLMAN HARDING, LEM (AT SEVENTEEN!)

This account of Stillman Harding is long and rich in detail, especially regarding his life after his CCC service, for two reasons. First, when I interviewed him in February 2016 he was one of the few CCC "boys" still alive and mentally sharp at the age of ninety-eight, and second, an account of his post-CCC experience is one that needs to be told since it demonstrates the loyalty, courage, and perseverance we like to think of as characteristic of those who survived those troubled times of which the Civilian Conservation Corps was a significant part.

Although most LEMs were somewhat older than the average enrollee, Stillman Harding reported that he had been taken on at the ripe old age of seventeen years. Just five months out of Box Elder High School he answered an ad on October 21, 1936, for "local experienced men" because

Figure 5.16. Stillman Harding, a veteran of the Great Depression and the Civilian Conservation Corps and a Purple Heart combat veteran of World War II, exemplifies all that is great about the "Greatest Generation."

at that particular time the CCC had an immediate need for truck drivers. He joined Company 736, one of the older companies from the Seventh Corps Area, which was made up primarily of young men from Missouri. The company was stationed at SCS-4 in his home town of Willard, just a few miles south of Brigham City. On entering the Corps Harding was immediately assigned as a truck driver.

Harding served at SCS-4 on the south side of Willard in the winter of 1936–37 until transferring to the Army detachment at Fort Douglas, in Salt Lake City. Beginning in March 1937, he drove trucks from district headquarters all over the Fort Douglas District, usually hauling supplies in convoys to various camps.

After six months in Salt Lake City he returned to SCS-4 around September 1937, where he resumed his truck driving responsibilities, usually stationed at either the spike camp in Willard Basin or the main camp in town. After about three months, however, he was transferred to Jericho camp DG-26 in Juab County southwest of Provo.

At Jericho Harding worked on cutting posts for building fences and corrals with Company 1967 until driving jobs opened. It was at Jericho that he became an assistant leader, which led to other opportunities—running the camp canteen and later serving as the camp first aid man.

He was discharged in April 1939, "when I came back to Willard to stay for awhile."

The following year he joined the 222nd Field Artillery Regiment of the Utah National Guard; when it was transferred to Fort Lewis, Washington, he applied for transfer to the Army Air Corps. After serving at various bases Harding was awarded his wings, and by February 1944 he was in North Africa, flying as a copilot on a B-24 Liberator.

During a mission over Austria in May 1944, his plane was seriously damaged by antiaircraft fire, which also wounded the twenty-three-year-old Harding. His refusal to be removed from the damaged cockpit "until the bombs were dropped" resulted in his being awarded the Distinguished Flying Cross, along with a Purple Heart.

As a result of being severely wounded, Harding was treated in three hospitals in Italy and received multiple surgeries for the loss of his left thumb and part of his left leg. He finally returned to the States, where he talked his way to being sent to Bushnell Army Hospital in Brigham City, about ten miles from where he had spent his life and where his wife, Madelyn, was waiting for him. Having been unsure of where he was going to be sent for recuperation, he had not yet notified Madelyn or his parents of his scheduled return to Utah.

In the meantime, wanting to do something more for the war effort than merely contribute her husband, Madelyn had enrolled in a Cadet Nursing program at Weber State College in Ogden. Coincidentally, she was on duty at Bushnell the weekend her husband was being transported by ambulance from Hill Air Corps Base outside Ogden after having been flown in from New York City. As she always did, she went out to greet the incoming wounded warriors and, like something out of a Hollywood movie, opened the ambulance door to be face-to-face with her husband. Who was the more surprised and delighted would be difficult to determine.

After being hospitalized for fourteen months in Italy and Utah Harding was medically discharged on July 28, 1945. As a wounded veteran he had the opportunity to enter government service in November 1945, and his later life was spent as an air traffic controller in Washington, D.C., and in Salt Lake City, for just over a quarter century. He retired in November 1971 and passed away on March 23, 2017, at the age of ninety-eight. Stillman Harding is truly a hero in every sense of the word.

PEST CONTROL: INSECTS, RODENTS, AND PLANTS

The environment of Utah has always been difficult to conquer. As the CCC crews struggled to overcome the difficulties posed by inhospitable terrain and unruly climate, the forces of nature occasionally threw hordes of animal and insect pests into the fray. Aside from trail-building and the construction of campgrounds, projects in which nearly every camp in Utah was engaged at some time or other, pests demanded a great amount of attention.

Insects

The enrollees of Company 962 found themselves engaged in fighting insects immediately on arrival at NP-3 in 1934 and carried on for several years. In 1934 alone, the company attacked the problem by cutting and burning more than 1,600 Douglas fir and about nine hundred ponderosa pine trees.[74] The company newspaper once carried an article entitled "Beetles, Not Bugs," by Dr. Donald DeLeon, who fought insects for many years. He described Company 962's fight against two different species of *Dendroctonus* beetles simultaneously, one of which killed Douglas fir and the other of which attacked ponderosa pines. The article included not only the remarks of Dr. DeLeon but also some doggerel attributed to Idaho lumberjacks who were also assigned to insect control in the neighboring state:

> *Here's to the genus* Dendroctonus
> *That lives in the bark of the pine;*
> *He lives on pitch,*
> *The son-of-a b____*
> *And he's harder to kill than a lion.75*

The two camps assigned to Zion National Park also fought this battle constantly. Every spring crews usually sprayed cottonwood and ash trees on the valley floor trying to control tent caterpillars and also, as at Bryce, found it necessary to cut down a few beetle-infested pine and Douglas fir trees.[76] A column in *Hi Life*, the newspaper of Company 4779 then at NP-2, described the process in considerable detail in its April 22, 1937, issue:

> Every year in Zion National Park the caterpillars become so thick that it becomes necessary to poison them. This is done to

> keep them from eating all the leaves from the trees. These caterpillars are hatched from the eggs of a moth which are laid in a tent or a cocoon. There are from one hundred to five hundred hatched in every tent.
>
> The poison that we use is a wet spray which is composed of lead arsenate and blood albumn [*sic*]. The lead arsenate is the poison and the albumn [*sic*] is the base which makes it stick to the leaves. The mixture is eight pounds of arsenate and six ounces of albumin to two hundred gallons of water.

Another insect problem involved the so-called Mormon crickets, which have given Utahns problems since pioneer days in the 1840s; they proved troublesome again in the mid-1930s. In late 1935 residents of little Scipio in eastern Millard County reported clouds of crickets descending upon the area from the northwest. The Forest Service, CCC crews, Works Progress Administration workers, and farmers battled the insects all through 1936, but the traditional methods failed to stem the tide. Spraying poison dust, burning with gasoline, and even pasturing turkeys failed to do more than bring about a "partially successful program. In the spring of 1937 the crickets still controlled the scene."[77]

Crickets also hit the Uinta Basin. A spike camp of twenty men from DG-31 was assigned to work on cricket control. The boys used bells and other noisemakers to attract the crickets and then sprayed them with a powder of arsenic and lime. Crews also burned sagebrush across the path of the insects in an attempt to destroy them. Still another method was to erect galvanized iron sheets ten inches high across the crickets' line of march. Gaps left in the barricade led into deep pits. Upon falling in, the cannibalistic insects began devouring each other. At the conclusion of the orgy, the pits were filled with dirt. In this manner more than 250 bushels of the voracious insects were eliminated, and hopes were high that another year in the infested area would see the problem permanently solved.[78] Unfortunately, that still hasn't happened.

DG-28 crews out of Clover Creek worked with farmers in Tooele County in constructing the ten-inch fences five hundred feet on either side of the pits into which the crickets fell. Perhaps unwilling to trust the crickets' cannibalism, workers then set the pits afire and reported a successful kill.[79] During the same period a twenty-five-man spike camp from Antelope Springs was stationed near Oak City to battle the pests.

Pictures from the Division of Grazing report of the period show how the five-man crews dusted the crickets with the poisonous arsenic dust. Wearing a handkerchief over his mouth and nose and with his pants legs tied at the ankle, an enrollee would venture into the field armed with a back-pump operated by a lever worked with his right hand. In licking the annoying powder off their legs the crickets would take the arsenic into their stomach. Death soon followed.[80]

Rodents

Even more time-consuming was the battle against rodents. The burrowing of a honeycomb of tunnels could make the ground surface unsafe for a galloping horse. Holes were equally hazardous, and the excavated dirt covered up valuable grass. Burrowing pests also attacked the sides of roads and reservoirs. Even more serious was the loss of vegetation as a result of the eating habits of the animals. Thirty-two ground squirrels could eat as much as one 120-pound sheep. The same amount of grass could be consumed by twelve jackrabbits or twenty-five prairie dogs or pocket gophers.[81] As grasses disappeared from the rangeland, unpalatable brush varieties sprang up to take their place. The rodents constituted a health menace as well, since the prairie dogs occasionally carried bubonic plague, and rabbits carried tularemia, both of which may be transmitted to humans.[82]

Kangaroo rats proved especially destructive against seeds, although they ate roots as well during their nighttime foraging. In infested areas over 80 percent of most grass seeds were generally destroyed—99 percent in some cases. Enrollees found one den in which a kangaroo rat had stored up to two quarts of seeds for its winter supply. Instead of storing food like the kangaroo rat, the Zuni prairie dog cultivates a layer of fat to see it through its long hibernation. These pests normally destroyed vegetation by eating the roots, rhizomes, and lower leaves of plants. Rock chucks, deer mice, and ground squirrels also caused trouble for the stockmen.[83]

To combat the rising menace, thought to be due to the decrease in the natural enemies of the pests, Director Robert Fechner announced on April 8, 1936, that an intensive program of rodent control would be carried out by the CCC. Purchases of supplies were to be made immediately, with Pocatello designated as the distributing point for camps in the intermountain area.[84]

Preston Q. Hale served as the rodent control foreman of DG-31 at Vernal and conducted one of the most active campaigns against the little animals. Normally CCC crews of the Division of Grazing worked only on government land, but eventually special concessions permitted adjacent private lands to be treated by the CCC. Farmers and stockmen east of Castle Dale appreciated the opportunity of working with Foreman Marion Oveson of camp DG-27 in poisoning rodents on their land. Here and elsewhere in the state crews used poisoned grain as the chief weapon. In the Uinta Basin a rodent control crew of DG-31 consisted of twelve men who would treat rolled oats with strychnine and place a few grains on hard surfaces near holes or along the regular paths to apparent feeding grounds. Enrollees spread the grain carefully to prevent livestock from getting poisoned. They soon learned that it was useless to put grain down the holes, as the animals got suspicious of food so easily obtained and it quickly went to waste.

By early June 1936, DG-31 had treated more than 1,500 acres, with a 90 percent kill rate of prairie dogs, kangaroo rats, and deer mice. Another project later that same summer resulted in the treatment of 5,580 acres and the death of 111,000 prairie dogs.[85]

Among the daily activities of Beaver camp F-14 was the scattering of forty pounds of poisoned carrots in an attempt to control pocket gophers. At DG-35, 15,000 acres were treated in one six-month period. The method used there was to place two grains of poisoned oats near each hole; when the pocket gopher or kangaroo rat emerged it would eat the grain and die in a few seconds.[86] The report of the Blanding camp for the same period is quite informative on the subject. During the six months from April through September 1936, enrollees under Foreman Ellsworth Lee Griner covered 77,665 acres with 16,860 pounds of prebait including cornstarch and syrup to attract the animals and 17,482 pounds of poison, both of which cost just over $1,000. Crews worked in a heavily infested area and at the conclusion of the period reported the killing of 2,229,958 prairie dogs and 1,500,000 kangaroo rats. They estimated that the vegetation destroyed by these animals would support 24,257 cattle or 141,800 sheep and that the protection provided to future growth would be impossible to evaluate. The total cost of the camp's rodent-control activities for the period was $3,296.26, a small price to pay for virtually doubling the range's carrying capacity.[87] On this particular project less than one-fourth of a pound of poison per acre was distributed. At Cedar City, on the other hand, 16,000 acres were treated with eight thousand pounds of poisoned grain over a two-month period, more than double the dosage given by the Blanding crew.[88] Some crews would broadcast the grain by scattering it loosely; others measured out the required tablespoonful of grain by taking a pinch as seized by their thumb and two fingers from a bag carried over their shoulder.[89]

The Castle Dale camp carried on two major rodent-control projects during the summer of 1936. Project 22 involved the treating of some 45,000 acres of Emery County rangeland. After an expenditure of 1,603 man-days, the crew reported a kill rate of 95 percent, with kangaroo rats, prairie dogs, and jackrabbits the principal victims. Project 22-A was smaller in scope, with only 4,500 acres covered and 330 man-days reported. A crew of about a dozen enrollees spent just over a month poisoning for rock chucks in Carbon County to the north of the camp.[90] In the West Desert, crews from DG-26 and DG-29 worked together under the supervision of the Bureau of Biological Survey to poison kangaroo rats and ground squirrels near Leamington and Lynndyl in northeast Millard County.[91]

In their ongoing battle to conserve the country's natural resources enrollees sometimes found themselves in positions that might seem paradoxical in later decades. Frank Jensen served as a foreman in the Brigham City camp, BS-1, from 1934 to 1941. He died in 1982, and when his widow, Minnie Jensen, was interviewed years later she told of what she identified as a rabbit roundup, a "grisly yet necessary task" carried out at the request of local livestock interests with varying degrees of frequency by more than one camp in Utah. Because the rabbits were eating hay and grain, there was no question at the time that the rabbits had to go. Enrollees were assigned to stand about twelve feet apart and move into a large circle into which men and women on horseback would begin driving rabbits: "Then the boys would start closing the circle by walking in and clubbing the rabbits as they went." While bemoaning the slaughter, Mrs. Jensen acknowledged that "without the roundup they would have overrun everything."[92]

Plants

The CCC carried on vigorous campaigns against plant pests as well. Cedar City enrollees grubbed out and burned huge piles of poison milkweed and silky lupine while clearing stock trails. Men from the Jericho

Figure 5.17. Treatment and removal of diseased trees was a significant part of Civilian Conservation Corps work projects.

camp worked to rid adjacent rangelands of the poisonous larkspur plant. In addition to trying to get rid of noxious plants, crews also fenced off infected areas. At Blacksmith Fork camp F-2 in Cache County fences and cattle guards were constructed to protect cattle from locoweed. Stockmen asked DG-28 to clear cockleburs from the driveway between Salt Lake City and Grantsville just before the annual drive to the winter range. The Blanding camp cleared 306 acres of burrs during one six-month period.[93]

The battle against various tree diseases lasted throughout the life of the CCC; white pine blister rust was one of the worst. Blister rust, a fungus that grows on white pine trees, apparently arrived from Europe around 1900 and spread rapidly. Control usually consisted of digging up gooseberry and currant bushes because these were the culprits through which the disease attacked the white pines. Grubbing the bushes was difficult and tiring work since the entire bush had to be removed, roots and all. Unfortunately, the problem is still not solved.

WATER STRUCTURES

In some parts of the year, Utah often suffered from an overabundance of water due to the spring runoff from the mountains. During the summer months, however, the lack of water was a more common problem, especially in the desert areas of the state along both the west and east borders. Huge herds of sheep and cattle grazed in what is generally referred to as the West Desert during the winter months, and facilities for livestock often ran in short supply. As a result nearly all the Division of Grazing camps spent much of their time and labor in constructing reservoirs, developing springs, and erecting water troughs.[94]

The work of constructing storage dams and reservoirs got off to a slow start in Utah. Only six such structures were built during the Second Enrollment Period. Although many more followed in the next two years, not until 1937 did dam construction really get under way. The Division of Grazing constructed seventy-two of the ninety-one somewhat larger storage dams built in Utah that year, a total considerably higher than in the three previous years combined. A total of 423 large impounding and diversion dams and 309 small reservoirs were built during the nine years, primarily by the Soil Conservation Service and Division of Grazing.[95]

Many different types of reservoirs were built to meet a variety of situations. The Milford camp built one of the most unusual near Granite Peak. There, a narrow gap about ten feet wide provided an outlet for a natural granite bowl into which water flowed from a spring. Enrollees built a concrete dam eighteen feet high that plugged the gap and provided for the easy storage of about 576,000 gallons of water. By April 1938, the reservoir filled, and water flowed over the top. A pipeline 357 feet long carried water to a flat below where crews had built troughs. When this was completed an entirely new range area was made available west of the Mineral Mountains between Milford and Beaver.[96]

The same camp built the Cove Fort Dam and also Wildcat Reservoir. The latter filled up quicker than expected, as crews worked rapidly to keep the sides of the reservoir rising faster than the water that flowed in, to eventually back up two miles behind the dam. Due to the inaccessibility of the site the men had to travel to their work by horse and buggy. Crews of DG-35 completed a total of twelve reservoirs that one winter alone.[97]

The dams were originally built of earth with a "core" running through its length. The core was usually dug out down to bedrock after the dam had been roughly shaped. It looked as if a giant slice had been taken out of the dam, leaving one portion facing upstream, and the other, downstream. The void was then filled with carefully selected clay that was mixed with water, or "puddle," as it was poured into the core. When dry, the core became almost as hard as adobe and nearly completely impervious.

The camp at Castle Dale built such a dam in the bottom of a wash twenty feet deep and 115 feet wide. The natural walls of the dam consisted of solid rock, and the ample clay on the bottom of the wash proved excellent for dam-building. Water was so scarce that crews had to haul it in by tank truck for puddling the core. The men gained much jackhammer experience as they had to cut out three hundred cubic yards of rock for the spillway as well as excavate three thousand cubic yards of earth for the dam.[98]

Later other types of cores were regarded as more successfully watertight and became, in their turn, standard for the region. Instead of earthen dams with a core of puddle clay, these were built of rock rubble or some form of dry masonry with the faces about four feet apart and capped with rock crowns. A cement mixer stirred the core material of sand and adobe clay, and men then puddled it into the gap. Sometimes a big drum would be left near one end of the core, to which it would be connected by a short ditch. The drum, in turn, was filled by a dump truck with another drum mounted on its bed, which would back up on an overhanging ledge so that the water could be discharged into the drum for the core.[99] After the core was filled, tractor operators drove their "cats" back and forth, packing it to adobe hardness. Thin layers of dirt were also spread over the entire dam, which would be further compacted by trucks.

The earth dams remained popular in many situations. The upstream side would be lined with rock, or riprapped, usually to a depth of at least one foot. If practical, the entire reservoir would be riprapped, as this reduced the erosion caused by the wave action of the water and also made it easier for livestock to drink without damaging the sides of the reservoir. Often the toe of the reservoir wall was also riprapped to prevent the erosion caused by backwash from the spillway. J. V. Bollwinkel, engineer of the Vernal camp, described the dams built by the CCC as having wide tops with flat sides, with the principal objectives in mind of reducing erosion and preventing seepage. Because of flooding, which often occurred during heavy rains, extrawide spillways proved essential. Sometimes these were dug out of solid rock; in some cases they were dug out of the earth and lined with rock. Dams and spillways were constructed to be able to handle the occasional big storm that might come only once every fifty years but which would have the destructive potential to wash out a less sturdy structure.[100]

Camp DG-30 constructed Big Hollow Reservoir about fifteen miles north of Cedar City. The dam stretched 760 feet across and impounded 112 acre-feet of water. Crews worked from December 1935 through the following March on the project, which was designed to take care of 500,000 sheep and five thousand cattle as they traveled between summer and winter ranges. Four months after the completion of the reservoir, several consecutive cloudbursts caused considerable damage. Floodwaters washed out a fifty-five-foot-wide swath, but by September the damage had been repaired, with the reservoir reportedly stronger than it had been before the flood.[101]

Although Division of Grazing camps carried on other projects, they usually devoted most of their attention to such projects as these for the development of water resources for livestock. Reservoir construction constituted the major concentration in number of men, finances, and sheer magnitude of the projects. As early as 1936, not a particularly big year for this type of activity, half of the six crews of DG-31 worked on reservoirs. One of these structures, officially known as Project Number 8, was popularly referred to as DeVed Reservoir in honor of Assistant Leader Charles DeVed, who drew up the plans and was one of the two supervisors on the project.

Crews at Castle Dale built five fourteen-foot troughs cut from logs to capture water brought from a higher spring at the rate of about two gallons a minute. They also installed four twenty-foot troughs of galvanized iron. The Clover Creek camp DG-28 used the two halves of a boiler to utilize a spring. Crews from Dalton Wells also used hewn logs for troughs to utilize the water of Seven-Mile Springs. The spring was developed by sinking a large steel cylinder into the bottom of a wash until it struck the water-bearing strata below. Water piped up from the gravel strata through the cylinder flowed to ten log troughs. The same camp also blasted holes in sandstone to make additional containers.[102]

Another major water development was the Cisco Spring pipeline, constructed by DG-32. Utilizing available drought-relief funds, the crews built a pipeline that carried water nearly seven miles across dry rangeland. Crews spent nearly four thousand man-days on the project, which cost a total of $8,601 in materials. A special thirty-five-man spike camp sprang up to build the pipeline, located about sixty-five miles from the main camp at Dalton Wells. To develop Painter Springs in western Millard County, crews from the Antelope Springs camp trucked in thirty-five miles in subzero weather. Fifty sheep outfits, running a total of 75,000 head, benefited.[103]

CORRALS

With water holes and stock trails provided, with successful inroads against nuisances ranging from cockleburs to ground squirrels, and with attempts under way to revitalize the rangeland with new strains of grasses, Utah stockmen had ample reason to bless the CCC. The construction of twenty to thirty corrals throughout the state each year was an added benefit. In addition to constructing reservoirs, DG-26 worked on corrals in the summer of 1937. The Goshen cattle corral east of Eureka was a cooperative venture. Local stockmen provided the hardware and lumber for the gates and chutes; aspen poles came from the Forest Service; the scale, lumber, cement, and other materials came from the State Road Commission; CCC enrollees under the Division of Grazing did the work. The Union Pacific Railroad aided in construction by donating old railroad ties for a sheep corral located about seven miles west of DG-26. In twenty-five days a crew of twenty boys under Foreman Neil Bunder erected a corral approximately three hundred feet square. Complete with pens, loading chutes, and rounded corners for easier handling of the stock, the corral was built with materials costing less than $200. Railroad ties were used on the chutes for another corral thirty-eight miles west of Jericho.[104]

A crew from Clover Creek camp also used ties on a corral built eight miles northwest of Delle in northern Tooele County.[105] More typical, perhaps, was the six-pen sheep corral built at Powder Wash in Uinta County by DG-31. Cedar posts stood in the ground twelve feet apart and supported the corral walls of six-inch pine poles cut to a length of six feet. This type of structure could be erected in about two weeks. By 1939 this camp had reportedly erected thirty-five corrals, nearly one-eighth of the Utah total over the entire life of the CCC.[106]

Cattle corrals, of course, required stronger construction. One built by DG-30 used nine-foot cedar posts sunk three feet into the ground and connected by six large aspen poles used for the rails of each panel. The structure contained 120 feet of chutes and approximately a dozen gates and required four hundred cedar posts, 450 aspen poles, and about three thousand feet of two-inch lumber. The cost of the corral ran slightly above $500, and it took just over a month to complete.[107]

The camp at St. George used cedar posts set in the ground only one and a half feet, but they lay only five feet apart and were connected by

Figure 5.18. Civilian Conservation Corps–built corral near Garrison in Millard County, typical of many still used by West Desert stockmen.

two strands of heavy barbed wire twisted between the posts about one foot below the top all around the corral. These wires were tightened further by twisting them between the posts, and the entire structure held together so tightly that it "couldn't be shaken by a strong man."[108] As an additional refinement, a single strand of smooth wire was laid along the top of the smooth-cut posts to prevent cowboys' lariats from getting snagged. Still other corrals were round in shape, with cedar posts placed vertically side by side to form the outer wall. One still in use today may be seen at the site of DG-117, about seven miles south of Garrison.

The most active corral-building year was 1941, when forty-one were erected. Although the Division of Grazing built most of the corrals, the Forest Service built at least two that year in Sevier County, one of which measured 350 by sixty-four feet and was located next to the county fairgrounds in Richfield.[109]

WILDLIFE

The Bureau of Fisheries of the Department of Commerce cooperated with the Forest Service by providing much of the technical supervision on CCC projects designed to improve streams and lakes for fishermen. In 1934 a Vernal CCC crew constructed a concrete box twenty by three by four feet for holding fish until such time as they were discharged into a five-mile stretch of river near the edge of the Ashley National Forest boundary.[110]

In 1937 enrollees from Soapstone camp F-6 traveled south to Sevier County for the purpose of "harvesting" aquatic plants off the bottom of Fish Lake. Specially constructed tools were used, and the three-man crew took special pains to get only the plants with long roots that would be best suited for transplanting in Mirror Lake in the Uinta Mountains. The crew, under the direct supervision of the camp superintendent, gathered thirty barrels of plants, which they used in an experiment to improve the fish habitat of Mirror Lake. As part of the project, the lake was fertilized with seven tons of phosphate and two tons of lime that they mixed with dirt and after a few days scattered over shallower portions of the lake. A week later enrollees took another trip south, this time to Panguitch Lake, for more fish plants. Before long, the crew at Mirror Lake had a motorized raft from which they spread their phosphate, lime, and dirt to treat the plants with slightly over one ton per acre of lake surface.[111]

The CCC also built fishponds and artificial pools and spent more than ten thousand man-days in developing lakes and ponds for Utah sportsmen. The National Park Service proved equally interested in the use of CCC labor on recreational projects. In the summer of 1941 enrollees of the Bryce camps transferred 16,000 legal-sized trout from an isolated rearing pond too far from any road to be fished very often to the more popular waters of Duck Creek Lake.[112]

The camps worked hard on behalf of hunters as well. The severe winter of 1936–37 threatened Chinese pheasants and quail with the loss of their normal food supply. The sportsmen of the Carbon-Emery Fish and Game Association appealed to their grazing district advisory committee for assistance, and soon a foreman and small crew were assigned to feed an estimated four thousand game birds. The state Fish and Game Department estimated the value of the birds at $2.75 each, so this amounted to a project valued at around $11,000.[113]

A deer pasture about four miles south of Kanosh is another example of a somewhat unusual CCC project, also thought to be the first of its kind in the country. Fifty men from Salina first built a deer enclosure in which a herd of the animals stayed for study by the Bureau of Biological Survey. An attendant lived right in the enclosure so that he might keep track of the eating and drinking habits of the animals. The next year experimental plots were fenced: one against cattle only and the other against deer as well. It soon became obvious that the deer herd in the area should be reduced by about half or the entire range was going to suffer to such an extent that the whole herd could starve during the course of one bad winter.[114]

Trying to balance wildlife numbers with the carrying capacity of the land was always an occasional chore. Hinton said that between October 1938 and February 1939, Zion Park camp NP-4 trapped 114 deer to ship out of the canyon to other areas, including Bryce Canyon, a practice that continued through 1941.[115]

CHAPTER 6

Two Major Concerns

Erosion and Flood Control

The CCC was the finest thing that could have happened to the youth of America during the Depression years.

—Jack A. Craghead, enrollee, F-30

In addition to the problem of unemployment in the country, it was equally apparent that work was needed on the land. In 1933 the U.S. Department of Agriculture estimated conservatively that soil erosion cost the country more than $200,000,000 annually and that 17,500,000 acres were even then beyond reclamation or cultivation.[1] This represented approximately six billion tons of topsoil that had been eroded by the forces of wind and water.[2] Unwise timber management had resulted in the waste and despoliation of millions of acres of forest resources, and in the western portion of the country, arid areas offered optimum utilization only if water resources could be developed. Programs of conservation and development provided an ideal opportunity to help alleviate the problem of unemployment in the American scene.

It should be no surprise that in the second-driest state in the country the two arguably most significant CCC activities—though often either unrecognized or taken for granted—involved water. On the one hand, soil erosion has always been a problem, due for the most part to the spring runoff of snow in the mountains down overgrazed slopes. On the other hand, most of the water found in Utah's beautiful mountains is usually located where it is not really needed except by wildlife and the ardent fishermen of the state. For that reason, attempting to keep water away from where it should *not* be and facilitating the movement of water to where

Figure 6.1. Rugged slopes of the canyons above Springville and Provo in Utah County created serious runoff problems.

it can do the most good to the most people are both major achievements of the Civilian Conservation Corps' nine years in Utah.

EROSION AND FLOOD CONTROL

The ravaging of the land was one of the main concerns of President Roosevelt and others when the CCC first began its work. In arid Utah, state and federal conservation agencies had also been worried about the twin problems of flooding and erosion for many years. Summer storms as well as the spring runoff of winter snows were the most common problems.

In 1924, flood-control barriers had been built in Willard and Farmington under an agreement involving federal, state, county, and private agencies. In the years following, similar structures were built at more than a dozen other sites in western and central Utah. Check dams became one of the more common devices utilized to check erosion.

Check dams became a staple element of erosion control utilized by the Corps. One of the best descriptions of these structures is found in the camp newspaper of Company 1256 while it was at Moab camp SCS-6. Apparently enrollee reporter Angelo Trupello was asked by the company's educational adviser to visit one of the projects and report on its progress:

> According to my estimation, check dams are structures built in water channels and gullies to slow down the movement of

> water and give it more time to soak into the ground. It also prevents the gullies from growing. There are many types of check dams, and construction is generally both simple and inexpensive. Logs, sod, wire netting brush, stone, or almost any other available materials may be used effectively according to the size of the channel or gully and the amount of water to be controlled. Many of these dams, especially the larger ones, serve the useful purpose of impounding water for livestock, and in the drier parts of the country water can be taken from them for irrigating small fields and sometimes fairly large fields.[3]

The motoring public and vacationers in Utah have reason to be grateful to the young lads of the Civilian Conservation Corps for the campgrounds, trails, roads, and bridges that they constructed in the 1930s. Of even greater significance, although less well known, was, from the very beginning of the program, the tremendous accomplishment in the control of floods and soil erosion alluded to elsewhere.

At a meeting with Washington officials early in April 1933, Regional Forester R. H. Rutledge and Preston Peterson of the Utah State Road Commission made a suggestion that would have implications for Utah down to the present day. They asked for fourteen camps of two hundred men each that were to function for a six-month period, engaged primarily in the control of soil erosion by reseeding denuded areas and building small dams.[4]

Prior to this time, most conservationists considered soil erosion to be a problem solely in the forests of America and believed that only some good reforestation practices would be necessary to attack the situation. The suggestion offered by Rutledge and Peterson, however, would result in the construction of camps on public lands outside the national forests. Officials estimated that sufficient work existed for 16,000 man-months. Under the initial proposal camps would be set up at sites including Willard, Price, Brigham, Castle Dale, Moab, Escalante, St. George, Springville, and Davis County.[5]

On May 13, Governor Blood named a committee "to decide on specific locations for State Flood and Erosion Control camps" and to determine the work to be done. Blood named C. L. Forsling of the Forest Service office in Ogden as chairman; the other members were Preston G. Peterson; George A. Fisher, executive secretary of the State Land Board;

Reed Bailey of Utah State Agricultural College—now Utah State University; and L. M. Winsor, an irrigation expert with the Bureau of Agricultural Engineering. The governor asked Rutledge to administer the state camps in addition to his own Forest Service camps since the work would be "more expeditionally [sic] handled and it would greatly clarify fiscal procedure." The committee was also informed that there were no funds allocated to them and that any personal expenses should be defrayed by their own departments.[6]

STATE CAMPS

Robert Fechner's office announced on May 29 that the fourteen state camps Rutledge and Peterson had requested for erosion control had been approved, although he did not indicate whether the additional 2,800 men required would be recruited in Utah or from out of state. Three days later, however, bad news arrived in the form of a wire from Chief Forester Robert Y. Stuart, ordering a cutback because so many camps had been requested across the country. Instead of fourteen, Utah was to receive only five state camps at that time, though the remainder might possibly be established when winter snows forced the closing of Forest Service camps at higher elevations.[7]

These camps carried the designation "SE," which stood not for "*Soil* Erosion" as might be expected but for "*State* Erosion," meaning that the camps were sited on public land outside the national forests. Although this meant that they were usually at lower elevations, they were still set up where they could most effectively carry out the work.

From the beginning, Utah officials planned that these camps be used only to combat soil erosion. Although they were referred to as state camps and the projects were selected by the state, the Forest Service actually administered them. The five camps that were finally selected by the committee were part of the original twenty-six assigned to Utah that first summer of 1933: SE-201 in Woods Cross, SE-204 in Brigham City, SE-206 in Hobble Creek Canyon east of Springville, SE-211 at Widtsoe in Garfield County, and SE-212 located at Alton, in Kane County. Companies from the Second Corps Area occupied all five camps about the middle of June.[8]

These five camps, although designated state camps, were, as Blood had requested, under the technical supervision of the U.S. Forest Service and included in Forest Service reports. The selection of projects was the distinguishing factor of state camps. Although they took the wishes of the state and the citizenry into consideration where practical, U.S. Forest Service officials determined the work of the regular Forest Service camps; the work of the state camps, on the other hand, was on projects selected by Blood's state committee. The two governments, state and national, worked together, however, as the Forest Service handled the fiscal responsibilities and was represented on the state committee.

This might be the time to attempt to minimize some confusion regarding the camps in Davis County in 1933 and 1934. Based on accounts of enrollees who served in the camps, newspaper articles, and official records, I have come to the following conclusions.

SE-201 was identified as the Woods Cross camp, although it was physically located in Bountiful, first at Mueller Park on the east edge of the city and later where Holbrook Elementary School is now located, a few blocks farther north. SE-201 operated only during the First Enrollment Period, with Company 232, made up of New Jersey and New York enrollees. Why this was ever referred to as Woods Cross I have not been able to determine, since the two locations of SE-201 were both in Bountiful, perhaps five miles distant from what might ever have been considered Woods Cross.

SE-205 was also called the Woods Cross camp, this time correctly. Its location on what is now the border between Woods Cross and Bountiful provided some justification for a bit of the confusion regarding Woods Cross camps. Although Bountiful had been a town since 1892, Woods Cross was not incorporated until 1935, two years after SE-205 was set up in what was an area of Bountiful apparently identified as Woods Cross. The campsite was located on the south side of Utah Highway 68 or 500 South separating the two communities. This may or may not have been the site of what many sources identified as the "old Woods Cross Cannery."[9] Thus it was that SE-205 was sometimes identified as the Woods Cross camp and other times as the Bountiful camp.

Although SE-201 was the source of some confusion in Period One, the other four camps were quite straightforward. Three of the five original SE camps were situated on the western slope of the north-south Wasatch Range, which bisects the northern part of the state.

Camp SE-204, identified as the Brigham City camp, was actually located closer to the little community of Mantua, a few miles to the southeast of Brigham City, county seat of Box Elder County in northern Utah.

Figure 6.2. Dock Flat, campsite of SE-204, First Enrollment Period. A sharp eye might detect a turkey casually strolling down the road.

About the middle of June 1933, a tent camp was constructed two miles farther south of Mantua at a spot known as Dock Flat. With the completion of roads to the camp and a two thousand-foot pipeline from a nearby spring, the New York lads of Company 1253 under the command of Captain A. M. Siler were ready for work.[10]

Company 1253, incidentally, was one of the five Second Corps Area companies to come to Utah to serve for the First Period only. The others were Company 232 at SE-201, 1254 at SE-206 in Hobble Creek Canyon, 1255 at SE-211 in Garfield County, and 1256 at SE-212 in Alton in Kane County just outside Dixie National Forest.

Although off to a somewhat lackluster beginning with only five camps that first period, the state's soil erosion program proved to be quite effective. Just over the first three months enrollees carried out erosion-control measures on 779 acres, built one hundred stone dams and twenty miles of surface ditches, constructed twelve firebreaks and twenty-four miles of truck trails, and replanted eighty-five acres with trees.[11] None of the five camps lasted past the First Period, however, but the vital work of erosion control received a major boost when the Second Period was dedicated almost entirely to the problem of soil erosion and flood control. The concern that had resulted in the establishment of erosion camps in the First Period definitely carried over to the Second, as that important work was carried on by other units.

Figure 6.3. Terraces constructed by Company 958 out of F-30 still in use today in the upper reaches of Slate, Rock, and Little Rock Canyons in Utah County.

Terracing

In addition to the rather simple technique of trying to plug a gully with rock, logs, and other debris to curtail excessive runoff, the two most effective ways of dealing with erosion were, not surprisingly, also much more labor-intensive. The techniques of erosion control evolved over the years. Initially, the plan was to merely try to *control* the runoff in the canyons coming down from the mountains. Working out of SE-206 above Springville, for example, Company 1254 built small dams at the mouths of the Utah County canyons between Springville and Provo to contain the water and mud from the rain and snow along the Wasatch Front.

Later, the idea of *preventing* the runoff was heard even more, as terracing began to come into its own.[12] The earliest mention of terracing I have found was from around 1930, when Clarence L. Forsling of the Intermountain Forest and Range Experiment Station in Ogden contacted Utah State Agricultural College geology professor and rangeland authority Dr. Reed W. Bailey, asking for his opinion regarding the erosion situation. Bailey initially felt that the runoff was simply the result of summer cloudbursts, but he later reversed his opinion to agree, along with others he contacted, that overgrazing was the problem, an opinion that was contradicted by others equally qualified, especially in the area of weather and geology, who argued "that such floods were prehistorically common and the natural results of geological conditions."[13] Bailey,

Figure 6.4. Sign describing terracing work in Willard Basin by SCS-4. Later, a spike camp was located near here to continue the work.

along with Forsling, George W. Craddock, and A. Russell Croft, prevailed, however. They suggested that digging a series of parallel trenches along the contours of mountainsides would slow the runoff and that replanting those hillsides would help tremendously in holding back the water.[14] Previously, funds were lacking for the Forest Service to carry out that recommendation.

Then, like a divine windfall, the labor of CCC enrollees became available after the New Deal began. Buoyed by this new source of help the Forest Service established the Davis County Experimental Watershed to put Bailey's plans into practice. Driving bulldozers to the mountain peaks above Davis County, CCC enrollees gouged out massive in-sloping trenches and replanted the ground.[15]

In that first summer of 1933 Bailey was serving in Forsling's experiment station but traveled widely throughout the state explaining the new process. In an address to the Springville Kiwanis Club in August 1933, he stated that SE-206 in Hobble Creek Canyon was serving as a government experiment in checking erosion and alluded to the concept of terracing at the *heads* of the canyons.[16]

At just about the same time Uinta National Forest Supervisor Charles DeMoisy spoke to the same group describing the new CCC program. Among other items of interest he mentioned that, in addition to building check dams in many gullies in the mountains, terracing was also being carried out, mostly at the head of Little Rock Canyon. "This terracing or contour ditching was the first work of this character done in Utah," under Bailey's direction, who was to have a profound influence on terracing projects in the state.[17]

Terracing on the gentler slopes of private lands was quite different from that on steeper mountainsides. With proper surveying and engineering the terraces so constructed, according to Salmond, "offered little problem to the farmer in planting, working, and reaping his crops."[18]

Following Bailey's guidelines, enrollees in various camps were put to work digging long ditches following the contour around the face of slopes to be protected.[19] These ditches, two to three feet deep and approximately six feet across, trapped the heavy downpours or the melting snow, permitting seepage into the ground and retention of the precious moisture. Bailey especially used Davis Mountain behind Bountiful as his laboratory to test various combinations of terracing methods, and after four years of study he published his findings, which became the standard of flood and erosion control in many parts of the west.

Bailey conceded that contour terracing certainly was not a new technique, but he felt that the trenching that he utilized did constitute a revolutionary approach. Under the earlier system about 75 percent of the rainfall ran off, but with the trenches the figures reversed, with 75 percent of the rainfall caught.

It wasn't too long before the larger trenches that are still visible today began to come under construction. CCC personnel constructed trenches about nine feet wide spaced about five to twenty feet apart. The steepness of the slope and the condition of the vegetation and soil determined the varying distances between the trenches. Instead of the trench being just one huge ditch it was divided into compartments or elongated reservoirs separated by low cross dams or "equalizers" constructed at right angles to the axis of the trench. These ran about four inches lower than the leading edge of the trench and permitted the transverse flow of water from one compartment to another before the trench itself overflowed. The standard depth of a trench was about three to four feet, with greater or lesser depths depending upon the degree of slope, with some depths as much as five or six feet.

The trenched terraces were designed to trap melting snow and torrential rains of up to two inches an hour, which, although they occurred very rarely, caused the most serious damage. Within three years the system had been enlarged to include approximately seven hundred miles of trenches, enough, as one of the foremen on the job pointed out, to construct a ditch from Bountiful to Los Angeles.[20] Company 940, Utah's oldest, worked on the project, first out of camp SE-205 and then for seven years out of F-48. Charlie Wehmeyer and, later, Roy White were the camp superintendents for most of this time. The men had only one tractor on the job and did most of the work with scrapers and teams of horses. Men with shovels added the finishing work.[21]

In addition to those in Davis and Utah counties, by 1940 the CCC had built such structures in Salina and Soldier canyons in Sanpete County, Denmark Wash and Chalk Creek in Sevier County, and nearly every similar canyon in the Wasatch. Men at Bountiful carried out the work to the ultimate in simplicity by simply leveling off hills and filling in gullies. Unfortunately, the circumstances in which this method could be used were limited.[22]

Riprapping

Terracing, of course, was not the only arrow in the erosion-control quiver; different problems required different solutions. Another source of soil erosion came from streams and rivers leaving their channels during flooding and washing away soil as new channels were created. While terracing was the principal method on the hillsides, riprapping was perhaps the most important channel-control procedure used in Utah, done by laying rock walls bound in heavy wire netting along the riverbanks. Although varying somewhat depending on the local situation, this process often began with enrollees sinking cedar posts about three and a half feet deep in the ground in two rows facing each other and about four feet apart.

The wire was then secured to both sides of the framework and along the ground between the rows of posts. Crews carefully filled the elongated basket-like affairs, or cribs, with rocks and lashed cedar posts across the top to complete the wall.[23]

Don Penrod described a variation of riprapping used on the Virgin River south of Washington camp PE-216 in the winter of 1934. Enrollees built what he described as "jetties" of posts and stones out into the river at an angle downstream, tying the structure together with steel wire mesh. Trash floating downstream would be trapped in the wire, and water would be diverted out into the center of the river:

Figure 6.5. Riprapped section of a riverbank in American Fork Canyon about seven feet high.

> We set the cedar posts in the sand. Using a small water pump and a small fire hose we placed the nozzle at the base of the post—as the post sank deep into the sand we would jerk the nozzle away and the sand would wash in around the post and it was set.[24]

Pleasant Grove historian Beth Olsen gives a dramatic explanation of the value of riprapping and the conditions in which crews worked beginning in 1936. Obviously, the best time to carry out riprapping in the river would be in the winter when the water was low. The work started in January and continued into February, with two foremen supervising the seventy enrollees who had "to stand in the frigid water to accomplish the work." The crews had to move a great deal of snow before they could remove the 11,000 cubic feet of earth from the streambed in order to lay "a deep foundation of various sizes of rocks placed together along the bottom and sides of the steams without mortar." What made the accomplishment even more noteworthy is that not one day of sick leave was required in spite of the adverse working conditions. Among other locations, the American Fork Canyon provides excellent views of these structures, which are proving their value even today.[25]

As strong as riprapping and other flood-control structures were, however, the destructive force of water could sometimes be stronger. On Sunday, July 18, 1937, heavy rains undermined a concrete diversion dam outside Kanarraville, located about twelve miles south of Cedar City in Iron County. Fortunately, twenty-five volunteers from Leeds SCS-7 and about twenty townsmen responded "on a moment's notice" to reinforce the temporary structure with about 2,700 sandbags.[26]

Blood's committee for state camps not only had selected the sites for the original five SE camps but continued for the eight erosion-control camps in Utah in the winter of 1933–34. The state also continued working with the Forest Service in the technical discussion and the determination of projects. The Bureau of Agricultural Engineering further assisted by making technical recommendations in the complicated matter of perfecting satisfactory devices for diverting floodwaters and controlling runoff.[27]

After SE-201 was closed down at the end of that first summer, its erosion-control work was continued in the Second Enrollment Period by Company 940 at the new camp SE-205. In October 1933, Company 940 had moved in to SE-205 under Captain L. E. Thompson after having vacated F-5 in American Fork Canyon. A small group of twenty to twenty-five enrollees remained behind and worked all winter at the Timpanogos Cave and the South Fork Ranger Station. The rest of the SE-205 enrollees under Superintendent Charles R. Wehmeyer spent about six months carrying on erosion-control work above Farmington that had been under way off and on since the early 1920s. The first stage of the CCC project was completed in 1934 at a cost of $30,000. Work also continued at the mouths of the canyons near Bountiful to the east as SE-201 had previously done, thus beginning Company 940's long association with erosion control in Davis County.[28]

Company 940 was to remain on the Davis County flood-control project for the entire life of the CCC, first at SE-205, next at F-48 in Bountiful, and finally at F-49 in Farmington Canyon. During winters the company confined most of its work to the lower mouths of Walton, Bair, Webb, Farmington, Davis, and Parrish canyons, but in the summers the men moved to higher elevations for terracing work.[29] The thousand miles of terracing by Company 940 remains today as one of its major accomplishments. The good work of the company was acknowledged by Secretary of Agriculture Henry A. Wallace when he visited their camp with Robert Fechner, Congressman J. Will Robinson, and other dignitaries when they were in Utah for the funeral of George A. Dern. The boys were praised for their work on erosion control and even told that President Roosevelt

Figure 6.6. Plaque marking the site of two Civilian Conservation Corps camps, SE-213 (1933–34) and DG-45 (1935–39), at the Dixie Redhills golf course in St. George.

had read of their good work. Officials from other camps often visited to see what types of erosion-control structures worked best in various circumstances, especially as plans were being laid for similar work in the Willard watershed.[30]

When NP-1 got going at Blue Springs on the Kolob Plateau in the northern part of Zion National Park, the control of erosion was a major objective. Crews from Company 962 also engaged in stream protection, channel change, and the construction of rock-filled crib dams along the North Fork of the Virgin River to protect stream banks and roads and other downstream developments from floodwaters. The *Washington County News* reported that in August 1933 there were five different ongoing projects for erosion prevention, primarily by lining washes with rocks, trees, and debris and planting trees on bare slopes.[31]

Most of the state's erosion-control camps of the Second Period were located in Washington County. The major project was that carried out by the St. George camp, SE-213. Crews soon began building a diversion dam on the Santa Clara River above the Shivwits Indian Reservation. Initially claimed to be solely for flood control, it was later decided that it could also impound water for irrigation purposes. The concrete and rock structure was two hundred feet long and thirty-three feet high, one of the larger projects to be attempted by the Corps up to that time.[32]

Of the eight erosion-control camps that Second Period, SE-213 and SE-205 were the only two to bear the SE designation, as a new category of camps came into existence.

"PRIVATE EROSION" CAMPS

The emphasis on erosion control during the Second Period was evident in the fact that eight of the eleven camps authorized in Utah had been assigned to that task. Of those eight, six bore the new designation of "PE."

Although they originally felt that doing government work on private lands might be exceeding the mission of the CCC, by the end of the First Enrollment Period Roosevelt and Fechner came to accept the concept as long as it could be established that the work done would be of *public* benefit, that is, of value to others besides just the immediate landowners. As a result of this slight concession, six of the state camps were designated PE, indicating that their assignment was "Private Erosion," or work done on privately owned lands. These six were numbered consecutively PE-214 in Moab, -215 in Santa Clara, -216 in Washington, -217 in La Verkin, and -218 in Orderville. The three Washington County camps, plus SE-213 in St. George, spent most of their time in bringing the Virgin River and its tributaries under control.

Living quarters for Company 958 were set up in an old cotton mill just off Highway 91 in downtown Washington until barracks, an administrative building, a mess hall, and an infirmary could be built as PE-216.[33] The three PE camps in Washington County were open only in the Second Period. Like the other Washington County camps, La Verkin camp PE-217 with Company 957 built a large dam and diversion canal on the Virgin above town in order to divert the devastating floodwaters that had previously threatened the community. In addition, another dam was planned below town to "protect farm lands from being washed into the

Virgin River."[34] Enrollees of PE-217 also worked on Ash and Hurricane creeks and the La Verkin River north of the camp. These tributaries were fitted with channel-control structures, as was the unruly Virgin, in what was to be typical of the never-ending campaign of the SE and PE camps.[35]

Even outside of Washington County, the Virgin proved to be one of the chief targets for still another camp, PE-218 in Kane County, located about halfway between Orderville and Glendale on land donated by Walter S. Carpenter, a prominent citizen of the latter community.[36] As was usually the case, local men from the relief rolls were used to construct the wooden buildings for the camp, which was dedicated on November 25, 1933. Perhaps the campsite was selected with the objective of keeping the men constantly reminded of the significance of their mission.[37] Enrollee Vaughn Killpack told me in 1968 that his company, 959, had moved in from Joe's Valley camp F-10 in November and built eighteen miles of rock wall, approximately six to eight feet high and about the same dimensions wide along the bed of the Virgin. He was quite proud of the fact that his crew won a prize for having constructed the straightest wall.

In addition to the Virgin and Santa Clara, other Utah rivers and streams also required attention. Camp PE-214, close enough to Moab to be able to use the town's lights and water, was yet another camp working primarily on erosion and flood control. Here, under Lt. John R. Elting, thirteen buildings rose in September 1933 at a cost budgeted at $25,000. In mid-October Captain Vernon Peterson brought in Company 1345 from its original encampment at F-20 near the Warner Ranger Station in the mountains to the east of town. An additional group of one hundred men transferred to PE-214 from Ferron camp F-11, while a smaller detachment from Moab moved to F-10 at Joe's Valley en route to a permanent winter camp at Orderville in southern Utah. In addition to working on the Pack Creek–Castleton Road, CCC crews also built settling ponds on Pack Creek and worked on protecting the banks of Mill Creek.[38]

PE-219 of Salina in Sevier County was a fairly typical CCC camp. In October Company 960 had transferred from F-12, located in Salina Canyon, to the new site just outside the city limits.[39] The assignment here was to carry out erosion-control projects in Salina Canyon and others, in addition to the somewhat more routine tasks of construction and maintenance of telephone lines, roads, and campgrounds. The excessive runoff that had previously been created by the unchecked streams caused extreme silting farther downstream in the valley of the Sevier River. Crews under Superintendent R. C. Parkinson attempted to alleviate this situation by building two erosion dams in Salina Canyon as well as other spillways and rock barriers necessary to bring Salina Creek under control.[40]

Company 960 served at PE-219 until it moved to Soapstone at the beginning of summer 1934, part of a reduction of state camps that left only SE-205 in the Bountiful/Woods Cross area in operation, the only state camp open more than two periods. While camp SE-205 was the only soil erosion camp open that summer, the coming of winter saw not only the continuation of SE-205 and the reopening of SE-213 in St. George and PE-214 in Moab but also the start of four new camps: PE-220 in Provo, PE-221 in Willard, PE-222 in Cedar City, and PE-223 in Mt. Pleasant.

Forest Service responsibility had covered the state erosion-control camps during the first two years of the Corps. After that, however, with the pending creation of the Soil Conservation Service in 1935, the short-lived SE and PE camps came to an end. PE-220 did survive at the Provo fairgrounds, however, into the Fifth Period, when it gave way to F-40.

Although of short duration, the SE and PE camps firmly established that control of soil erosion was one of the principal objectives of CCC work. Indeed, the state erosion-control camps helped launch some of the methods that were to prove so effective in that ongoing battle, and eight of the seventeen SE/PE camps were even eventually taken over by other agencies.

THE DIVISION OF GRAZING AND SOIL EROSION

Between 1933 and 1942 the CCC camps of the Forest Service, National Park Service, and Soil Conservation Service built check dams and did terracing in the mountainous areas of the state; in the desert regions of eastern and western Utah, the work was done by the Division of Grazing camps, which after 1935 carried out the challenging task of controlling soil erosion and flooding along with their other assignments.

Cloudbursts often damaged roads, threatened towns, and raised the possibility of rivers overflowing their banks. CCC personnel used many techniques in the constant battle against the harassment of nature. DG-33 at Henrieville built three rock diversion walls about four feet high to divert floodwaters that might threaten the little community of Cannonville.

The men of DG-30 in Cedar City worked in extreme winter conditions to build a similar structure. In this case the men first dug a trench about one foot deep and then installed the posts, wire, and boulders for a wall 1,365 feet long to divert stream waters from the old channel that flooded the town of Summit after each cloudburst.[41] The Milford camp DG-35 dug a three thousand-foot canal completely by hand to carry floodwaters from one large drainage basin to a natural reservoir a short distance away.[42] There were probably more cribs and other types of rock retaining walls built along the Virgin than along any other river in Utah. Crews from the Green River camp did considerable riprap work along the Green for the purpose of protecting farmland as well as the community itself.

In late November 1937, Regional Grazier D. D. McKay wrote to Governor Blood. He enclosed a report of the work done by the DG camps as of the first of the month. In addition to the fifty-nine bridges built, 103 springs developed, and twelve wells drilled, McKay wrote of erosion-control devices such as the 849 check dams, the seventy-two large diversion dams, and the 65,811 square yards of riprap.[43] The earliest devices were quite simple. Small check dams were usually built at the heads of canyons found along the western face of the Wasatch Range. Some of these dug into the canyon walls at each end and curved upstream just like a regular dam, but others were even more elementary and simply diverted water so that it would run out into the brush and dissipate its eroding force. This technique persisted for many years in one form or another.

SE-205 was one of the few Second Period camps to remain in its same location in the summer of 1934. It was, in fact, the *only* state erosion camp to operate in Utah that Third Period, as all the companies that had been in the SE and PE camps during the Second Period were assigned to regular Forest Service camps that summer.

SOIL CONSERVATION SERVICE

When originally conceived, the Soil Conservation Service (SCS) was basically the brainchild of Dr. Hugh Bennett, a respected and widely published pioneer in the idea of preserving the soil. Born in North Carolina in 1881, he vigorously and passionately fought all his life for erosion control. Bennett was a soil chemist with the Department of Agriculture with thirty years of experience. For many years he had recognized that erosion was a serious attack not just on forests but on agricultural lands as well and believed that steps to fight soil erosion should also be carried out on private farmlands. Although he himself was then involved in the creation of still another conservation agency, his ideas impacted Forest Service thinking.

Back in 1928 Bennett had written *Soil Erosion: A National Menace*, but his cries for scientific soil management had fallen on deaf ears. In 1933, however, Roosevelt's adviser Rexford Tugwell recognized the need for a separate government agency to attack the national problem of soil erosion. In August 1933, Tugwell brought about the appointment of fifty-two-year-old Bennett as the first director of what Congress initially approved as a temporary agency, the Soil Erosion Service within the Department of the Interior headed by its secretary, Harold Ickes.

Although the state erosion camps administered by the Forest Service had been in the Corps from the beginning and the private erosion camps had existed since October 1934, Bennett had difficulty getting acceptance for CCC camps under the new Soil Erosion Service. In fact, during its one-year existence there were only eighty-six CCC camps assigned to Bennett's Soil Erosion Service across the country, none of which was in Utah.[44]

A study published by the Soil Erosion Service in 1935 identified soil erosion as "one of the most serious problems facing American agriculture."[45] More articles and more congressional testimony were indicative of the growing concern over the problem.

By 1935 the eighteen SE and PE camps in Utah had established the validity of erosion control outside the forests, even on private lands. Then, in April 1934, Mother Nature began helping Bennett's cause considerably through the terrible storms that created the Dust Bowl in the Great Plains states and plagued the nation for the rest of the New Deal period. The dust clouds reaching clear to the Atlantic coast added impetus to the problem of soil erosion.

Hugh Bennett's influence in getting Forest Service recognition of the problem of soil erosion outside national forests soon resulted in an even bigger change. With the Forest Service administering the SE and PE soil erosion camps under the Department of Agriculture and the Soil Erosion Service having been set up under the Department of the Interior, the situation was ripe for conflict due to the unnecessary overlapping of erosion-control responsibilities. Salmond offers an interesting interpretation:

> The matter was brought to the conference table, where representatives of both departments recognized the division of

> responsibility but could not agree on a solution. The President intervened, strongly backed by Fechner, and the result was the transfer of the Soil Conservation Service to the Department of Agriculture, an administrative move which did nothing to improve relations between the secretary of the Interior and the director of the CCC.[46]

Congress then acted with decisive legislation. On April 27, 1935, Congress voted approval of the Soil Conservation Act to change the *temporary* Soil Erosion Service in the Department of the Interior to the *permanent* Soil Conservation Service in the Department of Agriculture. Unfortunately, this created yet another escalation of tensions, which still exist today between the two cabinet departments.[47]

In the first six-month enrollment period of its existence the newly organized Soil Conservation Service had its most camps ever, an impressive 544 camps in the entire country, 150 of which had been transferred from the Forest Service. Throughout the life of the CCC, the SCS maintained an average of 362 camps.[48]

Making the transition from the state erosion camps to the new agency took some time. The only two SCS camps approved for Utah for the Fifth Period, the summer of 1935, were SCS-2 in Gunlock and SCS-3 in Price. SCS-2 opened around August, but SCS-3 in Price did not actually get under way until the following period. In fact, Utah fared rather badly, with only eight SCS camps throughout the entire life of the CCC, from consecutively numbered SCS-2 in Gunlock to SCS-9 in Tremonton.[49] Still, the challenge of soil erosion continued to be taken seriously, and the battle went on.

Administratively, the soil conservation camps in Utah were under the direction of the regional conservator headquartered in Albuquerque, New Mexico. In September 1938, the Conservator's Office announced a reorganization that in Utah included three major areas, each under an area conservator who oversaw SCS activities, including soil conservation districts and the five CCC camps then in operation. Salt Lake City was the headquarters of the Weber River Project, which included SCS-4 in Willard; the Price River area was based in Price and included SCS-3 in Price and SCS-5 in Mt. Pleasant. SCS-7 in Leeds would come under the Virgin River area located in St. George. The Moab camp, SCS-6, was in a different sort of arrangement outside of the SCS area organization and was under the supervision of Thomas J. Snyder, based in Grand Junction, Colorado, who reported directly to the regional office in Albuquerque.[50]

Salmond describes three categories of work carried out by the SCS: "demonstration of practical methods of soil conservation to farmers, actual work upon private land in cooperation with landowners, and the development and improvement of erosion control techniques through research."[51] All three of these issues were addressed by the formation of SCS-2 in Gunlock, not far from the Nevada line in western Washington County. In cooperation with the local Grazing Advisory Board and local ranchers, SCS-2 set up demonstration areas in order that erosion- and range-control techniques such as strip cropping, contour plowing, and crop rotation could be observed. Alma A. Nelson, former manager of a store in Kanab who had more recently served as superintendent of Pine Valley camp F-17, was appointed superintendent of the new camp in Gunlock and immediately set to work with Company 585 educating his constituency on range management as well as water development.[52]

When SCS officials considered the work at Gunlock to have been successfully launched after two years of labor, Company 585 was moved in June 1937 to the vacant site of F-24 in Leeds, still in southern Utah's Washington County. Short-lived F-24 had been open only for the winter of 1933–34 and was then abandoned for three years until the SCS set up SCS-7. The CCC facilities at Gunlock continued to be used as a spike camp out of Leeds, however, until national CCC policy led to the dismantling of most wooden, semipermanent spike camps as being too expensive to maintain.[53]

SCS-3 opened in the summer of 1935, when Company 2562 moved down from Kalispell, Montana, and began fencing 48,000 acres of grazing land northeast of the city. Shortly, however, Company 2562 was replaced by Company 593 out of Fort Knox, Kentucky, and remained until July 1942.

Although the Forest Service continued erosion control on national forest lands, the SCS assumed responsibility primarily for land that lay outside those forests and which had been protected by the SE and PE camps. In fact, of the eight SCS camps eventually established in Utah, five of them were at sites originally set up by the Forest Service.

By the time the new SCS took over primary responsibility for controlling soil erosion outside national forests in April 1935, there had been seven SE camps and ten PE camps administered by the Forest Service. Some of the camps lasted only one period and had already been

Figure 6.7. Willard Basin, at the top of the ridge east of U.S. 89, received a lot of attention from SE-204, SCS-4, and even F-34.

shut down, including SE-211, SE-212, PE-216, and others. Some camps were taken over by other technical agencies, such as PE-220, becoming F-40 in Provo, and Salina camp PE-219, becoming F-32. The camps in St. George (SE-213) and Cedar City (PE-222) were taken over by the Division of Grazing, while the camps in Moab, Willard, and Mt. Pleasant were eventually reopened by the Soil Conservation Service.

During the winter of 1936–37 the Soil Conservation Service added two more camps by installing companies from the Seventh Corps Area at the former sites of state soil erosion camps in Willard (PE-221), which now became SCS-4, and Mt. Pleasant (PE-223), which reopened as SCS-5, as described later in this chapter.

Around the latter part of September 1934, the short-lived PE-221 was set up in an orchard just south of Willard and east of the highway in a major attempt to attack the erosion problem above the town. In an article apparently written by camp superintendent J. C. Mauk, he gave a detailed explanation of the project. Crews began work immediately building V-shaped deflectors or dividers, the first and largest at the mouth of Willard Canyon, followed by eight other structures. Men also constructed riprap for the canyon, the largest wall of which was 591 feet long. On what was described as the Roberts Project, two caterpillar crews working day and night shifts over a period of five weeks worked on the dike and the rock spillway, which may still be seen today in Willard on U.S. Highway 89.

Figure 6.8. Spillway on the east side of U.S. 89 in Willard, one of the more visible Civilian Conservation Corps flood-control projects to be seen today.

They also worked on the channel by building check dams to prevent the erosion of stream banks and did some terracing work with plows and horses until the camp vacated the following spring.[54] But this still wasn't enough.

Although the regional forester had been advising community and county officials that the Forest Service stood ready to act on the problem, nothing could be done until the land shifted to public control. Only after another disastrous flood on July 31, 1936, did the Utah State Road Commission and the commissioners of Box Elder County and Willard City succeed in acquiring the private holdings on the watershed.[55] Finally the Soil Conservation Service reached an agreement with the Forest Service to seriously attack the problem by reopening the former camp PE-221 to become camp SCS-4. The Soil Conservation Service would provide the manpower, while the Forest Service handled supervision and administration. Company 736, composed of enrollees from Kansas, Missouri, and Arkansas, arrived at Willard from near Yellowstone, where it had served a short time after leaving Moapa, Nevada. The SCS enrollees from the Midwest immediately began to fulfill the agreement with the Forest Service in Utah.[56]

By September Project Supervisor John J. Wise was dispatched from F-34 in Hyrum to join Company 736 along with four foremen and an engineer to set up a spike camp on the divide between the heads of Perry Canyon and the North Fork of the Ogden River to the south.[57] The purpose of the spike camp was to build a road about six miles long into the Willard Basin, where the erosion-control work was to take place at an elevation of about nine thousand feet. Although the enrollees, nearly all from Arkansas, had jackhammers and three caterpillar bulldozers for the roadwork, much of the terracing was done by those wielding picks and shovels. The road extended to the east rim of Willard Canyon by around October 1, and part of the crew drew assignments to work on the watershed rehabilitation. Two crews felled the dead trees in a burned-over area and lay them horizontally along the contour of the side slopes of Willard Canyon. The boys also planted several thousand conifers in the burned area, as well as smooth bromegrass and orchard grass. In the meantime the rest of the men continued the road into other parts of the basin.

There was some disagreement among personnel from the Cache National Forest and those from Dr. Bailey's Intermountain Forest and Range Experiment Station over the best type of terrace to use under the circumstances, the "V" type or the flat-bottom type. Wise reports that "considerable discussion" ensued before a decision was reached: "It was determined that the flat-bottom trenches with check dams installed at about 25' to 30' apart would be the better design for the area.... It was reasoned that the flat-bottom terraces provided a greater surface area for water to penetrate into the ground."[58]

An engineer carefully laid out the plans for the terraces, which were constructed in 1936 beginning at the top of the slope and working downhill in order that the completed terraces might protect the work going on below should any summer storms hit the area. On their completion, a crew immediately seeded the terraces with domestic ryegrass to provide quick ground cover and with perennial grasses such as smooth bromegrass and orchard grass to provide slower-growing but longer-lasting cover.

During the seeding operations an early snowstorm hit the area one Friday night and provided the enrollees with an adventure. According to J. J. Wise, most of the foremen had been permitted to leave the camp for the weekend. By the next day snow stood waist-deep, and men had to keep brushing it off the tents to prevent their collapse. Wise, in charge of the crew, sent a radio message that the road was impassable and they would wait another day or two. On Monday the boys received orders to prepare to walk out the next morning if it became necessary to evacuate the camp. Tuesday morning, after an early breakfast of frozen onions, the caravan of about eighty apprehensive Midwestern boys began its march. Two or three of the huskier enrollees led the group; about the same number of the more reliable trailed the column to prevent straggling. They left their clothes and equipment and took only their valuables. After an exhausting eight miles, eighty weary hikers reached the trucks that had been sent to meet them and returned to the comfort of the rescuers' base camp, F-34 in Hyrum. The crew returned after a partial thaw a few days later to continue the work.[59]

After scattering the final seeds on six inches of snow, the camp moved out on about November 20, 1936, after having completed the construction of a low-standard road, the rehabilitation of the burned-over area, and the terracing and seeding of about forty acres of the Willard Basin.[60]

Willard camp SCS-4 continued to work on fencing, terracing, and planting in the basin. On August 2, 1938, the City Commission of Willard unanimously approved the donation of its watershed lands to the federal government, and Company 736 completed the project in 1940 before being transferred to SCS-9 in Tremonton. The solicitor general of the United States accepted title to the tract of 1,807 acres on October 20, 1941.[61] That the entire Willard project was a success much appreciated by the town is summed up in one sentence from the 1999 county history: "Finally, in the 1930s, the Civilian Conservation Corps built a camp in Willard basin, terraced the mountainsides, built a dike and spillway at the mouth of the canyon, and saved the town below from further flooding."[62]

This might, however, be the time to insert the one negative opinion I received concerning the work done on Willard Mountain. One female correspondent from Brigham City—who shall remain otherwise unidentified—soon made it clear to me in correspondence in 1968 that she did not like President Roosevelt, the Democratic Party, the New Deal, or anything associated with it, including the Civilian Conservation Corps. To paraphrase her remarks concerning the earlier flooding experiences and any effect the project might have had: "What a waste! They brought those young men out here and had them dig those big ditches around the mountain. Spent all that time and money, and it really wasn't necessary; we haven't had flooding like that since then, anyhow!" My original suspicion that this might have been a tongue-in-cheek attempt at humor

Figure 6.9. Several buildings of SCS-7 in Leeds, looking today as they must have looked in the late 1930s.

was soon negated by the tenor of other acrimonious remarks. Somehow the concept of cause and effect seems to have escaped her.

SCS-6 in Moab is another of those units that provides some confusion. PE-214 had been there originally in Periods Two and Four; SCS-6 was on the same site in Periods Nine through Fourteen; and NP-7 served Arches National Monument during the last two years of the program, presumably from the same site. All of these were referred to at one time or another as the "Moab camp," as were DG-32 at Dalton Wells, actually thirteen miles north of Moab, and sometimes even DG-157 at Dry Valley, actually just outside Monticello to the south. The county centennial *History of Grand County* gives much more thorough CCC coverage than is found in most of the volumes in that series, but even it tells little of the work of SCS-6 and states that the camp was actually open only for Period Sixteen, from October 1940 to March 1941.[63] Unfortunately, neither official records nor local newspapers offer any help. Firmage does point out, however, that CCC work in the county "was predominantly conservation or reclamation-oriented . . . planting trees, constructing firebreaks and trails, reclaiming damaged land, or repairing watercourses and working on flood-control measures."[64]

Camp SCS-7 began in Leeds in mid-June 1937, when Company 585 was transferred from Gunlock camp SCS-2 to the old site of F-24 just off present I-15. Newspaper coverage of this camp was among the best in the state, as the enrollees had a regular "Leeds CCC Camp" article in the accommodating *Washington County News*.

In addition to the expected work of building diversion dams on tributaries of the Virgin River and improving stream flow in Shoal Creek and LaVerkin Creek, SCS-7 had some specific claims to fame.[65] Just two months after the camp was set up, the *Washington County News* told of the masonry terraces and buildings of red sandstone that had already been completed under Superintendent R. W. McBride. These buildings included a toolhouse and oil house that have lasted to the present day, establishing the Leeds camp as one of the best representations of a CCC camp in the entire country today.[66] Leeds was also the only camp of which I am aware in Utah that had an Explorer Scout post. Operating under the Utah National Parks Council the post carried out service projects and took trips to such places as Bryce National Park.[67] One final feather in the Leeds camp's cap was the fact that the boys, supervised by Army and SCS personnel, built a twenty-by-ninety-foot swimming pool during the summer of 1939. The water came from a nearby spring, which generous neighbors Lawrence McMullin and Frank Hartley allowed the enrollees to tap. In addition to the athletic events many camps were able to host, Leeds also held swim meets with other envious camps.[68]

It was June 24, 1940, when Company 1256 from Camp Dix, New Jersey, got off the train at the Thompson railhead and was then trucked ninety-four miles south to San Juan County. They came to set up SCS-8 on the former site of F-41 near Monticello, which the Forest Service had agreed two years before to turn over to the Soil Conservation Service. San Juan County was not new territory for the CCC, since, in addition to F-41, DG-34 had been at Blanding since 1935 and DG-157, another relatively new camp, was setting up at Dry Valley north of Monticello on what is now U.S. 163/191 toward La Sal Junction. The county historian reported that the need for help was great, as there was a loss of fertility "due to constant cropping and lack of crop rotation as well as loss of topsoil through wind erosion and torrential rainstorms and from plowing ground on too steep a slope."[69] McPherson thinks that the camp opened in 1939, but official records point out that Company 1256 occupied the camp on June 24, 1940, with 177 men mostly from New York and New Jersey.

The remaining Soil Conservation Service camp in Utah was located in Tremonton and got started in October 1939, when Company 736 moved over from a very successful stay at Willard camp SCS-4. Local residents did their best to welcome the company, with the Lions Club setting up a banquet with entertainment and a speaker. Methodist and Latter-day

Figure 6.10. Camp SCS-9 site today. The camp was located between this present Tremonton hospital and the Box Elder County fairgrounds just to the south.

Saints clergy provided Sunday services, and the Bear River High School band and other groups performed at the camp. Again, the construction of check dams, terraces, and structures for gully erosion control was the main work carried out under the newly organized Northern Utah Soil Conservation District.[70]

There is no doubt that erosion control was one of the major accomplishments of the CCC, and, as might be expected, the Soil Conservation Service was a major player. In spite of the rare negative comment out of Brigham City, throughout the state it was the flood- and erosion-control projects that were to bring the greatest acclaim to the CCC program. While many CCC activities resulted in higher visibility from the improved facilities for comfort and recreation, the work of the soil erosion camps meant the protection of homes and lands for many of the farmers and urban dwellers of Utah. In the nine-year history of the CCC this period saw the greatest extension of appreciation by grateful communities for the performance of the regularly assigned work. A comment by a former enrollee suggests why this may have been so: "That little valley was on its way to becoming a flood-torn gulch, but rock and wire net dams held back the top soil and increased the value of its farmland beyond measure . . . and today you can still see the value of those dams."[71]

The success of the Davis County terracing was demonstrated in July 1938, when what was described as the heaviest storm on record took place. Over an inch of rain fell in fifteen minutes, and the residents of

Bountiful feared a repeat of the disasters of 1923 and 1930 and, in fact, were preparing to flee their homes. Then, fortunately, the benefits of the enrollees' work in the preceding years kicked in: "But the water stuck where the CCC boys wanted it to: in the terraces."[72]

The CCC flood-control measures were effective for nearly half a century, "as evidenced by the small number of debris flows between 1935 and 1982." The winter of 1983–84, however, provided "record rainfall and rapid snowmelt [that] saturated soil on steep mountainsides and caused small landslides that transformed into debris flows that charged down gullies and stream channels all along the Wasatch Front."[73] How much worse it might have been had those old terraces not been there can never be known, of course, but it certainly demonstrated the power of nature's elements.

Unfortunately, it was in the area of flood control in Washington County that less than total success was achieved. Although enrollees worked long and hard for several years to bring the Virgin and Santa Clara rivers under control, Mother Nature refused to be subdued. In January 2005, devastating flooding of the Santa Clara caused more than $180,000,000 in damage in St. George and Santa Clara, as dozens of homes were either seriously damaged or completely destroyed as they went crashing into the river as eroding riverbanks crumbled. The fight goes on to the present day.[74]

THE CAUSE, CURSE, AND COURSE OF OVERGRAZING

The danger from erosion of hillsides stripped bare by overgrazing was a problem of long and lengthy concern. Along with most historians and conservationists, Arthur Schlesinger laid the blame squarely on the livestock industry:

> As long as western ranchers could remember they had used the public lands to graze their cattle or sheep without supervision or payment of fee. The predictable consequences had been overgrazing, with the gradual destruction of the grass cover and the spread of desert. For some time, conservationists had urged public regulation of private grazing in order to check erosion. But the stockmen had always successfully fought such seemingly subversive proposals.[75]

This danger, of course, was that the lack of vegetation in the mountains created a potential for devastating flooding in the lands below. Dr. Vasco Tanner's plea in 1933 that a camp be set up on the Provo fairgrounds was no doubt aided by his statement that the canyons above Provo and Springville "have become so denuded that flooding is a real menace."[76]

Erosion-control work was carried on at the Willard watershed in Box Elder County. Here, too, Forest Service officials had long known the need for rehabilitation of the bare slopes, laid waste by overcutting of timber and by overgrazing by livestock. One history of the county intimated that the problem might have been due to early Mormon settlers rejecting the advice of their ecclesiastical leader: "The pioneers had ignored the counsel of Brigham Young and had overgrazed both valleys and mountains.... Willard Basin, high up in the Wasatch range, had been overgrazed for years, and was a catastrophe waiting to happen." And happen it did, when "a heavy downpour of cloudburst proportions" hit the area on August 13, 1923, causing massive flooding resulting in the deaths of two women and the hospitalization of several other people. The runoff of soil and water through the community destroyed buildings, livestock, and more than three hundred acres of farmland and also blocked the highway through Willard for several weeks.[77] Another flood took place in 1930, but it was to be a while before any serious remedies were pursued.

Not only did some of the pioneers ignore the advice of the president of their church, but later generations ignored the president of their country, as well. In May 1903, President Theodore Roosevelt visited the state and made his major address in the Latter-day Saints Tabernacle in Salt Lake City. He told the enthusiastic, overflow crowd of his admiration of the work done in the area of irrigation; he also warned of the dangers of overgrazing. The president acknowledged the complexities of the problem but also emphasized the necessity of a solution.

He admitted that he was not sure of the best answer to the problem, and he remained unsettled about what was the best method of solving the issue: "The greatest objective of Roosevelt's forest and land policy was to provide families with a continuous supply of timber, grass, and most importantly, water, not only for their present use, but for future generations as well."[78] Although a progressive Republican, Roosevelt shared the conservation ideals of his progressive Democrat cousin three decades later.

In 1930, Governor George Dern was so concerned about the loss of lives and property in Davis County that he appointed a committee headed by Sylvester Q. Cannon to investigate the situation and come up with ideas for solutions. Cannon's committee reported that as a result of overgrazing, "particularly by sheep," canyons were being stripped. "Without vegetation, the watersheds could not hold and absorb the water falling in summer thunderstorms," such that "the flooding water gouged out dirt and rocks that deposited on the lands, buildings, and people below." The recommendation: that the Forest Service buy and restore the denuded watersheds in Davis County.[79]

Superintendent Mark Anderson of SE-206 told the Provo Lions Club that the terracing being done was the most successful means of erosion control. Then, in what later generations might describe as, for Utah, another most politically incorrect statement, he went on to give his opinion that perhaps it would be even more effective to take the lands out of private control and put them under complete government supervision since overgrazing by sheep and cattle was the chief cause of erosion.[80]

This sentiment was not new. Michael Sweeney's beautifully illustrated book on Logan Canyon describes the results of uncontrolled logging of timber and overgrazing of livestock. The damage caused by cattle was bad enough, but "nothing like the sheep that became the valley's primary livestock in the last two decades of the 18th century when the ovine population rose from 10,000 to 300,000." Finally, when it was observed that sheep "stripped Logan Canyon like locusts in an Old Testament plague," Cache Valley residents took action. Moved perhaps by President Theodore Roosevelt's conservation ethos, they requested that he intervene. He did so, sending Grazing Inspector Albert E. Potter to survey the situation in the summer of 1902. His report that the canyon had been "grazed almost to extinction" and was "barren of vegetation" led to Roosevelt's creation of Logan Forest Reserve in May 1903.[81]

In the early years of the twentieth century the argument that the locals know better than Washington bureaucrats how to manage the land in Utah was, like the land itself, beginning to erode, and the desirability of federal assistance took another small step forward. It was not until the 1930s, however, that full-scale intervention occurred, in which the Civilian Conservation Corps was a major player.

Today, however, the pendulum has swung again, and the arguments heard now from governors down to outspoken activists clamor for state supremacy over that of the federal government in the ownership and control of public lands. Politically charged, potentially violent actions in

Utah, Nevada, and Oregon now cast the federal conservation agencies as the "bad guys," quite a different picture than that of the 1930s, when the CCC-built terraces, roads, stock trails, reservoirs, corrals, and other structures were most welcome. (If all these were to somehow be magically removed from the state, I wonder who would complain the loudest.) The problems of national-state relations today have been exacerbated by overzealous presidents, sovereignty-protective governors, violence-prone and shortsighted activists, and occasionally overreaching federal agencies. Therefore, the battle goes on. In a recent editorial the *Deseret News* raised the question not over the morality of a possible transfer but over whether or not the necessary lawsuit by Utah would be financially feasible.[82]

In the meantime, who knows but how the federal government is responding to some of the attacks. In 2016, the Forest Service called for public input on the possibility of opening about one hundred thousand acres for sheep grazing permits in Duquesne and Summit counties in northeastern Utah.[83]

Still, statistics again prove that anything can be proved by statistics. In December 2015, poll results indicated that seven western states all opposed the transfer of federal lands to the states. Admittedly, Utah, with only a 6 percent difference between the two options, was much more evenly divided than the others.[84]

What is to be done about the situation is well beyond the scope of this book. My only hope is that the tremendously helpful erosion- and flood-control activities of the CCC will not be forgotten in the hubbub.

CHAPTER 7

Dams, Canals, and Irrigation

The Bureau of Reclamation

Don't do that [shut down a dismantling project]; they're nine-tenths done and nobody got hurt yet.

—E. O. Larson, Bureau of Reclamation chief engineer, re: BR-12

The Bureau of Reclamation (BR) had been heavily involved in building dams and irrigation facilities for water and soil conservation since 1902. Getting involved with the Emergency Conservation Work program during the Great Depression seemed a natural association, but that did not occur until the summer of 1934, apparently due to the fear that "the technical engineering nature of Reclamation's work raised questions about the applicability of the CCC program to Bureau activities." After seeing the enrollees in action for a year, however, that doubt disappeared, and bureau officials changed their tune, as one associate engineer explained in 1937 how such young men could handle the job:

> Because the CCC enrollees are not more than 17 to 19 years of age, on an average, and as most of them have had very little or no experience in construction or any kind of manual labor, the use of experienced foremen and skilled workmen has been found necessary in providing an opportunity for the enrollees to adapt themselves to the kind of work being done. It has been the practice, as far as possible, to train small groups of enrollees directed by one or two skilled workmen or foremen on the various types of work such as operation of tractors and other heavy machinery, building of structures, excavation, planing of

> embankments, and on other related work requiring skilled and semi-skilled labor.[1]

Accordingly, for the Third Enrollment Period, the bureau authorized its first nine CCC camps: two each in Wyoming, Utah, and New Mexico and one each in Nebraska, South Dakota, and Texas.[2] It was not surprising that seven of these first nine BR camps—including Utah's DBR-5 and DBR-6—were assigned as drought-relief camps, a designation that did not extend past Enrollment Period Five, the summer of 1935.[3]

Of the six Bureau of Reclamation camps created in Utah, two were DBR-5, at Currant Creek "in a rather remote area 23 miles east of Heber, Utah," in Wasatch County, and DBR-6, east of Ephraim in Sanpete County. These two camps, incidentally, were two of Utah's first half-dozen drought-relief camps, described in chapter 4.

Bureau of Reclamation historian Christine Pfaff explained what the bureau was all about in her book about the relationship between her organization and the CCC: "The mission of the Bureau of Reclamation is to manage, develop, and protect water and related resources in an environmentally and economically sound manner in the interest of the American public," done primarily by building dams to regulate the water and generate hydroelectric power.[4] Since its primary task was the provision of water to needy areas, the Bureau of Reclamation was confined to the western, more arid portion of the United States. During the depression years, the bureau had projects in every state west of the one hundredth meridian except for Kansas, ranging from one in Texas to ten or possibly eleven in Wyoming, to which the CCC contributed in varying degrees.[5]

Although the Bureau of Reclamation historian described the agency "as a minor recipient of CCC benefits," having only 1.7 percent of the total number of camps in 1937, the bureau always regarded the CCC as a positive experience, having come to the rescue "when western agriculture was in critical straits," especially in the rehabilitation of existing irrigation systems, construction of new canals, building of roads, and clearance of reservoir sites.[6] Leonard Arrington, one of Utah's outstanding historians, stated that "nearly half the population of Utah was benefited directly or indirectly by these reclamation projects."[7]

While most CCC camps in Utah could be described as multipurpose in their work assignments, a few have been here described as having a much narrower focus. It was arguably the Bureau of Reclamation, however, whose camps had the narrowest of responsibilities, namely, the movement and distribution of water from where it was available to areas where it wasn't and was sorely needed.

Although it is true that BR camps did engage in rodent control as well as battling invasive weeds and even preparing experimental plots for instructing farmers and ranchers in conservation methods, these activities should be viewed as subprojects of their major assignments, that is, those having to do with the movement of water. And, of course, in typical CCC fashion BR camps were always available for fighting wildfires, rescuing both humans and animals, and carrying out other emergency activities.[8]

Eventually BR camps even worked on the development of recreational facilities at some of its projects and, like enrollees in the other technical agencies, built trails and developed campgrounds with picnic shelters, tables, benches, stoves, and fireplaces. Skills developed on the job enabled the enrollees to build latrines, sewage disposal plants, and facilities for fishing, swimming, and boating. Still, it is irrigation for which the bureau should be remembered.

Three decades prior to the creation of the CCC, President Theodore Roosevelt, cousin of Franklin Roosevelt, who created the Corps, extolled the value of irrigation during his 1903 visit to Utah and praised the local citizenry for their work in that area. Less than a year prior to the president's visit the Reclamation Service had been set up to provide irrigation facilities. In his article on Theodore's 1903 visit, Michael Eldredge stated that "Roosevelt argued that private enterprise could not build the dams and canals needed for reclamation in the West; progressives believed this enormous undertaking to be an obligation of the federal government." Although of different parties, of course, his cousin Franklin shared Theodore's vision and, with the help of the CCC, began to carry it out.[9]

In Utah, Bureau of Reclamation work was confined to the north and eastern portions of the state for farmers and ranchers hoping to see irrigation brought to their dry lands, as well as providing water and power to cities along the Wasatch Front. Storage dams and irrigation projects offered hope for the future and reassurance in the aftermath of the dry and depressed conditions of the 1930s.

The major impetus for reclamation work took place, again, due to the troubling aspects of nature. Utah, the second-driest state in the country to begin with, was hit hard by the forces of nature. The average precipitation for the state was thirteen inches, but it was considerably below that figure from 1930 to 1934, when the most serious trouble began. Meteorologists declare a drought in effect when the precipitation is 75 percent of normal; Utah experienced 51 percent of normal that winter. Not only was the winter the driest on record, but it was also the warmest. When Governor Blood toured central and southern Utah he described the danger of a water shortage to be both unprecedented and terrifying.[10]

The problem was by no means confined to Utah; most of the country, especially in the Midwest and Great Plains area, was experiencing the same challenge. To somewhat alleviate the difficulty of livestock dying of thirst and starvation the federal government spent $112,000,000 buying sheep and cattle to slaughter. In Utah approximately 126,000 head of cattle and 206,000 sheep were killed. Needy families were allowed to cart away meat as long as the animals were not diseased.[11]

The national picture was bleak. In August 1933, however, $15,415,000 was approved in eight western states for fourteen projects, including $930,000 for a dam and a reservoir near Wellsville for what came to be identified as the Hyrum Project and another $3,000,000 for another dam and reservoir near Huntsville for the Ogden River irrigation project. Deer Creek, however, was to "come up later" in the allocation of funds. On a second trip to Washington in September, Governor Blood spent two months lobbying for another $40,000,000, of which $17,000,000 was to be earmarked for reclamation projects in Sanpete County as well as the Deer Creek and Moon Lake projects. Partly as a result of his efforts and the threat of a dry winter, plans for both Pineview and Deer Creek dams were upgraded to "urgent." Initially thwarted by Public Works administrator Harold Ickes, Blood, with the help of his predecessor, George Dern, secured FDR's "presidential blessing."

Even after getting Interior's reluctant approval for eventually spending up to $10,000,000 for Bureau of Reclamation work in Utah, Blood still had to battle the Department of Agriculture regarding irrigation projects to be carried out from Deer Creek. Secretary of Agriculture Henry Wallace and his assistant Rexford Tugwell offered "strenuous objections" to the work unless specific conditions were met, primarily that poor agricultural lands be purchased with federal funds to balance the value of other lands that would benefit from the irrigation projects proposed. As Utah historian Thomas Alexander put it, "Blood succeeded in wearing down Roosevelt's resistance and in getting the president to override a rather testy Harold Ickes and a decidedly reluctant Secretary of Agriculture Henry Wallace," who were hesitant about more land being brought into agricultural production. Ickes reluctantly approved the money for the projects to get under way, whereupon "a somewhat cranky Ickes figured that the efforts of Dern and Blood had netted Utah 270 percent of her per capita share of PWA [Public Works Administration] funds."[12] In addition to his challenges on the national level, Blood also persuaded the Utah legislature to come up with the required matching funds from the state by increasing the sales tax to 2 percent.[13]

Getting water from where it was available to places where it was needed was always a priority, especially in challenging circumstances. The summer of 1934 was such a time. Camps BR-5 and BR-6 were thrown into canal-building projects in Wasatch and Sanpete counties in Utah's back country to provide much-needed irrigation water to farmers in the valleys, basically a monumental task of getting water from one side of the mountains to the other. Supervising engineer E. O. Larson appointed fellow engineers E. W. Hoopes and Herbert J. Blake of Salt Lake City as work superintendents of BR-5 and BR-6, respectively, both of which were tent camps at high elevations where work was possible only during the summer months.

BR-5, CURRANT CREEK, STRAWBERRY VALLEY PROJECT

There was no question that the need for the bureau was great. In 1934, for example, the Strawberry River discharged less than 20,000 acre-feet of water, about 10 percent of what might be expected in a good year. To help remedy the situation along the western side of the Wasatch Front, on July 27, 1934, Company 1968 was organized at Fort Douglas as one of the half-dozen DBR companies created in Utah. The company under Captain John B. Cannon was immediately sent to set up DBR-5 as a tent camp on the headwaters of Currant Creek at about nine thousand feet elevation in Wasatch County, east of Heber. The enrollees spent the first summer cutting timber on a steep mountainside to clear a right-of-way for a five-mile canal to carry water from Currant Creek through a mountain tunnel into Co-Op Creek, which in turn emptied into the Strawberry River. The river emptied into Strawberry Reservoir, where water was diverted to the west slope of the Wasatch when not needed on the Uinta bench.[14]

Superintendent E. W. Hoopes directed the work, which by the end of September was regarded as only about two-thirds finished. Since by then it was recognized that work on the diversion canal right-of-way would not be completed that summer, thirty men were sent to the Uinta Basin to build a winter camp. Then, in October, BR-5 shut down for good, and Company 1968 moved to Bridgeland for the winter.[15] The site continued to be used, however, and remains of the camp can still be seen on the downhill side of Forest Road 083, approximately two miles north of where that road separates from 082 west of Currant Creek Reservoir. Although no longer in use, the major canal is visible as well.

Spike camps out of BR-12 in Huntsville continued on the project the two subsequent summers to carry on "canal excavation and the building of two rock emergency spillways and a small diversion dam." The canal was ready for use in 1937; the campsite was abandoned for good that fall, and the buildings were dismantled for use at BR-64 in Heber and elsewhere.[16]

BR-6, EPHRAIM, SANPETE PROJECT

DBR-6 was set up in July 1934, on the headwaters of Cottonwood Creek about twenty miles east of Ephraim in Sanpete County. The camp was manned by Company 1967 under Captain L. E. Thompson, previously commanding officer at the Woods Cross camp. BR-6's mission was almost exactly like BR-5's. The enrollees drew assignments for the construction of feeder canals near Spring City and Ephraim. Again like DBR-5, DBR-6 was to construct canals to move precious water from where it was plentiful west through the mountains to where it was scarce. Cottonwood Creek, a tributary of the San Rafael River, was the source, and the water was moved through two tunnels to the Ephraim and Spring City divisions of what came to be identified as the Sanpete Project on the western slope of the Wasatch Range. They built four small canals totaling five and a half miles in length, two for each of the two tunnels.[17] CCC truck drivers also hauled concrete, lumber, and other building materials for not only the small bridges and two small masonry dams but also the tunnels that were built under contract by construction firms.[18]

As the winter approached both the companies moved to more workable locations in October 1934. Neither company returned to the high mountains the following summer. Instead, Company 259 of New York and New Jersey boys moved into BR-6. By 1937, the camps were abandoned, and the buildings were utilized elsewhere. The next two BR camps were set up farther north just three months after BR-5 and BR-6 in October 1934.

BR-11, BRIDGELAND, MOON LAKE PROJECT

Bridgeland camp BR-11 was set up on the north side of the Duchesne River five miles east of Duchesne in Duchesne County, about 140 miles east of Salt Lake City in the northeast part of Utah. Designated DBR-11 as another drought-relief camp, the enrollees were tasked with helping the Bureau of Reclamation with its Moon Lake Project by providing water to the Uinta Basin from the Midview Reservoir and Moon Lake.

The Moon Lake Project developed in the Uinta Basin north of the Duchesne River and west of the Uinta River. The Bureau of Reclamation first became interested in the project in 1927, less than a quarter of a century after white settlers first moved into the region. The bureau conducted an investigation in cooperation with the Utah Water Storage Commission and submitted a report to the federal government in 1933. Funds for construction were allotted on November 29, 1933, and President Roosevelt approved the Moon Lake Project on November 6, 1935.[19]

The work was divided into two parts. A San Francisco construction firm built the Moon Lake Dam under private contract on the west branch of the Lake Fork River. The balance of the facilities—the Yellowstone Feeder Canal, the Midview Dam, the Midview Lateral, and the Duchesne Feeder Canal—were built by CCC enrollees under the general supervision of the bureau's E. O. Larson.[20]

Duchesne Feeder Canal

Company 1968 first began work on the Duchesne Feeder Canal shortly after settling into the Bridgeland camp and by the following summer had it largely completed. This canal was to be used to divert surplus water from the Duchesne River fifteen miles to the Lake Fork River, with a lateral running off into Midview Reservoir. The reservoir, formed by the dam and accompanying dike, impounded water from the Duchesne River for the purpose of providing water via the Midview Lateral to the Uinta and Ouray Reservation lands on the north side of the river. This would be done in exchange for Indian water, which would be diverted to other parts of the project farther upstream. After the Duchesne Canal reached completion the CCC company began work on the dike and, in November 1935, started construction on the Midview Dam itself.[21]

Midview Dam

The dike was constructed to cut off a low portion from the northeast corner of the reservoir area. It was about a half mile long and twenty-one feet high and was sloped and riprapped, or lined with gravel and boulders, just like the dam itself.

During January and February 1937, temperatures dropped to nearly −40 degrees, and work slowed down until March, but the dike was completed the following month. Construction work on the dam proceeded at the same time. Enrollees poured 139,000 cubic yards of earth into the fifty-four-foot-high structure. The crest was 670 feet long, with the top thirty feet wide. As the embankment rose it was thoroughly rolled and packed, and crews lined sand, gravel, and boulders on both the upstream and downstream faces to a maximum depth of fifteen feet to reduce wave action.[22]

The dam was dedicated on September 10, 1937, in a ceremony attended by Congressman Abe Murdock and officials from Fort Douglas, the Bureau of Reclamation, and the surrounding area. The enrollees of Company 1968 saw to it that the reservoir received the name Lake Bauram in honor of Charles L. "Chip" Bauram, killed while changing the blade on a bulldozer during construction of the dam in February 1936.[23]

Midview Lateral Canal

The Midview Lateral Canal was three feet deep and ran nine miles from the reservoir to north of the Lake Fork of the Duchesne River. Construction began in December 1935 and continued until the following April, when the excavating equipment moved to work on the Midview Dam and dike. When the weather became too cold for work on those projects the equipment returned to the canal, and the project resumed. In 1937 a total of forty minor structures had been built in connection with the canal, including a reinforced concrete siphon placed beneath the Lake Fork River to carry water to the Dry Gulch Canal on the other side.[24]

In 1936 some feared that work might be discontinued due to a decrease in CCC enrollment. Utah's other Bureau of Reclamation camp, BR-12 in Huntsville, closed, but BR-11 was not disturbed. Officials had hoped, however, that Company 259 might be transferred to Altonah from the abandoned BR-6 in Ephraim in order to work on the Yellowstone Feeder Canal, but a nationwide cutback of CCC camps took place, and Company 259 was not moved.[25]

Yellowstone Feeder Canal

In April 1938, crews began work on the final stage of the project, completion of the Yellowstone Feeder Canal between the east fork of Lake Fork and Cottonwood Creek twenty-two miles away. Because the work site was so far distant from BR-11, a spike camp was established at Altonah about twenty-five miles closer to the job.

First the crew improved the road so that materials could be easily transported; then work began on the canal. The men completed excavation in August 1939 and released water into the first portion of the Yellowstone Canal to check it for leaks. Because of excessive seepage, enrollees began lining the canal with clay, and the first section became completely operable in June 1940.[26] The other section of the canal was nine miles long, and enrollees commenced work there in October 1939. Work stopped during the winter because of extremely poor weather conditions. When work began again the difficulty of excavation postponed the Yellowstone Canal's completion until July 1940. It was immediately put into service and prevented serious crop failures that same season. The Moon Lake Water Users' Association constructed the last two miles of the canal; CCC forces did the balance of the canal construction. Although irrigation from the canals commenced in 1938, work on the Moon Lake Project continued until 1941.

The nature of the Bureau of Reclamation and its relationship to the purposes of the CCC came in for serious questioning in January 1938. In the latter half of 1937, President Roosevelt launched a spirited attempt to reduce government expenditures in order to secure a balanced budget. For the CCC it meant that 104 camps would have to shut down by the end of the year and another three hundred would have to close by July 3, 1938. In what might seem to be a move contrary to his usual support, the president added his personal influence to the problem by recommending to Congress that the organization be reduced in size. Congressional supporters of the CCC attempted to turn back the onslaught, but they proved unsuccessful, and the necessary cuts began.[27] The Bureau of Reclamation was singled out for immediate attention.

Robert Fechner planned to discontinue the BR camps because he felt that private interests were the principal recipients of the CCC labor of those camps, a situation contrary to the original intent of the program.[28] While this may have been permissible when public projects were in short supply, the reduced number of CCC personnel ensured that there were more than enough projects in the public domain to occupy the remaining 1,200 camps. Therefore Fechner found no justification for continuing work on private or quasi-private activities such as those in which the Bureau of Reclamation was engaged in Utah.

Moon Lake Dam

Although the Moon Lake Dam was built under contract in 1938, the CCC set up a spike camp at the site in May 1939 to build curb walls and a parapet 1,200 feet long and seven feet high along the crest of the dam. This project seemed to be a desirable assignment according to the camp newspaper, which advised, "For the men desiring to work on this job it would be well to show a little 'Umph' and get into the eyes of the men who make the selections."[29] Work on the dam discontinued in July 1939, however, due to a reduction in funds and the size of the available workforce. Work moved slowly throughout the entire project that year. A flood on July 30 could have caused serious delay, but enrollees braved the cold water to salvage most of the material. Another flood in September necessitated a change in transportation routes to supply materials to the site of one of the diversion dams.[30]

By this time, however, most of the project had been sufficiently completed, and in late September 1939, the company transferred to Pleasant Grove. Work continued, however, by the Altonah spike camp in 1940 on the 1,200-foot parapet on the Moon Lake Dam as well as on the Yellowstone Feeder Canal. But problems continued. In July a break in the Yellowstone Feeder Canal took time to repair, and the next month enrollees left the job to fight fires. Camp BR-11 suffered a final ignominy that same summer when a suit was filed and hearings were held in federal court, which resulted in foreclosure on the land occupied by the camp. As a result the buildings were transferred to camps of the Division of Grazing and the Forest Service, and camp BR-11 was no more.[31]

CCC participation on the Moon Lake Project came to an end in 1941. Only a few enrollees were available to work, and even these moved out to join BR-64 in Heber City on August 9, but the benefits continued. Today the project provides water to more than 75,000 acres, and farmers in the Uinta Basin annually harvest irrigated crops worth between $1,000,000 and $2,000,000.[32]

BR-12, HUNTSVILLE, OGDEN RIVER PROJECT

For the most part, very few Utah communities protested the establishment of a CCC camp in their vicinity. One of these rare situations developed in the fall of 1934 when Company 1967 was scheduled to transfer from BR-6 in Ephraim to the Ogden area. Plans had been under way for several years to construct a dam on the Ogden River and a canal system to provide cheaper irrigation and culinary water for Ogden City and adjacent farmlands and communities.

When Governor Blood made his first trip to Washington asking federal officials for money in April 1933, the Pineview Dam was one of the projects he had in mind. Designed to control and store Ogden River floodwaters, the dam was approved that August.

In September an advance crew arrived at the campsite two miles northwest of Huntsville and fourteen miles east of Ogden. Located on a little knoll on a small peninsula extending out into what is now the north end of Pineview Reservoir between Eden and Huntsville, the camp became operable on October 15, 1934, with enrollees of Company 1967.[33]

As BR-6 duplicated BR-5 in its mission, so also does BR-12 possess much the same history as BR-11, as they opened within days of each other. BR-11 worked on the Provo River Project and contributed to the construction of Deer Creek Dam; BR-12 worked on the Ogden River Project and contributed to the construction of Pineview Dam. They both cleared the reservoir sites and built fences and parapets around the dams, as well as building auxiliary canals, parapet walls, and reservoirs. They both were set up as drought-relief winter camps by enrollees from high-elevation summer camps. Both projects created controversy due to the uprooting of families and the destruction of homes and farms from the flooding necessary to create their respective reservoirs.[34]

The City Commission of Ogden demanded an investigation into why "outsiders" from New York and New Jersey made up the work crew, which

Mayor Harman W. Peery and others apparently felt should be composed of local residents. They also claimed that CCC labor on the project would violate the regulations against work being done that might compete with private enterprise. As the bureau's spokesman Larson explained, actually the dam itself was to be built under contract by Ogden's Utah Construction Company and the Morrison-Knudsen Company out of Boise, Idaho, while the CCC enrollees would only be clearing the dam site and rebuilding the pipeline below the dam, work not covered by the dam contract. The dam was completed in 1937 and was initially 105 feet high with a crest length of 550 feet. The storage of 5,175 acre-feet of water was a great boon to famers, who were able to irrigate more than 60,000 acres between Brigham City and South Ogden.

Larson stated that it would save the farmers of the area some $150,000 if the enrollees did the labor. He countered the "carpetbagger" allegation by pointing out that Company 1967 was strictly a Utah company and that it and its sister company 1968 employed some 150 men from Weber County. In response to the suggestion that the camp be relocated and do general work elsewhere in the county, BR officials emphasized that this was a special-purpose camp and would not be located in the county at all except for the purpose for which it was organized. In spite of the explanation, misunderstandings prevailed, and the commission, upon motion by the mayor, voted to send a protest to CCC officials in Washington urging the relocation of the camp.[35]

Telegrams, conferences, and telephone calls followed. Some asked Governor Blood to persuade the Ogden River Water Users' Association to try and have the request withdrawn. Blood lent his support by stating that the work done by the camps would be reflected in lower costs to farmers, who could barely afford to meet expenses even then. Fechner, with his labor background, of course, was sensitive to any charges that might indicate an antilabor pose by his organization. He was therefore apprehensive about the protest voiced by Utah's Senator William King, who charged that the Corps interfered with the labor movement.[36]

The stalemate broke when the main contingent of Company 1967 arrived on October 16, 1934, as the new buildings of BR-12 neared completion. Clearing of the reservoir basin was one of the first tasks assigned. Enrollees set about cutting and burning willows and underbrush and removing fences and buildings from the area. By October 1935, BR-12 had nearly completed clearing the area and was about ready to start building canals. Spike camps settled at Hyrum for the Ogden River Project and at Currant Creek for the Sanpete Project, and all seemed well.

That same month, however, Robert Fechner dropped a bombshell by announcing that a serious CCC cutback necessitated the closing of 489 camps across the country, and BR-12 was one of fourteen BR camps to be discontinued.[37] Again letters and telegrams flew as Blood urged Fechner to postpone, if not cancel, the removal order since the labor costs without the CCC would be prohibitive to the farmers. Senator Thomas, stout defender of the CCC, agreed, however, that Fechner was justified in his actions but promised to return the camp the following April. Thomas assured Blood that Fechner "is aware of and appreciated our problems."[38] Blood had to settle for this promise and extended his thanks to Fechner by stating, "In my opinion the emergency conservation work accomplished by the CCC camps in connection with the Bureau of Reclamation has been highly creditable to the Administration and of great and permanent value to the public."[39]

In November 1935, BR-11 shut down, and CCC work at BR-12 and the spike camps at Hyrum and Currant Creek also came to a halt. Fechner worked under continued pressure during the winter to further reduce the size of the Corps, but he still planned to reestablish BR-12. Assurances continued to flow from Fechner's office, and on April 1, 1936, Assistant Director James J. McEntee announced that BR-12 would be reestablished as promised.[40]

During the summer months of 1935 and 1936, a BR-12 spike camp worked on the Strawberry Valley Project begun in 1934 by BR-5, and another BR-12 camp worked from 1935 to 1937 on the Hyrum Project in Cache County to the north. In a draining of the Pineview Reservoir in the mid-1970s, the old CCC camp foundations—then underwater due to enlargement of the reservoir in the mid-1950s—were removed as a "perennial threat to boaters during low water."[41]

Many odd jobs not covered by the contract were performed by the CCC in 1936 and in 1937. The enrollees did considerable work around the dam proper, including sloping of embankments, bridging Wheeler Creek where it enters Ogden River just below the dam, and doing some riprapping. Other work carried on by CCC personnel included constructing stream gauging stations to determine water flow, building drains along the highway, and widening the highway in the canyon to provide viewing areas of the lake and to make it easier to remove winter snows.

When the project was dedicated on August 15, 1937, Governor Blood described it as a "wedding of soil and water." Although the governor was pleased, residents were not at all happy due to the deprivation of the artesian wells in addition to the homes and land they had lost, which they felt was a harsh violation of property rights.[42]

One of the more unique aspects of the job was dismantling an old seventy-two-inch pipeline running the length of the canyon below the dam and replacing it with a seventy-five-inch pipeline built of wooden staves. This Ogden Canyon Conduit had carried water about five miles from an outlet at the dam to the two canals that branched to the north and south from the mouth of the canyon. When a CCC inspector saw the hazardous work the enrollees were doing along the wall of the canyon, he threatened to take them off the job before they all got killed. As the supervising engineer, E. O. Larson, replied, "Don't do that; they're nine-tenths done, and nobody got hurt yet."[43]

Problems continued to plague Huntsville, however, for Company 4792 was moved in December 1937. The company had been working out of BR-12 but now transferred to set up BR-64 in Heber to begin work in connection with the new Deer Creek Project at the head of Provo Canyon. Thereafter work on the Ogden River Project building canals and small reservoirs was carried on by spike camps out of BR-64.[44] In 1941 and 1942 spike crews from BR-64 worked on the South Ogden Canal Extension and built additional reservoirs. The spike camp was probably on the site of the old SCS-4 camp in Willard after that camp's terracing project was completed and the company moved to Tremonton to set up SCS-9 in the fall of 1939. The spike camp lasted until BR-64 closed down in July 1942, one of the final seven camps to operate in Utah.

Considerable canal construction accompanied the building of the Pineview Dam. The South Ogden Highline Canal extended seven miles from the mouth of the canyon along the edge of the mountains to the southwest; the Ogden-Brigham Canal was constructed to take irrigation water from the canyon mouth twenty-five miles north to Box Elder County. These two projects were virtually completed by 1938.[45] Over the next three years, enrollees built distribution laterals and three concrete-lined equalizing reservoirs; they lined the canals with concrete; and they even removed part of the Ogden-Brigham Canal and rebuilt it. As the numbers of enrollees declined in 1941 other laborers were brought in, and the work ended that summer.[46]

Company 4792 transferred from Huntsville to Heber in December 1937; thereafter work on the Pineview projects was carried on by spike camps out of Heber camp BR-64. In early August 1938, the vacated BR-12 campsite was turned over to the U.S. Forest Service, which, after two years, set up F-51 in November 1939. Since 1949, the Weber Basin Conservancy District has operated the Ogden River Project.[47]

BR-64 AND BR-91, PROVO RIVER PROJECT

Utah's Bureau of Reclamation CCC camps seemed to operate in pairs, that is, BR-5 and -6 in central Utah and BR-11 and -12 a bit farther north. This listing would not be complete without linking the two camps on the Provo River Project, BR-64 and BR-91. The assignments for the two camps were, compared with the other two pairs, even more identical since they actually worked on the same project; the major difference is that, for the most part, they operated at different times.[48]

The Provo River Project was somewhat similar in concept to what was being done on the Ogden River farther north. The bureau planned for the distribution of domestic and irrigation water to the cities and some one hundred thousand acres of farmlands between Salt Lake City and Provo, the two major cities along the Wasatch Front.[49] Key to the entire project was the construction of Deer Creek Dam, approximately sixteen miles upstream and northeast of the city of Provo. The project also entailed the construction of dams, tunnels, and canals to move water from the Weber and Duchesne rivers into the Provo River watershed, from which a forty-two-mile aqueduct connected to Little Cottonwood Canyon in Salt Lake County.

BR-64, Deer Creek

Deer Creek camp BR-64 began when a cadre of enrollees from Company 4792 left BR-12 in Huntsville on October 11, 1937, to help build their new wooden camp in a field with a nearby apple orchard in Heber, Wasatch County.[50] The rest of the company moved in on December 20 and began work the same day. Similar to what both BR-11 and BR-12 were doing on the Ogden River Project, the assignment of BR-64 was to prepare the site for the reservoir and other necessary elements for the Provo River Project. Clearing away trees, brush, buildings, and fences was, as always the case, essential for the work to really get under way.

The first year that Company 4792 resided in Heber, the enrollees constructed the Deer Creek government camp near the dam site as residences and offices for the construction personnel. They also began work on a bridge across Round Valley Creek and installed some culverts in preparation for work on the Round Valley Road, which left the state highway about one mile above the dam. The CCC youths made 660 guardrail posts from poles of a dismantled telephone line that had been removed from the reservoir area. The dam contractor used about two-thirds of these on a temporary road near the dam; the balance was used on guardrails on the Round Valley Road. The enrollees cleared the reservoir site when they could be spared from other tasks. They burned willows and bushes and salvaged several buildings in addition to the phone line. By the end of 1939, the reservoir-clearing stood about 60 percent complete.[51]

BR-91, Pleasant Grove

By October 1939, Company 1968 had transferred from Bridgeland to Pleasant Grove and set up BR-91 on the abandoned site of F-43. Having completed most of the work in the Uinta Basin, Company 1968 moved out of BR-11 down into Utah County after a short stay at Fort Douglas. Spike camps were left behind at Altonah and Moon Lake to complete work on the Moon Lake Project.

With an experienced company that it was loath to lose and with additional work needed on the Provo River Project, having the F-43 site available was a windfall for the bureau. According to Company 1968's newspaper, *Bridgeland News Weekly*, the 110 enrollees were looking forward to their new assignment, described as being "impertinent" to the Deer Creek Project.

Preparatory Work

The development of the reservoir necessitated the relocation of several structures, providing the enrollees with the opportunity of developing a variety of skills. Enrollees strung nearly sixteen miles of five-wire barbed wire fence and built seven timber road crossings, fourteen cattle guards along the new right-of-way, and loading pens and corrals.

Admittedly quite out of the ordinary for reservoir-clearing work was the relocation of about nine miles of telegraph line under the supervision of Western Union personnel. At Charleston enrollees constructed the only CCC-built railroad depot in Utah. Another railroad-based project was the relocating of Denver and Rio Grande Railroad tracks. Supervised by railroad personnel, enrollees moved the tracks from alongside the Provo River at what is now the bottom of Deer Creek Reservoir to their present location, skirting the northwestern edge of the lake. And perhaps the most unusual assignment was raising the level of what is now Utah Highway 113 between Charleston and Midway by about twelve feet.

In addition to installing a sprinkling system and carrying on landscaping at the government camp at the dam site, the enrollees built another camp at the outlet of the Duchesne tunnel to house construction workers on that project. The six-mile-long tunnel carried water from the diversion dam on the North Fork of the Duchesne River about thirty miles east of Heber into the Provo River drainage basin. A CCC-built road more than five miles long provided access to the camp. Other work included further clearing of the reservoir area, riprapping along road embankments, hauling materials for government construction forces, building a gauging station on the Provo River, and building another access road to still another tunnel.[52]

The little community of Charleston was to be the center of considerable controversy in connection with the building of the dam and the reservoir it created. Since the highway between Charleston and Midway ran a few feet below the ultimate water level of the reservoir, it proved necessary to relocate about 3,200 feet of roadway. In 1939 workers dismantled a one hundred-foot bridge and reconstructed it on concrete pillars to serve the new road.[53]

However, it was the razing and removal of nearly all of Charleston's homes that caused the greatest difficulties and hard feelings, as well as the eventual departure of every business establishment in the community. The post office was closed, forcing the retirement of Postmaster Lorraine S. Wright, who had served for twenty-eight years.[54] Today Charleston is completely devoid of any commercial facilities except for an occasional and usually short-lived store of one sort or another along its main road. Building up the Charleston-Midway highway continued at least into 1941.

Local residents were not happy over seeing their lifetime homes and property east and south of the dam site condemned for what they perceived as a fraction of their true worth. Several court cases were filed, and bitterness continued. A publication of the Daughters of Utah Pioneers lamented that the reservoir "forced many from their homes, put many hundreds of acres of choice lands under water and brought decline to the community" and concluded, in a sacrificial tone, "Now the community has given of itself so that Utah may continue to be the star of the west and that the desert shall blossom as the rose."[55]

As the project engineer in charge of the bureau's projects in Utah, Larson lauded the employment opportunities provided by the Deer Creek Project, but in a 1993 interview Richard McGuire claimed that local men didn't need the employment, because they could live off the land or find work in mines.[56]

THE PROJECTS AND THE CORPS WIND DOWN

Enrollees also worked on other bureau projects away from Deer Creek such as the enlargement of the Weber-Provo Diversion Canal east of Heber, and crews were also sent north to work on the Ogden River Project. In 1941 and 1942 spike crews from BR-64 worked on the South Ogden Canal Extension and built additional reservoirs. As noted, the spike camp was probably on the site of SCS-4 after that camp's terracing project was finished and the company moved on to set up SCS-9.[57]

By mid-1941, declining numbers at BR-91 soon led to the Moon Lake spike camp shutting down on August 9, and on August 20, BR-91 also closed, and the remaining enrollees of Company 5715 left Pleasant Grove for BR-64.[58] Abandoned for the second time, the site of Pleasant Grove camps F-43 and BR-91 was a wartime casualty as it became a training facility for the Army Air Corps. In 1944 the Army returned use of the property to the Bureau of Reclamation; subsequently the bureau transferred that use to the Provo River Water Users' Association. The property is now divided between the two entities. At the back of the property were the old CCC mess hall and another building.[59]

Unfortunately, the agency decided that the space was too valuable, and the CCC buildings were demolished. Costs for possibly moving one of the buildings to the Leeds campsite were estimated as being in excess of $25,000, and the windy road up American Fork Canyon to the closer location at Granite Flat Campground would be extremely difficult to traverse without dismantling the building.

On July 25, 1942—still with Company 4792—BR-64 also ceased operations, along with the spike camp on the Ogden River Project. The buildings of what was one of the last CCC camps in the nation were turned over to the Army Corps of Engineers and soon wound up at an Army air base in Salt Lake City.[60]

The CCC worked on other reclamation projects in the state, although none of the magnitude of the Moon Lake, Pineview, and Deer Creek projects. A small spike camp from BR-12 situated itself at Hyrum for two months in late 1935. Two shifts of men a day worked at sluicing silt into the reservoir for the purpose of reducing seepage. They left when Company 1967 transferred to the Jericho camp and were not replaced when BR-12 reopened in 1936.[61]

Virtually the same thing happened at the spike camp at Currant Creek in 1935. The enrollees then worked on jobs related to the activities of BR-5 when it had been there two years before. In 1941 the Bureau of Reclamation hoped to get CCC forces for work in the area of the Gooseberry Reservoir and on the proposed Scofield Dam.

The Bureau of Reclamation projects were among the most significant to be attempted in Utah. Project engineers supervised every aspect of the work, and construction was carried out to strict specifications. Those associated with the direction of the projects spoke highly of the work of the enrollees, and the director's reports indicated official CCC satisfaction with their efforts. In addition to commenting on the assistance being given the Bureau of Reclamation, the director stated that "the enrollees have acquired a reputation for building sound and permanent structures, durability being the objective of all CCC construction of reclamation projects."[62]

Analysis of the financial value of the projects is difficult.[63] The value of the crops irrigated by the reclamation projects that the CCC constructed would total nearly $8,000,000 a year for the past thirty-odd years. The difficulty arises, of course, in attempting to determine the relationship between the existence of the CCC and the completion of a project. Some of the projects would have been completed anyway; others, perhaps, would not. The Midview Dam, for example, was built entirely with CCC labor, and reports at the time indicate that construction would not have been planned then had CCC labor not been available. The Moon Lake Dam, on the other hand, would have gone ahead in either case. Work on the Pineview and Deer Creek projects was done primarily by bureau or contract forces, and the CCC did only the secondary tasks necessary to implement the use of the dams proper. Had the Corps not existed the work would have been accomplished, but the cost would have been greater, as CCC labor was not charged to the projects.[64]

The terracing and road-building projects described in the chapter are more easily discussed. The Forest Service did not receive budgetary considerations comparable to those of the Bureau of Reclamation. The tangible benefits of a dam attract more support and financial assistance than the somewhat intangible benefits of savings in life and property that might occur in case a torrential downpour does take place at some vague time in the future. Had the CCC not been in existence, it is unlikely that state or local monies would have been available in sufficient quantities to carry out the erosion-control projects, even in make-work situations that might have been part of a state relief program.

Evaluation of the CCC is made more positive when the side effects of the program are considered. E. O. Larson, for example, estimates that some four hundred former enrollees were hired elsewhere as a result of experience gained on Bureau of Reclamation projects in Utah.[65] The ultimate benefits of CCC service would have to be applied in any evaluation, but to summarize succinctly, the larger projects were a major contribution to Utah and to the stature of the CCC program.

CHAPTER 8

Some Camps Were One or Two or Three of a Kind

With the aid of the U.S. Park Service and the CCC, we are sure that Utah Lake can be made the most popular recreation center in the Great Basin.

—Mark Anderson, superintendent, SE-206

Although most of Utah's 116 CCC camps would certainly be referred to as multipurpose in nature, a few were set up with only one project in mind. While enrollees in most camps might at some point in their service have found themselves building roads, trails, and campgrounds, planting trees, or poisoning animal or plant pests, some single-purpose camps were more narrowly focused, although the more traditional tasks could be pursued as deemed necessary.

DESERT RANGE EXPERIMENT STATION

Dr. George Stewart was working out of the Forest Service regional office in Ogden when he and Lt. Stephen W. Ackerman of Fort Douglas were assigned to select a campsite for F-15, the Desert Range Experiment Station. Often identified as being in Beaver County, since that is where access to the camp was located, most of the station is actually located in Millard County, roughly twenty-two miles east at Wah Wah Springs on the road back toward Milford, where, as a local historian later reported, the site was preferable because "the cold spring water at Wah Wah was too inviting." The entry gate, consisting of pillars built by the CCC, is about one mile north of where the access road leaves Utah Highway 21, some fifty-odd miles west of Milford on the road to Ely, Nevada, now State Route 21. This, perhaps, is the initial exposure to several somewhat confusing elements of this unusual camp. Not only was F-15 to be a new camp, but it also represented a new focus for the CCC in Utah.

At the May 25, 1933, welcoming ceremony in Milford for what were to be the two Beaver County camps described in chapter 4, Dr. Stewart spoke, along with the military leaders in charge. Stewart, formerly on the faculty at Utah State Agricultural College in Logan (now Utah State University) explained that F-15 was an example of CCC work expanding beyond the usual locations in national forests and that the needs of approximately two million sheep grazing in the West Desert for more than five months out of the year certainly had to be addressed. Based on his studies of rangeland in protected and unprotected areas, Dr. Stewart clearly explained the harmful effects of overgrazing. He stated that "protection and improvement of watersheds are major problems to be considered" as well as "the conservation of winter range." The next day, under the temporary command of Lt. J. C. Wade, Company 1340 headed out to their new assignment in the West Desert virtually straddling the Beaver-Millard county line. Here they were to replant overgrazed sheep land and conduct research on 55,000 acres of winter stock range.[1] Enrollees were soon at work erecting the fifty-two miles of fence that eventually enclosed the test area. One hundred plots of two hundred square feet each were inventoried to determine the forage therein, and a survey was also made of the vegetation within a twenty-five-mile radius.[2]

The work that was carried out by Company 1340, on the other hand, was confined to the actual station.[3] That summer of 1933 enrollees of Company 1340 built two four-room homes, a dormitory, a lab, an office building, a warehouse/shop, two two-car garages, a four-horse barn, and a 42,000-gallon reservoir to hold water from a well they also constructed.[4]

On June 7, 1933, Captain Holland S. Shamness, formerly attached to the ROTC program at Pomona College, Claremont, California, arrived at F-15 to relieve Lieutenant Wade of his temporary command, but the popular junior officer remained with the camp, soon named Camp Cahill for the highly respected Army First Sergeant W. J. Cahill, who had been with the company from its beginning. Although in CCC usage "first sergeant" came to be one of the terms identifying the enrollee serving as the company's senior leader, in this case it was Cahill's actual Army rank. He was described as a "typical regular Army non-com" who "has endeared himself to all the men and boys at the camp and likewise to all the townspeople who have contacted him."[5]

The camp leadership under Superintendent H. J. Blake included seven foremen in charge of fences, post-cutting, shipments, trucks and accounts, miscellaneous work, vegetation survey, and carpenter work. A camp mechanic and a University of Washington graduate trained in vegetation research from Spanish Fork completed the staff.[6]

Work at the station used test plots to compare different types of vegetation under different types of grazing conditions. In his summary of the work that summer, Dr. Stewart told of the extensive research being carried out. Although the unprotected areas had two-thirds as much plant cover as the controlled areas, the former had only one-third the forage value. Unfortunately, unpalatable grasses took over the overgrazed areas, crowding out the more nourishing forage. Stewart also showed that wind erosion of from two to six inches followed excessive grazing, leaving clumps of plant crowns rising above the surface.[7]

Shamness was at F-15 only five days before he, too, was replaced by Captain Timothy Sapia-Bosch, who arrived on June 12 from Fort Sam Houston. Leadership change among the military officers continued to be the pattern, as two months later Lieutenant Wade transferred to Ferron camp, F-11. Stability continued to elude F-15, as on September 28, most of the boys of Company 1340 left for their native Virginia in response to the governor's request for their return to work on projects closer to home.[8]

One month later, October 20, 1933, was a busy day at Camp Cahill, as F-15 prepared to close for the winter, a closure that proved to be permanent. Although a large group of enrollees from Company 1340 had already left for the east coast, 115 reenrolled to stay behind and were transferred to Beaver camp F-15. They joined Company 1338 just prior to that company's transfer south to the new Santa Clara camp SE-215 in Washington County. Another group of twenty-five—presumably LEMs—transferred to American Fork camp F-5, leaving only the Army officers and seven enrollees at Wah Wah Springs to welcome the 121 enrollees arriving from Montana that same day. Expecting to go to Lone Pine, California, the new arrivals were delighted to be greeted with a large chocolate cake inscribed "Montana CCC: Welcome to 1340," which again illustrates the confusion arising from distinguishing between camp numbers and company numbers. Perhaps hoping to leave their signature behind, the Virginia boys should really have extended the welcome to camp F-15 instead of Company 1340, since most of Company 1340 was by then back on the east coast; camp F-15, of course, remained in the West Desert.[9]

The Montana company hardly had time to unpack before they were again on their way to Lone Pine, California. Although most of the company left on October 30, the final detachment of thirty men didn't leave until November 21, 1933, when local unemployed workers hired by the National Recovery Administration took over the work at the experiment station.

CCC work at Desert Range was discontinued for nearly a year, until—according to a virtually illegible *Beaver Press* article of September 14, 1934—Lieutenant C. G. Frake and an advance party of twenty men from Company 1964 left F-14 at Beaver Mountain to construct barracks with the help of local carpenters, electricians, and other craftsmen from the county for camp F-33. Company 1964 had been organized as one of Utah's six drought-relief companies in July 1934 and served that summer at F-14 before moving to F-33 out in the desert for the Fourth Enrollment Period. This camp, also identified as Desert Range, was described as "fifty miles west of Milford in Pine Valley," actually on the experiment station itself, quite unlike F-15. Just over a month later the remaining 235 men and officers were transported from F-14 in trucks "taxed to capacity" to what was described as the company's winter camp.[10]

Several concrete foundations still mark the location of F-33, which can be seen about a quarter mile north of the buildings still used by the Forest Service, one of the few such research facilities in the country. Confusion again triumphed because F-33, in addition to being identified as the Desert Range camp, was also referred to as the Milford camp, that being the closest Utah town of any size.

F-33 was short-lived as well, as was its Company 1964, which lasted only about fifteen months as a CCC unit. Perhaps weary of the confusion of which it was a part, Company 1964 returned to F-14 on Beaver Mountain in July 1935, where the boys served about three months before transferring once again.

Instead of being attached to any particular national forest, the CCC camp and the experiment station were largely on their own. What has since been renamed the Desert Experimental Range is virtually autonomous today, operating out of the U.S. Forest Service Shrub Sciences Laboratory based in Provo.

To the initial confusion of F-15/Desert Range Experiment Station/Wah Wah Springs/Camp Cahill/Milford and F-33/Milford/Desert Range Experiment Station was added still another challenging layer of uncertainty when a Division of Grazing camp was tossed into the mix. The camp to which Company 1964 transferred from Beaver Mountain was to be the new DG-35, a third "Milford camp" located right in the southwest corner of town on what was described as "higher bench ground." Geographically, DG-35 certainly had more claim to the identity of a "Milford camp" than either F-15 or F-33. Here Company 1964 was disbanded on October 21, 1935.[11] Most of the men were scattered to other Utah companies, while twenty-six remained behind at DG-35, then primarily occupied by Company 2530, made up of boys from Kentucky and Ohio.

DG-35 opened in the fall of 1935 and continued until 1940, usually with Fifth Corps Area companies. Its association with Desert Range was minimal, providing no more than enrollees for a possible spike camp.

A misunderstanding of the status of spike camps created additional identification problems associated with F-14, F-33, and DG-35. Some of these temporary camps were occasionally located on the sites of earlier camps at either Wah Wah Springs or Desert Range and were erroneously identified by the name of that camp, when in fact the spike camp might have been affiliated with another regular camp then in existence, probably DG-35 in Milford or perhaps another camp out in the West Desert.

Back in 1902 the Manti Forest Reserve was founded as a result of public requests concerning the severe flooding problems caused by overgrazing in the previous century. The Transfer Act of 1905 actually created the Manti National Forest, which led in 1912 to the establishment of the Utah Experiment Station, now known as the Great Basin Experimental Range, to study the causes of the floods and how they might be prevented in the future with innovative revegetation techniques.

Like the Desert Range station in Utah's West Desert, this, too, benefited from the work of the Civilian Conservation Corps. In the 1930s CCC manpower erected buildings at the site east of Ephraim, repaired fences, and conducted range surveys as well as carrying out the more typical CCC work of developing springs, working on roads, and fighting the occasional wildfire. Three Forest Service camps from which enrollees might have carried out this work were F-10 at Joe's Valley, eighteen

Figure 8.1. Great Basin Experimental Range, probably near the site of BR-6.

miles to the east toward Orangeville; Seeley Creek camp, F-50, only about five miles away; and F-28 at Gooseberry, about thirty miles to the north.

The work of the Great Basin Environmental Education Center continues into the present time, to a large extent under the mantle of Snow College in nearby Ephraim. A comprehensive work compiled by three Forest Service scientists associated with the Great Basin Experimental Range at one time or another lists several works published about the station over the years.[12] Although there is no question that the annotated bibliography gives a much more scientific explanation of what was done at the station, I think that the delightful description offered by Albert Antrei is much more readable. He states that the station—in its study of rainfall patterns, plant development, species identification, sunshine and cloud patterns, the effect of rodents upon the landscape, soil runoff, and reseeding techniques—"generally poked into the biological vitals of the Wasatch Plateau in a seemingly never-ending probe into the mysteries of what makes it tick.... Be it botanical, meteorological, zoological, or geological."[13]

MA-1, PROVO RIVER

The fact that Utah's camp MA-1 was the only one of its kind in the country when it opened in Provo in November 1939 certainly justifies its status as an extremely unusual feature on the CCC landscape. This was the

Figure 8.2. Utah Lake State Park built by MA-1, 1939–41.

only "Metropolitan Area" camp the state ever had and as late as 1941 one of only sixteen in the entire country. Its joint sponsorship between two administrative bodies, one national and one municipal, marked a new level of governmental cooperation. Although the camp began as a National Park Service recreational project, joint sponsorship with the city of Provo led to its MA designation.[14]

Near the beginning of the twentieth century local sportsmen among the citizens of Provo began expressing interest in developing a yacht harbor on Utah Lake. In 1937 Mayor Mark Anderson announced that the Works Progress Administration was considering such a development, although nothing had yet gone beyond the conceptual stage. NPS then became involved, and it wasn't long before it was working with the city to develop a plan.[15]

In late January 1939, Mayor Anderson received an encouraging letter from Irving W. Trimbel, assistant head of Utah's fish resources agency and state supervisor for the National Park Service. While emphasizing that "nothing definite" was promised, he stated that the project was "looked upon with favor" and the Park Service could possibly staff a CCC camp for the project, which Anderson felt would result in the finest harbor in the intermountain region. This was followed just over a month later by Trimbel's report with ten recommendations including the formation of a state park at the mouth of the Provo River on the shores of Utah Lake.[16]

Anderson's association with the CCC, of course, began back in 1933, when he was superintendent of camp SE-206 in Hobble Creek Canyon east of Springville. No doubt he took extra pleasure in his announcement at a public planning forum held on March 16, 1939.[17]

A few days later NPS representative Trimbel and David H. Mattson, supervisor of Utah's fish resources, sent notice to the office of Governor Blood. The city of Provo had just learned that the Park Service was authorized to carry out the project if sanctioned by the state and "requested by responsible authority." Trimbel and Mattson's letter suggested that the state of Utah's Park Board go on record as the sponsoring body. This would be in name only, since the city would assume all financial responsibilities for the project, but it was pointed out that the state might command more respect and secure more cooperation than would the city of Provo. In any case the state had to endorse the idea and make the formal request. This was completed in May 1939.[18]

The area under consideration was a plot of about five hundred acres, which consisted of portions of land belonging to the state and to the city and two small holdings of private owners. Although it had long been used for boating, swimming, and picnics, the land was covered with underbrush and subject to flooding.[19]

Major Mose Kent of Fort Douglas and Roy Smith, Park Service representative from San Francisco, visited Provo in August 1939 and announced that a "Metropolitan Area" CCC camp would soon be under construction at the north end of the Provo airport.[20] As part of its financial responsibilities, Provo City had to provide a site for the camp and free water for camp use. In a letter to Mayor Anderson, Frank A. Kittredge, regional director of the National Park Service, pointed out the rest of the city's obligations: technical assistance for the preparation of the preliminary and final plans of the work program, providing the special or heavy equipment such as pile drivers and sand pumps that would not be generally available from Corps sources, helping in the hiring of skilled labor, and providing for special materials in cases where CCC funds for these purposes proved inadequate. It all became official with a letter to Blood from Conrad L. Wirth, superintendent of recreation and land planning of the National Park Service, stating that the recommendations had all been approved. The work was to be coordinated through the San Francisco office of the regional director of NPS Region Four, and the CCC camp would be set up as soon as all arrangements had been completed.[21]

Company 958 of F-40, across the airport from the new campsite, got the assignment of erecting MA-1, as the camp was designated. Located within a rock's throw of F-40 where the airport, county fairgrounds, and a golf course were located, the campsite was on what is now University Avenue where the Central Utah Vocational School was later set up. After several changes in name, this location and educational mission eventually became Utah Valley University.

The fact that a Department of Agriculture camp was involved in the construction of a Department of the Interior camp is another indicator of governmental cooperation. Delbert C. Brimhall, construction foreman of F-40, six carpenter-foremen, and a crew of forty enrollees began erecting one building a day from fifteen carloads of precut parts that had been made to specifications in Seattle. The camp, more expensive than most, was projected to cost about $30,000, but it would be equipped with five barracks, a mess hall, an infirmary, a latrine, a bathhouse, a laundry, a barbershop, an education building, four insulated garages, quarters for officers and for the technical service personnel, and two shops. The city provided gravel for the streets and walks and also installed the sewer system.[22]

The camp was completed in mid-November 1939, and soon Division of Grazing trucks brought Company 1662 to Provo from their previous station, Callao camp DG-116 in northwest Juab County. Reflecting the demilitarized aspect of the CCC then existing, the company newspaper identified the lieutenant in charge of the approximately two hundred enrollees, mainly from Illinois, as Mr. John Antoncheck. Physician Mr. David M. Parker, subaltern Mr. Basil B. Taylor, and Educational Adviser Norman Hamilton completed the officer corps. The "civilian" designations were not consistent, however, as a *Provo Daily Herald* article of a few days before identified Lieutenant Antoncheck as continuing commander at the new MA-1. The newly named company newspaper pointed out that since the project would be under the National Park Service, the Division of Grazing foremen were being transferred from Callao to another West Desert Division of Grazing camp, DG-155 at Black Rock in southern Millard County.[23]

Walter H. Anderson of Salt Lake City, formerly of the State Engineering Department, received the nod from the NPS to be the superintendent on the project. Joseph Nelson, also of Salt Lake City, was named as landscape specialist, and engineer Frank Fonnesbeck of Logan was selected to be the senior foreman. Two other regular foremen, Charles Love of Salt Lake City and Lawrence Beebe of Price, and junior foreman John

W. Goodman of Provo completed the roster temporarily; mechanics and blacksmiths were to be appointed later.[24] Interest ran high. On December 7, 1939, Superintendent Anderson was scheduled to be the principal speaker at the first of a series of weekly meetings held to present information on the project.

Construction officially began with Provo Mayor Mark Anderson turning over the first shovelful on the harbor site in early January 1940.[25] According to City Engineer E. A. Jacob, the harbor would be on the north side of the river from which an artificial channel 2,550 feet long and two hundred feet wide would extend into the lake. The river itself would be developed for rowboats and other small craft. A large vehicle bridge and several footbridges would be built over the river as well. The early planning also included the planting of 50,000 trees and bushes and the construction of a thousand-car parking lot.[26]

Within a few months enrollees had completed the vehicle bridge, improved fifteen acres of beach, and worked on the eradication of poisonous weeds on another 103 acres.[27] Intense interest in the proposed park continued. Throughout 1939 and 1940 the *Provo Daily Herald* gave detailed coverage of the activities on the lakefront. The city took great pride in its "million-dollar project" and looked forward to its completion five years hence.[28]

In July 1940, the Illinois boys of Company 1662 transferred to Nevada, and Company 6431 moved into MA-1. After the normal two-day firefighting course, the new group, primarily from South Carolina, immediately went to work dredging the river channel and carrying out other tasks. Foreman Lawrence Beebe served as acting superintendent for about three months following Walter Anderson's departure, but before long Wells L. Brimhall was named to head the project.

By August 1940, the enrollees had completed the deepening of the river channel and had laid plans to begin work on the harbor proper. A crew was then working in the Uinta Mountains cutting timber for pilings to be used along the river to hold the rock and wire riprapping baskets in place for the prevention of erosion. By now the plans even included the construction of a seaplane base.[29] In October 1940, Company 6431 transferred to California, and Company 5713 took its place and remained on the project until CCC participation was discontinued.[30]

In that year there was another threat to the Provo River Project. Paul Franke had replaced P. P. Patraw as superintendent of Zion National

Park and attempted to have some MA-1 men temporarily assigned to complete some projects started by emergency relief personnel at Timpanogos Cave National Monument in American Fork Canyon for which he, as Zion superintendent, had responsibility at that time. The request seemed reasonable, since both MA-1 and the national monument were both under the National Park Service and Timpanogos Cave was just a relatively short distance from Provo. The proposal was discussed for three months before Park Service regional officers refused the request. The acting regional director informed Franke that a spike crew from his own NP-4 camp at Zion National Park could work out of MA-1 if desired but that no personnel or funds could be spared from the Provo River Project.[31] Franke demurred, apparently feeling that a Zion spike crew working on a project more than three hundred miles away was not a good option.

The Provo River work went on through 1941 under Superintendent Brimhall and the Arkansas youths of Company 5713. The Provo City annual report that year described the project as "nearing completion." But there, as in so many other cases, the outbreak of World War II curtailed activities, and in April 1942, Company 5713 transferred. Although the excavation of the harbor was nearly achieved, the entire project reached only about 50 percent completion.[32]

In the early 1950s heavy flooding destroyed much of the work done by the CCC, and when the city of Provo began extensive improvements in the early 1960s little remained to be seen of the work previously completed. Provo, however, was unable to continue the project, and finally the state of Utah took it over and is now responsible for the present development of Utah Lake State Park.

NATIONAL BIRD REFUGES

The Forest Service, Park Service, and Division of Grazing had almost no single-purpose camps; the agency responsible for national bird refuges, on the other hand, had nothing but single-purpose camps, resembling the Bureau of Reclamation in this regard. Going by different names during the CCC era—Bureau of Biological Survey, Bureau of Fisheries, and Fish and Wildlife Service—that agency set up two federal bird refuges on the shores of Great Salt Lake, at Bear River and Ogden Bay, to develop game habitats, especially for migratory waterfowl.

Figure 8.3. BS-1, located on the western edge of Brigham City, worked on the Bear River Migratory Bird Refuge.

Historically, bird refuges across the country were sometimes under the administration of the Department of Agriculture and sometimes under the Department of the Interior. The Bureau of Biological Survey, often the sponsoring agency, was in both the Departments of Agriculture and the Interior at different times under a variety of names and departmental titles and locations.

For more than six decades these various entities evolved with different names and responsibilities, weaving in and out of the Departments of Commerce and Labor, Commerce, Interior, and Agriculture and usually identified as either bureaus or divisions. Then, on June 30, 1940, the Bureau of Biological Survey was combined with the Bureau of Fisheries to form the new Fish and Wildlife Service in the Department of the Interior.

BS-1, Bear River

The bird sanctuary to which the CCC made the most significant contribution operates today as the Bear River Migratory Bird Refuge just outside Brigham City in Box Elder County. What is now one of more than 550 similar facilities in the National Wildlife Refuge System, it began as the result of the concerns of sportsmen in northern Utah's Brigham City back in the 1920s.

During the 1930s wildfowl planners in Utah made four attempts to aid the hordes of migrating birds for which the Great Salt Lake is an important stopover during their annual migrations. Work had begun previously to impound freshwater from Bear River after almost a million ducks had died from botulism in 1929 alone.[33]

The natural flow of Bear River en route to the Great Salt Lake was being hampered, and the Bear River Duck Club attempted to bring additional water into Bear River Bay to flood the area. However, added to the concerns over the alkalinity of the water was the other problem of botulism, or western duck sickness, among the wildfowl in the area. The need for solutions to the two challenges finally led to an act of Congress creating the refuge in 1928, with an appropriation of $350,000 and the appointment of George Musbach as superintendent.[34] The following year saw the beginning of a program of riverine restoration in which the Civilian Conservation Corps was to play a major part in the years to come.

CCC camp newspapers are often of great help in identifying camp designations, but that is not usually the case in this situation. Issues of *Take Five* of the Brigham City camp have columns entitled "Biological Survey News" and make references to Biological Survey foremen while at the same time stating that it is the camp newspaper for BF-1, indicating a Bureau of Fisheries sponsorship. In fact, this bureaucratic dichotomy seems to have existed from 1934 until about 1940, during which the Bear River Migratory Bird Refuge was sometimes designated as BS-1, other times as BF-1, and finally as FWS-1.

In the annual director's reports of 1934, 1935, and 1937 the camp was listed as BS-1, a Biological Survey camp under the Department of Agriculture; the 1940 and 1941 reports showed it as FWS-1, under the Fish and Wildlife Service of the Department of the Interior. At the same time, in accounts apparently as reliable as the director's reports, the camp was identified as BF-1, indicating a Bureau of Fisheries administration. To add to the confusion, newspaper accounts identified the camp with both Brigham City and Bear River; either designation would be accurate. Regardless of designation, the work remained constant, and today the Bear River Migratory Bird Refuge under the U.S. Fish and Wildlife Service shows the value of the work done by CCC enrollees.

On October 11, 1934, 168 men under Captain John W. Davis arrived in northern Utah from Allen Ranger Station in the Missoula, Montana, District and set up camp BS-1 next to Pioneer Park in Brigham City. The CCC camp was originally planned to be located on the actual site of the bird refuge about two miles away, but the availability of pure water and electricity was such that the camp was instead placed right in town.[35]

After about six months the Montana company was replaced by Third Corps Area Company 1350—soon designated a "special" California company and renumbered 1985—which also served for only one enrollment period. The CCC remained in the vicinity for nearly seven years as camp BS-1, BF-1, or FWS-1 working on the refuge west of town. Finally, in October 1935, Company 2539 moved in and served until about August 1941, when the camp was closed and most of the company transferred to the Uinta Basin.[36]

Over the seven years of CCC work enrollees built dikes and roads, planted grasses and shrubs to serve as food and cover for the birds, and created artificial nesting islands from brush and rocks in their assault on botulism. In 1939 fewer than one hundred ducks died during the summer season; when the camp closed in 1941 the disease was regarded as virtually under control.[37]

BS-2, Ogden Bay

Camp BS-2, later FWS-2, at Hooper engaged in similar activity in developing the Ogden Bay Refuge a few miles to the south of the Bear River site. In 1937 the Weber County Wildlife Federation turned its lakeside property over to the state of Utah, thereby permitting the utilization of CCC personnel, and for the next two years spike camps from BS-1 worked on the project. The state applied for the first federal funds for an aid-to-wildlife program to continue the work, which went on until the end of 1939. Work stopped for about six months until June 18, 1940, when Company 794, made up primarily of youths from Missouri and Arkansas, set up camp at BS-2.[38]

The refuge lay about eleven miles west of Ogden where the Ogden-Weber River empties into Great Salt Lake. In 1941 camp superintendent William C. Oakden explained the plans to develop three units of the refuge, which would total about nine thousand acres. He announced two purposes: the same as those for BS-1, that is, control of the dreaded botulism and provision of a resting place for migratory birds. As one of the first steps, CCC crews fenced the entire area, followed by a campaign to eliminate skunks, weasels, coyotes, duck hawks, and other natural enemies of the wildfowl. When 170 guests from the Western States Wildlife

Federation visited the camp in June 1941, the project gained much praise and was described as "one of the finest man-made refuges in the world."[39] BS-2 existed for only seventeen months, however, as it was one of four camps in Utah to close down operations in November 1941.[40]

STATE BIRD REFUGES

In addition to Bear River and Ogden Bay, two other camps were planned as wildlife refuges in Utah. The National Park Service had just begun to provide technical supervision of CCC work in state parks across the country. In what was described as a historic "first," the federal government cooperated with the states in the development of their recreational programs.[41] Utah benefited from this in a somewhat unusual way. To identify two "state park" camps in Utah, however, is somewhat misleading. The only state park Utah had in 1933 was the city block in Fillmore where the territorial capital had once been located. During its tenure in Utah the CCC did no work on state parks as such, although enrollees carried out one project that eventually did end up in the Utah State Parks system. Most of the forty-three Utah state parks now in operation were not built until after World War II and the CCC had long departed. So, what, then, was it in which the two state park camps were involved?

As noted, the state of Utah was anxious to develop some of its waterfowl areas on the shores of Great Salt Lake. State erosion camps with their "SE" designation had been discontinued, however, so the "SP" initials identified the "State Park" CCC camps to be established, not to develop state parks but, rather, bird refuges. The National Park Service set up camps where enrollees worked under the limited supervision of the NPS and also the Utah Fish and Game Commission, which had nominal control of the refuges.

SP-1, Locomotive Springs

CCC Company 536 arrived at Locomotive Springs near Kelton on the northwest shore of Great Salt Lake in the summer of 1935.[42] Organized on May 19, 1933, at Fort Knox, Kentucky, by the time it was assigned to the new SP-1 in Utah, the company had previously worked at camps in Anza, California; in Lizard Creek, Wyoming; and finally in Moapa, Nevada. It wasn't long, however, before an outbreak of tularemia, informally known as "rabbit fever," from the bites of deerflies put approximately three dozen of the Kentucky and Ohio enrollees in the Army hospital at the Presidio in San Francisco.

The camp was shut down, and under company commander Captain Joseph R. Knowles, Company 536 transferred around the lake to Farmington Bay, where SP-2 was erected on land formerly owned by the Improved Brick Company.[43] In spite of initial protests by the National Park Service and the state of Utah over the removal from Locomotive Springs, this proved to be a most beneficial change.

SP-2, Farmington Bay

Commissioner Newell B. Cook and others in the Utah State Fish and Game Department had come up with the idea that the relatively worthless swamplands along Farmington Bay could be used as a refuge for wildfowl. After the plan was approved, the National Park Service was brought in to supervise the project. Camp SP-2 was set up to carry out the work under the administration of Utah's Division of Wildlife Resources as Farmington Bay State Park beginning in 1935.[44] The name "Farmington Bay State Park" was subsequently used to identify what is now the Farmington Bay Wildlife Management Area.[45]

Beginning on August 10, 1935, Walter W. Welton, project superintendent, directed the work of constructing a huge dike for "holding back the saline waters of Great Salt Lake" and for impounding freshwater from the Jordan River in three artificial lakes. The dike was to be from four to six feet high with a twelve-foot-wide road across the top.[46]

In an article written for the camp newspaper, Robert G. Bee, senior wildlife foreman attached to SP-2, stated that the camp would be involved in moving "approximately 600,000 cubic yards of earth fill... to impound waters to form 3600 acres of lakes when the job is finished." Also to be built were seventeen water-control structures to move water from one lake to another, thirteen miles of roads along the tops of the dikes, thirty islands for resting and nesting habitats for the fowl, pens for the treatment and convalescence of sick birds, an observation tower, and buildings for other administrative purposes. A major fencing project took place in 1939 when thirty-two miles of barbed wire, 2,500 fence posts, two hundred pounds of brace wire, and two hundred gallons of creosote were utilized to encircle the facility. In May 1940, the final project of using a dragline to build a three-mile-long canal to bring more water from the Jordan River during "the dry season" was under way.[47]

In describing the game sanctuary, the local newspaper stated, "It will be one of the west's finest hunting grounds."[48] The irony of protecting birds in order that they might be there for hunters to shoot the following season was never addressed.

The dragline became one of the busiest pieces of heavy equipment used in the project. Hopes ran high for a while in 1935 that the cancellation of SP-1 would provide another dragline for the Farmington Bay operations, but disappointment replaced those hopes when the machine was sent to Arizona instead. Without the proper equipment the available manpower could not be utilized in the optimum manner.[49] The work went on successfully, however, and officials regarded it as being of sufficient significance to merit special description in the CCC annual report in 1939: "This protected fresh-water areas, furnished suitable conditions for the growth of aquatic plants and provides ideal conditions for migratory waterfowl that had suffered in late years through lack of fresh-water areas along Great Salt Lake."[50] Company 536 carried out the work until May 1940, when the entire company transferred to the Moab area in eastern Utah.[51]

The flexibility of the CCC program is illustrated by the fact that three different scenarios played out with the bird refuge camps. Although there were agency name changes along the way, the Bear River Migratory Bird Refuge is still with the same federal body with which the camp started. The Ogden Bay camp of BS-2/FWS-2, on the other hand, is no longer under the U.S. Fish and Wildlife Service but, instead, under the Utah Division of Wildlife Resources. Finally, SP-1 and, for all intents and purposes, its continuation as SP-2 were state camps to begin with, and the refuges on which their crews worked still continue as wildfowl management areas under the Utah Division of Natural Resources. By the time it folded, the CCC had worked on nearly three-fourths of the current waterfowl refuges located around the Great Salt Lake, certainly no mean accomplishment.

Another one-of-a-kind project was only slightly connected to SP-2, in that housing was provided for some thirty enrollees from the Division of Grazing who were on detached duty with the Salt Lake Drafting Office of that agency. Enrollees were selected from Division of Grazing camps from across the country for their "capability, speed, and accuracy" in working on a highly specialized project. The office was divided into three parts. The Drafting Office was "chiefly engaged in keeping up-to-date the base maps making up the state of Utah," using maps from wherever they might be found. The Land Status Department used paints and colored pencils on maps to show established land ownership. Finally, members of the Map Reproduction and Photography Department were trained to use blueprinting and other machines, a darkroom, and other photographic facilities to show "the need of improvements of roads, bridges, streams, reservoirs, etc." The camp newspaper of SP-2 devoted space in two issues explaining the work of their Grazing Service guests and explained that all the work produced such as maps and plans would be used not only for the Grazing Service but for other agencies as well.[52]

CHAPTER 9

Emergencies

Fires, Blizzards, Search and Rescue

The fellows, every one, performed wonderfully, doing instantly everything asked of them and doing it well. They worked their shirt-tails off all night and until noon the next day when the fire was all out.

—James A. Brown, enrollee, project assistant, BS-1

FIREFIGHTING

Regardless of what type of project on which the CCC might be working, men were always available if a fire call came in. Enrollees in Utah spent more than 40,000 man-days fighting fire.[1] With so much of Utah consisting of range- and desert land, camp officials did not have the same threat of disastrous forest fires experienced in more heavily timbered states. There was, nevertheless, sufficient activity to make Utah ranchers, lumbermen, and conservationists thankful for having such a large body of trained men available.

Although the Civilian Conservation Corps came to be very highly regarded for the work done in fighting fires, that was not originally part of its job description. It was not until August 17, 1933, four months after the first camp was set up, that Director Robert Fechner officially authorized the utilization of CCC crews to fight fires in Montana, as Salmond points out, "thus beginning a long chronicle of CCC assistance in local and national emergencies."[2]

In Utah, at least, CCC crews jumped the gun on that official authorization by at least three weeks. Perhaps the first fire call took place late in July 1933, just a few weeks after Company 1347 had arrived at Blacksmith Fork camp F-2, east of Hyrum in northern Utah. The entire company was called out to fight fire all afternoon. Ironically, the boys themselves had started this one when they were burning brush at the bottom of Blacksmith Fork Canyon. It took five hours to bring the errant blaze back under control. Strangely, the newspaper account of the fire stated that the company's commanding officer, Capt. R. B. Smith, led the crew, nothing being said about either the camp superintendent or any of the foremen who would normally have had that assignment. The assumption may have been that since Capt. Smith was the commanding officer, he was in charge of all activities, a not uncommon misconception regarding the division of responsibility. On the other hand, under what might have been an unusual set of circumstances, Army personnel could well have been leading the crew, since, on occasion, that actually did take place.[3]

Being called out on a fire line happened so often that it was almost considered regular duty. But it still earned the young men a great deal of appropriate gratitude and acclaim.

The need for a well-trained fire crew is great in any area vegetated by forest- and grasslands. Except at the higher elevations, much of Utah is covered by low-lying pinyon pine and juniper trees, often little more than bushes, in what firefighters and conservationists refer to as "P and J" vegetation. Utah, like the rest of the intermountain area, suffered from fires every summer, and after 1933 those responsible for watershed and rangeland protection enthusiastically welcomed the appearance of CCC crews on the fire lines.

The technical agencies taught fire suppression techniques as soon as a new group arrived in camp, a fortunate practice since enrollees were involved in fighting fires from the very beginning. The Cache County camp F-1 up Logan Canyon got a workout when Ranger Joe Libby of Cache National Forest led a crew of more than one hundred enrollees out at 2 a.m. one morning. Fifty acres of timberland in Mill Canyon near Mt. Logan burned before the blaze was controlled about ten hours later.[4]

As the summer of 1933 advanced, the situation became even more dangerous as the temperatures soared and the land became parched by the long dry season. Firemen from Salt Lake City fought a fire in Upper

City Creek Canyon early in September. After three days, they sought additional help, and soon fifty boys from American Fork camp F-5 and ten more from the CCC detachment at Fort Douglas were on the fire line.[5]

Enrollees from state camp SE-211 outside of Widtsoe in Garfield County narrowly averted an extremely serious fire a few days later. About the middle of September 1933 a fire broke out just three miles south of the camp. The fire moved rapidly toward a stand of timber, and rangers called on the CCC for help. Right at the edge of the trees the fire was stopped. Instead of losing thousands of acres of timberland, the only loss was two hundred acres of brush. The local paper was most complimentary in its praise of the young firefighters.[6]

Fire destroyed more than five hundred acres east of Bountiful at about the same time. A fire burned for several days in Holbrook Canyon before Davis County firemen and CCC crews brought it under control. In the Uinta Basin a crew from Kaler Hollow camp F-3 fought a fire in the Little Hole area on September 23, 1933. Ranger Glen Lambert led other Forest Service personnel and seventy-five F-3 enrollees in a campaign lasting into the following night. The "inexperienced, but keen" workers saw three hundred acres of valuable Douglas fir burned and a complete watershed destroyed above Jackson Creek before they extinguished the blaze.[7]

Fires were a serious problem right into the end of October that first year, and the phrase "baptism by fire" took on an ominous double meaning. Assistant Regional Forester C. N. Woods had announced earlier that month that the district fire loss was already about 25 percent higher than the average of the years between 1925 and 1929.[8]

Early October also saw problems in the northern part of Manti National Forest, where three fires were burning at the same time. One of them was in Emery County, where sixty enrollees from Joe's Valley camp F-10 were battling another blaze in the Wasatch Mountains near Mt. Pleasant. Here flames consumed several hundred acres before crews established control.[9] There seemed to be little doubt throughout the state that the boys were earning their pay.

Since firefighting classes were always scheduled immediately after new enrollees arrived in camp, it would be very rare for anyone to go on a fire line without having had some exposure to firefighting techniques. Stringing phone lines and building fire lines—nearly always with hand tools—were part of the fire protection training the boys received. A major

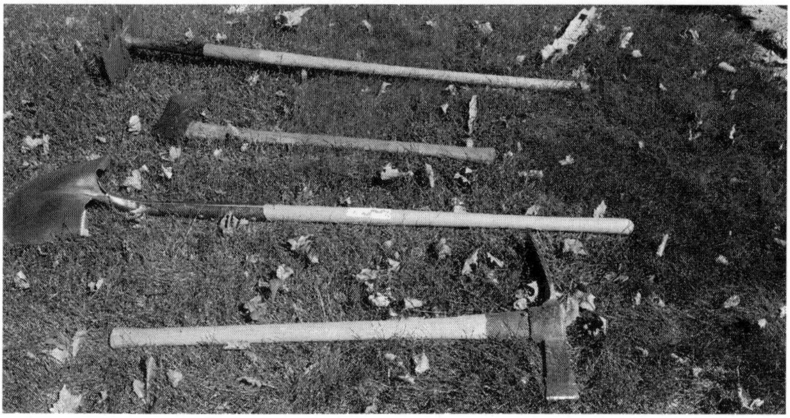

Figure 9.1. Basic tools of a Civilian Conservation Corps firefighter: (top to bottom) McLeod; ax; shovel; Pulaski.

exception to this rule was when twenty-year-old Owen Price of Ferron enrolled and reported to F-28 at Gooseberry on July 5, 1934. In an interview in 2003 regarding his first CCC job he recalled, "That was when the big fire was on in Huntington Canyon. The whole canyon was full of smoke," and he was sent along with the rest of the company: "Anyways, we went to fighting fire. Nowadays they wouldn't let you even hear about a fire on television without going and getting training for it. It's kind of funny how this worked out. We never lost a kid. We had brains enough."[10]

Brains, of course, are very helpful, but so is training, especially with the right type of equipment. One of the most useful tools utilized on a fire line was the Pulaski, a valuable piece of hardware similar to an ax. It has a double-bitted head with an ax-like blade on one side and an adze on the other, enabling one to chop through fairly thick roots; it was named for Edward C. ("Big Ed") Pulaski, the legendary forest ranger of Wallace, Idaho, who, if he did not actually design it, improved it so that after about 1913 it became the basic tool for fighting wildfires.[11] The McLeod was another helpful tool. Of lighter metal than the Pulaski, it has a longer handle and, again, a dual-purpose head. One side has heavy rake-like tines, and the other consists of a heavy blade one can use like a hoe. The shovel, familiar to all, is the old standby used for digging down through organic matter or duff to mineral earth and for throwing dirt on a blaze. In the absence of an ax it can even be used for chopping limbs or smaller trees.

As the second-driest state in the Union, Utah was used to long, hot, dry fire seasons, and the summers of the early 1930s proved no exception.

Rainfall at the Nephi dryland weather station measured 84 percent of normal in 1932, 73 percent in 1933, and only 65 percent in 1934.[12] In the summer of 1934 Utah as a whole was experiencing less than 25 percent of its normal water supply. The winter had started out with a good snowfall, but unfortunately, it was of short duration.

By that summer of 1934 central Utah was experiencing what many felt was the worst drought the state had ever experienced. Then, providing an indication of what lay ahead, a fire broke out in Payson Canyon in early July requiring twenty hours of suppression by thirty men from F-30 in Hobble Creek Canyon before the fire was out.

Early in the morning of Sunday, August 26, 1934, Captain Gestring of Company 957 at F-1 in Logan Canyon received an urgent request for help on a fire across the state line in timber country around fourteen miles southwest of Paris, Idaho. He replied that most of his men were on weekend leave, but he immediately dispatched about seventy-five, all he had available. By the time the two thousand-acre fire was subdued three days later, some two hundred Utah youths were on the fire line.[13] This was the worst fire year for the Forest Service in Utah, as 11,699 man-days, over one-fourth of the total for the full nine years of the CCC, was spent on fires that one year.[14]

Another of the bigger fires in Utah, which lasted even longer and probably caused more destruction than the Huntington Canyon fire, was the Smith-Moorehouse fire, six miles northeast of Kamas in 1935. F-6 was the only CCC camp on the fire, but the enrollees were aided by some temporary help hired by the Forest Service. Arnold Peterson, one of the CCC enrollees at the Smith-Moorehouse fire, had been born and raised in the little town of Scipio in northeast Millard County in central Utah. With six years of farmwork under his belt, he was able to join the CCC as a "local experienced man," although only eighteen years of age. He'd been in the Corps just over a year and was then stationed with Company 1979 at Soapstone camp F-6, east of Kamas on what is now Utah Highway 150. He was on the fire with his company for fourteen days, and had they been unable to prevent the fire from going over the ridge of a river canyon, he later said, "they might have been there a lot longer." His description of the fire would sound familiar to any who have been on a fire line at the end of the day: "At night it was lit up like a city and the burning trees would explode like giant firecrackers."[15]

In late July 1935, twenty F-30 men were called out for a fire in Daniel's Canyon above Heber in Wasatch County. When that number proved insufficient another fifty were sent up the next day. After the fire boss decided that they finally had the blaze under control, the original twenty and about half the fifty returned to their Hobble Creek camp. Unfortunately, the fire, which a U.S. Forest Service ranger described as one of the worst he'd ever seen, broke away again and burned "very hard and furiously." Finally, after another two days and with the help of rain, they brought the fire under control for good.[16]

The dry summer of 1936 caused continued difficulties. One of the largest fires ever fought in Utah was the Wah Wah Mountains fire of June 1936, out in the West Desert. All the personnel of Milford's DG-35 turned out under Superintendent Leslie Koch to battle the blaze burning in range- and timberland sixty miles west of the camp in central Utah. It was almost under control after three days, but strong winds pushed it over a ridge into dense timber and became what Koch said was "pronounced one of the largest ever fought in Utah." A crew of seventy-three men left Cedar City to respond to Milford's call for assistance; the young firefighters were supplied by pack animals and after ten days on the fire managed to get a line around the three thousand-acre blaze. The enrollees performed well without grumbling; the fire boss from the Fishlake National Forest reported that the lads had "conducted themselves as well as experienced firefighters."[17]

Finally, "darn near fagged out," as one of the enrollees later reported, forty-four were pulled off for a much-needed break. Thursday night the rested group was preparing to return to the line when the fire was finally out, and the entire group returned to Cedar City.[18]

The fires were not all big ones, but nearly every one during that long hot summer of 1937 had some feature that made it a little bit different. A sixty-acre fire in Rock Creek Canyon was fairly routine, and it was quickly suppressed by a ten-man volunteer crew from F-30 under Foreman Kingsley Thatcher.[19] Slightly more unusual, however, was one that took place near Duck Creek.

Lloyd Whitlock, educational adviser of F-16, was returning to camp when he saw smoke rising from the nearby woods. He drove on into camp and notified the superintendent. No foremen were available, so Whitlock took the crew himself to control the blaze. Shortly thereafter, a corral-building crew from DG-26 at Jericho was called upon to help control a stubble fire, action that resulted in saving a hay crop, a barn, and a thresher. Finally, on a Saturday morning, October 30, 1937, Superintendent D. M. Thompson and seventy-five enrollees of DG-45 were called out to fight another fire in the Dixie National Forest. Foremen Jim Bundy and Lester Parker, both with years of experience with the St. George camp, also led DG-45 crews before the fire was extinguished on Sunday afternoon, aided by fifty-one men from Bridge Mountain CCC crews from Zion National Park.[20]

A fire*break*, incidentally, is somewhat different from a fire *line*. A fire line is dug out on the spot in an attempt to confront the blaze head-on and is usually no wider than the fire boss feels necessary, perhaps as narrow as one or two feet, depending on the vegetation, terrain, size of the fire, and climatic conditions. A firebreak, on the other hand, may be either a permanent wide fixture or an ad hoc firefighting attempt from which a backfire might be started. Often rivers or roads could be used for this purpose; other times bulldozers could be thrown into the battle. Utah, unfortunately, had no counterpart to the CCC-built Ponderosa Way in California, a firebreak approximately eighty feet wide stretching nearly eight hundred miles along the lower elevations of the Sierra Nevada.[21]

George C. Larson, Uinta National Forest supervisor, described as "invaluable" the firefighting services of enrollees who fought a seven hundred-acre fire in Hobble Creek Canyon in August 1939. Larson and F-40 Superintendent Richard Greenland directed one hundred enrollees about ten days later on another fire between Provo and Rock canyons, also in Utah County. The blaze consumed almost two thousand acres of brush and grass as crews fought hard to keep fire out of the timbered slopes above. A turkey farmer was especially grateful to crews who trenched around his flock of one thousand turkeys, saving them from complete annihilation.[22]

Eastern Utah was hit hard the summer of 1940. Soon after the regular summer fire school was held at DG-31 in Vernal the boys had a chance to put their newly acquired training into practice. Their officers felt that they had indeed learned well when they suppressed a forty-acre fire in thirty minutes. They continued to receive plenty of practice as they fought seven fires in one forty-day period.[23] The Division of Grazing and Forest Service had a mutual assistance agreement, so fire crews from DG-31 of Vernal and F-35 of Manila saw each other quite often as the Ashley National Forest hit a new record high for number of fires.[24]

Few of the eastern lads had even seen a forest fire, and fighting one was never as glamorous as one might imagine. Professionals of the technical agencies usually took charge, although camp foremen generally gained enough experience after two or three fires that they were quite competent fire bosses. Some camps kept a standby crew always ready to respond when a fire call came. In many situations the entire camp was called out, in which case it might be necessary to recall crews from whatever work projects on which they were engaged. CCC regulations provided for equal time off for every day spent on a fire.[25] Some of the younger fellows even came to regard firefighting as a welcome break in the routine.

Many enrollees matured rapidly on the fire line. James Brown was the twenty-year-old son of a divorced mother when he joined the CCC in Toledo, Ohio, in 1939. About sixteen months later he was a leader and project assistant with Company 2539 at the Bear River Bird Refuge when the call came in that a fire was raging out of control on the west slopes of the Promontory Range, about forty miles west of Brigham City. Soon seventy-five young men of BS-1 sped across the alkali flats in four one-and-a-half ton stake-side trucks toward the mountains. Brown describes what happened:

> By the time we reached the east slopes of the Promontorys it was growing dark. We had to leave the trucks and proceed on foot, carrying tools, equipment, etc., up the mountain. A short time later the column stopped and word passed back that Jim Brown was wanted at the head of the group. When I got to where the three foremen who were in charge were waiting, one of them (no names will be mentioned since all three are now deceased) said to me, "Jim, you will have to take charge; take the men over the mountain and do what you can to control the fire until we can send someone to relieve you. We are too old to go any farther, so take charge and do your best." Then, as sort of an afterthought said, "Remember, there are about 75 young men here; we don't want anyone burned up."
>
> Anything that may have been said to me after that was purely a waste of breath. The statement about "75 young men" was the one thing that was in my mind from that moment on.
>
> The guys were superb. We crossed the mountain in almost total darkness and down the other side, where we met the fire,

> coming up the mountain. . . . [E]veryone performed wonderfully, doing instantly everything asked of them and doing it well. They worked their shirttails off all night and until noon the next day, when the fire was out.
>
> On the way down the mountain toward the nearest road we met the man who was sent to take charge of the detail on the way up. By the way, we had one man hurt. He slipped and fell while climbing on the truck to go back to camp. [He] sprained an ankle.[26]

There is little doubt about the adrenalin rush that accompanies duty on a fire line, especially for the first few fires of one's career. Although most boys initially welcomed a fire call as a break in the oft-monotonous work details, it would be difficult to say how many actually enjoyed the thrill and the danger involved. Some indicated that they were really frightened but were willing to carry on under the direction of experienced personnel, especially if they were professional foresters.[27]

Fortunately, Utah was spared the tragedy of neighboring states. Perhaps the worst of these was the Blackwater Fire, which took place in the Shoshone National Forest in northwest Wyoming. In mid-August 1937, what was only a two-acre lightning-sparked fire when it was first discovered exploded into a two hundred-acre inferno by nightfall. The next day, August 21, the fire took the lives of fifteen men, thirteen of whom were either enrollees or foremen of Company 1811 out of Texas stationed at Tensleep camp F-35 in the neighboring Bighorn National Forest.[28]

In what was then Nevada's Toiyabe National Forest—now Humboldt-Toiyabe—near the Oregon border, a fast-moving lightning fire on July 28, 1939, took the lives of five enrollees. In fleeing the eight thousand-acre fire, which was reported to have spread three and a half miles in less than forty minutes, one boy broke his ankle. His comrades tried to rescue him; all were burned to death. Less than two months later another neighboring state experienced the loss of a CCC firefighter in northern Idaho.[29] Fighting wildfires was definitely not child's play.

On July 17, 1941, Company 2558 was called from DG-160 in Hurricane to a fire on the Shivwits Indian Reservation west of St. George. The company had served at DG-45 in St. George since early November 1935 and so was back on familiar territory. County Sheriff Anton B. Prince suspected arson to be the cause of five fires on the reservation, the largest of which was about two thousand acres. According to the *Washington County News*, Sheriff Prince was most appreciative of "the fine help given to fighting the fires by the CCC boys and [Shivwits] Indians."[30]

It wasn't just in brush and timber country that CCC boys used their firefighting skills. Spontaneous combustion caused a fire in a hay barn in Castle Dale in July 1939, and enrollees of DG-27 joined the local fire department and other volunteers in suppressing the blaze. Although the barn and five tons of hay were lost, the firefighters kept the fire from igniting the house.[31]

The need to utilize whatever resources might be available led to the construction of what today is known as the Ute Mountain Fire Lookout Tower in the Ashley National Forest. Built by the CCC to provide visibility for the northeastern slope of the Uinta Mountains, it was perhaps the only such lookout tower in Utah until it was closed in 2008 due to decay in the legs and stairs of the structure. After six years of restoration work it was reopened for visitors in September 2014. Now little more than a historic artifact, it is a reminder that fires today are spotted quite differently than they used to be. It is located about nine miles southwest of Manila, seat of Daggett County, although the necessity of staying on Utah Highway 44 and various gravel Forest Service roads doubles the distance.[32]

In 1940 Regional Forester Rutledge issued a statement commending CCC crews for their great job in fire suppression, a characteristic that created a major part of the Corps' popularity. He described twenty-five-man "super squads" made up of young men selected for their "physique, endurance, spirit, and woodmanship" that constituted the first line of protection in the forests.[33]

In the early 1940s it didn't take long for the CCC firefighters to be missed when it became apparent that they might no longer be available. As the CCC was winding down a 1941 memo from the assistant regional forester of Region Four warned, "We have had a drastic cut in CCC camps and the prospects are that there will be a shortage of labor available for firefighting. There is a definite prospect that we may have great difficulty in manning our major fires." Although this "drastic cut" did not affect Utah immediately, the memo warned of the possible need "to enlist volunteer crews, even business men." It wasn't long, however, with only one or two CCC camps left, before this was soon echoed by John Burt, assistant state forester/fire warden, who expressed concern over the untrained firefighters who were expected to fill a significant gap. Burt lamented the loss of CCC fire crews, whom he described as "the only organized and trained manpower reserves available for fire work in many Utah areas." Unlike CCC firefighters, the new men employed to take their place failed to follow two basic rules of fire suppression: "Hit 'em while their [*sic*] small" and "Stay with them 'til they're out."[34]

BLIZZARDS OF 1936–37

Storms often created an environment for emergencies. Such was the case in abundance during the record-breaking winter of 1936–37. The fact that Utah experienced an unusually early snowfall around the first of November in 1936 was not, in itself, particularly alarming; after all, weather at that time of year between autumn and winter was often unpredictable. Nor was the fact that a CCC crew had to use a tractor to open Cottonwood Canyon, an indication of the tremendous effort that would be required by the organization. Even the news that three people had died as a result of the storm gave no indication of just what was to lie ahead, although the *Deseret News* describing the snowfall of November 1 after two days of steady rain was quite ominous: "Winter swooped down on Utah today, bringing the greatest snow depth for this time of year in the history of the U.S. Weather Bureau office in Salt Lake City."[35]

The defining moment came seven and a half weeks later on Christmas Day, when the *Ephraim Enterprise* reported that the normal snowfalls earlier in the month had provided lots of runoff, which softened the Russian thistles and other weeds, making excellent forage for all livestock wintering outside. December 21 had been an especially nice day, with the temperature at a balmy 52 degrees, a classic example of the calm before the storm! It was not until a three-day storm hit on Christmas night leaving record snow accumulation in its wake that people began to suspect that this winter was to be like no other experienced up to that time.

The search for survivors of an airliner that had gone down in central Utah the week before was called off when weather conditions became so bad that further efforts were not possible (see later in this chapter). The most serious storm damage was reported down in the southern part of the state. When the snowfall became so heavy that nineteen Southern Utah Power Company poles were broken in normally mild Washington County, leaving $1,100,000 in damages, the severity of the storm became apparent.[36] As a result power outages were common; St. George was without power for twenty-four hours and had power crews working around the clock. Veyo suffered in a similar manner as the heavy snow brought down wires and broke twenty-three poles, causing approximately $1,100,000 in damage to the power lines. Coal was also in short supply due to the mines being blocked with snow in what many newspapers described as the heaviest snowfall in years or, in some cases, ever.

The heavy snowstorm that Christmas night was followed two nights later by another one that seemed to put a meteorological coup de grâce on much of the state. Kanab, near the Arizona state line, was virtually isolated due to snow drift blocking all the access roads, preventing the mail from getting through.

With no mail and the phone system down, the little community was truly cut off from the outside world. Elsewhere in Washington County mail was being hauled on sleds, while up in Garfield County mail to Boulder was again being carried on horseback where two feet of snow lay on level ground and was piled ten feet deep in the drifts. The *Helper Journal* reported nearly twenty inches of snow in what old-timers described as the heaviest snowfall in fifteen years. Highway 91 between St. George and Cedar City was blocked by snow. Panguitch reported two feet of snow on the summit and one foot in the valley. The *Ephraim Enterprise* reported on New Year's Day that 1936 was the town's wettest year since record-keeping began in 1930: "Without even counting the most recent storm the 18.55" precipitation level in late December was 212% of what the average had been over the previous six years."[37]

By then highways were blocked with cars and buses, and even snowplows were marooned. On New Year's Eve, three people were stranded in their car between Enterprise and Newcastle for nearly twenty-four hours trapped by snowdrifts, suffering from exposure before finally being rescued. Snow depths were above normal throughout the state. Although southern Utah was hit most heavily, northern Utah was impacted as well. Ten inches fell in Weber County, and trains were delayed by fifteen inches of snow in Cache Valley just as they were in southern Utah.[38]

Even Bridgeland Bureau of Reclamation camp BR-11 was called into service twice in the month of January. In temperatures of −40 degrees, crews plowed a road to rescue a snowbound school bus at Arcadia, about ten miles northeast of camp. A call from Pleasant Valley sheepmen soon followed seeking help in getting to their stranded herds. Foremen and cat-driving enrollees volunteered and were soon working three eight-hour shifts daily to clear some fifty-two miles of roads.[39]

The winter of 1936–37 was generally regarded as the worst Utah had experienced up to that time. Conditions varied from place to place, of course, but overall, the consensus seemed to support that opinion. The situation started getting extremely serious when heavy snow started to fall on December 28, 1936, in the St. George area and throughout much of southwestern Utah and northern Arizona.

Southern Utah was hit especially hard. Three foremen and ten enrollees from one camp were assigned snow-removal chores in the Kanab area; former enrollee Arnold Peterson told of being one of those who came down all the way from the Salina Creek camp to bulldoze roads for two weeks in the same vicinity along the southern Utah border.[40]

It wasn't long, however, before most of the southern three-fourths of the state was affected. Snow-clearing operations began immediately, but it was impossible to keep the roads open. Rescue operations captured the attention of the entire state in connection with the terrible blizzards that winter.

The beginning of the new year brought no respite. It was on January 3, 1937, as Governor Blood was being inaugurated for his second term, that still another severe storm hit, bringing even lower temperatures. Between the years 1891 and 1937 the eighty-three stations tracking temperatures for the Department of Agriculture's Weather Bureau reported the mean January temperature for the state as 25 degrees. The previous lowest average temperature of 15.3 degrees had been recorded in 1917. January 1937 shattered that record, however, by a full five degrees, coming in at an average of 10.3 degrees for the month. On January 21 it was −44 degrees in Lewiston, in northern Cache County. The U.S. Weather Bureau showed admirable restraint in its description of "the most severely cold month in the 46 years of State climatic record." Except at a few scattered stations, the average temperature established an all-time record, while thirty-one stations had the lowest minimum ever observed, and eleven other stations matched their former record temperatures. The average precipitation over the state was 1.69 inches, nearly a half inch above the normal 1.21 inches. The average depth of snowfall, however, was 26.7 inches, nearly two and a half times as much as the average 11.3 inches, exceeded only by the 31.5 inches recorded in 1916.[41]

The falling snow continued to plague the state throughout January. Two and a half feet of snow blocked the highways near Cedar City. Traffic was blocked; buses were stalled on Highway 89, Utah's main north-south route, which was also blocked south of Panguitch. A hotel in Fillmore reported being so overflowing with customers that many travelers were being housed in private homes. The *San Juan Record* told of faithful church members wading up to a mile through the snow to get to church, while congregations were combining meetings to reduce the inconvenience. Nearly five feet of snow fell in Enterprise, where snowdrifts covered fence posts in places. The communities of Gunlock, Veyo, and Enterprise were snowed in for the first two weeks in January. Getting around in St. George was such a problem that the city ordered snowshoes and skis to help people run necessary errands.[42]

Low temperatures and more storms continued to bring new misery. Ephraim experienced –13 degrees on January 2, with an accumulated depth of twelve–sixteen inches of snow. Helper had nearly three feet. Record-breaking subzero temperatures for days at a time seemed to be the norm. Three deaths mentioned in the Provo newspaper were attributed to the –22 degree weather. Highway 91 south of Cedar City shut down, and traffic from St. George to Salt Lake City was routed via Mt. Carmel Highway to U.S. 89 through Richfield. This would have been a touch-and-go situation as well, since on January 15 that route via State Highway 9 was experiencing "the heaviest snowfall ever known in the history of Zion N.P.," with fifty inches between December 27 and January 6 and snowplows unable to keep up as high winds whipped the dry snow over the roads as fast as they were cleared. Gunlock was snowbound for the first time in its history, and residents of nearby Veyo were forced to burn fence posts for firewood, if they could find any that the snow had not covered. Up in Tooele County school buses were unable to break through to the southern part of the county, making it necessary for students to spend two nights in town.[43]

All in all, it was a most miserable winter, with record low temperatures and excessive snow depth and precipitation well distributed throughout the state and throughout the month. For most of the winter the weather elements were winning the battle, but finally, CCC crews and state highway maintenance men began fighting back.

Ironically, one of the earliest rescue missions carried out by the CCC was to go to the assistance of some of their own. There had been considerable apprehension in early January over some twenty-five men snowbound at the spike camp at Enterprise, where Superintendent Hyrum Kunz and a small group of foremen and Veyo enrollees were stranded with only a three-day supply of food to sustain them. The road was blocked by seven-foot drifts, and the entire state awaited news of the outcome.[44]

An article in the *Parks Post* of January 15 added another description of the severity of the situation when it mentioned that the state road engineer called Frank Rozelle, superintendent of NP-4 at Bridge Mountain, requesting that he bring snow equipment from his CCC camp in Zion National Park to help open the road from U.S. 91 to the stranded CCC camps. The communities of Veyo, Gunlock, and Enterprise and the two camps were experiencing "considerable suffering."[45]

Zion's NP-2 added its help as well. Within the camp, pipes were freezing and breaking; and snow-removal equipment was in constant use as large crews moved through the canyon removing snowdrifts from blocked roads. Still, when the call for help came, crews were dispatched outside the park. Superintendent Francis F. Raile reported NP-2's contribution: "Trucks, snow moving equipment and enrollees were rushed to the aid of snowbound areas of State highway near Anderson Junction. Also to snowbound areas on Arizona Strip to help haul feed to isolated bands of sheep. These enrollees worked long hours under bad weather conditions without complaint."[46]

Crews with horses and a snowplow were able to open the road to Newcastle, thirty miles from Cedar City, and then pushed on twelve miles further to rescue another eighteen Forest Service enrollees at Pinto. They continued on, rescued and fed the men, and sent them back via Newcastle to Cedar City. The rescuers then went on to Enterprise to pick up the thirty-four men at the spike camp there. DG-30 men, like crews all over Utah, also hauled feed in and, where possible, kept the roads open long enough to drive livestock out to safety. Thirty thousand sheep and two thousand cattle were saved in the process.[47] Former superintendent Hy Kunz described the event to me in a letter from June 18, 1970:

> We were snowed in both at Enterprise and Veyo. Foremen Henry Day and Edwin Higbee and myself undertook the task of opening a road from Enterprise, where we were, to Veyo with the help of a Cletrac Tractor with one missing cylinder. We took turns on this tractor for four days, never letting the machine stop. The

> temperature would often reach forty degrees below zero. We ran out of food, but, as luck would have it, a rancher by the name of George Lytle had left some salt bacon in his ranch home about ten miles from Enterprise, and this is what we survived on. Once we left, it was a one-way trip as we were snowed in behind us. We reached the main camp at Veyo at 4 a.m. on the fourth day and found them snowbound, also.
>
> I slept for a few hours. After talking with the foremen, I was informed that a tractor was coming in from Diamond Valley, but had only traveled a short distance and had been in lower Diamond Valley, about 10 miles from Veyo, for three days and could not break through the crust to continue.[48]

The difficulty of the operation was compounded by winds of fifty to sixty miles an hour, which filled in the roads behind the tractors as fast as they were cleared.

Captain W. G. Hines, assistant quartermaster of the Fort Douglas District, came down from Salt Lake City to take command of the rescue not only of the CCC camps and communities in southern Utah but also of five camps in Nevada that were also snowbound. Cooperation with the Utah state highway crews also made it possible for a very ill woman at Pinto to be taken to Cedar City for care, as well as the body of a woman in Newcastle to be taken to a cemetery for burial eleven days after her death. An Eighth Period report described other efforts carried out the first week of February: another thirty-three-mile trip to the railroad stop of Lund out on the Escalante Desert southwest of Cedar City to save another ten thousand sheep and five hundred cattle, where crews followed the usual practice of hauling feed in and creating a corridor to drive the animals out; and another eighteen miles to a ranch, which made it possible to free several hundred thousand head of stock as well as many children who had been unable to attend school for at least two weeks, earning still another letter of appreciation from General Sweeney.[49]

Crews at Henrieville, DG-33, dug themselves out of "the heaviest snowfall ever experienced." Enrollees opened the road from the camp into town, six miles away, and continued on the highway approximately thirteen more miles to Tropic. Altogether, Henrieville crews cleared 585 miles of roads and trails and reported hauling thirty-four loads of feed in to stranded herds and returning twelve loads of weakened stock back to safer surroundings. Crews spent two days shoveling snow to open a road to a spike camp where the "cat" crews lived. The tractor foreman and a helper waded two and a half miles farther on through waist-deep snow to where the tractor had been left on a road project, got it back to the spike camp after some severe trials, and eventually returned to the main camp after dark and without lights by following a man through the snow. Crews borrowed two additional machines as the operators worked thirteen-hour shifts seven days a week to try and keep the roads open.[50]

The "Eighth Period Report" for the camp contained many letters from stockmen expressing their appreciation for the help provided during the previous winter. I selected this one as representative:

> Henrieville, Utah
> February 18th, 1937
> Division of Grazing
> Federal Building
> Salt Lake City, Utah
>
> Gentlemen:
>
> I desire to make mention of the splendid work done by Supt. Chidester and his men of Camp DG-33, Henrieville, Utah.
>
> I have lived here for 47 years, during that time I have never seen as cold a spell from December 27th to January 28th, 1937. There was not a break in the weather, ranging from 10–28 below zero, snow from 2–4 feet deep and drifted badly.
>
> This camp, with the superintendent in the lead, saved several herds of sheep by breaking trails, hauling feed, supplies, etc. They broke trails for cattlemen and hauled our supplies so we could reach our cattle with packs.
>
> The towns in Cannonville, Henrieville and Tropic would of [*sic*] been snow-bound if it had not been for the help given by Supt. Chidester and his men. They kept the roads open so we all got our mail and moved feed and help to livestock.
>
> I commend them for it. In fact, we would have went out of business if it had not been for the help we received from the Henrieville CCC camp. I commend them for their efficiency and good judgment in snow and blizzards, the worst ever known in this country.

Yours very Truly,
E. M. Moore
Advisory Board Member, Dist. No. 5[51]

Camp DG-35 in Milford made arrangements with local stockmen to open roads so caravans of trucks could haul cotton cake and other feed to a central point for distribution to nearby herds by wagon and sled. Some herds were stranded as far as sixty miles from help. Trucks had to follow closely since it took but a short time for drifting snow to fill in the roads again, but eventually $200,000 worth of livestock was saved. As he saw a caravan of eight or nine trucks approaching his stranded herd, one stockman said, "Thank the Lord for the CCC." Maj. Gen. Simonds, Ninth Corps Area commanding officer, sent a letter of commendation to the camp:

> I have noted letters of appreciation from the Utah Woolgrowers and the Utah Livestock Association, and a copy of the resolution passed by the Wasatch Livestock Loan Co. regarding the excellent work done by enrollees of your company during the recent severe winter weather. These reports show that men from your company assisted by the Technical Service operating in the severest weather hauled food to snowbound herds in the vicinity of Minersville, Rocky Point, Dead Horse Point, Mineral Mt. area, Pine Valley and points almost to the Nevada state line.[52]

In early January Castle Dale camp DG-27 spent four days opening roads and on the last day stood just a mile from getting back to the highway when another blizzard hit, filling in the freshly cleared roads. The next day they began all over again. Still, the crews saved an estimated 13,000 sheep. Other camps were called into action, as well. Crews from Bridge Mountain camp NP-4 traveled in three trucks under Leader Virg Everett to St. George in late January. Here they picked up cattle feed to become part of a twelve-truck convoy to rescue herds in the snowbound Hurricane Valley. The crews made three trips and then also delivered coal to the CCC camp across the state line in Pipe Spring, Arizona. Using their seventy-five-horsepower "cat" they opened thirty-nine miles of roads to save an estimated 22,000 sheep and three thousand cattle.

Four men from Company 940 from F-49 in Bountiful spent seventeen days opening highways and roads to rescue some 17,500 sheep and one thousand cattle. Enrollees of Company 958 out of Provo's F-40 worked fourteen-hour days over a six-week period in their rescue efforts, earning them compliments from Gen. Sweeney at Fort Douglas, who was writing a great many letters of praise during that hectic period. Sweeney, by the way, recognized that cooperation was a two-way street and in a letter to the governor offered his thanks and those of the entire CCC organization for the help given by the Utah State Highway Commission in connection with road maintenance in southern Utah and clearing roads to snowbound camps.[53]

In the Uinta Basin, typically one of the colder areas in Utah, the residents were certainly getting their share of the miserable weather. That winter, which many considered the coldest in Vernal's history, provided many opportunities for the enrollees to gain even more respect from the community. The weather became so bad that all work stopped at DG-31 camp except for the "cat" crews working on snow removal. The *Vernal Express* first commented that crews had been operating twenty-four hours around the clock for several days in early January, but as the temperature dropped to thirty and forty degrees below zero, and thousands of sheep were in danger of starving, the articles increased in fervor over the enrollees' accomplishments. "Had it not been for the Vernal CCC boys of Camp DG-31," the paper stated on one occasion, "a great number of these sheep would have perished."[54]

Snow closed the roads, and the county commissioners visited camp superintendent James W. Orr to work out a plan for keeping the traffic moving. CCC bulldozers operated around the clock by a crew of seven enrollees opened the roads so that school buses and mail deliveries could go through. Roads to coal mines were cleared in order that people might have fuel. On its front page the *Express* declared, "These boys have gained the confidence and good will of the entire community for their ability and for their service over and above the line of duty."[55]

The DG-31 crews kept on clearing more than three hundred miles of roads in February and even continued into March. They hauled feed on sleds thirty-five miles to one ranch on the Green River to save starving sheep. They pushed their way through to another to rescue a sick and bedfast family who were so ill that they had not had a fire for thirty-six hours. Except for the CCC keeping roads open to the cemetery, it would have been impossible for the community even to bury its dead.[56] The commanding general of the Ninth Corps Area praised the camp after receiving letters of appreciation from both the Utah Woolgrowers and the Utah Livestock Production Credit Association for saving some thirty thousand sheep.[57]

On the occasion of the fourth anniversary of the CCC in April 1937, the *Vernal Express* carried a front-page letter from Uinta county commissioners congratulating the camp. "The people of Uinta County barely realize how much they owe to the CCC Camp for the manner in which the roads were kept open during the severe snow storms of the past winter," as enrollees worked around the clock for several days to keep the roads open and haul feed. Mayor R. C. Cooper also had a column praising the CCC both for the approximately $5,000 of financial help it brought to the community every month and, even more so, for the work accomplished, including, among other projects mentioned, keeping roads open to the cemetery, permitting the burial of the dead.[58] Another Uinta Basin camp, BR-11 at Bridgeland, opened twenty-six miles of road to help rescue about 50,000 head of sheep in Pleasant Valley south of Myton.[59] The stories go on and on.

For a while, it was thought that the worst was over, at least in some spots. Highway 91 finally opened after a week of being blocked. Stranded travelers who had been sent to a service station for shelter suffered from cold and exposure as they had to stand in one room to keep warm. When they realized that they were finally safe many broke down in tears.[60]

The danger to livestock out on windswept ranges was another major concern. Although stockmen had feed on hand, getting it to their herds proved virtually impossible. After doing all that could be done to save human lives, the CCC was pressed into service to rescue livestock, the chief means of livelihood for thousands of Utah residents. Three tractor crews from F-40 under Foremen Joseph Swain and Reed Christopherson worked near Delta and Jericho as far as 130 miles from their Provo camp and, along with DG-26 enrollees, saved some 21,000 sheep. Commanding officer Capt. Alvin Sessions, along with Superintendent Richard Greenland and the company's First Sergeant Val Hicks, traveled out to take supplies and equipment, at which time Greenland estimated the crews had about another ten days of work ahead of them.[61]

In January and February 1937, the men of Antelope Springs camp DG-29 were kept busy going to the rescue of snowbound herds, mostly near Kanosh. DG-29 opened four hundred miles of snowbound roads to bring food to starving sheep and also took weakened animals back to ranches for recovery. Even getting out of camp was difficult, as the roads were blocked by snowdrifts. The camp was isolated much of the time during this period, at one time even without any communication for nearly two months. Sheepmen were pleasantly surprised to learn that the great loss they expected in their herds due to starvation was actually very minimal, thanks to the work of the CCC.[62]

The situation in southern Utah was such that crews were called in from camps elsewhere in the state to help deal with the situation. Foreman W. Merrill Miller and four enrollees from Company 940 at F-48 in Bountiful spent seventeen days in southern Utah, where they opened highways and roads and reportedly assisted in the rescue of some 17,000 starving sheep and one thousand cattle.[63]

Governor Blood wired Washington and reported on the seriousness of the problem. Utah stockmen asked for financial help, not to buy feed but only to keep the state and CCC equipment supplied with gas and oil. In Washington, Utah congressmen met with Forestry and Grazing Service officials, and soon an emergency allocation of $25,000 was made, with more promised, if necessary, to keep the equipment operating.[64]

Escalante camp F-42 opened a thirty-nine-mile road to deliver feed to 22,000 sheep and three thousand cattle. In his report on the snow-removal operations, Regional Forester R. H. Rutledge reported that 115 enrollees and thirty-nine foremen from eleven camps had cleared three thousand miles of roads in Utah and Nevada, resulting in the relief of 428,000 sheep and 27,000 cattle.[65] Figuring the current market price of about $9.00 per sheep and $45.00 per cow, the enrollees saved livestock worth more than $5,000,000, or approximately $32,900 for each man involved in the rescue operations. One camp claimed that its enrollees saved some $200,000 worth of livestock just from the efforts of their one camp. A news account stated that several truckloads of cattle had been shipped from the southern community of Kanab just during the previous week to prevent them from starving to death.[66]

RESCUE ON THE ARIZONA STRIP

Perhaps the major challenge confronted by a Utah camp that entire winter took place not in Utah but just across the southern border on the Arizona Strip, where St. George camp DG-45 actually did most of its work, at least up to that time. The roads south from St. George were blocked with snow, isolating not only herds of sheep and cattle but also ranches and even little communities such as Bundyville and Mt. Trumbull.

Stockmen on the Arizona Strip asked Company 2558 and Superintendent Dan Thompson of DG-45 in St. George for assistance. After estimating that a 50–75 percent herd loss might be expected unless the stock could be fed soon, it was apparently of little difficulty to secure permission from the Salt Lake City regional office; immediately a relief expedition left for Little Tank, fifty-two miles south on the Arizona Strip. Led by an R-5 Caterpillar tractor, eight CCC and four private trucks with twelve tons of cottonseed cake and grain began their trek on January 7, 1937. Two days later they reached the spike camp at Wolf Hole (pronounced "Wufful" by the locals) twenty-eight miles south of St. George.[67]

Foreman Jim Bundy spent most of his five years in the CCC in charge of the Wolf Hole spike camp, usually involved in road-building. When the storm hit he was at home in Bundyville, several miles farther south on the road to Mt. Trumbull, but he immediately reported back to the spike camp and was heavily involved in the relief operations from then on.

The rescue caravan from DG-45 had been traveling about a mile an hour; after leaving the spike camp their progress slowed to three miles a day. Superintendent Daniel Thompson issued a special report in which he told the story of the ordeal:

> Since the need was so desperate to get some food and grain thru to Little Tank for both man and beast, we decided to hook the Cat onto one truck loaded heavily and attempt to drag it thru without breaking any road. Thus truck and Cat after two days of ceaseless effort arrived at Little Tank. Found the people there almost out of food and all grain gone.[68]

As it traveled through Main Street Valley, the caravan passed near a herd owned by a St. George judge and his two sons. One son was with the caravan; the other had been with the herd. The report continues:

> Hiram Cox, alone with the herd, had been thirty-six hours without food and had saddled his best horse to make a supreme effort to break thru the ten miles to Little Tank for food. He would

> probably not have reached there. However, just as he was starting he saw our truck and caterpillar coming over a hill about three miles away. Needless to say the relief was welcome there.[69]

The relief caravan reached Little Tank on January 15, having gone fifty-two miles in eight days of continuous travel. The feed was unloaded, and the caravan began its return to St. George immediately, apprehensive because of a broken bulldozer on the caterpillar and the possibility that they themselves might become stranded. Back in St. George by January 18, they learned that CCC forces had been mobilized throughout the state. Camp officials appealed to Salt Lake City and soon received a seventy-horsepower diesel caterpillar to help with their rescue work. With this new tractor and the faithful R-5 in the lead, another expedition was soon on its way to the strip. Eleven CCC trucks and eleven privately owned trucks and pickups arrived at Little Tank after six days and nights of steady travel with the CCC operators working in relays around the clock. The diesel "cat" continued on to Mt. Trumbull a week later and also started on to the relief of two herds farther south. However, rain began falling, the snow began to melt, and the herds survived. Apart from having to dig their equipment out of the mud several times on the way back to St. George, the ordeal was over.[70]

One highlight of the entire operation would make a great script for a Hollywood portrayal of the incident. On the second journey south from St. George, the rescue caravan reached Bundyville, around seven miles south of Little Tank. The tiny settlement included about seven families with perhaps another thirty people living within eight or ten miles who had come there to take refuge. Almost out of food, the settlement, including Foreman Jim Bundy's home, had been cut off for more than six weeks. Bundy's son Atwood told me on January 7, 2009, what a thrill it was for the fearful residents to hear the trucks coming, especially for him, as a seven-year-old lad, to see his father in the lead.[71]

Not only domestic livestock but wildlife as well were rescued during that severe winter. At a meeting of the Carbon-Emery Fish and Game Protective Association in January 1937, it was reported that CCC crews had fed three tons of whole and cracked corn to approximately 1,500 pheasant and quail in Carbon County and another four thousand in Emery County within the previous two weeks. In still another example of CCC and community cooperation the Fish and Game Association had paid for the grain, which was distributed daily by enrollees of SCS-3 to help keep the game birds alive.

In another Emery County project, Deputy Game Warden Fred Larsen supervised a $400 activity in which enrollees from Castle Dale camp DG-27 set out several thousand pounds of wheat and two tons of corn for the same purpose.[72] At the same time, enrollees from Company 736 in Willard's SCS-4 camp in northern Utah were assigned to keep deer out of the orchards of Utah's "fruit belt" just south of Brigham City. The CCC was also helping the Forest Service feed hay to an estimated five to six hundred deer that the storms had driven down from the mountains. The enrollee-driven camp bulldozer plowed roads to three feeding grounds to help keep the animals alive during that terrible winter.[73]

As noted above, in summarizing the work done the previous winter by just the eleven Forest Service camps, Regional Forester R. H. Rutledge reported that three thousand miles of roads were cleared in providing relief to 428,000 sheep and 27,000 cattle in Utah and Nevada: "And the work was done entirely with CCC enrollees and their foremen, a total of 115 men plus thirty-nine foremen, from eleven camps in addition to a number of forest supervisors and rangers." Twenty-six tractors operated a total of 4,100 hours, many in continuous shifts around the clock for three continuous weeks. The forty-six trucks and snowplows that were used traveled nearly 25,000 miles in clearing roads and hauling feed, which "prevented losses to stockmen the sum total of which will never be known." Rutledge concluded his report by emphasizing, "In spite of the difficulties and obstacles, the men carried on and their efforts added another colorful chapter in the history of the western livestock industry."[74]

Finally in February the worst was over, as most roads were reported open again and Utah livestock had "suffered only slight additional inconvenience [the] past week."[75] It would be difficult to overestimate the gratitude of the stockmen for the assistance given them. The Utah Livestock Association, Utah Woolgrowers, Wasatch Livestock Loan Company, and many other firms and individuals sent letters of appreciation and resolutions to Army officials in San Francisco and Fort Douglas; to Grazing and Forestry officials in Washington, Salt Lake City, and Ogden; and to the individual camps.

The story of the work done in that terrible storm was even recounted years later in a children's historical series in which CCC help in national disasters was described. Author Jennifer Savedge said that in addition to helping in flooding and hurricanes across the country the enrollees "assisted during winter blizzards in Wyoming, West Virginia, and Utah (actually saving 1 million sheep in the latter state that were separated from their farms and in danger of freezing in 1936)."[76]

Livestock rescue of quite a different sort took place the summer following the disastrous winter of 1936–37. The camp newspaper of DG-35 in Milford conveyed hero status on its survey and machine crews working in the vicinity of Iron Springs near Jockeys Reservoir when they rescued seventeen cattle trapped in a large concrete water tank: "Some of them bore evidence of having been there at least one week. They were all taken out saving a considerable loss to the owner, whoever he is."[77]

SEARCH AND RESCUE

Whether it was emergency work such as fighting wildfires or saving starving sheep or whether they were just painting a church, clearing a playground, or spending money in a depressed town, the CCC soon came to be regarded with considerably more favor than when it had originally arrived. Evidence indicates that the state quite overwhelmingly appreciated the presence of the enrollees—with qualifications, perhaps, but the appreciation still existed. Another facet of the CCC experience that created good feelings with local communities was the many times crews were called out on search-and-rescue missions. Just a few examples can illustrate the scope of their work.

Perhaps the major search-and-rescue operation carried out by Utah enrollees began just over a week before Christmas 1936 when a Western Air Express plane with seven aboard went missing in central Utah. It was December 16 when the flight from Salt Lake City to Los Angeles disappeared, initially thought to have gone down in the vicinity of Milford in Beaver County.[78]

Company 2531 of DG-29 was immediately called out and searched the House Range area between the camp at Antelope Springs and Tatow Knob about ten miles away. Four crews from Milford camp DG-35 tramped the Mineral Range for two days. Every man in camp F-40, including the off-duty kitchen personnel, came down from Provo to help in the search. Even F-40's spike camp in Hobble Creek Canyon went out searching, including tramping around Utah Lake, to no avail. The company newspaper, *Yell-A-Gram*, reported that between the main camp in Provo and the spike camp up Hobble Creek 750 man-days had been spent by Company 958 alone.

Brigadier General Walter C. Sweeney, CO of the Fort Douglas CCC District, placed the seven thousand men and resources of all forty-six camps in the district including Utah's thirty-one at the disposal of those directing the search. The Salina camp searched the foothills and mountains west and south of Salina and also sent fifty men to Kanosh for further assistance, as did the Mayfield camp.[79]

A CCC crew from Provo was to leave at daylight on December 21 to scale the 9,500-foot Provo Peak to investigate a bare patch where the plane might have crashed and burned. A finding of burned power poles on December 19 gave further evidence, which spiked intensification of the ground search then initiated. Enrollees assisted until a three-day snowstorm forced abandonment of the search on December 22.[80]

Finally, unsuccessful search efforts in the West Desert and recalculation of the plane's flight path suggested that the plane might have disappeared farther north than had been originally presumed. Captain Alvin Sessions, commanding officer of F-40 in Provo, was given the responsibility of coordinating the search for the downed aircraft and in early February received a personal note for his actions from Gen. Sweeney.[81] Finally, in May, with the snow almost gone, the search focused on northern Utah County.

From a plane flying overhead Sessions directed enrollees from F-40 and other CCC camps, along with soldiers and volunteers. On May 31, Sessions received a letter from Allan O. Barrie, vice president of Western Air Express, prompting Sessions to assign senior foreman Val Hicks to investigate the area northeast of the little community of Alpine nestled at the foot of the mountains. Hicks set up a camp at an elevation of about ten thousand feet supplied by two foremen leading a pack train. Four tents housed twenty-one enrollees, Western Air Express employees, and newspaper reporters for six days before the plane was found on the southeast slope of Lone Peak on the line between Salt Lake and Utah counties, about six miles due east of Draper, above Lake Hardy in what is now the Lone Peak Wilderness Area. A crew under Hicks and Foreman Ronald J. Dyches spent three days searching for bodies and bringing in the mail, for which they received high praise from U.S. postal authorities.[82]

As a result of the enrollees' assistance during the search, Western Air Express gave free plane rides to the boys of Company 958. It took three flights to take care of the fifty young men, most of whom were enjoying their first experience in the air. Enrollee Reid Carter, among those who first found the plane, was taken on two flights.[83]

Enrollees carried out a similar mission nearly four years later when an airliner crashed into the Wasatch Mountains near Centerville, not far from Bountiful. Again, the plane went down during a severe snowstorm; all ten aboard perished.[84]

Although perhaps not quite so dramatic, other search-and-rescue operations provided opportunities for CCC personnel to demonstrate their competence. Twenty enrollees from Soapstone camp F-6 rescued a woman lost near the headwaters of the Duchesne River near Mirror Lake in August 1934. Fifty Bridgeland CCC enrollees joined a search for the twenty-year-old librarian of Duchesne High School who walked out of a drunken party in disgust in March 1937 and tried to find her way home. She wandered through snow-covered hills in subzero temperatures for three days before her rescue, just five miles from where she had started walking.[85]

Two months earlier, in early January 1937, two Wyoming women skidded off the highway near the East Entrance to Zion National Park. A passing motorist rescued them from their car and brought them through the tunnel to safety. CCC Foreman Marion Willis and his dragline crew gathered ropes and chains and took off to try and save the car, now hanging precariously over a fifteen-foot bank. The CCC truck, aided by a tow truck from Springdale, succeeded in pulling the car back onto solid ground. Although no one got the women's names in all the excitement, the camp newspaper opined, "It's all in a day's work for the CCCers in winter," especially that terrible winter of 1937, when such rescues became almost routine.

Coincidentally, that same day a similar rescue was under way in the opposite end of the state. When state highway equipment couldn't handle the deep snow, Sardine Canyon between Brigham City and Wellsville, over the mountains in Cache County, became a treacherous nightmare. One young couple was trapped for seven hours in a "light roadster equipped only with side curtains." Wind drifted snow over the car before twenty-three enrollees from Huntsville camp BR-12 as well as a crew from BS-1, the Biological Survey camp at Bear River Bird Refuge, came to the rescue. They found the girl with a high fever and hysterical, but after being warmed up at the hospital in Brigham City, the couple was released. The car remained trapped for at least two more days. Four other cars and at least one intercity bus also had to be rescued in the canyon by twenty enrollees of BS-1, led by Capt. Warren D. Paul and Foreman Ken Murdock. Enrollees shoveled a pathway, and with boys pushing the cars got out, saving about twenty stranded people in the process.[86]

In addition to snow-clearing work in 1937 and again in 1939, the Vernal camp provided search and rescue crews several times: once to bring in a family marooned in a stalled car, another time to search for a couple drowned in Green River, and again to search for a lost three-year-old girl who had wandered away from her family on Little Brush Creek. After four hours, she actually "found" herself by walking up to a man working on his truck some two and a half miles away.[87] During a cold March in 1937 a foreman and a leader from Bridgeland camp BR-11 led forty volunteer enrollees in a successful search for another lost girl.[88] Enrollees from F-40 in Provo were called out and successfully rescued a boy who had fallen through the ice at the mouth of the Provo River in December 1938.[89]

One year later the other Provo camp, MA-1, was involved in one of the more bizarre searches, when a man fell into Utah Lake on another cold December day. A companion dragged him ashore and went for help but then couldn't remember where he had left his friend. Sheriff John S. Evans and other Utah County officers searched unsuccessfully before eighty CCC men were called out to help. Led by three foremen and three leaders, the enrollees searched about seven miles of shoreline, wading through deep mud, before the victim was found, suffering from hunger and exposure, about a hundred feet from where he had been left the day before.[90]

Two weeks later, just before Christmas, 1939, another group of one hundred men, mostly from the CCC, searched the area around Salina for a young farmer whom the sheriff feared might have been suffering from amnesia. In August 1940, enrollees were called out to help forest rangers and lawmen search for fourteen deer hunters trapped by a blizzard.[91]

Occasionally, it was a recovery operation rather than a rescue in which the CCC was involved. While at Panguitch Lake camp F-27 during the summer of 1934, Foreman Hyrum Kunz and about a hundred enrollees from Company 961 dragged the lake with grappling hooks for more than forty-eight hours before finding the body of a St. George businessman who had drowned. The boat carrying him and two others had capsized, and while his two friends made it to shore, he did not.[92] A search party of more than a hundred enrollees from Utah and Wyoming combed the Uinta Mountains for a lost government survey worker. Hope was abandoned, and the search was discontinued after two weeks.

A girl drowned when heavy floodwaters carried a car and its occupants about five hundred feet into Minersville Reservoir. The enrollees of the Milford camp participated in the search until they recovered the body four days later.[93]

Enrollees from the Big Cottonwood and Bountiful camps answered a call on New Year's Day, 1941, to try and rescue a skier trapped by an avalanche at Alta Ski Resort. His body was found after a two-day search.[94]

Well prepared, quickly mobilized, and highly organized with an enviable leadership structure, the CCC was a natural, "go-to" organization to meet emergency situations, whether fire, blizzard, or search and rescue. The fact that so many were used so often in so many different circumstances speaks well of the young men finding their way in life.

Plate 1. Enrollees of the Pleasant Grove camp lining up in formation outside their barracks for the daily flag ceremony.

Plate 2. Interior of a Civilian Conservation Corps mess hall with the tables set for a meal, Pleasant Grove.

Plate 3. Terraces in Davis County still in use eighty years later.

Plate 4. Planting trees, probably the work for which the "Tree Army" is best known.

Plate 5. Constructing identifying signs, a major Civilian Conservation Corps activity.

Plate 6. Entrance to Duck Creek Civilian Conservation Corps camp F-16, a typical tent camp.

Plate 7. Company 585 enrollees at Mountain Meadows, lining up behind a flatbed truck to get their lunch.

Plate 8. Hobble Creek camp enrollees with a horse pulling a wooden stoneboat loaded with rocks.

Plate 9. Construction progress on a spillway along a Utah river in Willard, Box Elder County, built by Civilian Conservation Corps Company 736 at SCS-4.

Plate 10. Civilian Conservation Corps built several amphitheaters, such as the Theater in the Pines at Aspen Grove in Provo Canyon.

Plate 11. Interior of Civilian Conservation Corps barracks, Pleasant Grove. This camp housed F-43 at first and then later BR-91.

Plate 12. Group of relaxing enrollees posing for a photograph outside one of the barracks at the Ferron Civilian Conservation Corps camp, F-11.

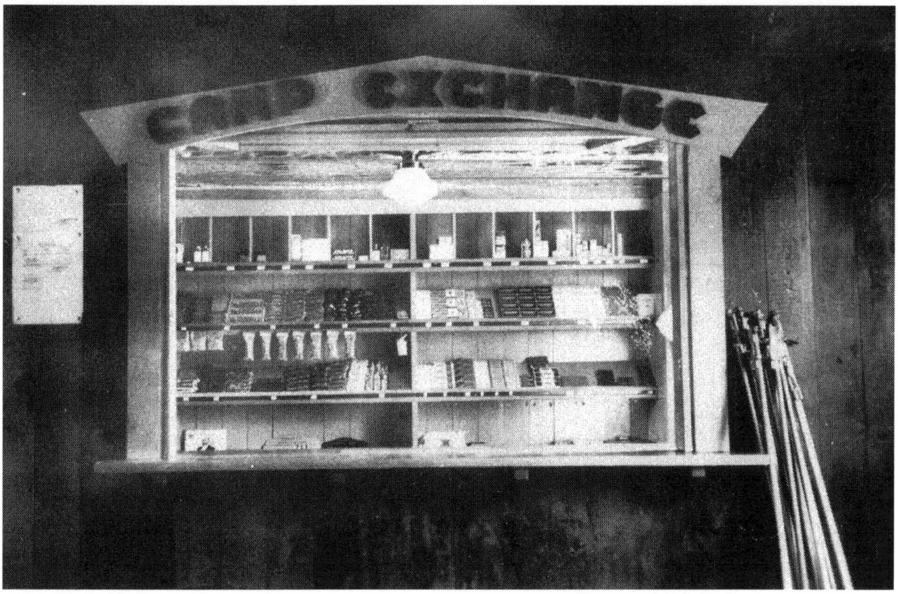

Plate 13. Merchandise available at a Utah Civilian Conservation Corps camp exchange counter, where enrollees could spend their remaining $5.00 after $25.00 of their $30.00 monthly wage was sent home to their families.

Plate 14. Sign and brick pylon marking the entrance to Zion National Park. Much of this monument was likely built by J. L. Crawford, who learned his skill as an enrollee.

Plate 15. Enrollees hauling two wagonloads of cut-down trees through a clearing near a Civilian Conservation Corps construction site, Hobble Creek camp.

Plate 16. Large rock structure, probably the Shivwits Dam on the Santa Clara River, built by Company 961, camp SE-213 of St. George.

Plate 17. Civilian Conservation Corps baseball team from Company 959 of Ferron camp F-11.

Plate 18. Crew of men working on a rock retaining wall at their Civilian Conservation Corps construction site.

Plate 19. Finished section of a flood-control embankment along the Virgin River in Zion National Park, at the east end of the canyon. This shows an example of "riprapping."

Plate 20. Bridge built over Sulphur Creek in Capitol Reef National Park, likely by enrollees of NP-7. Photograph courtesy of the National Park Service.

Plate 21. Built by the Civilian Conservation Corps, the ranger station at Sulphur Creek is now the superintendant's office at Capitol Reef National Park. Photograph courtesy of the National Park Service.

CHAPTER 10

Accidents, Health, and Safety

I remember one day we were out cutting trees that had been marked for felling. We cut one tree that didn't fall just as we had expected and it fell in such a way that it brought down three other large trees with it. Men ran in all directions. We were taught to be watchful at the cry of "Timber." One guy was hit by one of the trees in such a way that his thigh was split wide open from hip to just above the knee. It was squashed and not cut. We removed the tree and brought him into the open. The officer in charge had the first aid kit brought out and they just poured iodine into the open wound. The man gave just one loud yell and passed out. He was taken by truck down to Beaver, some 18 to 20 miles away.

—Lauritz Peterson, enrollee, F-14

Sergeant John B. Gresham of Fort Douglas was temporarily assigned to Logan camp F-1 when he became the recipient of a somewhat dubious distinction. Early in June 1933, just a few days after the CCC program got under way in Utah, he stepped out of a truck, slipped, fell, fractured his leg, and became the first reported casualty in any CCC camp in the Fort Douglas District.[1]

Accidents continued to be a serious problem, especially that first year. An enrollee at camp F-14 up on Beaver Mountain received a cut below his eye that required several stitches. It seems that a youth standing next to him in line had an ax over his shoulder and, when called by his foreman, turned around, wounding his unfortunate colleague. A short time later the ax-bearer had his turn; he suffered a cut and bruised head and was knocked unconscious when hit by a falling tree.

A nineteen-year-old enrollee at F-5 in American Fork Canyon fell over a ledge and received head and wrist injuries while working on a trail. A trail crew working on a hill near Springville dislodged a rock that rolled down, hitting the camp cook and breaking his leg. Ax injuries continued to plague F-14, even into October. A local enrollee, home on weekend leave, was cutting down a tree when his ax slipped; the split toe and gashed foot required sixteen stitches.

One of the first deaths in the district occurred at SE-213 in St. George. Thirty-four-year-old Wilford Humpherys of Salt Lake City, presumably an LEM, had just arrived in camp that day after being transferred from Blue Springs camp F-18 north of Escalante when he stepped on a thin outcropping at the edge of a gravel pit and was buried when tons of earth followed him into his grave.[2]

Escalante was near the site of another tragic accident in September 1935. F-42 had just been set up on the eastern edge of town and was working on the road connecting Boulder with the "outside" world. A spike camp had been located in Boulder and was working on the road north toward Grover. Highly respected Neil Forsythe from nearby Teasdale was the work foreman in charge when it was found necessary to blast a large tree from the projected roadway. The dynamite charge failed to explode, however, and when Forsythe went to investigate, an enrollee accidentally hit the detonating plunger, killing the popular foreman instantly. Following the funeral the next day Wanlass Alvey of Escalante was appointed foreman, and the work went on.[3]

Accidents involving motor vehicles became even more common. Two men had their knees badly injured when the truck on which they were riding passed too close to a parked vehicle. They were hospitalized for observation, although it appeared that no bones had been broken. A CCC driver returning to camp near Escalante swerved his truck to avoid hitting a squirrel. The truck overturned, and three enrollees suffered a variety of injuries including head and facial lacerations, a fractured hip, and a broken collarbone. The fate of the squirrel was not reported.[4]

In spite of injuries such as these, Director Fechner initially disapproved of a safety campaign because of excessive cost. The arguments of the Army and the technical services prevailed, however, resulting in a safety program being approved on April 9, 1934.[5]

The commanding generals were responsible for administering the safety program in each of the nine Corps Areas. The technical agency took charge of the safety program during work hours; the Army was responsible at all other times. Usually the superintendent named one of his more responsible foremen as camp safety officer. Safety meetings took place weekly with the leaders, assistant leaders, and truck drivers.[6]

Superintendents took their safety responsibilities quite seriously, since they realized they were being judged by the safety record of their crews. William E. Slade, superintendent of SP-2, was quite pleased to receive a congratulatory letter from CCC Director Robert Fechner, NPS Director Conrad Wirth, and Regional NPS Director Kittredge complimenting him on an accident-free year. Then, just five days later, an enrollee was seriously injured when dumping rubble from the truck he was driving on one of the dykes at the Farmington Bay bird refuge. When he reported the accident, Slade was then accused of "letting down" or relaxing his efforts to preserve his safety record![7]

The Utah State Department of Education also hired safety directors to oversee safety programs in the camps. Two-day safety conferences made a concerted effort to reduce accidents. Early in February 1938, one such conference opened in Salina, immediately followed by one in Hyrum; these involved Forest Service and CCC personnel from Idaho and Wyoming as well as Utah.[8]

Camps used various methods to acquaint the enrollees with the hazards of their jobs. Information was always available from the safety office on transportation, first aid, lifesaving, use of tools and equipment, scaffolding, excavation, electricity, handling explosives, firefighting, and so on. Local initiative also helped in developing safety awareness. At F-6 east of Kamas, safety men were delegated for each crew on a weekly rotating basis. These men looked for and reported problems to the safety committee, which met weekly. Camp F-43 at Pleasant Grove had a safety suggestion box mounted in the recreation hall, and the best idea submitted each month received a prize.[9] Company newspapers nearly always had one or more articles calling for the observance of safety measures as well as reporting on accidents.

A camp reporter for Moab camp SCS-6, for instance, in his article "SCS News," told of two enrollees injured while working "on rock and both had fractured fingers." One had a compound fracture that became infected, requiring his hospitalization at Fort Douglas, resulting in lost time of thirty-three days at the time of the article. The other lost only twenty-five days before his injury healed enough for him to return to work. The enrollee reporter concluded his article, "From the office... from the Garage, from every possible part of [the company] comes the request, even plea, to watch out, its [*sic*] you that are hurt and you who pay. Be Careful."[10]

In March 1935, falling rocks killed two men at Manila camp F-35 near the Wyoming border. The men were part of a blasting crew working on a road project in Flaming Gorge. After a charge had blown, the men returned to clear the debris when eight tons of rock came hurtling down, killing one man instantly and fatally injuring the other, who died while being removed from the scene. Another blasting accident resulted in the death of a Utah enrollee named Ray Tanner at Zion National Park. While on a road-sloping project of NP-4 he had been hit by flying rocks, and an immediate operation was attempted to save his leg. Amputation was necessary, however, and soon complications set in. Just over a month after the accident the seventeen-year-old enrollee passed away.[11]

A tractor at Zion Park camp NP-2 backed into an enrollee, crushing his heel. He was taken to St. George, but no surgical help was available there, so he was forwarded to Fort Douglas in an ambulance. Doctors originally planned to amputate his foot, but further investigation suggested other treatment, and the foot stayed on.[12] The danger of routine work and the concern displayed by conscientious foremen are both illustrated in this excerpt of a letter from a former enrollee:

> Bill Justen and I were on the "cat" one day starting the trail from the top of a long dugway down to meet two Cletracks that were working up. Bill was skinning and had just pushed over a small pine tree. A few passes later his lower track got on top of the tree and it rolled, throwing the "cat" down over the edge of a steep hill, about an 80° grade. He started to jump, then seeing that the "cat" had caught a balance he stayed on. After getting his breath he tried to pull it back but we decided the foreman should be consulted before we did something wrong and plunged that equipment to destruction and maybe a man with it to the bottom of that grade. George Allred was called and he wouldn't let either of us back on it but himself got on and after tedious and breath-taking struggle finally got it to take hold and slowly crawl back to safety.[13]

In spite of the dangerous work in which they engaged, it was still the ride to and from the work projects that was the most hazardous part of the day. A twenty-one-year-old enrollee from American Fork died when the truck he was driving met a school bus in a head-on collision. Another fatality took place when a truck hit a rut and the steering mechanism broke. The truck, out of control, plunged over a cliff into a canyon, killing a young man from Price and seriously injuring three others. A Park Valley enrollee died of a broken neck when a truck overturned on loose gravel. Box Elder County suffered another fatality of a similar nature just two weeks later. An enrollee from Ohio drew assignment as one of the drivers at the Brigham City camp. As he drove his truck loaded with gravel about five miles north of Brigham City, he leaped from the cab when it appeared that the truck would overturn. The truck slipped from the road, and the youth was crushed against the side of the embankment, suffering a fractured pelvis and broken ribs. He died in the Brigham City hospital. Trying to leap to safety cost the life of another enrollee north of St. George. The truck in which he was riding collided with an automobile and overturned, crushing the boy and injuring five others.[14]

One of the most serious CCC accidents in Utah took place on a recreational outing just east of Vernal when normal care was evidently lacking as a CCC driver rounded a corner too fast. His truck overturned. Two enrollees from Ohio died, in spite of attempts to save the life of one by amputating his mangled leg. Ten others in the truck received severe cuts and bruises. Another truck accident at Orderville proved less serious, although the two occupants of the truck did not escape injury. Trying to avoid an oncoming car, the enrollee swerved his truck, which rolled completely over, landing on its wheels.[15]

It was not just the enrollees who were involved in accidents. Chaplain Theodore Curtis was on his way to hold a religious service at Zion National Park when he crashed into a loaded truck, resulting in a broken jaw and lacerations about the head and arm. Foreman William Laursen of Manila camp F-35 had two automobile accidents in seventeen months—one, in hindsight, might be considered somewhat comical, but the other, unfortunately, was tragic. In May 1938 Laursen and two other foremen were driving up Provo Canyon on their way back to camp when a faulty steering mechanism caused their car to roll over, dumping them into the cold Provo River. Fortunately no one was injured. On October 8, 1939, Laursen again was returning to duty under similar circumstances. The sedan in which he was riding skidded into a culvert, killing the driver, another foreman from the Manila camp. The three passengers—Laursen, fellow foreman George Barron, and Superintendent Frank Hyde—sustained injuries.

That same day another Provo-area resident died in a Salt Lake City hospital as the result of another accident somewhat associated with the CCC. A nineteen-year-old youth not in the CCC was returning from delivering vegetables to a camp east of Farmington when his truck hit a soft shoulder and went over the side of a cliff, coming to rest three hundred feet below.[16]

As Hyde's experience indicates, even seasoned superintendents could fall victim. Forty-eight-year-old Ralph G. Parmelee, probably the most experienced man in DG-48 at Clover Creek, was returning from inspecting a spike camp when he apparently fell asleep and crashed through a guardrail four miles west of Grantsville.[17]

These incidents might suggest a lack of responsibility on the part of those associated with the program. Actually, the reverse is true. The drivers were carefully selected and were expected to keep their driving habits and their vehicles in excellent working condition at all times. The drivers at Jericho camp DG-26 attended a weekly lecture on Monday nights as well as a "laboratory" class on Saturday mornings. The camp mechanic, Lester M. Felt, instructed both sessions. A newsman visiting the Bountiful camp reported that Superintendent C. R. Wehymeyer had flagged down a passing driver and asked him to raise the hood on his truck. The engine was as "clean as a pin" and showed no evidence of dirt, rust, or surplus grease and oil. The six-year-old truck had traveled 62,942 miles over rough mountain roads. The newsman was impressed, not only with the truck but with the safety record in general. Enrollees from the camp had been working for the past year improving a steep road in the area. Trucks had been driven up and down grades for more than 125,000 miles without an accident. A large sign that read "Try your Brakes Here" located on the downgrade leading from the camp to the highway illustrated the safety awareness of the camp.[18]

Foremen and technical agency personnel exercised extreme caution in the selection and supervision of drivers. They were responsible to the point of losing their jobs should a driver under their command cause an accident. Foremen generally did not drive, but they always sat in the front seat with their drivers, seeing to it that drivers took no chances and obeyed all regulations.[19] Generally the better enrollees were selected as drivers, and they were thoroughly trained. One driving test included placing an egg behind a tire on a slight slope, loading thirty men into the truck, and driving away without first rolling back on the egg.

On one occasion a very dependable winch operator named Jackman approached his foreman asking for a driving job. Winch operators were hard to replace, so the foreman refused. After several more attempts the enrollee asked again when the foreman could not evade the issue. Hoping to discourage the young man once and for all the foreman gave him a test he considered impossible. He told the applicant to drive over a selected course up a steep grade and down again for about a mile without using his brakes. Jackman passed handily, and the foreman, with mixed emotions of pride and disappointment, began looking for a new winch operator.[20]

Safety slogans were displayed on the dashboards of CCC vehicles, and safety posters were very much in evidence around the barracks, garages, and workshops. A report of one of the camps spoke with pride of its membership in the National Safety Council and its active campaign to "best promote and maintain safety consciousness." The CCC issued Certificates of Proficiency to drivers who completed 25,000 miles without an accident. One such driver was Harry Hartman, the only one in F-43 in Pleasant Grove with the certificate, which he earned in July 1937. Just a month later he stopped his truck well clear of a curve on a dangerous mountain road to permit an automobile to pass. He must have been surprised when the car stopped and he was asked his name and camp. He must have been even more surprised a short time later when he received a commendation from the Utah State Road Commission, members of which had received a personal demonstration of his capabilities and caution.[21]

The men took great pride in their equipment and left their trucks parked in a neat line at the end of the day. Their natural pride was encouraged by the use of a demerit system. Demerits were given for such "offenses" as low tires, greasy engines, dirty truck beds, and so forth. For every demerit received the driver was "grounded" for one hundred miles of the truck's operation. Driving offenses resulted not in demerits but in instant dismissal.[22]

Unfortunately, drivers' skill and care did not always enable them to escape accidents. In one forest, traffic officers made two arrests of drivers who were subsequently convicted of colliding with CCC vehicles. In one case the driver and a CCC vehicle approached each other on a one-way road. On first coming into view of each other the two drivers were three hundred feet apart. The CCC driver stopped in thirty-three feet; the other driver closed the remaining 267-foot gap and collided with the CCC vehicle. In the other case, the CCC vehicle was unable to avoid a car that came around a blind curve on the wrong side of the road.[23] An enrollee from Pleasant Grove camp BR-91 was a passenger in a car that overturned in Provo Canyon and suffered injuries. Another "civilian" truck on the wrong side of the road hit and killed a CCC youth just outside of Tremonton in 1940. An enrollee in the Hobble Creek camp was scratched and bruised by a hit-and-run driver in Springville.[24]

Throughout the nation motor vehicle accidents proved responsible for approximately one-half of the nearly three hundred CCC deaths due to external causes in 1940.[25] A thorough search of Utah newspapers and available reports indicates that nearly all of the externally caused accidental deaths in Utah were also due to motor vehicle accidents. Drowning, railway accidents, suicide, homicide, and deaths due to fighting wildfires were the other major causes across the county; no record was found indicating that any of these were a problem in Utah.

An ever-increasing campaign against accidents proved effective. The Corps-wide accident rate per one thousand enrollees dropped from 16.81 in 1934 to 4.80 in 1940, and the rate of accidents per million man-hours of work fell to just over one-third what it had been. In 1939, 119 camps of the Soil Conservation Service operated the entire fiscal year without a single lost-time accident.[26] Safety consciousness was paying off.

In addition to combating accidents both on and off the job, the CCC authorities carefully studied ways and means of eliminating or controlling the effects of illness among the enrollees. Each camp was assigned a doctor, either a Reserve medical officer from one of the services or a civilian doctor from a nearby community working under contract.[27]

The surgeon, as he was officially known, was assisted by a first aid man, an enrollee with the rank of leader who was quartered right in the dispensary and expected to be on constant call. He assisted the doctor at sick call and on occasion had to take care of it by himself as contract doctors sometimes found it necessary to be elsewhere.

Occasionally a first aid man might let his sense of humor overcome his sense of duty. A story is told of the time when some new enrollees were receiving their physical examinations upon arriving at the Salina Canyon camp. One of the first aid men, "having nothing better to do," gave each enrollee two little brown "CCC Pills"—actually a highly potent laxative—with instructions to be sure to take them. One of the new men somehow received an extra administration of the pills, of which two were described as "guaranteed to move anything." The "victim" sat watching a poker game about four hours later when the double dosage began to take rapid effect. One of the onlookers described the occasion quite colorfully:

> He hurried out the barracks slowing down only for the four or five steps that led to the ground, then busted into a high lope. At the end of the barracks was the wash house and at the end of it, directly in line of his flight to the latrine below the hill, was a series of clothes lines. He caught one of these under the chin and landed flat on his back in the gravel. There was a long groan and a deep disgusted sigh and "Oh, G—, I wouldn't have made it anyway," as he crawled into the shower to take a bath.[28]

Most of the information herein concerning the activities of the first aid men and the medical procedures in camp came from Francis Welsh, who held that position for thirty of the thirty-three months that he served with Companies 1966 and 962 in Zion and Bryce national parks. Through two letters and two interviews he was most cooperative and informative concerning this phase of CCC life.

Francis was nineteen when he joined the Civilian Conservation Corps in Ogden in June 1934. Oddly enough, the family was not on relief since his father had employment with the Southern Pacific Railroad, but Francis himself was out of work and so was evidently considered eligible. The day after burying his mother he, along with close to one hundred other new Weber County enrollees, left the Ogden post office in late July 1934. After traveling south for about twenty hours in two chartered school buses they arrived in Zion National Park around 5:00 a.m. on July 28.

Welsh was assigned to drought-relief Company 1966 at what was then DNP-2 when the previous occupants, Company 962, had moved up to NP-3 at Bryce Canyon. He credited Captain Charles Kennedy with finally getting some straw ticks to replace the blanket-covered boards on which they originally slept. It was to be another few weeks before they were finally issued some outsized work clothing and the shaving kits they had been promised.

Welsh thoroughly enjoyed his first month serving as an assistant to Park Archaeologist Ben Weatherall. He described the work as "fascinating" and enjoyed staying up late at night cataloging the potsherds and other artifacts they collected while out in the field. Unfortunately, the funding for the archaeologist soon disappeared, and Welsh spent the next two months as what he called a subforeman, probably an assistant leader, building roads to the park quarry, where he learned to handle dynamite.

The floor of Zion Canyon can get extremely hot during the summers, and that summer of 1934 saw temperatures in the triple digits: "The barracks would get to about the temperature of a brick kiln." Captain Kennedy was a good sort, however, and granted permission to wet down the barracks with the fire hoses that were outside each barrack. Welsh explained the results:

> As could be expected of a bunch of high-spirited young men, there were some darn good water fights, too. One evening the C.O. came around one of the barracks and was boweled [*sic*] over with a stream of water, which didn't do his uniform or dignity any good. As a result only one barracks could use a hose at a time after that.[29]

When the camp surgeon was not in camp, the first aid man could exercise considerable influence, as Welsh did in Zion National Park during the miserably cold winter of 1936–37. The doctor was absent, so Captain Chauncey B. Whitney of NP-4 at Bridge Mountain asked Welsh whether he thought it safe for the men to go out to work. Several men were sick with influenza and bad colds, so the reply was negative. The camp commander then told the superintendent, who complained to Zion National Park Superintendent P. P. Patraw, who then called the camp commander. Captain Whitney replied that he could not go against the medical officer, even if he was just an enrollee. Patraw talked to the first aid man himself but to no avail. Next, he reportedly telephoned Fort Douglas, only to be told by the district surgeon that the enrollee status of the first aid man did not matter and that in the absence of the regular doctor he was to be considered the medical officer in charge and his orders regarding the health of the men were to be obeyed. As Welsh related it to me, "I was quite unpopular with P.P.P. for quite awhile until I had to take some fish-hooks out of his grandson's hand."[30]

First aid men had great responsibilities, of course, to go along with their power and were often called up by residents of nearby towns. On one occasion Welsh was on duty alone at the Zion camp when a Springdale man nearly severed his left thumb while getting a Christmas tree for his family. Another time at Bryce Canyon camp NP-3 Welsh treated a seven-year-old boy five hours after the lad had been bitten on his left hand by a rattlesnake. That one Welsh described as "pretty rough." The incident is described more completely in chapter 12.

Welsh served with Company 1966 for all four periods of its existence, always at NP-2 in Zion Canyon except during the summer of 1935, when it was at Cedar Breaks camp NP-5 or NM-1.[31] The company was disbanded on April 12, 1936, and the men moved across the Virgin River to join Company 962 at Bridge Mountain camp NP-4.

Admittedly, Welsh did some things that were outside the norm. For one thing, he had a six-foot-long pet gopher snake with which he terrorized new enrollees over a period of about four months before that activity was brought to a halt. Still his medical expertise enabled him to get away with things for which other enrollees might have experienced discipline.

On March 31, 1937, Welsh was discharged from the Corps with a rating of excellent to take a job with the Weber County Road Commission back up in his hometown of Ogden. When asked whether his CCC training had helped him get the job, he said, "Yes, that and politics." Welsh summarized his CCC experience as "about the most rewarding job I have ever had. Certainly not money-wise, but in more important ways. Certainly better than being senior non-com in a medical detachment with the Engineers in World War II."[32]

The duties of the first aid man included keeping the dispensary spotless; feeding the patients; looking after and driving the ambulance; assisting the doctor in inspections of the camp kitchen, washrooms, and latrines; making out requisitions and reports; and generally being on hand in case of emergencies as well as whatever other responsibilities the surgeon might wish him to have. He was usually designated as a leader, and either he or the camp surgeon was required to be at the camp at all times. If the surgeon was a contract civilian from a nearby community, the responsibility, of course, was that of the first aid man alone, including providing treatment and dispensing medicine.

Some camps had a separate dispensary and hospital constructed in a manner somewhat similar to the barracks, although on a smaller scale.

It was in the dispensary that sick call was held daily, usually in the late afternoon, and minor treatment was carried out. Patients' records, requisitions, and other office materials were kept in this area, as well. The camp hospital of eight to ten beds was usually just next to the dispensary, and here were kept the men too ill or injured to work but not so bad that they needed to be taken to a regular community hospital. Beyond this were located the first aid man's quarters and a one-bed isolation ward. In the summer camps two tents were often combined to provide the medical facilities.[33]

The medical problems created by the often hazardous work and the close confinement of two hundred young men sometimes proved severe. The newspapers of the period reveal that appendicitis was one of the major problems in Utah, especially during the First Enrollment Period. Within a span of one month in 1933 the hospital in Panguitch admitted five enrollees for appendectomies from the Blue Springs camp, F-18; two men suffering from acute appendicitis went to the hospital in Cedar City from the Alton camp, and two from Company 1342 near Vernal received operations.[34]

The following New Year's Eve proved a sad one for Company 1339 at Richfield when two of its members died of appendicitis within a few hours of each other, one just shortly before midnight following an operation in Salina and the other shortly after midnight at the hospital in Provo. Howard K. Nielsen of NP-2 was taken to Cedar City Hospital when his appendix ruptured. Apparently, no doctor there felt that he could handle it, so Captain Frank K. Root flew down from Fort Douglas to successfully operate.[35] Spinal meningitis took the life of a Zion Park enrollee after an illness of one week, also in August 1933.[36]

National records indicate that the Second Period was considerably worse than the First—206 deaths due to disease during the Second Period, compared with eighty-nine during the First. The severe winter and the fact that the Second Period involved more boys and covered a full six months have some bearing on the increase. On the other hand, during the same periods the death rate from injuries increased only from 138 to 178.[37]

The work program sometimes came to a virtual standstill when a major infection struck a camp. In November 1935, scarlet fever hit enrollees at a spike camp at Aspen Grove up American Fork Canyon, and quarantine was immediately imposed. The camp reporter described this as a "minor catastrophe" for the boys just preparing to return to the main camp at F-43 in Pleasant Grove for Thanksgiving dinner the following day. The considerate staff made the best of a bad situation by arranging for the turkey and trimmings to be sent out to the disappointed crew.[38]

A month later a similar experience almost befell the boys of DG-31 in Vernal. Eight Kentucky boys had spinal meningitis, and the doctor quarantined the entire camp. It appeared that Christmas would be celebrated under somewhat confining circumstances. However, only one serious illness developed, and the quarantine was withdrawn two weeks later, just two days before Christmas.[39] That company was quarantined again four months later when an influenza epidemic befell the camp. The same thing happened to Company 958 in Provo during the severe winter of 1936–37. As many as twenty-seven fell sick at once, including the camp commander, Captain Alvin Sessions. Finally the situation became so bad that the men stayed in camp until the return of better weather and less dangerous working conditions. In Provo that same week a twenty-year-old enrollee from Jericho camp DG-26 died as a result of the illness.[40] In one extreme case a camp was completely shut down as a result of sickness, when SP-1 at Locomotive Springs was abandoned due to the tularemia outbreak that took place in 1935.

Throughout the nation pneumonia proved the major cause of death from illness, although this does not appear to have been true in Utah. In October 1937 CCC authorities began an intensive program to curtail the hazard of the disease through the use of a vaccine. Jericho camp DG-26 reported receiving enough serum for seventy-five men and began inoculating volunteers to help determine its efficacy. By 1939 the prevention and treatment program had succeeded in reducing deaths to forty out of a total 806 cases that year, lower than usual for that age group.[41]

Utah enrollees were fortunate in living and working in quite a healthy environment and were spared the problems of malaria and venereal disease that plagued the southern and eastern regions. The Fourth Corps Area, for example, ranked highest in both these types of disease, and the Eighth Corps Area was also very susceptible to both. The Third experienced a great deal of venereal disease, and the Seventh suffered from a high incidence of malaria.[42] Generally a venereal disease was treated until the enrollee was cured, after which he was discharged from the CCC. Still, as the director acknowledged, it could have been worse: the 2,944 cases of venereal disease reported in the CCC in 1941, for example, was about one-third that of the Army.[43]

Former first aid man Francis Welsh recalled only one case of venereal disease from the two Utah companies he served. Diarrhea, on the other hand, proved a much more common problem, especially when nearly the entire camp was affected simultaneously. "Can you picture," asked Welsh, "150 men trying to get into a 16-toilet latrine at the same time?"[44]

The medical care provided for the enrollees was, perhaps somewhat surprisingly, of generally high quality. The men were encouraged to report for medical treatment immediately upon receiving the slightest injury or indication of illness "because the trivial illness usually disappears quickly with prompt treatment. Whereas, if unattended, it may become very serious."[45] Sick call was held first thing in the morning and again late in the afternoon. At this time injuries were redressed as necessary, and medication and treatment were prescribed and administered under the supervision of the camp doctor. If injured or sick, the enrollee spent an average of eight days under care. About 50 percent of the cases required hospitalization; the others received treatment in either camp dispensaries or the enrollee's quarters.

The rate of those absent from duty daily because of illness stood at 24.1 per thousand in 1940, slightly lower than the figure for white enlisted men in the Army.[46] Great importance was attached to success in keeping the men on the job, as indicated by a camp report that stated that, in spite of the fact that its men were untrained, the camp got through the winter without suffering any accidents or sickness.[47] During the first year of the CCC, the death rate among enrollees was only slightly lower than that of men in the same age group elsewhere; by 1941 the situation had improved considerably.[48] The constant emphasis on bodily cleanliness and the need for proper sanitation methods no doubt contributed to the improved health circumstances. From the beginning the physical development of the enrollees was regarded as one of the objectives of the program.

It's certainly true that there were occasional accidents during the often hazardous work in which the enrollees were engaged. Also, the sickness sometimes taking place among a large group of men living in close quarters could not have been pleasant. In spite of these negatives, the conditions under which they worked were usually quite positive, although at the time this might have been a subject for debate. Strenuous work in the fresh, pure air usually has a positive effect on one's physical condition. And then there was the food.

The Army pointed with pride to the records that showed that the average enrollee gained about ten pounds during his first period of work. Many enrollees, especially those from the cities, regarded this as a major accomplishment. Most of the men were eating the best meals they had encountered in several months—and for some, perhaps the best in their lives. The junior officer of the camp was usually detailed as mess officer, but specially appointed enrollees did the cooking. As long as they stayed within the allowance of approximately thirty cents a day per man, the cooks were allowed freedom and could generally determine their own menus.[49]

A fairly standard supper at the Bountiful camp, for example, was chicken, lettuce and tomato salad, creamed peas, mashed potatoes, ice cream, and lemonade, while salmon, salad, prunes, and iced tea formed the nucleus for dinner. Is it any wonder that a boy from Virginia or Pennsylvania at Diamond Fork camp F-8 was able to gain thirty-two pounds in six weeks?[50] Still, teenaged boys being what they are, when asked what they wanted the answer was usually, "More."

However, General Malin Craig of the Ninth Corps Area recommended that the meals be altered from day to day. For breakfast, he recommended that on one day the meal consist of oatmeal mush, milk, fried bacon, scrambled eggs, fried potatoes, bread, butter, and coffee. The second day the cook might serve fresh bananas, cornmeal mush, hash, milk, bread and butter, and coffee. Equal variety was suggested for dinner and supper. However, General Craig seems to have had the mealtime needs of the enrollees pretty well figured out: "Because the men will have completed only half of their day's work prior to the noonday meal, this meal will be lighter than the one served in the evening, at which time the workers will likely have a greater appetite and will have more time to enjoy the food."

The success of this objective is indicated by the increase in height and weight achieved by the enrollees. In April 1934, fifty-six men were discharged from Company 1339 at Richfield. Two of the men had lost weight; fifty-four had gained, one of them thirty pounds. The average gain per man was about ten pounds, the approximate mean in the camps across the country. Generally, enrollees from rural areas put on more weight and did so more rapidly than their companions from cities and larger towns. The increase in height was approximately a half inch for both rural and urban enrollees. The "typical enrollee" was described in a 1937 report as weighing approximately 147 pounds and standing five feet, eight and a half inches, seven pounds heavier and slightly taller than the 1940 figures would indicate.[51] CCC youths, on the average, showed greater increases in height and weight than did college students or soldiers in the Regular Army in the same age group.[52] The increase in their overall physical well-being and general muscular development was certainly one of the more significant accomplishments of the CCC program.

That the young men experienced a significant weight gain should not be surprising considering that, as previously mentioned, some of them were eating three good meals a day for the first time in their lives. In addition to preparing the nourishing fare of the regular meals, camp cooks usually went to great lengths to make holiday meals something quite extravagant. Although certainly not typical of regular repasts, the Christmas meal of Clover Creek camp DG-28 in 1936 is an example of what could be accomplished when the cooks really put their minds to it, to establish the claim that the 175 boys of Company 2517 were "the best fed 'woodpeckers' in the United States." Planned by enrollee William Angier, described as "formerly of a prominent restaurant," the meal included two hundred pounds of turkey, candied yams, tomatoes, two hundred pounds of Idaho potatoes, fifty dozen hot biscuits, the same number of French rolls, thirty dozen cinnamon rolls, forty pumpkin pies, and forty apple pies. To finance the gastronomical blowout, money had been saved from the regular food allowance over the previous weeks.[53]

In spite of the size of the regular meals many enrollees also had a desire for evening snacks. Enrollee Guy Pollock, according to his son, developed a liking for mayonnaise sandwiches. Since bread and mayo were the only eatables not locked up at night, young Pollock's raids on the kitchen soon developed into quite a craving for the somewhat unusual food item.[54]

In spite of the usual satisfaction, food was sometimes a catalyst for trouble in the camps. Company 1966 at Zion National Park experienced a minor incident one morning when one small plate of bacon was placed on each breakfast table to be divided among eight hungry enrollees. A former first aid man describes the scene:

> Nothing was said. The men just sat there. The head K.P. (kitchen police) ordered the mess-hall cleared. They just sat there and looked at him. The company clerk left to take care of the sick book

> and I left to take care of sick call at the dispensary. There were quite a few speeches made by both Army personnel, and ECW [Emergency Conservation Work] personnel, without results. When the "Pie Wagon" was dispatched to Cedar City to get emergency rations for dinner the men got up and left the mess hall. That afternoon they went back out on the projects. At no time was there any demonstration or noise. That was one of the times the Captain had the stem-winding hell scared out of him. It never did happen again.[55]

No regular dental service was provided for the enrollees prior to 1937. Treatment was limited to emergency service only "for the relief of pain or the repair of injuries sustained in the performance of duty."[56] Dentists from communities near the camps took care of this type of work as there were no dental officers on CCC duty. Beginning in February 1937, 168 Reserve dental officers drew calls to active duty and assignment to the various Corps Areas.[57] Four motorized dental teams were organized in the Fort Douglas District and visited the camps according to a schedule, staying about two weeks in each. The team consisted of an enrollee driver, an enrollee dental assistant, and a Reserve dental officer who administered emergency treatment in addition to regular dental work as time and facilities would permit. Treatment was available to enrollees only, although the dentists could extend treatment to other CCC personnel where relief from pain was desired.[58] On July 1, 1939, civilian dentists operating on a contract basis assumed responsibility for the dental care of the enrollees.[59]

Captain Willis C. Miner, assistant district dental surgeon of Fort Douglas District, made a typical visit to Provo in early 1937 and spent an entire day examining the men of Company 958 to determine the number of extractions and emergency fillings necessary. This was the first time the company had been treated with more time and attention than might otherwise have been the case. Officials estimated that six men could be treated each day and that it would take about six weeks to service the camps in Provo and Pleasant Grove. That first year there were 270,275 permanent fillings placed in CCC teeth across the nation and 169,730 teeth extracted, more than in either of the following two years.[60]

This systematic treatment was the first exposure to dental care that many of the enrollees had ever experienced, and the performance of remedial and preventive work on so many teeth of so many young Americans must rank as another success for the CCC program in improving the physical well-being of its men.

There were many accomplishments in this area: the increase in the height and weight of most of the enrollees, the instruction received in personal hygiene, the creation of attitudes regarding safety, and the development of skill in handling dangerous tools, equipment, and explosives in a relatively safe manner. In these physical ways the enrollee emerged from his experience a better man than when he went in.

CHAPTER 11

Life in the Camps—and Out

[In camp I spent my time] playing poker, checkers, chess, baseball, and taking pictures. Out of camp: chasing girls.
—Kenneth Bray, enrollee, camps NP-2, F-42, F-48

In an attempt to provide activities and to forestall any undesirable situations in camp, company officers encouraged lively recreational and educational programs. Chaplains or junior officers originally had responsibility for the loosely organized recreational activities. This was turned over to the educational advisers (EAs) when they became part of the camp leadership in 1934, and the recreational program then became more complete and varied—the variety usually limited only by the imagination of the EA and the wishes of the enrollees. The role of educational adviser is explained more thoroughly later in the chapter.

A quick survey of contemporary newspapers partially reveals the scope of the activities. The Logan Lions Club put on a program for F-34 complete with musical selections, tap dancing, and a speaker. A month later the choir from the Brigham City Second Ward of the Church of Jesus Christ of Latter-day Saints (LDS) performed at the same camp. At Jericho, DG-26 put on an amateur night and awarded prizes to the winners. Three weeks later, another was held at the same camp. There were performances on the cornet and harmonica, a magic act, dancing, and even a pie-eating contest.[1]

Across the state of Utah, camp and community newspapers served as a virtual CCC diary of the period by relating those incidents that seldom made their way into official reports. It is to these newspapers and to the personal accounts of the participants themselves that later generations must look to investigate one of the most interesting facets of this most interesting program, that is, just how life was lived in the CCC.

NEWSPAPERS: COMMUNITY AND CAMP

Local community newspapers generally cooperated with the CCC camps and often provided space for a regular column of camp news. "CCC Chatter" headed a front-page feature of the *Kane County Standard* in early 1934. In 1936, the same paper occasionally had articles on three or four camps in the same issue. The *Springville Herald* had a fairly regular column entitled "CCC Camp News Items" or sometimes just "CC Camp News" in 1934. The coverage given in 1935 was sparse, but in 1936, "Scenes from CC [or CCC] Camp" appeared with greater frequency. By 1937, however, Company 958 no longer returned to Hobble Creek Canyon for the summer, and the column disappeared completely. The *American Fork Citizen* included a weekly article on camp F-5 in 1933; the *Pleasant Grove Review* was equally cooperative with F-43 in 1937 and 1938. The *Eureka Reporter* included "Jericho CCC Camp News" among its regular features.

On May 20, 1933, two young men in Washington began publishing *Happy Days*, originally a twelve-page weekly that eventually became the official house organ of the CCC. Many of the camps followed suit with their own papers, either weekly, semimonthly, or monthly publications, usually between four and twenty quarto-sized multicolored pages. All the editors of the camp newspapers also acted as unofficial reporters of the parent *Happy Days*, to which they made frequent contributions.[2]

Utah had its share of camp newspapers, published by the enrollees with the assistance of the educational adviser. The *Southern Drawl* was published "on or about the fifteenth of each month" by Company 479 of F-32 in Salina. In March 1938, the staff consisted of fourteen enrollees, all gaining newspaper experience: an editor, an assistant editor, an associate editor, a circulation manager, five reporters, two cartoonists, a typist, and two pressroom operators. The twelve-page, quarto-sized paper had columns on camp projects, educational opportunities, poetry, stories, and camp news. The *CCC Courier* was, according to its own words, "published every Friday—Rain or Shine—by Camp F-1, Company 957." The single, eight-by-fourteen-inch sheet included stories about various enrollees and featured a "confidential" column by one "Dirthy Tix," all for the subscription price of one cent a copy.

Figure 11.1. Belden Lewis of Company 1966, inadvertently (though most deservedly) recognized on a statue plaque for his photographic and literary contributions to Civilian Conservation Corps history at Zion and Bryce national parks.

Quite often a journalism class at the camp prepared the newspaper. Such was the case with the *Bay Cross News* of SP-2 at Farmington Bay and the *Western Star*, put out by enrollees of Company 2558 at Hurricane camp DG-150. At Hurricane the journalism class elected the ten staff members for the camp paper. Volume 1, number 1, of the ten-page, quarto-sized mimeographed paper came out on December 25, 1939. Within a few days, however, the staff had decided to go for a one-page daily instead, appropriately renamed the *Daily Star*. Publication continued *almost* daily until at least April 12, 1940, which is the last issue found in Folder 9 of Box 8 of the camp newspapers at the Utah State Historical Society. Fortunately, most of Utah's CCC camp newspapers were sent almost immediately to the University of Illinois, where they were deposited until eventually ending up back in Utah.[3] A few of the CCC newspapers housed in the Utah State Historical Society carried advertisements, although this does not seem to have been the general rule.

The camp papers changed name, format, and personnel with considerable rapidity. The news staff at the Jericho camp planned to call their product the *Desert Breeze* after having given up the eight-page paper known as the *Spillway*. The following month, however, they announced that it was to be the *Wails of Jericho*, which would be published monthly. Further changes followed, and the imaginative title gave way to the *Jericho Journal* when it finally achieved publication in June 1938.[4]

Another company organ with a creative title was *Zionodak*, reflecting its current location as well as its origin: Zion National Park and North Dakota. This began publication on Christmas Day, 1936, by Company 4779, which had arrived about two months previously from, yes, North Dakota. It wasn't long, however, before the name was changed to the somewhat more prosaic *Hi Life*, but it continued under the able editorship of enrollee Belden Lewis, who was to have considerable experience in that position.[5]

One of the most regular of the camp publications was the *Vernal Journal*, which began in February 1936 as a biweekly newspaper for DG-31. Like most camp organs it was mimeographed, but for the special Mother's Day edition in 1939 the enrollee staff arranged to have it printed by the community's *Vernal Express*. On June 24, 1940, the *Journal*, by a now a fifteen-page monthly, proudly announced its upcoming status as a daily publication headed by seven coeditors.[6]

Pleasant Grove was another camp with an active newspaper program. Camp F-43 was originally located in that city, and enrollee A. F. Fischio became the first editor of the *Mt. Timpanogos Crier*, a successful publication run off on a mimeograph machine at the Pleasant Grove High School.[7] By November 1937, Fischio's company had left to be replaced by Company 3544. A new paper was organized, and four months later the first edition of the semimonthly news sheet was issued. The editors recognized the origins of the Fifth Corps Area camp by naming their paper *W.O.I.K.*, for West Virginia, Ohio, Indiana, and Kentucky.[8] This Forest Service camp closed in 1938, and by 1939 the camp was reopened by the Bureau of Reclamation as BR-91. Company 1968 moved down from Bridgeland, where it had already established a journalistic tradition.

The *Bridgeland News Weekly* had operated under the editorship of enrollee Grant Young, and this was followed by the *Bridgeland Bulletin*, published until the company transferred to Pleasant Grove in October 1939, where it became the short-lived *Timpanogos Gazette*. It was on Christmas, 1939, that the camp newspaper began its daily circulation as the *P.G. Bee*. Six reporters wrote for the single-page sheet. In January 1940, Glenn Ingalsbe, the camp barber and humor editor, began an informative column entitled "Who's Who in Camp," in which he presented interesting biographies on various members of the company. Sections entitled "Camp Notes" and "Something Interesting," occasional poetry, and a section on the educational program became regular features. The month after it commenced operations, the *P.G. Bee* was awarded a five-star rating by *Happy Days*, one of five daily camp newspapers to get this highest rating during the month of January.[9]

The *Longhorn Weekly* of DG-32 at Dalton Wells varied from the usual quarto format as a smaller six-by-eight-inch publication. What it lacked in size, however, it made up for in content. The May 14, 1939, issue boasted what I've perceived to be the maximum length of sixty pages. Some papers contained nothing but camp gossip and news of very little consequence. Most, however, had news describing the work projects and information about the technical agency. This issue of the *Longhorn Weekly* had an informative article by reporter Jack Davies, appropriately entitled "All in a Day's Work," in which he described the typical workday beginning at 6:00 a.m. and the activities of the day in two-hour segments through work, lunch, returning to camp, retreat, and evening activities until 10:00 p.m.: "Ten o'clock. The lights go out and the taps are blown. The echo echoes and re-echoes amongst the surrounding hills. The echo fades and he marks the end of another day in his life in the CCCs."[10] And with only minor alterations that is just about the way it was, at least at that camp at that time.

Some camp papers were very thorough in describing the work projects in which enrollees were engaged, much to the delight of those wanting to learn more about what the CCC actually did. Although the *Company 529 News* lacked a very imaginative title and even failed to put the date on its masthead, the content more than made up for these shortcomings. In mid-1938 the activities of DG-27 at Castle Dale were thoroughly described. The rodent control crew under Foreman Allen Lowry "has covered more acreage in the two seasons they have been at this type of work than any other Division of Grazing camp." Foreman Howard LeFevre's crew was building a rubble-rock dam in Sid's Hollow, working out of Calf Canyon spike camp. Foreman David Tuttle's crew was bringing aspen poles and red pine lumber out of Manti National Forest. Foreman Leslie Moffitt had one group from his crew on Dutch Flat Dam (about five miles southeast of Ferron) and the rest on Dry Wash Road.[11]

The *Weekly News* of DG-28 at Clover Creek under editor E. M. Gardner was a similar publication, both in the unimaginative name and in the value of the coverage. Reporters covered and described each of the six work projects then in the works, consisting of erecting a telephone line, constructing roads, and eradicating noxious weeds, along with the names of the foremen, size of the crews, and other items of interest.[12] In years to come, this type of journalism would be more likely to appeal to nostalgic CCC alumni than the jokes and gossip that were the usual fare of some of the publications seeking to provide instant laughs but little else.

LIBRARIES AND LETTERS

A camp newspaper, of course, was only one of a variety of after-hours activities with which an ambitious enrollee might get involved. There was initially some mention that welfare organizations such as the Young Men's Christian Association and the Knights of Columbus would supply recreational facilities for movies, baseball, and library services. As this didn't materialize, the Army again stepped in, usually beginning with a small reading area. In June 1933, Major General Malin Craig, commanding general of the Ninth Corps Area, ordered that 250 books be shipped to each camp. Reference books, dictionaries, pamphlets on forestry and related topics, textbooks, and general works were included in the shipment. An additional three "traveling libraries" of about one hundred books of fiction and travel were also assigned to the Fort Douglas District. Magazines and newspapers, including those from the company's home state, were supplied to each camp. Commercial businesses helped out as well, such as Peterson's Drug Store in Cedar City, which donated all its left-over magazines.[13] Even stationery was provided—enough to permit each enrollee to write two letters a week.[14]

Letter writing, in fact, developed into quite an art for many of the more expressive of the youths. One man, several years older than the others, was prevailed upon by several of his colleagues to write letters to their girlfriends at home. He discontinued this quickly, however, when some of the boys began receiving proposals of marriage.[15] At F-2, Max Schlegel, camp correspondent for the local newspaper, advertised similar secretarial help. He offered to take dictated letters in shorthand after which they would be typed and returned to the "author" for his signature. The work and the stationery would be provided for only five cents. The literary John Alden announced that his motto would be "Hear nothing, see nothing, say nothing."[16]

One of the more successful letter writers was Ray Martyne of Company 469 at DG-35. He participated in a contest sponsored by the national CCC newspaper, *Happy Days*, to respond to the question "What is the meaning of Practical Education?" His was judged the "best of the hundreds of letters." Although the *Milford News* carried the essay in its entirety, nothing was said of Martyne's prize.[17]

The impetus for letter writing might come from anywhere. Foreman E. W. Simons of Mt. Nebo camp F-9 had his men write an open letter containing their opinions of camp life. It seems that originally the men were concerned about the money they would make, but after two weeks their objectives expanded to include gaining good health, learning an occupation, and developing discipline. As their attitudes changed they expressed an interest in the forests and a desire to help in their conservation.[18]

It may be debated whether the following letter was seriously written, but it was presented in a Cache Valley newspaper as one from an enrollee to his friend back home. My guess is that the writer was enjoying a case of tongue-in-cheek:

> You know I wrote you about the ticks when I first landed here in Utah. The folks said these ticks would bite you and you'd turn all over spots and swell up and die. Boy, was I scared. I never seen a tick back in Jersey. I thought a tick was what a clock says. I tho't I saw a tick running up a tree one time and I tho't he was getting up there to jump on me and bite me and boy did I run! When I told the captain this tick had a bushy tail and jumped from branch to branch in the tree, boy, did he laugh and how!
>
> P.S. They've got the workingest sun in this country you ever saw. Sunset don't come till almost midnight and then the sun gets up again about one o'clock in the morning and it makes it hard for me to get enough sleep.[19]

Getting enough sleep could indeed be a challenge for the enrollee determined to take advantage of everything a camp had to offer.

EDUCATION PROGRAM

Since the Civilian Conservation Corps was organized to provide relief for thousands of unemployed young men and to help in the conservation of many of our natural resources, lawmakers had made no plan for an educational program in the original bill. In some cases, however, Utah enrollees themselves sought the opportunity of furthering their education while in the camps. In late July 1933, a group of young men in the Blacksmith Fork camp F-2 approached their commanding officer and Forest Service personnel about educational possibilities in the areas of fish and fishing, range use, erosion, fire hazards, geology, and horticulture, among others. Within a short time the Camp F-2 Research Club was organized and meeting twice a week.[20]

CCC historian John Salmond states that W. Frank Persons, the director of selection, "probably" should get credit for introducing the concept of using the Corps for educational purposes.[21] Director Robert Fechner was not originally impressed with the idea, nor was the Army, which reportedly feared the introduction of radical ideas among the men. It wasn't long, however, before the movement for education had grown stronger and quickly received support from many quarters, including the U.S. commissioner of education, universities, professional foresters, and even President Roosevelt.

Many military authorities in Washington openly resented the program, but little of this resentment found expression on the camp level, at least in Utah. Salmond feels that in spite of dissatisfaction in some quarters with the role of the Army, "the vesting of ultimate responsibility with the Department of War was the best practical solution."[22] Further fragmentation of authority in a camp could well have pushed inherently strained relations past the breaking point. As it was, the Army, although no doubt less skilled than professional educators, was considerably more enthusiastic in its support of a program of its own creation.

Forest Service personnel in Utah had begun making plans for classes as soon as the education idea was first mentioned. In December 1933, officials met at regional headquarters in Ogden to discuss the types of courses that would be offered in their camps. As yet unaware of just what educational resources would be available, the Forest Service wisely decided to limit its offerings to such basic courses as forestry and the operation of audiovisual equipment, courses that could easily be taught with the personnel then in the camps willing to teach after hours on a volunteer basis.[23]

Those responsible soon realized that the key to a successful educational program lay primarily in the hands of a capable educational adviser, an individual able to carry out a plan geared to a wide variety of needs and interests of young men expected to sit in a classroom after a day of hard work in the field. The educational adviser was expected to help each enrollee learn something of available occupations in order that he might be able to make some progress in selecting his life's vocation on his return to the "outside" world. In summary, the EA, as the educational adviser soon became known in CCC jargon, was expected to "help every enrolled man make the most constructive use of his capabilities."[24] Still another statement of suitable requirements suggested that he have a desire to help others, possess a sense of humor, have spiritual qualities without being a "sissy," refrain from being a "stool pigeon," be broad-minded, and possess initiative and financial integrity.[25]

One might well question the demands of such a task that would require a person of such tremendous capabilities. A "Handbook for Educational Advisors," first issued in January 1934, outlined his duties, and as the program developed subsequent instructions were given through conferences and visits by district and Corps Area supervisors. The educational adviser had the responsibility of administering the camp educational program, which entailed setting up sixteen to twenty classes to meet the needs and interests of two hundred young men, finding the camp personnel or local schoolteachers to staff the classes, and making out the multitude of reports for the camp commander and the district education officials. He served as a counselor and a coordinator. He was a liaison officer between the Army, the technical service, and the boys themselves and found himself occasionally in bad graces with at least one of the three groups. He acted as the camp's public relations expert and had to keep the local newspaper supplied with favorable articles. He often had great influence but actually had very little power, certainly not commensurate with his responsibility, as he could only recommend courses of action. He took many orders but gave very few.

Some men proved unable to cope with the demands of the position and left CCC employment at the first opportunity. Others carried on in an attitude of pessimism brought about by inadequate supplies and facilities, lack of cooperation from the local public schools, or unsympathetic camp leadership.

The EA, although a civilian, wore a military-type uniform and was attached to the Army rather than to the technical agency of his camp. He took over responsibility for the camp in the absence of the camp commander and junior officer, occasionally served as law enforcement officer, and took his turn in leading the morning exercises in addition to what might be considered the more routine activities of an educator.[26] For all this he had only one regular helper—an enrollee with the rank of assistant leader appointed on the EA's recommendation to the position of assistant educational adviser. Nevertheless, the educational advisers in Utah carried on doing the best they could under their particular circumstances. As one former EA put it after six years' experience, "Really, a good EA had to be a superman.... It was a tough but a noble job." In compensation the educational adviser received the use of a camp car and a driver, free lodging, meals at cost, and a salary of $1,980 a year. District EAs received the same salary when first authorized; they later were paid $2,750.[27] Had they but known, they could have taken comfort that in years to come many of their students would look back upon their efforts with gratitude and admiration.

Such educational activities were carried out even before the position of educational adviser had been set up on the camp level. The first educational advisers in the entire program were selected in February 1934 and at first were expected to serve two and sometimes three camps. On March 3, 1934, D. L. Pack became the first educational adviser in the Fort Douglas District and drew assignment to Company 940 at Woods Cross camp SE-205.[28]

The initial offerings were those classes with a direct application to the work assignments, although it wasn't long before the night school classes at one camp, at least, came up with plans for teaching mathematics and geology. The commanding officer even offered to teach a course in the elementary principles of aviation, and the Army chaplain proposed to make arrangements for a series of lectures by visiting college professors.[29]

Pack, in addition to serving as camp EA at SE-205, was appointed "educational coordinator" for the Fort Douglas District in October 1934.[30] Basically, however, the original twenty-one CCC districts of the Ninth Corps Area remained the direct educational responsibility of Corps Area Advisor John B. Griffing, formerly president of San Bernardino Junior College in California, until district advisers were authorized in July 1935.

Dr. Reynolds C. Merrill, then EA of Company 958 in Utah County, was tapped to actually become the first official educational adviser for the entire Fort Douglas District in April 1935. Leadership changes occurred rapidly, however, and the position was quite fluid until Norman Hamilton succeeded Edward H. Isenberg in early 1940. Hamilton had been a high school principal in Logan and in Carbon County before going to work for the CCC in 1935. He served at MA-1 in Provo and F-48 in Bountiful, but within a few weeks he became educational adviser over all thirty-nine camps of the Fort Douglas District.[31] Lloyd C. Whitlock graduated from Brigham Young University and was EA at Duck Creek camp F-16 in 1936 and 1937. He later worked at Escalante and moved to replace Hamilton at MA-1 in November 1939. He finished his CCC work by again following Hamilton into the office of district EA.

Soon after the program commenced each camp set up a "Committee on Education." The commanding officer, educational adviser, project superintendent, and one enrollee chosen by the camp commander met at least semimonthly for the purpose of reviewing progress and making plans.[32] The camp commander was expected to take an active part in the program and not merely assume titular responsibility while an overburdened educational adviser did all the work.

As just one example, it is worth detailing the service of one educational adviser, Karl Bunnell. Bunnell's breadth of experience in the CCC was probably as wide and varied as anyone's I contacted. In addition to serving as one of Utah's outstanding educational advisers he also worked as foreman and camp commander. His span of service could hardly have been longer, having served from 1933 until 1942. He worked in camps administered by the Forest Service, Bureau of Reclamation, and Soil Conservation Service as well as with companies of different Corps Areas. Most of the CCC information here has come from extensive correspondence with him in 1968 and 1969 and company newspapers in camps where he served. His son, Lee Bunnell, a retired professor and administrator of Dixie College in St. George, was very helpful in providing most of the personal information. He confirmed what I had expected about his father's excellent memory, being able to nail down exact dates that, in most cases, I was able to confirm from other sources.

Karl Bunnell was working for the U.S. Bureau of Fisheries when the CCC began but soon transferred to the Forest Service to begin his CCC experience as a foreman in Black's Fork camp F-7 in northeastern Utah on June 20, 1933. His work there was primarily in building roads with young men from Company 231 out of New York, although he spent about a month at a Mirror Lake spike camp stocking fish, an activity he was to duplicate about a year later.

His interest in the outdoor life could be traced to his growing up on a farm in Utah County. With his 225 pounds packed on a six-foot one-inch frame he was an asset to the football and track teams for Brigham Young University, where he graduated with a degree in botany. It was at university that he met Provo girl Helen Webster, whom he married on August 25, 1930, in Salt Lake City.

When F-7 closed at the end of that first summer of 1933 Bunnell was transferred to F-24 at Leeds at the opposite end of the state, again as foreman, again in building roads. Although Company 1335 was nominally a Third Corps Area company, the camp was staffed primarily by young men from Utah.

While at F-24 Bunnell was encouraged by Ed Gurr, supervisor of the Dixie National Forest, to develop a program of night classes to be taught by Army and technical service personnel for seven camps in southern Utah. Officially, however, he was still a foreman when he transferred to Soapstone camp F-6 east of Kamas on May 15, 1934, to spend the rest of the Third Period. He was still building roads, although he also worked on stream and lake improvement, including stocking fish in the Mirror Lake region. At the end of the summer of 1934, Bunnell was transferred with Company 960 to Salina camp F-32 for the following year, where again he built roads in addition to fences, corrals, and flood-control structures. The camp closed down around November 1, 1935, and Company 960 was dissolved, with the enrollees being distributed to other camps.

Bunnell later left his work as a Forest Service foreman and began a new phase of his CCC career on August 6, 1936. When the education scheme was officially instituted he applied for a position as an educational adviser and began his formal education work at Bridgeland camp BR-11. Here Bunnell replaced R. A. "Pop" Morris Jr. as EA when Morris transferred to BR-12 in Huntsville. In addition to having in-camp classes taught by Army and Bureau of Reclamation personnel, Bunnell had many correspondence classes offered by the University of California. All I learned of him at BR-11 came from the October 16, 1936, issue of *CCC Reflections*, the camp newspaper, which stated that the company was "very fortunate" in having Bunnell as EA and that "many improvements have taken place and we are proud of our camp educational department."[33]

Bunnell subsequently joined Company 958 at Provo camp F-40, where he spent the next five years. Here he arranged with Provo High School to offer credit for classes taken, enabling several of the enrollees to actually graduate from high school. He also received similar cooperation from Brigham Young University, which offered classes for the training of foremen, for which college credit was offered. Bunnell expanded his own education by taking a Red Cross lifesaving and water safety course and between 1938 and 1941 passed on that training to an estimated four hundred young men, as well as teaching first aid to another six hundred during his CCC years.

F-40 was abandoned on July 1, 1941, and Bunnell served brief periods as EA with the Soil Conservation Service at Mt. Pleasant camp SCS-5 until December 1941 and at Price camp SCS-3 for the following two months. With the advent of World War II most of the Reserve Army officers were being called to active military duty, so at the latter camp he was, in his words, "drafted" as company commander. Bunnell subsequently transferred to Big Cottonwood camp F-38 east of Salt Lake City, also as company commander, until he helped close it down on August 3, 1942.

After leaving the Corps in 1942 Bunnell worked nearly thirty years for Geneva Steel Company on the outskirts of Orem in Utah County and later for its parent company, United States Steel Corporation in Lander, Wyoming. At the time of our correspondence in 1968–69, Bunnell was superintendent of personnel services. After nearly thirty years in the steel industry he retired at the age of sixty-three, and subsequently he and his wife moved to St. George, Utah, where they had children living. Bunnell lived there another ten years before passing away on January 22, 1991, at the age of eighty-two. He is buried in Provo, where he was born and raised.

The filing of the "Monthly Educational Report" was among the regular responsibilities of the camp educational adviser. This listed the courses taught, the grade level of the course, the name of the instructor, the number of weekly meetings of the class, and the average attendance.[34]

At one time each enrollee was averaging ten hours of classes a week, all offered in the evening after work or by correspondence from the University of California.[35] The adult education program of the Provo schools made the camp educational program even more attractive since it offered several classes to which the enrollees were invited.[36]

Five different types of courses beckoned the men of F-34 in Hyrum. The "academic" program included English, mathematics, government, journalism, psychology, and nature study. The "vocational" program offered auto mechanics, radio, baking, cooking, landscape gardening, and photography. Fire supervision and forest operation were part of the "forestry" offerings, while bookkeeping and salesmanship made up the program for the "business vocational" program. "General" courses included first aid, singing, safety, personal hygiene, and leadership.[37] Although most of the camps had their educational programs in the evening, the Hyrum boys met at 7:30 a.m. to receive first aid instruction from the camp surgeon on Mondays, social science and government from the company commander on Tuesdays, and so on. The ever-popular first aid class always proved quite a favorite since a first aid certificate was required before one could qualify for a rating as assistant leader.[38]

The commanding officer of DG-26 taught a class in office procedure. The junior officer held a class in aviation. German, shorthand, typing, and history were also available, as well as courses in music and the handling of explosives. In addition to the offerings available in camp, about 50 percent of the enrollees worked on correspondence courses, the most popular being surveying, auto mechanics, and commercial law.[39]

Ninth Corps Area Educational Advisor Griffing initiated the Correspondence Extension Service, administered by the Bureau of Vocational Rehabilitation under the California Department of Education. Funds granted by the Federal Emergency Relief Administration helped finance the program, which in March 1935 reached 17,593 enrollees in the Ninth Corps Area. The first ten courses, each of which lasted for twelve lessons, included auto mechanics, business English, diesel engines, "How to Study," elementary aeronautics, forestry, blueprint reading, journalism, practical photography, and psychology.[40] Later courses in the Ninth Corps Area were distributed by such institutions as the University of California, one of forty across the country that did extension work for the CCC.[41] An enrollee of the Salina camp took a course in higher accounting that he found very helpful, and in 1968 he was the manager of a bank in Provo.[42] There were reportedly more correspondence courses under way in the Ninth than in all the other Corps Areas combined.[43]

The educational adviser had the responsibility of finding teachers for his classes. He generally taught several of the classes himself, and Army and technical service personnel usually conducted classes as well. Superintendent Walter A. Rupea of DG-103 taught eight different classes a week, varying from one to four hours of classroom instruction.[44] One EA with more than seven years' experience in the CCC reported, "In most cases the technical services personnel from all branches were very competent and in most cases, supported the educational program, both as to academic training and training on the job."[45] A study of available Division of Grazing reports indicates that each member of the staff averaged about eight hours a week of classroom teaching.

Local elementary teachers taught classes—some voluntarily, while others received payment. Mrs. Sadie Avery had seventy-two Southern boys, several of them illiterate. Few had gone beyond the fourth grade. She taught them history, reading, writing, and arithmetic, all without the aid of textbooks. Mrs. Avery thought that the enrollees were "real sweet boys," although she also felt that the local people didn't care much for them. She later commented that they all smoked until she asked them to quit for her sake; she reported the they all marched to the door, threw their cigarettes away, and never smoked in class again.[46]

Dedicated foremen, educational advisers, and camp officers often engaged in "extra mile" activities for the enrollees. Ellis Shurtz, a foreman at four different camps, stated, "With the help of the [local] first-grade teacher I held a class each day and taught reading, writing, counting of numbers, times tables, etc." While foreman at the Manila camp, William Laursen spent many nights teaching illiterate and homesick Kentucky boys to write their names and to tell time. Most proved eager to learn and were very appreciative of the help offered them.[47]

L. John Nuttall, superintendent of schools in Salt Lake City, studied eighteen camps in Utah and Idaho during the winter of 1934–35. He reported that of 3,502 enrolled, 28.6 percent had only elementary schooling, 64.6 percent had some high school, and 6.8 percent had some college. Of the 2,254 with only high school exposure, just 814 had entered their senior year. These figures compare quite favorably with national figures compiled that same year, which indicated that about 49 percent of all CCC enrollees had not progressed beyond an elementary education, 48 percent had had some high school experience, and only 3 percent had enrolled in college. The average enrollee had completed 8.7 years of education.[48] Nuttall reported that the boys did not want the traditional type of schooling, from which many of them had in fact run away. Perhaps due to the Latter-day Saint emphasis upon education, companies made up of Utahns generally had an educational level higher than the national average.

In her study of four not necessarily typical camps, Thora Bergeson reveals the results of a survey by R. C. Merrill, district educational adviser, on the educational attainment in the camps of the district. The Ninth Corps Area camp F-48, made up completely of Utahns, showed an attainment of 11.2 years of school, as compared with 10.0 years for the Second Corps Area camp F-38, 9.2 years for the Seventh Corps Area camp SCS-4, and 9.0 years for the Fifth Corps Area camp SP-2.[49]

The enrollee usually encountered the educational program when he first entered camp. In normal procedure, camp officials explained some of the aspects of camp life to a new group. At F-43 Superintendent Frank Hyde conducted interviews himself with the help of one clerk. As replacements joined the camp, Hyde talked to them about their previous training and experience, their wishes for education and employment, and their reasons for enrolling. The clerk placed the information in their permanent records, and the data were used in filling vacancies and planning classes. The enrollees appreciated the interest shown, and the personal concern of the superintendent had a positive effect on camp morale.[50]

In most camps, the educational adviser conducted individual interviews during which he encouraged enrollees to try and determine their vocational goals and then take classes that would help in their attainment. The enrollees filled out a four-page questionnaire containing information on themselves, their parents, school and work experience, and likes and dislikes in reading, sports, and use of leisure time.[51] Educational advisers used this information to get acquainted with the men and become better equipped to counsel them and to stimulate them educationally.

Camps administered by the Division of Grazing generally had quite active programs. Dalton Wells camp DG-32 in the remote eastern portion of the state announced that "for those with higher aspirations the equivalent of a college course is offered in Psychology and Journalism."[52] During the same period, an increase in educational activity advanced DG-27 at Castle Dale from thirty-first to third place among the Fort Douglas District camps. In addition to the usual academic and vocational offerings, courses were available in "correct attitudes, character development, and correct living."[53]

The reports of Hanksville camp DG-114 indicate that class enrollment varied from two enrollees taking blacksmithing to seventeen attending the class in leadership, generally one of the more popular classes throughout all the camps. In addition, a special class in English was conducted for twenty-three Spanish-speaking youths.[54] Instructors at Provo camp MA-1 provided fifty different classes, ranging from reading and writing for the four or five enrollees who had never attended school right up through the senior year of high school.[55]

In addition to classes conducted in each camp under the direction of the camp EA, special classes were also held at Fort Douglas and elsewhere under the supervision of the district educational adviser. A four-week school for cooks and bakers was held at Fort Douglas as early as 1936.[56]

Bert Huish, a craftsman in canvas repair, instructed enrollees in his trade at a district school held at F-40 in Provo. This was conducted under the auspices of the Central Utah Vocational School, which issued diplomas at the conclusion of the course.[57]

Abundant evidence is available illustrating the genuine efforts made to meet the educational needs of the enrollees. For example, most of the classes took place in the evening after working hours, but if this proved either inconvenient or unsuccessful, it was then left up to the ingenuity of the educational advisers and other camp officials to select a time both convenient and conducive to the enrollees' learning prospects. At the Jericho camp a regular class held at noon during the men's "leisure" time proved to be more successful than the evening classes.[58] In Brigham City, Bridgeland, and various other camps the EAs found it more advantageous to hold classes in the morning while the men were still fresh. In Pleasant Grove, officials found morning classes better suited for the technical courses, although the hobby classes and vocational training continued in the evening.[59]

There were several motivational factors to encourage enrollee participation in the classes that were offered. The camp commander at Vernal required a written excuse from any enrollee missing class. The excuse had to be handed in to the officer at noon on Saturday, just about the time that the rest of the enrollees might be leaving camp for the weekend. The camp commander usually managed to be "too busy" to read the excuse until about 4 p.m.; meanwhile the enrollee was confined to camp. This practice reportedly had quite a good effect on attendance.

There was continued wrangling over the future of the education component within the Corps. Salmond agrees that although the Corps did a masterly job of combating illiteracy and also providing opportunities for gaining a high school diploma, "education must be counted one of the less successful fields of CCC endeavor" and fell short of meeting the educational needs of the young men.[60] Academic courses, while doubtless interesting in themselves, were of limited practical value to youths who would almost certainly lead nonacademic lives, while one can legitimately question whether instruction in digging ditches and building dams was fitting the enrollees for life in an increasingly urbanized society. For these educational shortcomings Salmond spread the blame to include Roosevelt, Fechner, and educational officials.[61]

And still the fight continued. These complaints diminished somewhat in later years, although the education program remained the most vulnerable aspect of the CCC.

In the camps, EAs encouraged enrollees to continue in their vocational classes until they had mastered sufficient competency to satisfy the most discriminating employer. Unit certificates were issued to enrollees completing more than twelve hours in any course. The enrollee who successfully completed on-the-job training programs in a wide variety of fields received another type of card. These cards stated that the enrollee not only received the classroom instruction set out in the job-training manual for that course but also possessed "the necessary work experience." Still another type of award was the Certificate of Proficiency. The Division of Grazing awarded these to enrollees who satisfactorily completed fifty hours on a given project and the correlated training that went with it. Proficiency certificates were made available to whatever technical agencies wanted them throughout the Ninth Corps Area by Educational Advisor Dr. D. E. Weidman.

Former U.S. Forest Service Region Four forester R. H. Rutledge, by then director of the Division of Grazing of the Department of the Interior, preferred that the division have its own certificate with the buffalo insignia of the Department of the Interior in the center.[62] The certificate was given only under closely supervised circumstances and was designed to serve the enrollee as a meaningful document proving meritorious service in a vocational area.[63] On the back of the certificate was information regarding the boy's qualifications and the skill and initiative demonstrated in performing the tasks described.[64] At the 1939 district training conference, however, officials suggested that letters of recommendation be given departing enrollees since the proficiency certificates were not highly regarded by many employers.[65]

As repeatedly emphasized, the purpose of the educational plan was to enable the enrollee to improve himself to the extent that he might be more employable on leaving the Corps. Of course those continuing in some field of conservation would have received the greatest benefit from their training. Many enrollees became sufficiently skilled that they were hired by the technical agencies under which they had received their training. When Company 957 disbanded at Hyrum four of the enrollees with leader ratings got jobs as Forest Service foremen to serve with the new company that had just arrived from North Dakota. Others found jobs with mining or construction companies or became cooks or parachute riggers as a result of the education and training picked up in the Corps.

On the other hand, employment records of three Division of Grazing camps suggest that the training program of the CCC was not as beneficial as was (or is) generally assumed. Of twenty-six enrollees who left camp to accept employment, only six indicated that the CCC training had been of any help in securing their new job. Four of these, who had been, respectively, a cook, clerk, truck driver, and tractor operator in the CCC, found comparable jobs on the "outside." The tractor operator and the cook had cause to be grateful; the cook stated that his training had "vastly increased his knowledge" of food preparation, and the "cat skinner" had never driven a tractor before entering the CCC. Another of the six had been on a survey crew and left to start his own business in landscape gardening. The other, perhaps generously, indicated that his experience in general labor had prepared him to accept a job on a farm. The remaining twenty, however, including eight other potential "laborers," denied that their CCC work had added to their employability.[66] In 1968, of the sixty-three former enrollees who responded to the education segment of my questionnaire, only 38 percent felt that their CCC training helped them get their first job after leaving the Corps. This is admittedly based on a sampling too small to really be conclusive.

However, of thirty-three respondents I contacted who had taken or taught courses, 64 percent regarded them as "very helpful," 30 percent considered them "mildly helpful," and only 6 percent thought the courses of "little value." Although the transfer value of their education and experience remained less than either officials or enrollees might have desired, it is interesting to note that the program was quite well thought of by those who participated in it.

Part of the reason for the high regard for the educational scheme in the Utah camps may have been that so many people worked so hard in order that it might be successful. School officials made high school gymnasiums and auditoriums available, recommended books, and provided correspondence courses.[67] The school board in Eureka gave its surplus desks to DG-26. Within a week of the establishment of DG-31 in Vernal, Educational Advisor H. D. Miller made arrangements for evening classes at the local high school.[68] Sometimes facilities became available without cost; in other situations the schools would be paid about $200 a month to provide special instruction for the CCC enrollees.[69] In Utah the state director of vocational services offered the help of his teachers whenever they happened to be in areas where camps were located.[70]

A shortage of funds provided an additional handicap for the EAs. However, EAs and camp commanders were directed in no uncertain terms that lack of finances would not serve as an excuse for a poor educational program. An officer from Corps Area headquarters stated,

> If you have a good reason for using more, you will never be turned down. Corps does not want to save it; it is there to use. This business of piddling along and trying to be penny watchers is foolishness. Do not save a few dollars at the sacrifice of efficiency.[71]

With the passage of time and the setting of realistic objectives, the program improved. In spite of the attitude held by some of the enrollees toward conventional education, the Corps did what it could to encourage the youths to further their formal schooling. In 1937 a program began that enabled an enrollee to get a leave of absence from the Corps for as much as a year in order to return to school.[72]

Evaluation of the CCC educational program is difficult. As an institution of academic learning it proved less than successful, in spite of the hundreds of men who received high school and college diplomas through the program. In the preparation of men for their future life's work it was likewise not as successful as might be imagined, in spite of the tractor drivers and cooks it turned out. In most cases, the on-the-job training that, of necessity, accompanied the employment of inexperienced personnel would have produced the same results whether there had been any formal educational program or not.

There were areas, however, in which the program was extremely successful. In the first seven years of the program nearly 85,000 illiterate youths learned how to read.[73] This alone must rank as one of the outstanding accomplishments of the entire CCC operation. Furthermore, in 1940 approximately 150,000 young men took classes in first aid, safety, and lifesaving.

The enrollees indicated their approval of the educational program by the response showed in signing up for classes, usually after working hours. Most of the classes were held at night, although classes in cooking and mess management were held at ten in the morning, at least at DG-27 in Castle Dale.[74]

For the most part classes were completely voluntary, although commanding officers often established their own requirements. At the Castle Dale camp, all new enrollees were required to take a class on etiquette, taught by the CO himself. Those unable to read or write were required to take the literacy class, while all cooks and bakers had to sign up for cooking and mess management. On-the-job training was also offered in classes taught by camp foremen, even at the spike camps. The camp also had three optional groups—Academic, Vocational, and Miscellaneous—and enrollees were to select at least one class from each group.[75]

Very few camps in Utah had less than 90 percent of their complement enrolled. Several camps reported 100 percent enrollment; one former EA recalled that every man in his company took at least two classes. One youth at the Pleasant Grove camp received a certificate in 1940 showing that he had completed thirteen different correspondence courses thus far in his CCC service.[76] The enrollees were afforded the opportunity of sampling a veritable potpourri of educational and leisure time activities. Education came in a variety of guises.

Karl Bunnell, the longtime educational adviser of Company 958, stated that "on the whole, the education program in the CCC was helpful to probably 80% of the enrollees, there always being some who are unwilling to cooperate."[77] Admittedly the CCC education program was not quite the success that some of its adherents had in mind. Still, it was a benefit to many, even if it was one of the less bright stars in a galaxy of CCC accomplishments.

IDLE HOURS

Finding enough time for sleep could admittedly be a problem, especially for one who was determined to take advantage of every possible way to fill his leisure time. For the most part, the boys themselves were quite enthusiastic boosters of the Corps. About a month after the program started, two members of the Blacksmith Fork camp returned to their homes in Ogden over the four days off granted for the Fourth of July holiday.[78] They described the competition that existed between the various units to determine the superiority of the camps. Naturally, their camp was claimed as the most orderly, the one that served the best food, and in all other respects the superior camp in the area.[79] Their prejudice was not without foundation, however, as the eighteen-tent camp was entitled to fly the coveted blue pennant, signifying excellence in camp administration, cleanliness, and successful completion of work details for the month as the best tent camp in the Fort Douglas District. Coincidentally, the other Cache Valley camp, F-1 in Logan Canyon, also flew the other blue pennant for having the best "wooden" or barracks camp in the district.[80]

These pennants represented the Army's attempt to create pride in one's organization by recognizing the accomplishments of superior camps. Blue, red, and white flags were awarded to the camps that placed first, second, and third in the district based on their success in a variety of categories. Tent camps and "wooden" camps were ranked separately.

Camp PE-218 won the blue flag for having the highest efficiency rating in April 1934. This was a prized possession until the bugler overslept one summer day and blew calls at the wrong time; soon, the second place red flag flew in front of the camp. When I interviewed him more than three decades later, the delinquent bugler reported that he was assigned nothing but the dirtiest of details for the following month.[81]

The district and individual camp commanders both made awards for special accomplishments. One former enrollee reported that Company 1966 flew a blue flag for having the best athletic teams over a period of three years. Another remembered his crew winning an award for constructing the straightest wall during a work project along the Virgin River. The same man also lived in the winning tent in a camp landscape contest. Officers at Pleasant Grove awarded prizes for the best-made bed and for the cleanest barracks.[82]

Whether for competition or not, some of their leisure-time activities reflected pride in what they were doing. Quite often on their own some camps incorporated unusual features into their buildings and grounds right from the start, and many of these became established precedents that were to last the life of the program. Camp F-3, north of Vernal, was quite typical, with grass and flowers planted around the buildings and the flagpole. The initials "CCC" planted in flowers added to the elegance of the camp.[83]

Occasionally the boys found someone they could take on a "snipe hunt" and left him waiting all night with a sack and lantern for the elusive bird to be driven into the trap. An interesting variation of this activity took place when rookies were sometimes ordered into formation in the middle of the night and told to follow the "officer" into the woods. They would usually be found in the morning shivering and awaiting "further orders" by a genuine officer who perhaps had wondered whether most of his new men had deserted.[84]

These and other forms of initiation for the newcomers to the camps usually provided some entertainment for all except the initiates. A typical welcome backfired one night at the Salina Canyon camp, where three barracks were located side by side, with a group of newcomers placed in the middle building. A few days after the new boys arrived, the enrollees from the adjoining barracks each decided to raid the one in the middle and tear up their beds after the lights went out. One of the intended victims described what followed:

> Fortunately for us they didn't bother to inform each other of their plans and somehow the word got to us. So as they entered we stood back and watched while one group entered from each end and met in the center for a royal fight. When it was over we tossed the remains out the doors and went to bed. We got a reputation as a pretty tough bunch without an effort, since none of us showed any after-effects the next day and they did.[85]

A veteran of Bridge Mountain camp NP-4 told of getting involved in the dramatic activities of a church group in Springdale and putting on four or five plays over a two-year period. Enrollees at F-43 in Pleasant Grove organized their own drama club and presented musical items and comedy skits.[86] Many camps had glee clubs and dance bands that played at camp dances and in neighboring communities.

FIELD TRIPS

Camp educational advisers proved instrumental in creating not only educational opportunities but also morale-building situations by carrying on active programs of recreation, entertainment, and organized sports. They often arranged field trips or hikes for the enrollees on Saturdays and holidays. In October 1936, two truckloads of boys from F-43 and the Soapstone spike camp spent the day in Salt Lake City on an outing arranged by camp officers. The visitors toured Temple Square, listened to the organ recital in the Mormon Tabernacle, wandered about the state capitol building and Fort Douglas, and capped off the day with a free hour on their own in the downtown area of the city.

Almost immediately, another trip was planned, this time to Bingham Canyon copper mine, Great Salt Lake, and the Lake Crystal Salt Plant. In early 1938 F-43 visitors to the Mormon Tabernacle were pleased to find organist Frank Asper practicing. They were even more pleased when he played the well-known Mormon hymn "O, My Father" and followed this with "My Old Kentucky Home," which probably created some lumps in the throats of his listeners.[87]

Camp PE-218 of Orderville ran fairly regular trips to Zion and Bryce Canyon national parks and Boulder Dam during the winter of 1933–34. The boys at DG-31 had access to Dinosaur National Monument, which was a favorite destination for their outings. The eastern boys of this camp even enjoyed a visit to shearing sheds to learn just how sheep were divested of their woolen coats.[88]

Soon after Company 3544 transferred to F-6 for the summer of 1938, EA Paul B. Murdock and Lieutenant John H. Watson led a group of sixty enrollees to the summit of snow-covered Mt. Baldy. It was the first mountain-climbing experience for many of the eastern lads. And Washington's Birthday, 1936, was an active day for the enrollees of DG-31 at Vernal. Educational Advisor R. A. Morriss took a group of thirty-four into the hills to look for rocks, fossils, and Indian relics.

Visiting speakers gained grateful acceptance. Lee Kay, Utah State fish and game warden, was a popular guest, as he showed wildlife movies accompanied by personal lectures.[89] Merrill Christofferson, assistant Scout executive of the Provo District, was also a camp visitor, although the purpose of his visit to F-43 in February 1937 seems to have been quite unique. He addressed a group of twenty youths who had just organized a

Sea Scout "ship" at the Pleasant Grove camp under "Skipper" Lieutenant Charles H. Brown, junior officer of the company.[90]

One busy day at DG-31 in Vernal a pioneer of the area addressed the boys on local history. That night John W. Willis, a government trapper, told them of the work involved in capturing predatory animals.[91]

Enrollees within walking distance of a nearby town counted themselves fortunate since they could usually leave the camp two or three nights a week. Saturday morning was generally free time, although plenty of work beckoned around camp, such as planting shrubs, painting, or making minor repairs. There was never any project work on Saturday unless the men wanted to work then in order to get extra time over a holiday.[92] Saturday afternoon the enrollees were free to go into town or on one of the trips organized frequently. Sufficient numbers stayed in camp, however, to serve as a fire crew in case of emergency. Utah enrollees often hitchhiked home over the weekends since they did not have to be back until it was time to go to work Monday morning. Incidentally, it might be noted that hitchhiking was prohibited by CCC regulations as well as Utah state law, although enforcement, admittedly, was virtually nonexistent.[93]

Occasionally all the camps across the country took a holiday; sometimes a camp commander would make it possible for the boys to have time off for certain occasions. The men of Company 958 were all released for Armistice Day, 1936, and most of them took the opportunity to go pheasant hunting. Labor Day was another occasion when the enrollees got to visit celebrations in nearby towns. In 1939 several enrollees managed to get away on leave to visit the Golden Gate Exposition in San Francisco.[94]

Enrollees accumulated leave at the rate of one day for each month's service, but, as this could not be transferred into the next enrollment period, it actually amounted to one six-day leave per period. Emergency leave was usually granted in cases of illness in an enrollee's family, and occasionally an enrollee would try to arrange special leave. A young man in a Fifth Corps Area company stationed at DG-29, Antelope Springs, hoped to go home just before Christmas in 1935. He wrote, "Pappy, if I can get a furlough to come home for ten days at Christmas, I will come." Pappy supposedly answered, "Son, you stay off those furloughs; they might blow you to hell."[95]

RELIGIOUS ACTIVITY

That "hell" not be the destination of unfortunate enrollees concerned the chaplains assigned to the conservation camps and also many religious leaders of various denominations within the state. On Sundays the boys were free to attend church, although in many little Utah towns, the predominant Church of Jesus Christ of Latter-day Saints was the only religious institution available. Many CCC veterans came to Utah as young men from out of state and went through the process of being introduced to the church—usually as a result of marrying Mormon girls—and often joining the church themselves.

Religious activity in the CCC camps proved quite different from anything the youths might have experienced at home, nor was it comparable to that available in the military services. A chaplain generally had seven or eight camps for which he might be responsible and was usually on the move constantly. One veteran chaplain likened his fellows to the old-time circuit riders and felt that in the CCC chaplain "the soul of Francis Asbury marches on."[96] The typical CCC chaplain was either an Army Reserve officer called to active duty, a contract minister working part-time, or a volunteer clergyman from a nearby community. The latter were usually recruited by Army chaplains and generally received only enough to cover their transportation costs.[97]

Most of the chaplains found their work quite different from any type of religious activity with which they had previously been acquainted. Initially the chaplains did many of the tasks later assigned to the educational advisers, such as organizing clubs, encouraging vocational guidance work, assisting dischargees in their search for employment, and organizing recreational activities.[98] When the education program began the chaplain was freed to carry out the more spiritual aspects of his responsibilities.

Two Protestant, one Catholic, and two Latter-day Saint military chaplains were assigned to camps in the Fort Douglas District.[99] In addition, two Catholic priests served as contract chaplains in Utah. They were not all assigned specific areas and occasionally ran into each other in their travels. Lieutenant Frederick G. Lamb, the Catholic chaplain, visited the Bridge Mountain camp at Zion National Park early in December 1937, for example, and two days later Latter-day Saint Chaplain Captain Reuben E. Curtis arrived. They both showed movies and gave inspirational talks.[100] The Reverend Willard Spence of the Vernal Community Church worked closely with DG-31. In 1936 he assisted with the Easter services at the camp, and later in the year he took two of the enrollees with him on a weeklong hunting trip.[101]

Most of the volunteer clergymen who served the Utah camps were from the predominant Latter-day Saints Church. In addition to local Mormon leaders, general authorities of the LDS Church occasionally visited the camps to observe conditions and visit the enrollees. After such a visit to a few northern Utah camps in September 1934, David A. Smith of the LDS Church's Presiding Bishop's Office and Captain Theodore Curtis Jr., senior chaplain of the Fort Douglas District, reported that the men had few complaints and seemed to be sufficiently happy in their work that most planned on signing up again for another enrollment period.[102]

The Latter-day Saints Church did not oppose the CCC as such, although Corps officials realized that there was official displeasure with some practices, such as giving cigarettes as prizes in camp competitions. Mormon leaders initially favored the New Deal, but by 1936, the program was far less popular. Workers were told to keep their relief jobs as necessary but to get off relief rolls as quickly as they were able to do so. By 1941 only one Latter-day Saint chaplain served in the Fort Douglas District, and although it was implied that this might reflect church displeasure, there is nothing to verify this.[103]

Many newspapers and personal accounts tell of services conducted in the camps or of invitations accepted by both Mormon and non-Mormon enrollees alike to attend LDS services. Except in isolated instances, enrollees were made to feel welcome among the Mormons, although it must be admitted that the Utah boys were usually more cordially received than those from other areas. In October 1936, President W. W. Warnick of the Timpanogos Stake of the Church of Jesus Christ of Latter-day Saints spoke to a gathering at F-43 and invited the boys to take advantage of the opportunities available in the community of Pleasant Grove, especially the youth organizations of the churches. A committee was formed in the town to handle nonsectarian church services, designed to be instructive and entertaining. Major Lyman Johnson was one of the first speakers to participate when the services got under way.[104]

In 1936 twenty-six different church affiliations were represented in the Bountiful, Willard, Woods Cross, and Big Cottonwood camps of the Bergeson study. Company 940 was 80 percent Mormon, the two companies from the Second and Fifth Corps Areas were predominantly Catholic, and the Baptist Church was most highly represented in the Seventh

Corps Area camp, with 27 percent of the enrollees claiming membership. Of the total 546 enrollees in all four camps, the Mormons were the most numerous, followed in turn by the Catholics, Baptists, and Methodists.[105]

Religious diversity was generally the rule in all but the Utah camps. The Vernal camp had a Fifth Corps Area company and reported 130 Protestants and twenty-seven Catholics in its religious census in 1938. The Utah company at Bridge Mountain camp, on the other hand, had only one Catholic.[106] There is no indication that religious differences, per se, caused any difficulty among enrollees, except as another factor in their overall cultural differences, which contributed to interstate rivalries. In most cases wherever a boy hailed from, be it Utah, New York, or Arkansas, had more of a bearing on his relationships with his fellow enrollees than whether he was Mormon, Catholic, or Baptist.

Some of those who served in the CCC felt that the lack of more rigorous moral training was a serious defect. Others commented on the moral decline that often occurs among young men away from home and under the influence of peers whose habits are not in conformity with those previously observed. One veteran of the Bountiful camp pointed out that problems of this nature existed even among Utah companies:

> The camp was a place where any good moral training one had would be destroyed if one was willing to allow it. One had to be capable of standing alone against the crowd to survive, but there were quite a lot who were capable. Some were not and profited by having a better crowd to follow available. Some tried extensively to pull down and destroy all good principles.[107]

ANNIVERSARIES AND COMPETITIONS

One of the major activities of the year was the annual celebration of the founding of the CCC, held in early April. This provided an opportunity for the enrollees to show off their camps to the nearby communities as well as to have sporting events and other contests with other CCC camps. In addition to these annual affairs camps could also host similar athletic contests at other times.

The description of such an event held on September 6, 1941, illustrates the ingenuity displayed in the way of contests. Three different technical agencies were involved: Company 962 of NP-4 from Bridge Mountain in Zion National Park, Company 2558 of Hurricane's DG-160, and the host, Company 585 of SCS-7 in Leeds. Of course, having one of the few regular swimming pools among the Utah camps permitted the camp to hold an on-site swimming meet, while most of the other events were held at the community ballpark a quarter mile away. Starting at 9:15 a.m., the day was filled with interesting and challenging contests. One was the "truck-driving contest," with enrollees of the three camps exhibiting their skills by driving not only forward and backward but also around curves and on grades. Other events included softball throwing for accuracy and for distance, typing, posthole digging, wire splicing, log chopping, log sawing, and nail driving, as well as regular track and field events. The highlight of the day, however, according to the newspaper, was the retreat ceremony, when all three companies "stood in respect to the Flag of our country after an athletic battle of valor, but of peace and good will toward each other."

OTHER ACTIVITIES

In addition to enjoying the recreation planned by the officers or the nearby communities, the enrollees were quite adept at providing their own entertainment. Card playing, reading, and general "bull sessions" occupied much of their off-duty time.

Just a few days after arriving at F-34 in Hyrum, four enrollees of Company 2761 hiked up Blacksmith Fork Canyon about one and a half miles and discovered a cache of Indian beads and knives.[108] The enrollees of Company 958 had a pet elk named Peavie, which used to terrorize the golfers on the Provo City golf course next to camp F-40. The animal reportedly peered around the corner of a building, waiting until the golfers ventured out in the open. At the appropriate moment, Peavie would charge, and golfers would flee across the course seeking the safety of a tree, where they remained trapped until amused enrollees would come to their rescue.

Knowing the reputation of the Second Corps Area enrollees, it should have been no surprise to read of the opinion of Marshall Davis, a CCC artist who had come to Utah with the New York boys of Company 1253. In a letter to a Treasury Department official involved with the CCC art program, Davis offered his "candid impressions of CCC life": "the reigning impression of getting the other fellow before he got you.... I had seen mutiny, burning of tents, throwing of lye and set rat traps in bunks, fights every day and bloody nose army sergeant and finally a replacement of the Commanding Officer."[109] At the time Davis wrote the letter in 1934 he had been associated with camps in Utah, Florida, Mississippi, and Tennessee, the latter identified as "the best camp to which he had been assigned." I must confess, however, that I never read of the incidents he described in either camp or community newspapers.

Neither should it be a surprise that problems developed within the camps as a result of having a group of two hundred young men living and working together, especially considering the cultural differences and backgrounds of the enrollees. The Fifth Corps Area had perhaps the greatest internal challenges since there were Protestant farm boys from the hill country areas of Kentucky and West Virginia in camp with Catholic city dwellers from Ohio and Indiana. Sometimes fights would break out in camp or at work during the day, but leaders and foremen usually stopped them immediately. That night the disputants would be required to don boxing gloves and settle their disagreement in a series of two- or three-minute rounds in the ring.[110]

The urban/rural differences may have contributed to at least one serious fracas between Kentucky and Ohio enrollees in Pleasant Grove in 1936. An eyewitness related the incident as follows: "Windy," the company's senior leader from Ohio, got drunk one night. He went to the kitchen and demanded that the mess sergeant, a lad from Kentucky, give him the keys to the storeroom. "Windy" wanted to get into the vanilla extract, but the mess sergeant refused, and a fight broke out. Although guns were forbidden in camp, one suddenly appeared in the hands of one of the battlers when his opponent pulled a knife. The "top sergeant" was shot in the groin and went to the hospital, and both men were subsequently discharged from the Corps. The eyewitness who told me the story was at that time in charge of the camp canteen; to fill the vacancy created by the fight, he was promoted to mess sergeant and advanced to the rank of leader. The account that appeared in the local newspaper, however, was considerably different; nothing was said about the fight, and the canteen steward was reportedly named to replace a mess sergeant who had returned to his home in Indiana "to receive an Army commission as second lieutenant."[111]

A foreman at the camp recalled the trouble from still another point of view, although this may have been a subsequent incident arising from this or similar difficulties. Apparently trouble had been brewing for some time, and one night a foreman was called from his home in American Fork and asked to report to camp immediately. The camp officers quickly apprised him of the situation: Kentucky youths were barricaded in one barracks, and Ohio Buckeyes, in another. Both groups had promised to "get" the other and anyone else who tried to interfere. Both groups also announced that they were armed. The foreman, however, had friends and crew members in each contingent who had agreed to talk to him if he came into the darkened barracks alone. Over the protests of the camp commander he went in unarmed and emerged with a pistol from one barracks and a blackjack from the other. One ringleader from each group was sent home, and the trouble soon abated.[112]

Rules, of course, depended significantly on the certainty of disciplinary action for lack of obedience. Admonition, suspension of privileges, and extra duties were the most common forms of punishment. More serious offenses might gain the miscreant a deduction of cash allowances for as many as three days, while a dishonorable discharge might be meted out for refusal to work, being absent without leave, continued serious misconduct, and a general unwillingness to abide by the rules and regulations laid down by the War Department.[113]

Theoretically, no one with a criminal record was to be allowed into the Corps. Major General George Van Horn Moseley, outspoken commander of the Fourth Corps Area, created a stir when he refused admission to a youth who had been offered the alternative of joining the CCC or being sentenced to a chain gang.[114] Occasionally, however, enrollees were discovered who had changed their names in order to avoid being barred from the program. One ex-foreman told of having five confessed murderers in his crew, one of whom said he had killed three times in his native Kentucky. Although he deplored their actions, the foreman considered them among his best workers.[115] Unfortunately, I was unable to verify his account.

Punishment for either civilian or Corps violations could run the gamut from mild reprimand to confinement to camp or extra work details. In extreme cases, discharge from the Corps was administered for serious violations. Even nonviolence could bring such punishment as that doled out in August 1933, when officers discharged two boys from Hobble Creek camp SE-206 as agitators and nonworkers.[116]

Dissatisfaction with a commanding officer caused a protest at F-6 in the summer of 1934. Among the enrollees were some older union members, unemployed miners from Coalville and Park City, Utah. A protest precipitated over what was regarded as unsuitable food, and the men marched on the captain's office. The three Army officers strapped on their pistols, and it was an uncertain two or three hours before the matter was peacefully settled.[117] Although these situations created morale problems, most of the enrollees appear to have taken the difficulties in stride.

The occasional violence was only one small part of the CCC experience, albeit one often remembered. As in so many situations, the actions of a few tend to obscure the positive contributions of the many. Less remembered, perhaps, but of more positive worth were the recreational programs that were instituted and the religious activities that were pursued. It was from these latter areas that many of the men gained the experiences that they were to treasure in their future life.

SPORTS AND FIELD DAYS

An active sports program was an integral part of the recreation provided for the enrollees. Nearly every camp had baseball and basketball teams, and each usually entered town or church leagues in nearby communities. The Jericho camp played in the Utah-Juab baseball league twice a week under the tutelage of Lieutenant John R. Kurdy, junior officer.[118]

Camp F-1 in Logan Canyon had one of the better baseball teams in northern Utah. They posted an 11-1 record in 1933 and were well on their way to a successful season in 1934 in the Cache Valley Commercial League. They were in a first place tie at the end of the first half of play and were described as "one of the fastest teams in the state." Unfortunately, an interpretation of the league rules resulted in the demand that all games be played in Cache Valley, thereby ruling out the CCC field eighteen miles up Logan Canyon. Captain John Gestring, F-1 commanding officer, withdrew the team to comply with CCC regulations requiring home-and-home play in order to provide entertainment for the rest of the camp. In his withdrawal letter to league Vice President Kenneth Nyman, Gestring emphasized that he had no quarrel with the league and invited any interested team wanting home-and-home games to contact him. The camp posted a standing offer to provide transportation from Logan and provide dinner for the visitors after the games.[119]

Although baseball and basketball appear to be the sports of choice mentioned most often in camp newspapers, there were certainly others. An editorial in the Farmington Bay SP-2 newspaper boasted that, in addition to basketball and softball, the camp enjoyed boxing, ping-pong, badminton, and volleyball and also had "the best athletic camp in the district."[120]

The Vernal camp displayed a better-than-average sports program. In the summer of 1936, Company 1507 fielded both softball and baseball teams, both of which were reported as "doing well" in town and CCC competition. The local paper noted that the team was "to be commended for their fine spirit and clean sportsmanship which has manifest itself all season." Their 12-2 season and league championship earned all sixteen team members red sweaters with the company number in white numerals. With the baseball season out of the way, enrollees were getting ready for touch football, to be followed by basketball.[121]

Enrollees played basketball even more than either baseball or softball. Camps not only entered local competition but also engaged in a district-wide CCC league. In 1936 the district basketball league included teams from twenty-four camps and the headquarters detachment at Fort Douglas. The league included teams from Blanding to Brigham City and from Manila to Gunlock and was divided into four divisions, one of which separated further into two subdivisions. One team in each division was designated the "sponsoring team" and was responsible for seeing that the division play finished by March 14, in order that the league playoffs could be held March 20–21, 1936. Unfortunately, the district tournament wasn't held, although a similar league was organized the following year.[122]

On March 5, 1940, the camp newspaper of BR-91 in Pleasant Grove carried an optimistic story familiar in tone to those who have suffered defeat. The sports editor of the *P.G. Bee* announced that although the basketball team had indeed endured a losing season, nonetheless it was one that proved "interesting." He wrote, "An important factor in developing interest in basketball in this camp were the suits which this camp can boast of being nicer than any of the other teams that were played by the Dinys." He concluded by reminding his otherwise disappointed readers that the good sportsmanship of the Pleasant Grove team had "created a fine opinion by the surrounding communities."[123] The team ended on a good note, however, by defeating a team from the Pleasant Grove First Ward, 81 to 79, in what must have been an extremely exciting game in those days of low-scoring basketball.

On at least one occasion, a basketball game led to still another athletic activity. Two enrollees from the Leeds and Washington camps had a dispute over "how basketball should be played" and agreed to settle their differences in a four-round bout at one of the boxing matches sponsored by the St. George American Legion post in the Dixie College gymnasium. It was predicted that the grudge match would be a "knock-down, drag-out affair," which "should be vicious if not scientific."[124]

CCC boxers added excitement to boxing cards throughout the state as they participated in local events. There was also district competition, and in March 1940, boxers from throughout the Fort Douglas District gathered for a big tournament at the Greenriver camp.[125] Boxers from DG-31 entered the trials for a state meet, and one, James Bell, was picked as one of the four to represent Vernal in the State Amateur Athletic Union tournament.

Boxing and wrestling were always among the main events at intercamp field days. On these occasions several camps would get together and compete in a variety of contests.

In addition to sports, there was competition in music as well as art and handicraft exhibits at a field day held in Price for camps of southern and eastern Utah. Six camps in central Utah participated in a field day at Provo in May 1940. Camp MA-1 won the day, which included softball, track and field events, logging, chopping, horseshoes, badminton, sand shoveling, tug-of-war, and other activities.[126]

CCC companies engaged in track and field competition, both with other companies and with local schools and colleges. Within the camps, the boys participated in intramural competition. Volleyball proved a popular game, with competition also available in pool, horseshoes, ping-pong, billiards, soccer, tennis, bowling, swimming, checkers, and other games. Camp regulations prohibited tackle football, but some camps had touch football.

The approved age requirement remained in effect for the duration of the program. Throughout the life of the Corps, nearly 75 percent of the new enrollees came from the ranks of those under twenty-one years of age. Over half of those enrolling during the fall of 1935 and the spring of

1936 were either seventeen or eighteen years of age; less than one-tenth were over twenty-three.[127] In fiscal year 1939, 57 percent of the enrollees accepted nationally were either seventeen or eighteen, and less than 3 percent were twenty-three or older. The figures for 1940 were comparable, at 60 percent and 1.4 percent.[128]

Youths enrolled for a variety of reasons: to get away from home, to get a job, to help support their parents, to seek adventure. A few just sought the excitement of a ride across the country to a faraway camp, after which some cooperative relative would write, insisting that they were needed at home, thereby gaining their honorable discharge. The average stay for an enrollee was about nine months, although some of those exempt from service limitations stayed in for three or four years. Of the 350,350 enrolled in 1937, 142,205, or 40.5 percent, had been in six months or less; 14.2 percent, from seven months to a year; 31.1 percent, between one and two years; and 14.2 percent, more than two years. Utah enrollees stayed in much longer, on the average, than enrollees from outside the state.[129]

The boys who left for the CCC camps were a mixed lot. Their backgrounds varied; their reasons for entering the program were diverse. As a result of their different experiences their reactions might also be expected to have been dissimilar. Here, however, there was great agreement, as most men who worked in the CCC looked back upon their service with a fondness that cannot be entirely attributed to nostalgia. For some, the episode was governed strictly by financial necessity, and a few of them felt ashamed to be a part of the great mass of Americans unemployed or on relief. Both while in the program and later in retrospect, however, most took a more positive view and found their CCC experience quite enjoyable. For this to have been so, the program has to have provided more than merely a job and three square meals a day, or "three hots and a cot," as they put it. And so it did.

CHAPTER 12

Camp and Community Relations

At first they were welcomed like an epidemic of smallpox. Anyone who professed to be moral practically refused to walk on the same side of the street with any of the CCC boys. Parents were alarmed and stories were circulated to scare the young girls. Maybe this was justified.... It took several years to make much change but gradually the change came.... About 15 or 20 married and remained in the community of the state. Without exception they have been a positive addition in the community.

—Lela Robinson Rodabaugh, interested observer/girlfriend/wife, camp DG-29

Utah in the 1930s was a conservative, small-town, primarily Mormon society; in that respect Utah has changed very little in the past eighty years. Relations with the federal government had not been cordial during earlier Mormon history. Utah was denied statehood for half a century because of Washington's opposition to the Mormon practice of polygamy and the degree of theocracy found in the Utah territorial government. Less than four decades after receiving statehood, Utah, like the rest of the country, needed federal help. Officially, the state welcomed the New Deal and the agencies for which it provided. But how about the people of Utah? To what extent would suspicion, fear, provincialism, or intolerance affect the reception given the CCC program and those participating in it?

That the situation was indeed critical was recognized by Elder Melvin J. Ballard, one of the top officials in the Church of Jesus Christ of Latter-day Saints, when he spoke to a women's conference in October 1937. At the same time he was encouraging Latter-day Saints to try and get off relief programs, he acknowledged that had the government "not stepped in [in 1933] to aid the unemployed, America would have had a revolution."[1]

FINANCIAL IMPACT

It must be admitted that economic considerations were certainly a factor in the acceptance and popularity of the CCC among the businessmen in most communities. The merchants of Utah *understood* the financial impact the presence of the camps had upon the economy. An average camp cost nearly $20,000 to build, and at least $5,000 a month was spent in the nearby towns to maintain a camp.

It is true that accurate estimates are difficult for a variety of reasons. The camps themselves varied in cost of construction. The tent camps erected in 1933 cost about $2,800; the wooden camps were about $4,300. During the following year, on the other hand, fourteen new camps were built for $18,000 each, while it cost $2,000 just to repair those constructed previously. It was estimated that MA-1 in Provo, one of the later camps to be built, would cost around $30,000.

To start off, each of the camps was supplied with fifteen days' rations, and an additional thirty-day reserve for each camp valued at $224,000 was maintained at the Fort Douglas headquarters.[2] The daily consumption of a typical camp was nearly a half ton of staples, with twenty pounds of cornmeal, sixteen one-pound cans of evaporated milk, twenty-five gallons of fresh milk, twenty-five pounds of butter, 150 one-pound loaves of bread, twenty-five pounds of coffee, sixty-three pounds of sugar, 225 pounds of meat, 125 pounds of potatoes, six pounds of jam, nineteen pounds of canned pineapples, three pounds of cocoa, and twenty-five pounds of onions.[3] Purchasing in the district amounted to approximately $150,000 a month on food alone the first several months of the program.

Initially, the Army did most of its buying centrally, in Ogden or Salt Lake City, until Utah Congressmen Abe Murdock and William Robinson visited Secretary of War George Dern. After their successful appeal, regulations were altered to permit Army purchasing officers to buy meat locally, and soon the order was expanded so that *all* supplies for the camps were to be purchased locally as far as possible.[4] This established a sizable market for farm produce, as all farmers interested in selling beef, pork, mutton, poultry, potatoes, green vegetables, grain, and dairy products were urged to contact the county agent's office, enabling Army purchasing officers to procure the necessary provisions.[5]

Money spent by the officers and enrollees could easily yield another $2,000 to the coffers of the business community each month. In some of the smaller rural communities of the state, the money circulated as a result of the CCC was about all that was available.

The amounts of money spent in the community differ considerably in various reports. In 1934 Director Fechner reported that an average camp would spend between $3,000 and $5,000 locally each month on goods and services. This agrees quite closely with the figure given by Uinta National Forest Supervisor George C. Larson in 1939, when he stated that it cost about $40,000 annually to operate a camp. He further mentioned that a community would benefit financially by at least $50,000 every year *a camp was in the vicinity*. Mayor R. C. Cooper told Vernal residents that they received $60,000 annually as a result of the presence of DG-31 in town: $30,000 spent by the Division of Grazing and $30,000 spent by the officers and enrollees. The Army figured that for the forty-six camps of the Fort Douglas District in 1939, only thirty-one of which were in Utah, an average of $125,000 a month was spent locally for food and supplies; $10,000 for lumber, hardware, and repair materials; $5,000 for motor vehicle fuel and repairs; $8,500 for trucking and hauling; $4,800 for laundry services; and $105,000 annually for 13,800 tons of coal. This would average $5,615 per camp per month for these commodities.

Excluding the enrollees' pay, the Corps spent just over $500 annually per man for operating the camps, according to Major Mose Kent, commander, Fort Douglas District. For a two hundred-man camp, this would generate about $8,300 a month, much of that being spent in the immediate vicinity. The district commander of the five previous years, Brigadier General Pegram Whitworth, told a group that the Army spent about $12,000 monthly for each camp in the district. The community benefits ranged even higher using figures provided by a staff officer of the Ninth Corps Area, who stated that the average camp cost the government $20,000 each month. Again, however, not all of this was spent locally.[6]

A major spike in Army and CCC expenditures took place when camps were first set up. The three camps built in and near Dixie National Forest in southern Utah that first summer provided for contracts for $22,000 to firms in nearby communities. The Southern Lumber Company and the Cedar Lumber Company of Cedar City benefited most from the construction contracts. A local dealer, Petty Ford Company, provided many of the trucks purchased by both the Forest Service and the Army. A sale of such magnitude in a small community was so unusual that seventeen trucks had to be brought in from Chicago to consummate the sale.[7]

In addition to the monthly wages paid out to the officers, technical agency personnel, and enrollees, around $5,000 more was sent by government check to families of the enrollees out of the Fort Douglas finance office. And as a result of the program, the Army and Corps officials spent funds for a wide variety of purposes. On one occasion the Salt Lake Transportation Company received a check for $1,344 for delivering more than eight hundred youths to some sixteen camps throughout the state.

A need for work clothes resulted in a rush order to ZCMI of Salt Lake City for $16,320. The company was asked to deliver 20,400 sets of denim jumpers and trousers to the Army quartermaster in San Francisco. ZCMI was only one of several companies so engaged in producing 300,000 work suits for CCC camps on the West Coast. R. H. Rutledge, in what appears to have been a casual observation, estimated that for every man in a camp at least two more would receive employment supplying him with food, shelter, and equipment.[8]

COMMUNITY PROJECTS

Not only the merchants realized the impact of the CCC. The need for conservation work and for employment was so great, and the fulfillment of these needs by the Corps so dramatic, that resignation rapidly gave way to enthusiasm. The work projects carried out in the immediate vicinity of many of the towns gave definite proof of the physical possibilities available.

In addition to regular work projects that benefited the community, the CCC also created good public relations by participating in community work of a volunteer nature. On many occasions the boys gave up their Saturdays or worked after hours during the week just to perform a helpful task. Camp officials cooperated by making trucks and equipment available in these situations. Twenty volunteers from F-43 devoted several Saturdays to hauling dirt and preparing the grounds of the Pleasant Grove elementary school for the planting of lawns and shrubs.[9] The enrollees of three camps in Washington County participated in City Park Day in St. George by donating their own time to clearing away weeds,

Figure 12.1. Mutual Dell, owned by the Church of Latter-day Saints, benefited from Civilian Conservation Corps labor.

hauling gravel, and doing other odd jobs. A congratulatory editorial remarked that one youth worked so late mixing cement that he missed the truck back to camp and had to walk home. Four months later, enrollees in St. George cooperated with the community and Dixie College in cleaning up the local track and baseball diamond in preparation for a field day activity.[10]

Enrollees worked on some activities of community betterment as regular projects, although these were not what might be considered typical conservation or recreation projects for the general public. In his response to my 1965 questionnaire, longtime employee of the Soil

Conservation Service Scott Passey described some of the CCC volunteer activities in which enrollees became involved: "Many of the boys worked willingly during days off and Saturdays on community projects such as parks, beautification, and cleanups—especially helpful to widows and old people. I know of several churches constructed with considerable voluntary CCC labor."

Enrollees at F-5 in American Fork Canyon worked on two projects with the Church of Jesus Christ of Latter-day Saints in 1933. In one case, they assisted youth groups of the church in preparing the grounds and planting lawns at Mutual Dell, an LDS campground on the Alpine Loop along the back side of Mt. Timpanogos in Utah County. Just a few miles away was located Aspen Grove, since 1963 a family camp but then a summer school for students and faculty of Brigham Young University and one of the jumping-off points for the annual Mt. Timpanogos hike held at the time. Although a local newspaper incorrectly labeled F-5 as a "transient camp," it otherwise correctly praised the enrollees under Ford Poulsen for providing a "spacious roll of law[n]" and preparing the "Theatre of the Pines" for the pre-hike program to be held. That same summer of 1933 the CCC cooperated with Brigham Young University in installing five thousand feet of pipe for a new sprinkler system at Aspen Grove as well as working on parking spaces, stoves, campsites, and a new trail.[11]

The young men of the Corps also built the rock amphitheater with masonry benches described in chapter 5. The work at Mutual Dell was continued by Pleasant Grove camp F-43. As at Aspen Grove, enrollees built an amphitheater, which was dedicated on June 30, 1937, with a speech by Dr. Harrison R. Merrill of Brigham Young University and a formal presentation to the Church of Jesus Christ of Latter-day Saints by Wasatch National Forest Supervisor James E. Gurr. Pleasant Grove historian Beth Olsen offers a poetic description of the facility, still in use by church entities from miles around: "The outdoor theater, surrounded by pines, had a seating capacity of 800 in five sections of tiered, half-log benches, accessed by steps and isles [*sic*] of native stone, all facing a concrete, half-circle stage, constructed of native rubble-work."[12]

In August 1935 a spike camp of sixty-five men out of the Hyrum camp began building a small earth and rock dam to create an artificial lake one thousand feet long for the Boy Scouts at Camp Kiesel. Requests for assistance of this type were not always honored, however, as indicated by the denial of an appeal to have the CCC build a Girl Scouts camp

Figure 12.2. Amphitheater at Mutual Dell on the Alpine Loop, one of several built by enrollees, including ones in Logan Canyon and Zion National Park.

near Ogden.[13] And four months later Superintendent George Moyes announced that the four caterpillar tractors and nine trucks that were in use at Camp Kiesel were being moved back to Blacksmith Fork.[14] But when DG-27 men could not get to their projects during the 1937 blizzards, they endeared themselves to Castle Dale by shoveling snow from the city streets.[15]

In January 1937, the enterprising sports enthusiasts of DG-31 created an ice rink by digging out an area behind the mess hall into which water could be run and allowed to freeze. The following winter they endeared themselves to local residents by building a seventy-five-by-two-hundred-foot rink in the northeast corner of the town ballpark.[16]

This type of cooperation and mutual assistance was even evident in some regular CCC work projects when different levels of agencies worked together. During the summer of 1933 various groups met and decided to improve Navajo Lake near Panguitch by raising the impounding dike six feet. The Forest Service agreed to provide the labor through Duck Creek camp F-16; the Utah Fish and Game Department would provide $1,500 for materials and supplies; and the balance of the cost was to be provided by the counties that were affected by the lake's improvement.[17]

About ten miles east-southeast of Milford was the very popular Rock Corral park overseen by the Milford Lions Club, whose past president

J. R. Murdock first suggested an improvement project. District Grazier Dean H. Seely of Fillmore and Regional Grazier Chesley Seely based at Salt Lake City were instrumental in providing CCC labor for improving the facility.

In the summer of 1940 crews of DG-35 made a truck trail providing better access into the area, as well as building fences and a reservoir. The Lions then officially renamed the park the Seely-Murdock Recreational Area, honoring the men of the Grazing Service as well as their past president. A Lions Club resolution praised the CCC enrollees who carved the "ideal and easily reached park out of an area that was almost inaccessible" and who were "entitled to a large measure of credit."[18]

THE RACIAL SITUATION

The community of Brigham City had some problems with the CCC as well. The enrollees came from outside the state and were not too favorably received. The following letter from a mother in the community to Governor Blood indicates the degree of community concern—and perhaps some other characteristics as well:

> At present the War Department has stationed a very undesirable class of men, such as Mexicans, Philippians [*sic*] and, worst of all, Negroes. Imagine the social problems this incurs in our city. As a mother of two growing daughters, whose property and home joins this camp, I implore your support and influence in having this group of men moved from our community. . . . If a petition is necessary I know I could get the endorsement of every citizen in Brigham City, but that should not be necessary for surely you can see the injustice of it all. With the location of the camp as it is, please use your influence in seeing that we have a more desirable class of men stationed at this camp.[19]

As a matter of national CCC policy, by the mid-1930s African Americans were serving only in segregated companies, usually only in the South, although California eventually had five all-black companies. Historian Olen Cole Jr. points out that in the first years of the CCC, black enrollees in California served with white enrollees in integrated companies with less difficulty than might be imagined.[20] In the summer of 1935, however,

Ninth Corps Area headquarters at the Presidio in San Francisco ordered that, effective August 9, 1935, all black enrollees in California were to be transferred to "five colored companies," and for the duration of the CCC, Companies 2922, 2923, 2924, 2925, and 2940 served in seven camps in national forests, four in national parks, and two on state lands.[21]

According to Cole, in May 1935 there had been some black enrollees in a Ninth Corps Area company that had apparently been transferred back to Utah after service in California. Donald Hobart, a former camp commanding officer, wrote Cole on August 11, 1982, that "upon arrival, the local hostility was so great that the African-American enrollees wrote to President Roosevelt asking to be returned to California."[22] Since the letter from the disgruntled woman in Brigham City was written about the same time as the incident described by Cole, one might possibly guess that the two were connected, although I have no other sources to corroborate this.

Three years later, however, two black enrollees were serving with Company 1967 at DG-26 in Jericho, Juab County, until their transfer to an African American company in California in March 1938, and perhaps that is the situation to which Cole alluded.[23] The mayor of Brigham City also showed concern and "interest in the character of the personnel in the CCC camp," and Blood promised that the vexing problem would soon be resolved.[24]

Although there were no camps of Latin Americans as such, there was a large contingent of enrollees with Latino names in Company 962 stationed at Zion camp NP-4 in 1941. At the Zion Museum may be seen a photograph album called "CCC Snapshot Treasures, 'CCC Co. 962, Bridge Mt Camp NP-4, Springville, Utah, October, 1939.'" The photographer and apparent owner of the album is identified as John F. (Tim) Timmons of Salt Lake City. Company 962, of course, was a Ninth Corps Area company, and for most of its long existence the enrollees had been identified as Utahns. Captions in the album, however, identify many of those pictured with names such as Robert Arando, Manuel Garcia, George Trejo, Armando Lopez, and other similar names amid terms such as "Un Chingaso" and "Un Mejcano" and notes suggesting that they came from southern California. In one photo two enrollees carrying what appear to be pipes or rolls of some material are identified as "Ese burros," or "Those burros [donkeys]." There are also white enrollees in the photos, indicating a high degree of interracial camaraderie. One photo of fourteen enrollees bears the caption "Seeing a great bunch of fellows off, Lund, Utah, September 30, 1941"; eight of those fellows had obvious Spanish surnames, such as Mendez, Gallardo, Garcia, Rubio, and Cardona. The date, of course, was the last day of Period Seventeen, and with the CCC in its final days the structure of companies was not as rigid as had once been the case.

THE BOYS AND THE GIRLS

Many girls were quite pleased at the arrival of an extra two hundred available young men in their community, especially since the young men had money to spend. The local lads took exception to this interest and naturally resented the incursion of such a large group of rivals.

As might be expected, Utah parents worried about the impact upon their young daughters of two hundred young men, often with a background completely foreign to anything previously encountered. The girls who first indicated any interest in the new arrivals were looked down upon by the community and by their peers as "girls who couldn't care less about morals."

The threat of sexual promiscuity among both the enrollees and local girls provided the major fear. One observer complained that the enrollees "were always daytime, nighttime, anytime seducing the local females, many of them got pregnant [at a] much higher percentage than by the local boys."[25] An American Fork women remembered the Provo enrollees of Company 940 equivocally: "Some were nice, others not so nice."[26] The girls could be described with the same phrase. One former camp superintendent remarked that

> the Mormon people must teach their girls physical hygiene and the facts of life at an early age because the boys seemed to have a better time with less problems of V.D. [venereal disease] and pregnancies than did those camps that I was either camp engineer or superintendent of in New Mexico and Texas.[27]

Critics of the CCC made constant reference to the girls who became pregnant by "immoral" CCC youths. Defenders, on the other hand, pointed out that the girls involved bore a considerable share of the blame and that the boys were usually no worse than any collection of two hundred energetic young men looking for fun, excitement, and perhaps romance at the end of a hard day's work. Indeed, camp commanders occasionally had to eject some of the more aggressive females of the community when they turned up in camp after hours.[28]

Many of the boys soon learned that attending church was a good way to meet the more "respectable" local girls. Since the Mormons carried on quite an active recreational program for their young people, this provided the boys with opportunities for inexpensive social engagements.[29]

One Southern Baptist lad from Kentucky used to attend dances and church services in Bountiful. Years later he recalled,

> If a local girl was brave enough to take you, they accepted you. If you went alone you were given the cold shoulder.... Most of the residents tried to keep their daughters from associating with the boys from camp... but the boys who were known and acted like gentlemen were eventually accepted.[30]

A woman who grew up in American Fork later remembered that there was little fraternization between most of the girls she knew and the enrollees, largely due to parental disapproval. Admitting that this might reflect a minority attitude, she nevertheless maintained—probably correctly—"But as I think back to those days and life in that small Mormon town I suspect the attitude was rather widespread."[31]

Some townspeople realized that not all the enrollees were hoodlums, and respectable girls eventually began to date them. One young woman developed a nodding acquaintance with many enrollees as they passed by the window in front of her office desk. She became more closely acquainted when she was asked to prepare a program for the camp. The mess sergeant, Harry Rodabaugh from Mississippi, soon gained her respect; friendship ripened into romance; marriage followed. The girl's family approved of the match, but she was virtually ostracized by the community. Moving to another town eliminated most of the problems, especially when Rodabaugh joined her faith and rose to a position of respect.[32]

This happened frequently. Anthony Fischio was from Ohio and taught photography to his fellow enrollees of Company 536. He went into a store in Pleasant Grove to buy some chemicals and later began dating the salesgirl. The people of the community did not approve of such association, but the girl's mother remarked that the Mormon church sent missionaries all over the world and was overlooking a prime missionary opportunity right in Utah. The young couple married; in 1958 Fischio joined his wife's church, which he later served in a position of some responsibility.[33]

Nevertheless, one Salina resident of the period vividly described an encounter that arose out of a situation regarded as all too common by local communities: "L___ came home from a tour of duty in the navy to find his childhood sweetheart pregnant by a CCC boy. I watched as he knocked nine of them unconscious one after another as the local marshal stood there with drawn gun to maintain a semblance of order."[34]

TROUBLES IN THE TOWNS

Most of the CCC problems in the communities were blamed on the few enrollees who were naturally belligerent or had engaged in excessive drinking. Deciding that the drinking problem might be more easily solved than the belligerency, officials inside of camp and out tried to cut off the source as much as possible. Finally in 1936 the Utah Liquor Commission clamped down on liquor sales to minors among the enrollees. The camp officials were asked to provide the names of their minors to package agencies and liquor stores near the camps in an attempt to prevent the fraudulent obtaining of licenses.[35] This proved unsuccessful, however, and enrollees still got drunk.

This was illustrated quite poetically in the summer of 1935 when some enrollees from Utah Company 1966 at Cedar Breaks, including the head cook, were thrown in jail at Cedar City for drunkenness. A few of their comrades broke open the jail and freed the enrollees as well as some Indians in for the same offense.[36] The incident provided the impetus for the following song, written by the camp troubadour, Sammy Taylor:

I'm a stranger in your city, My name is Charlie Flynn,
I got drunk in town one night and the sheriff run me in.
I've got no money to pay my fine, no one to go my bail,
So I got soaked for ninety days in the Cedar City Jail.
Oh, hurry, Mr. Captain; Captain, bring back the key,
Hurry, Mr. Captain; give me my liberty.
Oh, what a bunch of hoodlums, the worst you ever saw
All robbers, thieves, and burglars, all breakers of the law.
They all sang songs the whole night through; their curses fell like hail,

I'll bless the day when they take me away from the Cedar City Jail.[37]

In Vernal the father of young Glade Sowards was the manager of a dance hall. In an interview Glade described what apparently was a fairly common occurrence:

> I would have been a seven–eight-year-old boy when they came in. I was frightened of them. They used to come to the dances when my father was managing the Imperial Hall.... [P]robably the worst problem that he had as a manager...was when the CC boys would get drunk. Of course a lot of these boys were handsome boys and they would want to date the local girls. The local boys resented this, and there would be fights and drinking and what-have-you. I remember that's probably another thing that maybe gave me the idea that there was something wrong with them because Dad would say, "Well, I had trouble with the CC boys tonight."[38]

The problems of law enforcement officers during the CCC years varied from town to town. Company 962, made up of Utah boys, moved into Zion camp NP-2 and held dedication exercises on Saturday, November 4, 1933. That night two enrollees from Salt Lake City stole two tires and rims. They were quickly caught, confessed, and returned the tires, for which a kind judge suspended $20.00 of their fines with the provision that they demonstrate "good behavior" for six months or during their stay at the camp.[39]

Russ C. Knowles, who retired in 1968 after forty years in police work, worked for the Logan City force while the CCC was in Cache Valley. He remembered no knifings or serious robberies, and except for occasional arrests for drunkenness or disturbing the peace, Logan was fairly quiet. No extra officers were hired. One night, however, he and another exasperated officer challenged an entire truckload of Blacksmith Fork enrollees. Fortunately, they did not accept, for, as Knowles recalled, "there were enough of them to eat us."[40]

Officers on duty alone often found themselves hard-pressed to keep the peace. On one occasion a Manti youth was recruited by the town marshal to help him capture two enrollees whom the marshal had managed to lock in the local firehouse. The marshal knocked one down and turned to assist his one-man posse when the first enrollee returned to the scrap with a heavy object in his hand. The "deputy" shouted a warning, and the marshal knocked his attacker out with his nightstick. The other enrollee then surrendered peacefully.

Public reaction sometimes favored the enrollees in their brushes with the law. In 1937 Washington County Sheriff A. B. Prince found it necessary to utilize a front-page article in the local newspaper to dispel rumors concerning the excessive use of force in quelling a disturbance. An enrollee from Veyo camp F-31 had twice been ejected from a dance; finally, the manager called the sheriff's office. The officers suggested that the enrollee wait in the camp truck, but he refused and tried to reenter the dance. The youth resisted when the officers then tried to place him under arrest, and two of his friends came to his assistance. In the melee the enrollee was injured. The story soon circulated that one officer had held the boy while another beat him over the head. The sheriff called the story false and said that the deputy regretted having to hurt the lad, who recovered handily and was by then back to work.[41]

A similar episode at Mammoth the next year was more serious. A deputy sheriff told a group of singing enrollees to keep their voices down, and an argument ensued. When the deputy attempted to arrest one of the offenders, two other enrollees waded in to attack. The lawman shot and killed one and wounded the other in the leg. A coroner's jury exonerated the deputy a week later following a deathbed admission of guilt by the fatally wounded enrollee.

Utah County law officers worried over a mystery in Hobble Creek Canyon that puzzled the area for more than six months. New York boys had been stationed at SE-206 in the summer of 1933. The nearby Holley ranch became a popular spot with the enrollees where they could play with the children, ride horses, and accompany Mr. Holley when he rode up into the hills taking supplies to his sheepherder. Several years later, two of the former enrollees returned to the area and stayed at the Holleys while looking for work. When one threatened the other with a knife, Mrs. Holley ordered him off the place. Six months later his horse was found tied to a tree: saddled, bridled, and dead. A jacket was found in the tree, and foul play was suspected. Sheriff John Evans investigated and soon received a letter from the missing man stating that he had been with his sister in New York for the past three months. Why he left the horse and how he got out of the canyon were never satisfactorily explained.

Camps with boys from out of state had the most difficulties. Newspaper accounts of crimes involving enrollees verify what might otherwise appear to be a statement of provincial prejudice. Cache County Sheriff Jeff Stowell arrested an Arkansas enrollee of F-34 in October 1936 for theft of government property. The youth, twenty-one years old, had deserted the Hyrum camp about two weeks previously and taken clothes, blankets, and other articles with him. A few months later an enrollee from Company 3796 of the same camp was found guilty of petty larceny in the Logan City Court and sentenced to thirty days in the county jail.[42] Nine months following, a company from the Second Corps Area was stationed at F-34. An enrollee from East Newark, New Jersey, entered and ransacked a house after cutting through a screen door. He stole two sets of silverware but was caught when the son of the homeowner came home and found the enrollee asleep after raiding the refrigerator. The son called the city marshal, and the enrollee went to trial for second-degree burglary.[43]

An enrollee drew a five-day jail sentence for disturbing the peace in Vernal. On his release, he was discharged from Company 1507 of DG-31 and returned to Kentucky.[44] A company from the Seventh Corps Area was at F-32 in Salina when a knifing incident took place. Two enrollees had a disagreement in town, and the next day one of them purchased a knife. He returned to camp at about 1:00 a.m. and, while his opponent was asleep in his bed, slashed him across the stomach. Although the wound was too shallow to cause injury to any vital organs, it was serious enough to require sixty-three stitches. The victim was treated at Salina hospital and soon returned to the job. The assailant was bound over to district court with bail set at $600.[45]

Troubles also involved enrollees from the farms, small towns, and cities of Utah, especially when turned loose on an otherwise fairly quiet community in order to seek diversion.[46] Warrants were issued in May 1934 for two Provo youths who were enrollees from Company 958 in Hobble Creek Canyon. They had kicked and beaten a man on the lawn of the Latter-day Saints Tabernacle in Provo, disturbed the peace at a local bar and on the street, used vile language to the night patrolman, and finally, broken into a girl's room. One received thirty days for battery; the other went to the state penitentiary.[47]

Reid Woolley was twenty-six when asked to take the job as town marshal of Escalante in 1936. His first five years were quite challenging, as nearly every weekend in the mid-1930s he had his hands full with errant CCC boys from two or more nearby camps. He stuck it out, however, and served as town marshal for thirty-eight years. Lacking a jail he considered safe during those CCC days, Woolley, with handcuffs he'd accumulated over the years from sympathetic highway patrolmen, would secure belligerent enrollees to telephone poles and call camp officials to come and get them.[48] On occasion, however, he also received CCC help. As Jerry Roundy points out, "Some of the enrollees from New York and Pennsylvania took a liking to Reid and would often back him up in his confrontations with the boys from the south."[49]

As a young man, Manti resident Brent Scott had some unpleasant experiences with out-of-state enrollees in town.[50] One night he was accosted by three of them who had come in to attend one of the popular open-air dances. The enrollees blocked his way as he attempted to cross a bridge over a swift stream next to the pavilion area, and the leader of the group, with whom Scott had previously exchanged words, told him that he would have to either fight or go around. Undeterred by the odds, Scott advanced, hit the youth in the face, and knocked him over the railing into the stream. Intent on watching the one in the water, he did not see another one of the enrollees slash at him with a knife. He moved slightly, however, and the knife just cut through his clothes and barely nicked his back, leaving a scar visible more than three decades later. The assailant fled, only to be halted by a young Mexican with whom he had quarreled on an earlier occasion. The Mexican, angered by the attack on his friend Scott, lunged at the enrollee and knifed him deep in the chest. The enrollee was hospitalized; the avenging Mexican was jailed for thirty days. Scott declined to press charges on the basis that his friend had evened the score for him.

Relationships between enrollees and local boys were not always violent, however. Blanding historian Gary Shumway tells of an incident when some Utah boys in good humor exploited the easterners' lack of information regarding the local fauna. They visited the camp with a tethered baby porcupine and sold some of the enrollees "porcupine eggs," assuring them that if "kept incubated in a warm, dry place," the "eggs" would indeed hatch out as the spiny creatures: "When the porcupine eggs in which they had invested failed to hatch after weeks of incubation, and the gullible young men found that they were actually cockleburs, the now-wiser eastern lads apparently took it all in the positive spirit that was intended," although many made a mental note never to trust the young men of the town again.[51]

ATTEMPTS AT HARMONY

Officials from both the CCC and the communities did their best to provide recreational activities that would minimize feelings of frustration or hostility. Unfortunately, these were not always successful and sometimes even backfired. It should be no surprise that problems developed within the camps as a result of having a group of two hundred young men living and working together, especially considering cultural differences and the variety of backgrounds.

Neither the Army nor CCC officials expected the financial benefits to a community to buy them the goodwill they sought with the residents. Camp leaders, responsible citizens, and church workers made a spirited attempt to improve the situation, and barriers finally began to sag. Sports provided a way to bridge any gaps of misunderstanding, as camp teams were invited into town leagues. In fact, before camp DG-35 in the West Desert railroad town of Milford had organized a baseball team, enrollees were invited to join the town team.[52]

From the beginning the CCC pursued an active program of positive community relations. This was primarily left to the ingenuity of the individual commanding officer and therefore varied from camp to camp. Officers often invited townspeople to visit the camp for dinner, though they occasionally cautioned apologetically that due to the small amount of money available for feeding the enrollees, the visitors might be expected to pay twenty-five cents a meal.[53]

In most parts of the state, the community, which in most cases meant the Mormon church as well, welcomed the enrollees and invited them to their homes and church gatherings. Many of the youths were practically adopted by families and cemented relationships that continued throughout their lives.[54]

The Smithfield First Ward of the LDS Church used to take one- and two-act plays up to F-1 in Logan Canyon. One former thespian recalled that no sooner was one play presented that rehearsals began immediately on the next.[55] A church group visited one camp occupied by a company from Alabama one Sunday evening. The enrollees reportedly felt "stiff from unaccustomed hill and mountain climbing and wrestling with under-brush on slippery, rocky trails." The entertainment for the evening began with community singing, and "America" was one of the first songs. One of the visitors recalled, "When it came to 'I Love thy rocks and rills, thy woods and templed hills,' a spontaneous groan of protest rose."[56]

Enrollees engaged in the dramatic activities of church groups and organized their own drama clubs, glee clubs, and dance bands.[57] They performed music and skits and played at camp and community dances.

These camp dances formed an important part of the CCC recreational program. Camp trucks, each under the command of a leader or assistant leader, were dispatched to nearby towns to pick up all the girls who wanted to attend. Dances were often held at the end of an enrollment period to bid farewell to those returning home; dances were also held at the beginning of enrollment periods to welcome the newcomers to camp. The boys also attended dances in town whenever possible.

Many communities capitalized on the very active sports program carried on in the camps, and almost immediately community and church leagues invited CCC teams to participate. League play in baseball and basketball was not the only type of recreation that brought camps and communities together. Soon after Company 962 shifted its location from Zion National Park to Blue Springs NP-1 about thirty miles north, they planned to stage a major field day of activities celebrating the Mormon Pioneer Day of July 24. Iron County livestock men were to cooperate in helping the boys put on a rodeo, which would provide a lively addition to the usual baseball game, races, and other athletic events. Still other camps had boxing, wrestling, horseshoes, and volleyball competitions as part of their after-hours activity.[58]

Musical programs by camps and neighboring communities helped provide entertainment. The community of Payson perhaps set the tone when it offered a program of songs and readings at the Currant Creek camp that first summer.[59]

One of camp SE-213's initial community activities when it was set up the following period was to present the first of several programs to the community in the local college auditorium in St. George. Aside from the fairly typical musical performances, readings, and a dancing act, one of the more unusual items scheduled was a boxing exhibition with the fighters on roller skates.[60]

The programs normally went very well, with return engagements often following. One evening, however, a tragicomic incident occurred at

Diamond Fork camp F-8 near Strawberry east of Provo. The people of the nearby community of Heber came to perform, and when the band played "My Old Kentucky Home" the Kentucky youths present almost broke down from homesickness. Although the commanding officer described it as "a hot time for awhile," it ended happily when the boys asked the church and community participants to make their visit a regular feature.

When possible, enrollees often went into a nearby town where the citizens based their reception on the previous attitudes and conduct of the boys. In Milford they were most welcome after some of the boys surrounded a building one night late in June to help capture two burglars.[61]

Utah residents often invited boys to their homes at Thanksgiving, Christmas, and other special times, according to a Provo resident then stationed at Zion National Park. An enrollee from Indiana—later mayor of the Utah community in which he settled—said that the enrollees felt "very welcome" in town and that the "people of Manila still think highly of the old CCC boys." An enrollee who traveled west with a Fifth Corps Area company stated that he "was accepted by the community whole-heartedly. I was included in all of their activities, at their homes, at church and away."[62]

Occasionally, residents of Toquerville went one step further and had groups of fifty boys from NP-2 to potluck dinners and dances in the little community. The boys were asked to pay forty-five cents each as their contribution to the expenses, and soon Toquerville became known among the enrollees as "Forty-five-cent-ville." With dinner, dancing, and a date all available for less than half a dollar, the boys had no complaints.[63] When the community of Springdale, possibly taking advantage of its closer proximity to the camp, raised the price of its dance to fifty cents, the enrollees of Zion Park rebelled. Feeling that 10 percent of their monthly wage was too much to spend on just a dance, sometimes the youths boycotted the community's affairs. The boys lolled around outside, while the girls danced with each other. On one occasion two enrollee "strikebreakers" went in, but their comrades hauled them out, stripped them, and turned them loose to make their way back to camp as best they could.[64] The town of Hurricane then sent word to the camp that the enrollees would be most welcome at their dances for only twenty-five cents; Springdale soon followed suit.[65]

Many camps had their own dance bands, which played at camp dances and in neighboring communities. Often camps held dances in their mess hall, recruiting girls from towns in the vicinity. Some of the officers in charge of the early recreational activities performed yeoman work in lining up partners for these dances, which soon became part of camp social life. Camp F-16 held its first such event at Duck Creek late in July 1933. Officers dispatched camp trucks, each under the command of a leader or assistant leader, to Cedar City and even to Panguitch, nearly forty miles away, to return with precious cargoes of young ladies. After dancing from nine to eleven, a break was taken for refreshments and a program, after which the dancers continued until midnight. The girls then began their long ride home, while the boys tumbled into bed to dream of their next encounter with the fair sex.[66]

OUT-OF-STATE ENROLLEES—A BAD RAP?

Although the Fifth and Ninth Corps Areas both had more companies in Utah, my research suggests that the Second Corps Area, with enrollees from New York, New Jersey, and Delaware, is represented most often in newspaper articles describing troubling incidents in which the CCC was involved. Five of Utah's original twenty-six companies were from the Second Corps Area and wasted no time in establishing a very poor reputation. One former CCC boy reported that the enrollees from New York were called the "Waterfront Boys" or "Coldwater Flat Boys" and were regarded by other enrollees and Utah residents with considerable fear and contempt. New York companies had been located near Alton and Widtsoe in 1933 and misbehaved to the extent that many Kane and Garfield County residents were reluctant to have the CCC in the area.[67]

That their reputation was less than sterling was acknowledged in a history of Company 1256 written in 1939. The writer quite deftly passed the buck for the problems to the Army, before concluding that when the Army overcame its poor beginnings, it wasn't so bad after all:

> It was at Alton that the company struggled through the convulsive throes common to an infant organization. Its existence is proff [*sic*] that the national organization has triumphed over the waste, mismanagement, and inefficiency which were the result of a lack of training personnel in the gigantic problems of housing, feeding, and clothing the members of the new conservation movement. There had been no occasion to cope with

> these problems previously and their weight was staggering. The administration was tenderly placed in the uneager hands of the U.S. Army and its Reserves. It is known that this allocation of responsibility was justified—the Army soon had things running smoothly and the CCC was ready to do the work of conserving the potentialities of the youth of America as well as the resources of the country.[68]

It may be tempting to blame camp problems entirely on those enrollees from out of state, since it does seem to be true that such camps had more challenges than camps with Utah personnel. However, not all the Utah boys were saints, by any means. As mentioned above, there were some homegrown ne'er-do-wells causing problems as well, as certain young Utah men also sought amusement in otherwise quiet communities.

A Utah company was stationed in Orderville around the same period as the Second Corps Area companies and suffered a classic case of "guilt by association." Orderville operated only during the Second Enrollment Period, and Company 959 was composed entirely of Utah enrollees. Still, the reputation of the CCC dropped quite low in the little community, largely because of some unpleasant experiences with the New York enrollees of Company 1256 in the nearby Alton camp during the previous summer. Although the local newspaper reported "remarkably little friction" with the Utah company, one former enrollee described the community reaction as "very cool," especially when compared with the "excellent" reception afforded the enrollees in Kanab, twenty-two miles away.[69] Several carloads of Orderville citizens visited PE-218 within a month of the company's arrival and requested that the Army establish a policing detail to keep order among its off-duty enrollees.[70] Both the Army and Forest Service had been apprehensive about locating a camp at Orderville in the first place, due both to local opposition and to technical problems associated with the campsite and the planned work projects.[71]

The hostility of Orderville was cited by city officials of Mt. Pleasant in their successful appeal to have the camp transferred to their own community for the following winter. Among the points made were the following: the people of Orderville had sent an official protest concerning the camp through high officials of the Church of Jesus Christ of Latter-day Saints, the enrollees were told to stay away from church services in town unless special permission had been granted by church officials, and the Army was unhappy with the unfriendly attitude of the people.[72] Apparently to everyone's satisfaction, the camp was moved and Orderville was spared any further inconvenience "either real or imaginary" by the CCC. When asked directly in 1968 about the attitude of the community of Orderville toward the CCC, a former enrollee of PE-218 and native of Utah gave an answer that reflected attitudes across the state:

> I don't deny that some people may have resented the C.C.C. boys there, but I think if an overall survey was taken, the value that was afforded that community as compared to the harm done would far outweigh [any negative feelings]. That little valley was on its way to becoming a flood-torn gulch, but rock and wire net dams held back [the] top soil and increased the value of its farm land beyond measure. I later lived in this area, and today you can still see the value of those dams. If I were to evaluate the CCC I would say 80% good, 10% bad and 10% indifferent or unchanged.[73]

COMMUNITY APPRECIATION—AND LACK THEREOF

Praise for the CCC program is to be found in nearly every publication covering those unfortunate depression years. Historian Richard Firmage refers to local newspaper coverage claiming that the CCC should be remembered "both for the work accomplished and for the behavior of the CCC recruits":

> The years that followed did not bring any altered reassessment: this was perhaps the most successful Federal program ever undertaken in the county, receiving high praise from almost all people, including those of the most radically differing political persuasions. Liberals and Conservative alike continue to hold the CCC in high esteem. As Bruce Louthian writes: "The CCC is one of the few federal programs ever viewed so universally in a positive way in this fiercely independent and isolated western community; it is perhaps the only federal program that fulfilled its promise."[74]

Many communities showed their appreciation with kindnesses of their own. Grateful towns gave banquets and dances for enrollees; organizations made presentations of books, magazines, and recreational equipment; the Provo Elks Lodge even donated a flagpole for the Provo River camp.[75]

Positive reactions from individuals, community organizations, and civic officials far outnumbered those of a derogatory nature. From the very start in 1933, newspaper editorials commented favorably on the program in general and on the work progressing throughout the state.[76] The *Washington County News* had many good things to say about the enrollees, as well. The editor asked local citizens to treat the boys well, be good neighbors, and neither tempt them nor blame them unwisely as people are inclined to do. And the problems that could arise would be kept to a minimum because "these men and boys are governed by as fine a set of officers as could be obtained."[77]

The Moab Lions Club issued a congratulatory resolution when PE-214 left the area in 1934. Among several other points made, the following is indicative of the community attitude:

> Whereas there have been remarkably few, if any, cases of law--breaking, hoodlumism or other examples of unworthy action on the part of the CCC enrollees or others connected with the CCC work in Moab, but on the other hand, these men and boys almost without exception conducted themselves as gentlemen while located in Moab. . . . The conduct of these officers has been an inspiring example to the men under their leadership, with the result that the discipline in this camp has been above reproach.[78]

In his semiannual report, camp superintendent Milton Greaves commented, "Public indifference and skepticism has changed to active and enthusiastic support with a strong demand for continuance of the work and the beginning of new and additional projects."[79]

In what might be regarded as a left-handed compliment the *Salt Lake Tribune* in 1937 heralded the program because "it taught discipline, decency, appreciations, and patriotism to potential vagabonds, felons, and traitors." But offering quite a different attitude than was the case back in the opening days in 1933, the *Tribune* editorialized in quite a positive manner: "It gave them a new outlook on life, revived their self-respect, awakened their purpose, aroused their courage, restored the love of country and ambition to succeed."[80]

The protests heard elsewhere in the country concerning the CCC program were, for the most part, lacking in Utah. There were, however, some negative letters to Governor Blood and newspaper comments that offered opposing views as compared with official reports, which usually presented only the positive. Although a few negative comments were found, the reactions in the great majority of instances were resoundingly upbeat.[81]

Vernal DG-31

Community opposition was negligible for the most part, especially in Vernal, which in spite of occasional dustups had perhaps the best record of positive community relations with its local camp of any in Utah. The *Vernal Express* did an outstanding job of covering the activities of the camp. Study of its pages discloses not only much about the life of the camp itself but also the attitude of the editor—and presumably the community—toward the CCC.

The Kentucky, Indiana, and Ohio boys of Company 1507 arrived in Vernal from duty at Priest's River, Idaho, in late October 1935 and moved into DG-31, consisting of $21,000 worth of buildings near the northeast corner of the county fairgrounds. The *Express* trumpeted, "Thousands of dollars in projects will be added to the public domain in Uinta County by the work of the camp."[82]

Community appreciation could come from unexpected circumstances. When a spinal meningitis quarantine was imposed on the camp, the paper praised the camp physician and the other officers and commented on the cooperation that had been extended by local medical and civic personnel. Both camp and town worked hard to cement good relations. The *Vernal Express* began a weekly column, "Vernal CCC News," and local officials were invited to inspect the facilities. The cooking class of the local high school visited the camp. Many of the enrollees, most of them from out of state, made their own contribution to public relations by marrying local girls. New arrivals to the camp expressed themselves positively about their good impressions and assured the community, "While we seem a little wild, we are nearly harmless." Mormon youth groups gave programs in camp; the camp quartet sang at the Vernal Congregational Church and the Myton Presbyterian Church, and Educational Adviser Frank J. Kennard sang the tenor solos in Vernal First Ward's Christmas cantata. Camp teams joined local athletic leagues, and the *Express* wrote, "The CCC boys are to be commended for their fine spirit and clean sportsmanship."[83]

Yet some negative feelings existed even in Vernal. This, of course, is quite surprising because Vernal's camp/community experiences were usually among the best in the state. Utah congressmen had received enough adverse mail from the Uinta Basin to indicate, "There is much sentiment in the community which would favor the removal of the camp." Although Congressman Murdock emphasized the absence of any direct action, he stated, "It is felt by some that the presence of the camp in such close proximity to this small city upsets the normal social and moral equilibrium of the community."[84]

This sentiment was echoed years later in an oral history interview:

> I remember that the local people were frightened because these boys would come in with a different standard of living. A lot of them would smoke and drink and they would come from a different part of the country and they'd be a different religion so the local people thought they would dilute the morals of their locals.

Although he maintained that there was some justification for certain negative reactions, the interviewee concluded by stating that many of the enrollees "turned out to be fine boys" and several married local girls, resulting in the fact that "a number of men that we have in our community today came in with the Civilian Conservation Corps."[85]

Vernal had gone all out in its praise when the camp celebrated the fourth anniversary of the CCC in April 1937. A front-page letter from the Uinta County commissioners commended the camp and asked that it be continued for the next twenty years. Further reference was made to the road-clearing feats of the previous four months. The mayor, the editor, and others all wrote in praise of the program, as did the paper's advertisers.[86] The anniversary celebrations of the CCC transpired more consistently and elaborately in Vernal than anywhere in Utah. Every year there was a band concert, a program, public visits to work projects, an inspection of the camp, and usually athletic events and a dance. In 1938 there was something extra. The local high school held an essay contest on the topic "What the Vernal CCC camp has done to benefit the Uintah Basin." The local banks, theater, and merchants donated prizes.[87]

The officers of Vernal camp DG-31 always participated actively in community affairs, and the community responded by supporting the CCC at every opportunity. At each April anniversary the *Vernal Express* devoted several pages to an accounting of CCC activities. In 1940, the mayor described the enrollees of Company 1507 as "clean, honest, sincere Americans," and the local American Legion Auxiliary presented a large number of books to the camp library.[88]

Mayor R. C. Cooper of Vernal declared in 1937, "We have found the entire personnel, with very few exceptions, to be the highest type of men and youths, sober and honest in their dealings, clean sports in their recreational contact, and their social entertainment of the highest order." A year later he followed up by saying that his city was

> more appreciative of the Vernal CCC camp being in our midst than I am able to express, for it was with doubts in our minds as to the ultimate good that could be derived from such a camp when we gave our consent for its establishment within the boundaries of our city.[89]

B. H. Stringham, president of the Ashley Woolgrowers Association, lavished equal praise on the program, which taught discipline and the value of work. He thought that it would be wise to compel all young men between eighteen and twenty-one to serve in "the best school in America."[90]

Never missing an opportunity to honor the CCC, Mayor Cooper spoke on "Americanism and the CCC" at the 1941 anniversary in Vernal, and B. H. Stringham, recognizing the threatening times, delivered "The CCC Camp and National Defense." This was the last of seven anniversaries spent in Vernal, however, as the camp moved the following November. The Vernal citizens had resisted earlier attempts to move the camp, but this time it was final.

Congressman Walter Granger tried to soften the blow by stating that the Division of Grazing had said that the camp had completed all the work it could, but he hinted at the same time that the camp would be kept in good repair and would possibly be used after the war. However, T. K. Ward, superintendent since he replaced Orr in December 1939, denied that the work was completed. Ward claimed that there was enough work within thirty miles to last the camp for six years and it would take ten years to accomplish all the projects within forty miles of the camp.

But the times, they were a-changing. A few days later the remaining sixty-five men transferred from Vernal to Arches National Monument.[91] The *Vernal Express* closed its pages on DG-31 with a brief article announcing the departure of Company 1507. This time it included no laudatory editorial; in fact, it made no mention of any farewell activities; DG-31 was no more.

Changing Opinions as Camps Opened, Moved, and Closed

Opening camp F-35 in Sheep Creek Canyon brought a new way of life to the residents of Manila and Daggett County up on the Wyoming border. Because of the huge discrepancy in the "before" and "after" circumstances, the somewhat wordy 1936 report written by camp superintendent John S. Bennett illustrates an impact unequaled in any other county in the state:

> Aside from the recreational facilities provided by campgrounds and excellent trout fishing streams, and the great benefit the sheep and cattle men received through the improvement of springs for watering livestock and the building of roads which can also be used as trails through country previously impenetrable, and the gradual raising of the cultural and educational standards of their sons through their stay at the CCC Camp, the people of Daggett County particularly value the Manila Camp for the social qualities it has provided for them.
>
> Moving pictures had never been shown in Daggett County before the Manila Camp came; now for the first time regular full-length motion picture programs with sound were available to these hardy pioneers who struggle for existence so far from the comforts of even small-city life—and they certainly do show their appreciation by regular patronage of the camp theater nicknamed, "The Primitive."[92]

After describing the camp's participation in the local basketball league in terms of "friendly competition" and "mutual good will," Bennett continued with his laudatory comments:

> Manila Camp also possess [*sic*] the unique distinction of having the only physician in Daggett County, the only 110 volt electric light plant, the only authorized telegraph office, the only newspaper and many other "onlys" which have during its short existence made the people of Manila and the surrounding territory almost universally state what one of the leading residents told the writer: "Since the CCC came, Daggett County has certainly become a better place to live in."—and they do consider the CCC part of their community and are for it—100%.[93]

Having a CCC camp in the vicinity also proved a blessing to the family of six-year-old Blaine Shakespeare of Tropic, in Garfield County. The curious lad had reached into a bird's nest and, instead of being nipped by a protective mother bird, was struck twice by an angry rattlesnake. It was not until his hand and wrist began to swell and turn dark, however, that snakebite was suspected. The closest medical attention available was at the Bryce CCC camp fourteen miles away, where Dr. Vern H. Anderson and First Aid Assistant Francis Welsh began treatment of the boy. They immediately administered serum, made fourteen incisions in the swelling, and for three hours applied suction to the cuts.

In spite of the efforts, the arm continued to swell up past young Blaine's elbow, and the doctor decided that the boy should be rushed to the hospital in Richfield, more than one hundred miles to the north. As the boy's father drove, Welsh sat in the back seat with the patient, looking after the tourniquet and continuing the suction until they arrived at Richfield at one o'clock in the morning. The local newspaper reported a few days later that the boy had a fifty-fifty chance of recovery, "the chance given him by the fast, steady work of Dr. Anderson and First Aid Man Francis Welch [*sic*]."[94]

Local officials protested almost every time a camp was scheduled to move. At the end of the very first enrollment period, the *Milford News* expressed dissatisfaction that F-19 was to be shut down. The main concern seemed to be the loss of the LEMS who were then part of Company 1340: "The apparent purpose of the present movement of reenlisted CCC men is to concentrate Utah's allotment of men in Utah's winter camps which is a laudable idea though open to criticism at this particular time."

Escalante residents complained on one occasion, not because they had lost a camp but only because of the transfer of a Utah company. A Democratic precinct chairman protested about the effect the disbanding of the company had on the enrollees: "Boys who never knew what a home was, have found friendship here and appreciated it very much."[95] During the 1937 deliberations on establishing the CCC as a permanent institution, the *Eureka Reporter* wrote—concerning a rumor that the CCC was to last until 1943—"If the CCC continues for that long, let's hope that Tintic will be able to hang on to its camp."[96]

The community of Pleasant Grove rallied to the support of F-43 when it appeared that the camp might be moved from its midst. Responding to an "Open letter to Utah County taxpayers" written by the Forest Service clerk at the camp, the Chamber of Commerce, Mayor Alma Kirk, and business and civic leaders fired off protests to Congressman Will Robinson. The story was carried in the local newspaper under a banner headline stretching across the front page: "Civic Leaders Oppose Closing of Triple C Camp." The mayor declared,

> We feel that the CCC camp is a vital asset to our community. Its closing would be a distinct loss to us. The CCC enrollees here are a very fine group and have accomplished a commendable work.... It would be with regret that we would regard the closing of the camp and we will make every effort to save it.[97]

Whenever a camp moved, other communities immediately put in their bids to have it settle in their neighborhood. Camp F-35 was scheduled to withdraw from Manila in 1937, and the community of Roosevelt—on the other side of the Uintas—rose virtually en masse to offer its hospitality and request that the company be transferred to the Uinta River to continue work begun there years previously, before the former camp had been discontinued.[98] Blood sympathized with the plea, but the Forest Service felt that it would be impractical to have a winter camp in the mountains.[99]

The continued existence of Jericho camp DG-26 was questionable in 1937 and 1938. Impacting factors included not only the wishes of the community and the national funding available but the concerns of the technical agencies, and again, politics entered the picture. In a response to a concerned constituent, Congressman Abe Murdock described the multiple influences. If the House bill then before the Senate allotting $21,000,000 to the CCC were adopted, the Jericho camp would stay. However, the Division of Grazing had its own concerns. Grazing "District Number 1 had never had a CCC camp, while District Number 2 then had had two for the previous two-and-one-half years, including the one at Jericho."[100]

Congressional districts were also part of the issue. Most of the Division of Grazing camps were in Murdock's district; Congressman Robinson opposed seeing another camp from his district given to Murdock. Murdock explained that the Division of Grazing was trying to be fair and that to bring this about it was necessary to move camps around occasionally, although he conceded that "everything possible was being done to retain the Jericho CCC camp."[101]

To the Juab County plea that there was more work that DG-26 needed to complete, Murdock answered that "even if retained for twenty-five years there would still be work to do."[102] The local paper was happy to report about seven weeks later that the additional funding had come through, enabling Fechner to revoke the order for a nine-camp reduction of Utah camps.[103]

The popularity of the CCC program was reaffirmed every time a community requested that a camp be either established, restored, continued, or allowed to expand its work projects. The city of Mt. Pleasant tried to overlook no one when it made its three-and-a-half page, single-spaced request listing several projects for which it sought attention by SCS-5. Letters reached each member of the state's congressional delegation, Regional Forester Rutledge, CCC Director Fechner, Fort Douglas Commanding General William Sweeney, Utah Relief Director Robert Hinckley, and Governor Blood.[104] For good measure an additional letter was sent to Senator Thomas the same day requesting that the rumor concerning the abandonment of SCS-5 and F-11 be proved false. Mayor Seely suggested that if SCS-5 did have to move, perhaps F-11 might be transferred to Mt. Pleasant to take its place, but that if the two were transferred, Sanpete County and the Manti National Forest would both be in difficulty.[105]

For the winter of 1933, Utah Company 957 moved to La Verkin from its summer camp, F-1 in Logan Canyon. Community and church leaders had admittedly been previously opposed to the camp. But one former enrollee described the situation as follows: "We did have a few problems at first but it was like a funeral when the camp moved from there."[106]

THE LAST DAYS

As enrollment began dropping off in 1941, civic organizations in the Salt Lake City area, such as the Murray Lions Club, Holladay Businessmen's Association, and Bountiful Junior Chamber of Commerce, demonstrated their support by undertaking some responsibility for recruiting local youths to enter the CCC.[107] As might be expected, the emergency activities of the camps as described in chapter 9 did much to create enthusiasm for the program. Although the not-in-my-backyard feeling was often the case initially, the combination of the financial impact, admiration of the work projects accomplished, appreciation of the community services performed by the boys on their own time, and realization that there were indeed some fine young men in the Corps, even from back east, led, in degrees, to tolerance, acceptance, respect, and, in many cases, affection.

The Utah boys of Company 959 seem to have made a most admirable impression on the residents of Mt. Pleasant during the winter of 1934–35. Although only at PE-223 for one enrollment period—with occasional visits from camp F-28 at Gooseberry about eighteen miles away during adjacent summers—the character of the camp and the men brought positive results. The blue flag won by the company for best wooden camp in terms of morale, cleanliness, and discipline in the Fort Douglas District in February 1935 spoke well of the enrollees, Forest Service personnel, and Army officers. Company participation in community sporting and artistic events and camp activities such as movies and dances to which the community was invited sparked intense goodwill.

The switch in community feelings toward the Corps was recorded by former enrollee Willard Smith in a company history written for the 1980 reunion of Company 959 in Ferron: "The City of Mt. Pleasant had fought hard to keep the CCC camp out of City Park when it was proposed to build it there [November 1934]. When word came that 959 was going to Ferron [November 1935] the town fought just as hard to keep us there." That sentiment was echoed by another former enrollee, ninety-two-year-old Owen Price, when he was interviewed in 2006 about his memories of the Corps: "When we first went into Mount Pleasant, the community didn't think they would like the CCC kids, but when it was time for us to leave, there wasn't a dry eye in [town]."[108]

Figure 13.1. The Hobble Creek (Springville) CCC Camp. Courtesy of the Utah Historical Society.

CHAPTER 13

Wrapping Up and Winding Down

I know that the CCC was one of the best things that Uncle Sam ever did for the boys of this country.

—A. E. Rocke, interested observer, camp SCS-9

As the war clouds in Europe and Asia darkened in the late 1930s the issue of militarism, not just in the CCC but in the entire country, came into sharper and contentious focus. Although there had been very little actual military drilling in the CCC, one or two camps did initiate the practice, but it was usually short-lived. However, with the coming of World War II there was no question that the CCC could well be overcome by higher priorities.

In spite of the debate over militarism in the camps, the work went on, although under somewhat less than full steam. With justification, by about 1938 CCC and Army officials were beginning to feel uncertainty concerning the future of the Corps in Utah.

Utah enrollments continued to decline in the late 1930s, although the number of camps remained fairly constant. Companies from the Second, Fourth, and Fifth Corps Areas continued to outnumber the Utah groups. Among those working at the thirty-four camps in Utah in the summer of 1940, only six could be identified as Utah companies.[1]

By September 30, 1939, exactly half of the forty-eight states were represented in Utah camps. State-wise, the most diverse camp at that time was DG-35 in Milford, where Company 1508, in addition to having enrollees from all four states in the Fifth Corps Area, also had men from two states each from the Fourth and Seventh Corps Areas. Twenty-nine of Utah's thirty-four camps had at least one Utah man in its ranks, while the only single-state camps were F-40, NP-4, and BR-91, with *only* Utah officers and enrollees.

Not only were half the nation's states represented in Utah, but nearly every Utah county could be added to the mix. Throughout the life of the CCC only Rich County in northeastern Utah on the Idaho and Wyoming borders never had a CCC camp. In 1939, twenty-two of Utah's twenty-nine counties had camps. Most had one or two camps then, but Box Elder, Utah, and Washington counties had three each.

Thirty Utah camps continued into the winter of 1940–41, but the total number of men kept declining, and by the end of the Fifteenth Period there were only 4,222 enrollees in Utah. The proportion of local youths continued at about one out of six but was also declining. There were 859 Utah enrollees in October 1940, but by the end of the period only 662 remained.[2] An influx of enrollees from the Fourth Corps Area occurred, however, as five companies, numbered 6426 and 6429 through 6432, moved into the state between July 9 and July 19, 1940, to occupy camps of every technical agency operating with the exception of the Bureau of Reclamation.[3]

In spite of the reductions going on in the summer of 1940, every technical agency still had camps: the Forest Service (eight), National Park Service (three), Division of Grazing (fourteen), Bureau of Reclamation (two), Soil Conservation Service (five), and Fish and Wildlife Service (two). As mentioned previously, one camp, MA-1, was under the joint administration of the NPS and the city of Provo. Numbers varied from two each under the Bureau of Reclamation and the Fish and Wildlife Service to fourteen under the Division of Grazing.

In 1940 Ashley National Forest Supervisor A. L. Taylor had hoped to get a camp reopened at Kaler Hollow and perhaps another in the vicinity of Dry Fork, about twelve miles northwest of Vernal on Dry Fork Canyon Road. The Forest Service debated plans for both camps, and rumor had it that companies from various places including Manila, Hyrum, Escalante, and Brigham City were going to be moved into the area. Kaler Hollow did reopen in late June 1941, but two months later the 106 enrollees transferred to a camp near Wells, Nevada, and F-3 closed for the last time.[4]

By then camps were closing all over the country, and by July 1941, arrangements were being made to gradually reduce the total number in the country to nine hundred or less. For the first time there were insufficient applications to bring the Corps to its authorized strength.[5] Grazing Service camps continued to close during the Sixteenth Period. Milford, Antelope Springs, and Castle Dale were abandoned in October

Figure 13.2. Camp ruins at DG-117, Garrison, Utah. Unsightly ruins still remain of camps, which sometimes were not reoccupied as planned due to the onset of World War II.

and November 1940. Many of the camps were dismantled; several were taken over by the Army.[6]

Due to the declining amount of unemployment applications for CCC enrollment, numbers continued to decline considerably. No new camps were authorized for the Seventeenth Enrollment Period in the summer of 1941, and in addition to the eight Forest Service camps that were closing, the other technical agencies were cutting back as well. Company 958 closed Provo camp F-40 in July and moved to F-51 in Huntsville.[7]

Camps that had operated for several years, including DG-31, SCS-3, F-38, FWS-2, and SCS-5, began closing rapidly during the eighteenth and final period, in the winter of 1941–42. With the exception of only three periods, there had been a camp in the Salina area since 1933, but in November 1941, F-32 shut down, never to reopen. Only two Forest Service camps remained, F-51 in Huntsville and F-38 in Big Cottonwood Canyon. Ogden Bay camp FWS-2 closed after three periods of work. Camp BR-91 in Pleasant Grove had terminated during the Seventeenth Period, and only Deer Creek camp BR-64 continued for the Bureau of Reclamation. Just three SCS camps, SCS-3, -5, and -9, remained; and the twelve grazing camps of the Seventeenth Period continued to close, dropping to eight in the Eighteenth Period.

DG-117 at Garrison, DG-158 at Willow Springs, and DG-160 at Hurricane shut down in late March 1942. When Regional Grazier Charles F. Moore announced the closures he pointed out that since 1935 more than

165,820 acres of rangeland had been reseeded and more than 2,200 miles of truck trails had been constructed. By the end of May 1942, only one Division of Grazing camp remained open, DG-157 in Dry Valley, which had received an extension to help build roads to some vanadium deposits in eastern Utah. Nearly all the remaining CCC camps closed within a few days of each other in July 1942. BR-64 in Deer Creek, SCS-5 in Mt. Pleasant, F-51 in Huntsville, and F-38 in Big Cottonwood Canyon all shut down, as did the Indian camps as well.[8]

During the hectic days of the Nineteenth Period the few remaining camps ceased operating. The Army Chemical Warfare Service took over the camps at Jericho and Lucin, and the Simpson Springs camp underwent a change of designation. The camp was originally scheduled to be turned over to the Army's Chemical Warfare Service with the others, and Company 2517 was to be transferred to DG-155 at Black Rock. The Army then requested that the company remain and continue to operate the camp for the Chemical Warfare Service. Floyd T. Baker became superintendent of this renamed camp, G(D)-1, at the Dugway Proving Grounds on the old Pony Express trail southwest of Tooele. This continued only briefly, however, and in July, the entire CCC came to a halt, with the camp turned over to the Army as originally planned.[9] The CCC had gone to war.

Some camps, of course, had been dismantled or moved much earlier, soon after they closed down. Some became equipment sheds, storage rooms, or even churches. A former LEM named Covington had worked at the Orderville camp, and when the camp closed in 1934 he obtained a contract to dismantle the camp in return for the wood. Much of the wood was used to build homes in Orderville, some of which are presumably still in use today.[10]

The Army Corps of Engineers took over much of the CCC heavy equipment, while the Navy had other equipment sent to Los Angeles. The Army tore down the camps at Garrison and Black Rock and used the lumber for construction near Ogden. Supervisor Gurr announced that F-48 in Bountiful would be occupied by Army engineers; the Pleasant Grove camp, once a Forest Service camp but by then BR-91, would be turned over to the Army Air Corps, while F-38 and F-49 would be salvaged. The technical agencies kept a few camps for storage purposes, and a few were given to their host communities, although the ten months of difficulty experienced by the city of Ferron in getting one building for Boy Scout use would have discouraged all but the most determined. Blanding was more fortunate, however, in getting one of the "left-over CCC barracks" to use as a temporary classroom/community center in a Navajo-Ute community on the edge of town.[11]

The Dalton Wells camp, DG-32, had an interesting post-CCC experience. On-site plaques about thirteen miles north of Moab incorrectly describe the "Moab Relocation Center" for the incarceration of Americans of Japanese ancestry who had been "relocated" from California, Oregon, and Washington. Moab was not, however, one of the eleven relocation centers set up by the government; Topaz in Juab County northwest of Delta was the only such center in Utah. Instead, Firmage correctly identifies it as the Moab Isolation Center, which was specially set up from January to April 1943 to temporarily house "about four dozen Americans of Japanese ancestry who had had the temerity to protest the treatment they and others of their race were receiving."[12]

The Japanese relocation, however, impacted another camp. Willow Springs camp DG-158 was located about two miles east of the Sevier County line. While some buildings and equipment from the camp were to be stored in Richfield, the barracks were dismantled and moved into Sevier County for Japanese workers to mine coal for the Topaz relocation camp.[13] Furthermore, Tremonton camp SCS-9 closed in November 1941 but did not remain empty for very long. German and Italian prisoners of war were housed there while working for nearby farmers.[14]

For most of the life of the Civilian Conservation Corps, Utah had between thirty and forty camps. Theoretically this meant that there should have been between six thousand and eight thousand enrollees in the state. Seldom, however, were the camps manned at full strength; in fact, during the closing years, many companies fell to less than one hundred men, especially in the Division of Grazing camps.

The departure of the Civilian Conservation Corps from the Utah scene in 1942 surprisingly created only a slight stir. There was no longer a Fort Douglas District; barely enough Utahns stayed in the Corps to staff two full camps; in fact, there were scarcely two camps left to be staffed. The Ohio and Kentucky boys, those from New York and New Jersey, and enrollees from Alabama and Arkansas had nearly all returned home. Most of the Reserve officers were once again in uniform and now on active duty for the duration of the war. America had a new set of priorities, and the CCC seemed irrelevant.

John Salmond suggests that the Corps had about reached the end of its existence in any case.[15] Still regarded by many as a temporary relief agency, the CCC had been experiencing internal strain for several years. Directors Fechner and, later, McEntee had been feuding with the Army over control of the organization; many disputes concerned the relative importance of relief and conservation and of work and education. As mentioned previously, employment was on the increase because of the war in Europe and the drive for preparedness at home. The military buildup, the draft, and a labor shortage in vital industries and on farms made it difficult to find unemployed youths for the camps. These various problems were coming to a head in late 1941, when the bombing at Pearl Harbor created an entirely new situation.

The Appropriation Bill of 1941–42 provided for the creation of a joint committee of Congress to look into all federal agencies whose continued existence might not be considered essential to the war effort. The committee contained few friends of the CCC and several enemies. Only two of the members, Senator Gerald Nye (R, N.D.) and Representative Clarence Cannon (D, Mo.), came from west of the Mississippi River. The committee report favored the elimination of the CCC, and Senator Kenneth McKellar of Tennessee, perhaps its most acid-tongued member, introduced legislation to initiate its demise by July 1, 1942. The measure never cleared the committee. Instead, the CCC went to its death by the simple method of suffocation when a congressional conference committee agreed to withhold further funds from the Corps, except for $8,000,000 to provide for its liquidation. On the fiftieth anniversary of the organization, an association of former CCC boys issued a pamphlet in which its history was summarized and the process was described: "Technically, the Corps was never abolished. It was far simpler for Congress just to refuse it any additional money."[16]

Still, the Civilian Conservation Corps had had a good run. In his summation of the CCC, David Kennedy, like most American historians, described it "as one of the most popular of all the New Deal's innovations." He cited the work that the three million "idle youngsters" accomplished, including building "firebreaks and lookouts in the national forests and bridges, campgrounds, trails, and museums in the national parks."[17] Like Kennedy, historian Gary Shumway echoed the sentiments of nearly every historian who ever wrote on the CCC, describing it as "one of the best conceived of the New Deal programs."[18]

Kennedy, although unfortunately failing to specify the agency responsible, stated that the New Deal had given many Americans "a sense of having a stake in their country" by the tremendous amount of work carried out. The CCC, of course, did almost all of the reforestation work and the erosion control of which he makes mention. The construction of several huge dams such as Grand Coulee, Bonneville, and Shasta was, admittedly, for the most part, outside the realm of CCC projects.[19] While giving high praise to the CCC in general, most historians generally accept that the end of the Great Depression was due less to the New Deal than to the onset of World War II.[20]

There is no doubt that many projects were carried out that could never have been attempted without the infusion of CCC funds and labor. Since the 1930s, never have the Forest Service, Park Service, and other technical agencies had the opportunity to carry out planned projects on such a scale. Fortunately, most of the agencies had long-range plans prepared so that when the CCC got under way there was little boondoggling or featherbedding.

K. C. Balcomb, regional CCC administrator for the Soil Conservation Service, described the accomplishments of his agency as follows:

> If one Utahn was to do the erosion-control work of the state's SCS camp over one year, he would have to work every day including Sunday for 643 years; if a crew of twenty men tried to accomplish the work done by the SCS between 1935 and 1941 it would take 104 years.[21]

Much of the work done by the CCC was monotonous; some of it was dangerous, such as firefighting, to which some enrollees looked forward as a relief from boredom. Some of it may have even been hastily planned and poorly directed, as some critics and even a few former participants have claimed. Deterioration has no doubt taken place. A quality analysis would be impossible to determine,[22] but over the years the work has been regarded as being of generally high standard; and the projects themselves, as most worthwhile. One Bureau of Land Management employee told me confidentially that projects built by the CCC eighty years ago were holding up better than similar projects built by other agencies—including his own—in more recent years.

A newspaper article in August 2014 identified a Sanpete County project that built on a CCC flood-control wall constructed near the small farming community of Wales back in the late 1930s, a wall "that has mostly withstood the onslaught of seasonal runoff and directed the water away from the town." Ron Francis, spokesman for the Natural Resources Conservation Service—formerly the Soil Conservation Service—paid this tribute to that seventy-five-year-old work carried out by a group of relatively inexperienced boys: "It's done a good job over the years, and the construction is amazing. This will help that [Civilian Conservation Corps] work and help keep this community safe from flooding." And in a statement one might expect to come out of the 1930s rather than the present time, the reporter wrote what could be considered "politically incorrect" by some today, but the latter half of the sentence reflects a widely held sentiment of the CCC era: "In rural Utah's political climate where the federal government is often cast as a foe, the conservation agency has earned the gratitude of locals who say the projects are critical to avert potential disasters down the road."[23]

My emphasis on the CCC should not convey the impression that I am unaware of projects carried out by other work-relief agencies during the Great Depression. The Reconstruction Finance Corporation, the Civil Works Administration, and the Works Progress Administration/Work Projects Administration made great contributions to the work that needed to be done, sometimes in conjunction with CCC work but more often on their own. Examples of Civil Works Administration activity include working on the Logan-Cache Airport as well as battling mosquitoes. Still another major project was the construction of what was then the longest bridge in the state out in Uinta County by a non-CCC working party, also in the first year of FDR's presidency. Later the *Vernal Express* told of the reservoirs and canals that had been constructed by other relief agencies.[24]

The Utah congressional delegation of that era, led by Senator Elbert D. Thomas, supported the CCC to the last. The Corps had been good to Utah, and the state was not about to desert an old friend. But it was too late. Another war raged, and this time there were enemies other than unemployment and an American wasteland, and the successes of the past gave way to concern for the future.

Arguably, most Americans of the twenty-first century have, unfortunately, never even heard of the Civilian Conservation Corps. "It's all well and good to hear about what a great outfit the CCC was," they might ask when told of the organization, "but just what did they *do*?"

During the nine years from 1933 to 1942 the Civilian Conservation Corps created an enviable legacy that has ensured its reputation for decades still to come. The dozens of fires suppressed in Utah and the thousands of trees planted endeared the organization to conservationists and foresters across the state. Untold numbers of those seeking recreation have enjoyed the campgrounds and hiking trails that were built and maintained. A smaller group of other Utah residents have benefited for eighty years from the pick, shovel, and tractor work carried out by the CCC.

In the latter years of the twentieth century the Division of State History of the Utah State Historical Society began collecting data to identify the structures built by the CCC. In an appeal to national and state conservation agencies within the state, Historic Preservation Coordinator Roger Roper asked for help. The admittedly incomplete list attached to his letter identified 447 such projects. Ignoring completely the campgrounds, roads, bridges, erosion-control structures, and ranger stations, there were at least 134 other projects including reservoirs, stock trails, corrals, spring development, and water tanks that would benefit *only* stockmen, making that group one of the major beneficiaries of CCC labor in the state in proportion to the group's size.[25]

While CCC labor in the Bureau of Reclamation camps was very significant, of course, those major projects were, for the most part, made possible only through the engineering and technical work of the bureau. The projects for the livestock industry, on the other hand, were carried out almost exclusively by CCC labor, hence my claim that, proportionately, stockmen benefited most. The irony, of course, as discussed earlier, is that today it is militant stockmen and -women in some cases who are leading the charge demanding that federal lands be turned over to state and/or local ownership.

Unfortunately, some of what was built by the CCC has been allowed to fall into disrepair due to a lack of funding and the manpower necessary for proper upkeep. In 2014 officials of the Ashley National Forest announced that about a dozen campgrounds in the Flaming Gorge and Vernal ranger districts might be closed due to maintenance problems.[26]

It should be acknowledged, however, that the law of "unintended consequences" does occasionally pop up, although, fortunately, not often, considering the amount of work that was done. Enrollees in the Zion

Table 13.1. Ten Highest States for Civilian Conservation Corps (CCC) Expenditures Per Capita, 1933–39.

State	CCC Expenditure Per Capita ($)	Percentage of Total Expenditure (%)
Nevada	213	19
Idaho	127	32
Wyoming	108	17
Arizona	101	17
New Mexico	101	19
Vermont	94	37
Utah	70	20
Montana	51	7
Colorado	41	11
Washington	36	10

Note: Arrington's table ranks forty-eight states in order of the per capita receipts of federal expenditures for the Reconstruction Finance Corporation, Federal Emergency Relief Administration, Civil Works Administration, Public Works Administration, Works Progress Administration, Rural Electrification Administration, loans, public roads, and the CCC. Other than loans, the largest single expense in forty-four of the states, CCC expenditures were the highest of all agencies listed for the first seven states listed above; in Montana, Colorado, and Washington, the Works Progress Administration ranked highest.

Nevada and Vermont may be considered aberrations. Nevada's per capita spending looms large because of the extremely small population; Vermont was the scene of the biggest CCC project in the country, the construction of three major flood-control dams along the Winooski River (Salmond, *Civilian Conservation Corps*, 128–29).

Source: Leonard Arrington, "The New Deal in the West: A Preliminary Statistical Inquiry," *Pacific Historical Review* 38 (August 1969): 315–16.

National Park camps did an outstanding job of controlling the Virgin River in the upper end of the canyon by building levees that have protected the road, campgrounds, and Zion Lodge from the spring floods. But the cottonwood trees that provide so much color to thrill park visitors are dying out as a result. The levees drastically altered the natural flow of the river. Instead of a meandering river that frequently changes channels in the springtime as it floods portions of the canyon, the Virgin River is now straight, fast, and especially energetic inside the artificial levees.

The problem is that cottonwood seeds "fall on inhospitable real estate if they land inside the levees" because the flooding river rips out any seedlings that have even managed to get a start. And it is even worse outside the levees since the seedlings require wet soil in which to take root and, outside the levees, that just doesn't happen.[27] Without CCC manpower, NPS hydrologist Dave Sharrow states that the $7,000,000 cost for a remedy to that problem "so far... has not reached the top of the priority list."

A final summation of the CCC in Utah must include some accounting of the financial effect the program had upon the state. With the exception of Vermont, only Utah's neighboring states had received a greater per capita share of CCC expenditures by 1939, and only Vermont and Idaho had had a greater share of the total federal expenditures spent for the CCC. Utah was treated well in this regard. The Federal Security Agency estimated that by the time active operations came to a halt in the summer of 1942, the CCC had spent $52,756,183 in Utah.[28]

The value, of course, would be increased if the project money supplied by the technical agencies could be calculated, in other words, the millions of dollars spent for trucks, bulldozers, draglines, bags of cement, and the pay for their own staffs. Economists marvel at the money spent, not only on the projects themselves but in infusing financial help into rural communities across the nation by constructing the camps and keeping them provisioned. Destitute families were aided by the $25.00 received monthly from their enrollee's wages, while the enrollee was able to spend the remaining $5.00 on himself, again to the financial betterment of many rural communities.

An even greater difficulty lies in determining the value received for the expenditure of these millions. How does one calculate the cost of a flood that did *not* occur, because of terracing done by CCC crews? How does one calculate the timber saved because a CCC "super squad" reached an isolated fire during the first critical minutes? What value can be placed on the enjoyment of families utilizing CCC-built campgrounds, campgrounds that might not have been built without the impetus of the CCC program and the availability of CCC labor? In 1969 James T. Patterson wrote: "It would be difficult to prove that the economic effects of

Table 13.2. Estimated Allotments to Dependants of Utah Enrollees, Fiscal Years 1933–42.

Year	Estimated Allotment ($)
1933	114,400
1934	734,448
1935	946,176
1936	727,584
1937	385,704
1938	325,248
1939	312,048
1940	297,528
1941	196,944
1942	126,004
Total	4,166,084

Source: Data compiled by multiplying an annual allotment of $264 (assuming a mean $22.00 monthly allotment in effect for most of the program) by the average number of Utahns in camps for the fiscal years, determined from *Reports of the Director.* The figure for 1942 is determined by subtracting the total through 1941 from the total given in U.S. Civilian Conservation Corps, "Total Work Completed during the Period—April, 1933 to June 30, 1942, Utah."

the New Deal were more beneficial to the West than elsewhere, but there is no doubt that the impact was considerable."[29]

Approximately $4,100,000 was returned to families from the monthly allotments of the 16,872 junior enrollees from Utah. The $264 a family received each year it had a member in the CCC helped considerably at a time when 65 percent of the families in the country received less than $1,500 a year.[30] The extra money, added to that saved because a family member was being clothed and fed by the government, made life a little easier for those still at home.

The relative value of the employment of Utah's 746 Indian enrollees and 4,456 supervisory personnel would be even more significant. In all, 22,074 Utah men were given employment by the CCC during the nine-year period. An additional 23,833 individuals were brought in from out of state to work in Utah, many of whom remained, although probably not the ten thousand referred to by one enthusiastic camp commander.[31]

Table 13.3. Employment Structure in Selected Industries in Utah, 1940.

Occupational Group	Percentage of Utahns Employed (%)
Agriculture	19.2
Metal mining	4.9
Civilian Conservation Corps	4.4
Banking and finance	3.0
Food processing	2.9
Nonferrous metal industry	2.4

Source: Compiled from table X, "Industrial Structure of the Mountain West, 1940," in Leonard J. Arrington, *The Changing Economic Structure of the Mountain West, 1850–1950*, Monograph Series, vol. 10, no. 3 (Logan: Utah State University Press, June 1963), 37. Arrington's data were taken from tables 74 and 75 in U.S. Department of Commerce, Bureau of the Census, *Sixteenth Census of the United States, 1940, Population, vol. III: The Labor Force, Parts L–5* (Washington, D.C.: U.S. Government Printing Office, 1943). The Civilian Conservation Corps figure is mine.

The employment contribution of the Corps may be seen by comparing CCC enrollment with those employed in other fields within the state. A few months before the 1940 Census, there were 6,179 enrollees in the Utah camps, in addition to approximately 340 others in supervisory positions as either military or technical agency personnel.[32] This amounted to 4.4 percent of the labor force as determined by the 1940 figures and compares very favorably with such significant and traditional Utah employers as metal mining and the nonferrous metal industry.

The Forest Service's Intermountain Region benefited more financially than any other sector of the nation. Utah ranked seventh in money spent, with $70.00 of CCC funding per capita. Although well below neighboring Nevada, Idaho, and Wyoming, ranked first to third, with $213, $127, and $108, respectively, Utah had no reason to complain, since CCC enrollment—also lower than in other intermountain states—as shown in Table 13.3, still ranked third in terms of percentage of the entire labor force in the state.[33]

The financial implications of the removal of the CCC presence were offset somewhat by the economic boost brought on by the war effort. In addition to the way the community benefited from the financial assistance provided and the work projects completed might be added another, less obvious gain: "that of accommodating…young men from different cultural, social, religious, and ethnic backgrounds who had a great deal to teach a group that had always been highly insular."[34]

Good things were being said about the benefits to the men of the Civilian Conservation Corps almost from the very beginning. An article in 1939 states that from the twenty-six states then represented in Utah camps, there were some "who never wore a pair of shoes, never saw a train, don't know how to read or write," and who had those shortcomings eliminated through their CCC service.[35]

In spite of the many high school diplomas and work course certificates that were granted, the Corps did not do as well as an establishment of formal education as had been hoped; as a vocational training institute its success was only slightly greater. Although most valued their CCC work experience for the feelings of accomplishment and mastery it provided, it actually proved to be of little lasting value in preparing very many men for their lifetime's vocation, the occasional cook and heavy equipment operator notwithstanding. Many a former CCC boy claimed that the major benefits to the participant were the intangibles in the realm of social development, that is, his own maturation and his ability to get along with his peers.

The following comments are representative of those offered when former enrollees were queried on the value of the CCC to them personally. An enrollee with five years' service commented:

> It made a man of me.…I learned how to take orders and give them in a way that could be understood.…I can say it was the most rewarding experience that I have ever had in my life.…A university professor felt that.…Overall it was a marvelous experience.…It helped me to mature and to weigh my values against others' values.

"I think it was the greatest experience a young fellow could enjoy," declared an ex-Floridian who stayed in Utah after his CCC experience. Another six-year veteran said that those were the "happiest years of my life [because the Corps] took me off the street as a boy and made a man of me."[36]

It was learning how to work, learning how to cooperate, and occasionally learning how to stand alone that the CCC provided for enrollees. So if the enrollee got less than was desired in the way of academic and vocational training, where was the benefit? Ultimately it was in that crucible of social development that the greatest good took place, a purpose for which the Corps had hardly been considered.

Francis Welsh, the former first aid man described in chapter 10, remarked, "For Roosevelt and the Democratic Party during those trying times, I thank God." He gave what I feel is a good summation:

> All the men I have talked to who were in the CCC have nothing but praise for it, and many of them say I sure wish I'd have stayed longer. During my tour with the CCC I seen many young men come into the camp, confused, some with a chip on their shoulder, Mama's boys spoiled rotten. Most of them away from home for the first time, and I've seen these same boys leave the camp as men, with a clear eye, and firm step, ready to face the world and life with confidence.[37]

The words of appreciation for their experience came not only from nostalgic old-timers reminiscing thirty years later. Many of the boys recognized at the time that they had a pretty good deal going for them. David Chicarelli of Company 536 was editor of the *Bay Cross News* and serving at SP-2 when he praised the CCC for (1) taking the boys off the streets and giving them a home, clothing, and food; (2) providing a proper education through night classes, which often led to a high school diploma; (3) giving them better training for getting a job at home; and (4) building "men out of boys."[38]

Max J. Schlegel was an enrollee at F-1 who wrote a column for the Logan newspaper where he described his feelings:

> Emergency conservation work is . . . a project essentially for restoring confidence, of building men through worthwhile work. . . . I have been given a chance to re-establish normal relations with life, to re-create faith in the future as well as the faith of relatives and friends, and an opportunity to send money home to help those who helped me and shared what little they had.[39]

Jim Brown served with Company 2539 at Brigham City's BS-1. He had been born in the backwoods of Tennessee in 1918 to a family described as "desperately poor." In 1939 he went to Toledo, Ohio, on an unsuccessful trip to find work in an auto factory. Seeing a flyer about the CCC, he endured three days of medical exams and shots and was soon on his way to Utah. He served twenty-seven months before joining the Marines when World War II broke out: "The training and discipline I learned in the C's were excellent preparation for the service. When I entered the Marines, my superiors couldn't believe I had never been in the military before."[40]

Another measure of the perceived value by those personally associated with the program, I feel, involves the responses given to a question on my questionnaire: "Would you like your son to have a chance to work in similar conditions and circumstances?" Admittedly, the sampling is too miniscule to be scientifically valid, but the results are still interesting. Of the eighty-seven former CCC and Army personnel and community observers who responded to that particular question, 78 percent answered yes—several quite emphatically—15.1 percent said no, and 6.9 percent said "only if necessary."

A question concerning their own personal enjoyment of their experience was answered by sixty-seven respondents, 70.2 percent of whom regarded their experience as "very pleasant"; 17.9 percent said that it was "only mildly pleasant"; 11.9 percent felt that it was "unpleasant." The latter figure I still find quite high considering the enthusiasm that those to whom I actually spoke felt about what they had done.

These were the boys who had become men during the Great Depression years and went on to even greater accomplishments during World War II. Most of them became those whom Tom Brokaw wrote about in his epic book:

> They faced great odds and a late start, but they did not protest. At a time in their lives when their days and nights should have been filled with innocent adventure, love, and the lessons of the workaday world, they were fighting, often hand to hand, in the most primitive conditions possible, across the bloodied landscape of France, Belgium, Italy, Austria. They fought their way up a necklace of South Pacific islands few had ever heard of before

> and made them a fixed part of American history—islands with names like Iwo Jima, Guadalcanal, Okinawa. They were in the air every day, in skies filled with terror, and they went to sea on hostile waters far removed from the shores of their homeland.
>
> ... This is the greatest generation any society has produced.[41]

In a news article written several decades later Lori Nawyn described the young men of the CCC in Box Elder County as "America's sweethearts, heroes to a country badly in need of a motivating force."[42] Young men who had previously been down and out began to take pride in themselves and in what they could do. Many felt the perspiration of an honest day's work for the first time and rejoiced in the satisfaction of it. It is these intangibles, these effects on the individuals, that CCC supporters meant when referring to the conservation of America's human resources. This is what Governor Blood probably had in mind when he described the changed outlook and attitudes of new enrollees:

> They were filled with hope and optimism; the spark of ambition had been re-kindled; they contemplated the future fearlessly and with little or no doubt as to its outcome.... In view of these facts I feel that immeasurable good has resulted from the establishment of these camps.[43]

Where, then, does one look for the monuments to the Civilian Conservation Corps in Utah? During its existence of less than a decade the CCC created a legacy that should ensure its acclaim for decades to come: if people only knew. Conservationists, foresters, and others commend it for the hundreds of fires suppressed and the millions of trees planted across the country. Many seeking recreation and outdoor activities have benefited from the campgrounds developed, the trails built and maintained, and the reservoirs constructed.

Such monuments might include the riprapping along the Virgin River, Lake Bauram, the bridge over the San Rafael Wash, the campgrounds up Logan Canyon, the Bear River Bird Refuge, the terracing overlooking much of the Wasatch Front, and the dozens of reservoirs and springs in the West Desert. All would qualify. In Utah, the 115 camps stretching from Lucin to Blanding and from Manila to St. George also built everything from massive irrigation projects, wildlife refuges, and cattle trails to parks and rodeo grounds. The young men in the camps, most of whom were nineteen or twenty years of age, were also available to provide emergency services in a variety of circumstances; snake-bitten children, lost hikers, and those rescued from capsized watercraft are but a few who had reason to be eternally grateful to the CCC.

The physical evidence exists in abundance. But, again, perhaps it would be best to turn again to the participants themselves and hear the words of some of Utah's human monuments:

> "It taught me to use good common sense.... The CCC was the finest thing that could have happened to the youth of America during the Depression years."
>
> "My enrollment in the Corps came at a time when everything I needed was lost to me, no home, financially unable to go to school and filled with despair."
>
> "It helped me to accept responsibility... taught me the importance of conservation [and] made me appreciate the outdoors more."
>
> "We were taught discipline, how to organize, get along and work and play together with a high moral outlook on life."
>
> "It took me out of the big city and factory district, taught me other ways of living and making a living."
>
> "One of the most enjoyable parts of my growing up."
>
> "The friends that were made will never be replaced."
>
> "I know that the CCC was one of the best things that Uncle Sam ever did for the boys of this country."

An unidentified reporter for the camp paper of Company 4779, then stationed at NP-2, added his testimonial concerning the program:

> After you have been in this organization for a few months you learn to shift for yourself and also along with your fellow-men. You learn to keep fit, clean, and healthy, and also learn to respect your Officers, Foremen, Leaders and other fellows with whom you deal with in everyday life.[44]

These positive feelings, for the most part, did not diminish with the passage of time. Speaking in 2006, former LEM Owen Price offered his view concerning the value of the program: "These CCC camps were the best thing that ever happened to boys that age. It kept them out of trouble and made men out of boys. They built character."[45]

Comments from out of state were equally effusive, although I include only two from personal contacts. In an undated typescript in my possession, Missouri resident Richard Crisinger shared his feelings about his CCC service in Wisconsin and Oregon more than six decades before and the CCC in general:

> My two years in the CCCs helped make a man of me, and it taught me skills which saved my life many times during a 34-year military career. The 3Cs allowed me to help build a better country. Millions of young people could become better citizens in a better country if the CCC could come alive again.

Until his death in his late nineties, retired U.S. Air Force Master Sergeant Crisinger was active in "CCC Legacy," the national organization of former CCC "boys," especially through his financial contribution of thousands of dollars for *CCC Worker* statues in several states, including Utah, until his death on January 12, 2017.

A similar sentiment was voiced by an information specialist with the Pennsylvania Game Commission in an article about an enrollee who served in the Keystone State:

> Tens of thousands of former CCC boys enlisted in the armed forces and went off to fight in World War II. The discipline, work ethic, and physical fitness training they received while with the CCC made this contingent of men uniquely prepared to meet the demands they were to face as soldiers, sailors, and Marines.[46]

The *Salt Lake Tribune* bade farewell to the Corps in an editorial on July 3, 1942, in which thanks were expressed for the physical accomplishments and recognition was granted for the human achievements as well:

> More than all else it aided youth to get a new grip on destiny and obtain a saner outlook on the need of the nation. It transformed

> millions of grumbling malcontents on the verge of revolution into heroes and patriots ready to fight for their birthright. The CCC may be dead but the whole country is covered with lasting monuments to its timely service.[47]

To set nostalgia, memories, and gratitude in their proper perspective, it would be well to consider the remarks published in an educational magazine in the 1960s:

> We were a better country for the CCC. Working on socially useful public projects, youth were given new health, new hope, new faith in the country and in themselves. . . . It left a tremendous legacy of good will and experience. Here is a program, an experiment, not to copy, but to recall and ponder as we rack our brains for new and fertile approaches to the problems of education, as we think of the plight of our inner cities, of our young people dissatisfied with school, of the long, hot summers ahead.[48]

The concept of work was not a political issue in the 1930s as it seems to be in the twenty-first century; rather, it was a matter of survival. Although few enrollees of the time had probably read of Alexis de Toqueville's 1831 visit to America, they would very likely have agreed with his observation that Americans are willing to work to get ahead—when that work is available. And although it was written in a politically conservative periodical of seven decades later, they would certainly have agreed, "Work is good for people."[49]

It would be extremely difficult to overestimate the popularity of the Civilian Conservation Corps, at least for anyone who knows anything at all about the program. Nearly every book concerning the depression years and the history of the New Deal as well as most local histories are extravagant in their praise of the organization. Writing in 2008, author Jen Jackson speaks from a strictly western point of view in a most positive manner: "In fact, the rural West, long known for its sagebrush rebels and local-versus-federal government attitudes, embraced the CCC like no other federal program before or since. And for good reason. Western states benefited greatly from the CCC's achievements."[50] And to bring that perspective into even more recent times, Olin Cole Jr. concludes his fine book on the African-American experience by conceding that although the CCC was of limited value to the subjects of his research, the value of the organization was still most positive and could, if continued, become part of a civil rights impetus.[51]

As a precedent, the image of the CCC is clear: it served as a basis for President John F. Kennedy's Peace Corps in the 1960s, as well as President Lyndon B. Johnson's Job Corps and similar "Great Society" programs. Indeed, the permanent testimony of the CCC and its work is the ability of the state to implement reform. The magnitude of the despair and hopelessness of the 1930s required state intervention, and the establishment of the CCC represented the nation-state's response to the problems of the youth. If the Civilian Conservation Corps represents an example of what the government can do for its jobless youth in times of depression, it is certainly worth the effort to put the New Deal to contemporary purposes.

The Civilian Conservation Corps will always stand as an outstanding example of what can be done in times of desperation. Perhaps one of the reasons for the failure, or, at least, the less-than-complete success, of recent CCC imitations has been that many of the participants have just not been "hungry" enough, and the availability of other, less demanding, alternatives has diluted enthusiasm for entering into strenuous physical labor in a strange environment. It may also be that the magnitude of the depression of the 1930s was such that not only the degree of unemployment was higher numerically but it consisted qualitatively of a wider spectrum of social and economic classes than is the case at present. For this reason "Middle America" was then inclined to be more sympathetic to the movement than it is now, when many people find it difficult to understand why, in these times of affluence, a person can't find work if he or she really wants to. Many oppose a revival of the CCC as a working organization because most of the vocational skills that young people would learn are unsuitable in the urban settings in which most of the nation's unemployed live. At a 1982 reunion in Ferron of Company 959 enrollees, Willard Smith, one of the reunion organizers, offered what might seem a cynical evaluation: "Kids today would laugh at you if you tried to hire them for what we did and offered them $500 a month."[52]

Although certainly a positive factor, the success of the program should not be measured by the absorption of specific skills. Rather, it consists in the creation of wholesome vocational attitudes, the feeling of making a positive contribution, the development of self-esteem and coming to grips with one's own self, and the establishment of rapport with one's fellow man and with society in general.

In short, those accomplishments achieved in the 1930s have led to the revival of several CCC-type organizations across the country. In retrospect, it may well be that of the activities that took place in Utah beginning more than eighty years ago, it was not the development of resources, or of monuments to conservation and recreation, but the creation of men that was the CCC's most significant contribution. Actually, I found that Arthur Schlesinger agrees with me—or I with him, since he wrote ten years before me: "The CCC left its monuments in the preservation and purification of the land, the water, the forests, and the young men of America."[53]

A similar sentiment was offered by Utah historian Robert McPherson in his contribution to the Utah Centennial County History Series. After reciting again a newspaper account of the physical products of the Civilian Conservation Corps—in constructing reservoirs, roads, trails, campgrounds, amphitheaters, and corrals; eliminating noxious weeds and rodents; thinning timber; fighting wildfires; and replanting forests and revegetating rangelands—he notes that perhaps its greatest accomplishment was "the reclamation of the American boy."[54] By that or most any other yardstick, those were an outstanding nine years of achievement.

Epilogue

The Beat Goes On

It was a very fine thing for both us youngsters and the conservation program and [I] wish it had continued.
—M. F. (Mike) Burson, enrollee, camp F-35

It isn't just the bridges, campgrounds, stock trails, and emergency work done by the CCC that have provided ways for the nation and the state of Utah to recall the tremendous impact of what was done by the Corps over the nine years between 1933 and 1942. Organizations have been created to perpetuate its legacy; signs have been erected to identify the location of CCC camps and projects, and many corps groups have been set up to carry on the actual work carried out by the enrollees in the 1930s.

CCC ALUMNI

National Association of Civilian Conservation Corps Alumni

That the great work of the CCC shall not be forgotten has, over the years, been the focus of several organizations, communities, and dedicated individuals. A major impetus was the creation of the National Association of Civilian Conservation Corps Alumni, set up in 1969 by men who had actually been in the Corps in their youth. From its headquarters in Missouri, the group's rallying cry was "Bring back the CCC."

CCC Legacy

As the National Association of Civilian Conservation Corps Alumni membership aged, however, and it appeared that their appeal for restoration of the Corps was falling on deaf ears, it began to fade from the scene;

Figure 14.1. One of the two field trips featured at the 2011 gathering of CCC Legacy in St. George stopped at Pine Valley, site of F-10, one of Utah's original twenty Forest Service camps.

and by 2008 it had merged with Camp Roosevelt CCC Legacy based in Edinburg, Virginia, carrying on the purpose of the original organization. Renamed CCC Legacy, the new organization received the support of the National Association of Civilian Conservation Corps Alumni, whose participants transferred their membership, loyalty, and interest to the new group. The goals of the organization were identified in a 2013 brochure: "Honor and remember the men of the CCC. Preserve the stories of the people and projects of the CCC. Develop CCC Interpretive displays. Develop educational programs that will reach citizens of all ages. Support the preservation of CCC heritage. Strengthen CCC Legacy."[1]

Headquartered near the site of the first CCC installation, Camp Roosevelt, CCC Legacy is administered by an executive board headed from its founding to at least 2018 by hardworking president Joan Sharpe. Initially local chapters were the foundation of CCC Legacy, but now only a few chapters remain, and it is just the general membership that keeps the organization functioning. The establishment of a CCC Museum, erecting commemorative pavers, and the construction of a replica CCC camp are projects pursued at the headquarters. Other ongoing projects include publication of the bimonthly twenty- to twenty-four-page *CCC Legacy Journal* and facilitating the annual "CCC Legacy gatherings," held

Figure 14.2. Only six of the surviving Civilian Conservation Corps "boys" were able to attend the 2016 gathering of CCC Legacy in Las Vegas.

around the country under the auspices of either local conservation agencies or dedicated CCC Legacy volunteers.

The first gathering was held in Virginia in 2008, and since then they have been held annually in order in Colorado, Missouri, Utah, Montana, Arizona, Minnesota, Connecticut, and Nevada. The 2011 Utah event was held in St. George, and on two days of field trips attendees visited thirteen of the fifteen CCC camps in Washington County, the most heavily "CCC-d" county in Utah. The 2016 gathering was held in Las Vegas, Nevada, September 22–25, and the 2017 gathering was in South Carolina.

A relatively new project in effect over the past few years has been the goal of placing a bronze, near-life-size *CCC Worker* statue in every state, on the grounds of a cooperating state park, national forest, or city park or even private property. Recently a statue was dedicated in Zion National Park, on September 26, 2016, the first to go up in Utah, although plans are currently afoot for another statue to be located in Salina, where an impressive sign is already in place on the site of PE-219 and F-32. This leaves fewer than a dozen states without a statue; Pennsylvania leads the field with seven.

Although the statue dedication was held the day after the gathering in Las Vegas in hopes that more CCC "boys" could attend, Sam Williams was the only one able to do so. Unfortunately, Sam passed away just over two weeks later.

Figure 14.3. Sam Williams was the only Civilian Conservation Corps "boy" to attend the dedication of the Zion National Park *CCC Worker* statue. He died just over two weeks later on October 14, 2016.

Figure 14.4. CCC Legacy President Joan Sharpe, at the dedication of the Zion National Park *CCC Worker* statue, listening to Zion Superintendent Jeff Bradybaugh tell of Civilian Conservation Corps work in the park.

The idea of using youth to carry out conservation projects did not completely die when the CCC folded in 1942. There have been many such groups to come and go with varying degrees of success. One of the earliest and certainly the longest-lived, largest, and most successful is the Student Conservation Association.

CARRYING ON THE WORK—THE "COPYCATS"

If imitation is the highest form of flattery, those associated with the Civilian Conservation Corps should feel well rewarded for the various organizations that have sprung up over the past eight decades that have taken the CCC as their model. Over the years there have been occasional cries to "Bring back the CCC," often espoused by CCC boys themselves, especially those who belonged to the National Association of Civilian Conservation Corps Alumni before it folded. Most of those voices have now been stilled, mostly because of the attrition of those nostalgic individuals who recall the tremendous impact the CCC had on their own lives and on the country in general.

Although the Job Corps began as a federally sponsored attempt to emulate the CCC, the program has experienced somewhat mixed results, with its emphasis on providing educational opportunities for disadvantaged youth and a lesser commitment to conservation. There are still a few of the "boys" in CCC Legacy, where there is a growing realization that rather than utilizing federal agencies, perhaps state and local conservation corps might be a better way to go. In 2008 there were 113 corps programs in forty-one states, operating under the umbrella of the Corps Network and providing employment opportunities for 21,000 young people annually in conservation work, which often leads to a career: "The CCC may be long gone, but a living legacy exists, continuing the environmental and societal work first implemented seventy-five years ago."[2] On conversing with members of different corps groups it appeared that their reasons for participating ranged from the need for employment, to resume-building for work in the conservation field, to a love of the outdoors, to a desire to just be part of something worthwhile.

AmeriCorps

In 2016 there were approximately 120 to 130 youth conservation groups in the United States, most of which exist under the umbrella of AmeriCorps, created by law in 1993. Of the three major segments of the organization, AmeriCorps State and National is the largest and casts a much wider net—including the approximately 130 various conservation corps—than the other two, AmeriCorps NCCC and AmeriCorps VISTA. Due to the unique characteristics of each conservation corps, there is no one-size-fits-all description of just how they are funded or how they operate.[3]

It would be safe to say, however, that the primary mission of the Corps Network is the education of corps enrollees, development of leadership skills, and preparation for future careers; the conservation work they do so well is more of a means to an end. In the CCC, on the other hand, the priorities were *relief*, followed very closely (almost equally, in fact) by *work*, with *education* further down the list of objectives, and sometimes it didn't show up at all.

Student Conservation Association

The national Student Conservation Association (SCA) is one of the oldest and certainly the largest of the youth conservation groups. If the one hundred-plus conservation corps that have existed over the years were spinoffs of the depression-era Civilian Conservation Corps, the SCA was itself a spinoff of a sort, from a college senior essay, no less.[4] Elizabeth Cushman was a student at Vassar College when, on December 1, 1954, she submitted her paper "Thesis on a Proposed STUDENT CONSERVATION CORPS." She recommended that her conservation corps, described in her introduction as a body that was "to be made up of, organized by, and planned for students," work in America's national parks. She conceded, however, that "if the Corps proves its value, it would do work in other needed areas."[5] Since then its value has been proved many times over, and today the Student Conservation Association partners with nearly every national land management agency as well as countless state and local groups.

In addition to giving her an *A* on her essay, Cushman's faculty adviser, Dr. A. Scott Warthin Jr., challenged her to spend two years doing something about the suggestions she had offered. Her response: "It was the funniest thing I'd ever heard. I mean, who'd listen to a girl with a paper in her hands?"[6] The paper in her hands, fortunately, was more than just a theoretical suggestion about the need for conservation work; it was virtually a nuts-and-bolts blueprint explaining how her plans could be carried out. She accepted the challenge, lined up some influential partners, and launched the Student Conservation Association. Cushman is still active in the organization sixty years after selecting her thesis topic and has found, to her great satisfaction, that many people, up to and including congressional committees, have been willing to listen to *that* girl, at least, with a paper in her hands.

The SCA record in Utah is impressive. Volunteers have served in all five of the national forests now existing in the state; every national park and national monument has benefited from the work they have done. In addition to the U.S. Forest Service and National Park Service, they have also worked for the Bureau of Land Management, the Bureau of Reclamation, and the Utah Division of Wildlife Resources. They have made their mark in three bird and wildlife refuges and three national recreation and historic areas, as well as agency headquarters and experiment stations.

In addition to being the target of SCA's first expansion, Utah figured in another "first" when volunteers were assigned to Dixie National Forest in the southern part of the state. It was "the organization's first foray beyond the park service."[7] It was also in Utah's Canyonlands National Park that a fifteen-year-old from New York and her crewmates traveled by jeep and river raft in 1975 to reach their summer campsite at Anderson Bottom on a bend of the Colorado River. After another SCA stint the following year, this teenager grew up to be Allison Whipple Rockefeller, for many years a commissioner with the New York State Office of Parks, Recreation and Historic Preservation.

Although trail-building has perhaps been the signature activity of SCA volunteers over the years, they have also served on a myriad of other assignments, from planting flowers in alpine meadows to working as interns with park biologists and naturalists, building bridges and outhouses, and constructing check dams. From the very beginning, Liz Putnam insisted that "the program must benefit both the park and the participants, as outlined in her original proposal."[8] The program has now moved into inner-city park work in some major metropolitan areas in the country. In addition to planting flowers and beautifying urban parks, SCA volunteers also helped in the aftermath of Hurricanes Sandy and Harvey.

One of the most massive projects in SCA history was the three-year Greater Yellowstone Recovery Corps, 1989–91. It was in the summer of 1988 that two "fairly typical forest fires were burning in different districts" of the park. In August the two fires merged, and not until the arrival of smothering snowfalls in November was the conflagration extinguished, leaving nearly half of the park's 2,200,000 acres in ashes. Jay Ashe had been a full-time SCA staff member since 1988 and in 1990 was serving as a coleader of "India-3," one of twenty alphabetically identified SCA crews of high school students who worked to restore Yellowstone along with other conservation corps and just plain citizens from not only forty-six states but fifteen other countries as well. Ashe later described the effort in a chapter of *Our Land. Our Youth. Our Future.*

Nearly 1,300 adult and teenaged volunteers worked at building miles of trails and sixty-three bridges along with various revegetation projects. Even fifty-six-year-old Liz Putnam spent time on the scene getting physically involved with the program she had conceived more than three decades before. Ashe summed up his summer experience as follows: "And after an exhilarating, challenging, and sometimes exhausting summer, my 'India-3' co-leader Meg Hafer and I pulled off the last crazy logistical feat of the year. We got married."[9]

In line with the need for trained firefighting professionals in 2010 SCA launched the Veterans Fire Corps in partnership with the U.S. Forest Service, designed primarily to help military veterans of service in Iraq and Afghanistan reenter civilian life. While liability concerns currently keep the veterans off active fire lines, crews do remove potential fire fuels in forested areas and also carry out prescribed burns to lessen the danger of destructive wildfires.[10]

SCA volunteers are just that—volunteers—and receive no pay for their services, in many cases buying some of their own equipment. The 2012 Annual Report shows that SCA was a $33,000,000 operation at that time and that the expenses of the organization are met by contributions from supportive citizens and from an esoteric list of partner organizations ranging from American Eagle Outfitters to Garden Club of America to Southwest Airlines to NASCAR. As high school and college students, SCA participants work primarily during the summer months.

SCA provides a great example of how a nongovernmental organization can work with government agencies—national, state, and local—on such a wide range of conservation projects as to be almost beyond description. The mission, of course, is to further the cause of conservation while helping the youth of America, as did its model, the Civilian Conservation Corps. The success of the program is reflected in an interview with SCA alumni Todd Nelson, now working as the volunteer coordinator at Grand Canyon National Park. When he was asked the number of SCA alumni employed at the park, his answer was impressive: "Forty. Ten percent of our staff. They're all over this place."[11]

Funding for programs varies from corps to corps. The SCA has the most aggressive fund-raising program, seeking public donations and offering annuities for long-term giving. While some locally based youth corps are now defunct, many are still operating. Only a few examples are offered here.

Utah Conservation Corps

In the Beehive State it is primarily the Utah Conservation Corps (UCC) that is carrying on the CCC tradition. This group, now one of about 140 across the country, began in January 2001, with about twenty young people and a grant from AmeriCorps. Theirs was a deliberate attempt to emulate the work of the CCC, and they felt strongly that its legacy was well worth preserving. In an e-mail to me on July 10, 2013, Sean Damitz, one of the original group members and the current director, emphasized that "our mission statement of 'developing the conservation leaders of tomorrow through service and education' reflects that commitment."[12]

The UCC is quite unique in that it is probably the only corps group in the country to actually be part of a university. Utah State University, formerly Utah State Agricultural College, began as a land-grant institution and is still pursuing the mission for which it was created. Administratively designated the Center for Civic Engagement and Service Learning within the university, the UCC receives funding from Utah State University, AmeriCorps, and the agencies for which projects are being carried out. The first project of the fledgling group began in 2001 at Capitol Reef National Monument in the south-central part of the state, where they constructed a trail to the requirements of the Americans with Disabilities Act.

Between 120 and 140 young adults, mostly between eighteen and twenty-five, go through the adult UCC program each year. The age limits can often be extended to include some slightly older members and even high school graduates who may not yet be eighteen. Unlike for the CCC, there is no relief requirement for the Utah Conservation Corps. Members, most of whom are students at Utah State University, are actually classified as employees and serve under the vice president for student services on the Logan campus, where the corps headquarters is located with the uninformative title of Student Sustainability Office. Open to both men and women, the UCC is also racially diverse, including African Americans, Latinos, and members of Southeast Asian backgrounds.

UCC's website describes the corps vision: "We strive to develop the conservation leaders of tomorrow through service and education, create partnerships to address environmental challenges, and inform civically-engaged citizens. We value leadership development and personal growth among Corps members and the inclusion of underserved populations."[13] The UCC is divided into a youth sector—which, incidentally, is bilingual in Spanish and English—and an adult sector. The former consists primarily of high school students who stay at their own home every night, while the adult group can remain away as long as necessary. After serving in the youth sector of the UCC students can advance to the adult crews, which Damitz has described as "pretty rewarding."[14]

Since 2010 there have even been three crews of military veterans who participate in regular UCC activities and, according to Damitz, seem quite happy to also be part of integrated crews, that is, mixed veterans and nonveterans. As mentioned, most of the UCC participants are students at Utah State University enthusiastically pursuing a major that will lead to some aspect or another of conservation.

The work carried out by the UCC consists of a variety of tasks: it has "maintained and restored over 3,055 miles of trails, built or maintained over 224 miles of fence, restored over 32,078 acres of habitat, provided environmental education for 244,000 students," in addition to fuel reduction, building check dams, and waging war on invasive plant species such as thistles, tamarisk, and Russian olives, the latter by cutting them down and then spraying the roots with herbicides.[15] There are some activities in which the CCC was heavily involved in which the UCC is not, such as firefighting, riprapping along streams, and rodent control. Crews are generally out in the field between March and November, although some replanting personnel may work year-round. While other corps across the country often have about a dozen in a crew, UCC crews generally have four, headed by a leader, either male or female. Crew members generally sign up for terms of three months to up to a year, with the possibility of reenlistment for up to two years.

Since its inception in 2001, the UCC has been quite popular, and there are usually more applicants than available positions. Participation in projects may be initiated by either the UCC or an agency needing its services, including nonprofit groups. In addition to getting contracts with national land management agencies, the UCC has also worked in city parks in Salt Lake City as well as carrying out work in neighboring

Wyoming and Idaho. In fact, UCC crews helped out with the aftermath of Hurricanes Katrina, Sandy, and Harvey.

In accordance with the standards set by AmeriCorps, its umbrella organization, UCC workers are paid a living allowance as well as a grant toward the pursuit of further education, meaning that during a summer tour from May to August, a student could earn a living allowance of more than $3,200 plus an education allowance of almost $1,500, usually tied to the federal Pell Grant for university students. There are also specific crews—one with a wheelchair-bound leader—who work on Americans with Disabilities Act projects.[16]

In the summer of 2016, UCC crews began working on the restoration of wetlands along the Jordan River Trail near Riverton in Salt Lake County. The project, administered by the Jordan River Commission, is a joint effort of the UCC; Utah Division of Forestry, Fire and State Lands; Salt Lake County; and Riverton City Parks and Recreation. The work involves the removal of puncture vine, thistle, and invasive phragmites through the application of herbicides followed by mowing treated areas along the steep, rocky banks of the Jordan River.[17]

Other Utah Corps Groups

Other corps groups in Utah include the Southern Utah University Intergovernmental Internship Cooperative, which places Southern Utah University students in land management agencies. The Canyon Country Youth Corps is another smaller group that operates out of the Four Corners School of Outdoor Education in Monticello in southeastern Utah, manned to a large extent by Native American and Latino young people between the ages of fifteen and twenty-five. Crews of eight carry out service projects on public lands such as construction and maintenance of trails, building and maintaining fences, restoration of habitat, and reduction of fuels in fire-prone areas. An educational component is pursued through the work experience so that participants in the Canyon Country Youth Corps "learn about the environment, career building, leadership, and communication." In an e-mail to me, program director Jake Deslauriers acknowledged the CCC connection, stating that his group was "thinking about putting a CCC exhibit in our new Canyon Country Discovery Center."[18]

Back Country Horsemen of America

Although claiming no link to the CCC and perhaps not realizing it, organizations such as the Back Country Horsemen of America are also carrying on the work of the CCC. For its own fortieth anniversary in 2013, about 150 Utah enthusiasts mounted on horseback or riding in wagons participated in a 150-mile, nine-day trek on the Skyline Drive along the crest of the mountains between Emery and Sanpete counties. Members and nonmembers of the national, nonprofit association carried out volunteer service projects for the Forest Service and Bureau of Land Management. Jeff Nichols, president of the Back Country Horsemen of America Utah County Chapter, said that the work done helps maintain and protect public lands to be sure that roads and trails are available to all. The main projects of the volunteers in 2013 were grubbing about five bags of noxious weeds from a meadow and dismantling abandoned corrals and fences, both projects on which enrollees worked eight decades before. Whether they knew they were on a road the CCC built back in the 1930s is not known, although there are a few signs to that effect in the vicinity.[19]

Southwest Conservation Corps

The Southwest Conservation Corps operates primarily in the Four Corners area of the country. "Approximately half of the participants" in the corps "could be labeled 'disadvantaged' youth," and their projects range "from day-long community service activities for 14-and-15-year olds to 11-month leadership programs for college graduates."[20]

Funding

Funding for these different corps organizations is as varied as the corps themselves. The SCA has an assertive fund-raising program that generates much of its money from private contributions as well as offering annuities for long-term income for those supporting the program.[21] Minnesota levies a small sales tax to help fund Conservation Corps Minnesota and Iowa, at least for those projects in Minnesota. The Utah Conservation Corps receives some of its funding from Utah State University, where it is housed. In most cases, however, nearly all of the corps are basically supported by income from the sale of their services, which they contract out to different public and private conservation entities when their bids on projects are accepted.

MEMORIALIZING THE CCC

It is perhaps fitting that the site of Utah's first Civilian Conservation Corps camp should also be among the top examples of paying homage to the enrollees and the accomplishments of the organization. Granite Flat Campground in American Fork Canyon was the site of F-5, which, although the first to open, was also one of the first to be discontinued, lasting only for the First Enrollment Period. Located in a beautiful setting at an elevation of more than six thousand feet a mile above Tibble Fork Reservoir, the beautifully maintained Forest Service campground has several signs explaining various aspects of CCC life. The eight camping areas are also identified by names associated with the CCC experience, such as Tree Army, Barracks, Mess Hall, Stonemason, Sandwagon, and Handshaker. Most of the terms are probably familiar to visitors, but the latter two might need explanation for those unfamiliar with CCC jargon. "Sandwagon" was a nickname for a wheelbarrow, while "handshaker" was the somewhat accusatory name given to an apple-polisher, or one trying to get in good with the boss.

After the CCC buildings were removed in 1937, the site became the Granite Flat Campground the following year. It soon became one of the most popular areas in the state for overnight camping as well as daytime activities, including use of the baseball diamond, the only CCC-built remnant visible today.

In 1993 the Uinta National Forest and Utah State Historical Society conducted a joint study of CCC campsites and CCC-built structures in Utah County in order to document the Corps' presence in the canyon. Mildred Sutch and Beth Olsen of the Pleasant Grove Historical Preservation Commission and Roger Roper, Utah state preservation historian, were assisted by Forest Service interns and volunteers in the project. As a result, the campground was closed briefly in 1994, while Forest Service personnel and volunteers carried out a major makeover of the site. In August 1995, a dedicatory service was held complete with a cake, a ribbon-cutting, and talks from two former enrollees of F-5 who told of their experiences in the camp.[22]

Another way the CCC is being remembered, although not as thoroughly as I would like, is through the refurbishing of guard stations by the Forest Service, which are then rented out to summer visitors. At the present time there are at least a half-dozen sites where this is being done, and in some cases it is acknowledged that they were constructed by the

Corps. One example is the Fork Guard Station about eleven miles east of Hyrum. Unfortunately, although the advertisements mention that the station was built in 1934, only the more knowledgeable would properly conclude that it was built by enrollees.[23] Guard stations at Seeley Creek, Tony Grove, Diamond Fork, and Payson Lakes are among others also scheduled to be part of the Forest Service's cabin rental program, where park visitors can appreciate the enduring workmanship of the CCC enrollees.

Appendix A

Army Corps Areas

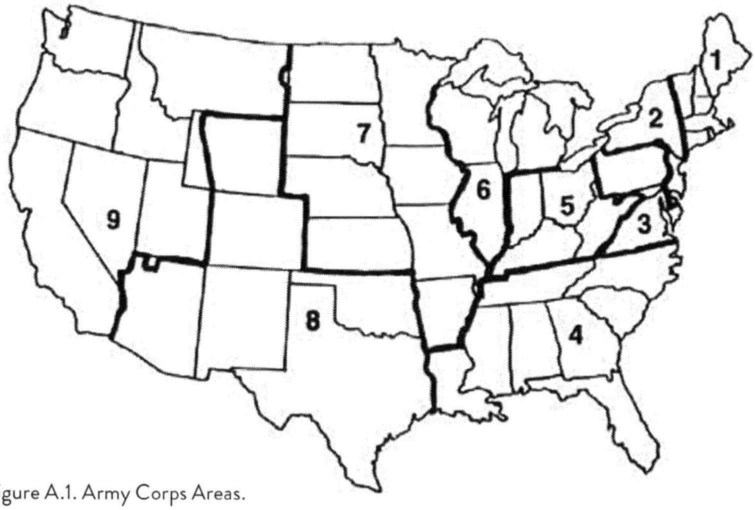

Figure A.1. Army Corps Areas.

Army Corps Area	States Included
First	Maine, New Hampshire, Vermont, Massachusetts, Rhode Island, Connecticut
Second	New York, New Jersey, Delaware
Third	Pennsylvania, Maryland, Virginia
Fourth	North Carolina, South Carolina, Tennessee, Mississippi, Louisiana, Alabama, Georgia, Florida
Fifth	Indiana, Ohio, West Virginia, Kentucky
Sixth	Wisconsin, Michigan, Illinois
Seventh	Missouri, North Dakota, South Dakota, Nebraska, Kansas, Minnesota, Iowa, Arkansas
Eighth	Oklahoma, Texas, New Mexico, Colorado, Arizona, Wyoming (partial)
Ninth	Montana, Idaho, Wyoming (partial), Utah, Nevada, California, Oregon, Washington

Appendix B

Utah Civilian Conservation Corps Camp Information

Table B.1. Civilian Conservation Corps Camps in Utah, Periods One through Eighteen.

Camp	Location	Company	County	Control
First Enrollment Period, April–September 30, 1933				
F-1	Logan Canyon	957	Cache	Cache National Forest (NF)
F-2	Blacksmith Fork	1347	Cache	Cache NF
F-3	Kaler Hollow	1342	Uinta	Ashley NF
F-4	Smith's Fork	230	Summit	Ashley NF
F-5	American Fork Canyon	940	Utah	Wasatch NF
F-6	Soapstone (Kamas)	1346	Summit	Wasatch NF
F-7	Black's Fork	231	Summit	Wasatch NF
F-8	Diamond Fork	1343	Wasatch	Uinta NF
F-9	Mt. Nebo (Nephi)	958	Juab	Uinta NF
F-10	Joe's Valley	959	Emery	Manti NF
F-11	Ferron	1341	Emery	Manti NF
F-12	Salina Canyon	960	Sevier	Fishlake NF
F-13	Fish Lake	1337	Sevier	Fishlake NF
F-14	Beaver	1338	Beaver	Fishlake NF
F-15	Desert Range Experiment Station	1340	Millard	U.S. Forest Service
F-16	Duck Creek	961	Kane	Dixie NF
F-17	Pine Valley	1335	Washington	Dixie NF
F-18	Blue Springs (Escalante)	1336	Garfield	Powell NF
F-19	Grover	1339	Wayne	Powell NF
F-20	Warner (Moab)	1345	Grand	La Sal NF
SE-201	Woods Cross	232	Davis	State Park
SE-204	Brigham City	1253	Box Elder	State Park
SE-206	Hobble Creek Canyon	1254	Utah	State Park
SE-211	Widtsoe	1255	Garfield	State Park
SE-212	Alton	1256	Kane	State Park
NP-1	Zion Canyon	962	Washington	National Park Service (NPS)
Second Enrollment Period, October 1, 1933–March 31, 1934				
F-24	Leeds	1335	Washington	Dixie NF

Table B.1. Civilian Conservation Corps Camps in Utah, Periods One through Eighteen.

Camp	Location	Company	County	Control
F-25	Richfield	1339	Sevier	Fishlake NF
SE-205	Woods Cross	940	Davis	State Park
SE-213	St. George	961	Washington	State Park
PE-214	Moab	1345	Grand	State Park
PE-215	Santa Clara	1338	Washington	State Park
PE-216	Washington	958	Washington	State Park
PE-217	Hurricane (La Verkin)	957	Washington	State Park
PE-218	Orderville	959	Kane	State Park
PE-219	Salina	960	Sevier	State Park
NP-2	Zion National Park	962	Washington	NPS
Third Enrollment Period, April 1–September 30, 1934				
F-1	Logan Canyon	957	Cache	Cache NF
F-3	Kaler Hollow (drought-relief camp [DR])	1965	Uinta	Ashley NF
F-6	Soapstone (Kamas)	960	Summit	Wasatch NF
F-9	Mt. Nebo (Nephi) (DR)	Vets[a]	Juab	Uinta NF
F-14	Beaver Mountain (DR)	1964	Beaver	Fishlake NF
F-18	Blue Springs (Escalante)	1339	Garfield	Powell NF
F-26	Maple Springs (Fillmore)	1338	Millard	Fishlake NF
F-27	Panguitch Lake	961	Garfield	Dixie NF
F-28	Gooseberry (Fairview)	959	Sanpete	Manti NF
F-29	Uinta River (Roosevelt)	1345	Uinta	Ashley NF
F-30	Hobble Creek (Springville)	958	Utah	Uinta NF
SE-205	Woods Cross	940	Davis	State Park
NP-2	Zion National Park (DR)	1966	Washington	NPS
NP-3	Bryce Canyon National Park	962	Garfield	NPS
BR-5	Currant Creek (Heber) (DR)	1968	Wasatch	Bureau of Reclamation
BR-6	Ephraim (DR)	1967	Sanpete	Bureau of Reclamation
Fourth Enrollment Period, October 1, 1934–March 31, 1935				
F-31	Veyo (DR)	Vets	Washington	Dixie NF
F-32	Salina Creek	960	Sevier	Fishlake NF
F-33	Desert Range (DR)	1964	Millard	U.S. Forest Service
F-34	Hyrum	957	Cache	Cache NF
F-35	Manila (DR)	1965	Daggett	Ashley NF
F-36	Kanosh	1979	Millard	Fishlake NF

Table B.1. Civilian Conservation Corps Camps in Utah, Periods One through Eighteen.

Camp	Location	Company	County	Control
F-37	Moon Lake (Duchesne)	2910	Duchesne	Ashley NF
SE-205	Woods Cross	940	Davis	State Park
SE-213	St. George	961	Washington	State Park
PE-214	Moab	1344	Grand	State Park
PE-220	Provo	958	Utah	State Park
PE-221	Willard	1350	Box Elder	State Park
PE-222	Cedar City	1339	Iron	State Park
PE-223	Mt. Pleasant	959	Sanpete	State Park
BF-1	Bear River	unknown	Box Elder	Biological Survey
BR-11	Bridgeland (DR)	1968	Duchesne	Bureau of Reclamation
BR-12	Huntsville (DR)	1967	Weber	Bureau of Reclamation
NP-2	Zion National Park (DR)	1966	Washington	NPS
NP-4	Bridge Mountain (Zion National Park)	962	Washington	NPS
Fifth Enrollment Period, April 1–September 30, 1935				
F-6	Soapstone (Kamas)	1979	Summit	Wasatch NF
F-11	Ferron	959	Emery	Manti NF
F-12	Salina Canyon	960	Sevier	Fishlake NF
F-14	Beaver	1964	Beaver	Fishlake NF
F-16	Duck Creek		Kane	Dixie NF
F-28	Gooseberry	959	Sanpete	Manti NF
F-30	Hobble Creek	958	Utah	Uinta NF
F-31	Veyo	Vets	Washington	Dixie NF
F-34	Hyrum	957	Cache	Cache NF
F-35	Manila	1965	Daggett	Ashley NF
F-36	Kanosh	3749	Millard	Fishlake NF
F-37	Moon Lake	2910	Duchesne	Ashley NF
F-38	Big Cottonwood	1339	Salt Lake	Wasatch NF
F-39	Mayfield	959	Sanpete	Manti NF
F-41	Indian Creek		San Juan	La Sal NF
F-42	Escalante	1980	Garfield	Powell NF
F-43	Pleasant Grove	2514	Utah	Wasatch NF
F-44	Aspen Grove	1339	Garfield	Powell NF
F-48	Bountiful	940	Davis	State Park
BF-1	Bear River	1350/1985	Box Elder	Biological Survey
SCS-2	Gunlock	585	Washington	Soil Conservation Service (SCS)
SCS-3	Price	2562	Carbon	SCS

Table B.1. Civilian Conservation Corps Camps in Utah, Periods One through Eighteen.

Camp	Location	Company	County	Control
BR-6	Ephraim	259	Sanpete	Bureau of Reclamation
BR-11	Bridgeland	1968	Duchesne	Bureau of Reclamation
BR-12	Huntsville	1967	Weber	Bureau of Reclamation
DG-28	Clover Creek	2517	Tooele	Division of Grazing
DG-30	Cedar City	1259	Iron	Division of Grazing
DG-34	Blanding	2516	San Juan	Division of Grazing
NP-2	Zion National Park (DR)	1966	Washington	NPS
NP-3	Bryce Canyon	962	Garfield	NPS
NP-4	Bridge Mountain	962	Washington	NPS
NP-5	Cedar Breaks	1966		
SP-1	Locomotive Springs (Kelton)		Box Elder	State Park
Sixth Enrollment Period, October 1, 1935–March 31, 1936				
F-11	Ferron	959	Emery	Manti NF
F-31	Veyo	Vets	Washington	Dixie NF
F-34	Hyrum	957/2761[b]	Cache	Cache NF
F-35	Manila	1965	Daggett	Ashley NF
F-36	Kanosh	3749	Millard	Fishlake NF
F-37	Moon Lake (Duchesne)	2910	Duchesne	Ashley NF
F-38	Big Cottonwood	?	Salt Lake	Wasatch NF
F-39	Mayfield	2937	Sanpete	Manti NF
F-40	Rock Canyon (Provo)	958	Utah	Uinta NF
F-41	Indian Creek (Monticello)	2515	San Juan	La Sal NF
F-42	Escalante	1980	Garfield	Powell NF
F-46	Pinto	1508	Washington	Dixie NF
F-48	Bountiful	940	Davis	Wasatch NF
BF-1	Bear River	2539	Box Elder	Biological Survey
SCS-2	Gunlock	585	Washington	SCS
SCS-3	Price	593	Carbon	SCS
DG-26	Jericho (Eureka)	1967	Juab	Division of Grazing
DG-27	Castle Dale	529	Emery	Division of Grazing
DG-28	Clover Creek	2517	Tooele	Division of Grazing
DG-30	Cedar City	1508/1259	Iron	Division of Grazing
DG-31	Vernal	1507	Uinta	Division of Grazing
DG-32	Dalton Wells (Moab)	561	Grand	Division of Grazing
DG-33	Henrieville	2529	Garfield	Division of Grazing
DG-34	Blanding	2516	San Juan	Division of Grazing
DG-35	Milford	2530	Beaver	Division of Grazing

Table B.1. Civilian Conservation Corps Camps in Utah, Periods One through Eighteen.

Camp	Location	Company	County	Control
BR-11	Bridgeland	1968	Duchesne	Bureau of Reclamation
NP-2	Zion National Park	1966/3238	Washington	NPS
NP-4	Bridge Mountain	962	Garfield	NPS
SP-2	Farmington Bay	536	Davis	State Park
Seventh Enrollment Period, April–October 1936				
F-16	Duck Creek		Kane	Dixie NF
F-30	Hobble Creek	958	Utah	Uinta NF
F-32	Salina Creek		Sevier	Fishlake NF
F-34	Hyrum	957/2761[b]	Cache	Cache NF
F-35	Manila	1965	Daggett	Ashley NF
F-36	Kanosh	3749	Millard	Fishlake NF
F-38	Big Cottonwood	?	Salt Lake	Wasatch NF
F-39	Mayfield	2937	Sanpete	Manti NF
F-42	Escalante	1980	Garfield	Powell NF
F-43	Pleasant Grove	2514	Utah	Wasatch NF
F-44	Aspen Grove	1339	Garfield	Powell NF
F-48	Bountiful	940	Davis	Wasatch NF
BF-1	Bear River (Brigham City)	2539	Box Elder	Biological Survey
SCS-2	Gunlock	585	Washington	SCS
SCS-3	Price	593	Carbon	SCS
BR-11	Bridgeland	1968	Duchesne	Bureau of Reclamation
BR-12	Huntsville		Weber	Bureau of Reclamation
DG-26	Jericho (Eureka)	1967	Juab	Division of Grazing
DG-27	Castle Dale	529	Emery	Division of Grazing
DG-28	Clover Creek	2517	Tooele	Division of Grazing
DG-29	Antelope Springs	2531	Millard	Division of Grazing
DG-30	Cedar City	1508	Iron	Division of Grazing
DG-31	Vernal	1507	Uinta	Division of Grazing
DG-32	Dalton Wells (Moab)	561	Grand	Division of Grazing
DG-33	Henrieville	2529	Garfield	Division of Grazing
DG-34	Blanding	3241	San Juan	Division of Grazing
DG-35	Milford	2530	Beaver	Division of Grazing
DG-45	St. George	2558	Washington	Division of Grazing
NP-2	Zion National Park	3238	Washington	NPS
NP-3	Bryce Canyon	962	Garfield	NPS
NP-5	Cedar Breaks	3238	Iron	NPS
SP-2	Farmington Bay (Woods Cross)	536	Davis	State Park

Table B.1. Civilian Conservation Corps Camps in Utah, Periods One through Eighteen.

Camp	Location	Company	County	Control
Eighth Enrollment Period, October 1936–March 1937				
F-16	Duck Creek	2910	Kane	Dixie NF
F-31	Veyo	4777	Washington	Dixie NF
F-32	Salina Creek	3749	Sevier	Fishlake NF
F-34	Hyrum	2761/3796	Cache	Cache NF
F-35	Manila	1965	Daggett	Ashley NF
F-39	Mayfield	4793	Sanpete	Manti NF
F-40	Rock Canyon	958	Utah	Uinta NF
F-41	Indian Creek	4776	San Juan	La Sal NF
F-42	Escalante	1980	Garfield	Powell NF
F-43	Pleasant Grove	2514	Utah	Wasatch NF
F-48	Bountiful	940	Davis	Wasatch NF
SCS-2	Gunlock	585	Washington	SCS
SCS-3	Price	593	Carbon	SCS
SCS-4	Willard	736	Box Elder	SCS
SCS-5	Mt. Pleasant		Sanpete	SCS
BR-11	Bridgeland	1968	Duchesne	Bureau of Reclamation
BR-12	Huntsville	4792	Weber	Bureau of Reclamation
DG-26	Jericho (Eureka)	1967	Juab	Division of Grazing
DG-27	Castle Dale	529	Emery	Division of Grazing
DG-28	Clover Creek	2517	Tooele	Division of Grazing
DG-29	Antelope Springs	2531	Millard	Division of Grazing
DG-30	Cedar City	1508	Iron	Division of Grazing
DG-31	Vernal	1507	Uinta	Division of Grazing
DG-32	Dalton Wells (Moab)	561	Grand	Division of Grazing
DG-33	Henrieville	2529	Garfield	Division of Grazing
DG-34	Blanding	3241	San Juan	Division of Grazing
DG-35	Milford	2530	Beaver	Division of Grazing
DG-45	St. George	2558	Washington	Division of Grazing
NP-4	Bridge Mountain (Zion National Park)	962	Washington	NPS
BS-1	Bear River	2539	Box Elder	Biological Survey
SP-2	Farmington Bay	536	Davis	State Park
Ninth Enrollment Period, April 1–October 1, 1937				
F-6	Soapstone	2514	Summit	Wasatch NF
F-11	Ferron	959	Emery	Manti NF
F-16	Duck Creek	2910	Kane	Dixie NF

Table B.1. Civilian Conservation Corps Camps in Utah, Periods One through Eighteen.

Camp	Location	Company	County	Control
F-32	Salina Creek	3749	Sevier	Fishlake NF
F-34	Hyrum	3796	Cache	Cache NF
F-35	Manila	1965	Daggett	Ashley NF
F-40	Rock Canyon	958	Utah	Uinta NF
F-41	Indian Creek	2515	San Juan	La Sal NF
F-44	Aspen Grove	4778	Garfield	Powell NF
F-49	Farmington		Davis	Wasatch NF
BS-1	Bear River	2539	Box Elder	Biological Survey
SCS-3	Price	593	Carbon	SCS
SCS-4	Willard	736	Box Elder	SCS
SCS-5	Mt. Pleasant		Sanpete	SCS
SCS-6	Moab	4776	Grand	SCS
SCS-7	Leeds	585	Washington	SCS
BR-11	Bridgeland	1968	Duchesne	Bureau of Reclamation
BR-12	Huntsville	4792	Weber	Bureau of Reclamation
DG-26	Jericho (Eureka)	1967	Juab	Division of Grazing
DG-27	Castle Dale	529	Emery	Division of Grazing
DG-28	Clover Creek	2517	Tooele	Division of Grazing
DG-29	Antelope Springs	2531	Millard	Division of Grazing
DG-30	Cedar City	1508	Iron	Division of Grazing
DG-31	Vernal	1507	Uinta	Division of Grazing
DG-32	Dalton Wells (Moab)	561	Grand	Division of Grazing
DG-33	Henrieville	2529	Garfield	Division of Grazing
DG-34	Blanding	3241	San Juan	Division of Grazing
DG-35	Milford	2530	Beaver	Division of Grazing
DG-45	St. George	2558	Washington	Division of Grazing
NP-2	Zion National Park	4779	Washington	NPS
NP-3	Bryce National Park	962	Garfield	NPS
SP-2	Farmington Bay (Woods Cross)	536	Davis	State Park
Tenth Enrollment Period, October 1, 1937–March 31, 1938				
F-11	Ferron	959	Emery	Manti NF
F-31	Veyo	4777	Washington	Dixie NF
F-32	Salina Creek	479	Sevier	Fishlake NF
F-34	Hyrum	3796	Cache	Cache NF
F-38	Big Cottonwood	3265	Salt Lake	Wasatch NF
F-39	Mayfield		Sanpete	Manti NF
F-40	Rock Canyon	958	Utah	Uinta NF

Table B.1. Civilian Conservation Corps Camps in Utah, Periods One through Eighteen.

Camp	Location	Company	County	Control
F-42	Escalante	2515	Garfield	Powell NF
F-43	Pleasant Grove		Utah	Wasatch NF
F-48	Bountiful	940	Davis	Wasatch NF
BS-1	Bear River	2539	Box Elder	Biological Survey
SCS-3	Price	593	Carbon	SCS
SCS-4	Willard	736	Box Elder	SCS
SCS-5	Mt. Pleasant	1965	Sanpete	SCS
SCS-6	Moab	4776	Grand	SCS
SCS-7	Leeds	585	Washington	SCS
BR-11	Bridgeland	1968	Duchesne	Bureau of Reclamation
BR-64	Deer Creek	4792	Wasatch	Bureau of Reclamation
DG-26	Jericho (Eureka)	1967	Juab	Division of Grazing
DG-27	Castle Dale	529	Emery	Division of Grazing
DG-28	Clover Creek	2517	Tooele	Division of Grazing
DG-29	Antelope Springs	482	Millard	Division of Grazing
DG-30	Cedar City	1508	Iron	Division of Grazing
DG-31	Vernal	1507	Uinta	Division of Grazing
DG-32	Dalton Wells (Moab)	234	Grand	Division of Grazing
DG-33	Henrieville	2529	Garfield	Division of Grazing
DG-34	Blanding	3241	San Juan	Division of Grazing
DG-35	Milford	2530	Beaver	Division of Grazing
DG-45	St. George	2558	Washington	Division of Grazing
NP-4	Bridge Mountain	962	Washington	NPS
SP-2	Farmington Bay	536	Davis	State Park
Eleventh Enrollment Period, April 1–September 30, 1938				
F-6	Soapstone	3544	Summit	Wasatch NF
F-11	Ferron	959	Emery	Manti NF
F-16	Duck Creek	4—	Kane	Fishlake NF
F-32	Salina Creek	479	Sevier	Dixie NF
F-34	Hyrum	3265	Cache	Cache NF
F-38	Big Cottonwood	3240	Salt Lake	Wasatch NF
F-40	Rock Canyon	958	Utah	Uinta NF
F-44	Aspen Grove	4778	Garfield	Powell NF
F-49	Farmington Canyon	940	Davis	Wasatch NF
F-1	Bear River	2539	Box Elder	Bureau of Fisheries
SCS-3	Price	593	Carbon	SCS
SCS-4	Willard	736	Box Elder	SCS

Table B.1. Civilian Conservation Corps Camps in Utah, Periods One through Eighteen.

Camp	Location	Company	County	Control
SCS-5	Mt. Pleasant	1965	Sanpete	SCS
SCS-6	Moab	1256	Grand	SCS
SCS-7	Leeds	585	Washington	SCS
BR-11	Bridgeland	1968	Duchesne	Bureau of Reclamation
BR-64	Deer Creek	4792	Wasatch	Bureau of Reclamation
DG-26	Jericho (Eureka)	1967	Juab	Division of Grazing
DG-27	Castle Dale	529	Emery	Division of Grazing
DG-28	Clover Creek	2517	Tooele	Division of Grazing
DG-29	Antelope Springs	482	Millard	Division of Grazing
DG-30	Cedar City	1508	Iron	Division of Grazing
DG-31	Vernal	1507	Uinta	Division of Grazing
DG-32	Dalton Wells (Moab)	234	Grand	Division of Grazing
DG-33	Henrieville	2529	Garfield	Division of Grazing
DG-34	Blanding	3241	San Juan	Division of Grazing
DG-35	Milford	2530	Beaver	Division of Grazing
DG-103	Park Valley	288	Box Elder	Division of Grazing
DG-45	St. George	2558	Washington	Division of Grazing
NP-3	Bryce	962	Garfield	NPS
SP-2	Farmington Bay (Centerville)	536	Davis	State Park
Twelfth Enrollment Period, October 1, 1938–March 31, 1939				
F-11	Ferron	959	Emery	Manti NF
F-31	Veyo		Washington	Dixie NF
F-32	Salina Creek	479	Sevier	Fishlake NF
F-34	Hyrum	3265	Cache	Cache NF
F-35	Manila	3544	Daggett	Ashley NF
F-38	Big Cottonwood	3240	Salt Lake	Wasatch NF
F-39	Mayfield		Sanpete	Manti NF
F-40	Rock Canyon	958	Utah	Uinta NF
F-42	Escalante		Garfield	Powell NF
F-48	Bountiful	940	Davis	Wasatch NF
BF-1	Bear River (Brigham)	2539	Box Elder	Bureau of Fisheries
SCS-3	Price	593	Carbon	SCS
SCS-4	Willard	736	Box Elder	SCS
SCS-5	Mt. Pleasant	1965	Sanpete	SCS
SCS-6	Moab	1256	Grand	SCS
SCS-7	Leeds	585	Washington	SCS
BR-11	Bridgeland	1968	Duchesne	Bureau of Reclamation

Table B.1. Civilian Conservation Corps Camps in Utah, Periods One through Eighteen.

Camp	Location	Company	County	Control
BR-64	Deer Creek	4792	Wasatch	Bureau of Reclamation
DG-26	Jericho (Eureka)	1967	Juab	Division of Grazing
DG-27	Castle Dale	529	Emery	Division of Grazing
DG-28	Clover Creek	2517	Tooele	Division of Grazing
DG-29	Antelope Springs	482	Millard	Division of Grazing
DG-30	Cedar City	1508	Iron	Division of Grazing
DG-31	Vernal	1507	Uinta	Division of Grazing
DG-32	Dalton Wells (Moab)	234	Grand	Division of Grazing
DG-33	Henrieville	2529	Garfield	Division of Grazing
DG-34	Blanding	3241	San Juan	Division of Grazing
DG-35	Milford	469	Beaver	Division of Grazing
DG-45	St. George	2558	Washington	Division of Grazing
DG-103	Park Valley	288	Box Elder	Division of Grazing
DG-114	Hanksville	298	Wayne	Division of Grazing
DG-115	Green River	3556	Emery	Division of Grazing
DG-116	Callao (November–January)	2529	Juab	Division of Grazing
DG-117	Garrison		Millard	Division of Grazing
DG-131	Kanosh (January–April)		Millard	Division of Grazing
NP-4	Bridge Mountain (Zion)	962	Washington	NPS
SP-2	Farmington Bay (Centerville)	536	Davis	State Park
Thirteenth Enrollment Period, April 1–September 30, 1939				
F-16	Duck Creek	959	Kane	Dixie NF
F-32	Salina Creek	479	Sevier	Fishlake NF
F-34	Hyrum	3265	Cache	Cache NF
F-35	Manila	3544	Daggett	Ashley NF
F-38	Big Cottonwood	3240	Salt Lake	Wasatch NF
F-40	Rock Canyon	958	Utah	Uinta NF
F-49	Farmington Canyon		Davis	Wasatch NF
F-50	Seeley Creek		Sanpete	Manti NF
BF-1	Bear River (Brigham)	2539	Box Elder	Bureau of Fisheries
SCS-3	Price	593	Carbon	SCS
SCS-4	Willard	736	Box Elder	SCS
SCS-5	Mt. Pleasant	1965	Sanpete	SCS
SCS-7	Leeds	585	Washington	SCS
SCS-8	Monticello		San Juan	SCS
BR-64	Deer Creek	4792	Wasatch	Bureau of Reclamation

Table B.1. Civilian Conservation Corps Camps in Utah, Periods One through Eighteen.

Camp	Location	Company	County	Control
BR-91	Pleasant Grove	1968	Utah	Bureau of Reclamation
DG-26	Jericho (Eureka)	1967	Juab	Division of Grazing
DG-27	Castle Dale	529	Emery	Division of Grazing
DG-28	Clover Creek	2517	Tooele	Division of Grazing
DG-29	Antelope Springs	482	Millard	Division of Grazing
DG-30	Cedar City	1508	Iron	Division of Grazing
DG-31	Vernal	1507	Uinta	Division of Grazing
DG-32	Dalton Wells (Moab)	234	Grand	Division of Grazing
DG-33	Henrieville	2558	Garfield	Division of Grazing
DG-34	Blanding	3241	San Juan	Division of Grazing
DG-35	Milford	2530	Beaver	Division of Grazing
DG-45	St. George	2558	Washington	Division of Grazing
DG-103	Park Valley	288	Box Elder	Division of Grazing
DG-114	Hanksville	298	Wayne	Division of Grazing
DG-115	Green River	3556	Emery	Division of Grazing
DG-116	Callao	2529	Juab	Division of Grazing
DG-117	Garrison		Millard	Division of Grazing
DG-131	Kanosh (January–April)		Millard	Division of Grazing
NP-3	Bryce Canyon	962	Garfield	NPS
SP-2	Farmington Bay (Centerville)	536	Davis	State Park
Fourteenth Enrollment Period, October 1, 1939–March 31, 1940				
F-31	Veyo	959	Washington	Dixie NF
F-32	Salina Creek	479	Sevier	Fishlake NF
F-38	Big Cottonwood	3240	Salt Lake	Wasatch NF
F-40	Rock Canyon	958	Utah	Uinta NF
F-42	Escalante	4723	Garfield	Powell NF
F-48	Bountiful	940	Davis	Wasatch NF
F-51	Huntsville	3265	Weber	Cache NF
BF-1	Bear River (Brigham)	2539	Box Elder	Bureau of Fisheries
SCS-3	Price	593	Carbon	SCS
SCS-5	Mt. Pleasant	1965	Sanpete	SCS
SCS-7	Leeds	585	Washington	SCS
SCS-8	Monticello		San Juan	SCS
SCS-9	Tremonton	736	Box Elder	SCS
BR-64	Deer Creek	4792	Wasatch	Bureau of Reclamation
BR-91	Pleasant Grove	1968	Utah	Bureau of Reclamation
DG-26	Jericho (Eureka)		Juab	Division of Grazing

Table B.1. Civilian Conservation Corps Camps in Utah, Periods One through Eighteen.

Camp	Location	Company	County	Control
DG-27	Castle Dale (to January 1940)	529	Emery	Division of Grazing
DG-29	Antelope Springs	482	Millard	Division of Grazing
DG-31	Vernal	1507	Uinta	Division of Grazing
DG-32	Dalton Wells (Moab)	234	Grand	Division of Grazing
DG-34	Blanding	3241[c]	San Juan	Division of Grazing
DG-35	Milford	794	Beaver	Division of Grazing
DG-114	Hanksville	298	Wayne	Division of Grazing
DG-115	Green River	3556	Emery	Division of Grazing
DG-117	Garrison	1508	Millard	Division of Grazing
DG-154	Simpson Springs	2517	Tooele	Division of Grazing
DG-155	Black Rock	3529	Millard	Division of Grazing
DG-156	Modena	1682	Iron	Division of Grazing
DG-158	Willow Springs	529	Emery	Division of Grazing
DG-160	Hurricane	2558	Washington	Division of Grazing
NP-4	Bridge Mountain	962	Washington	NPS
SP-2	Farmington Bay[d]	536	Davis	State Park
MA-1	Provo River	1662	Utah	NPS and Provo City
Fifteenth Enrollment Period, April 1–September 30, 1940				
F-6	Soapstone	940	Summit	Wasatch NF
F-16	Duck Creek	959	Kane	Dixie NF
F-32	Salina Creek	479	Sevier	Fishlake NF
F-35	Manila	3544	Daggett	Ashley NF
F-38	Big Cottonwood	3240	Salt Lake	Wasatch NF
F-40	Rock Canyon	958	Utah	Uinta NF
F-50	Seeley Creek	6432	Sanpete	Manti NF
F-51	Huntsville	6429/3265	Weber	Cache NF
FWS-1	Bear River	2539	Box Elder	Fish and Wildlife Service (F&WS)
FWS-2	Ogden Bay	794	Weber	F&WS
SCS-3	Price	593	Carbon	SCS
SCS-5	Mt. Pleasant	6430	Sanpete	SCS
SCS-7	Leeds	585	Washington	SCS
SCS-8	Indian Creek	1256	San Juan	SCS
SCS-9	Tremonton	736	Box Elder	SCS
BR-64	Deer Creek	4792	Wasatch	Bureau of Reclamation
BR-91	Pleasant Grove	1968/5715	Utah	Bureau of Reclamation
DG-26	Jericho (Eureka)	6426	Juab	Division of Grazing

Table B.1. Civilian Conservation Corps Camps in Utah, Periods One through Eighteen.

Camp	Location	Company	County	Control
DG-27	Castle Dale	529	Emery	Division of Grazing
DG-29	Antelope Springs	482	Millard	Division of Grazing
DG-31	Vernal	1507	Uinta	Division of Grazing
DG-32	Dalton Wells (Moab)	234	Grand	Division of Grazing
DG-34	Blanding	3241	San Juan	Division of Grazing
DG-35	Milford	1508	Beaver	Division of Grazing
DG-114	Hanksville	298	Wayne	Division of Grazing
DG-115	Green River	3556	Emery	Division of Grazing
DG-116	Callao	2529	Juab	Division of Grazing
DG-154	Simpson Springs	2517	Tooele	Division of Grazing
DG-156	Modena (Eight Mile)	6429	Iron	Division of Grazing
DG-160	Hurricane	2558	Washington	Division of Grazing
NP-4	Bridge Mountain	962	Washington	NPS
NP-7	Arches National Monument	6428	Grand	NPS
MA-1	Provo River	6431	Utah	NPS and Provo City
Sixteenth Enrollment Period, October 1, 1940–March 31, 1941				
F-31	Veyo	959	Kane	Dixie NF
F-32	Salina Creek	479	Sevier	Fishlake NF
F-38	Big Cottonwood	3240	Salt Lake	Wasatch NF
F-39	Mayfield		Sanpete	Manti NF
F-40	Rock Canyon	958	Utah	Uinta NF
FWS-1	Bear River	2539	Box Elder	F&WS
FWS-2	Ogden Bay	794	Weber	F&WS
SCS-3	Price	593	Carbon	SCS
SCS-5	Mt. Pleasant	6430	Sanpete	SCS
SCS-6	Moab		Grand	SCS
SCS-7	Leeds	585	Washington	SCS
SCS-9	Tremonton	736	Box Elder	SCS
BR-64	Deer Creek	4792	Wasatch	Bureau of Reclamation
BR-91	Pleasant Grove	1968/5715	Utah	Bureau of Reclamation
DG-26	Jericho (Eureka)	6426	Juab	Division of Grazing
DG-31	Vernal	1507	Uinta	Division of Grazing
DG-32	Dalton Wells (Moab)	234	Grand	Division of Grazing
DG-114	Hanksville	298	Wayne	Division of Grazing
DG-115	Green River	3556	Emery	Division of Grazing
DG-116	Callao	2529	Juab	Division of Grazing
DG-117	Garrison		Millard	Division of Grazing

Table B.1. Civilian Conservation Corps Camps in Utah, Periods One through Eighteen.

Camp	Location	Company	County	Control
DG-153	Lucin	1867 (?)	Box Elder	Division of Grazing
DG-154	Simpson Springs	2517	Tooele	Division of Grazing
DG-155	Black Rock	482?	Millard	Division of Grazing
DG-156	Modena (Eight Mile)	6429	Iron	Division of Grazing
DG-157	Dry Valley		San Juan	Division of Grazing
DG-158	Willow Springs	529	Emery	Division of Grazing
DG-160	Hurricane	2558	Washington	Division of Grazing
NP-4	Bridge Mountain	962	Washington	NPS
NP-7	Arches National Monument	536	Grand	NPS
MA-1	Provo River	5713	Utah	NPS and Provo City
Seventeenth Enrollment Period, April 1–September 30, 1941				
F-3	Kaler Hollow[e]		Uinta	Ashley NF
F-6	Soapstone		Summit	Wasatch NF
F-16	Duck Creek	959	Kane	Dixie NF
F-29	Uinta River		Uinta	Ashley NF
F-32	Salina Creek	479	Sevier	Fishlake NF
F-34	Hyrum (to May)		Cache	Cache NF
F-38	Big Cottonwood	3240	Salt Lake	Wasatch NF
F-40	Rock Canyon (to July)	958	Utah	Uinta NF
F-42	Escalante (to July)		Garfield	Powell NF
F-50	Seeley Creek		Sanpete	Manti NF
F-51	Huntsville (after July)	958	Weber	Cache NF
F-52	Dry Fork (never opened)		Uinta	Ashley NF
FWS-1	Bear River	2539	Box Elder	F&WS
FWS-2	Ogden Bay	794	Weber	F&WS
SCS-3	Price	593	Carbon	SCS
SCS-5	Mt. Pleasant	6430	Sanpete	SCS
SCS-7	Leeds	585	Washington	SCS
SCS-8	Indian Creek		San Juan	SCS
SCS-9	Tremonton	736	Box Elder	SCS
BR-64	Deer Creek	4792	Wasatch	Bureau of Reclamation
BR-91	Pleasant Grove (to August 1941)	1968/479	Utah	Bureau of Reclamation
DG-27	Castle Dale	529?	Emery	Division of Grazing
DG-31	Vernal	1507	Uinta	Division of Grazing
DG-32	Dalton Wells (Moab)	234	Grand	Division of Grazing
DG-114	Hanksville	298	Wayne	Division of Grazing

Table B.1. Civilian Conservation Corps Camps in Utah, Periods One through Eighteen.

Camp	Location	Company	County	Control
DG-115	Green River (to June)	3556	Emery	Division of Grazing
DG-116	Callao	2529	Juab	Division of Grazing
DG-117	Garrison		Millard	Division of Grazing
DG-153	Lucin (closed August)	1967	Box Elder	Division of Grazing
DG-155	Black Rock	482?	Millard	Division of Grazing
DG-157	Dry Valley		San Juan	Division of Grazing
DG-158	Willow Springs	529	Emery	Division of Grazing
DG-160	Hurricane	2558	Washington	Division of Grazing
NP-4	Bridge Mountain	962	Washington	NPS
NP-7	Arches National Monument	536	Grand	NPS
SP-2	Farmington Bay	794	Davis	State Park
MA-1	Provo River	5713	Utah	NPS and Provo City
Eighteenth Enrollment Period, October 1, 1941–March 31, 1942				
F-38	Big Cottonwood	3803	Salt Lake	Wasatch NF
F-51	Huntsville (after July)	958	Weber	Cache NF
FWS-2	Ogden Bay	794	Weber	F&WS
SCS-3	Price	593	Carbon	SCS
SCS-5	Mt. Pleasant	6430	Sanpete	SCS
SCS-9	Tremonton (closed November)	736	Box Elder	SCS
BR-64	Deer Creek	4792	Wasatch	Bureau of Reclamation
DG-31	Vernal	1507	Uinta	Division of Grazing
DG-117	Garrison		Millard	Division of Grazing
DG-154	Simpson Springs (to February)	2517	Tooele	Division of Grazing
DG-155	Black Rock (after February)	2517	Millard	Division of Grazing
DG-157	Dry Valley		San Juan	Division of Grazing
DG-158	Willow Springs	529	Emery	Division of Grazing
NP-7	Arches National Monument	536	Grand	NPS
MA-1	Provo River	5713	Utah	NPS and Provo City

a. A company of World War I veterans occupied F-9 and later F-31. The company number is not known.
b. Company 957 disbanded in January 10, 1936, replaced by Company 2761.
c. Moved to G-157 in January 1940 but returned to G-34 by March 1, 1940.
d. Moved to the Moab area, May 1940.
e. Moved to near Wells, Nevada, August 1941.

Table B.2. Total Work Completed in Utah during the Period April 1933–June 30, 1942.

Project Classification and Type of Job	Unit	New Work	Maintenance
Structural Improvements			
Bridges			
Foot and horse	Number	231	7
Vehicle	Number	478	80
Buildings, other than CCC camp			
Barns	Number	43	33
Bathhouses	Number	6	3
Cabins, overnight	Number	4	30
Combination buildings	Number	—	1
Dwellings	Number	117	197
Equipment and supply storage	Number	70	55
Garages	Number	74	37
Latrines and toilets	Number	445	187
Lodges and museums	Number	1	—
Lookout houses	Number	2	—
Lookout towers	Number	4	4
Shelters	Number	67	21
Other buildings	Number	634	186
Cribbing, including filling	Cubic yards	91,961	6,759
Impounding and large diversion dams	Number	423	139
Fences	Rods	662,054	252,208
Guardrails	Rods	6,877	150
Levees, dykes, jetties, and groins	Cubic yards	2,021,562	126
Power lines	Miles	9	—
Incinerators	Number	54	—
Sewage and waste-disposal systems	Number	17	36
Telephone lines	Miles	929	1,281
Water supply systems			
Fountains, drinking	Number	33	—
Open ditches	Linear feet	104,320	72,651
Pipe or tile lines	Linear feet	495,434	65,996
Storage facilities (in thousands)	Gallons	31,192	—
Wells, including pumps and pump houses	Number	154	154
Miscellaneous	Number	198	17
Other structural improvements			
Camp stoves or fireplaces	Number	1,242	358
Cattle guards	Number	189	15

Table B.2. Total Work Completed in Utah during the Period April 1933–June 30, 1942.

Project Classification and Type of Job	Unit	New Work	Maintenance
Corrals	Number	223	34
Seats	Number	284	24
Signs, markers, monuments	Number	9,128	377
Stone walls	Rods	440	—
Table and bench combinations	Number	1,884	568
Toolboxes	Number	255	9
Miscellaneous	Number	5,340	214
Radio stations	Number	11	—
Springs	Number	457	177
Water holes	Number	26	3
Small reservoirs	Number	309	38
Landing docks and piers	Number	—	—
Transportation Improvements			
Airplane landing fields	Number	—	—
Truck trails or minor roads	Miles	4,246	14,826
Trails, foot	Miles	58	82
Trails, horse or stock	Miles	515	513
Erosion Control			
Stream and lake bank protection	Square yards	10,983,407	120,234
Treatment of gullies			
Bank sloping	Square yards	76,986	—
Check dams, permanent	Number	7,971	97
Check dams, temporary	Number	13,760	217
Seeding and sodding	Square yards	432,360	100,000
Tree planting, gully	Square yards	1,621,508	1,500
Ditches, diversion	Linear feet	403,267	51,333
Terracing, channel construction	Linear feet	43,271	26,620
Terrace outletting			
Outlet structures	Number	717	1
Planting, seedlings, sodding	Square yards	120,431	—
Sheet erosion planting	Acres	215	—
Limestone, for liming soil			
Quarrying	Tons	3,659	—
Crushing	Tons	—	—
Hauling	Tons	3,995	—
Contour furrows and ridges	Miles	5,231	25

Table B.2. Total Work Completed in Utah during the Period April 1933–June 30, 1942.

Project Classification and Type of Job	Unit	New Work	Maintenance
Preparation for strip cropping	Acres	208	—
Road erosion demonstration	Miles	15	—
Wind erosion area treated	Acres	274	—
Water spreaders (rock, brush, wire)	Linear feet	1,213,098	—
Water spreaders (terrace type)	Linear feet	86,720	1,600
Flood Control, Irrigation, and Drainage			
Clearing and cleaning			
Channels and levees	Square yards	1,742,885	296,482
Residences, pond and lake sites	Acres	4,519	—
Lining of waterways	Square yards	52,565	—
Excavation of channels, canals, and ditches			
Earth	Cubic yards	1,855,497	3,292
Rock	Cubic yards	66,450	—
Pipelines, tile lines, and conduits	Linear feet	133,170	7,336
Riprap or paving			
Rock or concrete	Square yards	72,547	115
Brush or willows	Square yards	33,559	—
Water-control structures other than dams	Number	2,500	261
Concrete core walls other than dams	Cubic yards	1,947	—
Leveling of spoil banks	Cubic yards	3,405	—
Forest Culture			
Field planting or seeding (trees)	Acres	3,255	—
Forest stand improvement	Acres	1,223	12
Nurseries	Man-days	10,442	65
Tree seed collection			
Conifers (cones)	Bushels	12	—
Hardwoods	Pounds	27,676	—
Collection of tree seedlings	Number	65,576	—
Forest Protection			
Fighting forest fires	Man-days	40,007	—
Firebreaks	Miles	31	17
Fire hazard reduction			
Road- and trailside	Miles	577	5
Other	Acres	348	—
Fire presuppression	Man-days	15,589	—
Fire prevention	Man-days	1,481	—
Tree and plant disease control	Acres	2,657	—

Table B.2. Total Work Completed in Utah during the Period April 1933–June 30, 1942.

Project Classification and Type of Job	Unit	New Work	Maintenance
Tree insect pest control	Acres	155,600	10
Landscape and Recreation			
Beach improvement	Acres	15	—
General cleanup	Acres	4,273	1,619
Moving and planting trees, shrubs	Number	162,189	23,866
Landscaping, undifferentiated	Acres	1,209	63
Parking areas and parking overlooks	Square yards	143,085	6,039
Public campground development	Acres	2,688	3,587
Public picnic ground development	Acres	72	204
Razing undesired structures and obliterations	Man-days	16,275	—
Seed collection, other than tree	Pounds	122,043	—
Seeding or sodding	Acres	15,342	2
Soil preparation			
Topsoil, fertilizing, etc.	Acres	1,615	—
Vista or other selective cutting	Acres	—	60
Walks, concrete, gravel, cinder block, etc.	Linear feet	26,109	—
Range			
Elimination of predatory animals	Number	—	—
Range revegetation	Acres	214,290	846
Stock driveways	Miles	920	103
Pasture sodding	Acres	—	—
Pasture and range terracing	Acres	—	—
Wildlife			
Fish-rearing ponds	Number	48	1
Food and cover planting and seeding	Acres	194	5
Lake and pond development	Man-days	10,853	53
Stocking fish	Number	1,037,375	7
Stream development (wildlife)	Miles	50	—
Other wildlife activities	Man-days	10,040	—
Wildlife feeding	Man-days	953	—
Wildlife shelters	Number	18,627	—
Other Activities			
Education, guide, continuing station work	Man-days	6,779	—
Emergency work	Man-days	33,911	—
Eradication of weeds, poisonous or exotic plants	Acres	55,356	—
Experimental plots	Number	1,572	16

Table B.2. Total Work Completed in Utah during the Period April 1933–June 30, 1942.

Project Classification and Type of Job	Unit	New Work	Maintenance
Fighting coal fires	Man-days	—	—
Insect pest control	Acres	49,316	—
Maps and models	Man-days	34,948	—
Marking boundaries	Miles	3,941	—
Mosquito control	Acres	—	—
Preparation, transport of materials	Man-days	209,696	421
Reconnaissance and investigation			
Archaeological	Man-days	—	—
Other	Man-days	10,602	—
Restoration of historic structures	Number	—	—
Rodent and predatory animal control	Acres	1,654,269	—
Surveys	Man-days	52,726	—
Timber estimating	Acres	63,710	—
Tree preservation	Man-days	617	294
Equipment, repair or construction	Man-days	81,515	—
Hydraulic research	Man-days	1,267	—
Warehousing	Man-days	8,006	28
Technical service building	Number	204	218
Central repair shop labor	Man-days	4,851	—
Gas pipelines	Man-days	311	—
Unclassifiable	Man-days	—	—

Source: Typescript of reproduction of official report from the National Archives, in the author's possession.

Appendix C

Civilian Conservation Corps Camps in Utah

Table C.1. Civilian Conservation Corps Camps in Utah by Department/Agency.

Department/Agency	Number of Camps
Forest Service	46
Division of Grazing	24
State—Erosion Control	17
Soil Conservation Service	8
National Park Service	7
Bureau of Reclamation	6
Biological Survey	2
State Parks	2
Army	2
Metropolitan Area	1
Total	115

Table C.2. Utah Civilian Conservation Corps Camp Numbers and Locations.

Camp Department/Agency Designation and Number	Camp Location
Division of Grazing (DG-)	
26	Jericho
27	Castle Dale
28	Clover Creek
29	Antelope Springs (Delta)
30	Cedar City (formerly PE-222)
31	Vernal
32	Dalton Wells
33	Henrieville
34	Blanding
35	Milford
45	St. George (formerly SE-213)
103	Park Valley

Table C.2. Utah Civilian Conservation Corps Camp Numbers and Locations.

Camp Department/Agency Designation and Number	Camp Location
114	Hanksville
115	Green River
116	Callao
117	Garrison
131	Kanosh (formerly F-36)
153	Lucin
154	Simpson Springs
155	Black Rock
156	Modena
157	Dry Valley
158	Willow Springs
160	Hurricane
Forest Service (F-)	
1	Logan Canyon
2	Blacksmith Fork (Hyrum)
3	Kaler Hollow
4	Smith's Fork
5	American Fork Canyon
6	Soapstone (Kamas)
7	Black's Fork
8	Diamond Fork
9	Mt. Nebo (Nephi)
10	Joe's Valley
11	Ferron
12	Salina Canyon
13	Fish Lake
14	Beaver
15	Desert Range
16	Duck Creek
17	Pine Valley
18	Blue Springs
19	Grover
20	Warner (Moab)
24	Leeds (later SCS-7)
25	Richfield
26	Fillmore (Maple Springs)

Table C.2. Utah Civilian Conservation Corps Camp Numbers and Locations.

Camp Department/Agency Designation and Number	Camp Location
27	Panguitch Lake
28	Gooseberry (Fairview)
29	Uinta River
30	Hobble Creek (Springville)
31	Veyo
32	Salina Creek (formerly PE-219)
33	Milford
34	Hyrum
35	Manila
36	Kanosh (later DG-131)
37	Moon Lake
38	Big Cottonwood Canyon
39	Mayfield
40	Rock Canyon
	Provo (formerly PE-220)
41	Indian Creek
42	Escalante
43	Pleasant Grove
44	Aspen Grove (Escalante)
46	Pinto
48	Bountiful (formerly SE-205)
49	Farmington Canyon
50	Seeley Creek
51	Huntsville (formerly BR-12)
Soil Conservation Service (SCS-)	
2	Gunlock
3	Price
4	Willard (formerly PE-221)
5	Mt. Pleasant (formerly PE-223)
6	Moab (formerly PE-214)
7	Leeds (formerly F-24)
8	Indian Creek
9	Tremonton
State—Erosion Control (SE-)	
201	Bountiful
204	Brigham City

Table C.2. Utah Civilian Conservation Corps Camp Numbers and Locations.

Camp Department/Agency Designation and Number	Camp Location
205	Woods Cross (later F-48)
206	Hobble Creek Canyon
211	Widtsoe
212	Alton
213	St. George (later DG-45)
State—Private Erosion (PE-)	
214	Moab (later SCS-6)
215	Santa Clara
216	Washington
217	La Verkin
218	Orderville
219	Salina (later F-32)
220	Provo
221	Willard (later SCS-4)
222	Cedar City (later DG-30)
223	Mt. Pleasant (later SCS-5)
National Park Service (NP-)	
1	Zion (later Blue Springs)
2	Zion
3	Bryce Canyon
4	Bridge Mountain
5	Cedar Breaks
6	Capitol Reef
7	Arches
Bureau of Reclamation (BR-)	
5	Currant Creek (Heber)
6	Ephraim
11	Bridgeland
12	Huntsville (later F-51)
64	Deer Creek
91	Pleasant Grove (formerly F-43)
Biological Survey (BS-)	
1	Bear River (Brigham, formerly BF-1)
2	Ogden Bay
State Parks (SP-)	
1	Locomotive Springs

Table C.2. Utah Civilian Conservation Corps Camp Numbers and Locations.

Camp Department/Agency Designation and Number	Camp Location
2	Farmington Bay
Army	
G(D)-1	Dugway (formerly DG-154)
Army 1	Fort Douglas Detachment
Metropolitan Area (MA-)	
1	Provo River
Planned camps	
F-45	Woods Cross
F-52	Dry Fork
DG-159	Myton (later Bonanza)
NP-8	Bryce Canyon
BR-100	Fairview
BR-127	Scofield

a. Although they apparently never materialized, these camps were approved at various times for these locations.

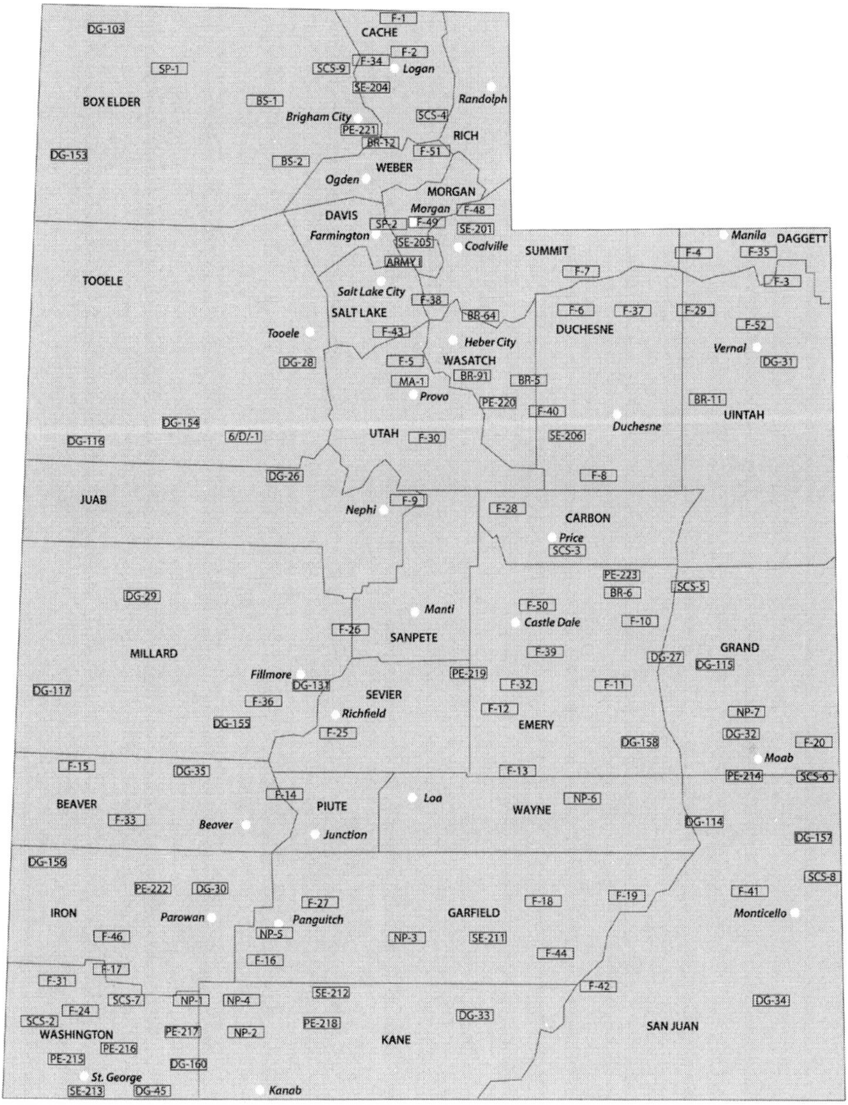

Figure C.1. Map of Utah Civilian Conservation Corps locations.

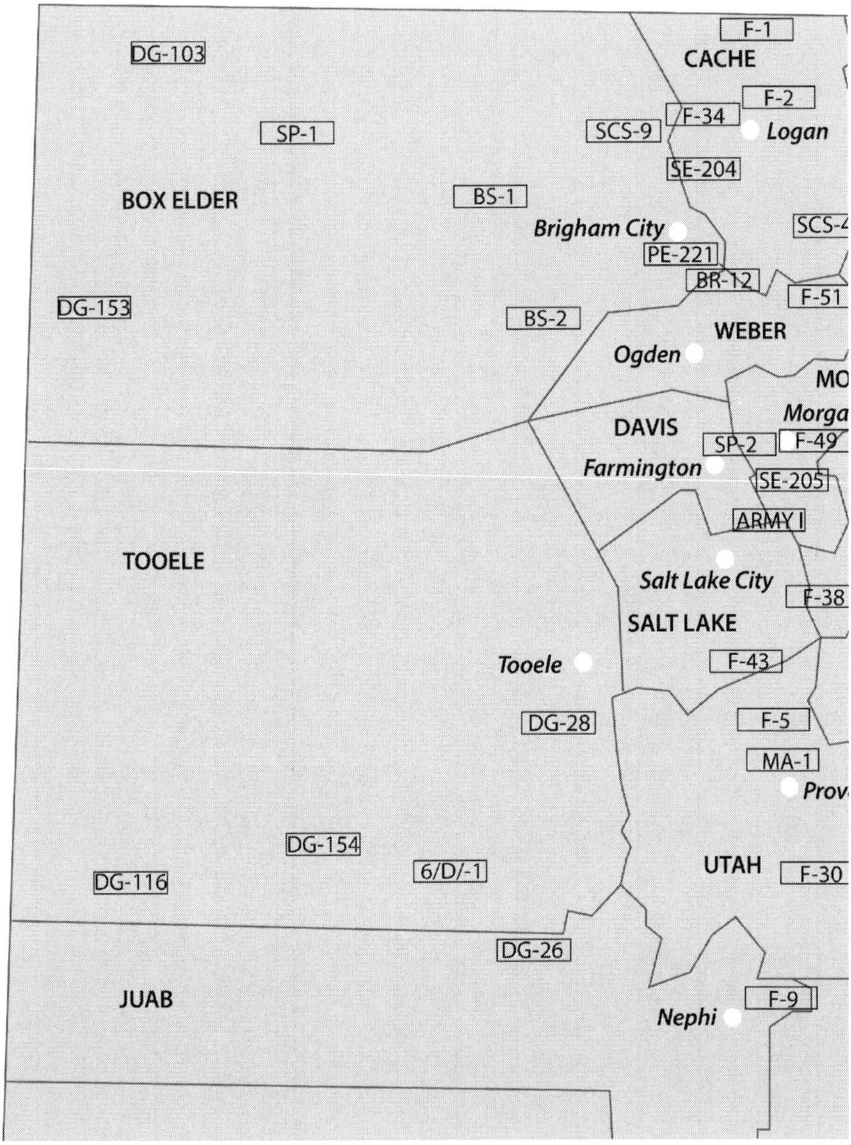

Figure C.2. Map of northeast Utah Civilian Conservation Corps locations.

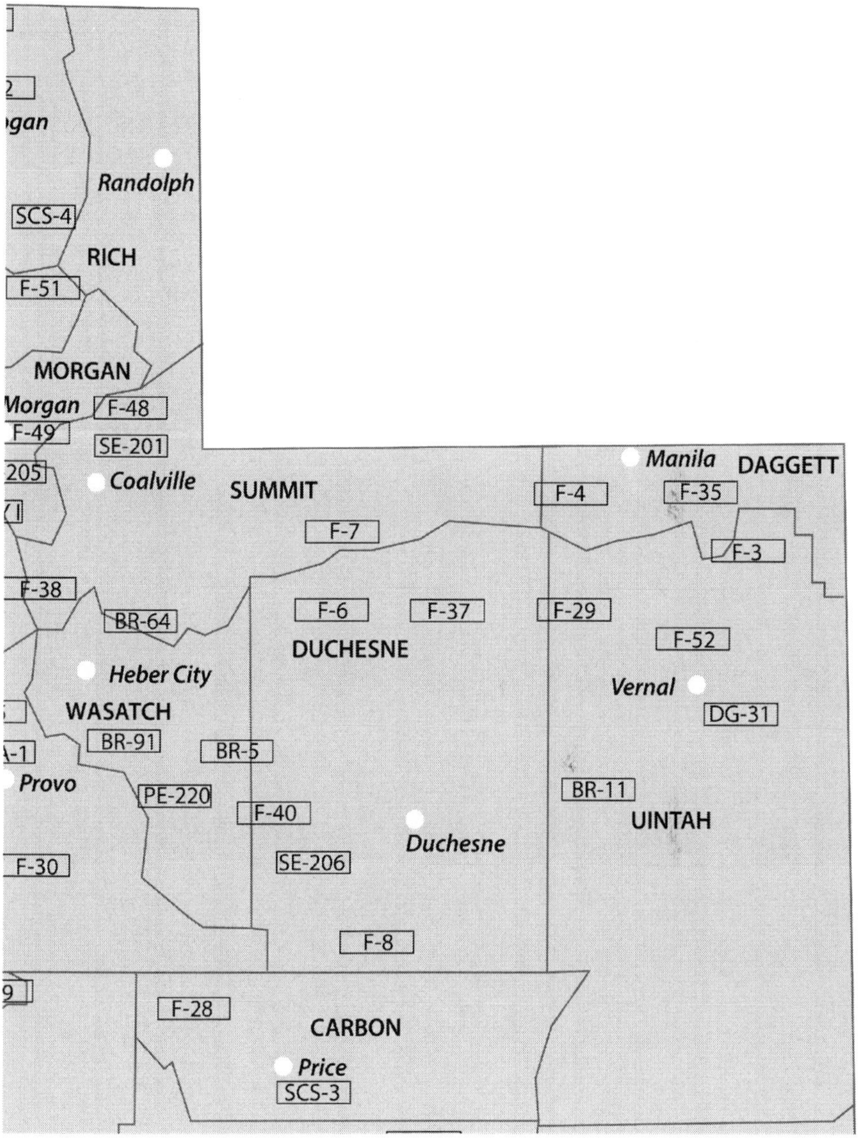

Figure C.3. Map of northwest Utah Civilian Conservation Corps locations.

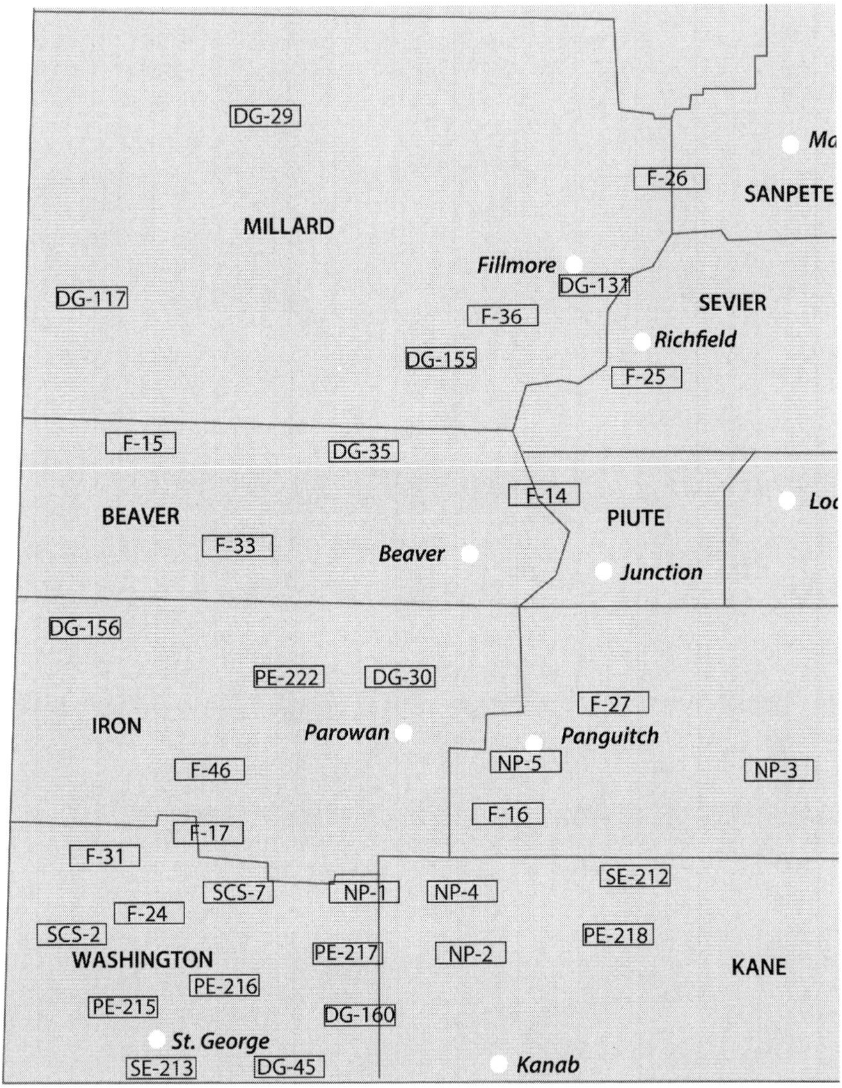

Figure C.4. Map of southeast Utah Civilian Conservation Corps locations.

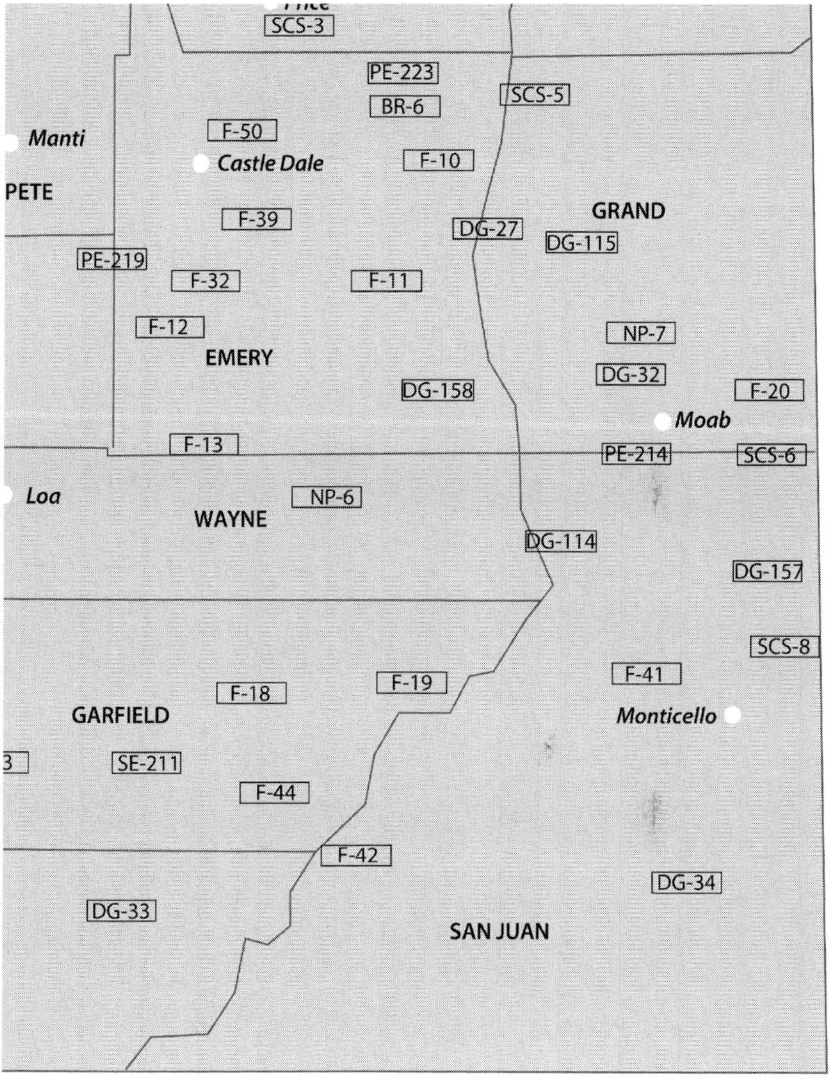

Figure C.5. Map of southwest Utah Civilian Conservation Corps locations.

Notes

CHAPTER 1

1. "484 Forest Lads Entrain for Home," *Deseret News*, October 4, 1933. The bill providing for the organization referred only to Emergency Conservation Work, and the official reports bore the designation "ECW." In its opening days the CCC was often referred to as the "reforestation army" or "job army," although Roosevelt's name for it, the Civilian Conservation Corps, was soon adopted. The organization was not officially designated as such by law until 1937. By then the nicknames had increased to include the "Three *C*'s," "Triple *C*'s," or simply "The *C*'s."
2. "Speaker Praises CC Flood Work," *Deseret News*, October 6, 1933; "Forester Lauds CCC Labors," *Deseret News*, October 18, 1933; "Camp Foresters Do Good Work Says Utah Chief," *Deseret News*, October 9, 1933.
3. "484 Forest Lads Entrain for Home"; "CCC Workers Get Fancy Winter Outfits," *Deseret News*, October 7, 1933.
4. David M. Kennedy, *Freedom from Fear: The American People in Depression and War, 1929–1945*, Oxford History of the United States, vol. IX, ed. C. Vann Woodward (New York: Oxford University Press, 1999), 99.
5. "Roosevelt to Speed Huge Jobless Relief Scheme to Congress," *Salt Lake Tribune*, March 11, 1933.
6. John A. Salmond, *The Civilian Conservation Corps, 1933–1942: A New Deal Case Study* (Durham, N.C.: Duke University Press, 1967), 24. Although Salmond treats too briefly the actual work of the CCC, the work covers like no other the various possibilities of what led to the president's championing of the idea of fighting not only to save the depleted natural resources of the country but also the specter of massive unemployment that was destroying the social and economic fabric of the nation.
7. Kennedy, *Freedom from Fear*, 99.
8. Raymond Moley, *After Seven Years* (New York: Harper and Brothers, 1939), 74.
9. Edgar B. Nixon, ed., *Franklin D. Roosevelt and Conservation, 1911–1934* (Washington, D.C.: National Archives and Record Service and the Franklin D. Roosevelt Library, 1957), I, 138; Moley, *After Seven Years*, 174; Arthur Schlesinger Jr., *The Age of Roosevelt, vol. II: The Coming of the New Deal, 1933–1935* (Boston: Houghton Mifflin, 1958), 287, 290, 292.
10. Salmond, *Civilian Conservation Corps*, 12.

11. U.S. Congress, An Act for the Relief of Unemployment through the Performance of Useful Public Work and for Other Purposes, Public Law 5, 73rd Cong., 1st Sess., 1933, 1.
12. For a detailed description of the debates on the bill, see U.S. Congress, Senate, Committee on Education and Labor, House, Committee on Labor, Joint Hearings on Unemployment Relief, S. 598, 73rd Cong., 1st Sess., 1933. The story of the passage is told very well in Salmond, *Civilian Conservation Corps*, chap. 1.
13. Schlesinger, *Age of Roosevelt*, 340.
14. U.S. Congress, 73rd Cong., 1st Sess., *Congressional Record* 77, pt. 1 (1933): 862–1013. "Foes Holding Out against Jobs Aid Bill," *Salt Lake Tribune*, March 23, 1933; "Senators Asked to Oppose Conservation Corps Bill," *Salt Lake Tribune*, March 23, 1933; "Miss Perkins, Dern Uphold Forest Work," *Salt Lake Tribune*, March 24, 1933; Salmond, *Civilian Conservation Corps*, 21. Salmond thoroughly describes the turmoil caused by the proposed wage (*Civilian Conservation Corps*, 15–23).
15. "Utah Forest Camps Build Men; Workers Happy Crowd," *Provo Evening Herald*, June 23, 1933.
16. Leland Livingston, "What Readers Think: Recruit Discusses Wage Scale in Forest Camps," *Deseret News*, July 3, 1933.
17. "Thomas Believes Program Will Work," *Salt Lake Tribune*, March 24, 1933; "Westerners Fail to See Forest Benefits," *Salt Lake Tribune*, April 9, 1933.
18. U.S. Congress, Senate, S. 598, 73rd Cong., 1st Sess., *Congressional Record* 77, pt. I (March 28, 1933): 929–36; (March 31, 1933): 1012–13.
19. Salmond, *Civilian Conservation Corps*, 23, 31; Samuel I. Rosenman, ed., *The Public Papers and Addresses of Franklin D. Roosevelt*, 5 vols. (New York: Random House, 1938–50), II, 107–8.
20. Salmond, *Civilian Conservation Corps*, 28.
21. "Job Recruiting Awaits List of County Agents," *Deseret News*, May 1, 1933; Rosenman, *Public Papers and Addresses of Franklin D. Roosevelt*, II, 107–8. The role of the Army was soon expanded to a position of nearly complete control, with the technical agencies being responsible for the men only during actual working hours. In 1939 the Labor Department gave up its seat on the Advisory Council when the enrollment of junior applicants was turned over to the Director's Office. The Veterans Administration, in charge of veteran enrollment almost from the very beginning, took Labor's place as the fourth member of the council.
22. Rosenman, *Public Papers and Addresses of Franklin D. Roosevelt*, II, 107–8.
23. The Corps Area organization was later altered by Chief of Staff Douglas MacArthur and completely changed during World War II. The system of numbering companies is more thoroughly explained in chapter 2.
24. "Roster of All Forest Camps Officers Filed," *Deseret News*, July 4, 1933.
25. "CCC News," *Herald Journal*, June 20, 1935; *Jericho Journal*, April 5, 1940. The *Jericho Journal* was one of more than eighty newspapers published

by CCC companies in Utah. These were short, usually weekly, of four to ten pages. The company newspapers cited in this book will be referenced by date only and are found in Manuscript Collection B540, "Civilian Conservation Corps Newspapers," Utah State Historical Society, Salt Lake City. Nearly all the papers bore the University of Illinois Library stamp, indicating that they were sent to that repository immediately after publication and subsequently sent back to Utah.

26. Salmond, *Civilian Conservation Corps*, 36.
27. Ibid., 36–37.
28. Schlesinger, *Age of Roosevelt*, 15.
29. Salmond, *Civilian Conservation Corps*, 37; William Seale, *The Presidents' House: A History* (Washington, D.C.: White House Historical Association, 1986), 932. It was not until January 1936 that Congress passed the long-delayed bonus bill, ironically over FDR's veto. Kennedy, *Freedom from Fear*, 279; Paul Dickson and Thomas B. Allen, *The Bonus Army: An American Epic* (New York: Walker Publishing Co., 2004), 213–20. Dickson and Allen provide an interesting description of the plight of the veterans and the outcome.
30. Salmond, *Civilian Conservation Corps*, 33–34.
31. Ibid., 34. For more on the LEMs, see chapter 5.
32. Ibid., 34–35. See Neil M. Maher, *Nature's New Deal: The Civilian Conservation Corps and the Roots of the American Environmental Movement* (New York: Oxford University Press, 2008). Using Salmond's figure, Maher thus calculated the number of LEMs in the Great Smoky Mountains as "approximately 200" by "multiplying the number of LEMs assigned each camp [8] by the number of camps in the Smokies during the years between 1933 and 1942" (*Nature's New Deal*, 22). He added a few to his figure to take personnel turnover into consideration (276 n. 150).
33. Paul Webbink, "Unemployment in the United States, 1930–1940," *Papers and Proceedings of the American Economic Association* 30 (February 1941): 248–72; Alfred C. Oliver Jr. and Harold M. Dudley, *The New America* (New York: Longmans, Green and Co., 1937), 30.
34. Kingsley Davis, *Youth in the Depression* (Chicago: University of Chicago Press, 1935), 7; Newton D. Baker, "Homeless Wanderers Create a New Problem for America," *New York Times*, December 11, 1932.
35. "National Forest Projects Will Employ Many Men This Winter," *Iron County Record*, November 16, 1933.
36. Maher, *Nature's New Deal*, 116.
37. *Pleasant Grove Review*, March 25, 1938.
38. "Miss Perkins Asks Utahn to Capitol," *Deseret News*, April 12, 1933.

CHAPTER 2

1. William E. Cheeseman, "Unemployment and Relief in Utah, 1929–1932" (master's thesis, Department of History, Brigham Young University, 1961), 59–60.
2. Ibid.
3. Edgar E. Robinson, *They Voted for Roosevelt* (Palo Alto: Stanford University, 1947), 41, 52.
4. R. Thomas Quinn, "Out of the Depression Depths: Henry H. Blood's First Year as Governor," *Utah Historical Quarterly* 54, no. 3 (Summer 1986): 217.
5. Logan City Commission, Minutes, May 16, 1933.
6. Paul C. Jones, Heber, Utah, to Governor Henry H. Blood, April 1, 1933, Box C, 1933, Governor Henry H. Blood's Correspondence, Utah State Archives, Salt Lake City; archive hereafter cited as "'CCC' [or relevant box], Blood Papers."
7. "Utah Federation of Labor Protests Roosevelt Bill," *Deseret News*, March 22, 1933; "The Conservation Corps," *Salt Lake Tribune*, March 23, 1933. International confusion concerning the proposal was indicated by a *Tribune* article on March 11 in which Mussolini's newspaper, *Popolo d' Italia*, was quoted claiming that Roosevelt's "assumption of extraordinary powers is evidence that dictatorial methods are superceding democratic government."
8. Ray Hoyt, *We Can Take It: A Short Story of the C.C.C.* (New York: American Book Company, 1935), 12; Rosenman, *Public Papers and Addresses of Franklin D. Roosevelt*, II, 109.
9. U.S. Emergency Conservation Work and Civilian Conservation Corps, *Reports of the Director* (Washington, D.C.: U.S. Government Printing Office, 1933–43), *Report of the Director, 1934*, 22; hereafter reports are cited as *Report of the Director* by year. For much of the time there were actually two Indian camps. They, however, operated so independently under the Bureau of Indian Affairs that, except where noted, their story remains outside the scope of this study.
10. Blood to Charles Lathrop Pack, n.d. [1933], "American Tree Association," Box 1, Blood Papers. As indicated in the previous note, these figures exclude the Indian camps.
11. The "state" camps involved in erosion and flood control are discussed in chapter 6; "local experienced men," or LEMs, are discussed in chapter 5.
12. *Report of the Director, 1934*, 25–26; "Utah Gets More Than Share of Forestry Men," *Salt Lake Tribune*, June 3, 1933.
13. Proposed wire to President Roosevelt, n.d. [1933], "CCC," Blood Papers. The only indication that the message was ever sent is a wire to Blood from Frank Persons received June 7, 1933, which appears to be an answer to that or a similar plea.
14. Frank Persons to Blood, June 5, 1933, "CCC," Blood Papers.

15. Gary L. Shumway, *This Part of the Vineyard: A Centennial Overview of the History of Blanding, Utah* (Yorba Linda: Shumway Family History Publishing, 2005), 79.
16. Deniane Gutke, "Open Arms? The CCC Invasion of San Juan County," *Blue Mountain Shadows* (Blanding, Utah) 1, no. 1 (Fall 1987). Thanks are due to Janet Wilcox of Blanding, who provided me additional information in a phone interview, January 1, 2016. Not one of the eavesdropping teenagers, Wilcox had had Gutke in one of her high school classes and was a founder of the publication in which her student's article appeared. Both Gutke and Wilcox acknowledged that several marriages took place between enrollees and local girls.
17. "My Brother's Keeper," *Washington County News*, November 16, 1933.
18. Wayne Hinton, "The New Deal Years in Utah: A Political History of Utah (1932–1940)" (master's thesis, Department of History, Utah State University, 1963), 93.
19. "Chief Executive Plans to Leave Later This Week," *Deseret News*, April 12, 1933.
20. Quinn, "Out of the Depression Depths," 227–29.
21. "Forest Recruits Lead Army Life," *Deseret News*, April 18, 1933.
22. "Job Army Quota Set for Utah," *Deseret News*, April 20, 1933.
23. *Report of the Director, 1934*, 2; "212 Men Selected for Forest Camps," *Salt Lake Tribune*, June 4, 1933.
24. "Reforestation Corps Agencies Will Be Chosen Wednesday," *Deseret News*, May 2, 1933.
25. "Applications for Forest Corps Work Will Be Received in S.L. Thursday," *Deseret News*, May 3, 1933; "Civilian Camps to Reach Full Quotas July 15th," *Iron County Record*, July 6, 1933; Salmond, *Civilian Conservation Corps*, 35. My research indicates that CCC procedures were often rather fluid, especially in the earlier days of the CCC.
26. "212 Men Selected for Forest Camps."
27. Major General Malin Craig, San Francisco, to Blood, wire, April 20, 1933, "CCC," Blood Papers; Leonard J. Arrington, "Utah's Great Drought of 1934," *Utah Historical Quarterly*, Summer 1986: 253; Quinn, "Out of the Depression Depths," 233.
28. King to Blood, March 3, 1933, and Blood to King, April 4, 1933, "Senator W. H. King," Box 6, Blood Papers.
29. "Job Recruiting Awaits List of County Agents."
30. *Frontier*, February 1940. My assumption is that W.O.D. means "Woolen, Olive Drab" and the John L's are "long johns" or winter underwear.
31. "Forest Work Attracts 4000 for 140 Jobs," *Deseret News*, May 4, 1933; "Conservation Army Goes into Training at Fort Saturday," *Deseret News*, May 5, 1933.
32. "Work Is Started on Reforestation Here," *Richfield Reaper*, May 11, 1933.

33. "Stations Set Up in All Utah Counties for Job Recruits," *Deseret News*, May 8, 1933; "Utah Deadline for Recruiting Job Army Set," *Deseret News*, May 12, 1933.
34. "Utah Deadline for Recruiting Job Army Set"; "Utah County Launches Recruiting for Job Army," *Deseret News*, May 10, 1933.
35. "County Recruiting for Forest Army to Start Monday," *Deseret News*, May 6, 1933; "Regional Forester Outlines Aims of Conservation Work," *Deseret News*, May 10, 1933.
36. "Forest Job Recruiting to Begin Thursday in Cedar City Area," *Deseret News*, May 9, 1933.
37. Mark J. Baird, Draper, correspondence with the author, March 31, 1968; "Utah Forest Camps Build Men; Workers Happy Crowd"; Elliott R. Killpack, San Pedro, Calif., correspondence with the author, May 16, 1968; Ken Haslam, Inglewood, interview by the author, August 19, 1969.
38. A. R. Standing to William Udink, June 21, 1933, in my possession.
39. Mrs. D. T. Guyman to Blood, July 3, 1933; Dick Titcomb to Blood, July 17, 1933; and Blood to Mrs. Nancy Allred, August 18, 1933, "CCC," Blood Papers.
40. William Carr, Provo, interview by the author, February 3, 1968.
41. "Officers Changed at Forest Camps," *Deseret News*, August 15, 1933.
42. Blood to Fechner, November 24, 1933, "CCC," Blood Papers.
43. "Forest Camps of West Have 15,758 on Jobs," *Deseret News*, June 7, 1933; "Hundred Veterans Wanted for Camps," *Deseret News*, June 9, 1933; "Veterans Forest Quota Received," *Salt Lake Tribune*, June 7, 1933; "Veteran Limit Fixed at 100," *Salt Lake Tribune*, June 5, 1933. Incidentally, Idaho's quota for veterans was also one hundred; Wyoming was eligible for fifty, and Nevada, twenty-five.
44. "Veteran Forest Corps Organized: Men Will Assemble at Fort Douglas on Wednesday," *Deseret News*, June 27, 1933. Company 1925 apparently stayed in California after the Utah men were returned to their home state. I never found the company of Utah veterans at either F-9 or F-31 identified by a company number; it was just the "veterans' company." During the Fourth Enrollment Period the veterans moved to F-31 in Veyo, where they stayed until the company was disbanded eighteen months later. After the Sixth Enrollment Period there was no more veterans' company in Utah, although veterans continued to serve in regular companies, usually as LEMs.
45. Frank G. Stone, Salt Lake City, interview by the author, July 17, 1968; Frank G. Stone to Blood, January 23, 1934, "CCC," Blood Papers.
46. "C. of C. to Buy Camp Supplies," *Deseret News*, May 2, 1933.
47. "Flood Control District Made by Commission," *Provo Evening Herald*, September 12, 1933.
48. "Five Millard County Towns Request Jobless Army Camp at Fishlake," *Deseret News*, April 27, 1933.

49. "Flood Dams Asked in Salina Canyon," *Deseret News*, May 10, 1933.
50. M. F. Murray to Blood, June 26, 1933, "CCC," Blood Papers. A camp was established in Salina Canyon in May, but Marysvale never did get one.
51. Fechner to Blood, wire, May 18, 1933, "CCC," Blood Papers; "Forest Camp Building Starts," *Deseret News*, May 30, 1933; "Forest Service Asks Bids on 50,000 Shovels," *Deseret News*, May 6, 1933; "Forest Office to Open Bids for Supplies," *Deseret News*, May 10, 1933.
52. Fred L. Rampton to Blood, June 30, 1933, "CCC," Blood Papers.
53. Salmond, *Civilian Conservation Corps*, 47. David P. Howells to Blood, August 18, 1933; Blood to Earl F. Dunn, September 16, 1933; Blood to William A. Miller, September 21, 1933; and Blood to Wayne County Commissioner, October 7, 1933, "CCC," Blood Papers.
54. Salmond, *Civilian Conservation Corps*, 30.
55. Ibid.; Blood to Fechner, November 24, 1933; John J. McEntee to C. C. Jeltman, January 14, 1941, "I (CCC) Camp—History—Utah—General," Grazing Service, Official File, Box 10858, Bureau of Land Management Records, Federal Records Center, Denver; archive hereafter cited as BLM Records.
56. Blood to C. L. Forsling and others, May 27, 1933, "CCC," Blood Papers.
57. "Quotas Set for State's Forest Units," *Salt Lake Tribune*, May 6, 1933; "State Names Committee to Select Camps," *Deseret News*, May 30, 1933; "Fourteen Special Forest Sites to Work on Flood Control," *Deseret News*, May 30, 1933.
58. Arnold R. Standing, interview by Merrill Nielsen, April 30, 1965, Accession #R-4-1680-92-0024-81, U.S. Forest Service Region 4 History Collection, Ogden; "Forest Men Visit Camps," *Salt Lake Tribune*, July 1, 1933.
59. "Regular Army Due to Erect Forest Camps," *Deseret News*, May 19, 1933.
60. "50 Called for Forest Work from 3 Areas," *Deseret News*, May 25, 1933.
61. "Forest Workers Leave for Camp," *Salt Lake Tribune*, June 4, 1933.
62. Deniane Gutke, "A CCC Enrollee a Day Kept Depression Away," *Blue Mountain Shadows* (Blanding, Utah) 1, no. 2 (Spring 1988): 78.
63. "Prevailing Wage Assured Builders of Forest Camps; Labor Federation Told Soldiers Will Not Be Used," *Deseret News*, June 8, 1933; "Union Laborers Urged for Camps," *Salt Lake Tribune*, June 4, 1933.
64. "Counties Get Allotments in Forest Corps," *Deseret News*, July 8, 1933; "Utah to Move 1400 to Camps in Next 2 Days," *Deseret News*, July 12, 1933. "1429 Additional Men Selected for CCC Camps," *Iron County Record*, July 13, 1933, said that Morgan County had a quota of only seven.
65. "Speed Ordered in Mobilizing Forest Camps," *Deseret News*, May 16, 1933; "Western Area Gets Third of Forest Camps," *Deseret News*, June 16, 1933.
66. Joseph Chez to Blood, July 8, 1933, and Blood to Holman, July 8, 1933, "H File, April–July," Box 5, Blood Papers.
67. Later in the program Bureau of Reclamation camps were designated "BR"; Soil Conservation Camps, "SCS"; Division of Grazing, "DG" or simply

"G"; and Biological Survey, "BS." The designation "SP" indicated camps in state parks, and "MA" was a special type of city-sponsored camp for a metropolitan area. Utah's only one of this latter type was camp MA-1 in Provo.

68. Wayne K. Hinton, *With Picks, Shovels, and Hope: The CCC and Its Legacy on the Colorado Plateau*, with Elizabeth A. Green (Missoula: Mountain Press Publishing Company, 2008).
69. Ibid., 103.
70. "Forest Army at Bullionville Do Road Work," *Vernal Express*, June 15, 1933; "CCC Camps at Bullionville and Smith's Fork Are Now Fully Manned," *Vernal Express*, June 29, 1933.
71. Advisory Council, Minutes, July 6 and 10, 1933, quoted in Salmond, *Civilian Conservation Corps*, 46.
72. *Canal Construction Chronicle*, April 6, 1936.
73. "Two Firms Get Contracts for Forest Camps," *Deseret News*, May 15, 1933; "Forest Camp in American Fork to Be Ready June 7," *Deseret News*, June 6, 1933. Camp F-1 in Logan Canyon was completed just a few days later and due to its designating number was sometimes erroneously cited as the first camp in Utah.
74. "First County Reforestation Camp to Be Started Monday," *Provo Sunday Herald*, May 14, 1933; "Canyon Forest Camp Is Ready," *Provo Evening Herald*, June 26, 1933; C. J. Olson, Ogden, to Blood, October 2, 1936, "CCC," Blood Papers; "Two Firms Get Contracts for Forest Camps"; "Forest Camp in American Fork to Be Ready June 7." See also Reid W. Gardner to Blood, June 7, 1933; M. R. Urie to Blood, June 9, 1933; James E. Gurr to Blood, June 10, 1933; L. C. Miles to Blood, June 13, 1933; W. R. Irish to Blood, June 20, 1933; Blood to Irish, June 23, 1933; and David S. Doggett to Blood, July 18, 1933, "CCC," Blood Papers.
75. "75 New Men at Canyon Camp," *Provo Evening Herald*, July 17, 1933. Since the numbers given of personnel added to the roster add up to three hundred rather than the normal company strength of two hundred, it appears that competency in mathematics was not required of those supplying the figures.
76. Beth Olsen, *Pleasant Grove Sesquicentennial History, vol. 3: American Fork Canyon, Pleasant Grove's Backyard* (Provo: Stevenson's Supply, n.d. [ca. 2008]), 111–13.
77. "Six Winter CCC Camps in Dixie," *Iron County Record*, September 28, 1933.
78. The work of the state's erosion control camps is covered in chapter 6.
79. "CCC Camp Is Now Finished for Men," *Washington County News*, October 19, 1933; "CCC Camp 961 Was Dedicated Saturday," *Washington County News*, November 2, 1933; "Mechanics Build St. George Camp," *Deseret News*, September 26, 1933.

80. "Camp PE-216 Holds Dedication," *Washington County News*, November 23, 1933; F. E. Moscon, "In and about PE-215," *Washington County News*, December 14, 1933; Heber C. Thompson, Laie, Hawaii, interview by the author, May 19, 1970.
81. Robert T. Hinckley to George Sutherland, September 7, 1933, "CCC," Blood Papers.
82. "Ft. Duquesne Ideal for CCC Winter Camp," *Vernal Express*, August 17, 1933.
83. Robert Hinckley to C. L. Forsling and Ernest Winkler, August 29, 1933, "CCC," Blood Papers.
84. "Forest Camps May Close in Two Months," *Herald Journal*, September 2, 1933; "CCC Workers Leave for Southern Camps," *Deseret News*, October 17, 1933; "Utah CCC Workers Entrain for East," *Deseret News*, October 26, 1933.
85. *Report of the Director, 1934*, 22. The Bureau of Indian Affairs, whose camps were not generally reported with the others, kept its two in the Uinta Basin.
86. "Work in Forest Camp Near End," *Provo Evening Herald*, September 26, 1933.
87. "Strawberry Road Nears Completion," *Provo Evening Herald*, August 17, 1933.
88. U.S. Department of Labor, "ECW Official Letter #51 to All State Directors of Selection of Men," August 25, 1933, "CCC," Blood Papers.
89. Blood to Frank A. Birkinshaw, November 2, 1933, "CCC," Blood Papers.
90. Rosenman, *Public Papers and Addresses of Franklin D. Roosevelt*, II, 322; "Expanding Human Resources," *Salt Lake Tribune*, December 15, 1933.
91. Charles S. Peterson and Linda E. Speth, *A History of Wasatch-Cache National Forest* ([Logan]: Utah State University, 1980), 103.
92. Max J. Schlegel, "News from CCC Camp," *Herald Journal*, September 13, 1933.
93. "What Readers Think: Idahoan Comments on Conditions in CCC," *Deseret News*, October 5, 1933.
94. "What Readers Think: Idahoan Comments on Conditions in CCC," *Deseret News*, May 15, 1933.
95. Jos. Hyrum Parry, "Parry Sees Blessing to Boys in Forest Camps," *Deseret News*, July 14, 1933.
96. Blood to Pack, n.d. [1933]; "Church Members Asked to Support Campaign of NRA," *Deseret News*, October 9, 1933.
97. Arrington, "Utah's Great Drought of 1934," 249.
98. Ovid Butler, ed., *Youth Rebuilds: Stories from the CCC* (Washington, D.C.: American Forestry Association, 1934), 140–41.
99. "The Forest Army," *Deseret News*, August 5, 1933.
100. James O. Stewart, "Ashley National Forest," *Roosevelt Standard*, December 14, 1933.

CHAPTER 3

1. Hoyt, *We Can Take It*, 35.
2. "Memorandum Number One—Company 959, Fort Douglas District, Civilian Conservation Corps, Apr. 15, 1935, Mt. Pleasant, Utah," Folder CCC 959, ECA 2003, 007-1, File 3.4, Emery County Archives, Castle Dale, Utah.
3. The Army structure of nine Corps Areas was discontinued in the early days of World War II.
4. "CCC News," *Herald Journal*, June 20, 1935; *Jericho Journal*, April 5, 1940.
5. "Marine Officers to Aid Local Forest Corps Men," *Salt Lake Tribune*, June 25, 1933.
6. "Roster of All Forest Camps Officers Filed."
7. U.S. Civilian Conservation Corps, "Location and Strength of Civilian Conservation Corps Projects and Work Companies in the Ninth Corps Area on September 30, 1940," 21, Leonard J. Arrington File, in my possession. This report, and others cited as part of the Leonard J. Arrington File, was photocopied by the late Professor Arrington, then of Utah State University, at the National Archives in Washington, D.C. In 1968 I expressed my personal appreciation to him for making these available.
8. Tamera Newman, "Tremonton Was Once Home to WW II POWs," in *Looking Back: Tremonton City's First 100 Years, 1903–2003* (Logan: *Tremonton Leader/Garland Times*, 2003), 65.
9. "Two Utah Reserve Officers Get Places in Forest Corps," *Deseret News*, May 9, 1933.
10. "Roster of All Forest Camps Officers Filed."
11. U.S. Congress, Senate, Committee on Education and Labor, House, Committee on Labor, Joint Hearings on Unemployment Relief, S. 598, 73rd Cong., 1st Sess., 1933, 41.
12. "Army Connection Denied in Reforestation Plan," *Deseret News*, April 12, 1933.
13. For a summary of the Army's relationships with Fechner and the CCC, see Salmond, *Civilian Conservation Corps*, 85–86, 172–75. See also Frances Perkins, *The Roosevelt I Knew* (New York: Holt, Rinehart and Winston, 1963), 179.
14. "Thousands Seek Forestry Jobs," *Salt Lake Tribune*, May 18, 1933.
15. "Army Speeds Machinery to Start Work in Mountains," *Deseret News*, May 10, 1933.
16. *P.G. Bee*, March 20, 1940.
17. Ned H. Dearborn, *Once in a Lifetime: A Guide to the CCC Camp* (New York: Charles E. Merrill Company, 1935), 237–38; "Roster of All Forest Camps Officers Filed."

18. Interview by the author, July 22, 1968. The interviewee did not wish to be identified.
19. Thora Bergeson, "A Survey of the Social Background of the Civilian Conservation Corps Enrollees of the Fort Douglas District" (master's thesis, Department of Sociology, University of Utah, 1937), 105.
20. Ibid., 107.
21. T. Carl Haycock, correspondence with the author, May 4, 1968.
22. J. Whitney Floyd, Logan, interview by the author, June 20, 1968; R. H. Rutledge, Radio Talk: CCC 4th Anniversary, 1937, 4, Accession No. R4-1680-1992-0031-14-48, U.S. Forest Service Region 4 History Collection, Ogden; *Yell-A-Gram*, July 19, 1935.
23. John Herrick Hiram Darling, "The C.C.C. Makes Good!" *Christian Century* 50 (October 25, 1933): 1334.
24. Raymond W. Cassell, Ogden, interview by the author, July 28, 1968.
25. U.S. War Department, *Civilian Conservation Corps Regulations* (Washington, D.C.: U.S. Government Printing Office, 1937), para. 40.
26. "CCC Camp Gets New Educational Advisor," *Pleasant Grove Review*, November 1, 1935.
27. *Report of the Director, 1936*, 5.
28. "Jericho CCC Camp News," *Eureka Reporter*, July 29, 1937; Francis P. Welsh, Ogden, correspondence with the author, April 14, 1968.
29. *Bridgeland Bulletin* (camp newspaper, BR-11), August 11, 1939.
30. Raymond Gram Swing, "Take the Army out of the CCC," *Nation* 140 (October 23, 1935): 459.
31. Edward L. Miller, North Ogden, correspondence with the author, April 7, 1968.
32. *Bridgeland Bulletin*, May 25, 1939.
33. "CCC Looks Back on Excellent Record as Sixth Birthday Nears," *Salt Lake Tribune*, April 2, 1939.
34. "Sixth Period Report, DG-30," March 31, 1936, Boxes 8606–7, BLM Records; hereafter reports are cited by title and date.
35. U.S. Civilian Conservation Corps, "Total Work Completed during the Period—April, 1933 to June 30, 1942, Utah."
36. "Many States Represented in Fort Douglas CCC District," *Eureka Reporter*, February 18, 1937.
37. U.S. Civilian Conservation Corps, "Location and Strength of Civilian Conservation Corps Projects and Work Companies in the Ninth Corps Area on September 30, 1940."
38. See Salmond, *Civilian Conservation Corps*, 116–20, 194–96.
39. U.S. Civilian Conservation Corps, *Standards of Eligibility and Selection for Junior Enrollees* (Washington, D.C.: U.S. Government Printing Office, June 15, 1939), 16.

40. Frank E. Hill, *The School in the Camps: The Educational Program of the Civilian Conservation Corps* (New York: American Association for Adult Education, 1942), 66.
41. James J. McEntee, *Now They Are Men: The Story of the CCC* (Washington, D.C.: National Home Library Foundation, 1940), 37. The suggestion that all personnel—including civilian supervisory staff—stand "Retreat" came not from the Army but from one of the technical agencies. *Training Conference, 1939*, 20, Box 10863, BLM Records.
42. Haslam, interview by the author, August 19, 1969.
43. Schlesinger, *Age of Roosevelt*, 339. See Joseph Cream, "The Genesis of the Civilian Conservation Corps" (master's thesis, Columbia University, 1955), 53; George R. Rawick, "The New Deal and Youth: The Civilian Conservation Corps, the National Youth Administration, the American Youth Congress" (Ph.D. dissertation, University of Wisconsin, 1957), 62, 106; Salmond, *Civilian Conservation Corps*, 117; "Million CCC Next Summer," *Washington County News*, January 18, 1934.
44. "Backbone of the U.S.A.," *Salt Lake Tribune*, February 21, 1933.
45. "Group Fights Army Drill for CCC Boys: Petition Signers Deny Any Connection with 'Red Network,'" *Salt Lake Tribune*, March 17, 1935.
46. "What Is the Motive?" editorial, *Salt Lake Tribune*, March 22, 1935.
47. Salmond, *Civilian Conservation Corps*, 118–19.
48. "Youth in the Shuffle," editorial, *Salt Lake Tribune*, February 17, 1937.
49. Salmond, *Civilian Conservation Corps*, 193.
50. "Militarization of CCC Bobs Up Again," editorial, *Provo Sunday Herald*, March 12, 1939.
51. *Report of the Director, 1939*, 4; Salmond, *Civilian Conservation Corps*, 179–80; *Bay Cross News*, June 1939.
52. *Report of the Director, 1940*, 17.
53. Ibid., 3.
54. U.S. Senate, Committee on Appropriations, Hearings, on H. J. Res. 544, A Joint Resolution Making Appropriations for Work Relief and Relief for the Fiscal Year Ending June 30, 1941, 76th Cong., 3rd Sess., 1941, 186–206, cited in Salmond, *Civilian Conservation Corps*, 193.
55. War Department, Washington, D.C., to Commanding General, Ninth Corps Area, October 7, 1940, Folder I, TRAINING: Instruction, Ninth Corps Area CCC Headquarters, Box 10863, BLM Records.
56. "CCC Men Get Army Drill," *Salt Lake Tribune*, August 17, 1941.
57. McEntee, *Now They Are Men*, 65–66.
58. Ibid., 67.
59. Blood to T. E. Gleaves, Annabella, Utah, May 6, 1935, "CCC," Blood Papers.
60. *Frontier*, February 1940.
61. "Tenth Period Report, DG-45," March 31, 1938.

62. U.S. Civilian Conservation Corps, *Standards of Eligibility and Selection for Junior Enrollees*, 4; "First It Was LEM's; Now It'll Be PA's," *Happy Days*, June 11, 1938.
63. *CCC Reflections*, October 16, 1936.
64. In the first six-month enrollment period, 516 of the 1,511 camps in the continental United States were in the states of California, Oregon, Washington, Utah, Nevada, Montana, Idaho, Arizona, New Mexico, Colorado, and Wyoming. *Report of the Director, 1934*, 21–22.
65. Patsy Stoddard, "A Look Back at the Ccc [*sic*] Camps," *Emery County Progress*, December 5, 2006.
66. Salmond, *Civilian Conservation Corps*, 34. For details on originally incorporating the LEM concept into the CCC program, see chapter 1.
67. Stephanie Jewett, "The Civilian Conservation Corps in Iron County and Surrounding Areas" (senior thesis, Southern Utah University, 1994), 5.
68. *Take Five*, June 21, 1935.
69. Michael J. Schultz, correspondence with the author, August 30, 2012. His book is Michael J. Schultz Jr., *The Civilian Conservation Corps in the Allegheny National Forest: A Traveling Companion* (Kane, Pa.: Kane County Historic Preservation Society, 2011).
70. Shumway, *This Part of the Vineyard*, 79.
71. Renée Corona Kolvet and Victoria Ford, *The Civilian Conservation Corps in Nevada: From Boys to Men* (Reno: University of Nevada Press, 2006), 27.
72. Ibid., 39; Salmond, *Civilian Conservation Corps*, 34–35.
73. Barbara W. Sommer, *Hard Work and a Good Deal: The Civilian Conservation Corps in Minnesota* (St. Paul: Minnesota Historical Society, 2007), 29.
74. "Examinations for CCC Applicants Set Monday," *Salt Lake Tribune*, July 8, 1933.
75. "Counties Get Allotments in Forest Corps."
76. "Tenth Period Report, DG-45," March 31, 1938.
77. U.S. Civilian Conservation Corps, *Standards of Eligibility and Selection for Junior Enrollees*, 4.
78. "Handbook for Enrollees, Company 536: A Pamphlet Published for Information and Instruction of All Enrollees of Company 536, CCC Camp SP-2, Woods Cross, Utah" (presumably around April 1939).
79. *Bay Cross News*, April 20, 1939. In SP-2, among other camps, he was designated "senior leader" on a roster on the military side. The technical agency side, in this case the National Park Service, included a senior foreman, junior foremen, and junior assistant technicians, among other positions. Determining ranks, responsibilities, and seniority was, admittedly, often a challenge.
80. My research suggests that where the positions were separate, the "canteen steward" was usually an assistant leader, while the "supply sergeant" seems

to have more often been ranked as a leader. This distinction, however, was not absolute.

81. *Frontier*, February 1940.
82. Ibid.
83. Shumway, *This Part of the Vineyard*, 84.
84. Ten pages of mostly handwritten notes in a folder headed "Civil [*sic*] Conservation Corps in Iron County," Special Collections, Gerald R. Sherratt Library, Southern Utah University, Cedar City. The first page has the name of Ron(?) Glass penciled in.
85. "Memorandum Number One—Company 959, Fort Douglas District, Civilian Conservation Corps, Apr. 15, 1935, Mt. Pleasant, Utah"; *Frontier*, February 1940.
86. "Quarterly Report on Emergency Conservation Work, CCC, DNP-2 Oct. 1–Dec. 31, 1934," ZION 15450, Zion National Park Service Museum, courtesy of the National Park Service.
87. *Veyo Scroll*, November 23, 1939. A look at other rosters yielded similar results.
88. "Political Patronage Barred in Civil Works," *Iron County Record*, November 30, 1933.
89. Benjamin Heywood, Logan, interview by the author, March 29, 1968. There was some question about whether the CCC was going to be reduced in the early part of 1938, but by April it had been determined that there would be no cutback. The tardiness of Heywood's selection, therefore, could not be blamed on internal economic difficulties.
90. *Spirit of '48*, April 1937, Folder 1, Box 4, MSS-B 540, Utah State Archives, Salt Lake City.
91. The term *pairing* is, as far as I know, my own and was never used by either the Corps or the technical agencies to describe the rotation between summer and winter camps. To me it seems like an appropriate word to describe the situation.
92. R. H. Rutledge to Blood, September 29, 1937, "CCC," Blood Papers.

CHAPTER 4

1. *Report of the Director, 1941*, 34.
2. Sommer, *Hard Work and a Good Deal*, 114. The work of the Soil Conservation Service and the bird refuges of the Fish and Wildlife Service are covered in chapters 6 and 8, respectively.
3. *Report of the Director, 1941*, 4.
4. Rutledge left the Forest Service in late 1938 to become head of the Grazing Service in the Department of the Interior. On January 11, 1939, he was replaced by Associate Regional Forester Clarence N. Woods, the first of three consecutive regional foresters to come up through the ranks

according to Brigham Young University professor Thomas G. Alexander and historian of Region Four. Thomas G. Alexander, *The Rise of Multiple-Use Management in the Intermountain West: A History of Region 4 of the Forest Service* (Salt Lake City: Brigham Young University and MESA Corporation, May 1987), chap. 6, n. 43 (page number not visible).

5. Morse's information provided by Richa Wilson, archaeologist, U.S. Forest Service Region Four, Ogden. Morse retired in December 1946 and passed away April 12, 1950.
6. The twenty camps do not include the five state soil-erosion camps operating in 1933, which, although administered by the Forest Service, operated under state guidelines. Rutledge, Radio Talk, 2.
7. "Army Speeds Machinery to Start Work in Mountains."
8. Stanley O. Nelson, Ogden, correspondence with the author, May 19, 1968; Maurice M. Marlor, Logan, correspondence with the author, April 6, 1968; "Forest Camps in Northern Utah May Close for Winter Season," *Deseret News*, August 23, 1933.
9. "Fifteen Recruits Join Forest Job Army Unit," *Deseret News*, June 15, 1933.
10. Identified in the *Utah Road and Recreation Atlas* (Medford, Ore.: Benchmark Maps, 2006) only as the Squaw Peak Trail, it has no number identifying it as a Forest Service road.
11. "Uinta County Men Taken to Forest Camp," *Vernal Express*, June 1, 1933, cited in U.S. Forest Service Region Four archaeologist Richa Wilson, *Cozy Cabins and a Hyperbolic Paraboloid* (Ogden: Forest Service Intermountain Region, June 2015). This is an excellent source for detailed information about the work carried out by CCC camps in Ashley National Forest and about F-3, F-29, F-35, and proposed camp F-52. Further mystery may be found in a token about the size of a silver dollar seen at the Regional Library in Vernal. On one side is printed "Bullionville, Utah, U.S. 1362," apparently the company number. On the opposite side is printed "CCC, 1937." However, Company 1362 never served in Utah, nor was there a camp at Bullionville in 1937. I have no explanation.
12. Wilson, *Cozy Cabins and a Hyperbolic Paraboloid*, 24.
13. "IMACS CONTINUATION SHEET," State No. 42UN826, Agency No. AS-0017, photocopy given to me by Ashley National Forest archaeologist Tara Hamilton, October 30, 2012.
14. A printed pamphlet by W. E. Hussey, "Brief History of Company 957, CCC," identifies Company 230 with Mountain View (4). A letter from Guy D. McKinney, Assistant to the Director, to Senator William H. King, June 6, 1940, lists all the camps that were ever established in Utah. Among them is listed F-4, located in Summit County. A few newspaper accounts provide further information: "CCC Camps at Bullionville and Smith's Fork Are Now Fully Manned"; "Forest Service Calls 45 More Recruits to Camp," *Deseret News*, June 16, 1933; "Forest Camps in Northern Utah

May Close for Winter Season"; "Utahns Honored by Selection as Forest Foremen," *Kane County Standard*, October 20, 1933.

15. "Forest Camps in Northern Utah May Close for Winter Season." An afternoon surveying Wyoming newspapers in the Evanston library indicated that the local media largely ignored F-4 and F-7, justifying their lack of coverage presumably because they were Utah camps.
16. What appears to be the actual site of F-9 is just off the Mt. Nebo Loop (Forest Road 015) in Juab County. Although a sign at the campground indicates that it was built in 1933, it unfortunately does *not* reveal that it was built by the CCC.
17. "C.C.C. Chatter," *Kane County Standard*, December 1, 1933; "80 Men Added to Ferron Camp," *Kane County Standard*, July 19, 1933. Emery County Commissioner James R. ("J.R.") Nelson showed me the original F-11 campsite, September 3, 2014.
18. George Alma Platt, Richfield, Utah, correspondence with the author, April 20, 1968.
19. "Hundreds Attend Dedication Day at CCC Camp," *Richfield Reaper*, July 27, 1933; "Foresters Control Pocket Gophers," *Deseret News*, August 23, 1933; "Fish Lake Camp, CCC Dedication Ready for July 22," *Deseret News*, July 18, 1933. Yes, *Fish Lake* (two words) is located in *Fishlake* (one word) National Forest.
20. "Foresters Ask Public to Camp," *Deseret News*, July 27, 1933. In addition to the appellations of Beaver Camp and Tusher Ranger Station Camp, F-14 was also identified in local newspapers at various times as Beaver River, Puffer Lake, and Camp Delano. To maintain consistency I will use Beaver Mountain and hopefully remove F-14 from the arena of confusion.
21. "CCC Boys Make Beauty Spot of Brush Area," *Iron County Record*, September 21, 1933; "U.S. Prepares to Move 4000 Foresters East for Discharge," *Deseret News*, September 9, 1933.
22. Jerry C. Roundy, *Advised Them to Call the Place "Escalante"* (Springville, Utah: Art City Publishing, 2000), 182.
23. Although it has been identified as the Grover camp, I'm starting to believe that F-19 was actually located in Torrey, several miles north on Highway 12. Roundy's note that this was the case as well as the presence of government buildings in Torrey and their absence in Grover support that belief.
24. "First Group Arrives for LaSal National Forest Camp," *Moab Times-Independent*, May 25, 1933; "CCC History on LaSal National Forest," an anonymous mimeographed copy bearing no date or place of publication, sent to me by Forest Supervisor Robert E. Terrill of the Manti–La Sal National Forest in November 1967.
25. "More Men Added to Warner CCC Camp," *Moab Times-Independent*, July 13, 1933; "100 New Men Added to Warner CCC Camp Crew," *Moab Times-Independent*, July 20, 1933.

26. "Winter Work Is Urged for CCC," *Milford News*, September 14, 1933.
27. Utah National Emergency Council, "Report of the Governor's Advisory Committee on Public Welfare and Emergency Relief for January, 1934" (Salt Lake City, 1934), table 2; Jay M. Haymond, "A Survey of the History of the Road Construction Industry in Utah" (master's thesis, Department of History, Brigham Young University, 1967), 2; "$5,000,000 Funds Released by U.S. for Utah Roads," *Deseret News*, June 15, 1933.
28. "Outline of Proposed Summer Camps," *Deseret News*, January 18, 1934.
29. Blood to Rutledge, January 22, 1934, "CCC," Blood Papers.
30. Blood to Senators William King and Elbert D. Thomas and Congressmen J. Will Robinson and Abe Murdock, telegrams, March 5, 1934, "CCC," Blood Papers.
31. Ibid.
32. Ibid.
33. "Appointees Chosen for CCC Camps," *Herald Journal*, April 11, 1934; "220 Seek Jobs Here with the CCC," *Herald Journal*, July 10, 1934.
34. Salmond, *Civilian Conservation Corps*, 55–56.
35. Ibid., 56.
36. "Utah County CCC Quota Is 226 Men," *Springville Herald*, July 5, 1934; Farrell Olsen, Richfield, Utah, correspondence with the author, April 26, 1968.
37. *Report of the Director, 1935*, 61.
38. Ibid., 57; "History of CCC Company Sketched on Eve of Return to Beaver Mountain Camp," *Milford News*, June 27, 1935; "CCC Camps Approved for Fifth Period (1935), State of Utah," Leonard J. Arrington File. ; "CCC to Enroll 1900 New Men on Thursday," *Salt Lake Tribune*, July 8, 1934. The new drought-relief camps were identified with the letters *DR* except for the ones run by the Bureau of Reclamation, which just used the letter *D*, apparently to reduce any possible confusion through having two *R*'s in the camp number.
39. "CCC Corps Assigned to Drouth [*sic*] Aid," *Salt Lake Tribune*, July 26, 1934.
40. "CCC to Enroll 1900 New Men on Thursday"; Stone to Blood, January 23, 1934; Richard Greenland, Richfield, Utah, correspondence with the author, September 20, 1969.
41. "Efforts Are Being Made to Move Two CCC Camps Here," *Richfield Reaper*, August 31, 1933; "Prospects Bright for Getting CCC Boys Located Here," *Richfield Reaper*, September 7, 1933.
42. "Dreams of Forest Officials Realized thru CCC Camp," *Richfield Reaper*, August 31, 1933; "CCC Camp to Be Definitely Stationed Here," *Richfield Reaper*, October 12, 1933.
43. "Rapid Progress Being Made on CCC Barracks," *Richfield Reaper*, October 26, 1933.

44. "CCC Men Due in Logan Thursday," *Herald Journal*, April 25, 1934; Hussey, "Brief History of Company 957, CCC," 4.
45. Olsen, correspondence with the author, April 26, 1968; Nels Bogh, Fillmore, Utah, correspondence with the author, February 17, 1969.
46. "CCC Men Move to Forest Camps for the Summer," *Richfield Reaper*, May 10, 1934.
47. W. Merrill Miller, Bountiful, interview by the author, July 22, 1968. Information came from a printed camp history in Miller's possession.
48. Arnold W. Peterson, Tooele, correspondence with the author, March 30 and April 15, 1968. A note filed with Winsor, "Flood Control in Utah," stated that Company 1338 was at Maple Springs. The *Richfield Reaper*, May 10, 1934, says that "the only Fishlake Forest camp for the summer will be at Maple Spring, near Fillmore." (There is a Maple Grove and a Maple Canyon east of Holden, which is about eleven miles north of Fillmore. My Utah atlas, however, shows neither a Maple Spring nor a Maple Springs.)
49. "Panguitch Lake to Have CCC Camp," *Kane County Standard*, April 6, 1934.
50. "CCC Camp near Panguitch Lake Named Best Unit in the Fort Douglas District," *Salt Lake Tribune*, July 29, 1934.
51. Robert E. Terrill, Supervisor, Manti–La Sal National Forest, correspondence with the author, May 31, 1968; Killpack, correspondence with the author, May 16, 1968; "CCC Boys Build Bridge; Beavers Chew Off Posts," *Salt Lake Tribune*, August 19, 1934.
52. "CCC Company No. 1345 Leaving for Uinta after Year at Moab," *Moab Times-Independent*, May 10, 1934; "Uinta Canyon Headquarters for CCC," *Vernal Express*, March 29, 1934.
53. Alexander, *Rise of Multiple-Use Management in the Intermountain West*, 104.
54. Thomas G. Alexander, *A Clash of Interests: Interior Department and Mountain West, 1863–96* (Provo: Brigham Young University Press, 1977), 182.
55. Ibid., 184.
56. Schlesinger, *Age of Roosevelt*.
57. Ibid.
58. The "Mighty Five" is the name by which Utah's southern national parks are sometimes known: Zion, Bryce Canyon, Capitol Reef, Canyonlands, and Arches. The CCC played a role in the development of all of them.
59. "Parks Work Included in Forest Plan," *Salt Lake Tribune*, April 24, 1933.
60. This Blue Springs camp, NP-1, should not be confused with the Blue Springs camp F-18, although that Forest Service camp was more often identified as either Box Canyon or Escalante.
61. *Parks Post*, January 10, 1936; "CCC Camp Moved from Zion to Blue Springs," *Iron County Record*, June 29, 1933; "All Zion CCC Boys Are Utah Residents," *Iron County Record*, July 20, 1933.

62. "Bryce Gets Zion Park CCC Camp," *Washington County News*, March 22, 1934.
63. "Public Invited to Visit C.C.C. Camps," *Kane County Standard*, July 13, 1934.
64. *Parks Post*, November 7, 1935, and March 20, 1937. Both of these issues were post hoc accounts of the history of Company 962.
65. "FY Annual (Zion's Superintendent) Report, July 1936–June 1937," ZION Box 9, Zion National Park Museum Collection, courtesy of the National Park Service; *Parks Post*, November 7, 1935.
66. *Parks Post*.
67. "FY Annual (Zion's Superintendent) Report, July 1935–June 1936," ZION Box 9, Zion National Park Museum Collection, courtesy of the National Park Service.
68. "FY Annual (Zion's Superintendent) Report, July 1936–June 1937"; *Report of the Director, 1934*, 21–22; *Happy Days*, May 20, 1933; U.S. Civilian Conservation Corps, "Total Work Completed during the Period—April, 1933 to June 30, 1942, Utah"; Cassell, interview by the author, July 28, 1968. About one month after the Indians joined his company at NP-2 in southern Utah, Lieutenant Cassell was transferred to another command, and his former company was moved to Wyoming. Some dispute arose, and the Indians decided to hang their new company commander. He escaped out the rear of his tent and took refuge in a nearby ranger station. The company was disbanded soon after. The incident took place outside Utah, so I did not pursue it further.
69. D. H. Beck, "Bi-annual Report on Emergency Conservation Work, Zion Canyon National Park, October 1, 1934 to March 31, 1935," ZION 18283, Zion National Park Museum Collection, courtesy of the National Park Service; "Narrative Report, NP-2, NP-4, April, 1937," ZION 15455, Zion National Park Museum Collection, courtesy of the National Park Service. Company 4779's newspaper, *Hi Life*, offered quite a detailed company history in its May 29, 1937, issue. In a July 28, 1968, telephone conversation, Cassell told me that he got along well with the Indian enrollees and found them to be good workers.
70. *Parks Post*, January 15, 1937.
71. "FY Annual (Zion's Superintendent) Report, July 1936–June 1937."
72. *Parks Post*, February 20, 1935.
73. "Seven Hundred Men Are Now in Nearby Camps," *Kane County Standard*, July 19, 1935.
74. "FY Annual (Zion's Superintendent) Report, July 1935–June 1936."
75. "Seven Hundred Men Are Now in Nearby Camps"; *Parks Post*, February 20, 1935.
76. *Parks Post*, June 23, 1936.

77. "FY Annual (Zion's Superintendent) Report, July 1935–June 1936"; Hinton, "New Deal Years in Utah," 66, 279; "Zion Canyon CCC Camp News Notes," *Kane County Standard*, April 10, 1936.
78. Hinton, "New Deal Years in Utah," 66; *Weekly Letter*, September 4, 1936. Hinton agrees that Cedar Breaks was a regular camp with its own company in the summer of 1936, although that company was 3238, not 3233 as he states on page 279.
79. G. A. Platt, correspondence with the author, April 28, 1968.
80. Hinton, "New Deal Years in Utah," 66, 279; "Zion Canyon CCC Camp News Notes."
81. G. A. Platt, correspondence with the author, April 28, 1968. Most of the work in that area was done by Works Progress Administration forces. Paul R. Franke, Superintendent, to Darrell J. Greenwell, Work Projects Administration Administrator, Salt Lake City, November 6, 1940, Folder 601-03.1 (ERA), Applications for Camps, Capitol Reef, Box 8759, NPS Records.
82. Hinton, "New Deal Years in Utah," 192.
83. Bradford J. Frye, *From Barrier to Crossroads: An Administrative History of Capitol Reel National Park, Utah*, Cultural Resources Selections, vol. 1 (Denver: Intermountain Region, National Park Service, 1998), 66; Hinton, "New Deal Years in Utah," 193.
84. Frye, *From Barrier to Crossroads*, 66; Hinton, "New Deal Years in Utah," 194.
85. Frye, *From Barrier to Crossroads*, 67. Capitol Reef was upgraded to a national park on December 18, 1971, when President Nixon signed Public Law 92207.
86. Another district was formed in 1939; by 1941 there were eleven. A typed list of grazing districts was found in an index of Grazing Service records, Box 10906, BLM Records.
87. "Tenth Period Report, DG-36," March 31, 1938.
88. "CCC Camps Approved for Fifth Period," 2.
89. Chesley P. Seely, Regional Grazier, Salt Lake City, to Kenneth Wolfe, San Francisco, August 28, 1939; and Seely to Director, CCC, January 14, 1941, I (CCC) Camp—History—Utah, Box 10858, BLM Records.
90. Christine Pfaff, *The Bureau of Reclamation's Civilian Conservation Corps Legacy: 1933–1942* (Denver: Department of the Interior, Bureau of Reclamation, February 2010), 3. Though this report was initially published in June 2000, the bureau republished a somewhat expanded edition ten years later.
91. U.S. National Park Service, *The CCC and Its Contribution to a Nation-wide State Park Recreational Program* (Washington, D.C.: U.S. Government Printing Office, 1937), 4.
92. Sommer, *Hard Work and a Good Deal*, 100.
93. *Report of the Director, 1941*, 63.

94. The work of SP-1, SP-2, and MA-1 is described in chapter 8.
95. Salmond, *Civilian Conservation Corps*, 33; *Report of the Director, 1933*, 2; *Report of the Director, 1934*, 21.
96. *Report of the Director, 1933*, 3; *Report of the Director, 1934*, 20; Salmond, *Civilian Conservation Corps*, 33; "US to Open Indian Camps during Week," *Deseret News*, July 4, 1933; Sommer, *Hard Work and a Good Deal*, 27.
97. In fact, after 1934 the *Reports of the Director* did not even contain information on the number of camps administered by the Bureau of Indian Affairs. Newspaper reports that referred to the number of camps within a state generally excluded those on Indian reservations. As a result, the usual sources of information on the CCC rarely yield much material on Indian camps.
98. *Report of the Director, 1933*, 4, 6.
99. "Half Million Dollars Expended on Reservation CCC Projects in Five Years Has Wiped Out 'Vanishing Indian' Lament, Supervisor Points Out," *Salt Lake Tribune*, March 18, 1939. The North Dakota/Minnesota company at NP-2 mentioned earlier in the chapter was *not* a Bureau of Indian Affairs company.
100. "Camp to Be Located at Ouray for Range Work," *Vernal Express*, May 30, 1935.
101. Kathryn L. MacKay, "The Uncompahgre Reservation and the Hill Creek Extension," *Utah Historical Quarterly* 83, no. 3 (Summer 2015): 180–93.
102. *Report of the Director, 1934*, 21–22; *Happy Days*, May 20, 1933; U.S. Civilian Conservation Corps, "Total Work Completed during the Period—April, 1933 to June 30, 1942, Utah"; *Salt Lake Tribune*, March 18, 1939.
103. *Report of the Director, 1933*, 4, 6; Stewart, "Ashley National Forest"; "Uinta Indian Camp No. 1 Is Real Model," *Roosevelt Standard*, November 16, 1933; "Uinta-Ouray Indian Agency: Fort Duchesne, Utah," *Roosevelt Standard*, December 14, 1933. The November 16 issue of the *Roosevelt Standard* gave a figure of 150 men working on a road to "Johnnie Star Flat"; the December 7 issue used "John Star flat"; and the December 14 issue said that there were approximately one hundred men working on a road to "John Starr Flat." Current maps use the John Starr name. "Half Million Dollars Expended on Reservation CCC Projects in Five Years Has Wiped Out 'Vanishing Indian' Lament, Supervisor Points Out."
104. John Collier, "Indian Family Camps Do Conservation Work," *New York Times*, August 27, 1933.
105. Ibid.
106. James B. Andrews, "IECW on the Uinta-Ouray Reservation," *Vernal Express*, July 23, 1936.
107. "Half Million Dollars Expended on Reservation CCC Projects in Five Years Has Wiped Out 'Vanishing Indian' Lament, Supervisor Points Out."

108. "Contracts Awarded for Eleven Winter Forestation Camps," *Deseret News*, September 29, 1933.
109. Lazelle Stucki, Santa Clara, Utah, correspondence with the author, February 23, 1970.
110. "Indian Works Projects Start at Reservation," *Kane County Standard*, July 19, 1935.
111. Andrews, "IECW on the Uintah-Ouray Reservation."
112. "Half Million Dollars Expended on Reservation CCC Projects in Five Years Has Wiped Out 'Vanishing Indian' Lament, Supervisor Points Out."
113. Rosenman, *Public Papers and Addresses of Franklin D. Roosevelt*, III, 207.
114. *Report of the Director, 1935*, 58.
115. "CCC Camps Approved for Fifth Period," 2. The establishment of camp F-45 in Woods Cross was far enough along in the planning to make the list of approved camps, although, in fact, it never opened. F-46 and F-47 were not even listed; in fact, nothing has been found in Governor Blood's correspondence, Forest Service records, or newspapers to indicate that a camp F-46 ever existed in Utah. Camp F-47 operated at Pinto during the Sixth Period and was approved to operate during the Tenth Period. "Sixth Period Report, DG-30," March 31, 1936; Rutledge to Blood, September 29, 1937.
116. *Report of the Director, 1934*, 2; *Report of the Director, 1936*, 22–23.
117. *Report of the Director, 1936*, 56.
118. "Non-residents in State CCC Outnumber Utahns," *Salt Lake Tribune*, October 5, 1936; "Many CCC Places Open within Utah," *Provo Evening Herald*, July 8, 1937.
119. "Non-residents in State CCC Outnumber Utahns."
120. Salmond, *Civilian Conservation Corps*, 149–53, 156.
121. "Youth in the Shuffle."
122. B. H. Stringham to Senator Elbert D. Thomas, August 23, 1937, "Folder 0207, Civilian Conservation Corps, G-31," Uinta County Regional History Center, Vernal, Utah.
123. "Two Agencies of New Deal Cite Progress," *Salt Lake Tribune*, January 10, 1937.
124. "The Future of the Forest Army," *Herald Journal*, September 15, 1933.
125. Salmond, *Civilian Conservation Corps*, 54.
126. Fechner to Blood, February 6, 1934, "CCC," Blood Papers.
127. "CCC Extended to Serve for Another Year," *Iron County Record*, December 14, 1933.
128. U.S. Civilian Conservation Corps, "A Brief Summary of Certain Phases of the CCC Program in Utah, April, 1933–August 31, 1936," Leonard J. Arrington File; "Intermountain CCC Camp News," *Salt Lake Tribune*, September 2, 1939; U.S. Civilian Conservation Corps, "Location and Strength of Civilian Conservation Corps Projects and Work Companies in the Ninth Corps Area on September 30, 1940."

129. "Backman Asks Retention of Utah CCC," *Salt Lake Tribune*, April 7, 1938.
130. Harold George Muhlestein and Fay Lunceford Muhlestein, *Monticello Journal: A History of Monticello until 1937* (Monticello, Utah: H. G. and F. L. Muhlestein, 1937), 239.
131. Salmond, *Civilian Conservation Corps*, 147–49; Hinton, "New Deal Years in Utah," 93.
132. McEntee, *Now They Are Men*, 53; Sommer, *Hard Work and a Good Deal*, 124.
133. Salmond, *Civilian Conservation Corps*, 171–76; "The Day in Washington," *New York Times*, February 16 and 27, 1940.
134. "Utah Receives Thirty-Four Camps in CCC for October, 1939, to March 31, 1940."
135. *Report of the Director, 1939*, 116.
136. *Report of the Director, 1941*, app. G.
137. Ibid., 4.
138. "U.S. Reviews CCC Merger," *Salt Lake Tribune*, August 20, 1941; "Utah Wages Battle to Retain CCC," *Salt Lake Tribune*, August 22, 1941; "S.L. Studies Site for CCC Offices," *Salt Lake Tribune*, August 25, 1941; "C of C Offers Land Plan to Keep CCC," *Salt Lake Tribune*, August 27, 1941; "Pocatello Becomes Center for District CCC Work," *Salt Lake Tribune*, February 2, 1942.

CHAPTER 5

1. Rosenman, *Public Papers and Addresses of Franklin D. Roosevelt*, II, 68.
2. J. H. Paul, "What Readers Think: What New Forest Policy Means to Utah and West," *Deseret News*, April 27, 1933; R. Beecher, "What Readers Think: R.B. Advocates Vast Public Works Program," *Deseret News*, May 10, 1933. Earl Dunn to Blood, September 16, 1933; David Howells to Blood, August 18, 1933; and A. O. Smoot, Provo, to Blood, April 2, 1933, "CCC," Blood Papers.
3. "Towns Seek Forest Roads," *Salt Lake Tribune*, October 12, 1934.
4. Smoot to Blood, April 2, 1933.
5. "Regional Forester Outlines Aims of Conservation Work."
6. "Sixth Period Report, DG-30," March 31, 1936.
7. Jack A. Garfield, Draper, correspondence with the author, March 29, 1968.
8. Floyd, interview by the author, June 20, 1968.
9. "News from the New Civilian Camp Located at Duck Creek," *Kane County Standard*, June 9, 1933; "Forest Service Takes Over Lake Dike Project," *Iron County Record*, September 21, 1933; "Report Rapid Progress at 961, Camp F-16," *Iron County Record*, June 15, 1933; "Reforestation Corps Assigned Quarters at Pine Valley," *Iron County Record*, June 1, 1933; "All Activities

with Boys of Camp F-16," *Iron County Record*, June 8, 1933; "Projects Galore Handled by CCC Camp Men," *Iron County Record*, August 10, 1933.

10. "Largest Forest Recreation Project in Intermountain West Developing in County," *Richfield Reaper*, May 20, 1937.
11. "FY Annual (Zion's Superintendent) Report, July 1935–June 1936."
12. J. L. Crawford, *Rock Structures of Zion: A Pictorial History* (Springdale, Utah: Zion Natural History Association, 1999), 14–16.
13. Michael S. Sweeney, *Last Unspoiled Place: Exploring Utah's Logan Canyon* (Washington, D.C.: National Geographic, 2008), 62.
14. William C. Davis, Ernest Wright, and Carl Hartley, *Diseases of Forest-Tree Nursery Stock*, Forest Publication No. 9 (Civilian Conservation Corps, February 1942), 47.
15. U.S. Civilian Conservation Corps, "Total Work Completed during the Period—April, 1933 to June 30, 1942, Utah"; "CCC Looks Back on Excellent Record as Sixth Birthday Nears."
16. "Many Trees Are Planted in Forest," *Kane County Standard*, May 10, 1940.
17. McEntee, *Now They Are Men*, 25.
18. Sommer, *Hard Work and a Good Deal*, 87.
19. Ibid., 89; "Planting Reconnaissance Report of the Willard Canyon Watershed," Forest Service Records, Box 230664, "Planting—Cache—General, 1916–1950," National Archives and Record Service, Denver.
20. "Activities of 940," *Davis County Clipper*, May 14, 1937.
21. "Drift Fence on Blue Mt. Being Built by Local CCC," *Vernal Express*, October 19, 1939; "Vernal CCC News," *Vernal Express*, March 28, 1940; "Ashley Forest News," *Vernal Express*, April 2, 1936.
22. *Report of the Director, 1940*; *Report of the Director, 1942*.
23. "Drift Fence on Blue Mt. Being Built by Local CCC."
24. "Reseeding of Grazing Land Progresses," *Richfield Reaper*, October 16, 1941.
25. "Jericho CCC Camp News," *Eureka Reporter*, December 16, 1937; "Jericho Camp May Be Moved," *Eureka Reporter*, April 7, 1938.
26. "Hobble Creek CCC Camp Progressing," *Provo Evening Herald*, July 13, 1933; "Camp Workers Building Road," *Provo Sunday Herald*, September 3, 1933.
27. Glade Sowards, oral history interview, Tape 116, n.d., Uinta County Regional History Center, Vernal, Utah, 1.
28. "Sixth Period Report, DG-28," March 31, 1936; Peterson, correspondence with the author, April 15, 1968.
29. "Sixth Period Report, DG-30," March 31, 1936.
30. "Eighth Period Report, DG-35," March 31, 1937. Both of the roads were still under construction one year later, as was another road from Milford to Black Rock. "Tenth Period Report, DG-35," March 31, 1938.
31. Michael R. Kelsey, *The Story of Black Rock, Utah* (Provo: Kelsey Publishing, 1996), 98.

32. "Restoration of Forest Road Funds Urged by Southern Utah Boosters," *Salt Lake Tribune*, April 9, 1936.
33. "Stock Driveway in Span. F. Canyon to Be Improved," *Provo Sunday Herald*, November 26, 1939.
34. "Stock Trail Construction Ready to Go," *Provo Daily Herald*, January 8, 1941; "Stock Trail Set-Up Signed," *Provo Daily Herald*, February 11, 1941.
35. "Sixth Period Report, DG-30," March 31, 1936.
36. "Ninth Period Report, DG-30" and "Ninth Period Report, DG-45," September 30, 1937.
37. "Eighth Period Report, DG-34," March 31, 1937.
38. "Seventh Period Report, DG-34," September 30, 1936; "Eighth Period Report, DG-34," March 31, 1937; "Ninth Period Report, DG-34," September 30, 1937.
39. "DeMoisy Reviews CCC Camp Projects," *Provo Evening Herald*, March 31, 1938.
40. Ibid. The Rock Canyon camp, by the way, was nowhere near Provo's Rock Canyon, which actually lies about three miles to the north of the CCC campsite. Beginning as state erosion camp PE-220 in 1934, the following year it had been designated F-40. The Utah County fairgrounds, airport, and city golf course—none of which are now located near where they were then—were all identified at one time or other with the location of the campsite, just a short distance west of where MA-1 was later built. This entire area would be found today along the east side of South University Avenue in Provo, just south of the railroad overpass.
41. Ibid.
42. "Ninth Period Report, DG-30," September 30, 1937.
43. "Forest Workers Stop Blaze on Mountain," *Deseret News*, July 19, 1933.
44. "Eighty CCC Men Who Had Been Camped on Mountain Are Back," *Davis County Clipper*, October 30, 1936.
45. Albert C. T. Antrei, ed., *The Other Forty-Niners: A Topical History of Sanpete County, Utah, 1849–1983* (Salt Lake City: Sanpete County Commissioners, Western Epics, 1982), 223.
46. Although very scenic, the road is quite rough and suitable for high-clearance vehicles only. Motorists are warned to avoid the road in wet weather.
47. Christian Nelson, Ferron, Utah, to Blood, March 14, 1934; Blood to Nelson, March 29, 1934; Milton E. Moody, St. George, to Blood, May 23, 1934; Edwin Dalton, Leeds, Utah, to Blood, August 7, 1934; and Blood to Willard Mackelprang, Kanab, Utah, August 20, 1934, "CCC," Blood Papers.
48. Robert Hyslop, "Three Years in Ferron," *Ferron Chatterbox*, October 1938. A structure similar to the Steven's Creek Dip may be seen about forty miles north at Boulger Reservoir off Utah Highway 31 in Huntington Canyon. A photo of that spillway may be seen in Stoddard, "Look Back at the Ccc [*sic*] Camps."

49. Dottie Grimes, "The Civilian Conservation Corps on the Manti Forest," Emery County Archives, Castle Dale, Utah.
50. Peterson, correspondence with the author, April 15, 1968.
51. "Sixth Period Report, DG-45," March 31, 1936; "Tenth Period Report, DG-45," March 31, 1938.
52. "Sixth Period Report, DG-29," March 31, 1936; "Seventh Period Report, DG-29," September 30, 1937.
53. "Eighth Period Report, DG-45," March 31, 1937.
54. Ibid.; "Ninth Period Report, DG-45," September 30, 1937.
55. "Sixth Period Report, DG-30," March 31, 1936.
56. "Eighth Period Report, DG-45," March 31, 1937.
57. "KHS News Flashes," *Kane County Standard*, October 30, 1936; "Dedication Held in Dixie at New Bridge," *Deseret News*, October 24, 1936; D. D. McKay to Blood, November 22, 1937, "CCC," Blood Papers.
58. "National Register of Historic Places Continuation Sheet," U.S. Department of the Interior, National Park Service, San Rafael Bridge, Emery County, Utah (ca. 1996).
59. "New Suspension Bridge on San Rafael River to Be Dedicated March 27," *Emery County Progress*, March 12, 1937.
60. Ibid.
61. "Grazing District Reaps Benefits of Program," *Salt Lake Tribune*, January 4, 1941; "Seventh Period Report, DG-27," September 30, 1937; George L. Moffitt, Orangeville, Utah, correspondence with the author, June 9, 1968; McKay to Blood, November 22, 1937, and Blood to D. D. McKay, November 23, 1937, "CCC," Blood Papers.
62. Most of the information on the San Rafael Bridge is found in "National Register of Historic Places Registration Form, San Rafael Suspension Bridge," Emery County Archives, Castle Dale, Utah; "National Register of Historic Places Continuation Sheet"; Wilson G. Martin to Kent Peterson, June 25, 1996, Folder ECA 2004.005.02 1932, "San Rafael 'Swinging Bridge' Historic Information," Emery County Archives, Castle Dale, Utah; "CCC Spike Camp to Be Established on Bitter Creek," *Emery County Progress*, May 29, 1936; "New Suspension Bridge on San Rafael River to Be Dedicated March 27."
63. Roundy, *Advised Them to Call the Place "Escalante,"* 136, 169, 182.
64. "Two CCC Camps Work on Road to Isolated Boulder," *Richfield Reaper*, September 7, 1933; Senator Elbert D. Thomas to Blood, April 4, 1933, "Elbert D. Thomas File," Blood Papers.
65. Roundy, *Advised Them to Call the Place "Escalante,"* 185.
66. Ibid.; "Pack Mule Starts the Last Year of Service on Boulder Mail Route," *Richfield Reaper*, September 8, 1938.
67. The unusual nickname, so Jerry Roundy reports, was given McInelly for his pedal-to-the-metal speed of driving the dirt roads around Escalante.
68. Roundy, *Advised Them to Call the Place "Escalante,"* 187.

69. Jack Shumate, Supervisor, Dixie National Forest, to David Rees, March 5, 1965, Leonard J. Arrington File. In 1965 Professor Arrington had Rees, a graduate assistant, contact several former forest supervisors and others who had been connected with the CCC. The letters in this file are the responses received. "Pack Mule Starts the Last Year of Service on Boulder Mail Route."
70. "Ruby's Inn Scene of Confab of Associated Civic Group," *Kane County Standard*, July 22, 1938.
71. "Civic Clubs Protest CCC Removal," *Richfield Reaper*, March 2, 1939; "CCC Camp Approved for Escalante," *Richfield Reaper*, September 21, 1939; "Utah Receives Thirty-Four Camps in CCC," *Vernal Express*, September 21, 1939.
72. "CCC Youths Get Roads in Shape," *Ogden Standard-Examiner*, April 11, 1940.
73. Beck, "Bi-annual Report on Emergency Conservation Work, Zion Canyon National Park, October 1, 1934 to March 31, 1935."
74. Hinton, "New Deal Years in Utah," 188.
75. *Parks Post*, May 12, 1937.
76. "FY Annual (Zion's Superintendent) Report, July 1935–June 1936."
77. "Mormon Crickets Making Appearances in This State," *Eureka Reporter*, April 8, 1937; "Juab to Battle Cricket Invasion," *Eureka Reporter*, April 15, 1937; Alison T. Otis, William D. Honey, Thomas C. Hogg, and Kimberly K. Lakin, *The Forest Service and the Civilian Conservation Corps, 1933–42* (Washington, D.C.: U.S. Department of Agriculture, 1986), 36.
78. "Vernal CCC News," *Vernal Express*, June 18, 1936; F. J. Kennard, "Range Improvement by CCC Camp Big Benefit to Basin Stockmen," *Roosevelt Standard*, August 6, 1936; Uintah County Regional History Center Staff, *Images of America: Ashley Valley* (Charleston, S.C.: Arcadia Publishing, 2011), 80.
79. "Seventh Period Report, DG-28," September 30, 1936.
80. "Seventh Period Report, DG-29," September 30, 1936. Other back-pumps, by the way, were operated with a push-pull motion of a pipe with a nozzle attached to the end of a three- to four-foot hose.
81. R. Scott Zimmerman, "Rodent Control: A Seasonal Project," *Utah Farmer*, April 10, 1934, p. 1.
82. "Seventh Period Report, DG-34," September 30, 1936.
83. Ibid.; "Ninth Period Report, DG-27," September 30, 1937.
84. "CCC to Wage Rodents War in West Areas," *Salt Lake Tribune*, April 9, 1936.
85. "Marion Oveson in Charge of CCC Rodent Control," *Emery County Progress*, May 29, 1936; "CCC and Farmers to Kill Rodents in Uinta Basin," *Vernal Express*, May 21, 1936; "Vernal CCC News," *Vernal Express*, June 4, 1936; "Crews Complete Rodent Control on Diamond Mt.," *Vernal Express*, August 20, 1936. The campaign against prairie dogs and rock

chucks continued for at least the following two summers. "Rodent Control Project on Diamond Mountain Completed by CCC Crew," *Vernal Express*, September 16, 1937; "Vernal CCC News," *Vernal Express*, July 14, 1938.

86. "Seventh Period Report, DG-35," September 30, 1936.
87. "Seventh Period Report, DG-34," September 30, 1936.
88. "Ninth Period Report, DG-30," September 30, 1937. Unfortunately, the report didn't indicate the success of the project.
89. Heywood, interview by the author, March 29, 1968. Heywood, with the Soil Conservation Service in 1968, was rodent control foreman at DG-34 from the autumn of 1938 until March 1939.
90. "Seventh Period Report, DG-27," September 30, 1936.
91. "Jericho CCC Camp News," *Eureka Reporter*, June 3, 1937.
92. Lori L. Nawyn, "CCC Camp Brought Jobs, Hope and Young Men to Brigham," three-page typescript in *CCC Camp by Lori L. Nawyn*, Box 3, Brigham City History, Brigham City Library, Brigham City.
93. "Seventh Period Report, DG-30," September 30, 1936; "Jericho CCC Camp News," *Eureka Reporter*, June 16, 1938; "Sixth Period Report, DG-28," March 31, 1936; Max J. Schegel, "News from CCC Camp: Outlines Work in Blacksmith Fork," *Herald Journal*, August 17, 1933; "Seventh Period Report, DG-34," September 30, 1936.
94. The Bureau of Reclamation projects of large dams for irrigation and culinary use are discussed in chapter 7.
95. *Reports of the Director, 1933–1942*; Utah National Emergency Council, "Photographic Reports of Representative Work Projects Being Done by Division of Grazing CCC Camps in Utah to November 1, 1937", "National Emergency Council, Civilian Conservation Corps," Box F-1, Utah State Archives, Salt Lake City.
96. "Ninth Period Report, DG-35," September 30, 1937; "Tenth Period Report, DG-35," March 31, 1938.
97. "Tenth Period Report, DG-35," March 31, 1938.
98. "Sixth Period Report, DG-27," March 31, 1936.
99. Both the Seventh and Ninth Period reports of Dalton Wells camp, DG-32, spoke of "new types" of dams. The prototype listed in the former report was identified as the Hook and Ladder Reservoir. A dam called Art's Pasture Tank was the "new type" referred to in the "Ninth Period Report." Also see "Tenth Period Report, DG-35," March 31, 1938.
100. "Ninth Period Report, DG-27," September 30, 1937; "Tenth Period Report, DG-27," March 31, 1938.
101. "Seventh Period Report, DG-30," September 30, 1936.
102. "Ninth Period Report, DG-27," September 30, 1937; "Ninth Period Report, DG-28," September 30, 1937; "Seventh Period Report, DG-32," September 30, 1936; "Sixth Period Report, DG-32," March 31, 1936.
103. "Eighth Period Report, DG-32," March 31, 1937; "Sixth Period Report, DG-29," March 31, 1936.

104. "Ninth Period Report, DG-26," September 30, 1937; "CCC Camp News," *Eureka Reporter*, June 3, 1937; "Jericho CCC Camp News," *Eureka Reporter*, August 12 and December 13, 1937; "CCC Looks Back on Excellent Record as Sixth Birthday Nears."
105. "Ninth Period Report, DG-28," September 30, 1937.
106. "Vernal CCC Crews Work on 9 Projects," *Vernal Express*, March 3, 1938; "35 Corrals Built on Public Domain by Vernal Camp," *Vernal Express*, March 30, 1939.
107. "Ninth Period Report, DG-30," September 30, 1937.
108. "Ninth Period Report, DG-45," September 30, 1937.
109. "Cattle Corral Construction Progresses," *Richfield Reaper*, February 27, 1941.
110. "CCC Builds Fish Dams in Uintah Canyon," *Vernal Express*, August 30, 1934.
111. "CCC News," *Pleasant Grove Review*, August 20, August 27, and October 1, 1937.
112. "Duck Creek Lake and Spring Open for Fishing Sunday," *Kane County Standard*, August 7, 1941.
113. "Eighth Period Report, DG-27," March 31, 1937.
114. "Feeding and Habits of Deer Studied," *Richfield Reaper*, May 2, 1940; "CCC Camp Observes Anniversary," *Richfield Reaper*, April 17, 1941; Albert Albertson, Cedar City, Utah, to David Rees, April 26, 1965, Leonard J. Arrington File. The irony of feeding the wildlife in the winter so that they could be shot the following season was, in my research, never addressed.
115. Hinton, "New Deal Years in Utah," 182.

CHAPTER 6

1. E. A. Sherman, "Saving Our Soil," *Nation* 136 (April 12, 1933): 401–3.
2. Salmond, *Civilian Conservation Corps*, 4.
3. *Frontier*, March 1940.
4. "Utahns Carry Job Plan to Capital," *Deseret News*, April 10, 1933.
5. Ibid.
6. Blood to Forsling and others, May 27, 1933, and Blood to R. H. Rutledge, June 6, 1933, "CCC," Blood Papers; "State Names Committee to Select Camps"; "Deer Creek Forest Projects to Aid Unemployment," *Provo Evening Herald*, May 31, 1933.
7. "State Names Committee to Select Camps"; "Utah Forestation Camps Slashed by 30 Per Cent," *Deseret News*, June 1, 1933.
8. "Forest Men Visit Camps." As mentioned previously, unless specially noted, the two Indian camps located in Utah are not included in camp tabulations.

9. *Wikipedia* provided the dates of incorporation and identified the cannery as operating between 1912 and 1980 at 200 South Depot Street. Located between 1200 and 1300 West in Woods Cross, the streets of the subdivision bear names such as Presidential, Governor, Mayor, Senator, and Councilman.
10. "New Work Camp Improves Canyon; Dock's Flat, near Mantua, Takes Appearance of a Tented City," *Deseret News*, June 23, 1933. The site was referred to as both Dock's Flat and Dock Flat. The latter name is that used on road signs today and the one I shall use hereafter, except where Dock's Flat is used in quotations.
11. U.S. Emergency Conservation Work, "Summary of Work, Utah State Camps," September 30, 1933, in my possession.
12. This conundrum brings to mind the philosophical riddle of which is best: to build guardrails at the top of the cliff or provide an ambulance down in the valley.
13. Alexander, *Rise of Multiple-Use Management in the Intermountain West*, 165.
14. Thomas G. Alexander, *Utah. The Right Place* (Salt Lake City: Utah State Historical Society, 1996), 322–23.
15. Ibid., 323.
16. "Work Starting on CCC Camp," *Provo Evening Herald*, April 27, 1934; R. H. Rutledge, "Review of State Camps which Have Been Established in Utah and the Work Done by Each by Six-Month Periods," October 20, 1934, "CCC," Blood Papers; "Work of Forest Camp Is Told at Kiwanis Meeting," *Provo Evening Herald*, August 5, 1933.
17. "Reforestation Plans Call for New Roads," *Deseret News*, June 3, 1933. The terracing at Little Rock and nearby Rock and Slate canyons is still visible today.
18. Salmond, *Civilian Conservation Corps*, 125.
19. Most of the material in the following paragraphs comes from a pamphlet Reed W. Bailey wrote with A. R. Croft, *Contour-Trenches Control Floods and Erosion on Range Lands* (Washington, D.C.: U.S. Government Printing Office, May 1937).
20. Ibid. W. M. Miller, interview by the author, July 22, 1968.
21. Bailey, *Contour-Trenches Control Floods and Erosion on Range Lands*. Davis Mountain was reterraced in 1964.
22. "Meeting Held at CC Camp," *Provo Evening Herald*, August 1, 1933; "CCC Camp States Public Program," *Richfield Reaper*, April 4, 1940; "CCC Looks Back on Excellent Record as Sixth Birthday Nears"; Earl F. Partridge, Orem, correspondence with the author, April 10, 1968; Moffitt, correspondence with the author, June 9, 1968.
23. "Ninth Period Report, DG-33," September 30, 1937.
24. Don Penrod, "Don Penrod Married Rosemary Smith," May 25, 1994, photocopy in my possession, given to me by LoAnne Barnes, CCC

historian in Leeds, Utah, in March 2011. Penrod, then of Grand Junction, Colorado, had been asked to write down some of his memories of his year in the CCC at F-9 in the summer of 1933 and PE-216 in the period following. The eighth of twelve children, he lied about his age and at sixteen joined the CCC to help support his widowed mother with seven children still at home.

25. Olsen, *Pleasant Grove Sesquicentennial History*, 118–19.
26. "Leeds CCC Camp Helps Kanarraville Build Dam," *Washington County News*, July 22, 1937.
27. Ernest Winkler to Robert Hinckley, October 28, 1933, "CCC," Blood Papers; "Contracts Awarded for Eleven Winter Forestation Camps."
28. Jack J. Baird, Draper, correspondence with the author, March 31, 1968; "Timpanogos Cave Now Open," *American Fork Citizen*, April 6, 1934; Winsor, "Flood Control in Utah," 2.
29. M. J. Baird, correspondence with the author, March 31, 1968; "Davis CCC Flood Control Work Ends," *Davis County Clipper*, November 15, 1935.
30. "Sec. Wallace Goes by 'Sky Line' to 'Spike Camp,'" *Davis County Clipper*, September 4, 1936; "Flood Control Work in Hills Brings Visitors," *Davis County Clipper*, September 25, 1936; "Dern Memorial Committee Maps Inspection Trip," *Salt Lake Tribune*, July 1, 1941.
31. "Zion's Park Camp F-1 Progressing and Producing," *Washington County News*, August 10, 1933.
32. "Inspect Dam Site on Clara Creek," *Washington County News*, November 16, 1933; Hinton, "New Deal Years in Utah," 146.
33. Penrod, "Don Penrod Married Rosemary Smith."
34. "Camp PE-216 to Hold Dedication," *Washington County News*, November 16, 1933; "CCC Camp PE-216 Deserves Praise," *Washington County News*, April 26, 1934.
35. "Dedication for CCC Camp PE-217," *Washington County News*, November 23, 1933. Some confusion is caused by the fact that "Roster of Company [957]," sent to me by former enrollee William Udink, identifies "Hurricane Camp PE-217, La Verkin, Utah." The camp was located near the border between the two communities and is not to be confused with Hurricane camp DG-160, the site of which was located in downtown Hurricane and which operated from 1939 to 1941.
36. "C.C.C. Chatter," *Kane County Standard*, December 1, 1933.
37. Photograph of camp in possession of Elliott R. Killpack, San Pedro, Calif.; Rutledge, "Review of State Camps"; "C.C.C. Chatter," *Kane County Standard*, January 8 and March 30, 1934.
38. Much of the information for PE-214 was found in "CCC History on La Sal National Forest," sent to me by Manti–La Sal National Forest Supervisor Robert B. Terrill, November 13, 1967. Unfortunately the document had no date or author listed. See also "13 Buildings for Winter CCC Camp," *Moab*

Times-Independent, September 28, 1933; "100 New CCC Men to Arrive Friday," *Moab Times-Independent*, October 19, 1933.

39. Bogh, correspondence with the author, February 17, 1969.
40. "CCC Workers Complete Two Dams to Control Floods in Salina Canyon," *Salt Lake Tribune*, April 29, 1934; Rutledge, "Review of State Camps"; Winsor to Winburn; Winsor, "Flood Control in Utah," 2.
41. "Sixth Period Report, DG-30," March 31, 1936.
42. "Sixth Period Report, DG-35," March 31, 1936.
43. McKay to Blood, November 22, 1937. A copy of the complete report may be found in Box F-1, 01.12, Utah State Archives, Salt Lake City.
44. Maher, *Nature's New Deal*, 61–63; Sommer, *Hard Work and a Good Deal*, 77–78; Schlesinger, *Age of Roosevelt*, 341–43.
45. *Supplementary Report of the Land Planning Committee to the National Resources Board*, pt. 5, *Soil Erosion: A Critical Problem in American Agriculture*, 105, cited in Maher, *Nature's New Deal*, 60.
46. Salmond, *Civilian Conservation Corps*, 83–84.
47. For an interesting account of the 1930s squabble between Harold Ickes and Secretary of Agriculture Henry Wallace over who should control conservation in general and the Forest Service in particular, see Schlesinger, *Age of Roosevelt*, 341–49. After 1933, control of the CCC became another factor in the ongoing dispute, in which, of course, Fechner became heavily involved. See Salmond, *Civilian Conservation Corps*, 83–84.
48. Maher, *Nature's New Deal*, 62.
49. I have found no evidence of an SCS-1; it may have never gotten off the drawing board.
50. "Conservation Service Changes Utah Setup," *Cache American*, September 13, 1938.
51. Salmond, *Civilian Conservation Corps*, 124, citing *Report of the Director, 1936*, 31.
52. "Former Kanab Store Manager Appointed Camp Supt," *Kane County Standard*, August 2, 1935.
53. "Gunlock CCC Camp Being Dismantled by Leeds Camp," *Washington County News*, December 22, 1938.
54. John J. Wise, Ogden, interview by the author, August 28, 1969; "The History of Willard Camp," *Box Elder County Daily Journal*, May 3, 1935. J. Whitney Floyd stated in an interview, June 20, 1968, that he thought the camp had some machinery, although hand labor was used on most of the work.
55. Arthur G. Nord, "Historical Information Concerning 'The Willard Watershed Rehabilitation Program,'" mimeograph copy in my possession.
56. Verner W. Sparks, Ogden, correspondence with the author, June 14, 1968; Verner W. Sparks, Ogden, interview by the author, August 26, 1969;

Nord, "Historical Information Concerning 'The Willard Watershed Rehabilitation Program,'" 2.

57. John J. Wise, "Historical Information Relative to the Willard Basin Watershed Rehabilitation Project," mimeograph copy in my possession. Wise, still working for the Forest Service in 1969, was project supervisor on the Willard Basin Project. Most of the material on this project comes from the accounts written by him and Supervisor Arthur G. Nord, who took over Cache National Forest in September 1936.
58. Ibid., 2–3.
59. Wise, interview by the author, August 28, 1969.
60. Wise, "Historical Information Relative to the Willard Basin Watershed Rehabilitation Project," 3.
61. Nord, "Historical Information Concerning 'The Willard Watershed Rehabilitation Program,'" 2.
62. Frederick M. Huchel, *A History of Box Elder County*, Utah Centennial County History Series (Salt Lake City: Utah State Historical Society/Box Elder County Commission, 1999), 240.
63. Richard A. Firmage, *A History of Grand County*, Utah Centennial County History Series (Salt Lake City: Utah State Historical Society/Grand County Commission, 1996), 283.
64. Ibid., 281.
65. "Leeds CCC News," *Washington County News*, January 13, 1938, and September 14 and October 19, 1939.
66. "Leeds CCC News," *Washington County News*, August 12, 1937.
67. "Leeds CCC News," *Washington County News*, February 10 and September 4, 1938.
68. "Leeds CCC News," *Washington County News*, August 13, 1939, and September 4, 1941. Other similar structures had been built at the West Desert camp of Modena as well as one in Escalante camp F-44—a rarity indeed.
69. Robert S. McPherson, *A History of San Juan County*, Utah Centennial County History Series (Salt Lake City: Utah State Historical Society/San Juan County Commission, 1995), 188.
70. Huchel, *History of Box Elder County*, 252; "CCC Boys to Start Conservation Work," *Bear River Valley Leader*, November 2, 1939, cited in Newman, "Tremonton Was Once Home to WW II POWs."
71. Roland E. Platt, Salt Lake City, correspondence with the author, July 6, 1968.
72. "CCC Looks Back on Excellent Record as Sixth Birthday Nears."
73. Mark Milligan, "What Are Those Lines on the Mountain? From Bread Lines to Erosion-Control Lines," Utah Geological Survey, January 2010, https://geology.utah.gov/map-pub/survey-notes/glad-you-asked/erosion-control-lines-on-the-mountains/, accessed January 21, 2015.

74. Stace Hall, "Residents Reflect on Changes since Devastating 2005 Flood," *Deseret News*, January 18, 2015.
75. Schlesinger, *Age of Roosevelt*, 345.
76. "Flood Control District Made by Commission," *Provo Evening Herald*, September 12, 1933.
77. Huchel, *History of Box Elder County*, 238–40.
78. Michael S. Eldredge, "All Hail to the President! Theodore Roosevelt Comes to Utah, May 29, 1903," *Utah Historical Quarterly* 82, no. 1 (Winter 2014): 34–35.
79. Alexander, *Utah*, 322.
80. "Speaker Praises CC Flood Work," *Deseret News*, October 6, 1933; "CCC Work Given Praise," *Provo Evening Herald*, October 6, 1933.
81. Sweeney, *Last Unspoiled Place*, 49, 52.
82. "Utah and Federal Lands," *Deseret News*, March 19, 2016.
83. "Forest Service to Evaluate Sheep in High Uintas," *Deseret News*, March 20, 2016.
84. "Salazar Says Bundys 'Out of Touch,'" *Deseret News*, January 12, 2016.

CHAPTER 7

1. L. R. Dunkley, "CCC Builds Reservoir and Canals, Moon Lake Project," *CCC Reflections*, April 3, 1937.
2. Pfaff, *Bureau of Reclamation's Civilian Conservation Corps Legacy*, 5–7, 20.
3. The drought-relief program is described in chapter 4.
4. Ibid., ii.
5. Ibid., E-1–E-7.
6. Ibid., 49.
7. Arrington, "Utah's Great Drought of 1934," 261.
8. Pfaff, *Bureau of Reclamation's Civilian Conservation Corps Legacy*, 28–29.
9. Eldredge, "All Hail to the President!" 41.
10. Arrington, "Utah's Great Drought of 1934," 252.
11. Ibid., 259.
12. Quinn, "Out of the Depression Depths," 237; "2 Utah Reclamation Projects Approved; $3,900,000 Allocated for Work Here," *Provo Evening Herald*, August 30, 1933; "CCC to Start Canal Work," *Salt Lake Tribune*, August 10, 1933; Alexander, *Utah*, 319–20.
13. Alexander, *Utah*, 319.
14. *Canal Construction Chronicle*, April 6, 1936.
15. "Payson Program at CCC Camp," *Provo Evening Herald*, September 26, 1933.
16. "CCC to Start Canal Work"; Pfaff, *Bureau of Reclamation's Civilian Conservation Corps Legacy*, A-30. Eric A. Stene, "Strawberry Valley Project," Bureau of Reclamation, 1995, 6, 16, https://www.usbr.gov/projects/

pdf.php?id=197, provides quite a detailed look at the entire multipurpose project carried out in the Strawberry Valley since its inception.

17. Pfaff, *Bureau of Reclamation's Civilian Conservation Corps Legacy*, A-29, A-31; Stene, "Strawberry Valley Project," 6.
18. Pfaff, *Bureau of Reclamation's Civilian Conservation Corps Legacy*, A-31.
19. U.S. Department of the Interior, Bureau of Reclamation, "Moon Lake Project," in *Reclamation Project Data* (Washington, D.C.: U.S. Government Printing Office, 1961), 528–29.
20. Ibid.
21. E. O. Larson, "Facts Concerning Moon Lake Reservoir Project," *Vernal Express*, August 1, 1935; U.S. Department of the Interior, Bureau of Reclamation, *History, Moon Lake Project, Utah*, I (1936), 7–8, Bureau Library, Salt Lake City. Six volumes of the *History* cover the project from 1936 until 1941 and are to be found in the library of the Bureau of Reclamation office at the Federal Building in Salt Lake City.
22. U.S. Department of the Interior, Bureau of Reclamation, "Abstract from Project History of Moon Lake Project," 1953, 2, Bureau Library, Salt Lake City, sent to me by W. L. Rusho, Public Information Officer of the Bureau of Reclamation, Region Four, Salt Lake City, November 9, 1967; U.S. Department of the Interior, Bureau of Reclamation, *History, Moon Lake Project, Utah*, II (1937), 8, 16.
23. "Midview Dam Dedicated at Bridgeland," *Vernal Express*, September 16, 1937; "Huge Lake, Dam Dedicated to Enrollee by CCC," *Salt Lake Tribune*, September 12, 1937; Glen A. Ingalsbe, Orem, interview by the author, April 11, 1968. Although Forest Service and Bureau of Land Management maps designate the reservoir today as Lake Bauram, all Bureau of Reclamation maps and printed information refer to it as the Midview Reservoir. One BR official said that he had never heard it called anything else, although E. O. Larson, engineer in charge of all the BR projects in Utah, remembered Lake Bauram as "the CCC name" for Midview Reservoir. E. O. Larson, Salt Lake City, interview by the author, July 22, 1968.
24. U.S. Department of the Interior, Bureau of Reclamation, "Abstract from Project History of Moon Lake Project," 6; U.S. Department of the Interior, Bureau of Reclamation, *History, Moon Lake Project, Utah*, II, 16.
25. T. H. Humpherys, Secretary, Utah Water Storage Commission, to Blood, October 14, 1935, "CCC," Blood Papers.
26. U.S. Department of the Interior, Bureau of Reclamation, "Abstract from Project History of Moon Lake Project," 8–9. It was eventually necessary to clay-line the entire section of the canal. This was done in the summer of 1941.
27. Salmond, *Civilian Conservation Corps*, 170.
28. J. W. Robinson to Blood, January 15, 1938, "CCC," Blood Papers.

29. U.S. Department of the Interior, Bureau of Reclamation, *History, Moon Lake Project, Utah*, IV (1939), 13, v, 8; *Bridgeland News Weekly*, April 28, 1939.
30. U.S. Department of the Interior, Bureau of Reclamation, *History, Moon Lake Project, Utah*, IV, 13, v, 8; *Bridgeland Bulletin*, August 10 and September 14, 1939.
31. *Bridgeland News Weekly*, September 14, 1939; U.S. Department of the Interior, Bureau of Reclamation, *History, Moon Lake Project, Utah*, V (1940), 8, 24.
32. U.S. Department of the Interior, Bureau of Reclamation, *History, Moon Lake Project, Utah*, VI (1941), 28, 529.
33. The story of the project is told in Leonard J. Arrington and Lowell Dittmer, "Reclamation in Three Layers: The Ogden River Project, 1934–1965," *Pacific Historical Review* 35 (February 1966): 15–34.
34. Pfaff, *Bureau of Reclamation's Civilian Conservation Corps Legacy*, A-67, A-75.
35. "Protest Aimed at CCC Camp," *Salt Lake Tribune*, September 19, 1934; "City Requests Change in Site of CCC Camp," *Salt Lake Tribune*, September 21, 1934.
36. William R. Wallace, Washington, D.C., to Blood, September 22, 1934, and Blood to Wallace, September 24, 1934, "CCC," Blood Papers. Fechner would have been especially concerned had he been alive to see a comment by a Ph.D. candidate on the subject: "The CCC not only maintained an open shop, it also prohibited strikes, hired scab labor, and refused employment to workers who went out on strike" (Rawick, "New Deal and Youth," 103).
37. U.S. Department of the Interior, Bureau of Reclamation, *Final Report on Design and Construction of Pineview Dam and Reservoir, Ogden, River Project, Utah* (Denver: Bureau of Reclamation, 1941), 38. T. H. Humpherys, Secretary, Utah Water Storage Commission, to Blood, Senator William King, and Congressman Abe Murdock, October 14, 1935; Robert Fechner to Ora Bundy, October 16, 1935; and Elwood Mead, Director, Bureau of Reclamation, to Blood, October 17, 1935, "CCC," Blood Papers.
38. Blood to Fechner, October 15, 1935, and Senator Elbert D. Thomas to Blood, October 16, 1935, "CCC," Blood Papers.
39. Blood to Fechner, October 23, 1935, "CCC," Blood Papers.
40. McEntee to Senator William King, April 1, 1936, "CCC," Blood Papers. For complete correspondence on this issue, see the 1935 and 1936 boxes.
41. Pfaff, *Bureau of Reclamation's Civilian Conservation Corps Legacy*, A-75; La Verna Burnett Newey, *Remember My Valley: A History of Ogden Canyon, Eden, Liberty, and Huntsville* (Salt Lake City: Hawkes Publishing Company, 1977), 345.

42. Richard C. Roberts and Richard W. Sadler, *Ogden, Junction City*, with the Ogden Area Chamber of Commerce (Northridge: Windsor Publications, 1985), 126; Newey, *Remember My Valley*, 339–40.
43. U.S. Department of the Interior, Bureau of Reclamation, "Ogden River Project," in *Reclamation Project Data* (Washington, D.C.: U.S. Government Printing Office, 1961), 562; Larson, interview by the author, July 22, 1968.
44. Pfaff, *Bureau of Reclamation's Civilian Conservation Corps Legacy*, A-273–74.
45. U.S. Department of the Interior, Bureau of Reclamation, *History, Ogden River Project, Utah*, VI (1938), 23, Bureau Library, Salt Lake City. Volumes IV through IX of the *History* cover the project from 1936 to 1941 and are to be found in the library of the Bureau of Reclamation office at the Federal Building in Salt Lake City. Also see U.S. Department of the Interior, Bureau of Reclamation, "Ogden River Project," 560.
46. U.S. Department of the Interior, Bureau of Reclamation, *History, Ogden River Project, Utah*, IX, 37. The facilities were subsequently enlarged under the Weber Basin project development from 1955 to 1957. Nearly 163,000 people were served with project water the following year. U.S. Department of the Interior, Bureau of Reclamation, "Ogden River Project," 562.
47. Pfaff, *Bureau of Reclamation's Civilian Conservation Corps Legacy*, A-76; Newey, *Remember My Valley*, 275.
48. This "pairing," of course, is quite different from the rotation of companies between summer and winter camps described in chapter 3.
49. U.S. Department of the Interior, Bureau of Reclamation, *History, Provo River Project, Utah, Deer Creek Division*, VII (1943), 25, Bureau Library, Salt Lake City. Volumes I through VII of the *History* cover the project from 1937 to 1943 and are to be found in the library of the Bureau of Reclamation office at the Federal Building in Salt Lake City. U.S. Department of the Interior, Bureau of Reclamation, "Provo River Project," in *Reclamation Project Data* (Washington, D.C.: U.S. Government Printing Office, 1961), 614.
50. Kathleen Denbow Pace (daughter), Heber City, Utah, conversation with the author, March 30, 2016.
51. U.S. Department of the Interior, Bureau of Reclamation, *History, Provo River Project, Utah*, II (1938), 71; III (1939), 87–88.
52. Ibid., IV (1940), 106; U.S. Department of the Interior, Bureau of Reclamation, "Provo River Project," 614–15.
53. U.S. Department of the Interior, Bureau of Reclamation, *History, Provo River Project, Utah*, III, 88, 90; IV, 106; V (1941), 70.
54. William James Mortimer, comp. and ed., *How Beautiful upon the Mountains: A Centennial History of Wasatch County* (Salt Lake City: Wasatch County Chapter, Daughters of Utah Pioneers, 1963), 1001.

55. "Many Apply for Work on Deer Creek," *Provo Evening Herald*, March 25, 1938; Jesse L. Embrey, *A History of Wasatch County*, Utah Centennial County History Series (Salt Lake City: Utah State Historical Society/ Wasatch County Commission, 1996), 178–79; Mortimer, *How Beautiful upon the Mountains*, 994, 1019. I am indebted to Steve Cain, facilities and land manager of the Provo River Water Users' Association, and Gerri Bradford of the Pleasant Grove office for helping me somewhat understand the intricacies of the water distribution mechanisms in Utah and Salt Lake counties.
56. Embrey, *History of Wasatch County*, 173. McGuire did acknowledge, however, that there were positive benefits from the infusion of "a lot of good new blood in the valley" from the outsiders who married local girls and added to the community.
57. Pfaff, *Bureau of Reclamation's Civilian Conservation Corps Legacy*, A-273–74. The spike camp lasted until BR-64 closed down in July 1942.
58. U.S. Department of the Interior, Bureau of Reclamation, *History, Provo River Project, Utah*, VII (1943), 25. The Salt Lake Aqueduct and the Deer Creek Powerhouse, now integral parts of the Deer Creek Project, were not constructed until the 1950s. U.S. Department of the Interior, Bureau of Reclamation, "Provo River Project," 165.
59. Pfaff, *Bureau of Reclamation's Civilian Conservation Corps Legacy*, A-385–86.
60. Ibid., A-274.
61. U.S. Department of the Interior, Bureau of Reclamation, *History, Hyrum Project, Utah* (1934), 38–39, Bureau Library, Salt Lake City.
62. *Report of the Director, 1940*, 42.
63. Cost figures usually include construction costs for private contracts, regular government workers, and CCC personnel all added in together. In 1952, however, Bureau of Reclamation accountants reported that a review—conducted in February 1942—of the final cost reports and related information concerning the Moon Lake Project revealed "a total CCC construction cost of $279,843.92 not included in Bureau of Reclamation costs." The construction cost to the bureau of projects on which the CCC did virtually all the labor amounted to $287,400; in 1952 the estimated cost of such projects amounted to $1,165,000. U.S. Department of the Interior, Bureau of Reclamation, "Abstract from Project History of Moon Lake Project."
64. Arrington and Dittmer, "Reclamation in Three Layers," 22.
65. Larson, interview by the author, July 22, 1968.

CHAPTER 8

1. "Welcome Given CCC Officials," *Milford News*, June 1, 1933; "Foremen Named for Camp Work," *Milford News*, June 8, 1933; "Forests Plant Grass to Halt Range Drouth [*sic*]," *Deseret News*, June 3, 1933.
2. "Camp Cahill Notes," *Milford News*, October 26, 1933.
3. Kelsey, *Story of Black Rock, Utah*, 97.
4. "CCC Camp Moves to Desert Range," *Milford News*, October 26, 1933.
5. "Veterans Forest Quota Received"; "CCC to Start Canal Work," *Salt Lake Tribune*, August 10, 1933; "Camp Cahill Boys Hold Election," *Milford News*, August 10, 1933; "CCC Camp Moves to Desert Camp," *Milford News*, October 25, 1934.
6. "Foremen Named for Camp Work."
7. S. R. DeBoer, *First Report on State Policies* (Salt Lake City: Utah State Planning Board, 1935), 31.
8. "Additional Men for Two Camps," *Milford News*, June 15, 1933; "Camp Cahill Notes," *Milford News*, September 28, 1933.
9. "All but Seven Men Leave Camp," *Milford News*, October 19, 1933.
10. "CCC Camp Moves to Desert Camp."
11. "Well Being Drilled for Milford CC Camp," *Milford News*, June 20, 1935.
12. E. Durant McArthur, Bryce A. Richardson, and Stanley G. Kitchen, *Great Basin Experimental Range: Annotated Bibliography*, Gen. Tech. Rep. GTR-305 (Fort Collins: U.S. Department of Agriculture, Forest Service, Rocky Mountain Research Station, 2013). Much of the information I have used comes from this compilation.
13. Antrei, *Other Forty-Niners*, 217.
14. "Nursery Is Planned at Utah Lake," *Provo Daily Herald*, April 25, 1940; *Report of the Director, 1941*, 63.
15. "Nursery Is Planned at Utah Lake."
16. "CCC Camp Favored for Harbor Project," *Provo Evening Herald*, February 1, 1939; "Official Urges System of State Parks," *Salt Lake Tribune*, March 8, 1939. Some confusion exists, as the April 25, 1940, *Provo Daily Herald* states that the project was to be turned over to the national government on completion. Ownership between the federal government and Provo City was debated for some time, however, before it was eventually handed over to the *state*; it is now Utah Lake State Park.
17. "Lake Harbor Project Is Considered," *Provo Evening Herald*, February 12, 1937; "Utah Lake Project to Be Recreational Attraction of Utah," *Provo Evening Herald*, March 17, 1939.
18. David H. Mattson and Irving W. Trimbel, Utah Department of Fish and Game, to Blood, March 22, 1939; and Blood to Arno Cammerer, Director of the National Park Service, Washington, D.C., May 3, 1939, "Provo Bay Recreation Harbor Project," P-R Box, Blood Papers.

19. Mattson and Trimbel to Blood, March 22, 1939; Blood to Cammerer, May 3, 1939.
20. "New CCC Camp to Be Located at Airport," *Provo Daily Herald*, August 10, 1939. The Provo airport was then located just south of the present overpass on the east side of South University Avenue.
21. "City Notified of Requirements in Harbor Project," *Provo Sunday Herald*, August 20, 1939; "Provo Officials Return from Trip to San Francisco," *Provo Sunday Herald*, December 10, 1939; Conrad L. Wirth to Blood, May 15, 1939, P-R Box, Blood Papers.
22. *Yell-A-Gram*, October 27, 1939; "Lake Harbor Camp Heads Appointed," *Provo Daily Herald*, October 30, 1939.
23. "183 Boys at CCC Camp to Begin Work," *Provo Daily Herald*, November 16, 1939; *Yell-A-Gram*, November 15, 1939; *Illini-Ute*, November 14, 1939.
24. *Yell-A-Gram*, November 2, 1939. Fonnesbeck's title, by the way, identified him as the actual senior technical service foreman and not the senior enrollee, as had been previously used in Company 958.
25. "Progress Made on New CCC Camp," *Provo Daily Herald*, October 17, 1939; "Elks Donate New Flag to CCC Camp," *Provo Sunday Herald*, February 4, 1940; "Elks Stage Flag Rites at CCC Camp," *Provo Daily Herald*, February 23, 1940; "Lake Harbor Camp Heads Appointed"; "Excavation of Harbor Underway," *Provo Daily Herald*, January 9, 1940.
26. "Western Boys Sought for New Utah Lake CCC Camp at Provo," *Provo Daily Herald*, September 19, 1939; "Lake Harbor Camp Heads Appointed."
27. *Report of the Director, 1940*, 46.
28. "Superintendent of Lake Project Is Forum Speaker," *Provo Daily Herald*, December 1, 1939; *Annual Report of the City of Provo, Utah, 1940*, Provo City Corporation, Special Collections, Provo City Library, Provo, 10; "$1,000,000 Project Starts at Utah Lake," *Provo Daily Herald*, January 10, 1940.
29. "Dredging Completed to Clear River Channel into Utah Lake," *Provo Daily Herald*, August 30, 1940; "Utah Lake Harbor Crews Excavate Channel, Revet Provo River Banks," *Provo Daily Herald*, December 12, 1940.
30. U.S. Civilian Conservation Corps, "Location and Strength of Civilian Conservation Corps Projects and Work Companies in the Ninth Corps Area on September 30, 1940," 23; "New CCC Youths Arrive in Provo," *Provo Sunday Herald*, July 21, 1940; "CCC Enrollees to Be Transferred to Redding, Cal.," *Provo Sunday Herald*, October 6, 1940; "Utah Lake Harbor Crews Excavate Channel, Revet Provo River Banks."
31. See Franke and the Regional Director, Region III, correspondence, October 28, 1940, to January 17, 1941, Folder 200 (ERA) Administration and Personnel—Timpanogos, Box 8776, NPS Records.
32. *Annual Report of the City of Provo, Utah, 1941*, Provo City Corporation, Special Collections, Provo City Library, Provo, 10; "Shift of CCC Hits

Project," *Salt Lake Tribune*, April 17, 1942; Luke Clegg, former Provo City commissioner, interview by the author, January 13, 1970.

33. Salmond, *Civilian Conservation Corps*, 125.
34. "Bear River Migratory Bird Refuge," in *Brigham City Centennial, 1867–1967*, comp. James H. Miller, 42, Brigham City Corp./Brigham City Chamber of Commerce, [1967], Box 3, Brigham City History, Brigham City Library, Brigham City; Lydia Walker Forsgren, *A History of Box Elder County* (Salt Lake City: Daughters of Utah Pioneers, 1927; repr. 2004), 251, 349.
35. "Montana CCC Men Arrive at Brigham City," *Salt Lake Tribune*, October 12, 1934; "Two CCC Camps for Box Elder County, One in Brigham and Another at Willard," *Daily Box Elder Journal*, August 3, 1934. The Box Elder paper gave the number as 166.
36. "Montana CCC Men Arrive at Brigham City"; "Two CCC Camps for Box Elder County, One in Brigham and Another at Willard."
37. "Montana CCC Men Arrive at Brigham City"; "Bear River Fowl Refuge Waits Sunday Caravan," *Salt Lake Tribune*, April 3, 1941; Whitney L. Johnson, Blacksburg, correspondence with the author, April 15, 1968; "Kaler Hollow CCC Camp Receives Brigham City Men," *Vernal Express*, July 10, 1941.
38. U.S. Civilian Conservation Corps, "Location and Strength of Civilian Conservation Corps Projects and Work Companies in the Ninth Corps Area on September 30, 1940," 21.
39. William C. Oakden, "The Ogden Bay Refuge Waterfowl Haven," *Utah*, June 1941, pp. 27–28; "Waterfowl Refuge Gives Employment to CCC Boys," *Ogden Standard-Examiner*, April 7, 1940.
40. *Report of the Director, 1940*, 49; *Salt Lake Tribune*, November 11, 1941.
41. U.S. National Park Service, *CCC and Its Contribution to a Nation-wide State Park Recreational Program*, 4.
42. As mentioned in chapter 4, the "SP" designation did *not* mean that Locomotive Springs and its successor SP-2 were state parks but, rather, only that the Utah State Parks Commission was the administering agency. The "park" was originally developed as a bird refuge and today bears the designation Locomotive Springs Wildfowl Management Area, operating under Utah's Division of Wildlife Resources. The same can be said of Farmington Bay camp SP-2.
43. "CCC Camps Approved for Fifth Period," 2; Blood to Conrad Wirth, November 20, 1935, and Herbert Evison, Acting Assistant Director, National Park Service, to Blood, November 22, 1935, "CCC," Blood Papers; "Utah CCC Youths Recovering on Coast," *Salt Lake Tribune*, September 20, 1935; "Rabbit Fever Epidemic Sends 35 CCC Men to Bed," *Davis County Clipper*, October 4, 1935; "Handbook for Enrollees, Company 536."
44. "Farmington Bay Waterfowl Management Area," https://wildlife.utah.gov/habitat/farmington_bay.php, accessed March 11, 2016.

45. "Utah CCC Camps Will Be Maintained for Present," *Eureka Reporter*, June 9, 1948.
46. Walter W. Welton, Sacramento, correspondence with the author, August 13, 1968; *Bird Haven Honker*, April 1940; Blood to Wirth, November 20, 1935.
47. *Bay Cross News*, April 20 and June 1939; *Bird Haven Honker*, May 1940.
48. "Camp News," *Davis County Clipper*, November 13, 1936. Today, online accounts of the history of Farmington Bay Waterfowl Management Area say nothing about CCC involvement, only that "several agencies and organizations joined forces with the original construction" ("Farmington Bay Waterfowl Management Area"). It is unfortunate that nearly six years of work by young men of the Corps should be so casually overlooked. On the other hand, in 2010, Rocky Mountain Power and the Utah Department of Natural Resources issued a pamphlet entitled "Birdmen: A History of the Civilian Conservation Corps Construction of the Farmington Bay Waterfowl Management Area" that is both enlightening and interesting. "Birdmen," incidentally, was the name given to the sports teams that competed in the area.
49. Evison to Blood, November 22, 1935, and Blood to Wirth, December 3, 1935, "CCC," Blood Papers.
50. *Report of the Director, 1939*, 65. Today the Farmington Bay Waterfowl Management Area consists of approximately ten thousand acres of impounded water and marshland in Davis and Salt Lake counties. The Utah Department of Fish and Game operates the area, which is used by the public for hunting waterfowl. Don M. Rees, Frank D. Arnold, Dean M. Andersen, and Glen C. Collett, *Multipurpose Management of Reusable Water in Utah*, Report No. 4 (Salt Lake City: University of Utah Institute of Environmental Biological Research Project, February 1966), 7.
51. "CCC Camps Approved for Fifth Period," 2; James T. Taylor, Bountiful, correspondence with the author, May 16, 1968.
52. *Bird Haven Honker*, April/May 1940.

CHAPTER 9

1. U.S. Civilian Conservation Corps, "Total Work Completed during the Period—April, 1933 to June 30, 1942, Utah." This lists 40,007 man-days spent fighting forest fires. Analysis of annual reports—covering only the five state camps for the first period—and figures issued by the assistant regional forester for 1934 reveals a total of 41,038 man-days. The summary figure is probably accurate within 5 percent.
2. Salmond, *Civilian Conservation Corps*, 46.
3. "Camp Workers Fight Small Fire," *Herald Journal*, August 3, 1933.
4. "Forest Fire Sweeps Mill Canyon," *Herald Journal*, September 2, 1933.

5. "City Creek Forest Fire Breaks Anew," *Deseret News*, September 6, 1933.
6. "Widtsoe CCC Boys Subdue Forest Fire," *Kane County Standard*, September 15, 1933. Although identified as Widtsoe, the camp was on what is now U.S. Forest Service 17 on the way to Escalante, approximately fifteen miles southeast of what was even then becoming the ghost town that it is today.
7. "Blaze Destroys 500 Acres of Davis Forest," *Deseret News*, September 20, 1933; "Men at Bullionville CCC Furnish Fire-Fighting Crew," *Vernal Express*, September 28, 1933.
8. "Fires Consume 17,699 Acres of Timbered Lands," *Deseret News*, October 12, 1933.
9. "Forest Officials Halt Manti Fire; Mt. Pleasant," *Deseret News*, October 30, 1933.
10. Grimes, "Civilian Conservation Corps on the Manti Forest."
11. Pulaski earned well-deserved hero status as a result of his courageous actions at the "Big Blowup" fire in the Northern Rockies in 1910, when his knowledge, bravery, calm leadership, and ready-to-use pistols saved the lives of all but six of his forty-five-man crew during one of the most disastrous wildfires in America. "Ed Pulaski," *Wikipedia*, https://en.wikipedia.org/wiki/Ed_Pulaski, accessed May 8, 2017; *The Big Burn*, dir. Ken Burns, PBS, 2015.
12. A. F. Bracken, "Lessons from the Drought," *Utah Farmer*, May 10, 1935, p. 1.
13. "CCC Workers Battle Raging Forest Blaze," *Salt Lake Tribune*, August 26, 1934; "Forest Blaze in Lakes Area under Control," *Salt Lake Tribune*, August 29, 1934.
14. Dana Parkinson, "The CCC Helps Farmers in Utah," *Utah Farmer*, March 25, 1935, p. 10; *Reports of the Director, 1933–1942*.
15. Killpack, correspondence with the author, May 16, 1968; Peterson, correspondence with the author, March 30, 1968, and April 22, 1970.
16. *Yell-A-Gram*, August 1, 1935.
17. "Seventh Period Report, DG-35," September 30, 1936; "Eighth Period Report, DG-35," March 31, 1937.
18. Leslie C. Koch, "Civilian Conservation Corps: A Community Benefit," *Milford News*. This article and photos from an undated segment of the *Milford News* were sent to me on November 23, 2013, by Fred Steinfels, son of Victor Steinfels, who was an enrollee at DG-35 in Milford.
19. *Yell-A-Gram*, July 6, 1936.
20. "Duck Creek CCC Camp News," *Kane County Standard*, July 23, 1937; "Jericho CCC Camp News," *Eureka Reporter*, September 16, 1937; "St. George Camp," *Washington County News*, November 4, 1937; Hinton, "New Deal Years in Utah," 82–83.
21. Otis et al., *Forest Service and the Civilian Conservation Corps, 1933–1942*, chap. 7, "Region 5—The California Region," accessed February 17, 2014. The purpose of the firebreak was to prevent fires spreading from the grass/

scrub oak/manzanita foothill vegetation to the coniferous firs and pines of the higher ranges.

22. "Kiwanians Hear Forest Chief," *Provo Daily Herald*, August 24, 1939; "Brush Fire on Mountainside Put Out; Vast Damage Noted," *Provo Sunday Herald*, September 3, 1939; "Brush Blaze Sweeps Mountainside," *Salt Lake Tribune*, September 2, 1939; "CCC Controls Provo Blaze," *Salt Lake Tribune*, September 3, 1939.
23. "Vernal CCC News," *Vernal Express*, June 26, 1941; "Vernal CCC Put Out Fire near Dry Fork Friday," *Vernal Express*, August 7, 1941.
24. "CCC Crews Battle Fire at Lambson Draw," *Vernal Express*, July 11, 1940; "Ashley Forest Fire Record at New High," *Vernal Express*, August 15, 1940.
25. U.S. War Department, *Civilian Conservation Corps Regulations*, para. 33.
26. James A. Brown, Brigham City, correspondence with the author, May 16, 1968.
27. "Fighting Fires in Forest Not Relished by Men in Camps," *Cache American*, August 22, 1933.
28. Karl Bruneis, "The James T. Saban Lookout—Shoshone National Forest," *CCC Legacy Journal*, May–June 2015, http://www.ccclegacy.org/CCC_Legacy_Journal.html; "1937 08/21 WY 15-Fatality Blackwater CCC," Always Remember, http://www.wlfalwaysremember.org/incident-lists/255-blackwater.html, accessed October 17, 2015.
29. *Preparatory Course for Fire Suppression Training* (Logan: School of Forestry, Utah State Agricultural College, 1940), 40; Kolvet and Ford, *Civilian Conservation Corps in Nevada*, 150–52. Enrollees and Forest Service personnel erected a monument near the town of Orovada honoring the young men on U.S. Highway 95 about three miles west of the Santa Rosa Range where the tragedy took place. "Enrollee Death Takes Forest Fire Total to Six," *Salt Lake Tribune*, September 3, 1939.
30. "Hurricane CCC Boys and Indians Fight Fires in Mountains West of Here," *Washington County News*, July 17, 1941.
31. *Buckhorn Breeze*, July 1939; "Leeds CCC Boys Praised for Work at Fire," *Washington County News*, March 13, 1941.
32. "Ute Mountain Tower to Be Rededicated," *Deseret News*, September 2, 2014.
33. Otis et al., *Forest Service and the Civilian Conservation Corps*, 36.
34. W. B. Rice to Forest Service personnel, Memo for Operation, "Control—Suppression—1941," Forest Service Records, Box 43986, National Archives and Record Service, Denver; "Warden Hits Lack of Fire Fighters; Expert Decries Elimination of CCC Crews," *Salt Lake Tribune*, July 12, 1942.
35. "Storms Add to Injuries on Highways" and "Utah's First General Snowstorm Today," *Deseret News*, November 2, 1936.
36. "More Snowfall Expected in Utah Areas," *Salt Lake Tribune*, December 31, 1936. The storm was so newsworthy that the *Washington County News*, December 31, 1936, carried two different articles on its front page:

"Heaviest Storm in Years Wrecks So. Utah Power Lines" and "Worst Storm in Years Blocks Highway; Wrecks Power Lines."

37. *Ephraim Enterprise*, January 1, 1937. "Southern Utah Has Heavy Snowfall," *Kane County Standard*, January 1, 1937; "Transportation at Standstill as Utah's Dixie Battles Snowstorms," *Washington County News*, January 7, 1937; "Boulder Notes," *San Juan Record*, January 7, 1937; "Record Snowfall Recorded Here," *Helper Journal*, December 31, 1936; "Valley Visited by Record Snowfall," *Garrison Valley News*, December 31, 1936; "Civic Clubs Meet Delayed by Storm," *Helper Journal*, January 15, 1937.
38. "Record Snowfall Recorded Here"; "Worst Storm in Years Blocks Highway; Wrecks Power Lines"; "Valley Visited by Record Snowfall," *Garrison Valley News*, December 31, 1936; "New Snow Storm Envelops State; Highways Closed," *Salt Lake Tribune*, January 1, 1937.
39. *CCC Reflections*, February 2, 1937.
40. "News from CCC Camp F-32," *Richfield Reaper*, January 28, 1937; Peterson, correspondence with the author, March 30, 1968.
41. "Maybe Season's Coldest Weather Hits Here," *Provo Sunday Herald*, January 3, 1937; U.S. Department of Agriculture, Weather Bureau, *Climatological Data*, vol. 39, no. 1 (Salt Lake City, January 1937), 1; David James, "How's the Weather in Provo in January," *Provo Daily Herald*, January 1, 2011.
42. "Snow Continues to Fall throughout Utah," *Millard County Chronicle*, January 7, 1937; "When Winter Comes," *San Juan Record*, January 7, 1937; "Snowshoes and Skis Ordered by City," *Washington County News*, January 7, 1937.
43. "Low Temperatures and Storms Feature Week's Weather," *Ephraim Enterprise*, January 8, 1937; "Manti Nat'l. Forest Snow Very Deep," *Helper Journal*, January 8, 1937; "Mercury Drops to 22 Below Here; Traffic Tied Up," *Provo Sunday Herald*, January 10, 1937; "Snow Conditions at Zion National Park," *Millard County Chronicle*, January 14, 1937; "Eighteen Inches Snowfall Brot [*sic*] in Tuesday's Storm: Highways to the South Are Blocked," *Transcript Bulletin*, January 22, 1937.
44. "Maybe Season's Coldest Weather Hits Here"; "Highway 91 Closed below Cedar City," *Provo Evening Herald*, January 7, 1937; "Mercury in Provo Drops to 14 Below," *Provo Evening Herald*, January 8, 1937; "Mercury Drops to 22 Below Here; Traffic Tied Up"; "Eighth Period Report, DG-35," March 31, 1937.
45. *Parks Post*, January 15, 1937.
46. "Narrative Report for the Month of January, 1937, NP-2," ZION 15454, Zion National Park Museum Collection, courtesy of the National Park Service.
47. "Eighth Period Report, DG-30 (Cedar Creek)," March 31, 1937.
48. Hyrum Kunz, correspondence with the author, June 18, 1970.
49. "Eighth Period Report, DG-30 (Cedar Creek)," March 31, 1937; *Parks Post*, January 15, 1937; "Storms Make Extra Work for CCC Men," *Washington*

County News, January 28, 1937; "CCC Boys Came to Rescue of Snowbound So. Utah," *San Juan Record*, June 21, 1937.

50. "Eighth Period Report, DG-33," March 31, 1937.
51. Ibid.
52. "Eighth Period Report, DG-35," March 31, 1937.
53. "Eighth Period Report, DG-27," March 31, 1937; *Parks Post*, February 1, 1937; "CCC Boys Fight Cold and Snow," *Kane County Standard*, February 5, 1937; "CCC Men Open Roads to Livestock; Save Sheep and Cattle," *Davis County Clipper*, February 12, 1937; *Provo Evening Herald*, February 13 and 15, 1937; Kenneth Bray, Provo, correspondence with the author, April 8, 1968; Sweeney to Blood, [ca. 1937], State Archives, Gen. W. C. Sweeney File, Correspondence S–Z Box, Blood Papers.
54. *Vernal Express*, January 7, 1937.
55. "Vernal CCC News," *Vernal Express*, January 7, 1937; "CCC Crews Open Roads to Save Stock," *Vernal Express*, January 14, 1937.
56. "Feed Hauled to Island Park by CCC Crew," *Vernal Express*, March 18, 1937.
57. "General Simonds Praises Vernal CCC for Work," *Vernal Express*, March 18, 1937; "CCC Looks Back on Excellent Record as Sixth Birthday Nears"; John W. Weaver, Byron Goodrich, and Ray G. Labrum, "City, County Officials Praise Work Projects of Vernal CCC Camp," *Vernal Express*, April 1, 1937.
58. "City, County Officials Praise Work Projects of Vernal CCC; Uinta County Receives Great Benefit from Vernal CCC Camp; Urge Continuation of Camp for 20-Year Program," *Vernal Express*, April 1, 1937.
59. Pfaff, *Bureau of Reclamation's Civilian Conservation Corps Legacy*, A-68.
60. "Winter Brings Snow to St. George," *Washington County News*, January 14, 1937.
61. *Yell-A-Gram*, January 29, 1937.
62. "Eighth Period Report, DG-29," March 31, 1937.
63. "CCC Men Open Roads to Livestock; Save Sheep and Cattle."
64. Blood to Congressman Abe Murdock, January 22, 1937, and Murdock to Blood, January 23, 1937, "Murdock File," Blood Papers.
65. "Forest Service Clears 3000 Miles of Snowbound Roads," *Salt Lake Tribune*, March 26, 1937.
66. "Eighth Period Report, DG-35," March 31, 1937; "Snow Causes Loss in Livestock," *Kane County Standard*, January 22, 1937.
67. D. M. Thompson, Superintendent of DG-45, "Report of Emergency Stock Relief on the Arizona Strip, DG-45, St. George, Utah, December 29, 1936 to February 15, 1937," 3, typescript in my possession.
68. Ibid.
69. Ibid., 4.
70. Ibid., 5–7.
71. Atwood Bundy (son), correspondence with the author, January 7, 2009.

72. “Intermountain News, Castle Dale, Utah,” *Beaver Press*, February 12, 1937.
73. “CCC Aid in Work of Feeding Wild Deer,” *Daily Box Elder Journal*, January 28, 1937.
74. “Forest Service Clears 3000 Miles of Snowbound Roads.”
75. “Weather Hits Normal Trend within State,” *Salt Lake Tribune*, February 11, 1937.
76. Jennifer Savedge, “Three Cheers for the CCC,” in *A Legacy of Labor: The Civilian Conservation Corps* (Peru, Ill.: Cobblestone, April 2005), 5.
77. *Sandstorm Sentinel*, July 15, 1937. Unfortunately, the article gave no clue as to how the extrication took place. I have been unable to locate either Iron Springs or Jockeys Reservoir near Milford.
78. “Search Goes On for Plane,” *Provo Evening Herald*, February 15, 1937.
79. “Local Camp Joins in Airplane Hunt,” *Salina Sun*, December 35, 1936.
80. “Search for Missing Air Liner Goes Forward,” *Deseret News*, December 26, 1936; “Eighth Period Report, DG-29,” March 31, 1937; “Eighth Period Report, DG-35,” March 31, 1937; “CCC Camp News,” *Springville Herald*, December 24, 1936; *Yell-A-Gram*, December 22, 1936, and January 8, 1937; “Plans to Enlarge Scope of Search Made by Officials,” *Salt Lake Tribune*, December 20, 1936; “Plane Search at Standstill,” *Provo Evening Herald*, December 31, 1936.
81. “Provo CCC Boys Win Compliments,” *Provo Evening Herald*, February 15, 1937.
82. *Yell-A-Gram*, June 14, 1937. The body of one of the women aboard was not dug out of the snow about 1,500 feet below the ridgeline until July 3. Again, search crews were about to abandon their attempt to find the last bodies since they were presumed to have been buried beneath the snow and rocks. “Woman’s Body Is Recovered from Plane Wreckage,” *Provo Sunday Herald*, July 4, 1937.
83. *Yell-A-Gram*, July 30, 1937.
84. “Ship Crashes in Mountain Region near Centerville,” *Provo Daily Herald*, November 4, 1940.
85. “CCC Workers Rescue Woman,” *Salt Lake Tribune*, August 15, 1934; “Lost Girl of Duquesne Found Alive Five Miles from Ranch,” *Salt Lake Tribune*, March 10, 1937; “Youth Missing in Mountains,” *Provo Daily Herald*, September 12, 1940.
86. *Parks Post*, January 15, 1937; “Couple Saved from Snow on Highway,” *Daily Box Elder Journal*, January 19, 1937.
87. “Vernal CCC News,” *Vernal Express*, July 9, 1936; “Searching Parties Called Out to Find Infant Lost in Forest,” *Vernal Express*, July 6, 1939.
88. *CCC Reflections*, March 12, 1937.
89. “Three Skaters Rescued from Icy Waters of Utah Lake,” *Pleasant Grove Review*, December 2, 1938.
90. “Missing Provo Man Found Alive Today Close to Utah Lake,” *Provo Daily Herald*, December 11, 1939.

91. "Posse Hunts for Lost Man," *Provo Daily Herald*, December 26, 1939; "Search Pressed for 14 Missing Hunters," *Provo Daily Herald*, October 28, 1940.
92. Elizabeth Kunz Jones, *Kunz Family History* (1995), 30.
93. "Hundreds Drag Lake for Body," *Salt Lake Tribune*, July 10, 1934; "Seventh Period Report, DG-35," September 30, 1936; "Eighth Period Report, DG-35," March 31, 1937.
94. "Women Wield Lusty Shovels as Rescuers Search Snow," *Salt Lake Tribune*, January 2, 1941; "Searchers Recover Body of Alta Snow Slide Victim," *Salt Lake Tribune*, January 4, 1941.

CHAPTER 10

1. "Sergeant Injured at Forest Camp," *Salt Lake Tribune*, June 8, 1933.
2. "Forest Worker Finds Trouble," *Deseret News*, July 31, 1933; "CCC Man Injured in Canyon," *American Fork Citizen*, August 4, 1933; "CCC Worker Slashes Foot on Home Visit," *Deseret News*, October 10, 1933; "CCC Worker Killed by Gravel Cave-In," *Iron County Record*, November 9, 1933.
3. Roundy, *Advised Them to Call the Place "Escalante,"* 201–2. An account of the construction of the roads to Boulder may be found in chapter 5. A more thorough telling, of course, is in Roundy's excellent chap. 11 on the CCC.
4. "CC Driver Swerves to Miss Squirrel, Injures 3 Workers," *Deseret News*, September 6, 1933.
5. Salmond, *Civilian Conservation Corps*, 55.
6. "Vernal CCC News," *Vernal Express*, May 7, 1936.
7. *Bay Cross News*, March 14, 1939.
8. "CCC News," *Pleasant Grove Review*, January 14, 1938; "CCC Safety Conference Held at Salina," *Richfield Reaper*, February 10, 1938; "Conduct Safety Meet at CCC Camp," *Herald Journal*, February 7, 1938.
9. "CCC News," *Pleasant Grove Review*, October 8, 1937, and May 20, 1938.
10. *Frontier*, February 1940.
11. "Manila CCC Cagers Capture State Laurels at Provo on Saturday," *Vernal Express*, March 21, 1935; "Springdale CCC Camp Boy Loses Left Leg," *Washington County News*, January 6, 1938; "Leg Injury Proves Fatal to CCC Enrollee," *Washington County News*, February 17, 1938; "Bridge Mountain CCC Camp News," *Kane County Standard*, January 7, 1938.
12. Francis P. Welsh, Ogden, interview by the author, August 28, 1969. Welsh stated that the enrollee later served in the infantry during World War II.
13. G. A. Platt, correspondence with the author, April 20, 1968.
14. "Injuries Fatal to CCC Youth," *Herald Journal*, July 10, 1936; "CCC Youth Is Accident Victim," *Herald Journal*, September 12, 1936; "CCC Enrollee Meets Death," *Provo Daily Herald*, September 8, 1939; "CCC Youth Killed

in Car Mishap," *Provo Sunday Herald*, September 24, 1939; "CCC Enrollee Dies in Crash," *Herald Journal*, August 29, 1940.

15. "Injuries Fatal to Two as CCC Truck Wrecks," *Vernal Express*, June 15, 1939; "Two Injured in Truck Wreck," *Kane County Standard*, April 6, 1934.
16. *Washington County News*, December 19, 1933; "Triple C Company Moves to Kamas, Starts Projects," *Pleasant Grove Review*, June 3, 1938; "CCC Foreman Killed in Auto Crash," *Vernal Express*, October 12, 1939; "Death Toll Boosted to 117 in Utah," *Provo Daily Herald*, October 9, 1939.
17. "Two Utahns Meet Death," *Provo Evening Herald*, July 1, 1937.
18. "Jericho CCC Camp News," *Eureka Reporter*, March 24, 1938; "CCC Looks Back on Excellent Record as Sixth Birthday Nears."
19. Floyd, interview by the author, June 20, 1968.
20. W. M. Miller, interview by the author, July 22, 1968.
21. "Seventh Period Report, DG-26," September 30, 1936; "CCC News," *Pleasant Grove Review*, August 27, 1937.
22. W. M. Miller, interview by the author, July 22, 1968.
23. "CCC Safety General Makes Pleas for Careful Driving," *Richfield Reaper*, July 28, 1938.
24. "CCC Enrollee Hurt in Crash," *Provo Daily Herald*, December 15, 1939; "Scenes from CCC Camp," *Provo Evening Herald*, June 7, 1934.
25. *Report of the Director, 1940*, 24.
26. *Report of the Director, 1941*, 8; *Report of the Director, 1939*, 20.
27. "Nine Officers Assigned to Forestation Work," *Deseret News*, May 29, 1933.
28. G. A. Platt, correspondence with the author, April 20, 1968.
29. Welsh, correspondence with the author, April 12, 1968.
30. Ibid.
31. The existence of two names for this camp is explained in chapter 4.
32. Welsh, correspondence with the author, April 12, 1968.
33. Welsh, interview by the author, April 14, 1968.
34. "Two CCC Boys Undergo Appendicitis Operation," *Deseret News*, July 15, 1933; "Forest Camp Worker Undergoes Operation," *Deseret News*, August 5, 1933; "Fifth Recruit at Camp Undergoes Operation," *Deseret News*, August 11, 1933; *Herald Journal*, August 22, 1933; Sgt. T. J. McCabe, "News Flashes from Bullionville," *Vernal Express*, August 10, 1933.
35. Welsh, interview by the author, August 28, 1969.
36. "News from the CCC Camp," *Richfield Reaper*, January 4, 1934; "CCC Worker Dies of Meningitis," *Iron County Record*, August 17, 1933.
37. *Report of the Director, 1934*, 6.
38. Arthur Woodworth, "Scarlet Fever Hits CCC Camp," *Pleasant Grove Review*, December 6, 1935.
39. "Vernal CCC Quarantined on Tuesday," *Vernal Express*, December 12, 1935; "Quarantine Lifted at Vernal CCC Camp on Monday," *Vernal Express*, December 26, 1935.

40. "Vernal CCC News," *Vernal Express*, April 2, 1936; "CCC Camp News," *Provo Evening Herald*, January 22, 1937; "Enrollee at Jericho Camp Died Monday from 'Flu,'" *Eureka Reporter*, January 21, 1937.
41. "Jericho CCC Camp News," *Eureka Reporter*, November 18, 1937; *Report of the Director, 1939*, 30.
42. *Report of the Director, 1939*, 31, 33.
43. Hill, *School in the Camps*, 57; *Report of the Director, 1941*, 21.
44. Welsh, interview by the author, August 28, 1969.
45. *Report of the Director, 1937*, 5.
46. *Report of the Director, 1940*, 24.
47. "Sixth Period Report, DG-29," March 31, 1936.
48. *Report of the Director, 1934*, 7; *Report of the Director, 1941*, 9.
49. "Utah Forest Camps Build Men; Workers Happy Crowd." In August 1933 the commanding officer of F-9 complained that the effect of the National Recovery Act had raised commodity prices so that it cost thirty-four cents a day per man rather than thirty-one cents as before.
50. "Chow for the CCC Boys," *Milford News*, June 8, 1933; "Forestry Camp Life Related," *Provo Evening Herald*, June 15, 1933. The noonday meal was identified as "dinner" rather than "lunch," although the latter term might actually be more appropriate for a meal that was often served on the job out of the back of a truck.
51. "News from the CCC Camp," *Richfield Reaper*, April 12, 1934; *Report of the Director, 1940*, 25; *Report of the Director, 1937*, 5.
52. *Report of the Director, 1941*, 19.
53. "Tables Groan under Camp Feast," *Salt Lake Tribune*, December 26, 1936.
54. Stan Pollock (son), Wellsville, Utah, e-mail to the author, January 15, 2016.
55. Welsh, correspondence with the author, April 12, 1968.
56. *Report of the Director, 1939*, 43.
57. Ibid.
58. "CCC Boys Get Dental Service," *Provo Evening Herald*, January 6, 1937.
59. *Report of the Director, 1941*, 20.
60. *Springville Herald*, March 11, 1937; *Report of the Director, 1940*, 25.

CHAPTER 11

1. *Springville Herald*, May 2 and June 10, 1935; "Jericho CCC Camp News," *Eureka Reporter*, November 12, 1936, and February 11, 1937; "CCC Chatter," *Kane County Standard*, January 19, 1934.
2. McEntee, *Now They Are Men*, 41.
3. *Bay Cross News*, June 1939.
4. "Jericho CCC Camp News," *Eureka Reporter*, December 3, 1936, and February 10, March 24, and June 2, 1938.
5. *Hi Life*, April 22 and May 29, 1937.

6. "Vernal CCC News," *Vernal Express*, February 27, 1936, and May 25, 1939; *Vernal Journal*, June 24, 1940.
7. Anthony F. Fischio, Salt Lake City, correspondence with the author, April 12, 1968.
8. "CCC News," *Pleasant Grove Review*, November 19, 1937; "Plans Made for Improvement of Central Grounds," *Pleasant Grove Review*, March 18, 1938.
9. *P.G. Bee*, February 15, 1940; Glen A. Ingalsbe, Orem, questionnaire, April 4, 1968.
10. *Longhorn Weekly*, May 14, 1939.
11. *Company 529 News*, n.d. [July 1938].
12. *Weekly News*, n.d. [November 1935].
13. Max J. Schegel, "News from CCC Camp," *Herald Journal*, August 21, 1933; "To Whom It May Concern," *Iron County Record*, July 13, 1933.
14. "Forest Workers to Get Library," *Herald Journal*, June 15, 1933.
15. William Udink, Ogden, correspondence with the author, April 5, 1968.
16. Max J. Schlegel, "News from CCC Camp—Bulletin Board," *Herald Journal*, August 3, 1933.
17. Hollie E. Tolar, "Milford CCC Notes," *Milford News*, February 2, 1939.
18. "Recruits Laud Benefits from Forest Camps," *Deseret News*, June 15, 1933.
19. "Letters from a CCC Boy to His Pal," *Herald Journal*, July 14, 1933.
20. "News from CCC Camp: Forest Workers Do Much Studying," *Herald Journal*, August 17, 1933.
21. Salmond, *Civilian Conservation Corps*, 47–48. For an account of the adoption of the educational program, see Salmond, *Civilian Conservation Corps*, 47–54; and Hill, *School in the Camps*.
22. Salmond, *Civilian Conservation Corps*, 51.
23. Karl Bunnell, Lander, Wyoming, correspondence with the author, August 28, 1968.
24. Ibid.
25. *Training Conference, 1939*, 10.
26. Evans J. Phillips, Roosevelt, Utah, correspondence with the author, April 15 and 20, 1970.
27. Phillips, correspondence with the author, April 20, 1970; Hill, *School in the Camps*, 21, 31.
28. Bergeson, "Survey of the Social Background of the Civilian Conservation Corps Enrollees of the Fort Douglas District," 28.
29. "CCC Chatter," *Kane County Standard*, December 1, 1933.
30. Bergeson, "Survey of the Social Background of the Civilian Conservation Corps Enrollees of the Fort Douglas District," 28–29.
31. Ibid.; "Hamilton Takes CCC Supervision," *Provo Sunday Herald*, January 21, 1940; "New Educational CC Advisor Named," *Provo Daily Herald*, November 28, 1939.
32. Colonel E. S. Adams, Adjutant General, Ninth Corps Area, to all District and Company Commanders, Ninth Corps Area, February 27, 1937, Folder

I, TRAINING: Instructions, Box 10863, BLM Records; Rutledge, Radio Talk, 9.

33. *CCC Reflections*, October 16, 1936.
34. Hill, *School in the Camps*, 23.
35. Bunnell, correspondence with the author, May 28, 1968.
36. "Adult School to Resume Classes in Provo Monday," *Provo Sunday Herald*, January 3, 1937.
37. "News Notes from CCC," *Herald Journal*, May 6, 1935.
38. "News Notes from CCC," *Herald Journal*, June 20, 1935.
39. "Jericho CCC Camp News," *Eureka Reporter*, February 25, 1937, and February 24 and August 5, 1938.
40. Hill, *School in the Camps*, 36.
41. Salmond, *Civilian Conservation Corps*, 53.
42. Glen M. Carlson, Orem, correspondence with the author, April 8, 1968.
43. Neal McMaster Nelson, "An Historical Inquiry into the Civilian Conservation Corps Movement, with Special Reference to the Ninth Corps Area" (master's thesis, University of Idaho, 1933), 96.
44. "October Report, DG-103," Utah Training Reports, 1938, Box 10866, BLM Records.
45. Bunnell, correspondence with the author, February 12, 1969.
46. Mrs. Sadie Avery, Provo, interview by the author, April 11, 1968.
47. Ellis Shurtz, Salina, Utah, correspondence with the author, 1968; William Laursen, American Fork, interview by the author, May 11, 1968.
48. L. John Nuttall Jr., "Possible Influences on the Public Schools of the CCC Educational Program," *School Review* 43 (September 1935): 508; Hill, *School in the Camps*, 6–7.
49. Bergeson, "Survey of the Social Background of the Civilian Conservation Corps Enrollees of the Fort Douglas District," 39.
50. "CCC News," *Pleasant Grove Review*, October 15, 1937.
51. "CCC Camp Director Notes Opportunities," *Richfield Reaper*, May 22, 1941; Hill, *School in the Camps*, 24.
52. "Sixth Period Report, DG-32," March 31, 1936.
53. "Sixth Period Report, DG-27," March 31, 1936.
54. "CCC Camp Director Notes Opportunities."
55. "213 Illinois Boys Enroll at New CCC Camp in Provo," *Provo Daily Herald*, February 2, 1940.
56. "Vernal CCC News," *Vernal Express*, May 28, 1936.
57. Bert Huish, Orem, correspondence with the author, June 7, 1968; William B. Lane, Provo, interview by the author, March 30, 1968.
58. "March Report, DG-26," Utah Training Reports, 1938, Box 10866, BLM Records.
59. "CCC Men to Study in Morning Classes," *Salt Lake Tribune*, April 25, 1937; *Bridgeland News Weekly*, April 28, 1939; "CCC News," *Pleasant Grove Review*, November 26, 1937.

60. Salmond, *Civilian Conservation Corps*, 155.
61. Ibid., 155–56, 167–68.
62. Chesley Seely, Salt Lake City, to R. H. Rutledge, February 28, 1940; and A. D. Molohon to D. D. McKay, April 19, 1940, File I (CCC), Training/Awards/Proficiency Certificates/General/1940, Box 10863, BLM Records.
63. U.S. Department of the Interior, Division of Grazing, "Project Training for Enrollees," 5, Training/Awards/Proficiency Certificates/General/1939, Box 10863, BLM Records.
64. R. H. Rutledge to Regional Graziers, December 7, 1940, Training/Awards/Proficiency Certificates/General/1940, Box 10863, BLM Records.
65. *Training Conference, 1939*, 11.
66. I (CCC), Training, Enrollee Employment, Utah, Box 10863, BLM Records.
67. Nuttall, "Possible Influences on the Public Schools of the CCC Educational Program," 509, 512–13.
68. "Jericho CCC Camp News," *Eureka Reporter*, February 18, 1937; "Vernal CCC Increased to 208 Men Sat.," *Vernal Express*, November 7, 1935.
69. "CCC Looks Back on Excellent Record as Sixth Birthday Nears."
70. *Training Conference, 1939*, 18.
71. Ibid.
72. "CCC Enrollment Is Offered Boys of Utah County," *Pleasant Grove Review*, October 1, 1937.
73. McEntee, *Now They Are Men*, 51.
74. *Buckhorn Breeze*, July 1939.
75. Ibid.
76. *P.G. Bee*, March 27, 1940.
77. Bunnell, correspondence with the author, May 28, 1968.
78. "Three-Day Holiday Slated for Many Salt Lake Workers," *Deseret News*, June 30, 1933.
79. "Job Army Unit Claims Distinction," *Deseret News*, July 5, 1933.
80. "Cache Forest Camps Win 2 Blue Banners," *Deseret News*, August 31, 1933.
81. "Orderville Camp Gets First Place in This District," *Kane County Standard*, April 13, 1934; Haslam, interview by the author, August 19, 1969.
82. Earl F. Partridge, Orem, correspondence with the author, April 10, 1968; R. Vaughn Killpack, South Ogden, correspondence with the author, May 17, 1968; *P.G. Bee*, January 22, 1940.
83. "Bullionville Camp to Receive Quota," *Vernal Express*, July 13, 1933.
84. Newman Harris, Logan, correspondence with the author, March 29, 1933; Hoyt, *We Can Take It*, 53.
85. G. A. Platt, correspondence with the author, April 20, 1968.
86. Ibid.; "CCC Camp News," *Pleasant Grove Review*, February 14, 1936.
87. "CCC Camp News," *Pleasant Grove Review*, October 2, 9, and 10, 1936, and January 28, 1938.

88. "CCC Chatter," *Kane County Standard*, February 2, 1934; "CCC Camp Is Building Fine Road," *Vernal Express*, December 5, 1935; "Vernal CCC News, Camp 1507," *Vernal Express*, May 13, 1937.
89. *Southern Drawl*, March 1938.
90. "CCC Camp News," *Pleasant Grove Review*, February 19 and 26, 1937.
91. "CCC Camp News," *Pleasant Grove Review*, July 1, 1938; *Vernal Express*, February 27, 1936.
92. *Kane County Standard*, May 31, 1936.
93. Lorell E. Roberts, Brookfield, Wisconsin, correspondence with the author, April 16, 1938; *P.G. Bee*, February 8, 1940. The hitchhiking issue was not confined to Utah. In Missouri, the *Columbian*, the CCC newspaper of Company 3745, described the situation in its January 1942 issue. The camp reporter acknowledged that "strict enforcement of the rule has never been accomplished" and that it might continue to be difficult to stop, since "the public in general is tolerant in its attitude." However, in the future "no violations will be allowed to go unpunished," as officials pointed out not only that it was dangerous to those involved but that "it is discreditable to the CCC in general."
94. Ray West, "CC Camp News," *Springville Herald*, November 19, 1936; "CCC Notes, Company 1507," *Vernal Express*, September 14, 1939.
95. "Sixth Period Report, DG-29," March 31, 1936.
96. Oliver and Dudley, *New America*, 116.
97. Renwick C. Kennedy, "Military Interlude," *Christian Century* 50 (September 13, 1933): 144.
98. Oliver and Dudley, *New America*, 129.
99. "Jericho CCC Camp News," *Eureka Reporter*, February 18, 1937.
100. "Bridge Mountain CCC Camp News," *Kane County Standard*, December 10, 1937.
101. *Vernal Express*, April 16 and October 29, 1936.
102. "CCC Crews to Re-enlist Say Officials," *Salt Lake Tribune*, September 5, 1934.
103. "Minutes of Enrollment Conference, Fort Douglas, Utah, September 25, 1941," Folder I—Supervision—War Department Regs—Fort Douglas District, Box 10898, BLM Records; "Melvin J. Ballard Urges Avoidance of Relief Rolls," *Richfield Reaper*, June 27, 1935; Hinton, "New Deal Years in Utah," 185–94.
104. "CCC Camp News," *Pleasant Grove Review*, October 30, 1936; *Church News*, November 20, 1936.
105. Bergeson, "Survey of the Social Background of the Civilian Conservation Corps Enrollees of the Fort Douglas District," 83–84.
106. *Vernal Express*, March 31, 1938; *Kane County Standard*, December 10, 1937.
107. Mark J. Baird, Draper, correspondence with the author, March 31, 1968.
108. Partridge, correspondence with the author, April 10, 1968; "Hyrum CCC Youths Find Indian Cache," *Herald Journal*, February 28, 1936.

109. Marshall Davis to Edward Rowan, September 29, 1934, cited in Kathleen Duxbury, *CCC ART: Artists of the Civilian Conservation Corps: Marshall Davis* (Ridgeway, N.J.: Duxbury Media, Inc., 2014), 48.
110. Scott Passey, Price, Utah, to David Rees, April 12, 1965, Leonard J. Arrington File.
111. "CCC Camp News," *Pleasant Grove Review*, July 17, 1936. Although the newspaper said that the mess sergeant was from Indiana, the eyewitness and a foreman who was involved both insisted that the two enrollees were from Ohio and Kentucky.
112. Laursen, interview by the author, May 11, 1968.
113. U.S. War Department, "CCC Circular Number 16," July 29, 1933, Blood Papers.
114. "CCC Camp Head Bans Convicted Youth's Joining," *Salt Lake Tribune*, July 8, 1934.
115. Laursen, interview by the author, May 11, 1968.
116. "CCC Youths Rebel in Western Camps," *New York Times*, February 25, 1941.
117. Carlson, correspondence with the author, April 8, 1968.
118. "Jericho CCC Camp News," *Eureka Reporter*, July 14 and 28, 1938.
119. "Elks to Meet CCC Tomorrow," *Herald Journal*, July 26, 1934; "CCC Takes Team out of League," *Herald Journal*, July 23, 1934.
120. *Bay Cross News*, April 20, 1939.
121. "Roosevelt Wins First Game of Season by Defeating Dinosaurs Sun[day]," *Vernal Express*, July 2, 1936; "Vernal CCC Holds Top Place in Basin Series," *Vernal Express*, August 20, 1936; "Vernal CCC Camp Wins First Place in Uintah Basin Baseball Series" and "Vernal CCC News," *Vernal Express*, August 27, 1936.
122. "CCC Camp Men in Utah Form Basket League," *Springville Herald*, January 23, 1936; "Zion Canyon CCC Camp News Notes."
123. *P.G. Bee*, March 5, 1940.
124. "Boxing to Make New Start Here," *Washington County News*, January 18, 1934.
125. *Happy Days*, March 30, 1940.
126. "Provo CC Camp Wins Field Day," *Provo Daily Herald*, May 28, 1940.
127. *Report of the Director, 1936*, 23.
128. *Report of the Director, 1939*, 16; *Report of the Director, 1940*, 16.
129. *Report of the Director, 1937*, 33; U.S. Civilian Conservation Corps, "Total Work Completed during the Period—April, 1933 to June 30, 1942, Utah."

CHAPTER 12

1. "Leader Urges LDS People to Quit Relief," *Deseret News*, October 7, 1938.
2. "Forest Corps Asks 73 Men for Camp," *Deseret News*, June 8, 1933.

3. "Conservation Army Men Must Eat 4500 Calories Daily to Keep Fit," *Deseret News*, June 19, 1933.
4. "Five Officers Selected for Forest Camps," *Salt Lake Tribune*, May 27, 1933.
5. "Forest Camp to Furnish Market for Farm Produce," *Richfield Reaper*, May 25, 1933.
6. "Forest Corps Asks 73 Men for Camp"; "$122,000 Granted for CCC Camps," *Salt Lake Tribune*, September 27, 1934; "Lake Harbor Camp Heads Appointed"; *Report of the Director, 1934*, 7; "CCC Camp for Lake Project Ready October 16," *Provo Sunday Herald*, September 10, 1939; "Well-Supervised Enrollees of Local CCC Camp Fit into Vernal City's Life," *Vernal Express*, March 31, 1938; "Camps and Projects Bring 100 Millions to Section," *Salt Lake Tribune*, April 2, 1939; *P.G. Bee*, March 8, 1940; "The Army and the CCC Camps in the United States," *Kane County Standard*, February 15, 1935; *Training Conference, 1939*, 20.
7. "Reforestation Corps Assigned Quarters at Pine Valley"; "Lumber Company Busy Furnishing Camp Materials," *Iron County Record*, June 8, 1933.
8. "ZCMI Gets CCC Order," *1933; News*, October 23, 1933; "Foresters Receive Average of $5 Each," *Deseret News*, July 7, 1933; "Forest Office to Open Bids for Supplies."
9. "Plans Made for Improvement of Central Grounds."
10. "CCC Makes Park Day Successful," *Washington County News*, November 9, 1933; "CCC Cooperates with Dixie College for Big Field Day," *Washington County News*, March 15, 1934.
11. Charlene Renberg Winters, "Mountain Memories," *BYU Magazine*, Summer 2013, pp. 54–55; "Erection of Rangers' Station at South Fork Progressing," *American Fork Citizen*, September 22, 1933; "Aspen Grove Work to Aid in Big Hike," *Provo Evening Herald*, July 17, 1933; "CCC Crew Aid Camping," *Provo Evening Herald*, August 25, 1933.
12. "Merrill to Speak at Canyon Event," *Provo Evening Herald*, June 30, 1937; Olsen, *Pleasant Grove Sesquicentennial History*, 62.
13. "CCC Rushes Work on Dern Marker," *Salt Lake Tribune*, April 2, 1941; Senator Elbert Thomas to Blood, May 19, 1936, and Senator William King to Blood, June 18, 1936, "CCC," Blood Papers.
14. "CCC Will Build Dam for Scout Camp Lake," *Vernal Express*, August 8, 1935; "CCC Workers Shift Projects," *Herald Journal*, December 11, 1935. The *Vernal Express* article said that there were twenty-five men.
15. "Eighth Period Report, DG-27," March 31, 1937.
16. "Vernal CCC News," *Vernal Express*, January 13, 1938; "Ice Skating Rink Built by CCC," *Vernal Express*, November 17, 1938.
17. "Navajo Lake Dike Meeting to Be Held Monday," *Iron County Record*, July 6, 1933.
18. "Lions Club Names Park for Persons Who 'Put It Over,'" *Milford News*, June 13, 1940. The new name never replaced the original name, by which it is still known today, Rock Corral Recreational Area.

19. Mrs. Leland Larsen, Brigham City, to Blood, April 26, 1935, "CCC," Blood Papers.
20. Olen Cole Jr., *The African-American Experience in the Civilian Conservation Corps* (Gainesville: University Press of Florida, 1999), 22.
21. Ibid., 28–29.
22. Ibid., 19.
23. "Jericho CCC Camp News," *Eureka Reporter*, March 10, 1938.
24. Blood to Mrs. Larsen, May 2, 1935, "CCC," Blood Papers. Company 2539 apparently arrived in Brigham City on October 22, 1935, although a newspaper account announced the arrival of a company a full year earlier. U.S. Civilian Conservation Corps, "Location and Strength of Civilian Conservation Corps Projects and Work Companies in the Ninth Corps Area on September 30, 1940," 22; "Montana CCC Men Arrive at Brigham City." This company, number unknown, evidently was the one that proved troublesome and was moved out to make way for Company 2539, which remained in Brigham until about August 1941.
25. Reid D. Bench, Roosevelt, Utah, correspondence with the author, April 15, 1968. It should be mentioned that most of those who commented on this topic, admittedly former enrollees for the most part, felt that the girls who got into trouble would probably have done so with or without the CCC. Many nonenrollees concurred with this. An accurate analysis would be somewhat difficult.
26. Mrs. Phillip Cave, American Fork, correspondence with the author, May 20, 1968.
27. Kermit Carson, Denver, to David Rees, April 12, 1965, Leonard J. Arrington File.
28. Sparks, correspondence with the author, June 14, 1968.
29. Mrs. Paul J. Fletcher, Ferron, Utah, correspondence with the author, June 14, 1968.
30. Taylor, correspondence with the author, May 16, 1968. While still in the CCC, Taylor married the daughter of a local LDS bishop. After twenty-nine years of married life and five children, Taylor remembered that at the time his mother-in-law was quite apprehensive about the match.
31. Mrs. C. D. Harris, Chicago, correspondence with the author, April 22, 1968.
32. Mrs. Rodabaugh, correspondence with the author, April 22, 1968.
33. Fischio, correspondence with the author, April 12, 1968; Anthony Fischio, Salt Lake City, interview by the author, July 15, 1968.
34. Bench, correspondence with the author, March 23, 1968.
35. "Ban Liquor Sales to CCC Minors," *Herald Journal*, July 15, 1936.
36. Earl Partridge, Orem, interview by the author, May 13, 1968.
37. Words and a corroborating account were sent to me by Francis P. Welsh, Ogden, April 14, 1968. After first appearing in my dissertation of 1971, this

has since appeared in other publications about the CCC. It's no problem; I just want it known that I used it first.

38. Sowards, oral history interview, [2].
39. "CCC Boys Punished for Tire Stealing," *Iron County Record*, November 9, 1933.
40. Russ C. Knowles, Logan, interview by the author, June 20, 1968.
41. A. B. Prince, "Correction of False Rumor about CCC Boy," *Washington County News*, May 6, 1937.
42. He was identified in the newspaper as a "former" enrollee, perhaps in anticipation of the Corps policy to issue a dishonorable discharge to anyone convicted of a crime. Twenty days of his sentence were suspended on the condition that he leave the state, another suggestion that he was an enrollee at the time of the offense.
43. "CCC Youth Jailed for Burglary," *Herald Journal*, January 5, 1938.
44. "In Justice Court," *Vernal Express*, May 20, 1937.
45. "CCC Boy Held in Jail after Bad Cutting Scrape," *Richfield Reaper*, November 19, 1936.
46. Although Utah has long been much more urbanized than popularly believed, it is still true that in 1940, 59.4 percent of the population were found on farms and in communities of less than six thousand people. U.S. Department of Commerce, Bureau of the Census, *County and City Data Book, 1949: A Statistical Abstract Supplement* (Washington, D.C.: U.S. Government Printing Office, 1952), 404. Utah's official urban population, i.e., from communities in excess of 2,500, was 55.5 percent, compared with Indiana's 55.1 percent and Ohio's 66.8 percent. U.S. Department of Commerce, Bureau of the Census, *Statistical Abstract of the United States, 1941* (Washington, D.C.: U.S. Government Printing Office, 1942), 7.
47. "Youths Sought by Officers," *Provo Evening Herald*, May 22, 1934; "Draws Jail Term on Battery Charge," *Provo Evening Herald*, June 7, 1934.
48. Roundy, *Advised Them to Call the Place "Escalante,"* 216–18.
49. Ibid., 219.
50. The name has been changed to preserve anonymity.
51. Shumway, *This Part of the Vineyard*, 81–82.
52. *Outdoor World*, April 13, 1936.
53. "Reforestation Men Fed for Only 31c Per Day," *Iron County Record*, June 22, 1933.
54. G. A. Platt, correspondence with the author, April 20, 1968; Mrs. Sam McKell, Fullerton, correspondence with the author, 1968; Fletcher, correspondence with the author, April 15, 1968; Fred S. Deffendol, Price, Utah, correspondence with the author, March 28, 1968.
55. Mrs. Hansen, Logan, interview by the author, June 20, 1968.
56. P. Budge, Logan, correspondence with the author, March 25, 1968.
57. G. A. Platt, correspondence with the author, April 20, 1968; "CCC Camp News," *Pleasant Grove Review*, February 14, 1936.

58. *Iron County Record*, July 6, 1933.
59. "CCC Workers at Hobble Creek Down Obstacles," *Provo Sunday Herald*, August 20, 1933; "Payson Program at CCC Camp," *Provo Evening Herald*, September 26, 1934.
60. "Inspect Dam Site on Clara Creek"; "CCC Camp 961 to Give Program," *Washington County News*, November 23, 1933.
61. "Milford Night Guard Foils Pair of Yeggs; Watchman Calls Forest Workers Who Aid in Capture of Duo," *Deseret News*, June 27, 1933.
62. Joseph Bernini, Eureka, Utah, correspondence with the author, March 30, 1968; Kenneth Bray, Provo, correspondence with the author, April 8, 1968; M. F. Burson, Sunset, Utah, correspondence with the author, May 20, 1968; Deffendol, correspondence with the author, March 28, 1968. Many similar comments were made by others.
63. Partridge, correspondence with the author, April 10, 1968.
64. Welsh, correspondence with the author, April 14, 1968.
65. Ibid.
66. "Many Attend Duck Creek Celebration," *Kane County Standard*, July 28, 1933.
67. Bray, correspondence with the author, April 8, 1968.
68. *Frontier*, October 1939.
69. "CCC Chatter," *Kane County Standard*, December 8, 1933; Killpack, correspondence with the author, May 16, 1968.
70. Haslam, interview by the author, August 19, 1969. Like Killpack, Haslam suggested that the delegation's fears were based on experiences with Company 1256 of SE-212, since Company 959 had so far done nothing to create any suspicions.
71. Rutledge to C. B. Morse, San Francisco, September 25, 1933, "CCC," Blood Papers.
72. Ed Johnston, Mayor of Mt. Pleasant, and others to Ernest Winkler, Forest Service, Ogden, and others, "Petition to Locate a CCC Camp at or near Mt. Pleasant, Utah," n.d., copy received in Governor's Office, September 19, 1934, "CCC," Blood Papers.
73. R. E. Platt, correspondence with the author, July 6, 1968.
74. Firmage, *History of Grand County*, 285, citing Bruce Louthian.
75. "Santa Clara, Ivins, Show Appreciation for CCC Work," *Washington County News*, April 5, 1934; "Vernal CCC News," *Vernal Express*, September 5, 1940; "Elks Donate New Flag to CCC Camp."
76. "The Forest Army," *Provo Evening Herald*, August 5, 1933; "Future of the Forest Army."
77. *Washington County News*, November 16, 1933; see also January 25, 1934.
78. "CCC Company No. 1345 Leaving for Uintah after Year at Moab."
79. "Seventh Period Report, DG-27," September 30, 1936.
80. "Civilian Conservation Corps," *Salt Lake Tribune*, January 4, 1937.

81. See Cream, "Genesis of the Civilian Conservation Corps," 49–50; Salmond, *Civilian Conservation Corps*, 192, 214–15.
82. "Lumber Arrives for CCC Camp at Fair Grounds," *Vernal Express*, July 25, 1935; "Men Arrive for Vernal CCC Camp," *Vernal Express*, October 31, 1935.
83. *Vernal Express*, December 26, 1935; "Local CCC Camp One of Best in Area," *Vernal Express*, January 9, 1936; "Vernal CCC News," February 6 and 20, March 5, May 7, June 4, and July 16, 1936, and January 7, 1937; "Vernal CCC Holds Top Place in Basin Series."
84. "Protest Removal of Vernal CCC Camp," *Vernal Express*, September 28, 1939.
85. Sowards, oral history interview, [1].
86. Mayor R. C. Cooper, "City, County Officials Praise Work Projects of Vernal CCC Camp," *Vernal Express*, April 1, 1937.
87. "Uintah High Students Win CCC Essay Prize," *Vernal Express*, March 31, 1938.
88. "Lions and Ladies Hold Banquet at CCC Camp," *Vernal Express*, April 20, 1939; "Community to Be Guest of CCC Saturday," *Vernal Express*, April 11, 1940; "Vernal CCC News," *Vernal Express*, September 5, 1940.
89. Cooper, "City, County Officials Praise Work Projects of Vernal CCC Camp"; "Well-Supervised Enrollees of Local CCC Camp Fit into Vernal City's Life."
90. "Stockman Tells of Value of CCC," *Vernal Express*, April 14, 1938; Cooper, "City, County Officials Praise Work Projects of Vernal CCC Camp."
91. "Vernal CCC Prepares to Close Camp," *Vernal Express*, November 13, 1941; "CCC Departure Is Postponed until Saturday," *Vernal Express*, November 20, 1941; "CCC Enrollees Transferred from Vernal to Moab," *Vernal Express*, November 27, 1941.
92. "CCC on the Ashley Forest in Daggett and Uinta County, Utah," *Vernal Express*, April 23, 1936.
93. Ibid.
94. "Rattlesnake Bites Tropic Boy," *Kane County Standard*, July 24, 1936. When questioned about the incident thirty-two years later, Welsh expressed surprise at the detailed newspaper coverage of the event. He was happy to report that the boy lived. Welsh, correspondence with the author, April 12, 1968; Welsh, interview by the author, August 28, 1969.
95. "All but Seven Men Leave Camp"; L. C. Christiansen, Escalante, Utah, to Blood, Senator Thomas, and Congressman Murdock, October 9, 1936, "CCC," Blood Papers.
96. See Salmond, *Civilian Conservation Corps*, 145–61.
97. "Civic Leaders Oppose Closing of Triple C Camp," *Pleasant Grove Review*, March 25, 1938.
98. Homer P. Edwards, President, Roosevelt Lions Club, and others to Blood, September 10, 1937; and Daniel F. Mitchell, State House of Representatives, to Blood, September 14, 1937, "CCC," Blood Papers.

99. Blood to Rutledge, September 24, 1937, and Rutledge to Blood, September 29, 1937, "CCC," Blood Papers.
100. "Murdock Writes on Jericho Camp," *Eureka Reporter*, April 21, 1938.
101. "Firemen Ask for New Equipment," *Eureka Reporter*, April 21, 1938.
102. "Murdock Writes on Jericho Camp."
103. "Utah CCC Camps Will Be Maintained for Present."
104. Justus O. Seely, Mayor of Mt. Pleasant, and others to Blood, March 14, 1938, "CCC," Blood Papers.
105. Justus Seely to Senator Thomas, March 14, 1938, "CCC," Blood Papers. The camps stayed: F-11 for another fourteen months and SCS-5 until July 1942.
106. Harris, correspondence with the author, March 24, 1968.
107. "Civic Groups Hear Praise of CCC Camps," *Salt Lake Tribune*, May 23, 1941; "J.C. Sponsors CCC Drive," *Salt Lake Tribune*, October 12, 1941.
108. Willard Smith, "Memories of Bygone Days," 1980; Stoddard, "Look Back at the Ccc [*sic*] Camps."

CHAPTER 13

1. This and the following paragraphs contain figures from U.S. Civilian Conservation Corps, "Location and Strength of Civilian Conservation Corps Projects and Work Companies in the Ninth Corps Area on September 30, 1940." As was nearly always the case, the two camps on the Uinta and Ouray Indian Reservation in northeastern Utah were not included in the tabulation.
2. Ibid.; *Report of the Director, 1941*, 65.
3. Only Companies 6426 and 6430 were kept for the Sixteenth Period, after which, with the possible exception of Company 482, all Fourth Corps Area companies were removed from Utah.
4. "Vernal CCC News," *Vernal Express*, June 27, 1940; "Construction at Kaler CCC Started," *Vernal Express*, July 4, 1940; "Dry Fork CCC Camp Ask by Ashley Forest," *Vernal Express*, August 15, 1940; "Kaler Hollow CCC May Be Lost Lest Community Acts," *Vernal Express*, April 3, 1941; "Forest Plans CCC Camp Transfer to Kaler Hollow," *Vernal Express*, April 17, 1941; "150 Assigned Kaler Hollow CCC Camp," *Vernal Express*, June 26, 1941; "Kaler Hollow CCC Camp Receives Brigham City Men"; "Kaler Hollow Camp Moves Out Today," *Vernal Express*, August 21, 1941. After World War II began, local officials, disappointed that the projected roadwork planned for Dry Fork was no longer on the Forest Service's drawing board, proposed unsuccessfully that Japanese internees be brought in to carry out the work. "Interned Japs May Construct Dry Fork Road," *Vernal Express*, February 19, 1942; "Jap Labor Proposed for Scenic Road," *Vernal Express*, February 26, 1942.
5. *Report of the Director, 1941*, 4.

6. C. Seely, Regional Grazier, to CCC Director, January 14, 1941. The I (CCC) CAMP History UTAH file with this letter also contains a "Form F Report on Disposition of CCC Camp Structures" for each of the DG camps operating.
7. *Report of the Director, 1941*, 68.
8. E. K. Berlew to Acting Director, Grazing Service, May 15, 1942, "Camp History, DG-157," Box 10858, BLM Records; "14 Grazing Camps Close in Utah," *Salt Lake Tribune*, June 1, 1942; "Order Closes Projects of Indian CCC," *Salt Lake Tribune*, July 12, 1942.
9. R. A. Breach to District Commander, CCC, Pocatello, February 11, 1942; Archie D. Ryan to E. K. Berlew, Assistant Secretary, Department of the Interior, May 19, 1942; H. E. Wetherwax to E. R. Greenslet, Division of Grazing, wire, May 23, 1942; and Kenneth Wolfe to Regional Grazier, Salt Lake City, July 15, 1942, "Camp History, G(D)-1, Utah, Dugway Proving Grounds," Box 10858, BLM Records.
10. Lewis K. Cox, Lindon, Utah, conversation with the author, December 28, 2012.
11. "Army Begins Shift of CCC Machines," *Salt Lake Tribune*, August 5, 1942; "CCC Crews Begin Dismantling CCC Barracks," *Salt Lake Tribune*, December 13, 1942; "CCC Set-Ups Wait Moving," *Salt Lake Tribune*, December 19, 1942. Twenty-two letters to and from officials of the city of Ferron, Forest Service, Division of Grazing, Soil Conservation Service, Department of the Interior, Treasury Department, Ninth Corps Area, and Director's Office of the CCC, dating between September 9, 1939, and June 22, 1940, may be found in a folder in Box 10858, BLM Records; Shumway, *This Part of the Vineyard*, 67.
12. Firmage, *History of Grand County*, 293.
13. "Sevier Gets CCC Camp to House Jap Workers," *Salt Lake Tribune*, December 13, 1942.
14. Newman, "Tremonton Was Once Home to WW II POWs," 66.
15. Salmond, *Civilian Conservation Corps*, 218–20.
16. Ibid., 210–17; Fred E. Leake, ed., *Roosevelt's Tree Army. A Brief History of the Civilian Conservation Corps* (Carmichael, Calif.: National Association of Civilian Conservation Corps Alumni, 1983).
17. Kennedy, *Freedom from Fear*, 144.
18. Shumway, *This Part of the Vineyard*, 79.
19. Kennedy, *Freedom from Fear*, 379.
20. Ibid., 57; Salmond, *Civilian Conservation Corps*, 210.
21. "Utahns Benefit from CCC Work," *Kane County Standard*, October 23, 1941.
22. A quantitative account may be found in appendix C.
23. Amy Joi O'Donoghue, "Floods, Fire and Hope in Sanpete," *Deseret News*, August 21, 2014.

24. "Outlook for County Work Good," *Milford News*, June 1, 1933; "CWA Employs 986 Cache Men," *Salt Lake Tribune*, December 14, 1933; "New Bridge Spanning Green River at Jensen Dedicated Armistice Day," *Roosevelt Standard*, November 13, 1933.
25. In sheer numbers, of course, farmers and other residents of the Wasatch Front would claim that distinction due to the dams and irrigation projects of the Bureau of Reclamation, as described in chapter 7.
26. "Ashley National Forest Mulls Decommissioning Facilities," *Deseret News*, March 2, 2014.
27. John Hollenhorst, "Zion's Trees Are Dying of Old Age," *Deseret News*, May 26, 2015.
28. U.S. Civilian Conservation Corps, "Total Work Completed during the Period—April, 1933 to June 30, 1942, Utah."
29. James T. Patterson, "The New Deal in the West," *Pacific Historical Review* 38 (August 1969): 320.
30. U.S. Department of Commerce, Bureau of the Census, *Statistical Abstract of the United States, 1941*, 348. The figures given are for fiscal year 1935–36.
31. U.S. Civilian Conservation Corps, "Total Work Completed during the Period—April, 1933 to June 30, 1942, Utah"; *Salt Lake Tribune*, July 12, 1942.
32. This figure might be as much as one thousand lower than the peak for the year, since it was taken just before the arrival of the October enrollees.
33. Alexander, *Rise of Multiple-Use Management in the Intermountain West*, 104.
34. Shumway, *This Part of the Vineyard*, 81.
35. "CCC Looks Back on Excellent Record as Sixth Birthday Nears."
36. Letters to the author: Harry W. Rodabough, Provo, November 11, 1968; Wilford E. Smith, Provo, March 4, 1968; Alva Weyburn, Layton, April 9, 1968; Ralph Peay, Springville, Utah, 1968.
37. Welsh, correspondence with the author, April 12, 1968.
38. *Bay Cross News*, April 20, 1939.
39. Sweeney, *Last Unspoiled Place*, 62.
40. Nawyn, "CCC Camp Brought Jobs, Hope and Young Men to Brigham."
41. Tom Brokaw, *The Greatest Generation* (New York: Random House, 1998), xix, xxx.
42. Nawyn, "CCC Camp Brought Jobs, Hope and Young Men to Brigham."
43. In the Blood File, 1934, "CCC," Blood Papers. The statement was neither addressed nor dated. It presumably was a response to a request from Melvin Ryder, *Happy Days* editor, June 22, 1934, for a statement on Blood's evaluation of the CCC.
44. *Hi Life*, April 22, 1937.
45. Stoddard, "Look Back at the Ccc [*sic*] Camps."
46. William A. Williams, "Charles Libby—A CCC Boy Returns to Camp," *CCC Legacy Journal*, May/June 2015.
47. *Salt Lake Tribune*, editorial, July 3, 1942.

48. Sol Cohen, "Remember the CCC?" *Phi Delta Kappan* 49 (March 1968): 372.
49. Reihan Salam and Richard Lowry, "The Party of Work," *National Review*, March 24, 2014, pp. 16–18, https://www.nationalreview.com/2014/03/party-work-reihan-salam-rich-lowry/.
50. Jen Jackson, "Salvation through Service: The Enduring Legacy of the Civilian Conservation Corps Celebrating 75 Years," *Inside/Outside Southwest*, April/May 2008, pp. 12–15, at 14.
51. Cole, *African-American Experience in the Civilian Conservation Corps*, 77.
52. "CCC Built Friendships, Families and Character," *Deseret News*, August 1982. Unfortunately, a thorough search of the Emery County Archives, Castle Dale, Utah, as well as the *Deseret News* has failed to produce the article, which, as my incomplete notes suggest, appeared in the first week of August 1982.
53. Schlesinger, *Age of Roosevelt*, 340.
54. McPherson, *History of San Juan County*, 225, citing "Sixth Anniversary of the Civilian Conservation Corps," *San Juan Record*, April 6, 1939.

EPILOGUE

1. Fred E. Leake, ed., *History of the Civilian Conservation Corps and Its Lasting Legacy*, 2nd ed. (CCC Legacy, 2013).
2. Jackson, "Salvation through Service," 14.
3. See https://www.nationalservice.gov/programs/americorps; Joel Holtrop, correspondence with the author, June 7, 2016. After a thirty-five-year career with the U.S. Forest Service including serving as one of the four deputy chiefs, Holtrop is now chair of the Corps Network.
4. Most of the material in this section comes from the paper Elizabeth Cushman, "Thesis on a Proposed STUDENT CONSERVATION CORPS" (master's thesis, Vassar College, 1954); and Kevin Hamilton and H. Montgomery, eds., *Our Land. Our Youth. Our Future: Commemorating Fifty Years of the Student Conservation Association* (Charlestown, N.H.: Student Conservation Association, 2008), both in my possession.
5. Cushman, "Thesis on a Proposed STUDENT CONSERVATION CORPS," 1.
6. Ibid.
7. Ibid.
8. Ibid.
9. Jay Ashe, in *Our Land. Our Youth. Our Future: Commemorating Fifty Years of the Student Conservation Association*, ed. Kevin Hamilton and H. Montgomery (Charlestown, N.H.: Student Conservation Association, 2008), 27–29.
10. "Innovation. Engagement; Impact: Student Conservation Association 2012 Annual Report," 7; *Greenway: SCA's Conservation Quarterly*, Fall 2012, p.

4; Hugh Montgomery, Student Conservation Association, correspondence with the author.

11. "Alumni Spotlight," *Greenway: SCA's Conservation Quarterly*, Spring 2016, p. 7.
12. Sean Damitz, correspondence with the author, July 10, 2013.
13. See https://servicecenter.usu.edu/communitypartners/utah_conservation_corps.
14. Ibid.
15. Utah Conservation Corps, https://ucc.usu.edu/, accessed June 3, 2016.
16. Sean Damitz, Logan, interview by the author, May 8, 2013; Sean Damitz, correspondence with the author, May 7, 2015.
17. "Project Aims to Restore Riverton Wetlands," *Deseret News*, October 16, 2016.
18. See https://serviceyear.org/ccyc/; Jake Deslauriers, correspondence with the author, May 8, 2015. Damitz describes Deslauriers as "an up-and-comer in the corps world."
19. Katie McKellar, "Tales from the Trail," *Deseret News*, August 5, 2013.
20. Jackson, "Salvation through Service," 14.
21. In pursuit of full disclosure, my wife and I have such an annuity.
22. Olsen, *Pleasant Grove Sesquicentennial History*, 115.
23. "Historic 1930s Guard Station Restored in Utah National Forest," *Cache Valley Daily*, May 26, 2015.

Bibliography

Alexander, Thomas G. *A Clash of Interests: Interior Department and Mountain West, 1863–96*. Provo: Brigham Young University Press, 1977.

———. "Conflict and Fraud: Utah Public Land Surveys in the 1850s, the Subsequent Investigation and Problems with the Land Disposal System." *Utah Historical Quarterly* 80, no. 2 (Spring 2012): 108–31.

———. *The Rise of Multiple-Use Management in the Intermountain West: A History of Region 4 of the Forest Service*. Salt Lake City: Brigham Young University and MESA Corporation, May 1987.

———. *Utah. The Right Place*. Salt Lake City: Utah State Historical Society, 1996.

Alford, Kenneth L. "Camp Douglas: Keeping a Watchful Eye on Salt Lake and the Saints." *Pioneer*, 2012, pp. 2–19.

Antrei, Albert C. T., ed. *The Other Forty-Niners: A Topical History of Sanpete County, Utah, 1849–1983*. Salt Lake City: Sanpete County Commissioners, Western Epics, 1982.

Arrington, Leonard J. *The Changing Economic Structure of the Mountain West, 1850–1950*. Monograph Series, vol. 10, no. 3. Logan: Utah State University Press, June 1963.

———. "The New Deal in the West: A Preliminary Statistical Inquiry." *Pacific Historical Review* 38 (August 1969): 311–16.

———. "Utah's Great Drought of 1934." *Utah Historical Quarterly*, Summer 1986: 245–64.

Arrington, Leonard J., and Lowell Dittmer. "Reclamation in Three Layers: The Ogden River Project, 1934–1965." *Pacific Historical Review* 35 (February 1966): 15–34.

Audretsch, Robert W. *Shaping the Park and Saving the Boys: The Civilian Conservation Corps at the Grand Canyon, 1933–1942*. Indianapolis: Dog Ear Publishing, 2011.

———. *We Still Walk in Their Footprint: The Civilian Conservation Corps in Northern Arizona, 1933–1942*. Indianapolis: Dog Ear Publishing, 2013.

Bailey, Reed W., with A. R. Croft. *Contour-Trenches Control Floods and Erosion on Range Lands*. Washington, D.C.: U.S. Government Printing Office, May 1937.

Bell, Patti. *Bryce Canyon National Park: The Early Years: 1916–1946*. Bryce Canyon Natural History Association, 2011.

Bergeson, Thora. "A Survey of the Social Background of the Civilian Conservation Corps Enrollees of the Fort Douglas District." Master's thesis, Department of Sociology, University of Utah, 1937.

Bluth, John, and Wayne Hinton. "The Great Depression." In *Utah's History*, edited by Richard Poll, Thomas G. Alexander, Eugene Campbell, and David E. Miller, 481–96. Provo: Brigham Young University Press, 1978.

Bradley, Martha Sontag. *A History of Beaver County*. Utah Centennial County History Series. Salt Lake City: Utah State Historical Society/Beaver County Commission, 1999.

———. *A History of Kane County*. Utah Centennial County History Series. Salt Lake City: Utah State Historical Society/Kane County Commission, 1999.

Brokaw, Tom. *The Greatest Generation*. New York: Random House, 1998.

Bruneis, Karl. "The James T. Saban Lookout—Shoshone National Forest." *CCC Legacy Journal*, May–June 2015. http://www.ccclegacy.org/CCC_Legacy_Journal.html.

Butler, Ovid, ed. *Youth Rebuilds: Stories from the CCC*. Washington, D.C.: American Forestry Association, 1934.

"CCC History of LaSal National Forest." Mimeograph in the author's possession.

Cheeseman, William E. "Unemployment and Relief in Utah, 1929–1932." Master's thesis, Department of History, Brigham Young University, 1961.

Cohen, Sol. "Remember the CCC?" *Phi Delta Kappan* 49 (March 1968).

Cohen, Stan. *The Tree Army: A Pictorial History of the Civilian Conservation Corps, 1933–1942*. Missoula: Pictorial Histories Publishing Co., 1980.

Cole, Olen, Jr. *The African-American Experience in the Civilian Conservation Corps*. Gainesville: University Press of Florida, 1999.

Crawford, J. L. *Rock Structures of Zion: A Pictorial History*. Springdale, Utah: Zion Natural History Association, 1999.

Cream, Joseph. "The Genesis of the Civilian Conservation Corps." Master's thesis, Columbia University, 1955.

Cushman, Elizabeth. "Thesis on a Proposed STUDENT CONSERVATION CORPS." Master's thesis, Vassar College, 1954.

Darling, John Herrick Hiram. "The C.C.C. Makes Good!" *Christian Century* 50 (October 25, 1933).

Davis, Kingsley. *Youth in the Depression*. Chicago: University of Chicago Press, 1935.

Davis, William C., Ernest Wright, and Carl Hartley. *Diseases of Forest-Tree Nursery Stock*. Forest Publications No. 9. Civilian Conservation Corps, February 1942.

Dearborn, Ned H. *Once in a Lifetime: A Guide to the CCC Camp*. New York: Charles E. Merrill Company, 1935.

DeBoer, S. R. *First Report on State Policies*. Salt Lake City: Utah State Planning Board, 1935.

Dickson, Paul, and Thomas B. Allen. *The Bonus Army: An American Epic*. New York: Walker Publishing Co., 2004.

Duxbury, Kathleen. *CCC ART: Artists of the Civilian Conservation Corps: Marshall Davis*. Ridgeway, N.J.: Duxbury Media, Inc., 2014.

Eldredge, Michael S. "All Hail to the President! Theodore Roosevelt Comes to Utah, May 29, 1903." *Utah Historical Quarterly* 82, no. 1 (Winter 2014).

Embrey, Jesse L. *A History of Wasatch County.* Utah Centennial County History Series. Salt Lake City: Utah State Historical Society/Wasatch County Commission, 1996.

Firmage, Richard A. *A History of Grand County.* Utah Centennial County History Series. Salt Lake City: Utah State Historical Society/Grand County Commission, 1996.

Forsgren, Lydia Walker. *A History of Box Elder County.* Salt Lake City: Daughters of Utah Pioneers, 1927; repr. 2004.

Frye, Bradford J. *From Barrier to Crossroads: An Administrative History of Capitol Reel National Park, Utah.* Cultural Resources Selections, vol. 1. Denver: Intermountain Region, National Park Service, 1998.

Gestring, Captain John F. "Special Orders No. 97." Typewritten, Company 957, Camp PE-217, January 1, 1934.

Gutke, Deniane. "A CCC Enrollee a Day Kept Depression Away." *Blue Mountain Shadows* (Blanding, Utah) 1, no. 2 (Spring 1988).

———. "Open Arms? The CCC Invasion of San Juan County." *Blue Mountain Shadows* (Blanding, Utah) 1, no. 1 (Fall 1987).

Hamilton, Kevin, and H. Montgomery, eds. *Our Land. Our Youth. Our Future: Commemorating Fifty Years of the Student Conservation Association.* Charlestown, N.H.: Student Conservation Association, 2008.

Harding, John Stillman (incorrectly identified as Stillman, John Harding). Oral history interview by Kathy Bradford, May 11, 2006. Brigham City Library Oral History Collection, MS 302, Brigham City.

Harvey, Mark W. T. *Symbol of Wilderness: Echo Park and the American Conservation Movement.* Albuquerque: University of New Mexico Press, 1994.

Haymond, Jay M. "A Survey of the History of the Road Construction Industry in Utah." Master's thesis, Department of History, Brigham Young University, 1967.

Hill, Frank E. *The School in the Camps: The Educational Program of the Civilian Conservation Corps.* New York: American Association for Adult Education, 1942.

Hinton, Wayne K. *The Dixie National Forest: Managing an Alpine Forest in an Arid Setting.* Cedar City, Utah: Dixie National Forest, n.d.

———. "The Economics of Ambivalence." *Utah Historical Quarterly* 54, no. 3 (Summer 1986): 268–85.

———. "The New Deal Years in Utah: A Political History of Utah (1932–1940)." Master's thesis, Department of History, Utah State University, 1963.

———. *With Picks, Shovels, and Hope: The CCC and Its Legacy on the Colorado Plateau.* With Elizabeth A. Green. Missoula: Mountain Press Publishing Company, 2008.

Hoyt, Ray. *We Can Take It: A Short Story of the C.C.C.* New York: American Book Company, 1935.

Huchel, Frederick M. *A History of Box Elder County.* Utah Centennial County History Series. Salt Lake City: Utah State Historical Society/Box Elder County Commission, 1999.

Hussey, W. E. "Brief History of Company 957, CCC." Pamphlet in the author's possession.

Hutchings, Selar S., Junior Range Examiner. Memorandum for Mr. Stahman, September 12, 1934. Fld. E—Int, NIRA, Supervision, Desert Range, Documents File, U.S. Forest Service, Shrub Sciences Laboratory, Provo.

Jackson, Donald Dale. "Life in the Civilian Conservation Corps." In *American Decades: The 1930s*, edited by Louise I. Gerdes. San Diego: Greenhaven Press, Inc., 2000.

Jackson, Jen. "Salvation through Service: The Enduring Legacy of the Civilian Conservation Corps Celebrating 75 Years." *Inside/Outside Southwest,* April/May 2008, pp. 12–15.

Jensen, Naomi Asay Anderson, Ada Valoy Cox, and Heather J. Miller. *Recollections and Snapshots: A Historical Sketch of Castle Dale.* 1997.

Jewett, Stephanie. "The Civilian Conservation Corps in Iron County and Surrounding Areas." Senior thesis, Southern Utah University, 1994.

Kelsey, Michael R. *The Story of Black Rock, Utah.* Provo: Kelsey Publishing, 1996.

Kennedy, David M. *Freedom from Fear: The American People in Depression and War, 1929–1945.* Oxford History of the United States, vol. IX, edited by C. Vann Woodward. New York: Oxford University Press, 1999.

Kennedy, Renwick C. "Military Interlude." *Christian Century* 50 (September 13, 1933): 1144–45.

Kolvet, Renée Corona, and Victoria Ford. *The Civilian Conservation Corps in Nevada: From Boys to Men.* Reno: University of Nevada Press, 2006.

Lambert, Roy. *High Uintas Hi!* Kamas, Utah: Roy Lambert, 1964.

Leake, Fred E., ed. *History of the Civilian Conservation Corps and Its Lasting Legacy.* 2nd ed. CCC Legacy, 2013.

———, ed. *Roosevelt's Tree Army. A Brief History of the Civilian Conservation Corps.* Carmichael, Calif.: National Association of Civilian Conservation Corps Alumni, 1983.

Leonard, Glen M. *A History of Davis County.* Utah Centennial County History Series. Salt Lake City: Utah State Historical Society/Davis County Commission, 1999.

Logan City Commission. Minutes of Meetings, 1933–34, Logan.

MacKay, Kathryn L. "The Uncompahgre Reservation and the Hill Creek Extension." *Utah Historical Quarterly* 83, no. 3 (Summer 2015): 180–93.

Maher, Neil M. *Nature's New Deal: The Civilian Conservation Corps and the Roots of the American Environmental Movement.* New York: Oxford University Press, 2008.

Mann, Walter E. "Memorandum to Mr. Norton, April 13, 1936." Folder R, Supply Uniforms, Documents File, U.S. Forest Service, Shrub Sciences Laboratory, Provo.

Massey, Peter, and Jeanne Wilson. *Utah Trails: Central Region*. Hermosa Beach, Calif.: Adler Publishing Co., 2006.

McArthur, E. Durant, Bryce A. Richardson, and Staley G. Kitchen. *Great Basin Experimental Range: Annotated Bibliography*. Gen. Tech. Rep. GTR-305. Fort Collins: U.S. Department of Agriculture, Forest Service, Rocky Mountain Research Station, 2013.

McEntee, James J. *Now They Are Men: The Story of the CCC*. Washington, D.C.: National Home Library Foundation, 1940.

McPherson, Robert S. *A History of San Juan County*. Utah Centennial County History Series. Salt Lake City: Utah State Historical Society/San Juan County Commission, 1995.

Miller, James H., comp. "Bear River Migratory Bird Refuge." In *Brigham City Centennial, 1867–1967*. Brigham City Corp./Brigham City Chamber of Commerce, [1967], Box 3, Brigham City History, Brigham City Library, Brigham City.

Milligan, Mark. "What Are Those Lines on the Mountain? From Bread Lines to Erosion-Control Lines." Utah Geological Survey, January 2010. https://geology.utah.gov/map-pub/survey-notes/glad-you-asked/erosion-control-lines-on-the-mountains/, accessed January 21, 2015.

Moley, Raymond. *After Seven Years*. New York: Harper and Brothers, 1939.

Mortimer, William James, comp. and ed. *How Beautiful upon the Mountains: A Centennial History of Wasatch County*. Salt Lake City: Wasatch County Chapter, Daughters of Utah Pioneers, 1963.

Muhlestein, Harold George, and Fay Lunceford Muhlestein. *Monticello Journal: A History of Monticello until 1937*. Monticello, Utah: H. G. and F. L. Muhlestein, 1937.

Nawyn, Lori L. "CCC Camp Brought Jobs, Hope and Young Men to Brigham." Three-page typescript in *CCC Camp by Lori L. Nawyn*. Box 3, Brigham City History, Brigham City Library, Brigham City.

———. "CCC Meant Gains for 'Boys,' Brigham Area through Projects." Four-page typescript in *CCC Camp by Lori L. Nawyn*. Box 3, Brigham City History, Brigham City Library, Brigham City.

Nelson, Neal McMaster. "An Historical Inquiry into the Civilian Conservation Corps Movement, with Special Reference to the Ninth Corps Area." Master's thesis, University of Idaho, 1933.

Newell, Linda King, and Vivian Linford Talbot. *A History of Garfield County*. Utah Centennial County History Series. Salt Lake City: Utah State Historical Society/Garfield County Commission, 1998.

Newey, La Verna Burnett. *Remember My Valley: A History of Ogden Canyon, Eden, Liberty, and Huntsville*. Salt Lake City: Hawkes Publishing Company, 1977.

Newman, Tamera. "Tremonton Was Once Home to WW II POWs." In *Looking Back: Tremonton City's First 100 Years, 1903–2003*. Logan: *Tremonton Leader/Garland Times*, 2003.

Nixon, Edgar B., ed. *Franklin D. Roosevelt and Conservation, 1911–1934*. Washington, D.C.: National Archives and Record Service and the Franklin D. Roosevelt Library, 1957.

Nord, Arthur G. "Historical Information Concerning 'The Willard Watershed Rehabilitation Program.'" Mimeograph copy in the author's possession.

Nuttall, L. John, Jr. "Possible Influences on the Public Schools of the CCC Educational Program." *School Review* 43 (September 1935): 508–13.

Oliver, Alfred C., Jr., and Harold M. Dudley. *The New America*. New York: Longmans, Green and Co., 1937.

Olsen, Beth. *Pleasant Grove Sesquicentennial History, vol. 3: American Fork Canyon, Pleasant Grove's Backyard*. Provo: Stevenson's Supply, n.d. [ca. 2008].

Otis, Alison T., William D. Honey, Thomas C. Hogg, and Kimberly K. Lakin. *The Forest Service and the Civilian Conservation Corps, 1933–42*. Washington, D.C.: U.S. Department of Agriculture, 1986.

Patterson, James T. "The New Deal in the West." *Pacific Historical Review* 38 (August 1969): 317–27.

Pedersen, Lyman C. "History of Fort Douglas, Utah." Ph.D. dissertation, Brigham Young University, 1967.

Perkins, Frances. *The Roosevelt I Knew*. New York: Holt, Rinehart and Winston, 1963.

Peterson, Charles S., and Linda E. Speth. *A History of Wasatch-Cache National Forest*. [Logan]: Utah State University, 1980.

Pfaff, Christine. *The Bureau of Reclamation's Civilian Conservation Corps Legacy: 1933–1942*. Denver: Department of the Interior, Bureau of Reclamation, February 2010.

Preparatory Course for Fire Suppression Training. Logan: School of Forestry, Utah State Agricultural College, 1940.

Quinn, R. Thomas. "Out of the Depression Depths: Henry H. Blood's First Year as Governor." *Utah Historical Quarterly* 54, no. 3 (Summer 1986): 216–39.

Rawick, George R. "The New Deal and Youth: The Civilian Conservation Corps, the National Youth Administration, the American Youth Congress." Ph.D. dissertation, University of Wisconsin, 1957.

Rees, Don M., Frank D. Arnold, Dean M. Andersen, and Glen C. Collett. *Multipurpose Management of Reusable Water in Utah*. Report No. 4. Salt Lake City: University of Utah Institute of Environmental Biological Research Project, February 1966.

Roberts, Richard C., and Richard W. Sadler. *Ogden, Junction City*. With the Ogden Area Chamber of Commerce. Northridge: Windsor Publications, 1985.

Robinson, Edgar E. *They Voted for Roosevelt.* Palo Alto: Stanford University, 1947.

Rosenman, Samuel I., ed. *The Public Papers and Addresses of Franklin D. Roosevelt,* 5 vols. New York: Random House, 1938–50.

Roundy, Jerry C. *Advised Them to Call the Place "Escalante."* Springville, Utah: Art City Publishing, 2000.

Rutledge, R. H. Radio Talk: CCC 4th Anniversary, 1937. Accession No. R4-1680-1992-0031-14-48, U.S. Forest Service Region 4 History Collection, Ogden.

Salam, Reihan, and Richard Lowry. "The Party of Work." *National Review,* March 24, 2014, pp. 16–18. https://www.nationalreview.com/2014/03/party-work-reihan-salam-rich-lowry/.

Salmond, John A. *The Civilian Conservation Corps, 1933–1942: A New Deal Case Study.* Durham, N.C.: Duke University Press, 1967.

Savedge, Jennifer. "Three Cheers for the CCC." In *A Legacy of Labor: The Civilian Conservation Corps.* Peru, Ill.: Cobblestone, April 2005.

Schlesinger, Arthur, Jr. *The Age of Roosevelt, vol. II: The Coming of the New Deal, 1933–1935.* Boston: Houghton Mifflin, 1958.

Schultz, Michael J., Jr. *The Civilian Conservation Corps in the Allegheny National Forest: A Traveling Companion.* Kane, Pa.: Kane County Historic Preservation Society, 2011.

Seale, William. *The Presidents' House: A History.* Washington, D.C.: White House Historical Association, 1986.

Shaw, Seth T. (Range Management Department). Letter to Dr. George Steward, Intermountain Forest and Range Experiment Station, Ogden, April 23, 1935. Fld. Supervision: Meetings, Documents File, U.S. Forest Service, Shrub Sciences Laboratory, Provo.

Sherman, E. A. "Saving Our Soil." *Nation* 136 (April 12, 1933): 401–3.

Shumway, Gary L. *This Part of the Vineyard: A Centennial Overview of the History of Blanding, Utah.* Yorba Linda: Shumway Family History Publishing, 2005.

Smith, Kathy Mays. *Gold Medal CCC Company 1538: A Documentary.* Paducah, Ky.: Turner Publishing Co., 2001.

Sommer, Barbara W. *Hard Work and a Good Deal: The Civilian Conservation Corps in Minnesota.* St. Paul: Minnesota Historical Society, 2007.

Stene, Eric A. "Strawberry Valley Project," Bureau of Reclamation, 1995. https://www.usbr.gov/projects/pdf.php?id=197, accessed July 20, 2015.

Swain, Donald C. "The Bureau of Reclamation and the New Deal, 1933–1940." *Pacific Northwest Quarterly,* July 1970: 137–46.

Sweeney, Michael S. *Last Unspoiled Place: Exploring Utah's Logan Canyon.* Washington, D.C.: National Geographic, 2008.

Swing, Raymond Gram. "Take the Army out of the CCC." *Nation* 140 (October 23, 1935): 459–60.

Thompson, D. M. "Report of Emergency Stock Relief on the Arizona Strip, DG-45, St. George, Utah, December 29, 1936 to February 15, 1937." Typescript in the author's possession.

Uintah County Regional History Center Staff. *Images of America: Ashley Valley*. Charleston, S.C.: Arcadia Publishing, 2011.

U.S. Civilian Conservation Corps. *Standards of Eligibility and Selection for Junior Enrollees*. Washington, D.C.: U.S. Government Printing Office, June 15, 1939.

U.S. Department of Agriculture, U.S. Forest Service. Records, Box 371685, Federal Records Center, Denver.

U.S. Department of Agriculture, Weather Bureau. *Climatological Data*, vol. 39, no. 1. Salt Lake City, January 1937.

U.S. Department of Commerce, Bureau of the Census. *County and City Data Book, 1949: A Statistical Abstract Supplement*. Washington, D.C.: U.S. Government Printing Office, 1952.

———. *Sixteenth Census of the United States, 1940, Population, vol. III: The Labor Force, Parts L–5*. Washington, D.C.: U.S. Government Printing Office, 1943.

———. *Statistical Abstract of the United States, 1941*. Washington, D.C.: U.S. Government Printing Office, 1942.

U.S. Department of Labor. "ECW Official Letter #51 to All State Directors of Selection of Men," August 25, 1933. Governor Henry H. Blood Papers, 1933–40, Utah State Archives, Salt Lake City.

U.S. Department of the Interior, Bureau of Land Management. Records, Federal Records Center, Denver.

Box 10858 Official File Grazing Service, Camp Histories.

Box 10863 Official File Grazing Service, Training.

Box 10866 CCC Reports, Utah.

Box 10882 Supply and Equipment, Condemned, Utah.

Box 10898 Supervision, War Department Regulations, Fort Douglas District.

Box 10923 Livestock Associations, Fire Protection, Utah, 1936–37.

U.S. Department of the Interior, Bureau of Reclamation. Bureau Library, Salt Lake City.

"Abstract from Project History of Moon Lake Project," 1953.

"Abstract from Project History of Sanpete Project."

History, Hyrum Project, Utah, 1934.

History, Moon Lake Project, Utah, vols. I–VI, 1936–41.

History, Ogden River Project, Utah, vols. IV–IX, 1936–41.

History, Provo River Project, Utah, Deer Creek Division, vols. I–VII, 1937–43.

———. *Final Report on Design and Construction of Pineview Dam and Reservoir, Ogden, River Project, Utah*. Denver: Bureau of Reclamation, 1941.

———. *Reclamation Project Data*. Washington, D.C.: U.S. Government Printing Office, 1961.

U.S. Department of the Interior, National Parks Service. Records, Federal Records Center, Denver.
 Boxes 8606–7, Camp Histories.
 Box 8750, Records, Zion National Park, Utah.
 Box 8751, Arches National Monument, Utah.
 Box 8759, Records, Capitol Reef National Monument, Utah.
 Box 8776, Timpanogos Cave National Monument (ERA).
 Box 81239, CCC General Files, 1934–44.
 Box 81246, NPS Files on Liquidation of CCC Projects.
 Box 99483, Timpanogos Cave National Monument.

U.S. Emergency Conservation Work. "Summary of Work, Utah State Camps." September 30, 1933. Report in the author's possession.

U.S. Emergency Conservation Work and Civilian Conservation Corps. *Reports of the Director*. Washington, D.C.: U.S. Government Printing Office, 1933–43.

U.S. National Park Service. *The CCC and Its Contribution to a Nation-wide State Park Recreational Program*. Washington, D.C.: U.S. Government Printing Office, 1937.

U.S. Office of the Director. *Civilian Conservation Corps Safety Regulations*. Washington D.C.: U.S. Government Printing Office, 1938.

U.S. War Department. "CCC Circular Number 16," July 29, 1933. Governor Henry H. Blood Papers, 1933–40, Utah State Archives, Salt Lake City.

———. *Civilian Conservation Corps Regulations*. Washington, D.C.: U.S. Government Printing Office, 1937.

Utah National Emergency Council. "Photographic Reports of Representative Work Projects Being Done by Division of Grazing CCC Camps in Utah to November 1, 1937." "National Emergency Council, Civilian Conservation Corps," Box F-1, Utah State Archives, Salt Lake City.

———. "Report of the Governor's Advisory Committee on Public Welfare and Emergency Relief for January, 1934." Salt Lake City, 1934.

Utah Road and Recreation Atlas. Medford, Ore.: Benchmark Maps, 2006.

Utah State Planning Board. "Boundary Map for Proposed Farmington Bay Project." Salt Lake City, December 8, 1934.

Webbink, Paul. "Unemployment in the United States, 1930–1940." *Papers and Proceedings of the American Economic Association* 30 (February 1941): 248–72.

Willard Centennial, 1851–1951. Compiled by the Willard Ward Genealogical Committee [1951], Box 5, Box Elder County History, Brigham City Library, Brigham City.

Williams, Gerald W. *The USDA Forest Service: The First Century*. Washington, D.C.: U.S. Department of Agriculture.

Williams, William A. "Charles Libby—A CCC Boy Returns to Camp." *CCC Legacy Journal*, May/June 2015.

Wilson, Richa. *Commodious Cabins and Handsome Structures: Administrative Facilities of the Manti La Sal National Forest, 1905–1962*. Draft, 2013.

———. *Cozy Cabins and a Hyperbolic Paraboloid*. Ogden: Forest Service Intermountain Region, June 2015.

Winsor, L. M. Letter to Slack W. Winburn, August 7, 1934, and untitled publication, "Flood Control in Utah." Utah Historical Society, Salt Lake City.

Winters, Charlene Renberg. "Mountain Memories." *BYU Magazine*, Summer 2013.

Wise, John J. "Historical Information Relative to 'The Willard Basin Watershed Rehabilitation Project.'" Mimeograph copy in the author's possession.

NEWSPAPERS/NEWSLETTERS

American Fork Citizen

Bay Cross News (camp newspaper of SP-2, Farmington Bay, Utah)

Bear River Valley Leader

Beaver Press

Bird Haven Honker (camp newspaper of SP-2)

Bridgeland Bulletin/Bridgeland News Weekly (camp newspaper of BR-11, Bridgeland, Utah)

Buckhorn Breeze

Cache American

Cache Valley Daily

Canal Construction Chronicle

CCC Reflections (camp newspaper of BR-11, Bridgeland, Utah)

Church News

The Columbian (camp newspaper of Company 3745)

Company 529 News (camp newspaper of Company 529, DG-27, Castle Dale, Utah)

The Compass (camp newspaper of Company 1508, DG-30, Cedar City, Utah; MSS-B 540, Manuscript Collections, Box 6, Fld. 4, Utah Historical Society, Salt Lake City)

Daily Box Elder Journal

Davis County Clipper

The Deseret News (Salt Lake City)

Emery County Progress

Ephraim Enterprise

Eureka Reporter

Ferron Chatterbox

Frontier (camp newspaper of Company 1256)

Garrison Valley News
Happy Days (newspaper of the Civilian Conservation Corps)
Helper Journal
Herald Journal (Logan)
Hi Life (camp newspaper of Company 4779)
Illini-Ute
Iron County Record (Cedar City, Utah)
Jericho Journal
Kane County Standard (Kanab, Utah)
Longhorn Weekly (camp newspaper of DG-32, Dalton Wells, Utah)
Milford News
Millard County Chronicle
Moab Times-Independent
New York Times
1933; News
Ogden Standard-Examiner
Outdoor World
The Parks Post (camp newspaper of Company 962)
P.G. Bee (camp newspaper of BR-91, Pleasant Grove, Utah)
Pleasant Grove Review
Provo Evening Herald/Provo Daily Herald
Provo Sunday Herald
Richfield Reaper
Roosevelt Standard
Salina Sun
Salt Lake Tribune
San Juan Record
Sandstorm Sentinel (camp newspaper of DG-35, Milford, Utah)
Southern Drawl (camp newspaper of Company 479)
Spirit of '48 (camp newspaper of Company 940)
Springville Herald
Take Five (camp newspaper of BS-1/BF-1/FWS-1, Brigham City/Bear River City, Utah)
Transcript Bulletin (Tooele)
Utah
Utah Farmer
Vernal Express
Vernal Journal
Veyo Scroll
Voice of Veyo (camp newspaper of Company 4777, nine pages, most double-sided, quarto, mimeograph)
Washington County News (St. George)

The Weekly Letter (camp newspaper of Company 1508, DG-30, Cedar City, Utah; MSS-B 540, Manuscript Collections, Box 6, Fld. 4, Utah Historical Society, Salt Lake City)

Weekly News (camp newspaper of DG-28, Clover Creek, Utah)

The Yell-A-Gram (camp newspaper of Company 948, three–six mimeographed pages, published at Provo camps PE-220 and F-40 and Springville camp F-30, sometimes weekly and sometimes biweekly; Utah State Historical Society, Salt Lake City)

Index

Note: page numbers in italics refer to figures; those followed by *t*, to tables, and by n, to notes, with note number. Numbers preceded by P are plate numbers.